Terrorism
A Documentary History

Bruce Maxwell

CQ PRESS

A Division of Congressional Quarterly Inc.
Washington, D.C.

For Barbara

CQ Press
1255 22nd Street, N.W., Suite 400
Washington, D.C. 20037

(202) 729-1900; toll-free, 1-866-4CQ-PRESS (1-866-427-7737)

www.cqpress.com

Printed and bound in the United States of America

06 05 04 03 02   5 4 3 2 1

"Explosion, Then Arms and Legs Rain Down," copyright © 2001, *USA TODAY.* Reprinted with permission.

Typeset by G&S Typesetters, Inc., Austin, Texas
Cover design by Naylor Designs

Library of Congress Cataloging-in-Publication Data

Terrorism: a documentary history.
    p.   cm.
Compiled by Bruce Maxwell.
Includes bibliographical references (p.   ) and index.
  ISBN 1-56802-767-2
  1. Terrorism—History—Sources.   2. Terrorism—History.   I. Maxwell,
Bruce
  HV6431 .T4594 2003
  303.6′25′09045—dc21

                                                2002151050

CONTENTS

CONTENTS

CONTENTS

CONTENTS

PREFACE

Attempting to make sense of the daily barrage of news about terrorism following the September 11, 2001, attacks on the World Trade Center and the Pentagon can be overwhelming. *Terrorism: A Documentary History* aims to help by offering some perspective. The documents and explanatory introductions in this book provide a frame of reference that is useful for understanding current events and for evaluating policy options that may profoundly affect the future of the United States and other nations.

Included in the book are one hundred documents—government reports, presidential directives, speech transcripts, newspaper articles, court rulings, and trial transcripts, among others that trace the modern history of terrorism around the world. The documents cover the thirty-year period from 1972, when international terrorism burst into the public consciousness with live TV pictures of Palestinian terrorists holding Israeli athletes hostage at the Munich Olympics, to August 2002, just before the first anniversary of the September 11 terrorist attacks in the United States.

The documents in this book constitute a historical record, but many also provide lessons for today's battle against terrorism. A few examples:

- In response to questions about whether intelligence failures led to the September 11 attacks, members of President George W. Bush's administration said no one had ever imagined that terrorists would crash planes into buildings. But a September 1999 report prepared for the Central Intelligence Agency said Osama bin Laden might attack Washington, D.C., by flying planes into the Pentagon, the White House, or the CIA headquarters building. News stories in May 2002 about the report's existence prompted renewed calls in Congress for a full investigation of what the government knew before September 11.
- Since 1987 the General Accounting Office (GAO), the investigative arm of Congress, has issued repeated reports warning about gaping holes in aviation security. The reports have focused on problems with screeners at airport security checkpoints. Fourteen years after the first GAO warning, nineteen hijackers passed through security checkpoints at three major airports and took control of four airliners.
- When Attorney General John Ashcroft announced in May 2002 that he was loosening restrictions on domestic surveillance by the FBI, critics

- pointed to past FBI abuses of the rights of Americans. Reports in this book from 1975, 1976, and 1990 document those abuses.
- After the September 11 attacks, some Americans called for rounding up Arab-Americans and placing them in internment camps. But in a February 1983 report, a congressional panel that examined the internment of Japanese Americans during World War II concluded that a "grave injustice" had been done to the internees and that their confinement had not improved national security.
- Starting in the mid-1990s, a growing chorus of reports by expert panels warned that the United States was ill-prepared to prevent terrorist attacks or to cope with their aftermath. These studies are getting fresh scrutiny as Congress examines the events leading up to September 11.
- Some critics have questioned whether the United States is consistent in fighting terrorism. Included in this book are a 1977 directive by President Jimmy Carter tacitly admitting that terrorists based in the United States had attacked Cuba; documents about President Bill Clinton's controversial clemency offer in August 1999 to sixteen Puerto Rican terrorists; and an October 2001 speech by Cuban president Fidel Castro asking why the United States had not prosecuted a Florida man who, the State Department said, masterminded the 1976 bombing of a Cubana Airlines plane that killed seventy-three people.
- With Congress appropriating tens of billions of dollars to fight terrorism, questions are arising about how to spend that money most effectively. Several reports recommend priorities for spending terrorism funds and document poor management of previous federal antiterrorism efforts.

Some of the documents provide insight into infamous terrorist acts committed decades ago. Included are the prosecutor's closing argument from the February 1994 trial of Byron De La Beckwith, who was convicted in the June 1963 murder of civil rights leader Medgar Evers; a statement about the January 2001 conviction of a Libyan intelligence agent for the December 1988 bombing of Pan Am Flight 103 over Lockerbie, Scotland, in which 270 people were killed; and the prosecutor's opening statement in the May 2002 trial of Bobby Frank Cherry, the last major suspect convicted in the September 1963 bombing of the 16th Street Baptist Church in Birmingham, Alabama, which killed four young girls as they prepared for the Sunday service.

Other documents in this book chronicle the rise of Osama bin Laden and his al Qaeda terrorist network, along with the fits and starts during the decades-long effort to end terrorist violence in the Middle East and Northern Ireland. Still others document specific incidents like the November 1972 taking of American diplomats as hostages in Iran; the October 1983 bombing of the U.S. Marine headquarters in Beirut, Lebanon, which killed 241 soldiers; the October 1984 assassination of Prime Minister Indira Gandhi of India; the July 1994 bombing of a Jewish community center in the heart of Buenos Aires, Argentina, which killed 86 people and wounded hundreds more; and the August 2001 suicide bombing of the Sbarro pizzeria in Jerusalem, which killed 15 people. And finally, some documents explore issues such as antiabortion violence, church arsons, militias, ecoterrorism, narcoterrorism, security threats to computer networks and other parts of the nation's infrastructure, efforts to stop terrorists from obtaining weapons of mass destruction, and the widespread availability of instructions for making bombs.

Brief introductions explain the documents' historical significance and context. Because of space restrictions many of the documents have been excerpted; all omissions are indicated by the customary ellipsis points. If the full text of a shortened document is available on the Internet, the URL is provided.

No claim is made that the reports, speeches, and other items included in this book constitute the one hundred most important documents about terrorism made public in the past three decades. I examined more than four hundred documents for possible inclusion; the ones that were selected are a representative sample, chosen because they are historically significant, illustrate major trends, or highlight important issues.

To help fill in the inevitable historical gaps between documents, a chronology at the back of the book briefly describes hundreds of selected terrorism-related events that occurred during the period this book covers. All chronology entries that pertain to documents in the book have cross-references to the relevant documents.

Further information about terrorism is available through the resources listed in the bibliography. As well as listing articles, books, and reports, it briefly describes nearly five dozen selected Web sites.

I am indebted to many people who helped make this book possible. At CQ Press, I am grateful to acquisitions editor Christopher Anzalone for taking on this unexpected project and handling it so gracefully, assistant editor Grace Hill for coordinating the electronic files, and the superb production staff, especially Belinda Josey, for creating a beautiful book. Special thanks go to freelance editor Kerry Kern for her careful and thoughtful editing of the manuscript and for her unwavering graciousness throughout the process.

For assistance in obtaining documents, I am grateful to Peter Kornbluh, senior analyst at the National Security Archive in Washington, D.C., and Robert Bohanan, chief archivist at the Jimmy Carter library in Atlanta, Georgia. I would also like to thank Kathleen Nadeau for her support and encouragement throughout this project, which were instrumental in making it possible.

As always with my books, my greatest thanks are reserved for my wife, Barbara. Every person who lives with a writer probably deserves consideration for sainthood, but Barbara is unquestionably the most deserving of them all.

INTRODUCTION

Before 8:46 a.m., the most striking thing about the morning of September 11, 2001, was its beauty. On the East Coast the day dawned exceptionally clear and bright, one of those seemingly perfect days that combines the last remnants of summer with the first traces of fall.

Then at 8:46 a.m. a huge fireball erupted high up in the 110-story North Tower of the World Trade Center in New York City. The first news reports were sketchy. As television pictures showed the building burning, anchors of the networks' morning shows said it seemed that a plane of some sort had hit the tower. But was it a private plane or something bigger? Were any passengers aboard? And how could a pilot run into the fifth-tallest building in the world on such a clear day?

As those questions hung in the air, startled viewers watching the live TV pictures at 9:03 a.m. saw another airliner cross their screens, bank sharply, and purposefully smash into the 110-story South Tower. The impact blew flames and debris out the other side of the building. Suddenly everyone knew this was no accident.

The horror of that reality was just starting to sink in when, at 9:40 a.m., a plane crashed into the Pentagon near Washington, D.C. The TV networks split their screens to show pictures of the World Trade Center, a symbol of the nation's economic strength, and the Pentagon, a symbol of its military strength, both burning.

After this third crash the Federal Aviation Administration shut down the nation's airspace for the first time in history. The agency ordered every plane in the sky to land immediately at the nearest airport.

As tens of millions of people in the United States and around the world sat transfixed in front of televisions, the pictures became even more horrific. They showed people on the highest floors of the towers, trapped by raging flames fed by jet fuel, jumping out windows to their deaths. At least two people jumped together, holding hands as they plummeted.

At 9:50 a.m. the unthinkable happened. The South Tower imploded, the weight of the top floors pancaking floor after floor as they fell. A massive cloud of dust and ash that billowed up and darkened the sky shrouded the last moments of the building's collapse.

Twenty minutes later a fourth airliner crashed, this one into a Pennsylvania field. Before the plane crashed some passengers called loved ones on cell phones, only to be told of the earlier crashes. Realizing that the men who took over their plane intended to use it, too, as a missile, a group of passengers apparently stormed the cockpit, attempting to wrestle control from the hijackers. At some point the airliner turned nose down and hurtled into the ground. Investigators later said the plane's intended target was the White House.

Nineteen minutes later, at 10:29 a.m., the North Tower of the World Trade Center collapsed. A soft "Oh my gosh" was the stunned reaction of ABC television anchor Peter Jennings as he and his viewers watched live pictures of the building crumbling floor by floor, starting at the top.

By the time most people ordinarily get their second cup of coffee in the morning, slightly more than three thousand people caught up in the madness in New York, Washington, and Pennsylvania were dead or dying.

What Is Terrorism?

Terrorism is not a new phenomenon. The word *terrorism* dates only to the French Revolution in the 1790s, but historians trace the first acts of terrorism to biblical times. In an irony of history, the first terrorist campaign was launched in A.D. 48 by members of a Jewish sect called the Zealots, who sought to drive the Roman occupiers out of Palestine. Their chief weapon was a short dagger called a *sica*, which they used to slash the throats of Roman legionnaires and Jews who collaborated with them. The Zealots hoped in vain that their attacks would lead to a general uprising against the Romans.

A millennium later came the Assassins, members of an Islamic sect who killed Muslims from other sects and the occasional Christian. In *The Terrorist Trap* Jeffrey D. Simon describes how the Assassins worked: "Through the use of selective murders, almost always by dagger, the fanatically loyal and secretive Assassins spread fear and terror throughout the Middle East. . . . The Assassins viewed their killings as a holy mission, much like contemporary Islamic fundamentalist terrorist groups. They were convinced they would be rewarded in the afterlife."

The most famous terrorist attack before September 11 was the 1914 assassination of Archduke Franz Ferdinand of Austria by a Serb anarchist, an event that historians generally agree helped trigger World War I. The anarchists were a bloody bunch. Two decades before the assassination of Ferdinand, over a seven-year period they assassinated the president of France, the empress of Austria, the prime minister of Spain, the king of Italy, and the president of the United States, William McKinley.

Throughout history terrorism has primarily been a tool used by the powerless to besiege the powerful. Over the centuries the factors motivating terrorists have remained largely the same: religion, nationalism, and politics. So, too, has the usual primary goal of terrorists: to make their message heard in the most public way possible. Terrorism expert Brian Jenkins put it best: "Terrorism is theater."

Yet a precise definition of terrorism remains elusive. Ask one hundred people to define terrorism and you will likely get one hundred different answers—whether you query people on the street or experts on the subject.

Is murdering a doctor who performs abortions an act of terrorism? Are Cuban exiles in Florida who help bomb Havana hotels terrorists? Are Palestinians who blow themselves up on Israeli buses terrorists? Are Israeli troops who hunt down and kill Palestinians suspected of directing the suicide bombings terrorists? Our answers to these questions are rooted in our individual backgrounds and political viewpoints, not in a universally accepted definition of terrorism.

Even the federal government cannot agree on what constitutes terrorism. Three federal statutes and regulations define terrorism—all differently:

- Terrorism is "the unlawful use of force and violence against persons or property to intimidate or coerce a government, the civilian population, or any segment thereof, in furtherance of political or social objectives," according to the federal regulation that spells out the duties of the FBI.
- Terrorism is "premeditated, politically motivated violence perpetrated against noncombatant targets by subnational groups or clandestine agents," according to a law that applies to the Department of State.
- Terrorism "means activities that involve acts dangerous to human life that are a violation of the criminal laws of the United States or of any State" and that "appear to be intended to intimidate or coerce a civilian population; to influence the policy of a government by intimidation or coercion; or to affect the conduct of a government by mass destruction, assassination or kidnapping," according to the law that defines federal crimes and criminal procedures.

Over the past thirty years the United Nations has repeatedly struggled to reach agreement on a definition of terrorism—and failed every time. UN secretary general Kofi Annan expressed his frustration only weeks after the September 11 attacks. "There can be no acceptance of those who would seek to justify the deliberate taking of innocent civilian life, regardless of cause or grievance," he said. "If there is one universal principle that all people can agree on, surely it is this."

Apparently not. In January 2002 diplomats from more than one hundred countries met at the United Nations to try to reach a consensus on what constitutes terrorism. The key issue: Should any attack targeting civilians, no matter the cause, be considered terrorism? The United States, the European Union, and many other countries said yes. Most Islamic countries said no, arguing that attacks on civilians by "national liberation movements" or as part of "resistance to foreign occupation" were justified and should not be considered terrorism. Their intent was to avoid having the terrorism label applied to attacks by Islamic terrorists against Israel and in the portion of Kashmir that is controlled by India. Neither side would yield, so the attempt to define terrorism failed once again.

The UN's effort to define terrorism is much more than an academic exercise. Without a definition, the UN cannot pass a comprehensive treaty requiring all member states to cooperate with each other in the fight against terrorism. And without a comprehensive treaty, nations have plenty of wiggle room to cooperate—or not—as they see fit on terrorism matters.

Countless papers and even small books have been devoted to the sole task of defining terrorism. For the purposes of this book, to be considered terrorism an incident must:

- involve violence or the threat of violence
- have a political motivation (broadly defined to include religious terrorists)
- target civilians, government officials, or off-duty military forces
- be committed by individuals or groups that are not part of a government, or by a government's covert agents in another country
- be designed to attract publicity and to scare a broad audience beyond the actual victims
- require planning instead of being a spur-of-the-moment act

The criteria ignore any claims by perpetrators that a particular attack is "justified" for some reason and should not be considered terrorism. In a civilized world political violence can never be justified—especially when it targets civilians.

The criteria eliminate some acts that may be considered terrorism under other definitions:

- The April 1999 shooting rampage by two seniors at Columbine High School in Littleton, Colorado, in which twelve students and a teacher were killed and twenty-three other people were wounded. The attack did not constitute terrorism because it was not politically motivated.
- Attacks by a government upon its own people. For example, the March 16, 1988, attack by Iraqi troops on the Kurdish city of Jalabja with mustard gas and other poisonous gases did not constitute terrorism, despite statements by the U.S. State Department that approximately 5,000 Iraqi civilians were killed and another 10,000 injured. Such internal attacks are more properly labeled repression, although the Jalabja attack also could be labeled genocide.
- The series of mail bombings by the so-called Unabomber. The attacks were motivated by the Unabomber's mental problems as much as anything else.
- The targeted killing by Israeli military forces of Palestinians who are suspected of directing suicide bombings against Israel. These acts may constitute anything from human rights violations to war crimes, but because a government commits them openly they are not terrorism.

Few people want to be called a terrorist, which is almost universally considered a pejorative term. Euphemisms abound: freedom fighter, guerrilla, militant, extremist, nationalist, holy warrior, revolutionary, insurgent, subversive, rebel, radical, gunman, attacker. All these words have more positive connotations than does the word "terrorist." "Freedom fighter" sounds heroic, "guerrilla" has romantic overtones, and "holy warrior" seems noble. Many of the others are so vague that they obscure the true horror of terrorism.

Euphemisms are especially popular with journalists. Some of these efforts approach absurdity. A Reuters story about the sentencing of four Palestinians convicted in the October 2001 assassination of an Israeli cabinet minister refers to the men as "four radicals." A headline on another Reuters story about a suicide bombing of a bus that killed eight Israelis says the "Hamas militant group" claimed credit. An Associated Press story about an attack in the disputed Kashmir region that killed ten civilians identifies the perpetrators as "suspected Islamic militants," "four guerrillas," "gunmen," and "suspected militants," but never once calls them terrorists.

In a few instances former terrorists have joined the mainstream and become respected political leaders. The most prominent example is Menachem Begin, who served as prime minister of Israel from 1977 to 1983. Begin's political career began in December 1943 when he took over leadership of the Irgun Zvai Luemi, a Jewish terrorist group that sought to drive the British rulers out of Palestine and create a Jewish state. "The Irgun's plan was not to defeat Britain militarily," Bruce Hoffman wrote in his book *Inside Terrorism*, "but to use terrorist violence to undermine the government's prestige and control of Palestine by striking at symbols of British rule." Their tactics ranged from bombing prominent buildings to assassinating British officials.

The most spectacular attack by the Irgun occurred in Jerusalem at the King David Hotel, which served as headquarters for British government officials and military forces. On July 22, 1946, bombs planted at the hotel by members of the Irgun exploded just after noon. The blast destroyed the hotel's south wing, killing ninety-one people and injuring forty-six. A year later the Irgun kidnapped two British sergeants after British forces captured three Irgun members. When the British executed the three terrorists, the Irgun retaliated by hanging the two sergeants. Slightly less than a year later the British left Palestine for good.

Trends in Terrorism

Terrorism today has a number of trends. Unfortunately, few of them are positive.

About the only favorable trend is that even though the level of terrorism remains high in hotspots such as the Middle East, Colombia, and Kashmir, the actual number of terrorist attacks around the world keeps declining. Yet even this bit of good news is deceiving. On the surface, it seems to indicate a decreased interest in using terrorism as a political tool. What it really indicates, though, is that terrorists are shifting their focus away from small attacks that can be arranged quickly in favor of larger, increasingly deadly efforts that require extensive planning.

Attacks are getting bigger because the nature of terrorism is changing. In the past, rogue nations such as Iraq, Iran, Libya, and Syria provided much of the financial and logistical support for international terrorist groups and for specific attacks. The best example is the December 1988 bombing of Pan Am

Flight 103 over Lockerbie, Scotland, which killed 270 people and was carried out by a Libyan agent. State sponsorship of terrorist groups and individual attacks has declined dramatically, mostly because of international pressure. Some terrorist groups that relied on state sponsorship have disappeared. Those that survived found new funding sources that lack the constraints previously imposed by state sponsors.

The rise of independent terrorist groups motivated by religious extremism, such as Osama bin Laden's al Qaeda terrorist network, also has fueled the increase in the size of terrorist attacks. Religious terrorists see themselves as holy warriors on a divine mission to rid the world of "infidels"—that is, anyone who does not share their religious beliefs. In this context, the greatest glory comes to those who kill the most people. It also clears the way for suicide attacks, because the terrorists believe they will be immediately rewarded in the afterlife.

Attacks are growing more deadly, too, because terrorists are becoming more sophisticated. They are able to make more powerful bombs that are more easily concealed, to manufacture phony passports that allow them to cross borders almost at will, to transfer money around the world that is almost impossible to trace, and to communicate across long distances with little fear of monitoring by police.

The growing sophistication of terrorists is also making them harder to capture. Groups like al Qaeda are organized in small, self-contained cells that have no contact with each other and only indirect contact with the group's leadership. This means that even if police discover a cell, the people they arrest cannot lead them to others outside their own cell.

Another disturbing trend is that the consequences of terrorist attacks, even small-scale efforts, are becoming increasingly serious beyond the immediate victims. After the December 2001 attack on India's parliament building by five terrorists believed to be from Pakistan, the two countries massed a million troops on their border and reached the brink of nuclear war. The September 11 attack triggered a war in Afghanistan by the United States, Great Britain, and allied countries that toppled the existing government; reductions in civil liberties long cherished by Americans; sharper divisions between the United States and many other countries; and serious problems for a world economy that was already teetering. In both attacks, the full consequences remain unknown because the repercussions continue.

The last trend is that governments are applying the label "terrorist" to just about anyone with whom they disagree. Governments quickly learned that if they paste the terrorist label on dissidents whose only crime is freely speaking their minds, they can crack down pretty much at will. The world will applaud their resolute action against terrorists, whereas it might have condemned the same action against people merely labeled dissidents. Likewise, governments have found that if they can somehow label an action or plan as being necessary to protect against terrorism, they can largely muzzle any opposition.

ELECTRONIC SURVEILLANCE IN DOMESTIC SECURITY CASES
June 19, 1972

The bombing of the Central Intelligence Agency's recruiting office in Ann Arbor, Michigan, on September 29, 1968, occurred amid growing concern about protecting domestic security. Within the previous year the nation had been rocked by massive protests against the Vietnam War, racial rioting, and the assassinations of Sen. Robert F. Kennedy and Martin Luther King Jr.

Federal authorities charged three members of the White Panther Party, a short-lived group formed largely to support the Black Panther Party, in the Ann Arbor bombing. Police had wiretapped the phone of one defendant. In an effort to see whether the government had illegally obtained evidence for the case, defense lawyers asked for disclosure of all information gained through the wiretap. Government attorneys refused, arguing that although no court had authorized the wiretap, it was lawful as a reasonable exercise of presidential power to protect national security. In a unanimous decision the U.S. Supreme Court disagreed, ruling that electronic surveillance without a court order violated the Fourth Amendment, which bars unreasonable searches and seizures. Justice Lewis F. Powell Jr., an appointee of President Richard Nixon with a record of previous support for wiretapping, wrote in the opinion that Fourth Amendment freedoms "cannot safely be guaranteed if domestic security surveillance may be conducted solely within the discretion of the executive branch." With the Supreme Court upholding the trial court's order to give the wiretap tapes to defense attorneys, government prosecutors dropped all charges in the case.

Ever since the Court's decision, law enforcement officers have been required to get judicial approval before placing wiretaps in domestic security cases involving American citizens and permanent resident aliens. However, Powell carefully noted in the ruling that it did not apply to "activities of foreign powers or their agents." This left the door open for Congress to pass the Foreign Intelligence Surveillance Act of 1978. It allows the president to authorize warrantless surveillance in sensitive national security cases involving citizens of foreign countries who are in the United States.

1

***Following are excerpts from the June 19, 1972, opinion of
the U.S. Supreme Court in the case of United States v. United
States District Court (407 U.S. 297):***

The issue before us is an important one for the people of our country and
their Government. It involves the delicate question of the President's power,
acting through the Attorney General, to authorize electronic surveillance in
internal security matters without prior judicial approval. Successive Presidents for more than one-quarter of a century have authorized such surveillance in varying degrees, without guidance from the Congress or a definitive
decision of this Court. This case brings the issue here for the first time. Its
resolution is a matter of national concern, requiring sensitivity both to the
Government's right to protect itself from unlawful subversion and attack and
to the citizen's right to be secure in his privacy against unreasonable Government intrusion. . . .

It is important at the outset to emphasize the limited nature of the question
before the Court. This case raises no constitutional challenge to electronic
surveillance as specifically authorized by Title III of the Omnibus Crime Control and Safe Streets Act of 1968. Nor is there any question or doubt as to the
necessity of obtaining a warrant in the surveillance of crimes unrelated to the
national security interest. Further, the instant case requires no judgment on
the scope of the President's surveillance power with respect to the activities
of foreign powers, within or without this country. The Attorney General's affi-
davit in this case states that the surveillances were "deemed necessary to protect the nation from attempts of *domestic organizations* to attack and subvert
the existing structure of Government" (emphasis supplied). There is no evidence of any involvement, directly or indirectly, of a foreign power.

Our present inquiry, though important, is therefore a narrow one. It addresses a question left open by *Katz [Katz v. United States* (1967)]: "Whether
safeguards other than prior authorization by a magistrate would satisfy the
Fourth Amendment in a situation involving the national security. . . ."

The determination of this question requires the essential Fourth Amendment inquiry into the "reasonableness" of the search and seizure in question,
and the way in which that "reasonableness" derives content and meaning
through reference to the warrant clause.

We begin the inquiry by noting that the President of the United States has
the fundamental duty, under Art. II, §1, of the Constitution, "to preserve, protect, and defend the Constitution of the United States." Implicit in that duty
is the power to protect our Government against those who would subvert or
overthrow it by unlawful means. In the discharge of this duty, the President—
through the Attorney General—may find it necessary to employ electronic
surveillance to obtain intelligence information on the plans of those who plot
unlawful acts against the Government. . . .

Though the Government and respondents debate their seriousness and
magnitude, threats and acts of sabotage against the Government exist in suffi-

cient number to justify investigative powers with respect to them. The covertness and complexity of potential unlawful conduct against the Government and the necessary dependency of many conspirators upon the telephone make electronic surveillance an effective investigatory instrument in certain circumstances. The marked acceleration in technological developments and sophistication in their use have resulted in new techniques for the planning, commission and concealment of criminal activities. It would be contrary to the public interest for Government to deny to itself the prudent and lawful employment of those very techniques which are employed against the Government and its law-abiding citizens.

It has been said that "the most basic function of any government is to provide for the security of the individual and of his property" [*Miranda v. Arizona* (1966)]. And unless Government safeguards its own capacity to function and to preserve the security of its people, society itself could become so disordered that all rights and liberties would be endangered. . . .

But a recognition of these elementary truths does not make the employment by Government of electronic surveillance a welcome development— even when employed with restraint and under judicial supervision. There is, understandably, a deep-seated uneasiness and apprehension that this capability will be used to intrude upon cherished privacy of law-abiding citizens. We look to the Bill of Rights to safeguard their privacy. Though physical entry of the home is the chief evil against which the wording of the Fourth Amendment is directed, its broader spirit now shields private speech from unreasonable surveillance. . . .

National security cases, moreover, often reflect a convergence of First and Fourth Amendment values not present in cases of "ordinary" crime. Though the investigative duty of the executive may be stronger in such cases, so also is there greater jeopardy to constitutionally protected speech. . . .History abundantly documents the tendency of Government—however benevolent and benign its motives—to view with suspicion those who most fervently dispute its policies. Fourth Amendment protections become the more necessary when the target of official surveillance may be those suspected of unorthodoxy in their political beliefs. The danger to political dissent is acute where the Government attempts to act under so vague a concept as the power to protect "domestic security." Given the difficulty of defining the domestic security interest, the danger of abuse in acting to protect that interest becomes apparent. . . . The price of lawful public dissent must not be a dread of subjection of an unchecked surveillance power. Nor must the fear of unauthorized official eavesdropping deter vigorous citizen dissent and discussion of Government action in private conversation. For private dissent, no less than open public discourse, is essential to our free society. . . .

Fourth Amendment freedoms cannot properly be guaranteed if domestic security surveillances may be conducted solely within the discretion of the executive branch. The Fourth Amendment does not contemplate the executive officers of Government as neutral and disinterested magistrates. Their duty and responsibility is to enforce the laws, to investigate and to prosecute. . . . But those charged with this investigative and prosecutorial duty should not be the sole judges of when to utilize constitutionally sensitive means in pursuing their tasks. The historical judgment, which the Fourth Amendment accepts, is that unreviewed executive discretion may yield too readily to pressures to obtain incriminating evidence and overlook potential invasions of privacy and protected speech. . . .

The independent check upon executive discretion is not satisfied, as the Government argues, by "extremely limited" post-surveillance judicial review. Indeed, post-surveillance review would never reach the surveillances which failed to result in prosecutions. Prior review by a neutral and detached magistrate is the time tested means of effectuating Fourth Amendment rights. . . .

We cannot accept the Government's argument that internal security matters are too subtle and complex for judicial evaluation. Courts regularly deal with the most difficult issues of our society. There is no reason to believe that federal judges will be insensitive to or uncomprehending of the issues involved in domestic security cases. Certainly courts can recognize that domestic security surveillance involves different considerations from the surveillance of ordinary crime. If the threat is too subtle or complex for our senior law enforcement officers to convey its significance to a court, one may question whether there is probable cause for surveillance.

Nor do we believe prior judicial approval will fracture the secrecy essential to official intelligence gathering. The investigation of criminal activity has long involved imparting sensitive information to judicial officers who have respected the confidentialities involved. Judges may be counted upon to be especially conscious of security requirements in national security cases. . . .

Thus, we conclude that the Government's concerns do not justify departure in this case from the customary Fourth Amendment requirement of judicial approval prior to initiation of a search or surveillance. Although some added burden will be imposed upon the Attorney General, this inconvenience is justified in a free society to protect constitutional values. Nor do we think the Government's domestic surveillance powers will be impaired to any significant degree. A prior warrant establishes presumptive validity of the surveillance and will minimize the burden of justification in post-surveillance judicial review. By no means of least importance will be the reassurance of the public generally that indiscriminate wiretapping and bugging of law-abiding citizens cannot occur. . . .

As of April 22, 2002, the full text of the Court's decision was available at http://www2.law.cornell.edu/cgi-bin/foliocgi.exe/historic/ query=[group+407+u!2Es!2E+297!3A]^[group+citemenu!3A]^ [level+case+citation!3A]^[group+notes!3A]/doc/{@1}/hit_headings/ words=4/hits_only?

THE "BLOODY FRIDAY" ATTACKS IN NORTHERN IRELAND
July 24, 1972

On January 30, 1972, some 10,000 people embarked on a civil rights march through the streets of Londonderry, Northern Ireland. They were protesting a decision the previous year by the British government that allowed soldiers to arrest people and jail them without trial. Some of the protesters clashed with British soldiers along the route, and the soldiers responded by opening fire on the crowd. Thirteen civilians died at the scene and another died later from his wounds. The soldiers claimed they had been fired upon, and a hasty government inquiry agreed. No evidence to support the claim was ever found, and Londonderry's coroner called the carnage "sheer unadulterated murder." The event became known as "Bloody Sunday." Within two months the British government abolished Northern Ireland's parliament and imposed direct rule from London.

The Irish Republican Army (IRA), which sought to drive the British from Northern Ireland, responded on Friday, July 21, by setting off about two dozen bombs around Belfast in just over one hour. Nine people—most of them civilians—died and 130 were wounded in the attack, which became known as "Bloody Friday." The sight of blood and mangled bodies all around the city caused public outrage. It also resulted in many people deciding that the IRA was a terrorist group instead of a legitimate political organization that should have a seat at any negotiations with the British.

Twenty years after Bloody Sunday, relatives of the dead and wounded called for a public inquiry into the shootings. British prime minister John Major, while declining their request, said that the people killed should be considered innocent of any crime. That was not enough for the relatives, who kept pressing for an inquiry. On January 29, 1998, Prime Minister Tony Blair announced that an inquiry would be conducted because there was "compelling new evidence." The main public hearings began in 2000, and the inquiry was still in progress in October 2002.

Following is a statement made July 24, 1972, by William Whitelaw, the Secretary of State for Northern Ireland, in the British House of Commons:

As the House will know, the City and people of Belfast suffered a murderous sequence of explosions last Friday. Most of the 27 explosions in Belfast that day occurred within a three-hour period in the afternoon—at a time when, and at places where high civilian casualties must have been expected and intended. No adequate warnings were given.

Seven civilians and two soldiers were killed and at least 130 civilians injured—many gravely. I hardly need point out that all sections of the community are indiscriminately affected by these outrages. Of the dead two were Roman Catholics. Of the 130 injured at least 40 were Roman Catholics. Fifty-three were men and boys, 77 women and children.

I am sure the whole House will wish to join with me in expressing sympathy to the families of all those involved in this wanton attack on innocent men, women and children.

After the appallingly bloodthirsty and criminal events of last Friday, there cannot be any remaining shred of support for the men who perpetrate them. Even those sectors of Roman Catholic opinion throughout the world which have traditionally identified themselves with and perhaps given the benefit of the doubt to any group of men who claimed to speak for the Irish Republican movement can surely no longer continue to uphold the men who were responsible for Friday's horrible catalogue of slaughter.

Supporters of the Republican movement in this country, in Northern Ireland, in the United States and elsewhere, will no doubt notice the revulsion in some circles in the Irish Republic.

Since Parliament at the end of March entrusted the Government with complete responsibility for all administration in Northern Ireland, we have made the most patient and reasoned effort to secure the end of violence.

No one can deny that Her Majesty's Government have now an absolutely unchallengeable right to ask this House, this country, and indeed the whole world for their support in an absolute determination to destroy the capacity of the IRA for further acts of inhumanity.

They have degraded the human race, and it must now be clear to all that their sole object is to promote their aims by violence and by violence alone.

Updates about the Bloody Sunday inquiry are available at its official Web site: http://www.bloody-sunday-inquiry.org.uk

MURDER OF ISRAELI ATHLETES AT THE MUNICH OLYMPIC GAMES
September 10, 1972

World attention was riveted by a hostage drama that occurred during the 1972 Olympic Games in Munich, West Germany. Just before dawn on September 5, eight members of the Palestinian group Black September stormed the Israeli quarters, killing two Israeli athletes and taking nine others hostage. The terrorists demanded that Israel release more than 200 jailed Palestinians. After a botched rescue attempt by German authorities, all the Israeli athletes were dead, as were five of the terrorists and a policeman.

Israel responded swiftly. On September 8 it launched an estimated fifty to eighty warplanes to attack ten suspected Arab guerrilla bases and naval installations deep within Syria and Lebanon. Two days later the United Nations Security Council met in emergency session to consider the Middle East situation but could not agree on a course of action. The United States, the Soviet Union, and China all vetoed various proposals. The resolution vetoed by the United States demanded that Israel end its air strikes. Ambassador George H.W. Bush, the future president who was then the U.S. representative to the UN, said the United States vetoed the resolution because it failed to include any reference to the Munich killings that had provoked the Israeli raids.

German authorities arrested the three terrorists who survived the rescue attempt in Munich. Only weeks later, though, two other Palestinian terrorists hijacked a Lufthansa flight from Beirut and demanded release of the three men. Germany complied.

Following are excerpts from the September 10, 1972, statement by Ambassador George Bush, U.S. representative to the United Nations, explaining the U.S. veto of a Security Council resolution calling for a halt to Israeli air strikes:

. . . We should all recall that until a few days ago the world had again dared to hope because a climate of reasonableness and realism seemed to be developing in the area [Middle East]. There were grounds to hope that new opportunities for progress towards peace in the Middle East were opening up before us. Then came "Munich"—the senseless act of terrorism there which cast a pall over these hopes. Yet we are now meeting on a complaint by Syria—a complaint that stands out for its unreality. It makes no reference to the tragic events at Munich. It gives no salve to the wounded conscience of an agonized world.

There is an obvious connection between the actions of which the Syrian government now complains and the tragic events which took place in Munich this past Tuesday. Did the Syrian government join in complaint or expressions of outrage when terrorists invaded the Olympic Village, in violation not only of law but of the spirit of Olympic brotherhood, and murdered innocent athletes? Did we hear even a word of condemnation from the government of Syria for this despicable act? No, quite the contrary. The Syrian government continues to harbor and to give aid and encouragement to terrorist organizations which openly champion such acts.

And the Syrian government is not alone in its encouragement of terrorism. Certain other governments in the area—whether by word or deed, or by silent acquiescence and failure to disassociate themselves from the acts of a minority that preaches and practices lawlessness and violence—cannot be absolved of responsibility for the cycle of violence and counterviolence we have again witnessed this past week. . . .

The United States will continue to work for a just and lasting peace in the Middle East. But one-sided resolutions of the type which this Council has so frequently adopted in recent times, do not contribute to the goal for peace; indeed, they create an atmosphere in no way conductive to peace by encouraging perpetrators and supporters of acts of terrorism to believe they can escape the world's censure.

Let us not put our heads in the sand and perpetrate the notion of "unreality" that is often assigned to the United Nations. Munich was so horrible, so vicious, so brutal, so detrimental to order in the world and to peace in the Middle East that we simply must not act here as if it did not exist.

We believe each member of the Council, indeed of the entire international community, should make it unmistakably clear that acts of terror and violence practiced against innocent people as a matter of policy are unacceptable in a civilized world. Each of us has a responsibility to make clear that those who practice such acts, or aid and abet them in any way, are the ones deserving of censure and condemnation. Only then will we begin to eliminate this scourge from the earth, and with it the acts of counterviolence to which history inevitably proves it gives rise. . . .

MESSAGES BY PATTY HEARST FOLLOWING HER KIDNAPPING
February 12 and April 3, 1974

The Symbionese Liberation Army (SLA) burst upon the American scene on November 7, 1973, when it claimed credit for the assassination the previous day of Marcus Foster, the superintendent of schools in Oakland, California. The SLA, a small group of black convicts and white radicals, said it killed Foster because of his supposed support for requiring all high school students to have photo ID cards. It was never clear how the slaying of Foster, a black man who was widely respected in his diverse community, fit within the group's avowed purpose of uniting downtrodden minorities.

In its short history the SLA's most notorious crime was the kidnapping of Patricia Hearst, granddaughter of the late newspaper magnate William Randolph Hearst, on February 5, 1974. In the months after the kidnapping California radio stations, newspapers, and Hearst's parents received a series of tape recordings and letters that discussed Patricia's status, conditions for her release, and her apparent conversion to SLA ideology. In an April 3 tape Hearst announced that she had "chosen to stay and fight" with the SLA for the "freedom of oppressed people." The authenticity of her decision was widely debated, but on April 15 she was photographed holding a sawed-off carbine during a San Francisco bank robbery by the SLA.

Six core SLA members died the next month in a confrontation with police, but it took the FBI until September 18, 1975, to capture Hearst and three other SLA members in San Francisco. Hearst was initially defiant, listing her occupation at her arrest as "urban guerrilla," but during her later bank robbery trial Hearst claimed that she had been brainwashed by the SLA. A jury found her guilty and sentenced her to seven years in prison, but President Jimmy Carter commuted her sentence after she served twenty-one months. In January 2002 five former SLA members were charged with killing a bank customer during a 1975 robbery. Hearst, who drove a getaway car for the heist, was not charged. On CNN's "Larry King Live" Hearst said she looked forward to testifying against the former SLA members at their upcoming trials.

Following are excerpts from two tape-recorded messages from Patricia Hearst, received February 12 and April 3, 1974:

FEBRUARY 12 MESSAGE

Mom, Dad, I'm okay. I had a few scrapes and stuff, but they washed them up and they're okay and I caught a cold, but they're giving me pills for it and stuff, I'm not being starved or beaten or unnecessarily frightened. . . .

The SLA has ideological ties with the IRA [Irish Republican Army], the people's struggle in the Philippines, and the Socialist people in Puerto Rico and their struggle for independence, and they consider themselves to be soldiers who are fighting and aiding these people.

I am a prisoner of war, and so are the two men in San Quentin.* I'm being treated in accordance with the Geneva Convention and one of the conditions being that I am not being tried for crimes which I'm not responsible for.

I'm here because I'm a member of a ruling-class family, and I think you can begin to see the analogy. The men in San Quentin are being held, and they're going to be tried simply because they are members of the SLA and not because they've done anything. Witnesses to the shooting of Foster saw black men and two white men have been arrested for that.

You're being told this so you'll understand why I was kidnapped. And so that you'll understand that whatever happens to the two prisoners is going to happen to me. You have to understand that I am held being innocent the same way that the two men in San Quentin are innocent, and they are simply members of the group and have not actually done anything themselves to warrant their arrest.

They apparently were part of an intelligence unit and never executed anyone themselves. The SLA has declared war against the government, and it's important that you understand that they know what they are doing and you understand what their actions mean and that you realize that this is not considered by them to be just a simple kidnapping, and that you don't treat it that way and say I don't know why she was taken. . . .

APRIL 3 MESSAGE

I would like to begin this statement by informing the public that I wrote what I am about to say. It's what I feel. I have never been forced to say anything on any tape. Nor have I been brainwashed, drugged, tortured, hypno-

---

Editor's note: The two were SLA members who were awaiting trial on charges of murdering Oakland School Superintendent Marcus Foster.

tized or in any way confused. As George Jackson wrote, "It's me, the way I want it, the way I see it."

Mom, Dad, I would like to comment on your efforts to supposedly secure my safety. The PIN giveaway [a Hearst food distribution program demanded by the SLA] was a sham. You attempted to deceive the people, the SLA, and me with statements about your concern for myself and the people. You were playing games—stalling for time—which the FBI was using in their attempts to assassinate me and the SLA elements which guarded me. . . .

Steven [Weed, Miss Hearst's fiancé], I know that you're beginning to realize that there is no such thing as neutrality in time of war. There can be no compromise, as your experiences with the FBI must have shown you. You have been harassed by the FBI because of your supposed connections with so-called radicals, and some people have gone so far as to suggest that I arranged my arrest. We both know what really came down that Monday night—but you don't know what's happened since then. I have changed—grown. I've become conscious and can never go back to the life we led before. What I'm saying may seem cold to you and to my old friends, but love doesn't mean the same thing to me anymore.

My love has expanded as a result of my experiences to embrace all people. It's grown into an unselfish love for my comrades here, in prison, and on the streets. A love that comes from the knowledge that "no one is free until we are all free." While I wish that you could be a comrade, I don't expect it—all I expect is that you try to understand the changes I've gone through.

I have been given the choice of (1) being released in a safe area or (2) joining the forces of the Symbionese Liberation Army and fighting for my freedom and the freedom of all oppressed people. I have chosen to stay and fight.

One thing which I learned is that the corporate ruling class will do anything in their power in order to maintain their position of control over the masses, even if this means the sacrifice of one of their own. It should be obvious that people who don't even care about their own children couldn't possibly care about anyone else's children. The things which are precious to these people are their money and power—and they will never willingly surrender either. People should not have to humiliate themselves by standing in lines in order to be fed, nor should they have to live in fear for their lives and the lives of their children. . . .

Dad, you said that you were concerned with my life, and you also said that you were concerned with the life and interests of all oppressed people in this country, but you are a liar in both areas and as a member of the ruling class I know for sure that yours and Mom's interests are never the interests of the people. Dad, you said you would see about getting more job opportunities for the people, but why haven't you warned the people what is to happen to them—that actually the few jobs they still have will be taken away.

You, a corporate liar, of course will say that you don't know what I am talking about, but I ask you then to prove it, tell the poor and oppressed people of this nation what the corporate state is about to do, warn black and poor people that they are about to be murdered down to the last man, woman, and child. If you're so interested in the people, why don't you tell them what the

11

energy crisis really is. Tell them how it's nothing more than a manufactured strategy, a way of hiding industry's real intentions. Tell the people that the energy crisis is no more than a means to get public approval for a massive program to build nuclear power plants all over this nation.

Tell the people that the entire corporate state is, with the aid of this massive power supply, about to totally automate that entire industrial state, to the point that in the next five years all that will be needed will be a small class of button pushers. Tell the people, Dad, that all of the lower class and at least half of the middle class will be unemployed in the next three years, and that the removal of expendable excess, the removal of unneeded people has already started. I want you to tell the people the truth. Tell them how the law and order programs are just a means to remove so-called violent (meaning aware) individuals from the community in order to facilitate the controlled removal of unneeded labor force from this country, in the same way that Hitler controlled the removal of the Jews from Germany.

I should have known that if you and the rest of the corporate state were willing to do this to millions of people to maintain power, and to serve your needs you would also kill me if necessary to serve these same needs. How long will it take before white people in this country understand that what happens to a black child must sooner or later happen to a white child? How long will it take before we all understand that we must fight for our freedom?

I have been given the name of Tania after a comrade who fought alongside Che [Guevara] in Bolivia for the people of Bolivia. I embrace the name with the determination to continue fighting with her spirit. . . .

ARAFAT'S SPEECH BEFORE THE UN GENERAL ASSEMBLY
November 13, 1974

Despite his leadership of groups that had carried out numerous terrorist attacks against Israel, on October 14, 1974, the United Nations General Assembly invited Yasir Arafat, leader of the Palestine Liberation Organization (PLO), to address it during an upcoming meeting about the question of Palestine. The invitation was a historic departure from United Nations tradition, since Arafat represented no government. The Israeli delegate denounced the invitation, calling it virtual capitulation "to a murder organization which aims at the destruction of a state member of the United Nations."

During his speech on November 13, where he was accorded the privileges of a head of state, Arafat called for dissolution of the state of Israel and its replacement by a new Palestinian state comprised of Muslims, Christians, and Jews. "When we speak of our common hopes for the Palestine of tomorrow," Arafat said, "we include in our perspective all Jews now living in Palestine who choose to live with us there in peace and without discrimination." At the end of the speech he made a statement that seemed a combination plea and warning: "Today I have come bearing an olive branch and a freedom fighter's gun," Arafat said. "Do not let the olive branch fall from my hand."

Arafat's speech appeared to deliver a setback to Secretary of State Henry A. Kissinger's efforts to bring the Middle East parties to a settlement on the long-standing disputes over territory. Stirred by the PLO leader's remarks, Palestinians demonstrated in Israel. Palestinian groups also staged several terrorist raids, and Israel retaliated with raids of its own. Nonetheless, less than ten days after Arafat's speech, the UN General Assembly passed a resolution in which it reaffirmed "the inalienable right of the Palestinians to return to their homes and property from which they have been displaced and uprooted. . . ." In a separate resolution passed the same day, the General Assembly granted the PLO observer status for all of its future meetings.

*Following are excerpts from the speech by Yasir Arafat de-
livered November 13, 1974, before the United Nations General Assembly:*

. . . This is a very important occasion. The question of Palestine is being re-
examined by the United Nations, and we consider that step to be a victory for
the world Organization as much as a victory for the cause of our people. It indicates anew that the United Nations of today is not the United Nations of the
past, just as today's world is not yesterday's world. Today's United Nations
represents 138 nations, a number that more clearly reflects the will of the international community. Thus today's United Nations is more nearly capable of
implementing the principles embodied in its Charter and in the Universal Declaration of Human Rights, as well as being more truly empowered to support
causes of peace and justice. . . .

The roots of the Palestinian question reach back into the closing years of
the 19th century, in other words, to that period which we call the era of colo-
nialism and settlement as we know it today. This is precisely the period during which Zionism as a scheme was born. Its aim was the conquest of Palestine
by European immigrants, just as settlers colonized, and indeed raided, most
of Africa. This is the period during which, pouring forth out of the west, colo-
nialism spread into the furthest reaches of Africa, Asia, and Latin America,
building colonies, everywhere cruelly exploiting, oppressing, plundering the
peoples of those three continents. . . .

As a result of the collusion between the mandatory Power [Great Britain]
and the Zionist movement and with the support of some countries, this General Assembly early in its history approved a recommendation to partition our
Palestinian homeland. This took place in an atmosphere poisoned with questionable actions and strong pressure. The General Assembly partitioned what
it had no right to divide—an indivisible homeland. When we rejected that decision, our position corresponded to that of the natural mother who refused
to permit King Solomon to cut her son in two when the unnatural mother
claimed the child for herself and agreed to his dismemberment. Furthermore,
even though the partition resolution granted the colonialist settlers 54 percent of the land of Palestine, their dissatisfaction with the decision prompted
them to wage a war of terror against the civilian Arab population. They occupied 81 per cent of the total area of Palestine, uprooting a million Arabs. Thus
they occupied 524 Arab towns and villages, of which they destroyed 385, completely obliterating them in the process. Having done so, they built their own
settlements and colonies on the ruins of our farms and our groves. The roots
of the Palestine question lie here. Its causes do not stem from any conflict
between two religions or two nationalisms. Neither is it a border conflict between neighboring states. It is the cause of people deprived of its homeland,
dispersed and uprooted, and living mostly in exile and in refugee camps. . . .

It pains our people greatly to witness the propagation of the myth that its
homeland was a desert until it was made to bloom by the toil of foreign set-

tlers, that it was a land without a people, and that the colonialist entity caused no harm to any human being. No: such lies must be exposed from this rostrum, for the world must know that Palestine was the cradle of the most ancient cultures and civilizations. Its Arab people were engaged in farming and building, spreading culture throughout the land for thousands of years, setting an example in the practice of freedom of worship, acting as faithful guardians of the holy places of all religions. . . .

If the immigration of Jews to Palestine had had as its objective the goal of enabling them to live side by side with us, enjoying the same rights and assuming the same duties, we would have opened our doors to them, as far as our homeland's capacity for absorption permitted. Such was the case with the thousands of Armenians and Circassians who still live among us in equality as brethren and citizens. But that the goal of this immigration should be to usurp our homeland, disperse our people, and turn us into second-class citizens— this is what no one can conceivably demand that we acquiesce in or submit to. Therefore, since its inception, our revolution has not been motivated by racial or religious factors. Its target has never been the Jew, as a person, but racist Zionism and undisguised aggression. In this sense, ours is also a revolution for the Jew, as a human being, as well. We are struggling so that Jews, Christians, and Muslims may live in equality, enjoying the same rights and assuming the same duties, free from racial or religious discrimination. . . .

Those who call us terrorists wish to prevent world public opinion from discovering the truth about us and from seeing the justice on our faces. They seek to hide the terrorism and tyranny of their acts, and our own posture of self defense.

The difference between the revolutionary and the terrorist lies in the reason for which each fights. For whoever stands by a just cause and fights for the freedom and liberation of his land from the invaders, the settlers, and the colonialists cannot possibly be called terrorist, otherwise the American people in their struggle for liberation from the British colonialists would have been terrorists, the European resistance against the Nazis would be terrorism, the struggle of the Asian, African, and Latin American peoples would also be terrorism, and many of you who are in this Assembly hall were considered terrorists. This is actually a just and proper struggle consecrated by the United Nations Charter and by the Universal Declaration of Human Rights. As to those who fight against the just causes, those who wage war to occupy, colonize, and oppress other people, those are the terrorists. Those are the people whose actions should be condemned, who should be called war criminals: for the justice of the cause determines the right to struggle.

Zionist terrorism which was waged against the Palestinian people to evict it from its country and usurp its land is registered in our official documents. Thousands of our people were assassinated in their villages and towns, tens of thousands of others were forced at gunpoint to leave their homes and the lands of their fathers. Time and time again our children, women, and aged were evicted and had to wander in the deserts and climb mountains without any food or water. No one who in 1948 witnessed the catastrophe that befell the inhabitants of hundreds of villages and towns—in Jerusalem, Jaffa, Lydda,

15

Ramle, and Galilee—no one who has been a witness to that catastrophe will ever forget the experience, even though the mass blackout has succeeded in hiding these horrors as it has hidden the traces of 385 Palestinian villages and towns destroyed at the time and erased from the map. The destruction of 19,000 houses during the past seven years, which is equivalent to the complete destruction of 200 more Palestinian villages, and the great number of maimed as a result of the treatment they were subjected to in Israeli prisons, cannot be hidden by any blackout. . . .

Need one remind this Assembly of the numerous resolutions adopted by it condemning Israeli aggressions committed against Arab countries, Israeli violations of human rights, and the articles of the Geneva Conventions, as well as the resolutions pertaining to the annexation of the city of Jerusalem and its restoration to its former status?

The only description for these acts is that they are acts of barbarism and terrorism. And yet, the Zionist racists and colonialists have the temerity to describe the just struggle of our people as terror. Could there be a more flagrant distortion of truth than this? . . .

I am a rebel and freedom is my cause. I know well that many of you present here today once stood in exactly the same resistance position as I now occupy and from which I must fight. You once had to convert dreams into reality by your struggle. Therefore you must now share my dream. . . .

In my formal capacity as Chairman of the Palestine Liberation Organization and leader of the Palestinian revolution I appeal to you to accompany our people in its struggle to attain its right to self-determination. This right is consecrated in the United Nations Charter and has been repeatedly confirmed in resolutions adopted by this august body since the drafting of the Charter. I appeal to you, further, to aid our people's return to its homeland from an involuntary exile imposed upon it by force of arms, by tyranny, by oppression, so that we may regain our property, our land, and thereafter live in our national homeland, free and sovereign, enjoying all the privileges of nationhood. Only then can we pour all our resources into the mainstream of human civilization. Only then can Palestinian creativity be concentrated on the service of humanity. Only then will our Jerusalem resume its historic role as a peaceful shrine for all religions.

I appeal to you to enable our people to establish national independent sovereignty over its own land.

Today I have come bearing an olive branch and a freedom fighter's gun. Do not let the olive branch fall from my hand. I repeat: Do not let the olive branch fall from my hand. . . .

ROCKEFELLER REPORT ON THE CIA'S DOMESTIC ACTIVITIES
June 10, 1975

The banner headline on the front page of the New York Times *on December 22, 1975, was startling: "Huge CIA Operation Reported in U.S. Against Antiwar Forces, Other Dissidents in Nixon Years." In the story, Pulitzer prize-winning reporter Seymour Hersh wrote that the Central Intelligence Agency had amassed files on American citizens and engaged in illegal "break-ins, wiretapping and surreptitious interception of mail" that far exceeded its statutory authority. These charges, along with subsequent revelations, prompted a series of unprecedented government investigations into the entire U.S. intelligence community. Each probe devoted a major part of its efforts to examining whether intelligence agencies violated the rights of Americans while investigating everything from terrorism to antiwar protests.*

The first official report came June 10, 1975, with release of the findings from a presidential commission chaired by Vice President Nelson A. Rockefeller. The Rockefeller panel found that certain domestic activities of the CIA were "plainly unlawful and improper invasions of the rights of Americans." But it concluded that the "great majority" of the agency's domestic activities complied with provisions of the 1947 act creating the CIA. Although the commission confirmed to a large extent the newspaper accounts of domestic improprieties, it considered such abuses to be lapses in judgment rather than indicative of a coordinated domestic program.

On February 18, 1976, President Gerald Ford issued an executive order, based partly on recommendations in the Rockefeller report, that restructured the federal government's foreign intelligence operations and established an oversight board to prevent illegal or improper activities by intelligence agencies within the United States. However, the Rockefeller report and Ford's order were quickly overshadowed by congressional investigations of U.S. intelligence agencies. (Intelligence Activities and the Rights of Americans, p. 22)

17

Following are excerpts from the report released publicly June 10, 1975, by the Commission on CIA Activities Within the United States:

Chapter 1: The Fundamental Issues

In announcing the formation of this Commission, the President noted that an effective intelligence and counterintelligence capability is essential to provide "the safeguards that protect our national interest and help avert armed conflicts."

While it is vital that security requirements be met, the President continued, it is equally important that intelligence activities be conducted without "impairing our democratic institutions and fundamental freedoms."

The Commission's assessment of the CIA's activities within the United States reflects the members' deep concern for both individual rights and national security.

A. Individual Rights

The Bill of Rights in the Constitution protects individual liberties against encroachment by government. Many statutes and the common law also reflect this protection.

The First Amendment protects the freedoms of speech and of the press, the right of the people to assemble peaceably, and the right to petition the government for redress of grievances. It has been construed to protect freedom of peaceable political association. In addition, the Fourth Amendment declares:

> The right of the people to be secure in their persons, houses, papers, and effects, against unreasonable searches and seizures, shall not be violated.

In accordance with the objectives enunciated in these and other Constitutional amendments, the Supreme Court has outlined the following basic Constitutional doctrines:

1. Any intrusive investigation of an American citizen by the government must have a sufficient basis to warrant the invasion caused by the particular investigative practices which are utilized;
2. Government monitoring of a citizen's political activities requires even greater justification;
3. The scope of any resulting intrusion on personal privacy must not exceed the degree reasonably believed necessary;
4. With certain exceptions, the scope of which are not sharply defined, these conditions must be met, at least for significant investigative intrusions, to the satisfaction of an uninvolved governmental body such as a court.

These Constitutional standards give content to an accepted principle of our society—the right of each person to a high degree of individual privacy.

In recognition of this right, President Truman and the Congress—in enacting the law creating the CIA in 1947—included a clause providing that the CIA should have no police, subpoena, law-enforcement powers or internal security functions.

Since then, Congress has further outlined citizen rights in statutes limiting electronic surveillance and granting individuals access to certain information in government files, underscoring the general concern of Congress and the Executive Branch in this area. . . .

Chapter 3: Summary of Findings, Conclusions, and Recommendations

As directed by the President, the Commission has investigated the role and authority of the CIA, the adequacy of the internal controls and external supervision of the Agency, and its significant domestic activities that raise questions of compliance with the limits on its statutory authority. This chapter summarizes the findings and conclusions of the Commission and sets forth its recommendations.

A. Summary of Charges and Findings

The initial public charges were that the CIA's domestic activities had involved:

1. Large-scale spying on American citizens in the United States by the CIA, whose responsibility is foreign intelligence.
2. Keeping dossiers on large numbers of American citizens.
3. Aiming these activities at Americans who have expressed their disagreement with various government policies.

These initial charges were subsequently supplemented by others including allegations that the CIA:

- Had intercepted and opened personal mail in the United States for 20 years;
- Had infiltrated domestic dissident groups and otherwise intervened in domestic politics;
- Had engaged in illegal wiretaps and break-ins; and,
- Had improperly assisted other government agencies.

In addition, assertions have been made ostensibly linking the CIA to the assassination of President John F. Kennedy.

It became clear from the public reaction to these charges that the secrecy in which the Agency necessarily operates, combined with the allegations of wrongdoing, had contributed to widespread public misunderstanding of the Agency's actual practices.

A detailed analysis of the facts has convinced the Commission that the great majority of the CIA's domestic activities comply with its statutory authority.

Nevertheless, over the 28 years of its history, the CIA has engaged in some activities that should be criticized and not permitted to happen again—both in light of the limits imposed on the Agency by law and as a matter of public policy.

Some of these activities were initiated or ordered by Presidents, either directly or indirectly.

Some of them fall within the doubtful area between responsibilities delegated to the CIA by Congress and the National Security Council on the one hand and activities specifically prohibited to the Agency on the other.

Some of them were plainly unlawful and constituted improper invasions upon the rights of Americans.

The Agency's own recent actions, undertaken for the most part in 1973 and 1974, have gone far to terminate the activities upon which this investigation has focused. The recommendations of the Commission are designed to clarify areas of doubt concerning the Agency's authority, to strengthen the Agency's structure, and to guard against recurrences of these improprieties.

B. The CIA's Role and Authority

The Central Intelligence Agency was established by the National Security Act of 1947 as the nation's first comprehensive peacetime foreign intelligence service. The objective was to provide the President with coordinated intelligence, which the country lacked prior to the attack on Pearl Harbor.

The Director of Central Intelligence reports directly to the President. The CIA receives its policy direction and guidance from the National Security Council, composed of the President, the Vice President, and the Secretaries of State and Defense.

The statute directs the CIA to correlate, evaluate, and disseminate intelligence obtained from United States intelligence agencies, and to perform such other functions related to intelligence as the National Security Council directs. Recognizing that the CIA would be dealing with sensitive, secret materials, Congress made the Director of Central Intelligence responsible for protecting intelligence sources and methods from unauthorized disclosure.

At the same time, Congress sought to assure the American public that it was not establishing a secret police which would threaten the civil liberties of Americans. It specifically forbade the CIA from exercising "police, subpoena, or law-enforcement powers or internal security functions." The CIA was not to replace the Federal Bureau of Investigation in conducting domestic activities to investigate crime or internal subversion.

Although Congress contemplated that the focus of the CIA would be on foreign intelligence, it understood that some of its activities would be conducted within the United States. The CIA necessarily maintains its headquarters here, procures logistical support, recruits and trains employees, tests equipment, and conducts other domestic activities in support of its foreign intelligence mission. It makes necessary investigations in the United States to maintain the security of its facilities and personnel.

Additionally, it has been understood from the beginning that the CIA is permitted to collect foreign intelligence—that is, information concerning foreign capabilities, intentions, and activities—from American citizens within this country by overt means.

Determining the legal propriety of domestic activities of the CIA requires the application of the law to the particular facts involved. This task involves consideration of more than the National Security Act and the directives of the National Security Council; Constitutional and other statutory provisions also circumscribe the domestic activities of the CIA. Among the applicable Constitutional provisions are the First Amendment, protecting freedom of speech, of the press, and of peaceable assembly and the Fourth Amendment, prohibiting unreasonable searches and seizures. Among the statutory provisions are those which limit such activities as electronic eavesdropping and interception of the mails.

The precise scope of many of these statutory and Constitutional provisions is not easily stated. The National Security Act in particular was drafted in broad terms in order to provide flexibility for the CIA to adapt to changing intelligence needs. Such critical phrases as "internal security functions" are left undefined. The meaning of the Director's responsibility to protect intelligence sources and methods from unauthorized disclosure has also been a subject of uncertainty.

The word "foreign" appears nowhere in the statutory grant of authority, though it has always been understood that the CIA's mission is limited to matters related to foreign intelligence. This apparent statutory ambiguity, although not posing problems in practice, has troubled members of the public who read the statute without having the benefit of the legislative history and the instructions to the CIA from the National Security Council.

The evidence within the scope of this inquiry does not indicate that fundamental rewriting of the National Security Act is either necessary or appropriate.

The evidence does demonstrate the need for some statutory and administrative clarification of the role and function of the Agency.

Ambiguities have been partially responsible for some, though not all, of the Agency's deviations within the United States from its assigned mission. In some cases, reasonable persons will differ as to the lawfulness of the activity; in others, the absence of clear guidelines as to its authority deprived the Agency of a means of resisting pressures to engage in activities which now appear to us improper.

Greater public awareness of the limits of the CIA's domestic authority would do much to reassure the American people.

The requisite clarification can best be accomplished (a) through a specific amendment clarifying the National Security Act provision which delineates the permissible scope of CIA activities, as set forth in Recommendation 1, and (b) through issuance of an Executive Order further limiting domestic activities of the CIA, as set forth in Recommendation 2. . . .

As of June 3, 2002, the full text of the Rockefeller report was available at http://www.aarclibrary.org/publib/church/rockcomm/ contents.htm

INTELLIGENCE ACTIVITIES AND THE RIGHTS OF AMERICANS
April 26, 1976

During a fifteen-month investigation prompted by newspaper revelations of widespread abuses by American intelligence agencies, the Senate Select Committee to Study Governmental Operations with Respect to Intelligence Activities issued more than a dozen reports. One of the last—and most important—reports examined violations of the constitutional rights of Americans by intelligence agencies such as the Central Intelligence Agency, the Federal Bureau of Investigation, and the Defense Intelligence Agency, among others. A presidential commission had earlier examined domestic abuses by the CIA, but the Senate committee had a much broader mandate to investigate the more than five dozen federal intelligence and law enforcement agencies then in existence. (Rockefeller Report on the CIA's Domestic Activities, p. 17)

The Senate committee, known as the Church committee because Senator Frank Church (D-Idaho) chaired it, found a wide range of abuses in domestic intelligence activities that were conducted in the name of protecting national security. These included creating files on thousands of individuals and groups that had done nothing but dissent from government policies, conducting illegal wiretaps and break-ins, and undertaking covert actions to disrupt groups that were engaged in First Amendment activities. "We have seen segments of our Government, in their attitudes and action, adopt tactics unworthy of a democracy, and occasionally reminiscent of the tactics of totalitarian regimes," the committee said. "We have seen a consistent pattern in which programs initiated with limited goals, such as preventing criminal violence or identifying foreign spies, were expanded to what witnesses characterized as 'vacuum cleaners,' sweeping in information about lawful activities of American citizens." Less than a month after the committee issued its last report, the Senate followed its recommendation and created a permanent committee to oversee intelligence activities.

The 1976 Church report's warnings about abuses in domestic intelligence investigations took on new relevance a decade later when it was revealed that the Federal Bureau of Investigation had violated the rights of

Americans when it investigated the Committee in Solidarity with the People of El Salvador. And when Attorney General John Ashcroft in 2002 relaxed restrictions on domestic spying by the FBI in counterterrorism cases, opponents cited the warnings in the Church report. (FBI Admits Terrorism Probe Violated First Amendment, p. 107; FBI Gets Expanded Authority to Monitor Americans, p. 421)

> ***Following are excerpts from the Conclusions and Recommendations section of "Intelligence Activities and the Rights of Americans," a report released April 26, 1976, by the U.S. Senate Select Committee to Study Governmental Operations with Respect to Intelligence Activities:***

The findings which have emerged from our investigation convince us that the Government's domestic intelligence policies and practices require fundamental reform. We have attempted to set out the basic facts; now it is time for Congress to turn its attention to legislating restraints upon intelligence activities which may endanger the constitutional rights of Americans.

The Committee's fundamental conclusion is that intelligence activities have undermined the constitutional rights of citizens and that they have done so primarily because checks and balances designed by the framers of the Constitution to assure accountability have not been applied.

Before examining that conclusion, we make the following observations.

—While nearly all of our findings focus on excesses and things that went wrong, we do not question the need for lawful domestic intelligence. We recognize that certain intelligence activities serve perfectly proper and clearly necessary ends of government. Surely, catching spies and stopping crime, including acts of terrorism, is essential to insure "domestic tranquility" and to "provide for the common defense." Therefore, the power of government to conduct *proper* domestic intelligence activities under effective restraints and controls must be preserved.

—We are aware that the few earlier efforts to limit domestic intelligence activities have proven ineffectual. This pattern reinforces the need for statutory restraints coupled with much more effective oversight from all branches of the Government.

—The crescendo of improper intelligence activity in the latter part of the 1960s and the early 1970s shows what we must watch out for: In time of crisis, the Government will exercise its power to conduct domestic intelligence activities to the fullest extent. The distinction between legal dissent and criminal conduct is easily forgotten. Our job is to recommend means to help ensure that the distinction will always be observed.

—In an era where the technological capability of Government relentlessly increases, we must be wary about the drift toward "big brother government." The potential for abuse is awesome and requires special attention to

23

fashioning restraints which not only cure past problems but anticipate and prevent the future misuse of technology.

—We cannot dismiss what we have found as isolated acts which were limited in time and confined to a few willful men. The failures to obey the law and, in the words of the oath of office, to "preserve, protect, and defend" the Constitution, have occurred repeatedly throughout administrations of both political parties going back four decades.

—We must acknowledge that the assignment which the Government has given to the intelligence community has, in many ways, been impossible to fulfill. It has been expected to predict or prevent every crisis, respond immediately with information on any question, act to meet all threats, and anticipate the special needs of Presidents. And then it is chastised for its zeal. Certainly, a fair assessment must place a major part of the blame upon the failures of senior executive officials and Congress.

In the final analysis, however, the purpose of this Committee's work is not to allocate blame among individuals. Indeed, to focus on personal culpability may divert attention from the underlying institutional causes and thus may become an excuse for inaction.

Before this investigation, domestic intelligence had never been systematically surveyed. For the first time, the Government's domestic surveillance programs, as they have developed over the past forty years, can be measured against the values which our Constitution seeks to preserve and protect. Based upon our full record . . . the Committee concludes that:

> *Domestic Intelligence Activity Has Threatened and Undermined The Constitutional Rights of Americans to Free Speech, Association and Privacy. It Has Done So Primarily Because The Constitutional System for Checking Abuse of Power Has Not Been Applied.*

Our findings and the detailed reports which supplement this volume set forth a massive record of intelligence abuses over the years. Through a vast network of informants, and through the uncontrolled or illegal use of intrusive techniques—ranging from simple theft to sophisticated electronic surveillance—the Government has collected, and then used improperly, huge amounts of information about the private lives, political beliefs and associations of numerous Americans.

Affect Upon Constitutional Rights—That these abuses have adversely affected the constitutional rights of particular Americans is beyond question. But we believe the harm extends far beyond the citizens directly affected.

Personal privacy is protected because it is essential to liberty and the pursuit of happiness. Our Constitution checks the power of Government for the purpose of protecting the rights of individuals, in order that all our citizens may live in a free and decent society. Unlike totalitarian states, we do not believe that any government has a monopoly on truth.

When Government infringes those rights instead of nurturing and protecting them, the injury spreads far beyond the particular citizens targeted to untold numbers of other Americans who may be intimidated.

Free government depends upon the ability of all its citizens to speak their minds without fear of official sanction. The ability of ordinary people to be heard by their leaders means that they must be free to join in groups in order more effectively to express their grievances. Constitutional safeguards are needed to protect the timid as well as the courageous, the weak as well as the strong. While many Americans have been willing to assert their beliefs in the face of possible governmental reprisals, no citizen should have to weigh his or her desire to express an opinion, or join a group, against the risk of having lawful speech or association used against him.

Persons most intimidated may well not be those at the extremes of the political spectrum, but rather those nearer the middle. Yet voices of moderation are vital to balance public debate and avoid polarization of our society.

The federal government has recently been looked to for answers to nearly every problem. The result has been a vast centralization of power. Such power can be turned against the rights of the people. Many of the restraints imposed by the Constitution were designed to guard against such use of power by the government.

Since the end of World War II, governmental power has been increasingly exercised through a proliferation of federal intelligence programs. The very size of this intelligence system multiplies the opportunities for misuse.

Exposure of the excesses of this huge structure has been necessary. Americans are now aware of the capability and proven willingness of their Government to collect intelligence about their lawful activities and associations. What some suspected and others feared has turned out to be largely true— vigorous expression of unpopular views, association with dissenting groups, participation in peaceful protest activities, have provoked both government surveillance and retaliation.

Over twenty years ago, Supreme Court Justice Robert Jackson, previously an Attorney General, warned against growth of a centralized power of investigation. Without clear limits, a federal investigative agency would "have enough on enough people" so that "even if it does not elect to prosecute them" the Government would, he wrote, still "find no opposition to its policies." Jackson added, "Even those who are supposed to supervise [intelligence agencies] are likely to fear [them]." His advice speaks directly to our responsibilities today:

> I believe that the safeguard of our liberty lies in limiting any national police or investigative organization, first of all to a small number of strictly federal offenses, and secondly to nonpolitical ones. The fact that we may have confidence in the administration of a federal investigative agency under its existing head does not mean that it may not revert again to the days when the Department of Justice was headed by men to whom the investigative power was a weapon to be used for their own purposes.

Failure to Apply Checks and Balances—The natural tendency of Government is toward abuse of power. Men entrusted with power, even those aware of its dangers, tend, particularly when pressured, to slight liberty.

Our constitutional system guards against this tendency. It establishes many different checks upon power. It is those wise restraints which keep men free. In the field of intelligence those restraints have too often been ignored.

The three main departures in the intelligence field from the constitutional plan for controlling abuse of power have been:

(a) *Excessive Executive Power*—In a sense the growth of domestic intelligence activities mirrored the growth of presidential power generally. But more than any other activity, more even than exercise of the war power, intelligence activities have been left to the control of the Executive.

For decades Congress and the courts as well as the press and the public have accepted the notion that the control of intelligence activities was the exclusive prerogative of the Chief Executive and his surrogates. The exercise of this power was not questioned or even inquired into by outsiders. Indeed, at times the power was seen as flowing not from the law, but as inherent in the Presidency. Whatever the theory, the fact was that intelligence activities were essentially exempted from the normal system of checks and balances.

Such Executive power, not founded in law or checked by Congress or the courts, contained the seeds of abuse and its growth was to be expected.

(b) *Excessive Secrecy*—Abuse thrives on secrecy. Obviously, public disclosure of matters such as the names of intelligence agents or the technological details of collection methods is inappropriate. But in the field of intelligence, secrecy has been extended to inhibit review of the basic programs and practices themselves.

Those within the Executive branch and the Congress who would exercise their responsibilities wisely must be fully informed. The American public, as well, should know enough about intelligence activities to be able to apply its good sense to the underlying issues of policy and morality.

Knowledge is the key to control. Secrecy should no longer be allowed to shield the existence of constitutional, legal and moral problems from the scrutiny of all three branches of government or from the American people themselves.

(c) *Avoidance of the Rule of Law*—Lawlessness by Government breeds corrosive cynicism among the people and erodes the trust upon which government depends.

Here, there is no sovereign who stands above the law. Each of us, from presidents to the most disadvantaged citizen, must obey the law.

As intelligence operations developed, however, rationalizations were fashioned to immunize them from the restraints of the Bill of Rights and the specific prohibitions of the criminal code. The experience of our investigation leads us to conclude that such rationalizations are a dangerous delusion. . . .

As of June 3, 2002, the full texts of all of the Church committee's reports were available at http://www.aarclibrary.org/publib/church/reports/contents.htm

ISRAELI PRIME MINISTER RABIN ON THE ENTEBBE AIRPORT RAID
July 4, 1976

Shortly after an Air France plane resumed its flight from Tel Aviv to Paris after a stopover in Athens, Greece, on June 27, 1976, four members of the Popular Front for the Liberation of Palestine hijacked the plane. They eventually ordered the plane, which carried 246 passengers, to land at Entebbe Airport in Uganda. The hijackers said they would blow up the plane and kill the passengers unless Israel and four other countries released convicted Palestinian and pro-Palestinian terrorists held in their prisons. Three of the countries—Germany, Switzerland, and France—emphatically rejected the hijackers' demands. The situation was complicated by the apparent cooperation of Uganda's military with the hijackers.

The hijackers released two groups of captives over the next several days but kept all the Israelis and Jews as hostages. That left about 100 hostages being held in the airport's terminal building. Israel's military had been preparing for a possible rescue almost since the moment the plane had been hijacked. In the middle of the night on July 3, four transport planes filled with Israeli commandos swooped down on the Ugandan airport. In a daring operation based on the element of surprise, commandos from the first plane stormed the terminal while commandos from the other planes secured the area. All the terrorists were killed by gunfire, as were three hostages and a commando leader. The Israeli troops shepherded the remaining hostages aboard the transport planes for the trip back to Tel Aviv. From landing to takeoff, the entire raid lasted just fifty-eight minutes.

The raid was a spectacular success, and further cemented Israel's 1969 policy of refusal to negotiate with terrorists. On July 4, amidst national rejoicing, Israeli prime minister Yitzhak Rabin lauded the commandos' bold counterattack against international terrorism in a speech delivered before a specially convened session of the Israeli parliament.

Following is Israeli prime minister Yitzhak Rabin's speech before the Israeli parliament on July 4, 1976:

In a bold, skillful, and resourceful operation the Israel Defence Forces carried out the decision of the government of Israel to rescue and liberate from captivity the passengers of the Air France plane, who were hijacked by Palestinian terrorists and kept prisoner in Uganda in danger of their lives. In the course of the rescue three of the Israeli passengers of the plane were killed and one officer fell in the fight.

The decision to undertake this rescue operation was taken by the government of Israel, and on its sole responsibility. We did not consult any other government in advance, nor shall we lay responsibility on any other country or government.

Anti-Israel terrorism has become a matter of international significance and we do not exempt any government from the duty to fight for the eradication of terrorism—but above all, we shall persist in this struggle, even alone.

An Air France plane that left from Israel en route to France was hijacked a week ago after a stopover in Athens. The hijackers forced the French pilots to land first at Benghazi, in Libya, and afterwards at the Entebbe Airport in Uganda.

The Government of Israel took all possible measures while urging on the government of the other countries whose citizens were in the plane to save the hijacked passengers.

Since the hijacked plane belonged to the French national airline, it was natural to regard the French government as bearing the immediate principal responsibility to do everything required for the release of all the passengers. We got in touch immediately with the French government, which accepted this responsibility. In addition, we approached other governments and institutions to do their utmost to ensure that no harm befell the hijacked passengers and to expedite their release. The terrorists transmitted their ultimative demands to the governments of Israel, France, Germany, Kenya and Switzerland—but it became clearer and clearer that the attack against the Israeli and Jewish passengers was the principal objective of the operation. The demands were accompanied by the threat that the hijacked passengers would be killed if the governments did not carry out the terrorists' demands for the freeing of murderers, terrorists, and accessories to terrorism who had been apprehended and imprisoned for their crimes.

Self defence against the attacks of the terrorist organizations and the war against the terrorists within our own borders and abroad, in complex and unusual circumstances and by various methods, have been part of our daily bread for years. When the terrorist organizations found themselves unable to operate on our territory they tried to attack us on foreign soil, and under conditions that placed inestimable difficulties in the way of protection, rescue, and reaction. There are cases where the terrorist organizations operate against us in countries where we enjoy the cooperation of the authorities, but the operational conditions are particularly difficult for us in countries where we have no access because of hostility, the absence of diplomatic relations, or even governmental cooperation with the Palestinian terrorist organizations. On more than one occasion, we have found ourselves faced with appalling dilemmas, each alternative being more difficult than the other, with our dear ones held captive far away, isolated, and without any possibility of our speeding aid or acting for their release.

In the hijacking of the Air France plane to Entebbe, all indications showed that the President of Uganda cooperated with the terrorists, under a cloak of deception and false pretences. This was the situation on the eve of 1 July 1976: the time of expiration of the ultimatum drew increasingly closer. The release of non-Israeli passengers more and more exposed the evil conspiracy against Israeli citizens. The political efforts bore no fruit. The sand in the hourglass was about to run out, leaving no possibility for an independent rescue effort. Under these conditions, the government of Israel decided unanimously to take the only way left to rescue our people and to declare its readiness to release terrorists detained in Israeli prisons. Following the cabinet's decision we accordingly informed the French government, through which the negotiations were being conducted with the terrorists. We were prepared to adopt even this alternative—in default of any other—to rescue our people.

This was not a tactic to gain time and had this choice alone been left—we would have stood by our decision, as a last resort.

Throughout the entire time since the capture of the plane we sought ways and means to foil the terrorists' scheme by our own means. The I.D.F. [Israel Defense Forces] and the intelligence services did not lose a single hour required for thinking, planning and preparation. When the opportune moment arrived the plan was submitted for the cabinet's consideration. The cabinet approved the operation unanimously.

This rescue operation is an achievement of great importance in our struggle against terrorism. This is Israel's contribution to humanity's struggle against terrorism as an international manifestation—but it should not be viewed as an epilogue. It will assist us as we continue our efforts but the struggle is not over, and new efforts, new methods, and unremitting sophistication will be required. Terrorism will find us neither immobile nor slaves to routine.

The operation that rescued our dear ones from captivity will be a subject for research, for song, and for legend, and it will be written about in the annals of the nation. I know the Israel Defense Forces, I know its qualities and achievements. Yet, all the same, this time I feel a personal need to express special thanks and appreciation to the I.D.F., the Chief of Staff, the General Staff, the several arms and those who personally participated in the operation for risking their lives in fulfillment of their duty as Jews and human beings, and for being an example and a source of pride to us all.

PRESIDENTIAL DIRECTIVE/NSC-6 ON RELATIONS WITH CUBA
March 15, 1977

Since Fidel Castro became leader of communist Cuba in 1959, the United States and Cuba have repeatedly traded accusations of engaging in terrorism. Both have claimed that the other supports terrorism in various countries and harbors terrorists on its soil. Cuba has especially emphasized its allegation that the U.S. government turns a blind eye to Cuban exiles in Miami who launch terrorist attacks aimed at overthrowing Castro.

President Jimmy Carter implicitly acknowledged that terrorists based in the United States had attacked Cuba in Presidential Directive/NSC-6, dated March 15, 1977. In the classified memo, Carter instructed a handful of top administration officials to take actions to start the process of normalizing relations with Cuba. Carter specifically instructed the attorney general to "take all necessary steps permitted by law to prevent terrorist or any illegal actions launched from within the United States against Cuba. . . ." Many years later a declassified version of the directive was made public by the National Security Archive, a nonprofit research center that has the world's largest nongovernmental collection of declassified documents.

Three days after Carter issued the directive, the U.S. government lifted its ban on travel to Cuba (it has since been reinstated). A few weeks later the two countries agreed to open diplomatic "interests sections" in each other's capitals. But by mid-1979 relations had soured again. Carter issued a new directive aimed at isolating Cuba, and the war of words resumed and continued into the next millennium. At a massive rally held October 6, 2001, to commemorate the twenty-fifth anniversary of the terrorist bombing of a Cuban plane in which 73 people were killed, Castro criticized the United States for allowing the two alleged masterminds of the attack to live without prosecution on its soil. (Castro Accuses United States of Inconsistency on Terrorism, p. 361)

Following is a declassified version of Presidential Directive/NSC-6, signed by President Jimmy Carter and dated March 15, 1977:

30

After reviewing the results of the meeting of the Policy Review Committee held on Wednesday, March 9, 1977, to discuss U.S. policy to Cuba, I have concluded that we should attempt to achieve normalization of our relations with Cuba.

To this end, we should begin direct and confidential talks in a measured and careful fashion with representatives of the Government of Cuba. Our objective is to set in motion a process which will lead to the reestablishment of diplomatic relations between the United States and Cuba and which will advance the interests of the United States with respect to:

— Combating terrorism;
— Human rights;
— Cuba's foreign intervention;
— Compensation for American expropriated property; and
— Reduction of the Cuban relationship (political and military) with the Soviet Union.

The issues we should raise in the exploratory talks include: fisheries and maritime boundaries; the anti-hijacking agreement; human rights conditions in Cuba (including release of American citizens in Cuban jails, visitation rights, and emigration rights); Cuba's external activities in Angola and elsewhere; Cuba's activities with regard to Puerto Rico; sports, cultural and scientific/technical exchanges; compensation for American property which was expropriated by the Cuban Government; the possibility of trade relations; and the establishment of an American Interest Section in the Swiss Embassy.

To implement this new policy and to negotiate in pursuit of these objectives, the Secretary of State should designate officials to begin exploratory talks with Cuba with the intention that they will lead to appropriate, reciprocal and sequential steps looking toward normalization of relations between our two countries. Following an exploratory round of discussions, the National Security Council should make recommendations to me on how we should proceed.

The Secretary of State should insure that the NATO Governments, Japan and various Latin American Governments are informed of U.S. initiatives toward Cuba, as appropriate.

The Attorney General should take all necessary steps permitted by law to prevent terrorist or any illegal actions launched from within the United States against Cuba and against U.S. citizens and to apprehend and prosecute perpetrators of such actions.

As of May 24, 2002, a PDF version of the original Presidential Directive/NSC-6 was available at the National Security Archive Web site at http://www.gwu.edu/~nsarchiv/news/20020515/cartercuba.pdf

PRESIDENT CARTER COMMUTES SENTENCES FOR 1950S ATTACKS
September 6, 1979

On November 1, 1950, two supporters of independence for Puerto Rico, a U.S. territory since 1898, approached police officers guarding Blair House, where President Harry Truman was staying during repairs to the White House. One of the men pulled out a gun and started shooting. In the ensuing gun battle a police officer and an attacker were killed and one police officer was wounded. The attackers had apparently planned to assassinate Truman. A little more than three years later, on March 1, 1954, three other Puerto Rican nationalists stood up in the visitors' gallery in the U.S. House of Representatives and started shooting at the 200 representatives below, wounding five of them. The four surviving terrorists from the two assaults all received long prison sentences.

On September 6, 1979, President Jimmy Carter commuted the sentences of all four to time served and they were released from prison. In a press release, the White House said that Carter commuted the sentences because the four had served an unusually long time in prison (between twenty-five and twenty-eight years each), they posed little risk, and their release would be a humanitarian gesture. The press release made it clear that the move should not be seen as softness on terror. "To the extent that clemency might, under other circumstances, be viewed as leniency toward terrorists, no such conclusion could be drawn here in light of the length of the sentences served," it said.

While the other assailants died or gave up public political activity, Lolita Lebron, who shouted "Free Puerto Rico Now!" as she shot at representatives in 1954, became a beloved figure in Puerto Rico and has continued her efforts to gain independence for the island. In a 2001 interview with the New York Times, *Lebron said she had renounced violence in favor of civil disobedience. But of her crime nearly fifty years earlier, she said: "We feel honored to have defended the nation."*

Following is a press release issued by the White House on September 6, 1979, announcing President Jimmy Carter's sentence commutation for four Puerto Rican nationalists:

President Carter today commuted the sentences of four Puerto Rican Nationalists to time served. These individuals have been serving prison terms for Federal convictions stemming from their participation in shootings that occurred at the Blair House in 1950 and the U.S. House of Representatives in 1954.

The four individuals are Oscar Collazo, 67; Rafael Cancel Miranda, 49; Irving Flores Rodriguez, 54; and Lolita Lebron, 59.

Mr. Collazo has been eligible for parole since April 1966, and Mrs. Lebron has been eligible since July 1969. Messrs. Cancel Miranda and Flores Rodriguez became eligible for parole in July 1979. However, none has applied for parole because of their political beliefs.

The president based his decision on a favorable recommendation of the Attorney General to commute the sentences of these individuals to time served. The Attorney General's letter of advice to the President cited the following reasons in support of the recommendation:

1. Each of the four has served an unusually long time in prison, and the Attorney General believes that no legitimate deterrent or correctional purpose is served by continuing their incarceration. Mr. Collazo has served over 28 years; Ms. Lebron and Messrs. Rodriguez and Miranda have each served over 25 years. Bureau of Prison reports show that in recent times only three inmates have served more time in Federal custody than these four.

2. Humane considerations militate against retaining in custody persons who have served (according to Bureau of Prison records) prison terms of far greater length than the terms normally served by those convicted of equally or even more heinous offenses.

3. It is the consensus of the law enforcement officials consulted that commutation would be appropriate and would pose little substantial risk of the defendants' engaging in further criminal activity or becoming the rallying point for terrorist groups. To the extent that clemency might, under other circumstances, be viewed as evidence of leniency toward terrorists, no such conclusion could be drawn here in light of the length of the sentences served.

In addition, the President concurred with the judgment of the Secretary of State that the release of these four prisoners would be a significant humanitarian gesture and would be viewed as such by much of the international community.

The four prisoners will be released from Federal prison immediately upon completing routine administrative discharge procedures for their release.

THE BEGINNING OF THE IRAN HOSTAGE CRISIS
November 12 and December 4, 1979

Amid growing pressure for his ouster as Iran's leader, Shah Mohammed Reza Pahlavi fled the country on January 16, 1979. Opposition to the shah centered on his repressive rule, a widespread belief that he allowed the United States to meddle in internal Iranian affairs, and a desire for Iran to be ruled by Islamic law. The shah's departure paved the way for Ayatollah Ruhollah Khomeini, a Muslim cleric who had been exiled since 1963, to assume power, sever Iran's ties with Western nations, and impose Islamic rule. Many Iranians were outraged when the administration of President Jimmy Carter on October 22 allowed the shah to enter the United States for treatment of lymphatic cancer. They suspected that the shah's hospital stay was a ruse to get him inside the United States, where he would remain.

During a demonstration in Tehran on November 4, a group of Iranian militants forced their way into the U.S. embassy compound and took everyone inside hostage. All the non-Americans were quickly released, and all blacks and women were released thirteen days after the takeover, at Khomeini's request. That left fifty-two hostages at the embassy. The Carter administration accused the Khomeini government of standing by and allowing the hostage-taking without moving to prevent it, in contravention of accepted international codes. Khomeini later endorsed the action of the captors, including their demand that the United States extradite the shah so he could be put on trial. The United States refused, offering instead to consider the shah's alleged crimes only after the hostages were released.

The embassy takeover posed a grave dilemma for the Carter administration, which labeled the captors "Marxist terrorists." The use of military force by the United States, officials believed, not only posed serious risks to the hostages but also might trigger a convulsive reaction throughout the volatile Muslim world. In addition, cutting Iran's oil production by military action might result in hardship to U.S. allies, and the introduction of American military power into Iran might provoke countermeasures by the Soviet Union. Instead of taking military measures, the Carter administration embargoed future oil shipments from Iran, froze Iranian assets in the

United States, and ordered the deportation of Iranians found to be in the United States illegally, but these actions seemed to have little effect on the captors. The Carter administration also appealed to the United Nations Security Council and the International Court of Justice for help. In December both groups said the hostages should be released, but to no avail. Even the shah's departure from the United States on December 15 failed to win the hostages' release. They would end up spending 444 days in captivity. (Rescue Attempt and Release of U.S. Hostages in Iran, p. 40)

Following are President Jimmy Carter's statement November 12, 1979, about the hostages; the Ayatollah Khomeini's request November 17, 1979, that female and black hostages be released; President Carter's opening statement November 28, 1979, at a news conference about the hostages; and United Nations Security Council Resolution 457 demanding release of the hostages, adopted on December 4, 1979:

PRESIDENT CARTER'S NOVEMBER 12 STATEMENT

We continue to face a grave situation in Iran where our Embassy has been seized and more than 60 American citizens continue to be held as hostages in an attempt to force unacceptable demands on our country. We're using every available channel to protect the safety of the hostages and to secure their release.

Along with the families of the hostages, I have welcomed and I appreciate the restraint that has been shown by Americans during this crisis. We must continue to exhibit such constraint, despite the intensity of our emotions. The lives of our people in Iran are at stake.

I must emphasize the gravity of the situation. It's vital to the United States and to every other nation that the lives of diplomatic personnel and other citizens abroad be protected and that we refuse to permit the use of terrorism and the seizure and the holding of hostages to impose political demands.

No one should underestimate the resolve of the American Government and the American people in this matter. It is necessary to eliminate any suggestion that economic pressures can weaken our stand on basic issues of principle. Our position must be clear. I am ordering that we discontinue purchasing of any oil from Iran for delivery to this country.

These events obviously demonstrate the extreme importance of reducing oil consumption here in the United States. I urge every American citizen and every American business to redouble efforts to curtail the use of petroleum products. This action will pose a real challenge to our country. It will be a test of our strength and of our determination.

I've directed Secretary [of Energy Charles] Duncan to work with the Congress and with other Federal, State, and local officials, and with leaders of industry to develop additional measures to conserve oil and to cope with this new situation. We will strive to insure equitable and fair distribution of petroleum products and to insure a minimum of disruption of our Nation's economy.

These American measures must be part of an effective international effort, and we will consult with our allies and with other oil-consuming nations about further actions to reduce oil consumption and oil imports.

America does face a difficult task and a test. Our response will measure our character and our courage. I know that we Americans shall not fail.

AYATOLLAH KHOMEINI'S REQUEST

The center of espionage and conspiracy called the American Embassy and those people who hatched plots against our Islamic movement in that place do not enjoy international diplomatic respect.

The extensive threats and propaganda of the American Government will not have the slightest significance to our nation. Neither is its military threat wise, nor its economic embargo significant.

Carter makes one mistake and that is that he thinks that all governments are standing with their eyes closed to do his bidding. This great mistake will soon be made clear to him, too, and its first signs can already be seen.

The Iranian nation has arisen so that dens of espionage will not be able to continue their shameful deeds. This den of espionage and those professional spies will remain as they are until Mohammed Reza Pahlevi is returned to be tried and until he has returned all that he has plundered.

However, since Islam has a special respect toward women, and since the blacks, who have spent ages under American pressure and tyranny, may have come to Iran under pressure, therefore mitigate their cases if it is proved that they have not committed acts of espionage.

Dear students, please hand over the blacks and the women whose spying is not proved to the Ministry of Foreign Affairs so that they may be immediately expelled from Iran.

The noble Iranian nation will not give permission for the release of the rest of them, who will therefore remain under arrest until the American Government acts according to the wish of the nation.

PRESIDENT CARTER'S NEWS CONFERENCE

For the last 24 days our Nation's concern has been focused on our fellow Americans being held hostage in Iran. We have welcomed some of them home to their families and their friends. But we will not rest, nor deviate from our efforts, until all have been freed from their imprisonment and their abuse.

We hold the Government of Iran fully responsible for the well-being and the safe return of every single person.

I want the American people to understand the situation as much as possible, but there may be some questions tonight which I cannot answer fully, because of my concern for the well-being of the hostages.

First of all, I would like to say that I am proud of this great Nation, and I want to thank all Americans for their prayers, their courage, their persistence, their strong support, and patience.

During these past days our national will, our courage, and our maturity have all been severely tested, and history will show that the people of the United States have met every test.

In the days to come our determination may be even more sorely tried but we will continue to defend the security, the honor, and the freedom of Americans everywhere. This Nation will never yield to blackmail.

For all Americans, our constant concern is the well-being and the safety of our fellow citizens who are being held illegally and irresponsibly hostage in Iran. The actions of Iran have shocked the civilized world.

For a government to applaud mob violence and terrorism, for a government actually to support and, in effect, participate in the taking and the holding of hostages is unprecedented in human history. This violates not only the most fundamental precepts of international law but the common ethical and religious heritage of humanity. There is no recognized religious faith on Earth which condones kidnapping. There is no recognized religious faith on Earth which condones blackmail. There is certainly no religious faith on Earth which condones the sustained abuse of innocent people.

We are deeply concerned about the inhuman and degrading conditions imposed on the hostages. From every corner of the world, nations and people have voiced their strong revulsion and condemnation of Iran and have joined us in calling for the release of the hostages.

Last night, a statement of support was released and was issued by the President of the United Nations General Assembly, the Security Council, on behalf of all its members. We expect a further Security Council meeting on Saturday night, at which more firm and official action may be taken to help in obtaining the release of the American hostages.

Any claims raised by government officials of Iran will ring hollow while they keep innocent people bound and abused and threatened. We hope that this exercise of diplomacy and international law will bring a peaceful solution, because a peaceful solution is preferable to the other remedies available to the United States. At the same time we pursue such a solution with grim determination. The Government of Iran must recognize the gravity of the situation which it has itself created, and the grave consequences which will result if harm comes to any of the hostages.

I want the American people to know and I want the world to know that we will persist in our efforts, through every means available, until every single American has been freed. We must also recognize now, as we never have before, that it is our entire Nation which is vulnerable, because of our overwhelming and excessive dependence on oil from foreign countries. We have got to accept the fact that this dependence is a direct physical threat to our national security, and we must join together to fight for our Nation's energy freedom.

We know the ways to win this war: more American energy and the more efficient use of what we have. The United States Congress is now struggling with this extremely important decision. The way to victory is long and difficult, but we have the will, and we have the human and the natural resources of our great Nation.

However hard it might be to see into the future, one thing tonight is clear: We stand together. We stand as a Nation unified, a people determined to protect the life and the honor of every American. And we are determined to make America an energy-secure Nation once again. It is unthinkable that we will allow ourselves to be dominated by any form of overdependence at home or any brand of terrorism abroad. We are determined that the freest Nation on Earth shall protect and enhance its freedom.

UN SECURITY COUNCIL RESOLUTION

The Security Council

Having considered the letter dated 25 November 1979 from the Secretary General (S/13546),

Deeply concerned at the dangerous level of tension between Iran and the United States of America, which could have grave consequences for international peace and security,

Recalling the appeal made by the President of the Security Council on 9 November 1979 (S/13616), which was reiterated on 27 November 1979 (S/13652),

Taking note of the letter dated 13 November 1979 from the Foreign Minister of Iran (S/13626) relative to the grievances of Iran,

Mindful of the obligation of States to settle their international disputes by peaceful means in such a manner that international peace and security, and justice, are not endangered,

Conscious of the responsibility of States to refrain in their international relations from the threat or use of force against the territorial integrity or political independence of any State, or in any other manner inconsistent with the purposes of the United Nations,

Reaffirming the solemn obligation of all States Parties to both the Vienna Convention on Diplomatic Relations of 1961 and the Vienna Convention on Consular Relations of 1962 to respect the inviolability of diplomatic personnel and the premises of their missions,

1. *Urgently calls on* the Government of Iran to release immediately the personnel of the Embassy of the United States of America being held in Teheran, to provide them protection and allow them to leave the country;

2. *Further calls* on the Governments of Iran and of the United States to take steps to resolve peacefully the remaining issues between them to their mutual

satisfaction in accordance with the purposes and principles of the United Nations;

3. *Urges* the Governments of Iran and the United States to exercise the utmost restraint in the prevailing situation;

4. *Requests* the Secretary General to lend his good offices for the immediate implementation of this resolution and to take all appropriate measures to this end;

5. *Decides* that the Council will remain actively seized of the matter and requests the Secretary General to report urgently to it on developments regarding his efforts.

RESCUE ATTEMPT AND RELEASE
OF U.S. HOSTAGES IN IRAN
April 25, 1980 and January 20, 1981

Frustrated by its inability to secure through diplomacy the release of the fifty-two Americans held hostage by militants in Iran, the administration of President Jimmy Carter finally decided to launch a rescue attempt by the military. Planning for a possible rescue had begun shortly after the hostages were seized on November 4, 1979. (The Beginning of the Iran Hostage Crisis, p. 34)

The rescue attempt began April 24, 1980, when eight helicopters took off from the aircraft carrier Nimitz *to rendezvous at a desert landing site in Iran with six C-130 transport planes that were carrying ninety commandos. The commandos were to board the helicopters, fly to a hidden staging area outside Tehran, and then the next evening rescue the hostages at the American embassy. But two helicopters had to turn back because of mechanical failure before reaching the desert landing site, and a third suffered a hydraulic failure that could not be repaired at the site. With three helicopters out of commission, the task force commander contacted his superiors in Washington and Carter canceled the operation. To make matters worse, eight American soldiers were killed and five wounded when a helicopter that was being refueled for the flight out of Iran smashed into one of the transport planes, triggering an explosion and fire. Carter announced the mission's failure in a nationally televised address the morning of April 25, 1980. A subsequent high-level report prepared for the Joint Chiefs of Staff said the mission would have been more likely to succeed had the planners been more willing to sacrifice a margin of secrecy and had they utilized an existing task force, rather than assembling a special unit for the rescue.*

In November Carter lost to Ronald Reagan in the presidential election, and many U.S. political observers felt that the hostage issue was a major factor in Carter's defeat. Yet negotiations for the hostages' release continued, possibly spurred on by Iran's fear that Reagan might take stronger measures than Carter to end the crisis. On Inauguration Day, with only minutes left in Carter's presidency, an agreement was finally reached. Under the complex deal, the United States agreed to unfreeze Iranian assets in American

40

banks and to stay out of Iran's affairs, among other actions. In a final snub to Carter, the hostages' planes did not leave the Tehran airport until just minutes after the presidency officially transferred from Carter to Reagan. Carter flew home to Georgia, where he made a statement about the hostages' release. The next day, at Reagan's request, he flew to West Germany to greet the hostages when they arrived at an air force hospital in Wiesbaden for rest and tests.

Following are President Jimmy Carter's televised address April 25, 1980, announcing the failed hostage rescue attempt and excerpts from former president Carter's statement January 20, 1981, about the release of the Iran hostages:

PRESIDENT CARTER'S TELEVISED ADDRESS

Late yesterday, I cancelled a carefully planned operation which was underway in Iran to position our rescue team for later withdrawal of American hostages, who have been held captive there since November 4. Equipment failure in the rescue helicopters made it necessary to end the mission.

As our team was withdrawing, after my order to do so, two of our American aircraft collided on the ground following a refueling operation in a remote desert location in Iran. Other information about this rescue mission will be made available to the American people when it is appropriate to do so.

There was no fighting; there was no combat. But to my deep regret, eight of the crewmen of the two aircraft which collided were killed, and several other Americans were hurt in the accident. Our people were immediately airlifted from Iran. Those who were injured have gotten medical treatment, and all of them are expected to recover.

No knowledge of this operation by any Iranian officials or authorities was evident to us until several hours after all Americans were withdrawn from Iran.

Our rescue team knew and I knew that the operation was certain to be difficult and it was certain to be dangerous. We were all convinced that if and when the rescue operation had been commenced that it had an excellent chance of success. They were all volunteers; they were all highly trained. I met with their leaders before they went on this operation. They knew then what hopes of mine and of Americans they carried with them.

To the families of those who died and who were wounded, I want to express the admiration I feel for the courage of their loved ones and the sorrow that I feel personally for their sacrifice.

The mission on which they were embarked was a humanitarian mission. It was not directed against Iran; it was not directed against the people of Iran. It was not undertaken with any feeling of hostility toward Iran or its people. It has caused no Iranian casualties.

Planning for this rescue effort began shortly after our embassy was seized, but, for a number of reasons, I waited until now to put those rescue plans into effect. To be feasible, this complex operation had to be the product of intensive planning and intensive training and repeated rehearsal. However, a resolution of this crisis through negotiations and with voluntary action on the part of the Iranian officials was obviously then, has been, and will be preferable.

This rescue attempt had to await my judgment that the Iranian authorities could not or would not resolve this crisis on their own initiative. With the steady unraveling of authority in Iran and the mounting dangers that were posed to the safety of the hostages themselves and the growing realization that their early release was highly unlikely, I made a decision to commence the rescue operations plans.

This attempt became a necessity and a duty. The readiness of our team to undertake the rescue made it completely practicable. Accordingly, I made the decision to set our long-developed plans into operation. I ordered this rescue mission prepared in order to safeguard American lives, to protect America's national interests, and to reduce the tensions in the world that have been caused among many nations as this crisis has continued.

It was my decision to attempt the rescue operation. It was my decision to cancel it when problems developed in the placement of our rescue team for a future rescue operation. The responsibility is fully my own.

In the aftermath of the attempt, we continue to hold the Government of Iran responsible for the safety and for the early release of the American hostages, who have been held so long. The United States remains determined to bring about their safe release at the earliest date possible.

As President, I know that our entire Nation feels the deep gratitude I feel for the brave men who were prepared to rescue their fellow Americans from captivity. And as President, I also know that the Nation shares not only my disappointment that the rescue effort could not be mounted, because of mechanical difficulties, but also my determination to persevere and to bring all of our hostages home to freedom.

We have been disappointed before. We will not give up in our efforts. Throughout this extraordinarily difficult period, we have pursued and will continue to pursue every possible avenue to secure the release of the hostages. In these efforts, the support of the American people and of our friends throughout the world has been a most crucial element. That support of other nations is even more important now.

We will seek to continue, along with other nations and with the officials of Iran, a prompt resolution of the crisis without any loss of life and through peaceful and diplomatic means.

CARTER STATEMENT ON HOSTAGE RELEASE

. . . Just a few moments ago, on Air Force One before we landed at Warner Robins, I had received word, officially, for the first time, that the aircraft carrying the 52 American hostages had cleared Iranian airspace on the first leg of the journey home and that every one of the 52 hostages was alive, was well and free.

It's impossible for me to realize—or any of us—how they feel on that plane because they recognize that they are hostages no more, they are prisoners no more, and they are coming back to this land that we all love.

Our diplomats will be arriving sometime in the near future—I can't yet tell you exactly when—in Algiers. The Algerians, the last few weeks, have been real heroes. They have literally worked day and night—from their President, their Foreign Minister, the president of their national bank, and others—to try to gain the freedom of the American hostages.

And I want to express my personal, and also my political, official, and public thanks to the people of Algeria.

They'll be flying on two Algerian planes—they are now. They'll refuel in Athens, Greece; after they land in Algiers, they will transfer to an American plane and they will fly from there to Germany, land near Frankfurt in a military air base, and go from there about 30 miles away to the hospitals in Wiesbaden, Germany, where American doctors and others will be waiting for them.

Former Secretary [of State] Cyrus Vance will be there to shake their hands and to put his arms around them when they come down from the airplane. I had the plane standing by in Washington, with Secretary Vance in charge. And I directed that the plane take off the moment the hostage planes' wheels cleared the ground.

After a brief rest in Germany—three or four days, probably—then the hostages will come back home to be reunited with their families.

As suggested yesterday morning by our new President Reagan, early tomorrow morning I will leave for Germany to welcome our hostages to freedom. And I know I will take with me the joy and the relief of our entire nation.

Throughout this time of trial, we Americans have stood as one, united in our prayers, steadfast in our concern for fellow Americans in peril.

I doubt that at any time in our history more prayers have reached heaven for any Americans than have those given to God in the last 14 months.

We've achieved, at the end of this crisis, the two objectives that I set for this nation, and for myself, when they were first seized: to secure their safety and their ultimate release, and to do so on terms that would always preserve the honor and the dignity and the best interests of our nation.

As I said a few hours ago in a brief press announcement, the essence of this agreement is that as our people are freed, we're releasing a part of the assets belonging to Iran, which I froze by Presidential order after our embassy was seized and the hostages were taken.

There will also be established a firm, established procedure, involving binding arbitration completely in accordance with American law, and international law, to resolve any remaining claims that might exist by American people against Iran, or vice versa.

Our people held captive, and their families here at home, have borne this ordeal with courage and with honor.

Our nation acted as a great nation ought to act: not only with justified outrage at a despicable and illegal act, but with purpose and constant restraint in the face of severe provocation; working always to uphold the law in the face of lawlessness in Iran. We've kept faith with our principles and our people and as a result, we've reached this day of joy and thanksgiving. . . .

THE ATTEMPTED ASSASSINATION OF POPE JOHN PAUL II
May 13 and 17, 1981

In November 1979 a twenty-three-year-old Turkish citizen, Mehmet Ali Agca, escaped from a maximum-security Turkish prison where he was being held following his conviction for the terrorist murder of a newspaper editor. Agca left behind a letter threatening the life of Pope John Paul II if the pope visited Turkey in late 1979, as planned. The pope made the trip with increased security precautions and there were no incidents.

However, on May 13, 1981, Agca shot and seriously wounded the pope in St. Peter's Square in Vatican City. The sixty-year-old head of the Roman Catholic Church was shot twice, suffering wounds in the abdomen, arm, and hand. Two American women who were among the 10,000 worshipers in the square that day also were wounded. The pope immediately underwent surgery that lasted more than five hours. He spent twenty-two days in the hospital following the surgery, returned to the hospital August 5 for more surgery, and continued a lengthy recuperation period into the fall. Worldwide reaction to the shooting was swift and sharp, with President Ronald Reagan and other political and religious leaders issuing immediate statements of support for the pontiff.

Agca was captured at the scene and on July 22, 1981, he was convicted in an Italian court of attempting to kill the pope and the two American women who were wounded. The judges and jury did not accept the defense attorney's argument that Agca was a misguided, psychopathic "religious fanatic" who could not be held accountable for his actions. Sentenced to life in prison, Agca spent nearly twenty years in an Italian prison before being moved to a Turkish prison in 2000, where he started serving a seventeen-year sentence for murdering the newspaper editor and robbing an Istanbul factory. Agca's motive for shooting the pope is unknown. It was never proven that Agca was part of a conspiracy aimed at the pope, although Turkish military authorities reported that Agca had established links with the Nationalist Action Party—an extreme right-wing group in Turkey.

Following are a statement made by President Ronald Reagan concerning the May 13, 1981, attack on Pope John Paul II, and a public message delivered May 17, 1981, by Pope John Paul II, his first statement following the shooting:

STATEMENT BY PRESIDENT REAGAN

Pope John Paul II, a man of peace and goodness—an inspiration to the world—has been struck today by a would-be assassin's bullet. The world is horrified, and all of us grieve over this terrible act of violence.

Pope John Paul II was wounded today while doing what he had done so well and so often throughout his travels—reaching out to others, offering hope, light and the peace of God.

We are grateful that he has been spared. We pray that all of us will heed Pope John Paul's call for a "world of love, not of hate"; that we will hear his words reminding us that all men are brothers, that they must forever forsake the ways of violence and live together in peace.

The people of the United States, whose unbounded affection for Pope John Paul II was shown in our city streets a year and a half ago, join millions throughout the world in fervent prayer for his full and rapid recovery.

MESSAGE FROM POPE JOHN PAUL II

Praised be Jesus Christ!

Beloved brothers and sisters, I know that during these days and especially in this hour of the Regina Coeli you are united with me. With deep emotion I thank you for your prayers and I bless you all.

I am particularly close to the two persons wounded together with me. I pray for that brother of ours who shot me and whom I have sincerely pardoned.

United with Christ, priest and victim, I offer my sufferings for the church and for the world.

To you, Mary, I repeat: *"Totus tuus ego sum"* (I belong entirely to you).

THE ASSASSINATION OF EGYPTIAN PRESIDENT ANWAR AL-SADAT
October 6 and 9, 1981

During his presidency of Egypt from 1954 until 1970, the flamboyant and charismatic Gamal Abdel Nasser aligned his country firmly with Russia and repeatedly waged war against Israel, a nation he considered to be a usurper of Arab and Islamic rights. Nasser, who ruled the most powerful Arab nation, died of a heart attack in September 1970. He was succeeded by a relative unknown in Egypt and the West—Anwar al-Sadat—who, in the space of eight years, turned Egypt's foreign policy around 180 degrees, forging an alliance with the United States and a peace agreement with Israel. Those moves cost him his life.

On October 6, 1981, as Sadat sat at a reviewing stand during a military parade, a car in the parade suddenly stopped in front of him. Four men in military uniforms leaped out and opened fire with automatic weapons and hand grenades. Sadat was mortally wounded. The attackers were affiliated with al-Jihad, also known as the Egyptian Islamic Jihad, an extremist Islamic group that seeks to overthrow the Egyptian government and replace it with an Islamic state. The group also has attacked United States and Israeli interests in Egypt and abroad. In recent years al-Jihad has closely aligned itself with al Qaeda, the terrorist organization headed by Saudi Arabian exile Osama bin Laden.

Sadat's isolation in the Arab world was at no time more apparent than in death. Palestinians and Arab hard-liners—primarily the Libyans, Syrians, Iraqis, and members of the Palestine Liberation Organization (PLO)— took to the streets to rejoice at the death of a leader they considered to be a traitor to the Arab cause. Those demonstrations of joy, although shocking to the Western world, were vivid reminders that many Arabs had indeed come to view Sadat very differently than did those outside the region. For the Palestinians, Sadat's persistent willingness to negotiate with the Israeli government of Menachem Begin was ample proof of Egypt's "betrayal" of their cause. Vice President Hosni Mubarak, Sadat's closest adviser, was elected president exactly one week after Sadat died.

Following are Egyptian vice president Hosni Mubarak's October 6, 1981, announcement of the assassination of President Anwar al-Sadat and a description of the assassination released October 9, 1981, by the Egyptian Defense Ministry:

MUBARAK'S ANNOUNCEMENT

In the name of God, the compassionate, the merciful:

To the righteous soul will be said: O (thou) soul, in (complete) rest and satisfaction: come back thou to thy lord, well pleased (thyself), and well-pleasing unto him: Enter thou, then, among my devotees! [Koranic verse] Everything is true which the almighty God says!

I am at a loss for words, and while full of emotion, I announce to the Egyptian nation, to the Arab and Islamic peoples and to the whole world the death of the struggling leader and hero, Anwar al-Sadat.

The leader, to whose love millions of hearts were attached, has been martyred! The hero of war and of peace has been martyred! The man, who had given his nation since his youth his blood, sweat and life has been martyred! The struggler, who had not ceased struggling for a split second for the sake of great principles, sublime values and immortal standards, has been martyred! The leader, who has freed the will of his homeland and who has given his nation an unparalleled glory, was martyred while he was standing aloof, looking at his greatest achievements on the day of the great glory, the glory of October—the symbol of strength and the base of peace!

God almighty has so willed that the leader should be martyred on a day which, in itself, symbolizes the leader. God almighty has also willed that the field in which he fell a martyr should be among his soldiers and heroes and among the millions of sons of the people, while these millions were celebrating with pride the anniversary of the great 10 Ramadan, the anniversary of the day on which dignity and greatness were restored for the Arab nation. This victory was bestowed only by God. It was achieved through the will of the people, through the thinking and decision of the leader and commander, and through the heroism of the armed forces.

A sinful and treacherous hand has assassinated the leader. Although we have lost the leader and commander, we derive our consolation from the fact that the whole Egyptian people—in their millions throughout the country, its cities and countryside alike—are now being torn apart by sorrow and pain. The Egyptian people declare that we will proceed on the path charted by the leader and that we will follow your course without deviation, the course of peace, out of our belief that this is the path of righteousness, justice and freedom!

We will proceed on the leader's path, the path of democracy and prosperity.

We tell the leader, while he is with his lord: The people who have believed in your leadership will proceed forward, guided by the beacon of the principles and values which you have entrenched, believing in democracy and the supremacy of the law, and seeking to achieve development and prosperity.

We tell the leader, may God rest his soul: We stand in one united, solid and coherent front around all the banners you have raised.

Oh great people of Egypt, oh peoples of our Arab nation: The calamities of history have accustomed us to reconcile ourselves to the fact that great leaders disappear from the scene of history who, through their struggle, write history's events and chart its course.

We also grew accustomed to dress our wounds, to overcome our pain, to be patient and to believe in the will of God almighty, and to continue the procession with determination and persistence!

Oh great people of Egypt, I announce in the name of the soul of the late great and in the name of the people and their constitutional institutions and armed forces that we will adhere to all the international charters and treaties and commitments signed by Egypt. We will not stop pushing the wheel of peace in fulfillment of the message of the commander and leader.

We will also remember him with all pride when his hope will be achieved; that is, when our flags will be raised all over Sinai, and when comprehensive peace will be achieved on the two sides of the borders in the whole region.

Rest assured, our great leader, Egypt will continue to exist as the state of the institutions, of the supremacy of the law, of stability, of security and peace and of prosperity. The desert will be cultivated and the edifice will rise high and the good and green revolution will be completed! Egypt will continue to raise its head. It will remain immune thanks to the strong arms of its sons and to its army. Egypt will remain dignified through its principles, strong through its authenticity and proud of its history and ancient civilization.

Oh leader and commander: Your people will remember you forever as an epitome of overwhelming heroism, of surging dignity and pride, of perspicacity and sound viewpoints and of wisdom and good example. Your people will remember you as an example of nobleness and faithfulness, of ethics and values, of authenticity and sacrifice and redemption. Your people will remember you as an epitome of Egypt's grandeur and glory!

Oh great people, since our Constitution stipulates in Article 84 that when the post of the president of the republic becomes vacant, the presidency is assumed temporarily by the People's Assembly speaker. The People's Assembly announces the vacancy of the post of the president of the republic and a president is chosen within a period not exceeding 60 days. Therefore, the post of the president has been temporarily assumed by Dr. Sufi Hasan Abu Talib, speaker of the People's Assembly.

The People's Assembly has also been summoned for an extraordinary session to be held at noon tomorrow, 7 October 1981, to declare the post of the president of the republic vacant and to begin to take the constitutional measures required for electing the president of the republic.

Oh great people, our leader has fallen in the field of struggle. The best honor we can render him and his noble memory is to cling steadfastly to God's rope, all of us and without allowing our ranks to be divided. We can also honor the leader by continuing to struggle so that Egypt will always be lofty, strong and steadfast, proud and amply dignified!

May God have mercy on the soul of the great and believing leader. May he give the leader abode in paradise with the martyrs and the truthful. May God endow his family, the Egyptian people and Arabism, the Islamic world and the whole world with patience at the loss of a hero of peace and a hero who ranks among the makes [sic] of history.

Long may Egypt live and long may its great people live! Peace be with you.

DEFENSE MINISTRY STATEMENT

The annual armed forces celebrations marking the anniversary of their victory in the 6 October war included the holding of a big military parade at the parade grounds in An-Nasr City. Symbolic units of the main branches of the armed forces participated in the parade. A few days before the parade, these units assembled in the open air areas near the stadium to prepare for the parade and carry out the necessary rehearsals.

One of the small units, which it was decided would participate in the parade this year, was under the command of first lieutenant named Khalid Ahmad Shawqi al-Islambuli. He is the brother of one of those who were recently arrested and who belonged to the Society of Repudiation and Renunciation [Takfir].

Blinded by black hatred, the aforesaid officer exploited these circumstances and agreed with three misled youths to participate in committing the crime. He provided them with the opportunity of riding with the crew members of the car allocated to him wearing military uniforms. He gave leave to three soldiers who were among the original members of the crew on the morning of the parade, claiming that they were sick. He replaced them with the reservist forces for the parade to complete the crew. It was natural that his partners should get the weapons allocated to the original members of the crew.

In view of the fact that the existing instructions forbid the armed forces participating in military parades from carrying any ammunition to avoid any mistakes, the traitors managed to obtain a quantity of bullets and four offensive and defensive hand grenades . . . from sources outside the armed forces.

Just before the unit moved to participate in the military parade column, First Lieutenant Khalid secretly distributed the ammunition and grenades among his partners and kept some for himself.

When the car reached the main reviewing stand, First Lieutenant Khalid ordered the driver to stop. He was sitting next to the driver and he threatened to kill him if he disobeyed. When the driver hesitated, the aforesaid officer pulled the handbrake and the car stopped. He alighted first and was followed by the three others who were riding in the back and who had their weapons with them.

At first everyone thought that the car had developed trouble and that these individuals were going to try to push it forward. However, the traitorous criminals began hurling their bombs and shooting in the direction of the main reviewing stand. The firing continued despite the fact that the president's special guards exchanged fire with them. When the criminals tried to escape, they were arrested after being wounded.

The president and some of those who were in the main reviewing stand were wounded. His excellency was immediately moved by a helicopter to the armed forces hospital in Al-Ma'adi' where his pure soul departed.

The military prosecution is continuing its investigation of the criminals. The public interest dictates that no other information be disclosed now about the perpetrators of the incident.

THE WORLD WAR II INTERNMENT OF JAPANESE-AMERICANS
February 24, 1983

Mass hysteria swept across the United States following Japan's sneak bombing attack on Pearl Harbor on December 7, 1941. People of Japanese descent living in the United States—even those who had been born there—were suddenly widely viewed as potential saboteurs and terrorists. On February 19, 1942, President Franklin D. Roosevelt signed Executive Order 9066, which authorized the internment of Japanese-Americans. Within months approximately 120,000 men, women, and children living on the West Coast had been rounded up and transported to internment camps. Many remained there until the prohibition against returning to their homes was lifted in December 1944.

Nearly forty years later, on February 24, 1983, a panel created by Congress to examine the internment period issued a stinging indictment in a 467-page report titled "Personal Justice Denied." The Commission on Wartime Relocation and Internment of Civilians concluded that a "grave injustice" had been done to the internees. "The record does not permit the conclusion that military necessity warranted the exclusion of ethnic Japanese from the West Coast," the panel said. A few months later, on June 16, 1983, the commission recommended that the government pay $20,000 to each of the 60,000 internees who were still alive "as an act of national apology."

That recommendation became reality on August 10, 1988, when President Ronald Reagan signed the Civil Liberties Act of 1988. The bill required payment of $20,000 and a formal apology to each of the surviving internees. The bill also created the Civil Liberties Public Education Fund to teach children and the public about the internment period.

Following are excerpts from "Personal Justice Denied," the report of the Commission on Wartime Relocation and Internment of Civilians, released February 24, 1983:

On February 19, 1942, ten weeks after the Pearl Harbor attack, President Franklin D. Roosevelt signed Executive Order 9066, which gave to the Secretary of War and the military commanders to whom he delegated authority, the power to exclude any and all persons, citizens and aliens, from designated areas in order to provide security against sabotage, espionage and fifth column activity. Shortly thereafter, all American citizens of Japanese descent were prohibited from living, working or traveling on the West Coast of the United States. The same prohibition applied to the generation of Japanese immigrants who, pursuant to federal law and despite long residence in the United States, were not permitted to become American citizens. Initially, this exclusion was to be carried out by "voluntary" relocation. That policy inevitably failed, and these American citizens and their alien parents were removed by the Army, first to "assembly centers"—temporary quarters at racetracks and fairgrounds—and then to "relocation centers"—bleak barrack camps mostly in desolate areas of the West. The camps were surrounded by barbed wire and guarded by military police. Departure was permitted only after a loyalty review on terms set, in consultation with the military, by the War Relocation Authority, the civilian agency that ran the camps. Many of those removed from the West Coast were eventually allowed to leave the camps to join the Army, go to college outside the West Coast or to whatever private employment was available. For a larger number, however, the war years were spent behind barbed wire and for those who were released, the prohibition against returning to their homes and occupations on the West Coast was not lifted until December 1944.

This policy of exclusion, removal and detention was executed against 120,000 people without individual review, and exclusion was continued virtually without regard for their demonstrated loyalty to the United States. Congress was fully aware of and supported the policy of removal and detention; it sanctioned the exclusion by enacting a statute which made criminal the violation of orders issued pursuant to Executive Order 9066. The United States Supreme Court held the exclusion constitutionally permissible in the context of war, but struck down the incarceration of admittedly loyal American citizens on the ground that it was not based on statutory authority.

All this was done despite the fact that not a single documented act of espionage, sabotage or fifth column activity was committed by an American citizen of Japanese ancestry or by a resident Japanese alien on the West Coast.

No mass exclusion or detention, in any part of the country, was ordered against American citizens of German or Italian descent. Official actions against enemy aliens of other nationalities were much more individualized and selective than those imposed on the ethnic Japanese.

The exclusion, removal and detention inflicted tremendous human cost. There was the obvious cost of homes and businesses sold or abandoned under circumstances of great distress, as well as injury to careers and professional advancement. But, most important, there was the loss of liberty and the personal stigma of suspected disloyalty for thousands of people who knew themselves to be devoted to their country's cause and to its ideals but whose repeated protestations of loyalty were discounted—only to be demonstrated beyond any doubt by the record of Nisei [the first generation of ethnic Japanese born in the United States] soldiers, who returned from the battlefields of Europe as the most decorated and distinguished combat unit of World War II, and by the thousands of other Nisei who served against the enemy in the Pacific, mostly in military intelligence. The wounds of the exclusion and detention have healed in some respects, but the scars of that experience remain, painfully real in the minds of those who lived through the suffering and deprivation of the camps.

The personal injustice of excluding, removing and detaining loyal American citizens is manifest. Such events are extraordinary and unique in American history. For every citizen and for American public life, they pose haunting questions about our country and its past. . . .

The exclusion and removal were attacks on the ethnic Japanese which followed a long and ugly history of West Coast anti-Japanese agitation and legislation. Antipathy and hostility toward the ethnic Japanese was a major factor of the public life of the West Coast states for more than forty years before Pearl Harbor. . . .

Contrary to the facts, there was a widespread belief, supported by a statement by Frank Knox, Secretary of the Navy, that the Pearl Harbor attack had been aided by sabotage and fifth column activity by ethnic Japanese in Hawaii. Shortly after Pearl Harbor the government knew that this was not true, but took no effective measures to disabuse public belief that disloyalty had contributed to massive American losses on December 7, 1941. Thus the country was unfairly led to believe that both American citizens of Japanese descent and resident Japanese aliens threatened American security. . . .

Having concluded that no military necessity supported the exclusion, the Commission has attempted to determine how the decision came to be made.

First, [Lieutenant] General [John L.] DeWitt [commanding general of the western defense command] apparently believed what he told Secretary [of War Henry L.] Stimson: ethnicity determined loyalty. Moreover, he believed that the ethnic Japanese were so alien to the thought processes of white Americans that it was impossible to distinguish the loyal from the disloyal. On this basis he believed them to be potential enemies among whom loyalty could not be determined.

Second, the FBI and members of Naval Intelligence who had relevant intelligence responsibility were ignored when they stated that nothing more than careful watching of suspicious individuals or individual reviews of loyalty were called for by existing circumstances. In addition, the opinions of the Army General Staff that no sustained Japanese attack on the West Coast was possible were ignored.

Third, General DeWitt relied heavily on civilian politicians rather than informed military judgments in reaching his conclusions as to what actions were necessary, and civilian politicians largely repeated the prejudiced, unfounded themes of anti-Japanese factions and interest groups on the West Coast.

Fourth, no effective measures were taken by President Roosevelt to calm the West Coast public and refute the rumors of sabotage and fifth column activity at Pearl Harbor.

Fifth, General DeWitt was temperamentally disposed to exaggerate the measures necessary to maintain security and placed security far ahead of any concern for the liberty of citizens. . . .

With the signing of Executive Order 9066, the course of the President and the War Department was set: American citizens and alien residents of Japanese ancestry would be compelled to leave the West Coast on the basis of wartime military necessity. For the War Department and the Western Defense Command, the problem became primarily one of method and operation, not basic policy. General DeWitt first tried "voluntary" resettlement: the ethnic Japanese were to move outside restricted military zones of the West Coast but otherwise were free to go wherever they chose. From a military standpoint this policy was bizarre, and it was utterly impractical. If the ethnic Japanese had been excluded because they were potential saboteurs and spies, any such danger was not extinguished by leaving them at large in the interior where there were, of course, innumerable dams, power lines, bridges and war industries to be disrupted or spied upon. Conceivably sabotage in the interior could be synchronized with a Japanese raid or invasion for a powerful fifth column effect. This raises serious doubts as to how grave the War Department believed the supposed threat to be. Indeed, the implications were not lost on the citizens and politicians of the interior western states, who objected in the belief that people who threatened wartime security in California were equally dangerous in Wyoming and Idaho. . . .

The history of the relocation camps and the assembly centers that preceded them is one of suffering and deprivation visited on people against whom no charges were, or could have been, brought. The Commission hearing record is full of poignant, searing testimony that recounts the economic and personal losses and injury caused by the exclusion and deprivation of detention. No summary can do this testimony justice.

Families could take to the assembly centers and the camps only what they could carry. Camp living conditions were Spartan. People were housed in tar-papered barrack rooms of no more than 20 by 24 feet. Each room housed a family, regardless of family size. Construction was often shoddy. Privacy was practically impossible and furnishings were minimal. Eating and bathing were in mass facilities. Under continuing pressure from those who blindly held to the belief that evacuees harbored disloyal intentions, the wages paid for work at the camps were kept to the minimal level of $12 a month for unskilled labor, rising to $19 a month for professional employees. Mass living prevented normal family communication and activities. Heads of families, no longer providing food and shelter, found their authority to lead and to discipline diminished.

The normal functions of community life continued but almost always under a handicap—doctors were in short supply; schools which taught typing had no typewriters and worked from hand-me-down school books; there were not enough jobs. . . .

After the war, through the Japanese American Evacuation Claims Act, the government attempted to compensate for the losses of real and personal property; inevitably that effort did not secure full or fair compensation. There were many kinds of injury the Evacuation Claims Act made no attempt to compensate: the stigma placed on people who fell under the exclusion and relocation orders; the deprivation of liberty suffered during detention; the psychological impact of exclusion and relocation; the breakdown of family structure; the loss of earnings or profits; physical injury or illness during detention. . . .

BOMBING OF THE U.S. MARINE
HEADQUARTERS IN LEBANON
December 19, 1983

The U.S. Marine Corps landed in Lebanon in September 1982 as part of a multinational force that eventually also included troops from France, Italy, and Great Britain. The force was designed to discourage further military action and violence in the war-torn country. The specific mission of the U.S. troops was to "establish an environment that would facilitate the withdrawal of foreign military forces from Lebanon and to assist the Lebanese Government and the Lebanese Armed Forces (LAF) in establishing sovereignty and authority over the Beirut area," according to a later Department of Defense report about the deployment. Yet even after the marines deployed, the political and military situations in Lebanon continued to deteriorate. Concerns about the safety of all Americans in Lebanon, including the marines, were heightened on April 18, 1983, when terrorists used a pickup truck laden with explosives to blow up the U.S. embassy in Beirut. Sixty-three people died in the explosion, including seventeen Americans.

As most of the marines slept early on the morning of October 23, 1983, a truck loaded with explosives crashed into their Beirut headquarters, killing 241 U.S. servicemen. The heavy loss of American lives in the suicide terrorist attack exceeded the casualties produced by any single action of the Vietnam War. At almost the same moment that the marine compound was attacked, another explosives-laden truck blew up at a French barracks only two miles away. Fifty-eight French soldiers were killed in the blast. Western diplomats blamed the attacks on a militant, pro-Iranian Shi'ite Muslim group known as the Party of God, and the New York Times *reported that the White House believed the Iranian government played a key role in the bombings. In December separate reports from the Investigations Subcommittee of the House Armed Services Committee and a special Defense Department commission both pointed to critical failures on the part of marine commanders in Beirut and officers above them in failing to prevent the marine headquarters attack.*

The day after the attack, President Ronald Reagan said he would not withdraw the marines as long as the American mission in Lebanon was incomplete. He changed course approximately three months later, however, announcing on February 7, 1984, that the marines would leave Beirut for their ships offshore. The announcement came amid a sharply deteriorating situation in Lebanon and the collapse of the government of Lebanese president Amin Gemayel.

Following is the summary of findings and conclusions from "The Adequacy of U.S. Marine Corps Security in Beirut," a report released December 19, 1983, by the Investigations Subcommittee of the House Armed Services Committee:

1. There were inadequate security measures taken to protect the Marine Unit from the full spectrum of threats. The truck bomb that transited and exploded in the Battalion Landing Team (BLT) headquarters building, with the loss of 240 lives, rolled through a concertina wire fence that was primarily a personnel barrier; it went between guard posts where the guards had their guns unloaded and had no opportunity to fire before the truck got past them; it went through a gate that was generally left open and was almost assuredly open that morning; iron pipes in front of the building were not large enough to stop the vehicle and had an opening the vehicle could drive through. It is by no means certain that defenses protecting the BLT building would have been adequate to repel a car bomb attack.

2. While the subcommittee fully recognizes it is easy to be wise after the fact, it finds that the commander of the Marine Amphibious Unit (MAU) made serious errors in judgment in failing to provide better protection for his troops within the command authority available to him. As the commander, he bears the principal responsibility for the inadequacy of the security posture at the BLT headquarters.

3. The Amphibious Task Force commander, as the commanding officer of the amphibious sea and land forces in the area, shares responsibility for the inadequate security posture of the MAU.

4. The subcommittee found no evidence of the military chain of command or the diplomatic and political leadership denying any requests for material or assistance with regard to security of the Marine detachment at Beirut International Airport or attempting to influence the deployment and actions of the battalion for political/diplomatic reasons in a way that would limit the security precautions the unit might take.

5. While the higher elements of the chain of command did not deny any requests for support from the MAU, the subcommittee concludes that these higher command elements failed to exercise sufficient oversight of the MAU. Visits by higher level commanders were commonly familiarization briefings and appeared not to provide positive oversight, such as directions to improve security. The change in security effective with the guidance of higher headquarters since the bombing is indicative of what that higher command influence might have done before the bombing. The subcommittee is particularly

concerned that the higher level commanders did not reevaluate the MAU security posture in light of increasing vulnerability of the unit in the weeks before the bombing.

6. While of necessity calling attention to the failures of local commanders within their area of responsibility, the subcommittee must also call to account the higher policy-making authority that adopted and continued a policy that placed military units in a deployment where protection was inevitably inadequate.

7. Both the Marine ground commanders who testified, consistent with the view of the Marine Corps leadership, interpreted the political/diplomatic nature of the mission to place high priority on visibility and emphasized visibility to the extent of allowing greater than necessary security risks. The subcommittee was particularly distressed to find that the security of the MAU was less than that provided at the interim U.S. embassy in Beirut.

8. The individuals attached to the MAU performed their duties with skill, courage and extraordinary fortitude. The subcommittee believes these individual Marines are worthy of high commendation for outstanding performance under extremely adverse circumstances. Despite the fact that these are our most-ready fighters, they are functioning well in a role that is more political than military.

9. The MAU in Lebanon did not receive adequate intelligence support dealing with terrorism. Serious intelligence inadequacies had a direct effect on the capability of the unit to defend itself against the full spectrum of threat. The Marines did not possess adequate capability to analyze the massive amount of data provided them. The chain of command should have provided a special intelligence officer, with expertise in terrorism, capable of assembling all-source intelligence in a usable form for the commander.

Notwithstanding the inadequacy of intelligence support, the subcommittee believes the Marine command erred in failing to consider the possibility of a large bomb-laden truck as a significant threat while it was receiving information on, and attempting to be prepared for, numerous car bomb threats. The failure is particularly inexplicable in view of numerous other threats considered (such as bomb-laden speedboats or airborne kamikaze-type planes that might attack the fleet) and in view of the fact that an intelligence survey in the summer of 1983 recommended that trucks be visually inspected for explosive devices.

10. The information, complete with diagrams, provided by the Marine Corps in Beirut four days after the explosion, and the initial testimony given to the Armed Services Committee by the Marine Corps Commandant and other Marine Corps and administration witnesses eight days after the explosion, was found by the subcommittee to be often inaccurate, erroneous and misleading. While not intentionally misleading, this testimony hindered the subcommittee and delayed its inquiry. Further, this first explanation provided the Congress and the American people thus presented a misleading picture of what actually took place on October 23.

11. The rejection of an Israeli offer for medical assistance on October 23 was a decision made solely by the commander of Task Force 61, the Amphibi-

ous Task Force that include[s] the MAU and naval amphibious units. The subcommittee finds that the decision was based solely on operational and medical considerations and has found no evidence of political considerations. The subcommittee found no evidence that the death of any U.S. personnel could be attributed to the matter of providing medical evacuation and medical care.

The message offering assistance to the Task Force commander did not come to his attention until several hours after the explosion and after he had made decisions regarding medical evacuation and had aircraft on the way that had been requested hours earlier. When the Task Force commander needed body bags he had no hesitancy in requesting them from Israel and they were supplied. The subcommittee commends the Task Force commander for his decision and also for the manner in which the medical evacuation was carried out.

12. Most witnesses insisted that the policy in the Middle East and the mission of the Marines has [sic] not changed. But between objectives, policy, mission and conditions—something has changed. The subcommittee urges in the strongest terms that the administration review the policy in Lebanon from the standpoint of how the Marine mission fits into that policy to determine if continued deployment of the Marine unit, as part of the Multinational Force (MNF) of French, Italian, British and American units, is justified.

Sustained deployment of personnel in the situation of almost certain further casualties should only be undertaken if the policy objectives are visible, profoundly important and clearly obtainable. Failure of the administration to adequately reexamine its policy and relate it to present conditions will only mean that such reexamination will have to be done by Congress.

13. Diplomatic pressure of the most serious sort must be brought to bear on the [Amin] Gemayel government to reach an accord with the warring factions. The solution to Lebanon's problems will only be found at the bargaining table. We must not in any way encourage the perception that a solution can be found on the battlefield with the participation of U.S. armed forces.

SPEECH ON TERRORISM BY SECRETARY OF STATE SHULTZ
October 25, 1984

During the 1980 presidential campaign, Republican nominee Ronald Reagan repeatedly castigated President Jimmy Carter for allowing Americans to be held hostage by Iranian militants and for the failure of the U.S. government's attempted rescue of the hostages. Carter's failure to resolve the Iran crisis was widely credited with helping Reagan defeat him in the 1980 election. Shortly after taking office, Reagan pledged to retaliate against major acts of terrorism, like the taking of hostages in Iran. Yet continued terrorist attacks, such as the 1983 bombing of the Beirut Marine headquarters that killed 241 U.S. servicemen, taught Reagan—as they had other presidents both before and since—that effectively striking back at small, nebulous bands of terrorists was far from easy. (The Beginning of the Iran Hostage Crisis, p. 34; Rescue Attempt and Release of U.S. Hostages in Iran, p. 40; Bombing of the U.S. Marine Headquarters in Lebanon, p. 57)

In a speech October 25, 1984, to the Jewish Community Relations Council in Manhattan, Secretary of State George P. Shultz said the United States should make preemptive strikes against terrorists and retaliate for any attacks—even if the actions kill innocent people. The secretary asked for broad public support for using military force to fight terrorism. There will be no time for a national debate after every terrorist attack, Shultz said, and "we cannot allow ourselves to become the Hamlet of nations, worrying endlessly over whether and how to respond." He added that the government might often have to act before "each and every fact is known."

Shultz's forceful speech caught the White House by surprise. A State Department spokesman said the speech reflected administration policy, but Vice President George Bush disagreed with the secretary's contention that the public should be ready to accept some loss of innocent life. When later questioned about the strident nature of Shultz's speech, Reagan said: "I don't think it was a statement of policy." But thirty minutes after Reagan spoke, White House spokesman Larry Speakes issued a clarification. "Shultz's speech was administration policy from top to bottom," Speakes said. As for Shultz, he flew to India days after his speech to attend the funeral of Indian prime minister Indira Gandhi, who was assassinated by religious extremists. (The Assassination of Indian Prime Minister Indira Gandhi, p. 65)

Following are excerpts from Secretary of State George P. Shultz's speech about terrorism on October 25, 1984, before the Jewish Community Relations Council:

Someday terrorism will no longer be a timely subject for a speech, but that day has not arrived. Less than two weeks ago, one of the oldest and greatest nations of the Western world almost lost its Prime Minister, Margaret Thatcher, to the modern barbarism that we call terrorism. A month ago the American Embassy Annex in East Beirut was nearly destroyed by a terrorist truck bomb, the third major attack on Americans in Lebanon within the past two years. To list all the other acts of brutality that terrorists have visited upon civilized society in recent years would be impossible here because that list is too long. It is too long to name and too long to tolerate.

But I am here to talk about terrorism as a phenomenon in our modern world—about what terrorism is and what it is not. We have learned a great deal about terrorism in recent years. We have learned much about the terrorists themselves, their supporters, their diverse methods, their underlying motives, and their eventual goals. What once may have seemed the random, senseless, violent acts of a few crazed individuals has come into clearer focus. A pattern of terrorist violence has emerged. It is an alarming pattern, but it is something that we can identify and, therefore, a threat that we can devise concrete measures to combat.

The knowledge we have accumulated about terrorism over the years can provide the basis for a coherent strategy to deal with the phenomenon, if we have the will to turn our understanding into action.

We have learned that terrorism is, above all, a form of political violence. It is neither random nor without purpose. Today we are confronted with a wide assortment of terrorist groups which, alone or in concert, orchestrate acts of violence to achieve distinctly political ends. Their stated objectives may range from separatist causes to revenge for ethnic grievances to social and political revolution. Their methods may be just as diverse: from planting homemade explosives in public places to suicide car-bombings to kidnappings and political assassinations. But the overarching goal of all terrorists is the same: they are trying to impose their will by force—a special kind of force designed to create an atmosphere of fear. . . .

They succeed when governments change their policies out of intimidation. But the terrorist can even be satisfied if a government responds to terror by clamping down on individual rights and freedoms. Governments that overreact, even in self defense, may only undermine their own legitimacy, and they unwittingly serve the terrorists' goals. The terrorist succeeds if a government responds to violence with repressive, polarizing behavior that alienates the government from the people.

We must understand, however, that terrorism, wherever it takes place, is directed in an important sense against us, the democracies—against our most basic values and often our fundamental strategic interests. Because terrorism relies on brutal violence as its only tool, it will always be the enemy of democracy. For democracy rejects the indiscriminate or improper use of force and relies instead on the peaceful settlement of disputes through legitimate political processes. . . .

Terrorism is a step backward; it is a step toward anarchy and decay. In the broadest sense, terrorism represents a return to barbarism in the modern age. If the modern world cannot face up to the challenge, then terrorism, and the lawlessness and inhumanity that come with it, will gradually undermine all that the modern world has achieved and make further progress impossible. . . .

While terrorism threatens many countries, the United States has a special responsibility. It is time for this country to make a broad national commitment to treat the challenge of terrorism with the sense of urgency and priority it deserves.

The essence of our response is simple to state: Violence and aggression must be met by firm resistance. This principle holds true whether we are responding to full-scale military attacks or to the kinds of low-level conflicts that are more common in the modern world. . . .

But part of our problem here in the United States has been our seeming inability to understand terrorism clearly. Each successive terrorist incident has brought too much self-condemnation and dismay, accompanied by calls for a change in our policies and our principles, or calls for withdrawal and retreat. We *should* be alarmed. We *should* be outraged. We *should* investigate and strive to improve. But widespread public anguish and self-condemnation only convince the terrorists that they are on the right track. It only encourages them to commit more acts of barbarism in the hope that American resolve will weaken. . . .

We must reach a consensus in this country that our responses should go beyond passive defense to consider means of active prevention, preemption, and retaliation. Our goal must be to prevent and deter future terrorist acts, and experience has taught us over the years that one of the best deterrents to terrorism is the certainty that swift and sure measures will be taken against those who engage in it. We should take steps toward carrying out such measures. There should be no moral confusion on this issue. Our aim is not to seek revenge, but to put an end to violent attacks against innocent people, to make the world a safer place to live for all of us. Clearly, the democracies have a moral right, indeed a duty, to defend themselves. . . .

There is no question about our ability to use force where and when it is needed to counter terrorism. Our nation has forces prepared for action—from small teams able to operate virtually undetected, to the full weight of our conventional military might. But serious issues are involved—questions that need to be debated, understood, and agreed if we are to be able to utilize our forces wisely and effectively. . . .

The heart of the challenge lies in those cases where international rules and traditional practices do not apply. Terrorists will strike from areas where no governmental authority exists or they will base themselves behind what they expect will be the sanctuary of an international border. And they will design their attacks to take place in precisely those "gray areas" where the full facts cannot be known, where the challenge will not bring with it an obvious or clear-cut choice of response.

In such cases we must use our intelligence resources carefully and completely. We will have to examine the full range of measures available to us to take. The outcome may be that we will face a choice between doing nothing or employing military force. We now recognize that terrorism is being used by our adversaries as a modern tool of warfare. It is no aberration. We can expect more terrorism directed at our strategic interests around the world in the years ahead. To combat it we must be willing to use military force.

What will be required, however, is public understanding *before the fact* of the risks involved in combatting terrorism with overt power.

The public must understand *before the fact* that there is potential for loss of life of some of our fighting men and the loss of life of some innocent people.

The public must understand *before the fact* that some will seek to cast any preemptive or retaliatory action by us in the worst light and will attempt to make our military and our policy-makers—rather than the terrorists—appear to be the culprits.

The public must understand *before the fact* that occasions will come when their government must act before each and every fact is known—and that decisions cannot be tied to the opinion polls.

Public support for U.S. military actions to stop terrorists before they commit some hideous act or in retaliation for an attack on our people is crucial if we are to deal with this challenge. . . .

If we are going to respond or pre-empt effectively, our policies will have to have an element of unpredictability and surprise. And the prerequisite for such a policy must be a broad public consensus on the moral and strategic necessity of action. We will need the capability to act on a moment's notice. There will not be time for a renewed national debate after every terrorist attack. We may never have the kind of evidence that can stand up in an American court of law. But we cannot allow ourselves to become the Hamlet of nations, worrying endlessly over whether and how to respond. A great nation with global responsibilities cannot afford to be hamstrung by confusion and indecisiveness. Fighting terrorism will not be a clean or pleasant contest, but we have no choice but to play it. . . .

As we fight this battle against terrorism, we must always keep in mind the values and way of life we are trying to protect. Clearly, we will not allow ourselves to descend to the level of barbarism that terrorism represents. We will not abandon our democratic traditions, our respect for individual rights, and freedom, for these are precisely what we are struggling to preserve and promote. Our values and our principles will give us the strength and the confidence to meet the great challenge posed by terrorism. If we show the courage and the will to protect our freedom and our way of life, we will prove ourselves again worthy of these blessings.

THE ASSASSINATION OF INDIAN PRIME MINISTER INDIRA GANDHI
October 31, 1984

In the early 1980s Sikh religious extremists who wanted to create a separate Sikh state in the Punjab region of northern India started launching terrorist attacks that killed hundreds of people. In an effort to break the separatist drive, on June 6, 1984, Indian prime minister Indira Gandhi ordered the military to storm the Golden Temple of Armistar, the Sikhs' holiest shrine. Sikh extremists had been using the temple as a base for terrorist operations, and Sikh militant leader Jarnail Singh Bhindranwale and hundreds of his followers were inside the temple when the raid started. During thirty-six hours of fierce fighting nearly 600 people were killed, including Bhindranwale.

In apparent retaliation for the raid, two of Gandhi's trusted Sikh bodyguards shot the prime minister at close range with a submachine gun and a pistol on October 31, 1984, as she walked from her home to her office in New Delhi. Gandhi, whose body was riddled with nearly a dozen bullet wounds, was pronounced dead at a nearby hospital. Loyal guards killed one of the assassins and captured the other.

The assassination touched off a major political crisis. Outraged Hindus attacked Sikhs across India, and more than 1,200 people were reported killed in the two weeks after Gandhi was murdered. Many Sikhs fled their homes to go into hiding. Hours after her death Indira's son, Rajiv, was sworn in as the new prime minister, and he immediately appealed for calm. As the rioting continued, his mother was cremated in a traditional Hindu funeral ceremony attended by tens of thousands, including nearly one hundred foreign leaders and dignitaries.

Following are speeches made October 31, 1984, by Rajiv Gandhi, as the newly sworn-in prime minister of India following his mother's assassination, and by President Giani Zail Singh:

RAJIV GANDHI'S ADDRESS

Indira Gandhi, India's Prime Minister, has been assassinated. She was mother not only to me but to the whole nation. She served the Indian people to the last drop of her blood. The country knows with what tireless dedication she toiled for the development of India.

You all know how dear to her heart was the dream of a united, peaceful and prosperous India. An India in which all Indians, irrespective of their religion, language or political persuasion live together as one big family in an atmosphere free from mutual rivalries and prejudices.

By her untimely death her work remains unfinished. It is for us to complete this task.

This is a moment of profound grief. The foremost need now is to maintain our balance. We can and must face this tragic ordeal with fortitude, courage and wisdom. We should remain calm and exercise the maximum restraint. We should not let our emotions get the better of us, because passions would cloud judgement.

Nothing would hurt the soul of our beloved Indira Gandhi more than the occurrence of violence in any part of the country. It is of prime importance at this moment that every step we take is in the correct direction.

Indira Gandhi is no more but her soul lives. India lives. India is immortal. The spirit of India is immortal. I know that the nation will recognise its responsibilities and that we shall shoulder the burden heroically and with determination.

The nation has placed a great responsibility on me by asking me to head the Government. I shall be able to fulfill it only with your support and cooperation. I shall value your guidance in upholding the unity, integrity and honour of the country.

PRESIDENT SINGH'S ADDRESS

My Dear Countrymen,

On this the saddest day of my life I speak to you when I am totally overtaken by the dark cloud of cruel fate. Our beloved Mrs. Indira Gandhi is no longer with us. I have lost my dearest friend; we have all lost one of the greatest leaders our country has ever produced; and the world has lost a harbinger of peace who was undoubtedly the greatest woman leader mankind has ever produced.

My association with her family spans over four decades. Panditji's [Indira Gandhi's father] passing away was my first personal bereavement. The loss of Mrs. Gandhi is for me unbearable. In spite of her preoccupation with her official duties we met often. For me each such meeting was a memorable experience. She was gentle, soft spoken, brilliant and above all an epitome of culture. She was a daughter Panditji would have been proud of.

Now all that has ended. The dastardly act of assassins which is not only heinous but a crime against humanity itself, has put the nation to test at an extremely critical juncture of our history. The unity and integrity of the nation is being challenged. Let our grief not cloud our good sense and maturity both as individuals and a nation. God shall grant us the strength to meet the new challenges. Let us rally behind the ideals we have inherited from our forefathers. Let us demonstrate to the world that India's stability cannot be jeopardised by a handful of subhuman assassins.

RELEASE OF THE HOSTAGES FROM TWA FLIGHT 847
June 30, 1985

One of the most dramatic terrorist incidents in 1985 started on June 14 when two gunmen carrying a grenade and an automatic pistol burst into the cockpit of Trans World Airlines Flight 847, which was en route from Cairo to Rome. They forced the plane to fly to Beirut. After landing, the terrorists read their demands, which included the release of more than 700 prisoners, mostly Shi'ite Muslims, that Israel had captured during its occupation of southern Lebanon. The plane then flew to Algiers, back to Beirut, back to Algiers, and back to Beirut again. At several stops some passengers were released, although during the second Beirut stop the hijackers dumped out the body of passenger Robert D. Stethem, a U.S. Navy diver. Shortly after the plane returned to Beirut June 16 for the third and final time, the remaining passengers were taken off the plane and dispersed throughout Beirut, to make any rescue more difficult.

On June 30 complex negotiations apparently spearheaded by Syrian president Hafez al-Assad culminated in release of the thirty-nine Americans still held hostage. Two days later, Israel released 300 of the 735 Lebanese and Palestinians it had taken prisoner in southern Lebanon. Israel and the United States insisted there was no connection between the two events. "The United States gives terrorists no rewards and no guarantees," President Ronald Reagan said in a nationally televised address announcing the release of the American hostages. "We make no concessions; we make no deals."

Seven Americans who had been kidnapped previously in Lebanon remained in captivity, including two who had been missing for more than a year. They included a U.S. embassy officer, two clergymen, a journalist, and three staffers at the American University in Beirut. The Reagan administration had tried unsuccessfully to obtain their release during the hijacking negotiations. The only good news about the remaining hostages came September 14 when Rev. Benjamin Weir, a Protestant missionary, was released. Administration officials said Weir was released as a result of intensive but unspecified diplomatic efforts.

Following is a nationally televised address by President Ronald Reagan on June 30, 1985, announcing the release of the thirty-nine Americans held hostage following the hijacking June 14 of TWA Flight 847:

Good afternoon. The 39 Americans held hostage for 17 days by terrorists in Lebanon are free, safe, and at this moment, on their way to Frankfurt, Germany. They'll be home again soon. This is a moment of joy for them, for their loved ones, and for our nation. And America opens its heart in a prayer of thanks to Almighty God.

We can be thankful that our faith, courage, and firmness have paid off. But this is no moment for celebration. Let it be clearly understood that the seven Americans still held captive in Lebanon must be released along with other innocent hostages from other countries; that the murderers of Robert Stethem and of our marines and civilians in El Salvador must be held accountable; that those responsible for terrorist acts throughout the world must be taken on by civilized nations; that the international community must ensure that all our airports are safe and that civil air travel is safeguarded; and that the world must unite in taking decisive action against terrorists, against nations that sponsor terrorists, and against nations that give terrorists safe haven.

This drama has reminded us how precious and fragile are the freedoms and standards of decency of civilized societies; how greatly civilized life depends on trust in other human beings; but how those values we hold most dear must also be defended with bravery—a bravery that may lie quiet and deep, but that will rise to answer our call in every time of peril. Freedom, democracy, and peace have enemies; they must also have steadfast friends.

The United States gives terrorists no rewards and no guarantees. We make no concessions; we make no deals. Nations that harbor terrorists undermine their own stability and endanger their own people. Terrorists, be on notice, we will fight back against you, in Lebanon and elsewhere. We will fight back against your cowardly attacks on American citizens and property.

Several countries have been actively involved in efforts to free our fellow citizens. Syria has had a central responsibility. The efforts of the Algerian Government were likewise an example of constructive cooperation against the direct challenge of lawless terrorists. King Hussein spoke out early and forcefully in condemning the hijacking. Saudi Arabia also made an effective contribution. Throughout the past 17 days, we have also been in close touch with Israel and a number of governments in Europe and the Middle East, as well as with international organizations—all of which displayed great concern for the safety and release of the hostages.

We will remember and offer our thanks to all who helped us and who stood with us. And, yes, we'll remember those who did not. We will not rest until justice is done. We will not rest until the world community meets its responsibility. We call upon those who helped secure the release of these TWA passengers to show even greater energy and commitment to secure the release of all others held captive in Lebanon. And we call upon the world community to strengthen its cooperation to stamp out this ugly, vicious evil of terrorism.

I just want to inject a personal note here that, like all of you, Nancy and I have been living with all these 17 days, and like you, we have both been praying for what has now taken place. And like you, we thank God and wait with bated breath their final arrival here on our shores.

Thank you.

PRESIDENT REAGAN CHARGES FIVE NATIONS WITH TERRORISM
July 8, 1985

The month before President Ronald Reagan's July 8, 1985, speech about terrorism at the American Bar Association's national convention in Washington, D.C., had been especially bloody. Just more than a week before he spoke, the last 39 American hostages had been released by the hijackers of TWA Flight 847 after seventeen days in captivity and the killing of passenger Robert D. Stethem, a U.S. Navy diver. And on June 23 all 329 people aboard an Air India flight over the Atlantic Ocean had died in an explosion blamed on Sikh terrorists. (Release of the Hostages from TWA Flight 847, p. 68)

In his July 8 speech Reagan singled out five nations—Libya, Iran, North Korea, Cuba, and Nicaragua—as ringleaders of "a new, international version of Murder Incorporated" that had instigated "outright acts of war" against the United States. Notably absent from his condemnation was Syria, a nation that had frequently appeared on the State Department's list of countries that it said had "repeatedly provided support to acts of international terrorism." White House officials said the omission was an indirect acknowledgement of Syria's intervention on behalf of the United States to obtain the June 30 release of the thirty-nine U.S. airline hostages held in Beirut. Reagan said the five nations he cited sought "to cause us to retreat, retrench, to become Fortress America." While he did not call for military reprisal against such "acts of war" by "this confederation of criminal governments," the president said that "under international law, any state which is the victim of acts of war has the right to defend itself."

Although the United States was thwarted in its efforts to capture the TWA hijackers and bring them to justice, Reagan's actions in the hijacking of an Italian cruise ship four months later were more successful. Four young Palestinian terrorists had seized the ship after it set sail from Genoa, Italy, on October 3. With the liner moored outside Port Said, PLO and Egyptian officials negotiated an arrangement with the hijackers that allowed them to leave Egypt safely in return for release of the passengers. Subsequently, however, it was learned that the terrorists had murdered an elderly American passenger, and as the Egyptian plane carrying the hijackers departed for Tunisia, Reagan ordered Navy F-14 jets to intercept it, forcing it to land at an Italian military base. Although Egyptian president Hosni Mubarak strongly criticized the action, other allies as well as members of Congress praised the move. Yet terrorist attacks continued. In November terrorists killed 5 people during the hijacking of an Egyptair flight, and 59 more died when Egyptian special forces stormed the plane. On December 27 gunmen from the renegade Palestinian group Abu Nidal killed 14 people and wounded more than 110 in attacks on El Al airport ticket counters in Rome and Vienna.

Following are excerpts from President Ronald Reagan's July 8, 1985, speech to the American Bar Association's annual convention in Washington, D.C., in which he accused five nations of engaging in terrorism:

. . . There is a temptation to see the terrorist act as simply the erratic work of a small group of fanatics. We make this mistake at great peril, for the attacks on America, her citizens, her allies, and other democratic nations in recent years do form a pattern of terrorism that has strategic implications and political goals. And only by moving our focus from the tactical to the strategic perspective, only by identifying the pattern of terror and those behind it, can we hope to put into force a strategy to deal with it.

So, let us go to the facts; here is what we know: In recent years, there has been a steady and escalating pattern of terrorist acts against the United States and our allies and Third World nations friendly toward our interests. The number of terrorist acts rose from about 500 in 1983 to over 600 in 1984. There were 305 bombings alone last year—that works out to an average of almost one a day. And some of the most vicious attacks were directed at Americans or United States property and installations. And this pattern has continued throughout 1985, and in most cases, innocent civilians are the victims of the violence.

At the current rate, as many as 1,000 acts of terrorism will occur in 1985. Now, that's what we face unless civilized nations act together to end this assault on humanity.

In recent years, the Mideast has been one principal point of focus for these attacks—attacks directed at the United States, Israel, France, Jordan, and the United Kingdom. Beginning in the summer of 1984 and culminating in January and February of this year, there was also a series of apparently coordinated attacks and assassinations by left-wing terrorist groups in Belgium, West Germany and France—attacks directed against American and NATO installations or military and industrial officials of those nations.

Now, what do we know about the sources of those attacks and the whole pattern of terrorist assaults in recent years? Well, in 1983 alone, the Central Intelligence Agency either confirmed or found strong evidence of Iranian involvement in 57 terrorist attacks. While most of these attacks occurred in Lebanon, an increase in activity by terrorists sympathetic to Iran was seen throughout Europe: Spain and France have seen such incidents, and in Italy, seven pro-Iranian Lebanese students were arrested for plotting an attack on the U.S. Embassy, and this violence continues.

It will not surprise any of you to know that, in addition to Iran, we have identified another nation, Libya, as deeply involved in terrorism. We have evidence which links Libyan agents or surrogates to at least 25 incidents last year. Colonel Qaddafi's outrages against civilized conduct are, of course, as infamous as those of the Ayatollah Khomeini. The gunning down last year— from inside the Libyan Embassy—of a British policewoman is only one of many examples.

Since September 1984, Libyan-backed terrorist groups have been responsible for almost 30 attacks, and, most recently, the Egyptian government aborted a Libyan-backed plot to bomb our Embassy in Cairo. It was this pattern of state-approved assassination and terrorism by Libya that led the United States a few years ago to expel Libyan diplomats and has forced other nations to take similar steps since then. But let us, in acknowledging his commitment to terrorism, at least give Colonel Qaddafi his due. The man is candid: He said recently that Libya was—and I quote—"capable of exporting terrorism to the heart of America. We are also capable of physical liquidation and destruction and arson inside America. . . ."

Now three other governments, along with Iran and Libya, are actively supporting a campaign of international terrorism against the United States, her allies, and moderate Third World states.

First, North Korea. The extent and crudity of North Korean violence against the United States and our ally, South Korea, are a matter of record. Our aircraft have been shot down; our servicemen have been murdered in border incidents and two years ago, four members of the South Korean Cabinet were blown up in a bombing in Burma by North Korean terrorists—a failed attempt to assassinate President Chun [Doo Hwan]. This incident was just one more of an unending series of attacks directed against the Republic of Korea by North Korea.

Now, what is not readily known or understood is North Korea's wider links to the international terrorist network. There is not time today to recount all of North Korea's efforts to foster separatism, violence, and subversion in other lands, well beyond its immediate borders, but to cite one example, North Korea's efforts to spread separatism and terrorism in the free and prosperous nation of Sri Lanka are a deep and continuing source of tension in South Asia.

And this is not even to mention North Korea's involvement here in our own hemisphere, including a secret arms agreement with the former communist government in Grenada. I will also have something to say about North Korea's involvement in Central America in a moment.

And then there is Cuba, a nation whose government has, since the 1960s, openly armed, trained, and directed terrorists operating on at least three continents. This has occurred in Latin America. The OAS [Organization of American States] has repeatedly passed sanctions against Castro for sponsoring terrorism in places and countries too numerous to mention.

This has also occurred in Africa. President Carter openly accused the Castro government of supporting and training Katangan terrorists from Angola in their attacks on Zaire. And even in the Middle East, Castro himself has acknowledged that he actively assisted the Sandinistas in the early 70s when they were training in the Middle East with terrorist factions of the PLO.

And finally there is the latest partner of Iran, Libya, North Korea, and Cuba in a campaign of international terror—the communist regime in Nicaragua. The Sandinistas not only sponsor terror in El Salvador, Costa Rica, and Honduras—terror that led recently to the murder of four United States Marines, two civilians, and seven Latin Americans. They provide one of the world's principal refuges for international terrorists.

Members of the Italian government have openly charged that Nicaragua is harboring some of Italy's worst terrorists. And we have evidence that, in addition to Italy's Red Brigades, other elements of the world's most vicious terrorist groups—West Germany's Baader-Meinhoff Gang, the Basque ETA, the PLO, the Tupamaros, and the IRA have found a haven in Nicaragua and support from that country's communist dictatorship.

In fact, the communist regime in Nicaragua has made itself a focal point for the terrorist network and a case study in the extent of its scope.

Consider for just a moment that in addition to establishing strong international alliances with Cuba and Libya, including the receipt of enormous amounts of arms and ammunition, the Sandinistas are also receiving extensive assistance from North Korea. Nor are they reluctant to acknowledge their debt to the government of North Korea dictator Kim Il-Sung. Both Daniel and Humberto Ortega have recently paid official and state visits to North Korea to seek additional assistance and more formal relations.

So we see the Nicaraguans tied to Cuba, Libya, and North Korea. And that leaves only Iran. What about ties to Iran? Well, yes, only recently the Prime Minister of Iran visited Nicaragua, bearing expressions of solidarity from the Ayatollah for the Sandinista communists. . . .

So there we have it—Iran, Libya, North Korea, Cuba, Nicaragua—continents away, tens of thousands of miles apart, but the same goals and objectives. I submit to you that the growth in terrorism in recent years results from the increasing involvement of these states in terrorism in every region of the world. This is terrorism that is part of a pattern, the work of a confederation of terrorist states. Most of the terrorists who are kidnapping and murdering American citizens and attacking American installations are being trained, financed, and directly or indirectly controlled by a core group of radical and totalitarian governments—a new, international version of "Murder, Incorporated." And all of these states are united by one, simple, criminal phenomenon—their fanatical hatred of the United States, our people, our way of life, our international stature.

And the strategic purpose behind the terrorism sponsored by these outlaw states is clear: to disorient the United States, to disrupt or alter our foreign policy, to sow discord between ourselves and our allies, to frighten friendly Third World nations working with us for peaceful settlements of regional conflicts, and finally, to remove American influence from those areas of the world where we're working to bring stable and democratic government. In short, to cause us to retreat, retrench, to become "Fortress America." Yes, their real goal is to expel America from the world.

And that is the reason these terrorist nations are arming, training, and supporting attacks against this nation. And that is why we can be clear on one point: These terrorist states are now engaged in acts of war against the government and people of the United States. And under international law, any state which is the victim of acts of war has the right to defend itself. . . .

The American people are not—I repeat, not—going to tolerate intimidation, terror and outright acts of war against this nation and its people. And we're especially not going to tolerate these attacks from outlaw states run by the strangest collection of misfits, looney tunes and squalid criminals—since the advent of the Third Reich. . . .

As of May 19, 2002, the full text of Reagan's speech was available at http://www.reagan.utexas.edu/resource/speeches/1985/70885a.htm

NATIONAL SECURITY DIRECTIVE ON TERRORISM
January 20, 1986

United States policy for fighting terrorism evolved through the 1970s and early 1980s in bits and pieces, with no single plan tying everything together. The need for a more formal policy became apparent in the early 1980s as terrorists launched increasingly bold attacks against Americans and American interests. These included the 1983 Marine barracks bombing in Beirut that killed 241 U.S. servicemen and the 1985 hijacking of TWA Flight 847 that resulted in the death of a U.S. Navy diver and the holding of thirty-nine Americans as hostages for more than two weeks. In June 1985 President Ronald Reagan appointed the vice president head of a task force to examine U.S. policies and programs on combatting terrorism. That task force, which included such senior administration officials as the secretary of state and the director of the Central Intelligence Agency, presented its classified report to Reagan in December 1985. (Bombing of the U.S. Marine Headquarters in Lebanon, p. 57; Release of the Hostages from TWA Flight 847, p. 68)

In response to the report, on January 20, 1986, Reagan signed National Security Decision Directive Number 207, titled "The National Program for Combatting Terrorism." The classified directive formalized U.S. terrorism policy. One of its key provisions forcefully restated the U.S. position of making no concessions to terrorists. "The USG [United States Government] will pay no ransoms, nor permit releases of prisoners or agree to other conditions that could serve to encourage additional terrorism," it said. "We will make no changes in our policy because of terrorist threats or acts." Ironically, Reagan signed the directive only three days after he signed an executive order that permitted covert arms sales to Iran in an effort to free American hostages held in Lebanon. Directive 207 also reaffirmed that the State Department would be the lead agency in responding to international terrorist incidents and that the Federal Bureau of Investigation, through the Department of Justice, would be responsible for domestic incidents. The directive, which was partially declassified in 1992, remained in effect until President Bill Clinton issued a new directive in 1995. (President Reagan's

Speech on the Iran-Contra Affair, p. 88; New Presidential Directive on Terrorism Policy, p. 166)

The report of the Vice President's Task Force on Combatting Terrorism and the resulting directive disappointed some experts because they did not call for appointing a "czar" to oversee all federal terrorism efforts. Then, as now, federal terrorism efforts were frequently criticized for lacking coordination. Two task force recommendations that were not included in the directive were frequently echoed after the September 11, 2001, terrorist attacks on New York City and Washington, D.C. They called for increasing the collection of human intelligence and creating a consolidated center to analyze all terrorism intelligence obtained by federal departments and agencies.

Following are excerpts from the declassified portions of National Security Decision Directive Number 207, "The National Program for Combatting Terrorism," dated January 20, 1986:

The Vice President's Task Force on Combatting Terrorism has completed an in-depth review of our current policies, capabilities, and resources for dealing with the terrorist threat. I have reviewed the Task Force Report and accompanying recommendations and concluded that our strategy is sound. I have determined that we must enhance our ability to confront this threat and to do so without compromising our basic democratic and human values.

Terrorists undertake criminal acts that involve the use or threat of violence against innocent persons. These acts are premeditated, intended to achieve a political objective through coercion or intimidation of an audience beyond the immediate victims. U.S. citizens and installations, especially abroad, are increasingly being targeted for terrorist acts. Our policy, programs and responses must be effective in ameliorating this threat to our people, property and interests.

Policy

U.S. policy on terrorism is unequivocal: firm opposition to terrorism in all its forms whether it is domestic terrorism perpetrated within U.S. territory, or international terrorism conducted inside or outside U.S. territory by foreign nationals or groups. The policy is based upon the conviction that to accede to terrorist demands places more American citizens at risk. This no-concessions policy is the best way of protecting the greatest number of people and ensuring their safety. At the same time, every available resource will be used to gain the safe return of American citizens who are held hostage by terrorists.

The U.S. Government considers the practice of terrorism by any person or group a potential threat to our national security and will resist the use of terrorism by all legal means available. The United States is opposed to domestic and international terrorism and is prepared to act in concert with other nations or unilaterally when necessary to prevent or respond to terrorist acts.

States that practice terrorism or actively support it, will not be allowed to do so without consequence. Whenever we have evidence that a state is mounting or intends to conduct an act of terrorism against us, we have a responsibility to take measures to protect our citizens, property, and interests. The USG [United States Government] will pay no ransoms, nor permit releases of prisoners or agree to other conditions that could serve to encourage additional terrorism. We will make no changes in our policy because of terrorist threats or acts. The United States is determined to act against terrorists without surrendering basic freedoms or endangering democratic principles. We oppose asylum, sanctuary, or safehaven for terrorists and will make every legal effort to extradite and prosecute terrorists. The USG encourages other governments to take similar strong stands against terrorism.

The National Program

The national program to combat terrorism is designed to provide coordinated action before, during, and after terrorist incidents. Our program includes measures to deter, resolve and, when necessary, respond proportionately to terrorist attacks. The implementation of this strategy requires an organization compatible with the overall structure of the U.S. Government, and relies on the authorities and responsibilities of the various departments and agencies.

The coordination of the Federal response to terrorist incidents will normally be the responsibility of the Lead Agency. The Lead Agency will be that agency with the most direct operational role in and responsibility for dealing with the particular terrorist incident at hand. The Lead Agency will coordinate all operational aspects of the incident, including press and intelligence. The Lead Agency will normally be designated as follows:

— The Department of State for international terrorist incidents that take place outside of U.S. territory.
— The Department of Justice for terrorist incidents that take place within U.S. territory. Unless otherwise specified by the Attorney General, the FBI will be the Lead Agency within the Department of Justice for operational response to such incidents.
— The FAA for aircraft hijackings within the special jurisdiction of the United States.

The Assistant to the President for National Security Affairs will resolve any uncertainty on the designation of the Lead Agency or on agency responsibilities.

The entire range of diplomatic, economic, legal, military, paramilitary, covert action, and informational assets at our disposal must be brought to bear against terrorism. To ensure that these measures are fully integrated and mutually supportive, the following interagency groups will assist the Lead Agencies in the coordination of our national program to combat terrorism.

1. The Terrorist Incident Working Group (TIWG). To support the Special Situation Group (SSG) during a terrorist incident, a Terrorist Incident Working Group has been established. This group consists of representatives from State, Treasury, DOD, Justice, CIA, JCS, FBI, the Office of the Vice President,

and the NSC staff, with augmentation from other agencies as required. The TIWG will be activated by the Assistant to the President for National Security Affairs or at the request of any of the members. The NSC staff will provide a senior representative to chair the TIWG, and a staff member to serve as the Executive Director of the TIWG and chair the Operations Sub-Group (OSG) of the TIWG to review ongoing non-crisis operations/activities. The TIWG will normally remain convened for the duration of a terrorist incident. The Ambassador-at-Large for Counter-Terrorism will serve as the Vice Chairman of the TIWG.

2. The Interdepartmental Group on Terrorism (IG/T). The Interdepartmental Group on Terrorism, chaired by the Ambassador-at-Large for Counter-Terrorism, is responsible for the development of overall U.S. policy on terrorism, including, inter alia, policy directives, organizational issues, legislative initiatives, interagency training activities, coordinated budget/programs, and policy direction of the Anti-Terrorism Assistance Program. Membership will include all departments and agencies supporting the national program to combat terrorism. Vice Chairmen of the IG/T will be the Department of Justice and the Executive Director of the TIWG.

3. [Withheld from public release]. . . .

As of May 21, 2002, a declassified version of National Security Decision Directive Number 207, "The National Program for Combatting Terrorism," was available by searching the National Archives and Records Administration's Archival Research Catalog (http://arcweb. archives.gov/arc/basic_search.jsp)

PRESIDENT REAGAN ON MILITARY STRIKES AGAINST LIBYA
April 14, 1986

Various incidents during the 1970s and 1980s caused relations between the United States and Libya to steadily deteriorate. As early as 1972 there was speculation that Libyan leader Muammar Qaddafi, who gained power following a 1969 military coup, was aiding various terrorist and guerrilla groups, including the Palestine Liberation Organization and the Irish Republican Army. In May 1981 the United States ordered the Libyan Embassy in Washington closed, citing "Libyan provocations and misconduct, including support for international terrorism." In August 1981, responding to Libyan provocation over American military maneuvers in the Gulf of Sidra off Libya's coast, U.S. Navy fighter planes shot down two Libyan SU-22s after a brief dogfight. Soon after, the United States charged that Libya planned to send "hit teams" to attack President Ronald Reagan and other senior officials. The administration next focused its efforts on trying to isolate Qaddafi through economic sanctions, and in a July 8, 1985, speech Reagan kept up the rhetorical heat by singling out Libya and four other nations as supporters of terrorism. (President Reagan Charges Five Nations with Terrorism, p. 71)

On April 14, 1986, Reagan announced in a televised address that American forces had launched military strikes against Libya. Two events apparently precipitated the strikes. The first occurred on March 24, 1986, when U.S. Navy planes were attacked by Libyan surface-to-air missiles while flying over international waters that Qaddafi claimed as national territory. The planes responded by destroying the missile-guiding radars and damaging two Libyan patrol boats. Then on April 5, evidently in retaliation for the navy attacks on Libyan forces, a bomb exploded in a West Berlin discotheque frequented by U.S. military personnel. One U.S. soldier and a Turkish woman were killed, and more than 200 persons, including 60 Americans, were injured. Claiming unequivocal evidence that Qaddafi sponsored the Berlin bombing, Reagan reportedly gave initial secret approval for the air strike on April 9. During the raid five days later, American bombers attacked five different military targets in Libya.

The raids did not halt Qaddafi's embrace of terrorism. On December 21, 1988, an agent of Libya's intelligence service blew up Pan American Airways Flight 103 as it flew over Lockerbie, Scotland, killing all 259 people on board and 11 more on the ground. That attack caused Libya and Qaddafi to become further isolated in the world community. It also resulted in the United Nations Security Council repeatedly demanding that Libya hand over the suspected bombers for trial, which it finally did in 1999. (The Bombing of Pan Am Flight 103 over Scotland, p. 102)

Following is President Ronald Reagan's televised address on April 14, 1986, announcing military strikes against Libya:

My fellow Americans, at 7 P.M. this evening Eastern Time air and naval forces of the United States launched a series of strikes against the headquarters, terrorist facilities and military assets that support Muammar Qaddafi's subversive activities. The attacks were concentrated and carefully targeted to minimize casualties among the Libyan people with whom we have no quarrel.

From initial reports, our forces have succeeded in their mission. Several weeks ago in New Orleans I warned Colonel Qaddafi we would hold his regime accountable for any new terrorist attacks launched against American citizens. More recently I made it clear we would respond as soon as we determined conclusively who was responsible for such attacks.

On April 5th in West Berlin a terrorist bomb exploded in a nightclub frequented by American servicemen. Sergeant Kenneth Ford and a young Turkish woman were killed and 230 others were wounded, among them some 50 American military personnel.

This monstrous brutality is but the latest act in Colonel Qaddafi's reign of terror. The evidence is now conclusive that the terrorist bombing of LaBelle discotheque was planned and executed under the direct orders of the Libyan regime. On March 25th, more than a week before the attack, orders were sent from Tripoli to the Libyan People's Bureau in East Berlin to conduct a terrorist attack against Americans to cause maximum and indiscriminate casualties. Libya's agents then planted the bomb. On April 4th the People's Bureau alerted Tripoli that the attack would be carried out the following morning. The next day they reported back to Tripoli on the great success of their mission.

Our evidence is direct; it is precise; it is irrefutable. We have solid evidence about other attacks Qaddafi has planned against the United States' installations and diplomats, and even American tourists.

Thanks to close cooperation with our friends, some of these have been prevented. With the help of French authorities we recently aborted one such attack—a planned massacre, using grenades and small arms, of civilians waiting in line for visas at an American embassy.

Colonel Qaddafi is not only an enemy of the United States. His record of subversion and aggression against the neighboring states in Africa is well documented and well-known. He has ordered the murder of fellow Libyans in countless countries. He has sanctioned acts of terror in Africa, Europe and the Middle East, as well as the Western Hemisphere.

Today we have done what we had to do. If necessary, we shall do it again. It gives me no pleasure to say that and I wish it were otherwise.

Before Qaddafi seized power in 1969, the people of Libya had been friends of the United States. And I'm sure that today most Libyans are ashamed and disgusted that this man has made their country a synonym for barbarism around the world. The Libyan people are a decent people caught in the grip of a tyrant.

To our friends and allies in Europe who cooperated in today's mission, I would only say you have the permanent gratitude of the American people. Europeans who remember history understand better than most that there is no security, no safety in the appeasement of evil. It must be the core of Western policy that there be no sanctuary for terror and to sustain such a policy, free men and free nations must unite and work together.

Sometimes it is said that by imposing sanctions against Colonel Qaddafi or by striking at his terrorist installations we only magnify the man's importance—that the proper way to deal with him is to ignore him. I do not agree. Long before I came into this office, Colonel Qaddafi had engaged in acts of international terror—acts that put him outside the company of civilized men. For years, however, he suffered no economic or political or military sanction, and the atrocities mounted in number, as did the innocent dead and wounded. And for us to ignore by inaction the slaughter of American civilians and American soldiers, whether in nightclubs or airline terminals, is simply not in the American tradition. When our citizens are abused or attacked, anywhere in the world, on the direct orders of a hostile regime, we will respond so long as I'm in this Oval Office. Self-defense is not only our right, it is our duty. It is the purpose behind the mission undertaken tonight, a mission fully consistent with Article 51 of the United Nations Charter.

We believe that this pre-emptive action against his terrorist installations will not only diminish Colonel Qaddafi's capacity to export terror, it will provide him with incentives and reasons to alter his criminal behavior. I have no illusion that tonight's action will bring down the curtain on Qaddafi's reign of terror. But this mission, violent though it was, can bring closer a safer and more secure world for decent men and women. We will persevere.

This afternoon, we consulted with the leaders of Congress regarding what we were about to do and why. Tonight, I salute the skill and professionalism of the men and women of our armed forces who carried out this mission. It's an honor to be your Commander in Chief.

We Americans are slow to anger. We always seek peaceful avenues before resorting to the use of force—and we did. We tried quiet diplomacy, public condemnation, economic sanctions and demonstrations of military force. None succeeded. Despite our repeated warnings, Qaddafi continued his reckless policy of intimidation, his relentless pursuit of terror. He counted on America to be passive. He counted wrong.

I warned that there should be no place on Earth where terrorists can rest and train and practice their deadly skills. I meant it. I said that we would act with others, if possible, and alone if necessary to ensure that terrorists have no sanctuary anywhere. Tonight, we have.

Thank you and God bless you.

PRIME MINISTER CHIRAC ON FRENCH ANTITERRORIST LAWS
September 14, 1986

Ten people were killed and more than 160 wounded in a series of terrorist bombings at Paris stores, restaurants, and public buildings between September 8 and 16, 1986. French authorities were tightlipped about who might be responsible for the blasts. They were believed to be the work of the Lebanese Armed Revolutionary Faction (FARL), a group with ties to Syria that had been implicated in the assassinations of several Western and Israeli diplomats in Europe. The group's leader, Georges Ibrahim Abdullah, was imprisoned in France, and it appeared that the Paris blasts were aimed at gaining his release.

Any thoughts French authorities might have about attacking Syria in retaliation for the bombings were dampened by the fact that extremist Shi'ite Muslim groups with their own ties to Syria were holding French hostages in Lebanon. Any attack on Syria would undoubtedly bring harm to the hostages. Instead, President Jacques Chirac initiated a stringent antiterrorist plan that he outlined on the television program "Grand Jury," a joint production of the network Radio-Television-Luxembourg and the newspaper Le Monde. *The extensive plan, which primarily aimed to keep terrorists out of France, included identity checks, new visa requirements, border and airport patrols by the military, intensified intelligence efforts, more active surveillance by local police, expulsion of illegal aliens, and improved coordination of government antiterrorism efforts, among other measures.*

Critics accused Chirac's government of negotiating with terrorists and their host countries. Some government officials and Paris police suspected that Chirac's government was moving toward cooperation with Syria to end the Paris attacks and win release of the hostages in Lebanon. Chirac denied conducting any negotiations. Nonetheless, two French hostages were released in November and another in December, apparently because of negotiations with Syria, Iran, Algeria, and Saudi Arabia. Other nations also tangled with Syria in 1986. In October the United Kingdom broke diplomatic relations with Syria after a British jury convicted a Jordanian-born Palestinian of unsuccessfully attempting to blow up an El Al airliner. The

British government said it had "conclusive evidence" that the man had ties to the Syrian government. The United States and Canada withdrew their ambassadors from Syria in support of Britain's action, and the United States also imposed economic and political sanctions. The next month, the West German government refused to name an ambassador to Damascus and ordered the Syrian embassy to reduce its staff after a court found that two Syrian officials had helped carry out a March bombing in West Berlin.

Following are excerpts from French prime minister Jacques Chirac's televised statement September 14, 1986, on "Grand Jury," a joint production of the network Radio-Television-Luxembourg and the newspaper Le Monde:

Since our election and the formation of this government we have been working on a series of bills that are now ready. The laws on security and particularly on terrorism that were voted on during the last session were promulgated a few days ago according to the democratic legislative process for passing laws. We will implement their provisions immediately and with the greatest authority. What do these laws provide for? First of all, improvement of prevention by extension of police custody, general identity checks, and searches on premises.

On the question of identity checks I ask every one of our citizens to understand that, in the current situation, the constraint that these controls represent should be accepted with, so to speak, good humor. It is necessary for everyone's security.

These laws also centralize investigations and legal proceedings in Paris, in the hands of specialists, in order to be more effective in the prosecution of those who are implicated of direct or indirect involvement in terrorist acts.

They also include a measure new to our system, although it is classic and has been effective in several countries. It is the law concerning those who repent and which allows total exoneration of punishment for sentenced persons who aid in preventing a crime, and partial exoneration if they denounce and aid in the capture of terrorists or those who commit attacks.

This measure, which is employed in most of the great democracies, has been especially effective in Italy and Germany.

Finally, the law on foreigners permits an important improvement in our control over our borders and it will accelerate the procedures of expulsion.

The second set of decisions we have taken will naturally aggravate a certain number of our foreign friends visiting France. We have in effect decided to require a mandatory visa for all foreigners entering France, regardless of their origin, with the exception, of course, of the European Community and Switzerland.

But for all others, no matter what their origin, the North or the South, Asia or Africa, from tomorrow on visas will be required, albeit with a few days' delay, for technical reasons, before actual implementation begins. The visas will be issued by our consulates around the world and will enable us to prohibit entry into France to all sorts of people who appear at the borders and enter the territory with passports which, as everyone knows, are all too often irregularly issued, or are forgeries that we cannot verify.

I ask all our foreign friends to understand that, in the crisis situation in which we find ourselves, this measure is necessary. Unfortunately it is likely to provoke some problems when enforced, such as delays in airports or at points of entry into France, but these are inevitable incidents in the implementation of this type of measure.

Certainly the very few nations with whom we have agreements (about the movement of persons) should understand this measure which, I add, is taken for six months. . . .

The third point concerns a very important reinforcement of control at our borders. Terrorism thrives on the possibility of illegally entering and leaving our country with impunity. We have decided to strengthen our means of control. You know that border control is ensured partly by the air and border police—although the means at its disposal are not sufficient to control all our borders—and partly by the customs service. This leaves some very large sectors that are in fact not under surveillance and which are used as passageways. I have therefore decided to ask the armed forces to assume their responsibility.

In this way the armed forces, through permanent patrols, will ensure the control of our borders. They will carry out their mission on the German and Belgium-Luxembourg border with appropriated forces, naturally in conjunction with the air and border police who are to retain responsibility of action. In the central and eastern Pyrenees the paratroops division will carry out their mission, and in the Alps, the Alpine division will do so. This will alleviate the burden on the air and border police and the customs officials, who can concentrate on the flow at the traditional points of entry into our country. I hope this will be an element of dissuasion, even of crackdown if need be, against the crossing of our borders.

More than a thousand soldiers are going to patrol the different borders, without counting those that are assigned to the assistance and command of these troops. Moreover, the minister of defense will deploy a few hundred soldiers to reinforce the security at the points of entry into France, especially the airfields.

Finally, the gendarmerie [local police] has been ordered to extensively improve identity checks around airports and in border zones, and to intensify its intelligence missions. . . .

My next point concerns checks and, where necessary, expulsion. Everyone knows that the police have an eye on a certain number of people whom they suspect, but cannot accuse, of belonging to what I would call the terrorist organizations' sphere of influence. We have decided to strengthen considerably checks on and surveillance of all those active in the terrorist movements' sphere of influence, hence the series of arrests which you have probably heard about in the last few days and which will result in expulsion—and which has in the last two days resulted in the expulsion of persons whose presence in

France we consider a danger to the public order. That has begun, will continue and be carried out with the greatest determination and the greatest firmness.

Finally, there is the problem of security in public places. As you saw earlier, reports have just come in, and will perhaps be corrected since this occurred virtually as we were coming into the studio, of a dubious package apparently, I say apparently being discovered in the Renault Pub, a place where there are a lot of people, and being taken down into the basement, where it unfortunately exploded, wounding three policemen: that clearly illustrates the vulnerability of public places. They must have proper security. I am mayor of Paris, I see what happens in the close vicinity of my City Hall. Everyone who enters the Bazar de l'Hotel de Ville [a large department store] with a package, even a small one, has to open it. I tell you that this has not caused the slightest problem nor created the slightest incident in the last three or four years. And this has made the Bazar de L'Hotel de Ville a very safe place. Other stores, like the Galeries Lafayette and others as well, do the same thing. I want private places frequented by the public to enforce those security measures, which are a very considerable deterrent.

I ask all our fellow citizens to understand that such measures are useful and in their own interest. Tomorrow the minister of the interior or the minister of security and the minister with responsibility for trade, the artisan industries and services will meet at the ministry of the interior with the leaders of the professional organizations involved, particularly those concerned with large shopping areas, places of entertainment and other premises of a like nature, to tell them that it is absolutely vital for them to organize a security system, as some of their competitors or colleagues have done: the number of entrances must be limited where there are large numbers of people and all packages or bags brought into the premises checked. We are going to take similar measures, either permanent or temporary depending on the case and nature of the service, in all the public services.

There you have a certain number of measures, those that can be announced. I tell you right away that there are others, but these others are the sole responsibility of the public authorities and, because of their nature, are not being publicized and I shall not answer questions or comment on them. However, they are also being taken in the context of this calm, firm fight against this veritable scourge of modern times that is terrorism.

In conclusion, I shall say that everyone must feel he or she has a part to play in these matters. Everyone's safety is at stake. Terrorism is, by definition, blind and spares no one, not you, me or anyone. . . .

I would like everyone to be certain that the day, and it will inevitably come, there's no doubt about that, when we catch a terrorist in the act, he will talk and those manipulating him must clearly realize that they will receive draconian retribution, that we shall be pitiless, regardless of the consequences. They must realize that.

PRESIDENT REAGAN'S SPEECH ON THE IRAN-CONTRA AFFAIR
November 13, 1986

Relations between the United States and Iran virtually ended in November 1979 after Iranian militants stormed the U.S. Embassy in Tehran, subsequently holding fifty-two Americans hostage for 444 days. The United States imposed an arms embargo on Iran in 1979 and urged other nations to suspend weapons sales to Iran as well. In a July 1985 speech to the American Bar Association, President Ronald Reagan denounced Iran as one of five nations that engaged in terrorism. Yet on January 17, 1986, Reagan signed an executive order approving covert arms sales to Iran—even though the U.S. arms embargo remained in effect and Reagan had trumpeted the American policy of making no concessions to terrorists. Administration officials involved in the arms sales hoped that in return for the weapons, Iran would help gain release of American hostages held in Lebanon by pro-Iranian terrorists. (The Beginning of the Iran Hostage Crisis, p. 34; President Reagan Charges Five Nations with Terrorism, p. 71)

Press reports in early November disclosed the sales, and Reagan went on national television November 13 to admit that the United States had, indeed, shipped arms to Iran. However, he labeled as "wildly speculative and false" press claims that the arms were payment for Iran's help with the hostages. "We did not—repeat—did not trade weapons or anything else for hostages—nor will we," he said. Reagan said the weapons were sent to Iran as a signal "that the United States was prepared to replace the animosity between us with a new relationship." A few American hostages in Lebanon had been released during the course of the arms shipments, although others were not freed and groups linked to Iran had even abducted three more Americans in Beirut in September and October.

In a bombshell announcement November 25, the administration revealed that profits from the arms shipments of between $10 million and $30 million had been diverted to the U.S.-backed contra guerrillas who were attempting to overthrow the communist Sandinista government in Nicaragua. That diversion violated a congressional ban on direct or indirect aid to the rebels. Meanwhile, in a televised address March 4, 1987, Reagan acknowledged that *the primary intent of the Iran arms sales was to gain the hostages' release. "A few months ago I told the American people I did not trade arms for hostages," he said. "My heart and my best intentions still tell me that is true, but the facts and the evidence tell me it is not." Numerous administration officials pleaded guilty or were convicted of crimes related to the Iran-contra affair. Ultimately, however, two had their convictions overturned on constitutional grounds and President George H. Bush—who had served as Reagan's vice president—pardoned six others in December 1992, one month before leaving office.* (Independent Counsel's Report on the Iran-Contra Affair, p. 137)

Following are excerpts from President Ronald Reagan's nationally televised address on November 13, 1986, announcing that he had authorized some covert arms sales to Iran—even though the U.S. arms embargo remained in effect:

Good evening.

I know you have been reading, seeing, and hearing a lot of stories the past several days attributed to Danish sailors, unnamed observers at Italian ports and Spanish harbors, and especially unnamed government officials of my administration. Well, now you're going to hear the facts from a White House source, and you know my name.

I wanted this time to talk with you about an extremely sensitive and profoundly important matter of foreign policy. For 18 months now we have had under way a secret diplomatic initiative to Iran. That initiative was undertaken for the simplest and best of reasons: to renew a relationship with the nation of Iran, to bring an honorable end to the bloody 6-year war between Iran and Iraq, to eliminate state-sponsored terrorism and subversion, and to effect the safe return of all hostages. Without Iran's cooperation, we cannot bring an end to the Persian Gulf war; without Iran's concurrence, there can be no enduring peace in the Middle East. . . .

The charge has been made that the United States has shipped weapons to Iran as ransom payment for the release of American hostages in Lebanon, that the United States undercut its allies and secretly violated American policy against trafficking with terrorists. Those charges are utterly false. The United States has not made concessions to those who hold our people captive in Lebanon. And we will not. The United States has not swapped boatloads or planeloads of American weapons for the return of American hostages. And we will not. . . .

During the course of our secret discussions, I authorized the transfer of small amounts of defensive weapons and spare parts for defensive systems to Iran. My purpose was to convince Tehran that our negotiators were acting with my authority, to send a signal that the United States was prepared to replace the animosity between us with a new relationship. These modest deliveries, taken together, could easily fit into a single cargo plane. They could not, taken together, affect the outcome of the 6-year war between Iran and Iraq nor could they affect in any way the military balance between the two countries.

Those with whom we were in contact took considerable risks and needed a signal of our serious intent if they were to carry on and broaden the dialog. At the same time we undertook this initiative, we made clear that Iran must oppose all forms of international terrorism as a condition of progress in our relationship. The most significant step which Iran could take, we indicated, would be to use its influence in Lebanon to secure the release of all hostages held there.

Some progress has already been made. Since U.S. Government contact began with Iran, there's been no evidence of Iranian Government complicity in acts of terrorism against the United States. Hostages have come home, and we welcome the efforts that the Government of Iran has taken in the past and is currently undertaking.

But why, you might ask, is any relationship with Iran important to the United States?

Iran encompasses some of the most critical geography in the world. It lies between the Soviet Union and access to the warm waters of the Indian Ocean. Geography explains why the Soviet Union has sent an army into Afghanistan to dominate that country and, if they could, Iran and Pakistan. Iran's geography gives it a critical position from which adversaries could interfere with oil flows from the Arab States that border the Persian Gulf. Apart from geography, Iran's oil deposits are important to the long-term health of the world economy.

For these reasons, it is in our national interest to watch for changes within Iran that might offer hope for an improved relationship. Until last year there was little to justify that hope.

Indeed, we have bitter and enduring disagreements that persist today. At the heart of our quarrel has been Iran's past sponsorship of international terrorism. Iranian policy has been devoted to expelling all Western influence from the Middle East. We cannot abide that because our interests in the Middle East are vital. At the same time, we seek no territory or special position in Iran. The Iranian revolution is a fact of history, but between American and Iranian basic national interests there need be no permanent conflict. . . .

This sensitive undertaking has entailed great risk for those involved. There is no question but that we could never have begun or continued this dialog had the initiative been disclosed earlier. Due to the publicity of the past week, the entire initiative is very much at risk today.

There is ample precedent in our history for this kind of secret diplomacy. In 1971, then-President Nixon sent his national security adviser on a secret mission to China. In that case, as today, there was a basic requirement for discretion and for a sensitivity to the situation in the nation we were attempting to engage.

Since the welcome return of former hostage David Jacobsen, there has been unprecedented speculation and countless reports that have not only been wrong but have been potentially dangerous to the hostages and destructive of the opportunity before us. The efforts of courageous people like Terry Waite have been jeopardized. So extensive have been the false rumors and erroneous reports that the risks of remaining silent now exceed the risks of speaking out. And that's why I decided to address you tonight.

It's been widely reported, for example, that the Congress, as well as top executive branch officials, were circumvented. Although the efforts we undertook were highly sensitive and involvement of government officials was limited to those with a strict need to know, all appropriate Cabinet officers were fully consulted. The actions I authorized were, and continue to be, in full compliance with Federal law. And the relevant committees of Congress are being, and will be, fully informed.

Another charge is that we have tilted toward Iran in the Gulf war. This, too, is unfounded. We have consistently condemned the violence on both sides. We have consistently sought a negotiated settlement that preserves the territorial integrity of both nations. The overtures we've made to the Government of Iran have not been a shift to supporting one side over the other, rather, it has been a diplomatic initiative to gain some degree of access and influence within Iran—as well as Iraq—and to bring about an honorable end to that bloody conflict. It is in the interests of all parties in the Gulf region to end that war as soon as possible.

To summarize: Our government has a firm policy not to capitulate to terrorist demands. That no concessions policy remains in force, in spite of the wildly speculative and false stories about arms for hostages and alleged ransom payments. We did not—repeat—did not trade weapons or anything else for hostages nor will we. Those who think that we have gone soft on terrorism should take up the question with Colonel Qaddafi.

We have not, nor will we capitulate to terrorists. We will, however, get on with advancing the vital interests of our great nation—in spite of terrorists and radicals who seek to sabotage our efforts and immobilize the United States. Our goals have been, and remain, to restore a relationship with Iran; to bring an honorable end to the war in the Gulf; to bring a halt to state-supported terror in the Middle East; and finally, to effect the safe return of all hostages from Lebanon.

As President, I've always operated on the belief that, given the facts, the American people will make the right decision. I believe that to be true now. I cannot guarantee the outcome. But as in the past, I ask for your support because I believe you share the hope for peace in the Middle East, for freedom for all hostages, and for a world free of terrorism. Certainly there are risks in this pursuit, but there are greater risks if we do not persevere.

It will take patience and understanding; it will take continued resistance to those who commit terrorist acts; and it will take cooperation with all who seek to rid the world of this scourge.

Thank you, and God bless you.

TESTIMONY ON INEFFECTIVE AIRPORT PASSENGER SCREENING
June 18, 1987

After a rash of airplane hijackings in the early 1970s, the Federal Aviation Administration (FAA) in January 1973 began requiring airlines to screen all passengers and their carry-on baggage. Passengers walked through metal detectors and their carry-on items were scanned, procedures aimed at stopping terrorists or anyone else from taking guns, explosives, and other weapons onto planes. But as early as 1979 a joint study by the FAA and the airline industry found many problems with screening personnel, who typically worked for private security firms under contract to the airlines. The screener problems included high turnover, low wages, and inadequate training.

FAA tests where inspectors tried to get weapons past screeners at major airports turned up widely varying results, according to testimony on June 18, 1987, before a congressional subcommittee by Kenneth M. Mead of the General Accounting Office (GAO), the investigative arm of Congress. The detection rates ranged from a low of 34 percent to a high of 99 percent, Mead said. He added that those numbers were probably artificially high because the FAA's tests were too simple and were often conducted by local FAA inspectors who the screeners knew. Mead recommended that the FAA establish performance standards for screeners and fine airlines that failed to meet them.

Shortly after Mead testified, the FAA established performance standards and fines as he had recommended. However, his testimony was just the first in a long line of GAO reports and congressional appearances by GAO officials that cited continuing problems with screeners and the FAA's overall security program. The GAO's recital of ongoing failures continued through and beyond the attacks of September 11, 2001, when hijackers who passed through security screenings were able to take over four commercial airliners. (Vulnerabilities in the Aviation Security System, p. 210)

Following are excerpts from the testimony of Kenneth M. Mead of the General Accounting Office before a subcommit-

tee of the House Committee on Government Operations on June 18, 1987:

We appreciate the opportunity to testify on the preboard passenger screening process—a critical component of the Federal Aviation Administration's (FAA) Civil Aviation Security Program. The purpose of passenger screening at U.S. airports is to prevent firearms, explosives, and other dangerous weapons from being carried on board an airplane and presenting a danger to the traveling public.

Our testimony today covers the preliminary results of our work on FAA's testing of preboard passenger screening. This work was done as part of a more comprehensive assignment currently underway, also at the Subcommittee's request, to evaluate domestic airport security. Our observations are based on work at six major airports, an analysis of about 2400 of FAA's recent passenger screening tests, discussions with FAA program officials, and a review of FAA documentation. We did not validate FAA's test data.

FAA considers the passenger screening process effective in deterring criminal acts against civil aviation. According to FAA data, since 1973, over 38,000 firearms have been detected and at least 117 potential hijackings and related crimes may have been averted by FAA required security measures. Overall, we believe this aviation security program plays a significant deterrent role and promotes the safety of the traveling public. However, we believe the passenger screening process can be made more effective. We found that there are shortfalls in the passenger screening program and, based on FAA test results, wide variations in the frequency with which weapons are detected. FAA is working to improve preboard passenger screening, but the program continues to experience many of the personnel-related problems—high turnover, low wages, inadequate training—identified in a 1979 FAA/industry study.

FAA also has not been satisfied with the overall results of the tests it has performed, but there are no standards setting goals or stipulating the levels of performance for passenger screening. To help strengthen the program, we believe FAA should establish performance standards to define for air carriers what is expected. Additionally, standards would provide FAA with a management tool for monitoring and enforcing the passenger screening aspects of the Civil Aviation Security Program.

Preboard Passenger Screening and How It Works

The current process for screening aircraft passengers and their carry-on baggage began in January 1973 following the issuance of an emergency regulation by FAA. FAA established the process to curb the growing number of aircraft hijackings that were occurring in the early 1970s and to insure safety. In 1974, the process was made statutory.

FAA prescribes screening regulations, provides overall guidance and direction for the program, and reports semi-annually to Congress on the effectiveness of screening procedures. The air carriers are responsible for screening passengers and their carry-on baggage; however, private security firms under contract to air carriers typically do the screening. Both the air carriers and FAA monitor a security firm's performance.

Screening personnel rely on equipment consisting primarily of walk-through metal detectors and X-ray inspection systems to screen carry-on items. Hand-held metal detection devices are used as backup support for the walk-through detectors. In addition, screening personnel may require physical searches for items in carry-on baggage that appear suspicious when X-rayed. Each of the components of the process—X-ray, metal detector, and physical search—are periodically tested by the airline and FAA. While there have been some technological improvements to screening equipment, for the most part the process operates essentially the same today as it did when implemented in 1973.

FAA Test Results: Absence of Performance Standard

FAA has periodically tested preboard passenger screening and has not been satisfied with test results. However, the Air Carrier Standard Security Program, which establishes preboard passenger screening requirements and is approved by FAA, does not establish a performance standard for measuring the effectiveness of the process. FAA officials told us that they are considering incorporating such a standard in the Security Program. Without a standard, FAA cannot take enforcement actions, which range from warning letters to fines, when air carriers' screening stations fail to detect test weapons.

The results of about 700 tests of X-ray screening operations conducted during 1978 showed a detection rate of approximately 87 percent. The fact that 13 percent of the test weapons passed through the X-ray system were not detected was considered "significant and alarming" by both FAA and the airline industry. In 1981 and 1982, tests of both X-ray and metal detector screening operations showed an overall weapon detection rate of 89 and 83 percent, respectively.

In tests conducted by FAA from September through December 1986, screening personnel detected approximately 79 percent of the test weapons for X-ray tests, 82 percent for metal detector tests, and 81 percent for physical search tests. Detection rates varied significantly among FAA regions, ranging from a low of 63 percent to a high of 99 percent. For major airports, the detection rate ranged from a low of 34 percent to a high of 99 percent.

Moreover, our analysis shows that FAA test results may overstate the screening process' success in detecting weapons for at least two reasons: First, FAA test procedures are designed to favor detection of test weapons. For example, FAA inspectors are allowed to place only two or three objects such as a sweater, book, and shirt with a test weapon in the carry-on bag to be tested in an X-ray device. The tester cannot hide the test object among other objects in the carry-on bag or place other metal objects in the bag, as a saboteur might.

Second, screening personnel may be aware they are being tested. This is because FAA inspectors in some locations are well known to screening station personnel. FAA is aware of this problem and has acknowledged that high detection rates in certain locations may indicate the screeners recognized the FAA inspector.

Personnel-Related Factors

Following the 1978 tests of the screening process, a task group of FAA and airline security personnel studied ways to improve performance at passenger screening checkpoints. This task group's report, referred to as the "Human Factors Study," recommended several actions which were endorsed by both FAA and the airlines. For the most part, these recommendations focused on the personnel-related aspects of the process such as high employee turnover rates, low pay, and inadequate training. Although FAA and the industry endorsed the study's recommendations, the air carriers have not yet fully implemented them.

We visited six major airports and found that many of the problems addressed in the human factors study still exist. For example, security firm managers said that screening employees are still being paid at or near minimum wage and that low pay contributes to high turnover—in some cases, about 100 percent annually—and problems in hiring capable people.

We found that training was generally provided as required by the Air Carrier Standard Security Program. However, we noted that problems continue to exist in the training area. For example, at one screening firm's training session, we were advised that instructors did not attend the training and that trainees simply viewed the 5-part FAA "Safety through Screening" series by themselves. They then signed a statement to attest that they had attended. As a result, no one was available to answer questions as recommended by the Human Factors study group. In another case, we observed that trainees were tested on the training they received but were not graded. Thus, there was no measurement of the trainees' comprehension of the subject matter.

In addition, FAA's 1986 physical search test results show that screeners could not identify test weapons in 47 of 249 cases. During our work, we observed one case where the FAA test weapon—a mock pipe bomb—was initially identified as suspect by the X-ray operator. However, when the required physical search was made by another screener, the screener did not recognize the pipe bomb as a weapon and replaced it in the carry-on baggage. The screener then cleared the tester to proceed to the aircraft boarding gate.

Research and Development Efforts

As a final note, technological advances also may offer in the next several years the potential for enhancing the passenger screening process. During the past two fiscal years, FAA has increased spending for research and development to put new technology "on the shelf," thereby making improved security systems available for air carriers to purchase. FAA funding on research and development for security equipment increased from between $1 million and $2 million prior to 1985 to between $11 and $12 million per year during the past two fiscal years.

FAA expects to test a vapor system for detecting plastic explosives on passengers or in carry-on luggage in the summer of 1988. If successful, this system could be available for use in late 1989 or early 1990. FAA officials said this new technology will supplement the current screening process. . . .

As of May 28, 2002, the full text of Mead's testimony was available at http://161.203.16.4/d39t12/133425.pdf

COURT ON CLOSING THE PLO'S MISSION TO THE UNITED NATIONS
June 29, 1988

In 1974 the United Nations General Assembly granted permanent observer status to the Palestine Liberation Organization (PLO), even though some people labeled the PLO a terrorist organization. The PLO then opened quasi-diplomatic offices at the United Nations and in Washington, D.C. But more than a dozen years later, during the final days of the 1987 session of Congress, lawmakers approved a bill that formally declared the PLO a "terrorist" organization. The Anti-Terrorism Act of 1987 also required federal officials to close the PLO's two offices in the United States. Passage of the bill created a quandary for federal officials because it conflicted with the Headquarters Agreement, a treaty in which the United States—as host country for the United Nations—guaranteed the rights of UN diplomats to maintain offices in New York. The PLO's Washington office was closed with no problem, but 143 nations voted in favor of a UN General Assembly resolution declaring that closing the PLO's New York office would violate international law. The Justice Department asked a Manhattan judge to grant an injunction ordering the PLO office to close, and the PLO in turn challenged the law's validity. (Arafat's Speech Before the UN General Assembly, p. 13)

On June 29, 1988, U.S. District Court Judge Edmund Palmieri ruled that the Anti-Terrorism Act did not override the Headquarters Agreement. "The Agreement, along with longstanding practice," he wrote, "leaves no doubt that it places an obligation upon the United States to refrain from impairing the function of the PLO observer mission." The Justice Department did not appeal the case, apparently at the urging of President Ronald Reagan and the State Department.

Only months later, on November 15, 1988, the Palestine National Council met in Algiers and declared the establishment of an independent Palestinian state. The council, a de facto parliament in exile for the Palestinian movement, issued the declaration as part of a broad political program aimed at recovering land occupied by Israel. Nonetheless, on November 26 the Reagan administration announced that it would not grant PLO leader Yasir Arafat a visa to enter the United States to address the UN General As-

sembly, contending that he "knows of, condones and lends support to" acts of terrorism. UN Secretary General Javier Perez de Cueller called the visa denial a violation of the Headquarters Agreement, and the General Assembly held a special session in Geneva on December 13 to hear Arafat.

> **Following are excerpts from the order and opinion issued by Judge Edmund L. Palmieri in U.S. District Court, Southern District of New York, on June 29, 1988, in which he ruled that the United States must refrain from impairing the function of the PLO observer mission:**

The Anti-terrorism Act of 1987 (the "ATA"), is the focal point of this lawsuit. At the center of controversy is the right of the Palestine Liberation Organization (the "PLO") to maintain its office in conjunction with its work as a Permanent Observer to the United Nations. The case comes before the court on the government's motion for an injunction closing this office and on the defendants' motions to dismiss.

Background

The United Nations' Headquarters in New York were established as an international enclave by the Agreement Between the United States and the United Nations Regarding the Headquarters of the United Nations (the "Headquarters Agreement"). This agreement followed an invitation extended to the United Nations by the United States, one of its principal founders, to establish its seat within the United States. . . .Today, 159 of the United Nations' members maintain missions to the U.N. in New York. . . . In addition, the United Nations has, from its incipiency, welcomed various non-member observers to participate in its proceedings. . . .Of these, several non-member nations, intergovernmental organizations, and other organizations currently maintain "Permanent Observer Missions" in New York.

The PLO falls into the last of these categories and is present at the United Nations as its invitee. . . .The PLO has none of the usual attributes of sovereignty. It is not accredited to the United States and does not have the benefits of diplomatic immunity. There is no recognized state it claims to govern. It purports to serve as the sole political representative of the Palestinian people. . . .The PLO nevertheless considers itself to be the representative of a state, entitled to recognition in its relations with other governments, and is said to have diplomatic relations with approximately one hundred countries throughout the world. . . .

The Anti-Terrorism Act

In October 1986, members of Congress requested the United States Department of State to close the PLO offices located in the United States. That request proved unsuccessful, and proponents of the request introduced legislation with the explicit purpose of doing so.

The result was the ATA. It is of a unique nature. We have been unable to find any comparable statute in the long history of Congressional enactments. The PLO is stated to be "a terrorist organization and a threat to the interests of the United States, its allies, and to international law and should not benefit from operating in the United States." The ATA was added, without committee hearings, as a rider to the Foreign Relations Authorization Act for Fiscal Years 1988–89, which provided funds for the operation of the State Department, including the operation of the United States Mission to the United Nations. The bill also authorized payments to the United Nations for maintenance and operation.

The ATA, which became effective on March 21, 1988, forbids the establishment or maintenance of "an office, headquarters, premises, or other facilities or establishments within the jurisdiction of the United States at the behest or direction of, or with funds provided by" the PLO. . . .

Personal Jurisdiction Over the Defendants

. . .The PLO does not argue that it or its employees are the beneficiaries of any diplomatic immunity due to its presence as an invitee of the United Nations. We have no difficulty in concluding that the court has personal jurisdiction over the PLO and the individual defendants.

The Duty to Arbitrate

Counsel for the PLO and for the United Nations and the Association of the Bar of the City of New York, as *amici curiae*, have suggested that the court defer to an advisory opinion of the International Court of Justice. That decision holds that the United States is bound by Section 21 of the Headquarters Agreement to submit to binding arbitration of a dispute precipitated by the passage of the ATA. Indeed, it is the PLO's position that this alleged duty to arbitrate deprives the court of subject matter jurisdiction over this litigation.

In June 1947, the United States subscribed to the Headquarters Agreement, defining the privileges and immunities of the United Nations' Headquarters in New York City, thereby becoming the "Host Country". . . . Section 21(a) of the Headquarters Agreement . . . provides for arbitration in the case of any dispute between the United Nations and the United States concerning the interpretation or application of the Headquarters Agreement. Because interpretation of the ATA requires an interpretation of the Headquarters Agreement, they argue, this court must await the decision of an arbitration tribunal yet to be appointed before making its decision. . . .

. . .[T]his court cannot direct the United States to submit to arbitration without exceeding the scope of its Article III powers. What sets this case apart from the usual situation in which two parties have agreed to binding arbitration for the settlement of any future disputes, requiring the court to stay its proceedings, is that we are here involved with matters of international policy. This is an area in which the courts are generally unable to participate. These questions do not lend themselves to resolution by adjudication under our jurisprudence. . . .[It] is a question of policy not for the courts but for the political branches to decide. . . .It would not be consonant with the court's duties for it to await the interpretation of the Headquarters Agreement by an arbitration tribunal, not yet constituted, before undertaking the limited task of interpreting the ATA with a view to resolving the actual dispute before it. . . .

The Anti-Terrorism Act and the Headquarters Agreement

If the ATA were construed as the government suggests, it would be tantamount to a direction to the PLO Observer Mission at the United Nations that it close its doors and cease its operations *instanter*. Such an interpretation would fly in the face of the Headquarters Agreement, a prior treaty between the United Nations and the United States, and would abruptly terminate the functions the Mission has performed for many years. This conflict requires the court to seek out a reconciliation between the two.

Under our constitutional system, statutes and treaties are both the supreme law of the land, and the Constitution sets forth no order of precedence to differentiate between them. Wherever possible, both are to be given effect. Only where a treaty is irreconcilable with a later enacted statute and Congress has clearly evinced an intent to supersede a treaty by enacting a statute does the later enacted statute take precedence. . . .

The long standing and well-established position of the Mission at the United Nations, sustained by international agreement, when considered along with the text of the ATA and its legislative history, fails to disclose any clear legislative intent that Congress was directing the Attorney General, the State Department or this Court to act in contravention of the Headquarters Agreement. This court acknowledges the validity of the government's position that Congress *has the power* to enact statutes abrogating prior treaties or international obligations entered into by the United States. However, unless this power is clearly and unequivocally exercised, this court is under a duty to interpret statutes in a manner consonant with existing treaty obligations. This is a rule of statutory construction sustained by an unbroken line of authority for over a century and a half. . . .

We believe the ATA and the Headquarters Agreement cannot be reconciled except by finding the ATA inapplicable to the PLO Observer Mission. . . .

. . . The United States has, for fourteen years, acted in a manner consistent with a recognition of the PLO's rights in the Headquarters Agreement. This course of conduct under the Headquarters Agreement is important evidence of its meaning. . . .

It seemed clear to those in the executive branch that closing the PLO mission would be a departure from the United States' practice in regard to observer missions, and they made their views known to members of Congress who were instrumental in the passage of the ATA. In addition, United States representatives to the United Nations made repeated efforts to allay the concerns of the U.N. Secretariat by reiterating and reaffirming the obligations of the United States under the Headquarters Agreement. . . .

. . .[T]he language, application and interpretation of the Headquarters Agreement lead us to the conclusion that it requires the United States to refrain from interference with the PLO Observer Mission in the discharge of its functions at the United Nations. . . .

We have interpreted the ATA as inapplicable to the PLO Mission to the United Nations. The statute remains a valid enactment of general application. It is a wide gauged restriction of PLO activity within the United States and, depending on the nature of its enforcement, could effectively curtail any PLO activities in the United States, aside from the Mission to the United Nations. We do not accept the suggestion of counsel that the ATA be struck down. The federal courts are constrained to avoid a decision regarding unconstitutionality except where strictly necessary. . . .

Conclusions

The Anti-Terrorism Act does not require the closure of the PLO Permanent Observer Mission to the United Nations nor do the act's provisions impair the continued exercise of its appropriate functions as a Permanent Observer at the United Nations. The PLO Mission to the United Nations is an invitee of the United Nations under the Headquarters Agreement and its status is protected by that agreement. The Headquarters Agreement remains a valid and outstanding treaty obligation of the United States. It has not been superceded by the Anti-Terrorism Act. . . .

THE BOMBING OF PAN AM FLIGHT 103 OVER SCOTLAND
May 15, 1990

On December 21, 1988, Pan American World Airways Flight 103 exploded at 30,000 feet over Lockerbie, Scotland. All 259 people on board—including 189 Americans—were killed, as were 11 people on the ground. Investigators determined that a small amount of the plastic explosive Semtex concealed in a radio cassette player that had been placed inside a checked suitcase brought down the plane, which was en route from Frankfurt to New York. Families of the victims were not content with the global criminal investigation that was launched to determine who was responsible for the crime. They insisted that President George H. Bush appoint a commission to examine whether security lapses led to the crash, and he reluctantly created the President's Commission on Aviation Security and Terrorism in August 1989.

In a 182-page report issued May 15, 1990, the commission called the aviation security system "seriously flawed" and concluded that the bombing of Pan Am 103 "may well have been preventable" if luggage had been screened properly at airports in Frankfurt and London where passengers boarded the plane. The commission faulted Pan Am's security procedures at both airports and the Federal Aviation Administration for lax enforcement of its security regulations and blasted both for allowing the problems to continue long after the bombing. In its most controversial recommendation, the panel said the United States should be prepared to take preemptive or retaliatory military action against terrorists.

The criminal investigation resulted in charges against two Libyan intelligence agents, but Libyan leader Muammar Qaddafi refused to turn them over for trial. After more than a decade of economic sanctions imposed by the United States and the United Nations, Qaddafi finally allowed the agents to be tried by a Scottish court sitting in the Netherlands. The trial ended January 31, 2001, with one man convicted and the other acquitted. The judges concluded that the Libyan government was behind the bombing. They did not cite a motive, but it was widely believed that Qaddafi ordered the bombing in retaliation for U.S. air strikes against Libya in 1986. Those air strikes were themselves retaliation for Libyan attacks on U.S. Navy planes flying over international waters and for Libya's involvement in the bombing of a West Berlin discotheque frequented by U.S. military personnel that killed a U.S. soldier and a Turkish woman. (President Reagan on Military Strikes Against Libya, p. 80; Verdict in the 1988 Bombing of Pan Am Flight 103, p. 336)

Following are excerpts from the Executive Summary of the report by the President's Commission on Aviation Security and Terrorism, issued May 15, 1990:

National will and the moral courage to exercise it are the ultimate means for defeating terrorism. The President's Commission on Aviation Security and Terrorism recommends a more vigorous U.S. policy that not only pursues and punishes terrorists but also makes state sponsors of terrorism pay a price for their actions.

With other nations of the free world, the United States must work to isolate politically, diplomatically and militarily the handful of outlaw nations sponsoring terrorism. These more vigorous policies should include planning and training for preemptive or retaliatory military strikes against known terrorist enclaves in nations that harbor them. Where such direct strikes are inappropriate, the Commission recommends a lesser option, including covert operations, to prevent, disrupt or respond to terrorist acts.

Rhetoric is no substitute for strong, effective action.

The Commission's inquiry also finds that the U.S. civil aviation security system is seriously flawed and has failed to provide the proper level of protection for the traveling public. This system needs major reform.

The Commission found the Federal Aviation Administration to be a reactive agency—preoccupied with responses to events to the exclusion of adequate contingency planning in anticipation of future threats. The Commission recommends actions designed to change this focus at the FAA.

Pan Am's apparent security lapses and FAA's failure to enforce its own regulations followed a pattern that existed for months prior to Flight 103, during the day of the tragedy, and—notably—for nine months thereafter. . . .

The Commission . . . conducted a thorough examination of certain civil aviation security requirements, policies and procedures surrounding Flight 103. It is a disturbing story.

The destruction of Flight 103 may well have been preventable. Stricter baggage reconciliation procedures could have stopped any unaccompanied checked bags from boarding the flight at Frankfurt. . . . Stricter application of passenger screening procedures would have increased the likelihood of intercepting any unknowing "dupe" or saboteur from checking a bomb into the plane at either airport. . . .

This Report contains more than 60 detailed recommendations designed to improve the civil aviation security system to deter and prevent terrorist attacks. Before new laws are passed and more regulations are promulgated, existing ones must be fully enforced and properly carried out. The Commission emphasizes that no amount of governmental reorganization or technological developments can ever replace the need for well-trained, highly-motivated people to make the security system work. . . .

At the end of an October 1988 inspection of Pan Am's security operations at Frankfurt, the FAA inspector was troubled by the lack of a tracking system for interline bags transferring from other airlines and the confused state of passenger screening procedures. Overall, the inspector wrote, "the system, trying adequately to control approximately 4,500 passengers and 28 flights per day, is being held together only by a very labor intensive operation and the tenuous threads of luck." Even so, the inspector concluded, "it appears the minimum [FAA] requirements can and are being met."

Passenger/baggage reconciliation is the bedrock of any heightened civil air security system. Under current FAA requirements for international flights, implemented since Pan Am 103, every bag carried on an aircraft must belong to someone who is also on that flight.

A key focus of the Commission's inquiry was the FAA written regulation in effect in December 1988 that unaccompanied baggage should be carried only if it was physically searched.

When Pan Am Flight 103 pushed away from the gate at Frankfurt and again at Heathrow, on December 21, 1988, no one knew whether the plane was carrying an "extra" interline bag that had been checked through to Pan Am from another airline. Months before Pan Am stopped reconciling or searching interline baggage and began simply X-raying this luggage.

Records examined by this Commission indicate that Pan Am Flight 103 might have carried one such interline bag that did not belong to a passenger on a flight. While this extra bag would have been X-rayed, the explosive Semtex cannot be reliably detected by X-ray used at airports.

Pan Am officials told the Commission that the FAA Director of Aviation Security had given the airline verbal approval to X-ray interline bags rather than searching or reconciling them with passengers. The FAA official denied this.

Passenger screening procedures required by FAA at Frankfurt and Heathrow included questioning to identify for additional screening those fitting a "profile" as most likely—knowingly or unknowingly—to be carrying an explosive in any manner, including checked baggage.

The subsequent FAA investigation of Pan Am 103 found that several interline passengers who boarded at Frankfurt were not even initially screened. Several others identified at the check-in counter for further screening did not receive that additional screening at the gate. . . .

The FAA investigation of the Pan Am 103 disaster began immediately and concluded on January 31, 1989. While the results were not announced for over three more months, the FAA proposed fines totaling $630,000 against Pan Am for violations of regulations, both on December 21 and during the five-week period thereafter.

The FAA, significantly, did not cite Pan Am for substituting X-ray for interline passenger/baggage reconciliation. The official FAA report made no reference to the fact that the investigation had found that one interline bag loaded on Flight 103 could not be accounted for in any passenger records. The agency also noted in its announcement that none of the violations cited by its investigation had contributed in any way to the bombing. . . .

Separate from the Flight 103 probe, the FAA found numerous security discrepancies by Pan Am at Frankfurt and London in January and February of 1989 but took no official action against the airline.

In a major inspection conducted May 8–23, 1989, the FAA found that major security violations still existed in Pan Am's Frankfurt operations.

One FAA inspector wrote in the report dated June 7, 1989, that while the operations of the four other U.S. carriers operating at Frankfurt were "good," Pan Am was "totally unsatisfactory."

Wrote the FAA inspector: "Posture [of Pan Am] considered unsafe, all passengers flying out of Frankfurt on Pan Am are at great risk."

When the FAA Associate Administrator with responsibility for the security division learned of the May inspection results, he called a June 14 meeting with Pan Am officials, who presented a plan for corrective action while contesting some of FAA's allegations.

Still, the security violations and deficiencies at Pan Am's Frankfurt station continued. An unannounced inspection in August of 1989 found that many of the same security problems from the May inspection remained uncorrected, especially unguarded airplanes and failure to search personnel maintaining the aircraft.

Pan Am came to a September 12 meeting with FAA on security at Frankfurt with yet another "action plan." A later gathering, however, included a private session between the FAA Administrator and the chief executive officer of the airline. That same evening, a team of high-level Pan Am managers, accompanied by FAA security inspectors, flew to Frankfurt.

Within one week, personnel changes at the station had been ordered and all security violations and deficiencies corrected. At the next FAA regular inspection, Pan Am at Frankfurt was rated a model station. This corrective action occurred nine months after the Flight 103 bombing.

The bombing of Flight 103 occurred against the background of warnings that trouble was brewing in the European terrorist community. Nine security bulletins that could have been relevant to the tragedy were issued between June 1, 1988, and December 21, 1988. One described a Toshiba radio cassette player, fully rigged as a bomb with a barometric triggering device, found by the West German police in the automobile of a member of the Popular Front for the Liberation of Palestine–General Command (PFLP-GC). The FAA bulletin cautioned that the device "would be very difficult to detect via normal X-ray," and told U.S. carriers that passenger/baggage reconciliation procedures should be "rigorously applied". . . .

The Commission also finds that the FAA's research and development program should be significantly intensified to keep pace with the changing terrorist threat to civil aviation. Under a contract awarded in 1985 to Science Applications International Corp. (SAIC), the FAA has purchased six thermal neutron analysis (TNA) machines to detect plastic explosives.

These machines, by design specification and by actual performance as observed by the Commission at JFK Airport in New York, will detect plastic explosives in an operational mode only in amounts far greater than the weight of the most sophisticated bombs actually used by terrorists. For example, the bomb that destroyed Pan Am Flight 103 is believed to have weighed half or less than the amount the TNA machine would reliably detect in an operational mode at an international airport.

Despite these limitations, FAA has announced a program to require U.S. airlines operating internationally to purchase 150 TNA machines (or the equivalent, although there is no competing equipment available) and to install them at 40 international airports at an estimated cost of $175,000,000. The Commission recommends that this program be deferred, pending development of more effective TNA machines or an alternative technology. . . .

FBI ADMITS TERRORISM PROBE VIOLATED FIRST AMENDMENT
September 7, 1990

Based largely on a tip from an informant who it later determined never should have been trusted, in March 1983 the Federal Bureau of Investigation launched a three-year investigation of the Committee in Solidarity with the People of El Salvador (CISPES). The informant told the FBI that CISPES, an American group that strongly opposed Reagan administration policies in Central America, provided money to a foreign terrorist group and was preparing for terrorist strikes of its own in the United States. During the investigation, which involved FBI offices around the country, files were created on 2,375 individuals and 1,330 groups. FBI headquarters closed the investigation in June 1985 after finding that "CISPES appears to be involved in political activities involving First Amendment activities but not international terrorism." No criminal charges were ever filed in the CISPES investigation, which CISPES contended was politically motivated.

Two congressional committees investigated the FBI's conduct in the CISPES case, and one asked the General Accounting Office (GAO)—the investigative arm of Congress—to review the FBI's international terrorism program. In a report dated September 7, 1990, the GAO said that between January 1982 and June 1988 the FBI closed about 19,500 international terrorism investigations. In about 12 percent of the cases the FBI monitored First Amendment-type activities, but the GAO said it was unable to determine whether that monitoring violated the law because the FBI had denied it access to many documents.

The FBI ultimately took mild disciplinary actions against six employees for "mistakes in judgment" in the CISPES cases, changed thirty-three policies and procedures in international terrorism investigations, and removed all files created during the CISPES investigation and turned them over to the National Archives and Records Administration. The final chapter in the case occurred in December 1997 with the settlement of a lawsuit that CISPES had filed eight years earlier against the FBI and the Justice Department. In the settlement, the government agreed to improve training of FBI agents about respecting First Amendment activities and to pay the

*group's legal costs of $190,000. The government also agreed to a consent de-
cree that said in part: "The FBI, in investigating United States persons,
shall not employ any techniques designed to impair their lawful and constitutionally protected political conduct or to defame the character or reputation of a United States person."*

**Following is the executive summary from "International
Terrorism: FBI Investigates Domestic Activities to Identify
Terrorists," a report released September 7, 1990, by the
General Accounting Office:**

Purpose

In carrying out its responsibilities for investigating possible terrorist activities, the Federal Bureau of Investigation (FBI) must balance its investigative
needs against the need to respect individuals' First Amendment rights, such as
the freedom of speech and the right to peaceably assemble. The difficulties in
trying to balance between the two was exemplified in an investigation of the
Committee in Solidarity with the People of El Salvador (CISPES). According
to the FBI, it opened an investigation on the basis of an informant's information that CISPES was involved in terrorist activities. CISPES alleged that
the FBI investigated it because it opposed the Reagan administration's Central
American policies. The release of documents obtained under the Freedom of
Information Act raised questions about the FBI monitoring of American citizens exercising their First Amendment rights.

Because of the issues raised about the FBI's investigation of CISPES, the
Chairman, Subcommittee on Civil and Constitutional Rights, House Judiciary
Committee, asked GAO to review the FBI's investigation of possible interna-
tional terrorism activities to determine

- the basis on which the FBI was opening investigations,
- the scope and results of the investigations,
- whether the FBI had monitored First Amendment activities during the investigations, and
- the reasons the investigations were closed.

Background

The FBI is responsible for detecting, preventing, and reacting to international terrorism activities that involve the unlawful use of force or violence to
try to intimidate a government or its civilian population for political or social
objectives. The FBI maintains a general index system in support of its investigative matters. The FBI identifies various information it obtains during its
investigations and enters it into the system for future retrieval. This process,
known as indexing, records such information as individuals' and organizations' names, addresses, telephone numbers, and automobile license plate

numbers. The FBI has policies governing indexing and the period of time indexed information is retained.

The allegations raised about the FBI's CISPES investigation prompted an internal FBI inquiry of that investigation. The internal study found that the FBI had properly opened the investigation, but the study also found that the FBI had substantially and unnecessarily broadened the scope of the investigation and had mismanaged the investigation. In response to the study's finding, the FBI Director implemented a number of policy and procedure changes regarding international terrorism investigations.

Between January 1982 and June 1988, the FBI closed about 19,500 international terrorism investigations. The FBI completed GAO questionnaires about various aspects of 1,003 cases randomly selected by GAO (e.g., the reasons cases were opened and closed, the subjects of investigations, the monitoring of First Amendment activities, and the use of indexing). GAO is generalizing the results of its questionnaire analyses to an adjusted universe of 18,144 closed international terrorism cases. On the basis of the questionnaire responses, GAO randomly selected 150 cases for review. Eight more cases were added at the request of the Subcommittee. However, the FBI limited GAO's access to data by removing from the case files information it believed could potentially identify informants, ongoing investigations, and sensitive investigative techniques. The FBI also removed information it received from other agencies.

Results in Brief

GAO estimates that about half of the 18,144 cases were opened because the FBI suspected that individuals or groups were involved in terrorist activities. U. S. citizens and permanent resident aliens were the subjects in 38.0 percent of the 18,144 cases. The FBI monitored First Amendment-type activities in about 11.5 percent of these 18,144 cases. The FBI indexed information about (1) individuals who were not the subjects of the investigations in about 47.8 percent of the cases and (2) groups not the subjects of the investigations in about 11.6 percent of the cases. The FBI closed about 67.5 percent of the cases because it did not develop evidence to indicate that the subjects were engaging in international terrorist activities.

The questionnaire and case file data show that the FBI did monitor First Amendment-type activities during some of its international terrorism investigations. Because of the limitations placed on its access to files, however, GAO cannot determine if the FBI abused individuals' First Amendment rights when it monitored these activities or if the FBI had a reasonable basis to monitor such activities.

GAO's Analysis

Reasons Cases Were Opened

From an adjusted universe of 18,144 closed international terrorism investigations from January 1982 to June 1988, GAO estimates that the FBI opened

9,507 cases (52.4 percent) because it had obtained information indicating that someone was engaged in or planning international terrorist activities.

The reasons cases were opened were essentially those stated in broad categories listed on GAO's questionnaires, which were completed by FBI personnel. To develop more detailed descriptions of the reasons cases were opened, GAO reviewed 158 cases and identified whether the information in the files indicated that the subject was or may have been (1) involved in or planned a terrorist act, (2) a leader or member of a terrorist group, or (3) associated with or linked to a terrorist group. The results of GAO's review showed that the FBI opened 70 of the 158 cases because of information indicating the subjects were associated with or linked to a terrorist group. For example, the information obtained may have indicated that the individual's phone number had been called by another person under investigation. Of these 70 cases, U.S. citizens and permanent resident aliens were the subjects in 37 cases.

Monitoring of First Amendment Activities

The FBI observed First Amendment-type activities to obtain information about the subjects of investigations. Information on such activities was also obtained through informants or from other law enforcement agencies.

On the basis of its questionnaire results, GAO estimates that the FBI monitored or observed First Amendment activities in 2,080 (11.5 percent) of its international terrorism cases. Of these 2,080 cases, 951 were investigations of U. S. citizens or permanent resident aliens.

Indexing of Names in Terrorism Investigations

On the basis of its questionnaire results, GAO estimates that the FBI indexed information about individuals, other than the subjects of investigations, in 8,671 (47.8 percent) of its international terrorism cases. Of these 8,671 cases, 3,354 were cases involving indexing of U.S. citizens or permanent resident aliens. Similarly, GAO estimates that 2,105 cases involved indexing of groups during the investigations. Of these 2,105 cases, 913 were cases involving indexing of groups with U.S. citizens or permanent resident aliens.

Reasons Cases Were Closed

GAO estimates that the FBI closed 12,240 cases (67.5 percent) because it found no evidence linking the subject to international terrorist activities. Of the investigations, another 4,015 cases (22.1 percent) were closed because the subject moved or could not be located. The remaining 1,889 cases (10.4 percent) were closed for other reasons, such as the subject was arrested or the case was transferred to another FBI field office.

Recommendations

The FBI removed information it considered sensitive from the closed case files before giving the files to GAO to review. Further, the FBI denied GAO access to open cases. Because of these limitations—information being removed from the files and no access to open cases—GAO is not making any recommendations. Also, GAO could not evaluate changes the FBI had made to its international terrorism program because of the lack of access to open cases.

Agency Comments

GAO requested, but did not receive, written FBI comments on the report. However, GAO discussed the report with FBI officials who generally agreed with the facts. GAO incorporated other views of the officials where appropriate.

As of May 31, 2002, the full text of the General Accounting Office's report was available at http://161.203.16.4/d22t8/142382.pdf

STATEMENTS BY HOSTAGES UPON THEIR RELEASE IN LEBANON
November 18 and December 4, 1991

Beginning in the early 1980s, various radical Arab groups in Lebanon with links to Iran started kidnapping Westerners—primarily Americans— and taking them hostage. Lebanon was in the midst of a civil war between Muslim and Christian militias, and a number of terrorist groups vied for recognition and popular allegiance. One of the most effective tools for achieving those goals was to kidnap prominent Westerners in Beirut, the capital. Between 1982 and 1988 more than twenty hostages were seized— instructors and administrators at the American University of Beirut, members of the clergy, relief workers, and journalists, among others. Some were only held for days, but most endured years of captivity before being released. A few were killed by their captors.

The final break in the hostage crisis came September 11, 1991, when United Nations Secretary General Javier Perez de Cuellar met with Iranian president Hashemi Rafsanjani and reportedly persuaded him to use Iran's influence to seek freedom for the hostages. That same day Israel announced the release of fifty-one Arab prisoners and the bodies of nine slain Arab guerrillas, and a steady trickle of Western hostages then started being released. Some of the last hostages freed were British clergyman Terry Waite and American educator Thomas Sutherland, who were freed November 18, and American Terry Anderson, chief Middle East correspondent for the Associated Press, who was released December 4 after enduring the longest captivity of any hostage: 2,454 days. Anderson's freedom came nearly six years after President Ronald Reagan signed an executive order that permitted covert arms sales to Iran in an effort to free the Americans held in Lebanon. (President Reagan's Speech on the Iran-Contra Affair, p. 88)

Only weeks after the joyful homecomings of Waite, Sutherland, and Anderson, a somber ceremony was held December 30 at Andrews Air Force Base upon the return of the bodies of two American hostages who were killed in Lebanon by their captors. William Buckley, the Central Intelligence Agency's station chief in Beirut, was apparently killed in October 1985 after eighteen months of captivity. William Higgins, a Marine Corps lieu-

tenant colonel who was kidnapped February 17, 1988, while serving on a United Nations truce-observer team, was killed allegedly in retaliation for the abduction of a Muslim spiritual leader by Israeli commandos in Lebanon.

Following are excerpts from remarks by Terry Waite and Thomas Sutherland at a news conference November 18, 1991, in Damascus, Syria, upon their release from captivity and by Terry Anderson at a news conference December 4, 1991, in Damascus upon his release:

REMARKS BY TERRY WAITE

Your Excellence, ladies and gentlemen, I think first of all I would like to say to the Syrian Government our grateful thanks for their hospitality and care during the last few hours. Of course, there are so many people we need to thank—the British Government, the United Nations, churches, and more especially I think ordinary people around the world who have kept the name of the hostages and others alive, and that to us has been supremely important.

This afternoon, when we were sitting together in our cell, chained to the wall, as we have been chained to the wall for the last five years—and in some cases, as Tom and others, for seven years, 23 hours and 50 minutes today, one of our captors came in and told us that Tom and myself would be freed this evening. He also said to me: We apologize for having captured; we recognize that now this was the wrong thing to do, that holding hostages achieves no useful, constructive purpose. He went on to say that before the end of the month, Joseph Cicippio and Alann Steen would be released, we hope within the next five days.

He furthermore said that by the end of the month Terry Anderson would be set free. . . .

REMARKS BY THOMAS SUTHERLAND

. . . As some of you may know, I'm an old college prof from way back, and when I get up to speak, I generally get 50 minutes—which is about five times longer than I've had to go to the bathroom every day for the last seven years, but that's another story.

I would like to especially thank. . .the Government of Syria for all of the work that they have done in those past months and years on our behalf. And I can tell you that in the past hour or so—hour and a half perhaps—we have been treated very, very nicely by some of the representatives of the Government of Syria. And we've had a very happy time joking with them and laughing out loud for the first time for a long time. . . .

Mr. Giandomenico Picco from the U.N. has also apparently played a reasonably key role in all of these negotiations and we are very, very grateful to him and to Secretary General de Cuellar. . . .

Like Terry Waite, I would say that his job is not done because we left Terry Anderson about three or four hours ago in Lebanon, and he is no longer chained to the wall, thank God, but he's still in a room that has very little fresh air and no daylight whatsoever. . . .

Also to Iowa State University in Ames, Iowa. I was very, very moved when I heard on VOA [Voice of America] a recording of "The Bells of Iowa State," which I particularly appreciated hearing when I was a student there on the campus. Walking to class every morning from quarter to 8 until 8, those bells played, so when I heard them ring out 72 bells on the occasion of my 72nd month, I was extremely happy.

So to Iowa State, I would say, keep the bells ringing, friends back there. . . .

Without Terry Anderson, I couldn't have made it six and a half years. Terry Anderson for me was a very big challenge for the first couple of years. He's very, very, very bright, and it was humiliating to me to have to cope with his tremendous brain. After a couple of years I came to grips with that, came to terms with it, and after that our sailing was free. . . .

And so I would just simply say to all of the friends of Terry Anderson, he is a man of whom all of you can be proud. He is in good health right now. He's in very good spirits. . . .

But he's a man who never should have been kidnapped. He was. . .doing his very best for the world and for Lebanon and reporting objectively about what was happening in Lebanon. And they never should have picked any of us up because I agree with Terry Waite that kidnapping is a great evil and that those who perpetrate it—I don't think they really thoroughly understand, many of these young men, what they were doing to us, putting those chains back on our legs every day. And Terry Anderson just said a couple of days ago, I simply couldn't do that to another human being; I simply couldn't do it. . . .

REMARKS BY TERRY ANDERSON

I'm going to try to shake as many people's hands as I can after we get finished here. I mean you're all my friends, but I can't get to you all.

You can't imagine how glad I am to see you. I've thought about this moment for a long time. And now it's here, and I'm scared to death. I don't know what to say.

I have, of course, to thank the Syrian, Lebanese and Iranian governments for their cooperation and their work in helping to free so many hostages recently. I feel the deepest gratitude to Mr. [Giandomenico] Picco and the [UN] Secretary General [Javier Perez de Cuellar]. I don't know how to express it. I mean thanks just doesn't cover it.

Your support, all my colleagues, journalists, has been very important. I've heard so many things over the years—on the radio, in the few magazines and newspapers we've gotten—about your work for me. Again, I just can't say how grateful I am.

Also, for thousands and thousands of people, whom I don't know, never met, who don't know me, who I know have been working and praying for us all, all the hostages, your support, your prayers were important. They made a big difference, they made a difference for us in some very dark times.

My family, of course, my incredible sister, Peg, I will be thanking shortly myself and personally. . . .

And I'd also like to thank my Lebanese colleagues, in the television and newspapers both, because each year they brought a message to me from my family on my birthday, on Christmas, and sometimes elsewhere. And they did this in the midst of their own terrible troubles. And that shows a depth of concern and support that again, I just keep saying, I'm very grateful for. . . .

I'll try to answer a few questions, although you'll understand I have a date with a couple of beautiful ladies, and I'm already very late.

Press: Can you tell about your journey here and when you were actually freed?

Yesterday afternoon, my captors came in, brought some new clothes, new shoes—my first in seven years, and they hurt my feet, by the way—and they said that I would be going home today. . . . Spent the night awake mostly. Today, I spent the day pacing the room and playing solitaire and waiting. I think this last 24 hours has been longer than the whole 6½ years beforehand. I was taken from my cell about 6:20 or 6:30, and driven to a nearby place, turned over to Syrian officers, and brought, with a couple of brief stops, here and to face you. . . .

Press: Tell us something more about what it's been like in captivity.

Oh Lord. Um, it would take a book. That's an idea, by the way.

Press: How do you feel about your title of longest-held hostage?

It's an honor I would gladly have given up a long time ago. . . .

Press: What kept you going?

Well, my companions. I was lucky enough to have other people with me most of the time. My faith. Stubbornness, I guess. You just do what you have to do. You wake up every day, and you summon up the energy from somewhere, even when you think you haven't got it, and you get through the day. And you do it day after day after day. . . .

U.S. ON THE BOMBING OF THE ISRAELI EMBASSY IN ARGENTINA

June 2, 1992

Argentina has a long history of anti-Semitism dating at least to the 1930s, and after World War II it gave refuge to a number of Nazi war criminals. Yet by the early 1990s it was also home to about 250,000 Jews—the largest Jewish population in Latin America—and more than 750,000 people of Arab descent.

On March 17, 1992, the Jewish community's peace was shattered by a car bomb that destroyed the Israeli embassy in Buenos Aires, killing 29 and wounding more than 250. Islamic Jihad, the clandestine wing of the Iran-backed terrorist group Hizballah, claimed responsibility for the attack. The bombing was the first indication to U.S. intelligence officials that Islamic fundamentalists had been organizing in Latin America. Further evidence came July 18, 1994, when a truck bomb blew up the Jewish community center in the heart of Buenos Aires, killing 86 and wounding hundreds more. Intelligence officials blamed that attack on Hizballah as well. (Iran Accused of Supporting Terrorism in Latin America, p. 172)

Investigations of both bombings languished for years, but in May 1998 Argentine authorities announced they had conclusive proof that Iran was behind both attacks and they expelled seven Iranian diplomats. The strongest evidence came from a former high-ranking Iranian security official who said that the cultural attaché at the Iranian embassy had played a key role in planning both bombings. Iran denied involvement in the attacks. The next year Argentina issued an international arrest warrant for Imad Fayez Mugniyah, an alleged leader of Hizballah who had been implicated in a long series of terrorist attacks. The investigation continued to take new twists. In 2000 there were reports that Syria had been involved in the embassy bombing. In perhaps the strangest twist yet, in March 2002 Argentina president Eduardo Duhalde said he believed that Osama bin Laden's al Qaeda network was responsible for both bombings in his country. Duhalde further claimed that al Qaeda and Hizballah had formed an alliance. Nonetheless, by June 2002 no one had ever been charged in the 1992 embassy bombing.

Following is House Concurrent Resolution 297, passed by the U.S. House of Representatives on June 2, 1992, in reaction to the bombing of the Israeli embassy in Buenos Aires, Argentina:

Whereas a terrorist bomb destroyed the Embassy of Israel in Buenos Aires, Argentina, on March 17, 1992;

Whereas at least 24 innocent individuals died and 250 innocent individuals were wounded as a result of the detonation of the bomb;

Whereas the terrorist organization Islamic Jihad has claimed responsibility for the bombing; and

Whereas the bombing is an atrocity: Now, therefore be it

Resolved by the House of Representatives (the Senate Concurring), That the Congress—

(1) condemns the bombing of the Embassy of Israel in Buenos Aires, Argentina, on March 17, 1992;

(2) mourns the victims of the bombing;

(3) extends its condolences to the families and friends of the victims; and

(4) declares that the Government of the United States should *continue to cooperate fully* with the Government of Argentina and the Government of Israel in identifying and bringing to justice all of the individuals responsible for the planning, preparation, and execution of the bombing.

PERUVIAN PRESIDENT ON THE ARREST OF TERRORIST LEADERS
September 13, 1992

In the 1980s and early 1990s frequent and brutal attacks by two rebel groups terrorized Peru, virtually paralyzing the nation's economy and resulting in the deaths of some 25,000 people. The Shining Path, known in Spanish as Sendero Luminoso, and the smaller Tupac Amaru Revolutionary Movement were guerrilla movements that frequently engaged in terrorist acts such as indiscriminate car-bomb attacks in major cities and assassinations of village officials in rural areas. Both groups, which operated separately, sought to overthrow the existing Peruvian government and replace it with a communist regime.

The worst single attack occurred in July 1992 when the Shining Path set off two car bombs in the capital of Lima, killing 20 people and wounding more than 250. But only two months later, on September 12, the authorities captured Shining Path founder Abimael Guzman Reynoso and several other rebel leaders. In a television broadcast to the nation the next day, President Alberto Fujimori called Guzman "a perpetrator of genocide" who had subverted a part of Peru's population and fooled numerous foreign governments. In October a newly created military court convicted Guzman of treason and gave him the maximum sentence of life in prison without parole.

Guzman's arrest was a huge blow to the Shining Path. Its popularity plummeted, as did the number of terrorist attacks committed by its members. However, starting in 2001 there were signs that the Shining Path was regrouping and reemerging. In November 2001 Peruvian authorities announced they had thwarted a Shining Path plan to attack the U.S. embassy in Lima. On March 20, 2002, a car bomb blew up across the street from the U.S. embassy, killing nine people and injuring thirty. The attack, which was widely attributed to the Shining Path, came just three days before President George Bush was to visit Peru. Bush made the trip despite the bombing, saying that "two-bit terrorists" would not interrupt his plans.

Following are excerpts from Peruvian president Alberto Fujimori's September 13, 1992, televised address to the nation on the capture of Shining Path founder Abimael Guzman Reynoso and several other rebel leaders:

Good evening, my fellow citizens:

We Peruvians are all deeply aware of the significance of the apprehension of Abimael Guzman, alias "Comrade Gonzalo," because we know what his terrorist group, the Shining Path, stands for—destruction, death, drug trafficking.

This sinister character is the true embodiment of the means and ends used by his bloodthirsty organization. He has an extraordinarily complex and contradictory mind. A little more than a year ago, the people of Peru were able to meet Abimael Guzman through a video, and instead of the mythical revolutionary leader they expected, they saw a drunken individual, dancing clumsily, surrounded by a group of young women, also inebriated, against the backdrop of portraits of the founders of communism.

Since then, the intelligence services and Dincote [the elite anti-terrorist corps of the National Police] have tracked Guzman and the members of his entourage. Once again, his weaknesses did him in, and made this new and important success possible. It is interesting, how even the most cunning of criminals are taken by surprise in this manner and the leader of the Shining Path was no exception.

The National Police fell upon one of his hideouts when some of the top leaders of the Shining Path were engaging in pleasure-seeking activities which the members of an organization of this sort would have found to be inconceivable. It is indeed difficult to relate the marches of the militant members of the Shining Path, with their Maoist rituals, observed in the past in the jails and part of their export propaganda, with the debauchery of their top leaders, the parties where Greek music and Scandinavian vodka flowed in the midst of other luxuries and sophistication.

That is the moral fiber of this man, the same man who recruited young boys and young men by force to transport bombs and take part in suicide operations. That is Abimael, the exterminator, but it is also Abimael, the debauchee. In sum, a monster. We are before a monster. This is also the man who, with inhuman cold-heartedness, ordered the crime against Mrs. Moyano, the killing at Tarata Street and as well as numerous genocidal raids against young people and peasant populations, where men and women were beheaded and mutilated.

This is the man who forsaking the principles enshrined in his revolutionary creed became the foremost hired assassin of drug trafficking in Peru.

The proceeds from drug-related activities, in addition to financing his personal luxuries and eccentricities and those of the closest members of his entourage, also financed narcoterrorist diplomacy in Europe.

Because part of the immense contribution from the drug cartels financed Shining Path ambassadors abroad, such as Adolfo Olaechea in Great Britain, Alberto Ruiz Eldredge Jr. in France, Luis Arce in Belgium, Javier Mujica Contreras in Spain, Carlos La Torre Cordova in Sweden and many others throughout different European nations.

However, Guzman has led his youngest followers, those who truly bear the brunt of their struggle, to believe that his ties with drug trafficking are lies concocted by the Fujimori administration. And those young men, who are cannon fodder, have never seen or even dreamed of the luxuries of their leaders, and still believe that there is no connection between their movement and drug trafficking.

But we must acknowledge that Abimael Guzman is a diabolical genius. For 12 years he has been able to fool not only a sector of Peru's youth but also democratic governments and even international organizations which lent him their support in a number of ways, including the granting of asylum for his assassins.

It has taken the international community twelve years to realize that it was before a war criminal, a perpetrator of genocide, one who is on a par with the fascist war criminals of the Second World War.

During those 12 years, this wicked genius, "Comrade Gonzalo," planted the seeds of death and destruction under the protective mantle of silence of human rights organizations while Peru counted its dead, buried its dead, and remained impotent. The human rights of this terrorist and genocidal gang were more important than those of 22 million Peruvians.

Let the world know that that has been the cost we Peruvians have had to pay. Let the world hear and express its solidarity towards a people yearning for the advent of peace. Let the civilized governments of the world close their doors to those who have not only violated but desecrated human rights, these genocidal terrorists who under the guise of a Peruvian revolutionary movement have joined forces with the drug cartels and exterminated any who opposed them. This is the man, who with this shameful background, claimed to be the architect of a new democracy.

Fellow citizens:

I have pledged to defeat all terrorist groups by 1995. This should not be interpreted as "triumphalism." We must not be "triumphalist" for even a second or let down our guard against these fanatic criminals. We must at all times be realistic, but we must be convinced that with this new strategy and our firm resolve to come out victorious we will defeat an enemy which is becoming increasingly visible.

In spite of what some may say on television, presumably moved by their political interests, I know that you are aware of the fact that there is a new strategy and that it is bearing fruit. As long as you believe this we will continue implementing this strategy. I cannot provide you with any details, but you already know that this strategy rests on winning over the support of the population for its government, for its armed forces. Because if the population and the authorities are on a different course we will be incapable of defeating terrorism. . . .

The distrust and even rejection of the forces of law and order which existed in the past years are giving way to genuine trust and collaboration. In each of those places, places never visited by a president, there is no longer a fear of terrorists.

I am not saying that the people support me, this is not propaganda, I am simply stating that the people no longer feel that their government has forsaken them.

When we aired the now famous video of the Guzman hideout some time ago, I made an appeal to the population indicating that the people of Peru, numbering some 22 million, are dealing with a small group of fanatics. Today we Peruvians know that it is impossible for a small and drug-crazed sect to defeat a country.

Naturally, changes in an important set of conditions were necessary in order for the citizens to start believing in themselves. We must not ignore the fact that one of those apprehended with Guzman was Meche Zambrano, famous for having been set free prior to the fifth of April by the judiciary and the pseudo-democratic system prevailing at that time.

Since April the fifth, with our new antiterrorist legislation, these criminals no longer enjoy sham trials where they can threaten, as they in fact did, the authorities, but rather are judged by military tribunals, so that they can be speedily sentenced and if found guilty, jailed. . . .

All of these actions have been complemented by a new anti-terrorist legislation which, for the first time, prevents the fruit of police and law enforcement efforts from going up in smoke. The previous legislation, with its loopholes and contradictions, its ambiguities and evident obsolescence, served the Shining Path's interests. In this connection, we must not forget the number of terrorist criminals absolved in the most absurd of ways by the judicial branch. . . .

Fear has long been left behind. It has been replaced by indignation. I know that there is a victim of the Shining Path in every one of you. Not only because your loved ones may have fallen prey to those criminals, but also because you have also lost much or part of the fruit of your hard work. Twelve years of frenzied and savage destruction, and losses amounting to more than 20 billion dollars have taken a toll on this impoverished country, making it even poorer. To that we add the loss of 25 thousand lives.

I believe I can sense what fate the population wishes for this criminal, who has done such harm to Peru. You will not be disappointed. Have no doubt that he will have received the maximum sanction possible.

Fellow citizens:

We witness the birth of a new country, a country which believes in itself. We Peruvians are ready to put an end to this terror. Since the fifth of April the population stands united. Large majorities have rejected the vice and flaws of a false democracy and now embrace a genuine democracy to put an end to the greatest scourge in our republic's history once and for all.

On behalf of the nation of Peru, I extend my congratulations to Dincote, agency of the national police for its efficient and committed efforts.

And I again pay tribute to all the victims of the terrorist madness. My promise to the relatives left behind, orphan children, widowed mothers, is that their crimes will not go unpunished.

I thank you very much.

THE 1993 BOMBING OF THE WORLD TRADE CENTER
March 9, 1993

It was lunchtime on a Friday afternoon—12:18 P.M. on February 26, 1993—when a Ryder rental van carrying a bomb weighing 1,200 to 1,500 pounds exploded in the parking garage under the 110-story World Trade Center towers in New York City. The massive blast killed six people and injured more than 1,000 others. Property damage alone was estimated at nearly $300 million.

Less than two weeks later, on March 9, 1993, a subcommittee of the House Judiciary Committee conducted the first hearing into the bombing. Law enforcement officials testified that they suspected a terrorist group was responsible, although they did not accuse any particular group. FBI director William Sessions tried to calm fears of additional attacks. "This suspected act of terrorism should not be viewed as an opening act of a coming wave of terror," Sessions said. Raymond Kelly, police commissioner in New York City, provided sometimes riveting testimony about initial efforts by firefighters, police officers, and emergency medical services personnel to help the injured and evacuate more than 50,000 people from the Trade Center complex.

Four Islamic extremists were convicted in 1994 of taking part in the bombing, and in 1997 two others—including Ramzi Yousef, the plot's alleged mastermind and a terrorist with links to Osama bin Laden and his al Qaeda network—were also convicted. Yousef reportedly told a federal agent that the bombers had intended to topple one of the twin towers into the other, killing everyone in the two buildings. In 1996, a year before his trial for the World Trade Center bombing, Yousef was found guilty of conspiring to blow up a dozen American airliners as they flew over the Pacific Ocean. And in a separate trial that ended in 1996, Egyptian cleric Sheik Omar Abdel-Rahman and nine other Islamic extremists were convicted of conspiring to simultaneously bomb five targets in New York City: the United Nations, a building housing the FBI, the Lincoln and Holland tunnels, and the George Washington Bridge that connects New Jersey and Manhattan. Prosecutors said Abdel-Rahman and the nine other men also were involved in the attack on the World Trade Center. Eight years after the 1993 bombing Islamic extremists attacked the World Trade Center again, crashing commercial airliners into the twin towers and causing both to collapse. (Terrorist Plot to Blow Up American Planes in Flight, p. 187; Bush on Terrorist Attacks Against the United States, p. 351)

Following are excerpts from the March 9, 1993, testimony of Raymond Kelly, police commissioner in New York City, before the Crime and Criminal Justice Subcommittee of the House Judiciary Committee:

On behalf of the New York City Police Department, I want to thank you for giving me the opportunity to testify today about the bombing at the World Trade Center. I am also the emergency management coordinator for the City of New York, and I'm also your witness in that capacity as well.

As you know, the World Trade Center includes two of the tallest office buildings in the world. Up until February, approximately 90,000 people worked and visited there every weekday. At least five of them were killed as a result of the bombing. A thousand more were injured, and the lives of tens of thousands more were severely disrupted. Estimates vary, but the loss incurred by businesses and individuals at the World Trade Center are in the neighborhood of $1 billion.

The World Trade Center bombing was the largest such attack experienced within the borders of the United States. As such, it has implications far beyond the New York metropolitan area. It has implications that Congress certainly will want to address. But before I touch on that let me tell you what happened, how the police department and other agencies responded to the immediate emergency, and how our joint investigation with the FBI and other federal agencies is going forward.

On Friday, February 26th, at 12:18 P.M. an explosion ripped through six underground parking levels of the World Trade Center located immediately underneath the Vista Hotel and between the two twin towers. Within minutes of the explosion, the street in front of the World Trade Center was filled with responding emergency equipment from the New York City Police Department, the New York City Fire Department, emergency medical services, and of course the Port Authority of New York and New Jersey, which owns the center.

As hundreds of victims suffering from smoke inhalation streamed out of the twin towers and the Vista Hotel, emergency equipment and personnel were already on hand to treat them at the scene, or to evacuate them to nearby hospitals.

Over 450 people were sent to area hospitals.

Another 170 were treated at the scene. Four hundred more walked into nearby hospitals on their own. Four New York City Police Department helicopters made 40 rooftop landings on towers one and two of the World Trade Center between 12:30 P.M. and 11:00 P.M.

During these first flights 25 New York City police officers rappelled from helicopters to the roof of tower one, where a landing zone was established and where immediate search and rescue efforts were launched.

Fighting high winds and nightfall, police department pilots delivered a total of 125 rescue personnel to the roofs. Over 30 people were evacuated to safety aboard the helicopters. Underground we established a temporary headquarters across from the World Trade Center at West and Liberty streets. We established a temporary landing zone at West and Vesey streets, and a temporary laboratory at the police academy.

A host of police, fire, and EMS equipment was deployed, including mobile light generators, gasoline and diesel refueling trucks, large electrical generators, decontamination vehicles, 125 ambulances, and 119 pieces of firefighting apparatus.

Uniformed officers from our police task forces scattered throughout the five boroughs were mobilized and brought to bear in the emergency. In all, 2,000 police, fire, and EMS personnel were on the scene. The search of the twin towers and the Vista Hotel by police, fire, and Port Authority personnel began immediately and continued through the night. Between 9:30 P.M. and 2:50 A.M. both towers of the World Trade Center were searched for a second time, floor by floor, to make certain no one was left behind.

The fire department and Port Authority personnel searched the first 50 floors of the twin towers, and the police department searched from the 51st floor to the roofs.

While search and rescue were still underway, the simultaneous turning of our attention to the blast site took place. Working with agents of the FBI and ATF [Bureau of Alcohol, Tobacco, and Firearms], here is what we found.

The explosion took place on the B-2 level of the underground garage. The blast was so strong that it produced a crater six stories deep and about 200 feet wide.

The explosion penetrated upward to the B-1 level, to the street 1 level here [shown in a slide], where it punched a hole in the lobby of the Vista Hotel. It blasted downward another four levels, taking out the World Trade Center's communication system and other vital equipment. . . .

You can see in the pictures of these twisted wrecks [of cars in the parking garage] that a tremendous amount of heat was produced at the center of the blast and the heat was one of the factors that led us to the conclusion early on that a bomb had been exploded.

The chassis of a van used in the blast was blown away from the center of the crater. It contained the partial vehicle identification number that eventually led to the arrest of Mohammed Salameh at a truck rental agency in New Jersey.

From the pictures you can get a good idea of how the vertical beams, as we said, were left without any lateral support, and workers are now welding lateral supports in place so that we can go forward with our search for evidence and for the missing employee, Wilfredo Mercado, Jr.

The successes in the investigation to date extend directly in my judgment from the fact that the New York City Police Department and the Federal Bureau of Investigation have a long working relationship. Our joint bank robbery task force was the first cooperative effort in the nation, and remains a national model. Our joint terrorist task force is now 13 years old and we work cooperatively every day of the year. We share resources.

The police department uses the expertise and assistance of the FBI, ATF, and other federal agencies, and they in turn can borrow the expertise of the New York City Police Department's own intelligence division, our arson explosion squad, and of course the bomb squad, which is the nation's largest and oldest, dating back to 1903.

The cooperative relationship is such that over 100 New York City detectives are assigned to various joint efforts with federal law enforcement agencies.

I would suggest that the tremendous resources being brought to bear in the World Trade Center investigation, both city and federal, will result in such significant costs that the Congress may want to consider defraying them as an investment in the nation's security.

As police commissioner, I certainly welcome the chairman's efforts to seek legislation to strengthen the federal role in combating terrorism. Certainly anything that can help us prevent a single terrorist act from occurring, or in apprehending those responsible, merits serious examination by Congress.

While obviously we would never welcome such attacks, we know that in New York City we are prepared to deal with them. Anyone contemplating such an act should know that the best law enforcement personnel in the world will be on their case for as long as it takes.

We are in the business of tracking down killers and locking them up, and we don't forget. New York City will never forget. . . .

REMARKS ON PEACE AGREEMENT BETWEEN ISRAEL AND THE PLO
September 13, 1993

In a secret exchange of letters in 1993 between Israel prime minister Yitzhak Rabin and Palestine Liberation Organization (PLO) chairman Yasir Arafat, Israel and the PLO agreed to recognize each other's legitimacy. Arafat's letter also said the PLO, which had a long history of launching terrorist strikes against Israel, acknowledged Israel's right "to exist in peace and security," renounced the use of terrorism, and pledged to discipline Palestinians who continued to commit acts of violence.

The letters, along with secret talks throughout the spring and summer of 1993, finally resulted in Israel and the PLO signing a "Declaration of Principles" on September 13, 1993. The accord promised limited self-government for Palestinians living in the occupied Gaza Strip and the West Bank town of Jericho and committed both sides to resolve their differences by peaceful means. Of equal or perhaps even greater significance was the psychological breakthrough represented by Arafat and Rabin standing on a platform at the signing ceremony in Washington, D.C., and sealing the agreement with a handshake before a beaming President Bill Clinton. One of the major factors prompting the agreement was the intifada, *the armed resistance by Palestinians to Israeli rule in the occupied territories. The Israelis had grown weary of the incessant armed strife, while Arafat found himself losing influence to a new generation of militant Islamic leaders.*

Terrorist attacks, shootings, retaliatory strikes, and arrests remained daily occurrences in Gaza and the West Bank after the signing, a sober reminder that implementing the declaration would be excruciatingly difficult. To complicate matters, militant factions on both sides vehemently opposed any peace deal. Nonetheless, on September 28, 1995, Rabin and Arafat continued moving the peace process forward by signing a new agreement that gave the Palestinians control over much of the West Bank of the Jordan River, which Israel had occupied since 1967. Five weeks later, Rabin was assassinated in Jerusalem by an Israeli who accused him of forsaking his nation. (The Assassination of Israeli Prime Minister Rabin, p. 182)

Following are remarks at the peace agreement signing ceremony September 13, 1993, by Israel prime minister Yitzhak Rabin, Palestine Liberation Organization chairman Yasir Arafat, and President Bill Clinton:

REMARKS BY RABIN

President of the United States, your excellencies, ladies and gentlemen:

This signing of the Israeli-Palestinian declaration of principle here today—it's not so easy—neither for myself as a soldier in Israel's war nor for the people of Israel, not to the Jewish people in the diaspora, who are watching us now with great hope mixed with apprehension. It is certainly not easy for the families of the victims of the war's violence, terror, whose pain will never heal, for the many thousands who defended our lives in their own and have even sacrificed their lives for our own. For them this ceremony has come too late.

Today on the eve of an opportunity, opportunity for peace and perhaps end of violence and war, we remember each and every one of them with everlasting love. We have come from Jerusalem, the ancient and eternal capital of the Jewish people. We have come from an anguished and grieving land. We have come from a people, a home, a family that has not known a single year, not a single month, in which mothers have not wept for their sons. We have come to try and put an end to the hostilities so that our children, our children's children, will no longer experience the painful cost of war: violence and terror. We have come to secure their lives and to ease the soul and the painful memories of the past—to hope and pray for peace.

Let me say to you, the Palestinians, we are destined to live together on the same soil in the same land. We, the soldiers who have returned from battles stained with blood; we who have seen our relatives and friends killed before our eyes; we who have attended their funerals and cannot look in the eyes of their parents; we who have come from a land where parents bury their children; we who have fought against you, the Palestinians—we say to you today, in a loud and clear voice: enough of blood and tears. Enough.

We have no desire for revenge. We harbor no hatred towards you. We, like you, are people—people who want to build a home. To plant a tree. To love—live side by side with you. In dignity. In empathy. As human beings. As free men. We are today giving peace a chance—and saying to you and saying again to you: enough. Let us pray that a day will come when we all will say farewell to the arms. We wish to open a new chapter in the sad book of our lives together—a chapter of mutual recognition, of good neighborliness, of mutual respect, of understanding. We hope to embark on a new era in the history of the Middle East. Today here in Washington at the White House, we will begin a new reckoning in the relations between peoples, between parents tired of war, between children who will not know war.

President of the United States, ladies and gentlemen, our inner strength, our high moral values, have been the right for thousands of years, from the book of the books. In one of which, we read: To everything there is a season and a time to every purpose under heaven: a time to be born and a time to die, a time to kill and a time to heal, a time to weep and a time to laugh, a time to love and a time to hate, a time of war and a time of peace. Ladies and gentlemen, the time for peace has come.

In two days the Jewish people will celebrate the beginning of a new year. I believe, I hope, I pray that the new year will bring a message of redemption for all peoples—a good year for you, for all of you; a good year for Israelis and Palestinians; a good year for all the peoples of the Middle East; a good year for our American friends who so want peace and are helping to achieve it.

For Presidents and members of previous Administrations, especially for you, President Clinton, and your staff, for all citizens of the world, may peace come to all your homes. In the Jewish tradition it is customary to conclude our prayers with the word Amen. With your permission, men of peace, I shall conclude with the words taken from the prayer recited by Jews daily, and whoever of you who volunteer, I would ask the entire audience to join me in saying Amen. [Speaking in Hebrew] May He who brings peace to His universe bring peace to us and to all Israel. Amen.

REMARKS BY ARAFAT

In the name of God the most merciful, the compassionate. Mr. President, ladies and gentlemen:

I would like to express our tremendous appreciation to President Clinton and to his Administration for sponsoring this historic event, which the entire world has been waiting for. Mr. President, I am taking this opportunity to assure you and to assure the great American people that we share your values for freedom, justice, and human rights—values for which my people have been striving.

My people are hoping that this agreement, which we are signing today, marks the beginning of the end of a chapter of pain and suffering which has lasted throughout this century. My people are hoping that this agreement which we are signing today will usher in an age of peace, coexistence and equal rights. We are relying on your role, Mr. President, and on the role of all the countries which believe that without peace in the Middle East, peace in the world will not be complete.

Enforcing the agreements and moving toward the final settlement, after two years to implement all aspects of U.N. resolutions 242 and 338 in all of their aspects, and resolve all the issues of Jerusalem, the settlements, the refugees and the boundaries, will be a Palestinian and an Israeli responsibility. It is also the responsibility of the international community in its entirety to help the parties overcome the tremendous difficulties which are still standing in the way of reaching a final and comprehensive settlement.

Now, as we stand on the threshold of this new historic era, let me address the people of Israel and their leaders, with whom we are meeting today for the first time. And let me assure them that the difficult decision we reached together was one that required great and exceptional courage.

We will need more courage and determination to continue the course of building coexistence and peace between us. This is possible. And it will happen with mutual determination and with the effort that will be made with all parties on all the tracks to establish the foundations of a just and comprehensive peace. Our people do not consider that exercising the right to self-determination could violate the rights of their neighbors or infringe on their security. Rather, putting an end to their feelings of being wronged and of having suffered an historic injustice is the strongest guarantee to achieve coexistence and openness between our two peoples and future generations.

Our two peoples are awaiting today this historic hope. And they want to give peace a real chance.

Such a shift will give us an opportunity to embark upon the process of economic, social and cultural growth and development. And we hope that international participation in that process will be as extensive as it can be. This shift will also provide an opportunity for all forms of cooperation on a broad scale and in all fields.

I thank you, Mr. President. We hope that our meeting will be a new beginning for fruitful and effective relations between the American people and the Palestinian people.

I wish to thank the Russian Federation and President Boris Yeltsin. Our thanks also go to Secretary [of State Warren] Christopher and Foreign Minister [Andrei V.] Kozyrev [of Russia], to the Government of Norway and to the Foreign Minister of Norway, for the positive part they played in bringing about this major achievement.

I extend greetings to all the Arab leaders, our brothers, and to all the world leaders who contributed to this achievement.

Ladies and gentlemen, the battle for peace is the most difficult battle of our lives. It deserves our utmost efforts because the land of peace, the land of peace yearns for a just and comprehensive peace.

Mr. President, thank you. Thank you. Thank you.

REMARKS BY CLINTON

We have been granted the great privilege of witnessing this victory for peace. Just as the Jewish people this week celebrate the dawn of a new year, let us all go from this place to celebrate the dawn of a new era, not only for the Middle East but for the entire world.

The sound we heard today, once again as in ancient Jericho, was of trumpets toppling walls, the walls of anger and suspicion between Israeli and Palestinian, between Arab and Jew. This time, praise God, the trumpets herald not the destruction of that city but its new beginning.

Now let each of us here today return to our portion of that effort, uplifted by the spirit of the moment, refreshed in our hopes and guided by the wisdom of the Almighty, who has brought us to this joyous day. Go in peace. Go as peacemakers.

PRIME MINISTERS ON BRINGING PEACE TO NORTHERN IRELAND
October 29 and November 29, 1993

Between 1969 and 1993 more than 3,100 people died in the latest round of "The Troubles," as the ongoing violence in Northern Ireland between Protestants and Catholics was called. Northern Ireland was a British province, and Britain had assumed direct rule of Northern Ireland in 1972 because of the ongoing violence. British rule was just fine with most of the province's Protestants, but most Catholics were committed to driving out the British so that Northern Ireland could be united with the Republic of Ireland. Paramilitary groups sprung up on both sides. This meant that when the latest round of "troubles" started in 1969, what had been largely a war of words became a war punctuated by blasts from plastic explosives and automatic weapons.

The British and Irish governments stepped up negotiations in 1993, and on October 29 British prime minister John Major and Irish prime minister Albert Reynolds issued a statement promising that "new doors could open" toward peace if the Irish Republican Army (IRA) would end its campaign of violence. The wording of the statement appeared to provide a place in peace negotiations for Sinn Fein, the political wing of the IRA, if the IRA stopped its bombings and other terrorist attacks. Four weeks later, on November 29, the British government issued an extraordinary statement admitting that emissaries of Prime Minister Major and the IRA had conducted secret talks, despite Major's earlier denial of such meetings. Responding to the anger of those who opposed any contacts with the IRA, British officials said they had a duty to take risks to seek an end to the conflict. The secret talks, like the October statement by the British and Irish prime ministers, were aimed at stopping the IRA's violence so that peace talks could be held.

Although there initially was no formal announcement, the violence stopped. On August 31, 1994, the IRA issued a statement announcing "a complete cessation of military hostilities," and six weeks later the Protestant side announced its own ceasefire. On October 21, 1994, Major promised to open exploratory talks with Sinn Finn if the IRA continued its ceasefire. (Talks with IRA Promised If Ceasefire Continued, p. 151)

Following are excerpts from the October 29, 1993, joint statement by British prime minister John Major and Irish prime minister Albert Reynolds and from the November 29, 1993, statement by Sir Patrick Mayhew, secretary of state for Northern Ireland, on peace initiatives between the Irish Republican Army and the British government:

OCTOBER 29 JOINT STATEMENT

The [British] Prime Minister and the Taoiseach [Irish Prime Minister] discussed a range of matters of common interest, with particular focus on Northern Ireland.

They condemned the recent terrorist outrages as murderous and premeditated acts which could serve no other end than to deepen the bloodshed in Northern Ireland, and they expressed their deep sympathy to the innocent victims, children, women and men who had been injured or bereaved.

The Prime Minister and Taoiseach called for restraint from all members of the Community in Northern Ireland, expressed their support for the security forces in their fight against all forms of terrorism, and noted the recent successes of cross-border security cooperation.

They utterly repudiated the use of violence for political ends. Their two Governments were resolute in their determination to ensure that those who adopted or supported such methods should never succeed. . . .

Against this background the Prime Minister and the Taoiseach reaffirmed that:

- The situation in Northern Ireland should never be changed by violence or the threat of violence.
- Any political settlement must depend on consent freely given in the absence of force or intimidation.
- Negotiations on a political settlement could only take place between democratic Governments and parties committed exclusively to constitutional methods and consequently there can be no talks or negotiations between their Governments and those who use, threaten or support violence for political ends.
- There could be no secret agreements or understandings between Governments and organisations supporting violence as a price for its cessation.
- All those claiming a serious interest in advancing the cause of peace in Ireland should renounce for good the use, or support for, violence.
- If and when such a renunciation of violence has been made and sufficiently demonstrated, new doors could open, and both Governments would wish to respond imaginatively to the new situation which would arise.

The Prime Minister and the Taoiseach renewed their support for the objectives of the talks process involving political dialogue between the two Governments and the main constitutional parties in Northern Ireland. They regard that process as vital and its objectives as valid and achievable. They urged the Northern Ireland parties to intensify their efforts to find a basis for new talks. The Taoiseach and the Prime Minister agreed that the two Governments will continue their discussions to provide a framework to carry the process forward.

MAYHEW'S NOVEMBER 29 STATEMENT

With permission, Madam Speaker, I will make a statement about messages between the IRA leadership and the Government.

There has for some years been a means of communication by which messages could be conveyed indirectly, between the Government and the IRA leadership. Clearly such a chain could only function if its secrecy was respected on both sides.

At the end of February this year a message was received from the IRA leadership. It said:

> The conflict is over but we need your advice on how to bring it to a close. We wish to have an unannounced ceasefire in order to hold dialogue leading to peace. We cannot announce such a move as it will lead to confusion for the volunteers because the press will misinterpret it as a surrender. We cannot meet Secretary of State's public renunciation of violence, but it would be given privately as long as we were sure that we were not being tricked.

That message came from Martin McGuinness. Madam Speaker, I have placed in the Library and the Vote Office all consequent messages which HMG [Her Majesty's Government] has received and despatched.

The Government had a duty to respond to that message. I will read to the House the substantive response which, after an intermediate exchange, we despatched on 19 March. The text published yesterday was no more than instructions as to how this was to be transmitted. The message was in these terms:

1. The importance of what has been said, the wish to take it seriously, and the influence of events on the ground, have been acknowledged. All of those involved share a responsibility to work to end the conflict. No one has a monopoly of suffering. There is a need for a healing process.
2. It is essential that there should be no deception on either side, and also that no deception should, through any misunderstanding, be seen where it is not intended. It is also essential that both sides have a clear and realistic understanding of what it is possible to achieve, so that neither side can in the future claim that it has been tricked.
3. The position of the British Government on dealing with those who espouse violence is clearly understood. This is why the envisaged se-

quence of events is important. We note that what is being sought at this stage is advice, and that any dialogue would follow an unannounced halt to violent activity. We confirm that if violence had genuinely been brought to an end, whether or not that fact had been announced, then dialogue could take place.

4. It must be understood, though, that once a halt to activity became public, the British Government would have to acknowledge and defend its entry into dialogue. It would do so by pointing out that its agreement to exploratory dialogue about the possibility of an inclusive process had been given because—and only because—it had received a private assurance that organised violence had been brought to an end.

5. The British Government has made clear that:
   - no political objective which is advocated by constitutional means alone could properly be excluded from discussion in the talks process
   - the commitment to return as much responsibility as possible to local politicians should be seen within a wider framework of stable relationships to be worked out with all concerned
   - new political arrangements would be designed to ensure that no legitimate group was excluded from eligibility to share in the exercise of this responsibility
   - in the event of a genuine and established ending of violence, the whole range of responses to it would inevitably be looked at afresh.

6. The British Government has no desire to inhibit or impede legitimate constitutional expression of any political opinion, or any input to the political process, and wants to see included in this process all main parties which have sufficiently shown they genuinely do not espouse violence. It has no blueprint. It wants an agreed accommodation, not an imposed settlement, arrived at through an inclusive process in which the parties are free agents.

7. The British Government does not have, and will not adopt, any prior objective of "ending of partition." The British Government cannot enter a talks process, or expect others to do so, with the purpose of achieving a predetermined outcome, whether the "ending of partition" or anything else. It has accepted that the eventual outcome of such a process could be a united Ireland, but only on the basis of the consent of the people of Northern Ireland. Should this be the eventual outcome of a peaceful democratic process, the British Government would bring forward legislation to implement the will of the people here. But unless the people of Northern Ireland come to express such a view, the British Government will continue to uphold the union, seeking to ensure the good governance of Northern Ireland, in the interests of all its people, within the totality of relationships in these islands.

8. Evidence on the ground that any group had ceased violent activity would induce resulting reduction of security force activity. Were violence to end, the British Government's overall response in terms of security force activity on the ground would still have to take account of the

overall threat. The threat posed by Republican and Loyalist groups which remained active would have to continue to be countered.

9. It is important to establish whether this provides a basis for the way forward. We are ready to answer specific questions or to give further explanation.

It is clear that this message was consistent with our declared policy: namely that if such people wanted to enter into talks or negotiations with the Government they first had genuinely to end violence. Not just temporarily, but for good. If they did, and showed sufficiently that they meant it, we would not want, for our part, to continue to exclude them from political talks. That remains our policy. . . .

The House will appreciate from what I have read out, and from the other messages when they have time to study them, that our main objective has been to reinforce and spell out in private our publicly stated positions.

It is for the IRA and their supporters to explain why they have failed to deliver the promised ending of violence. They should do so at once. Murder in Northern Ireland is no more tolerable than murder anywhere else in the United Kingdom. We must never lose sight of the fact that it is the terrorists who must answer for the deaths, destruction and misery of the last 25 years.

It lies therefore with the IRA, and with them alone, to end their inhuman crimes. It is for them and those who support and justify them to explain why they have wickedly failed to do that.

I promise the House and the people of Northern Ireland that, for our part, we shall not cease our efforts to bring violence to a permanent end. As my right Hon. Friend told the House on 18 November, if we do not succeed on this occasion we shall keep exploring again and again the opportunities for peace. Peace, properly attained, is a prize worth risks.

If a genuine end to violence is promised, the way would still be open for Sinn Fein to enter the political arena after a sufficient interval to demonstrate that they mean it. Our message of 5 November again spelt that out.

The key to peace is in the hands of the IRA.

INDEPENDENT COUNSEL'S REPORT ON THE IRAN-CONTRA AFFAIR
January 18, 1994

Only weeks before leaving office, President George H. Bush on December 24, 1992, pardoned former defense secretary Caspar W. Weinberger and five other Reagan administration officials who were facing trial or sentencing for their involvement in the Iran-contra affair. The scandal, which became public in late 1986, involved the Reagan administration secretly selling arms to Iran in the hope that it would help gain the release of American hostages held in Lebanon by pro-Iranian terrorists and then diverting profits from the sales to U.S.-backed contra guerrillas in Nicaragua. Bush's pardons of the six men were angrily denounced by Lawrence E. Walsh, the special prosecutor who had been investigating Iran-contra since 1986. "The Iran-contra coverup, which has continued for six years, is now complete," Walsh said. (President Reagan's Speech on the Iran-Contra Affair, p. 88)

Just over a year later, on January 18, 1994, Walsh released his long-awaited report on the scandal. At the press conference where he released his findings, Walsh said although there was "no credible evidence" that former president Ronald Reagan violated any law, impeachment "certainly should have been considered." The report said that once the arms sales to Iran and diversion of profits to the contras became public, "Reagan administration officials deliberately deceived the Congress and the public about the level and extent of official knowledge of and support of these operations." The report also sharply criticized Bush, who was Reagan's vice president and succeeded him in office. "Contrary to his public pronouncements, [Bush] was fully aware of the Iran arms sales and he participated in discussions to obtain third-country support for the contras," the report said. And it criticized Bush's pardon of Weinberger, who had been indicted on five counts of obstruction of justice, perjury, and making false statements. The report called the pardon "an act of friendship or an act of self-protection."

During his seven-year, $36 million investigation, Walsh filed criminal charges against fourteen people, many of them senior officials in the Reagan administration. However, Bush pardoned six, two had their convictions *overturned on constitutional grounds, and one had his case dismissed because of national security. The remaining five either pleaded guilty or were convicted.*

Following are excerpts from the executive summary of the report released January 18, 1994, by Independent Counsel Lawrence E. Walsh on the Reagan administration's involvement in the Iran-contra scandal:

Overall Conclusions

The investigations and prosecutions have shown that high-ranking Administration officials violated laws and executive orders in the Iran/contra matter. Independent Counsel concluded that:

- the sales of arms to Iran contravened United States Government policy and may have violated the Arms Export Control Act;
- the provision and coordination of support to the contras violated the Boland Amendment ban on aid to military activities in Nicaragua;
- the policies behind both the Iran and contra operations were fully reviewed and developed at the highest levels of the Reagan Administration;
- although there was little evidence of National Security Council level knowledge of most of the actual contra-support operations, there was no evidence that any NSC member dissented from the underlying policy— keeping the contras alive despite congressional limitations on contra support;
- the Iran operations were carried out with the knowledge of, among others, President Ronald Reagan, Vice President George Bush, Secretary of State George P. Shultz, Secretary of Defense Caspar W. Weinberger, Director of Central Intelligence William J. Casey, and national security advisers Robert C. McFarlane and John M. Poindexter; of these officials, only Weinberger and Shultz dissented from the policy decision, and Weinberger eventually acquiesced by ordering the Department of Defense to provide the necessary arms;
- large volumes of highly relevant, contemporaneously created documents were systematically and willfully withheld from investigators by several Reagan Administration officials; and
- following the revelation of these operations in October and November 1986, Reagan Administration officials deliberately deceived the Congress and the public about the level and extent of official knowledge of and support for these operations.

In addition, Independent Counsel concluded that the off-the-books nature of the Iran and contra operations gave line-level personnel the opportunity to commit money crimes.

Prosecutions

In the course of Independent Counsel's investigation, 14 persons were charged with criminal violations. There were two broad classes of crimes charged: Operational crimes, which largely concerned the illegal use of funds generated in the course of the operations, and "cover-up" crimes, which largely concerned false statements and obstructions after the revelation of the operations. Independent Counsel did not charge violations of the Arms Export Control Act or Boland Amendment. Although apparent violations of these statutes provided the impetus for the cover-up, they are not criminal statutes and do not contain any enforcement provisions.

All of the individuals charged were convicted, except for one CIA official whose case was dismissed on national security grounds and two officials who received unprecedented pre-trial pardons by President Bush following his electoral defeat in 1992. Two of the convictions were reversed on appeal on constitutional grounds that in no way cast doubt on the factual guilt of the men convicted. The individuals charged and the disposition of their cases are:

1. Robert C. McFarlane: pleaded guilty to four counts of withholding information from Congress;
2. Oliver L. North: convicted of altering and destroying documents, accepting an illegal gratuity, and aiding and abetting in the obstruction of Congress; conviction reversed on appeal;
3. John M. Poindexter: convicted of conspiracy, false statements, destruction and removal of records, and obstruction of Congress; conviction reversed on appeal;
4. Richard V. Secord: pleaded guilty to making false statements to Congress;
5. Albert Hakim: pleaded guilty to supplementing the salary of North;
6. Thomas G. Clines: convicted of four counts of tax-related offenses for failing to report income from the operations;
7. Carl R. Channell: pleaded guilty to conspiracy to defraud the United States;
8. Richard R. Miller: pleaded guilty to conspiracy to defraud the United States;
9. Clair E. George: convicted of false statements and perjury before Congress;
10. Duane R. Clarridge: indicted on seven counts of perjury and false statements; pardoned before trial by President Bush;
11. Alan D. Fiers Jr.: pleaded guilty to withholding information from Congress;
12. Joseph F. Fernandez: indicted on four counts of obstruction and false statements; case dismissed when Attorney General Richard L. Thornburgh refused to declassify information needed for his defense;
13. Elliott Abrams: pleaded guilty to withholding information from Congress;
14. Caspar W. Weinberger: charged with four counts of false statements and perjury; pardoned before trial by President Bush.

At the time President Bush pardoned Weinberger and Clarridge, he also pardoned George, Fiers, Abrams, and McFarlane.

The Basic Facts of Iran/Contra

The Iran/contra affair concerned two secret Reagan Administration policies whose operations were coordinated by National Security Council staff. The Iran operation involved efforts in 1985 and 1986 to obtain the release of Americans held hostage in the Middle East through the sale of U.S. weapons to Iran, despite an embargo on such sales. The contra operations from 1984 through most of 1986 involved the secret governmental support of contra military and paramilitary activities in Nicaragua, despite congressional prohibition of this support.

The Iran and contra operations were merged when funds generated from the sale of weapons to Iran were diverted to support the contra effort in Nicaragua. Although this "diversion" may be the most dramatic aspect of Iran/contra, it is important to emphasize that both the Iran and contra operations, separately, violated United States policy and law. The ignorance of the "diversion" asserted by President Reagan and his Cabinet officers on the National Security Council in no way absolves them of responsibility for the underlying Iran and contra operations.

The secrecy concerning the Iran and contra activities was finally pierced by events that took place thousands of miles apart in the fall of 1986. The first occurred on October 5, 1986, when Nicaraguan government soldiers shot down an American cargo plane that was carrying military supplies to contra forces; the one surviving crew member, American Eugene Hasenfus, was taken into captivity and stated that he was employed by the CIA. A month after the Hasenfus shootdown, President Reagan's secret sale of U.S. arms to Iran was reported by a Lebanese publication on November 3. The joining of these two operations was made public on November 25, 1986, when Attorney General Meese announced that Justice Department officials had discovered that some of the proceeds from the Iran arms sales had been diverted to the contras.

When these operations ended, the exposure of the Iran/contra affair generated a new round of illegality. Beginning with the testimony of Elliott Abrams and others in October 1986 and continuing through the public testimony of Caspar W. Weinberger on the last day of the congressional hearings in the summer of 1987, senior Reagan Administration officials engaged in a concerted effort to deceive Congress and the public about their knowledge of and support for the operations.

Independent Counsel has concluded that the President's most senior advisers and the Cabinet members on the National Security Council participated in the strategy to make National Security staff members McFarlane, Poindexter and North the scapegoats whose sacrifice would protect the Reagan Administration in its final two years. In an important sense, this strategy succeeded. Independent Counsel discovered much of the best evidence of the cover-up in the final year of active investigation, too late for most prosecutions. . . .

The White House and Office of the Vice President

As the White House section of this report describes in detail, the investigation found no credible evidence that President Reagan violated any criminal statute. The OIC [Office of Independent Counsel] could not prove that Reagan authorized or was aware of the diversion or that he had knowledge of the extent of North's control of the contra-resupply network. Nevertheless, he set the stage for the illegal activities of others by encouraging and, in general terms, ordering support of the contras during the October 1984 to October 1986 period when funds for the contras were cut off by the Boland Amendment, and in authorizing the sale of arms to Iran, in contravention of the U.S. embargo on such sales. The President's disregard for civil laws enacted to limit presidential actions abroad—specifically the Boland Amendment, the Arms Export Control Act and congressional-notification requirements in covert-action laws—created a climate in which some of the Government officers assigned to implement his policies felt emboldened to circumvent such laws.

President Reagan's directive to McFarlane to keep the contras alive "body and soul" during the Boland cut-off period was viewed by North, who was charged by McFarlane to carry out the directive, as an invitation to break the law. Similarly, President Reagan's decision in 1985 to authorize the sale of arms to Iran from Israeli stocks, despite warnings by Weinberger and Shultz that such transfers might violate the law, opened the way for Poindexter's subsequent decision to authorize the diversion. Poindexter told Congress that while he made the decision on his own and did not tell the President, he believed the President would have approved. North testified that he believed the President authorized it.

Independent Counsel's investigation did not develop evidence that proved that Vice President Bush violated any criminal statute. Contrary to his public pronouncements, however, he was fully aware of the Iran arms sales. Bush was regularly briefed, along with the President, on the Iran arms sales, and he participated in discussions to obtain third-country support for the contras. The OIC obtained no evidence that Bush was aware of the diversion. The OIC learned in December 1992 that Bush had failed to produce a diary containing contemporaneous notes relevant to Iran/contra, despite requests made in 1987 and again in early 1992 for the production of such material. Bush refused to be interviewed for a final time in light of evidence developed in the latter stages of OIC's investigation, leaving unresolved a clear picture of his Iran/contra involvement. Bush's pardon of Weinberger on December 24, 1992 preempted a trial in which defense counsel indicated that they intended to call Bush as a witness. . . .

GAO ON THE RISK OF TERRORIST ATTACKS ON AVIATION
January 27, 1994

The deaths of 270 people in the December 1988 bombing of Pan Am Flight 103 over Lockerbie, Scotland, prompted increased interest in protecting planes from terrorists. A presidential commission that investigated the bombing called the aviation security system "seriously flawed" in a 1990 report, and the General Accounting Office (GAO), which conducted investigations for Congress, had found problems in the passenger screening system since at least 1987. (Testimony on Ineffective Airport Passenger Screening, p. 92; The Bombing of Pan Am Flight 103 over Scotland, p. 102)

In a report released January 27, 1994, the GAO urged the Federal Aviation Administration (FAA) to pay closer attention to the threat posed by terrorists. It quoted officials from the Federal Bureau of Investigation as saying that terrorist groups had established networks inside the United States. The GAO acknowledged that government officials believed the terrorist threat was far greater overseas than in the United States, but pointedly noted that less than one year earlier—in February 1993—terrorists had bombed the World Trade Center in New York City, sending "a signal that it is possible for terrorists to operate in the United States." One line in the report is particularly chilling in light of the hijackings of four planes on September 11, 2001: "Although FAA, airports, and airlines have taken measures to strengthen domestic security, FAA and FBI officials believe that airports and aircraft will remain an attractive target for terrorists well into the foreseeable future."

In congressional testimony more than two years later—on September 11, 1996, exactly five years before the devastating hijackings of 2001—a senior GAO official once again expressed concerns about the aviation security system's "numerous vulnerabilities" to terrorists. "Nearly every major aspect of the system—ranging from the screening of passengers, checked and carry-on baggage, mail, and cargo as well as access to secured areas within airports and aircraft—has weaknesses that terrorists could exploit," the GAO official said. (Vulnerabilities in the Aviation Security System, p. 210)

Following are excerpts from the introduction of "Aviation Security: Additional Actions Needed to Meet Domestic and International Challenges," a report issued January 27, 1994, by the General Accounting Office:

On December 21, 1988, a terrorist bomb destroyed Pan Am Flight 103, killing all 259 passengers and crew aboard along with 11 residents of Locker-bie, Scotland. Since that time, remarkable geopolitical changes have occurred. The dissolution of the Soviet Union and success of the coalition forces led by the United States against Iraq in the Persian Gulf War have resulted in a lessening of global tensions. According to a recent Department of State report, international terrorism in 1992 fell to the lowest level since 1975. Despite this positive trend, experts at the State Department, Central Intelligence Agency, and Federal Bureau of Investigation (FBI) stress that the terrorist threat remains quite real. It is against this backdrop that the current threat from international terrorism needs to be assessed.

Aviation Security Improvement Act Mandates Significant Changes

In the aftermath of Pan Am 103, the President's Commission on Aviation Security and Terrorism was established to examine the nation's aviation security system. The Commission issued its final report in May 1990 and concluded that the U.S. civil aviation security system was seriously flawed and failed to provide the proper level of protection for the traveling public. The Commission also concluded that the Federal Aviation Administration (FAA) had been too reactive in its approach to aviation security and ill-equipped to anticipate future threats. The Commission made 65 recommendations to improve U.S. aviation security, many of which were subsequently included in the Aviation Security Improvement Act of 1990. The act mandated sweeping changes in FAA's and the Department of Transportation's (DOT) approach to aviation security. For example, the act mandated the following changes:

- DOT was required to establish an Office of Intelligence and Security to enhance communication, cooperation, and information sharing between DOT, FAA, and the intelligence community.
- FAA was required to establish several new positions, including the Assistant Administrator for Civil Aviation Security, to elevate security within FAA. The act also required FAA to establish Federal Security Managers (FSM) to serve as the focal points for security at the 19 category X [high-risk] airports and Security Liaison Officers (SLO) to cover high-risk airports abroad.
- FAA and the FBI were required to jointly assess the threats to and vulnerabilities of the nation's airports.

- FAA was required to review the security programs of foreign air carriers and approve those that provide a level of protection similar to that provided by U.S. carriers serving the same airport.
- FAA was required to study the need for additional measures to safeguard the transportation of cargo and mail by passenger aircraft.
- FAA was directed to support the acceleration of research to develop explosive detection equipment.

The Threat to Domestic Airports Is Low, But Concerns Exist

Since the early 1970s, FAA has based its domestic security program on the assumption that hijacking by other than terrorists is the major domestic threat. Indeed, terrorist acts inside the United States are rare. In 1992, the last year that the FBI published data on the subject, the United States experienced four incidents; three involved the use of explosive or incendiary devices. None resulted in the loss of life.

According to FBI officials, networks exist for some terrorist groups inside the United States that could support terrorist activities. These networks are important because they supply the necessary equipment, logistics, training, and financial aid to potential terrorist groups. Because information on these individuals, groups, and their networks is classified, we are precluded from discussing these issues in greater detail in this report. Although FAA, airports, and airlines have taken measures to strengthen domestic security, FAA and FBI officials believe that airports and aircraft will remain an attractive target for terrorists well into the foreseeable future.

However, the terrorist threat is continually evolving and presenting unique challenges to FAA and law enforcement agencies. For example, after FAA responded to the rash of hijackings in the 1970s by deploying metal detectors at domestic airports, terrorists began to board aircraft and leave explosive devices in the aircraft via carry-on baggage at various overseas locations. Similarly, after FAA began examining carry-on baggage, terrorists were successful in placing explosive devices on board aircraft via checked baggage without actually boarding the aircraft at foreign airports. At each level, terrorists have made it more difficult for FAA and law enforcement authorities to identify the perpetrators. Because of the uncertain nature of terrorist acts, FAA and the FBI have great difficulty in assembling a long-term view of the threat to aviation security, which underscores the need to continually reassess threats to aviation.

Terrorist Threat Is Greater Overseas

FBI, State Department, FAA, DOT, and airline officials maintain that the terrorist threat is still far greater overseas. Terrorists are more comfortable operating closer to home and closer to their infrastructure. According to experts, some terrorist groups seek a high body count. To this end, civil aviation is a tempting target—but one more likely to be located in Europe rather than the United States.

State Department officials point to the terrorist threat emanating from Latin America because of both the growing animosity of so-called "drug lords" to U.S. interdiction policies and their financial wherewithal to sponsor "narco-terrorism." According to the 1992 State Department report on terrorism, the continued threat of international terrorism to Americans and U.S. interests abroad is illustrated by the fact that, while the number of terrorist incidents has declined in recent years, attacks against American targets, both in real terms and as a percentage of the total, have increased. In addition, despite official beliefs that terrorists will continue to operate closer to home (most notably in Europe), the World Trade Center bombing in New York in February 1993 sends a signal that it is possible for terrorists to operate in the United States. . . .

As of June 3, 2002, the full text of the GAO report was available at http://archive.gao.gov/t2pbat4/150614.pdf

TRIAL REMARKS ON THE MURDER OF CIVIL RIGHTS LEADER EVERS
February 4, 1994

As civil rights leader Medgar Evers walked from his car to his home in Jackson, Mississippi, on the night of June 12, 1963, a single, fatal shot hit him in the back. Evers had been the first Mississippi field secretary for the National Association for the Advancement of Colored People (NAACP), a job that in the late 1950s and early 1960s involved extreme danger. In nearby bushes police found a rifle that belonged to Byron De La Beckwith, a well-known racist in a state where a black person who attempted to register to vote might be pistol-whipped or worse, and the gun had his fingerprint. Beckwith was charged with murdering Evers, but two all-white juries deadlocked and he walked away a free man. During jury selection for Beckwith's first trial in 1964, the tone was set by a question from the prosecutor: "Do you believe it is a crime to kill a nigger in Mississippi?" Any potential juror who hesitated in answering the question was immediately excluded.

In 1989 an article in the Clarion Ledger *newspaper in Jackson prompted Hinds County district attorney Ed Peters to reopen the case. The investigation found new witnesses and Beckwith, who remained an unrepentant segregationist, was indicted again in 1990. During the new trial that began in early 1994, six people testified that Beckwith had told them, either directly or indirectly, that he had killed Evers. It took the jury of eight blacks and four whites only six hours to convict Beckwith of murder. Beckwith died in January 2001 while serving a life sentence in prison.*

Beckwith's conviction led to the reopening of other decades-old cases where civil rights workers in the South had been murdered by terrorists who sought to retain segregation. In 1998 Sam Bowers, former imperial wizard of the Ku Klux Klan, was convicted of the 1966 killing of an NAACP leader. In May 2002 Bobby Frank Cherry became the last of three ex-Klansmen convicted of killing four black girls in the 1963 bombing of the Sixteenth Street Baptist Church in Birmingham, Alabama. (Last Major Suspect Convicted in 1963 Church Bombing, p. 411)

Following are excerpts from the official transcript of the closing argument of Hinds County assistant district attorney Bobby DeLaughter on February 4, 1994, in the Circuit Court of the First Judicial District of Hinds County, Mississippi, in the trial of Byron De La Beckwith for the murder of Medgar Evers:

When we started the testimony a little over a week ago now, I stood before you and I told you what the evidence would show in this case. I told you then that when all the evidence was in, you would see what this case was about; you would see what this case was not about; and now that you have all the evidence before you; now that the judge has instructed you on the law, then you know what this case is about. And you know that what it is about is about an unarmed man, arriving home the late hours of the night, having been working, coming home to his family, his wife, three small children that were staying up, waiting on him to get home inside the home there, getting out of his automobile with his back turned, and being shot down by a bushwacker from ambush. And that he dropped T-shirts in his arms, and he crawled from that automobile where he was gunned down, down the side of that carport, into the carport, trying to make it to his door, in this puddle of blood, with his keys in his hand, and his wife and children coming out when they hear the shot, and his three children stating over and over, "Daddy, daddy, please get up." And that's what the case is about. This man being gunned down and shot down in the back in the dark from ambush, not able to face his self-appointed accuser, his judge, and his executioner. . . .

. . . [T]his assassination by a sniper from ambush is something that's timeless. This is something that spans the races. It is something that every decent human being should absolutely be sickened by, whether you be black, white, Hispanic; it doesn't matter. Murder by ambush is the most vile, savage, reprehensible type of murder that one can imagine. And that's what you've got here.

This isn't about black versus white or white versus black. This is about something that is reprehensible to decent minds. This is about society, civilized society, versus the vile, society versus the reprehensible, society versus the shocking. This, ladies and gentlemen, is about the State of Mississippi versus this defendant, Byron De La Beckwith. . . .

His gun. His scope. His fingerprint. His car. And lastly, but certainly not least, his mouth. When he thought he had beat the system 30 years ago, he couldn't keep his mouth shut with people that he thought were gonna be impressed by him, and that he thought were his buddies and comrades, two of them from the Klan, one in Florida, one from Mississippi testified. At least six people have given you sworn testimony that at various times in different locations, none of whom knew each other or came across each other at any time, told you what he has said about this. He wants to take credit for what he has claimed should be done, but he just don't want to pay the price for it. And so he hasn't been able to keep his mouth shut.

And so not only do we have his car, his gun, his scope, his fingerprint, his mouth, we've got his own venom. His venom has come back to poison him just as effectively as anything else.

And why did this happen? Why did any of this happen? For what reason was Medgar Evers assassinated? For what he believed. Not in necessary self-defense was this done. Medgar Evers didn't do anything of a violent nature to this defendant. What he did was to have the gall, the uppitiness to want for his people. Things like what? To be called by name, instead of boy, girl. . . .To go in a restaurant, to go in a department store, to vote, and for your children to get a decent education in a decent school. For wanting some degree of equality for himself, his family, and his fellow man, and for them to be accepted as human beings with some dignity. This kind of murder, ladies and gentlemen, no matter who the victim, no matter what his race; this kind of murder, when you're talking about somebody that's assassinated, shot down in the back for what they believe, for such meager things as wanting some dignity, when that kind of murder happens, there is just a gaping wound laid on society as a whole. And even where justice is fulfilled, that kind of murder, that kind of wound will always leave a scar that won't ever go away. We have to learn from the past, folks, and where justice is never fulfilled—justice has sometimes been referred to as that soothing balm to be applied on the wounds inflicted on society—where justice is never fulfilled and that wound can never be cleansed, all it does is just fester and fester and fester over the years.

And so it is up to the system; it's up to the law-abiding citizens, and the law of the State of Mississippi that the perpetrator of such an assassination be brought to justice. This defendant. So that the decent law-abiding people of this state will maintain a new respect for the value of human life, and that our state will truly be one that is of the people, for the people, and by the people, no matter what your race, color or creed is.

One of the defense attorneys early on in the jury selection process asked whether or not any of you had heard something to the effect of the eyes being on Mississippi or Mississippi on trial. Mississippi is not on trial. And I'm not sure what eyes are on Mississippi, but this I do know. Justice in this case, in whatever case, is what the jury says it is. Justice in this case is what you twelve ladies and gentlemen say it is. So in this case, in effect, you are Mississippi. So what is Mississippi justice in this case, ladies and gentlemen? What is Mississippi justice for this defendant's hate-inspired assassination; assassination of a man that just desired to be free and equal? . . .

And so on behalf of the State of Mississippi, I'm gonna do what I told you I was gonna do in the very beginning. I'm gonna ask you to hold this defendant accountable. You have no part in sentencing. That's something that the law will take care of. It's up to the Court. But to hold him accountable, find him guilty, simply because it's right, it's just, and Lord knows, it's just time. He has danced to the music for 30 years. Isn't it time that he pay the piper? Is it ever too late to do the right thing? For the sake of justice and the hope of us as a civilized society, I sincerely hope and pray that it's not.

THE CAPTURE OF CARLOS THE JACKAL
August 18, 1994

In the 1970s and 1980s the terrorist known as Carlos the Jackal gained international notoriety for a series of shootings, bombings, and kidnappings across Western Europe. Carlos—born Ilich Ramirez Sanchez in Argentina—was associated with a number of terrorist groups devoted to Palestinian independence. His most notable attack came in December 1975, when he and five other terrorists rushed into a meeting of the Organization of Petroleum Exporting Countries (OPEC) in Vienna, Austria, killing three people and taking sixty others hostage. Carlos and his gang eventually released the hostages in return for a ransom in the tens of millions of dollars and safe passage. Carlos claimed that during the 1970s and 1980s he killed more than eighty people and wounded hundreds more.

After Carlos spent two decades on the run, French authorities tracked him to a hideout in Khartoum, Sudan, in August 1994. According to newspaper accounts, French security agents—working with at least the tacit cooperation of Sudanese officials—grabbed Carlos, threw him in a burlap bag, and hustled him to France on a private jet. In December 1997 a French court convicted him of the June 1975 murders of two French counterintelligence agents and an informer. The court sentenced Carlos to life in prison. He claimed the trial was the work of an Israeli conspiracy directed by the United States.

In June 1999 France's highest court rejected a final appeal filed by Carlos. He gained renewed attention in late 2001 when it was learned he had become engaged to his attorney, Isabelle Coutant-Peyre, who had represented accused terrorists for two decades. The couple planned to marry in 2002.

Following is an editorial broadcast on the Voice of America, a radio network operated by the U.S. government, on August 18, 1994, announcing the capture of Carlos the Jackal:

This week, French authorities won a major victory in the war against international terrorism with the arrest in Sudan of Ilich Ramirez Sanchez—alias Carlos. One of the world's most wanted terrorists, Carlos will go on trial for crimes committed in France.

Born in Venezuela, the son of a prominent Marxist lawyer, Carlos was named Ilich after the founder of the Soviet Union, Vladimir Ilich Lenin. Drawn by communist ideology, Carlos studied at Patrice Lumumba University in Moscow. In 1970, he was recruited by a Marxist Palestinian terrorist group, the Popular Front for the Liberation of Palestine, or PFLP. He was trained in Lebanon under terrorist leader Wadi Haddad.

After Haddad's death in 1978, Carlos helped organize three terrorist groups—the PFLP Special Command, the Lebanese Armed Revolutionary Faction, and the 15 May Organization. Around 1978, Carlos organized another terrorist network—the Organization of the Armed Arab Struggle. Over the years, Carlos lived in Syria and Libya, and received protection from several Soviet-bloc governments.

Carlos is wanted for numerous terrorist attacks carried out in the 1970s and 1980s. They include the wounding of a British millionaire in 1973; the bombing of a Paris drugstore in 1974; the 1975 killing of two French intelligence officers investigating Carlos's failed rocket attack on an El Al plane at a Paris airport; a 1975 attack on OPEC headquarters in Vienna, in which three people were killed and 11 oil ministers were taken hostage; the 1982 bombing of a Paris passenger train that killed five people; and railroad bombings around Marseilles that killed six people and wounded 80 in 1983.

Law enforcement authorities in many nations—especially France—were relentless in their efforts to bring him to justice. "We never gave up," said French Interior Minister Charles Pasqua. The United States applauds the government of France for its successful pursuit of one of the world's most dangerous criminals. The arrest of Carlos serves notice on all international terrorists that their crimes will not go unpunished.

TALKS WITH IRA PROMISED
IF CEASEFIRE CONTINUED
October 21, 1994

In 1993 the British and Irish governments stepped up negotiations over the future of Northern Ireland, where more than 3,100 people had been killed since 1969 in the latest round of terrorist violence between Protestants and Catholics. Those negotiations bore fruit on October 29, when the British and Irish prime ministers issued a joint statement promising that "new doors could open" toward peace if the Irish Republican Army (IRA) stopped its campaign of violence. The next month the British government stunned all parties involved when it admitted that representatives of the government and the IRA had conducted secret talks aimed at stopping the bloodshed. A shaky peace then took hold, and the IRA eventually helped solidify it by announcing a ceasefire on August 31, 1994. The Protestant side announced its own ceasefire six weeks later. (Prime Ministers on Bringing Peace to Northern Ireland, p. 132)

The seven-week-old IRA ceasefire set the stage for a speech October 21, 1994, by British prime minister John Major to a business group in Belfast, Northern Ireland. In his speech Major promised to open exploratory talks with Sinn Fein, the political arm of the IRA, if the IRA ceasefire continued. "If we continue reasonably to assume that Sinn Fein is establishing a commitment to exclusively peaceful methods; if the IRA continues to show that it has ended its terrorism; then we shall be ready to convene exploratory talks before this year is out," Major said.

With the ceasefire continuing to hold, on December 10 representatives of the British government and Sinn Fein met in Belfast for historic talks. These were simply the exploratory talks that Major had promised, but they represented the first time the two sides had ever talked together in public. Peace continued until February 9, 1996, when the IRA accompanied an announcement ending its ceasefire with a bombing in London that killed two people. Four months later the prime ministers of Britain and Ireland launched multiparty negotiations involving nine of Northern Ireland's political parties, but they excluded Sinn Fein because the IRA had resumed its violence. The IRA restored its ceasefire in July 1997, and a permanent peace seemed possible until a bomb attack August 15, 1998, in Omagh, Northern Ireland, by a splinter group calling itself the "Real IRA" killed twenty-nine people. ("Real IRA" Claims Credit for Omagh Blast, p. 257).

Following are excerpts from a speech by British prime minister John Major on October 21, 1994, at a meeting in Belfast, Northern Ireland, of a business group known as the Institute of Directors:

Mr. Chairman,

From the moment I stepped into Downing Street, I believed that the overwhelming majority of the people of Northern Ireland wanted peace.

Over the years they have demonstrated this in countless ways—the remarkable peace movement of the 1970s, the many groups and individuals who have worked so hard to heal community divisions. . . .

Seven months after I last spoke to you, seven weeks after the IRA [Irish Republican Army] ceasefire, seven days after the Loyalist paramilitary ceasefire, Northern Ireland is at peace. There is a different atmosphere.

Fear has been lifted from daily life.

People have begun to take the bars off their windows.

Trade in the High Street has gone up by 6 percent in one month.

Even sceptical commentators—with years of history to support their scepticism—are beginning to wonder whether, perhaps, a corner has been turned.

As to that, we shall see. But there has been a very encouraging beginning.

Now we have to move on. Towards a full return to democratic life. Towards a time when violence will be no more than a bad memory. Towards a just and lasting peace.

We have practical obstacles to overcome. Some of them will be difficult. We also have history to overcome and that will be even harder. Old enmities, old suspicions, old fears still swirl around and obscure opportunities that may lie ahead.

We are right to be cautious. But there is no entirely risk-free approach. With care and with calculation we must judge the art of the possible and deliver it.

I cannot guarantee success. But I do believe the chances of success are better than for generations.

Let me set out, therefore, the next steps I propose to take.

Our task is to make sure that the violence is over for good. We must aim to make a return to violence unthinkable.

Throughout these seven weeks, Sinn Fein and the IRA have sought to convey the impression that the ceasefire is permanent, but they have not stated this unambiguously. Because they left scope for doubt, I resisted pressure to set an early date for exploratory talks.

Instead, we have reviewed their actions. These have been more compelling than their words.

As a result, I am now prepared to make a working assumption that the ceasefire is intended to be permanent. This means we can move carefully towards the beginning of dialogue between Sinn Fein and the Government.

The basis for this dialogue is unchanged. There must be a genuine commitment by Sinn Fein to use and support only peaceful methods in a democratic political arena. We shall expect to see continuing practical evidence of this commitment. We shall not be able to proceed if it is called into question.

If we continue reasonably to assume that Sinn Fein is establishing a commitment to exclusively peaceful methods; if the IRA continues to show that it has ended its terrorism; then we shall be ready to convene exploratory talks before this year is out.

This preliminary dialogue between representatives of the Government and of Sinn Fein will be crucial.

It will explore how Sinn Fein can make a transition to normal political life. How it would be able to play the same part as the existing constitutional parties. How it could enter the political talks process.

And we shall discuss the practical consequences of ending violence—most obviously how illegal weapons and explosives are going to be removed from life in Northern Ireland. Peace cannot be assured finally until the paramilitaries on both sides hand in their weapons. This is a difficult issue but it cannot be ducked. We must consider therefore how guns and explosives can best be deposited and decommissioned. These weapons are both North and South of the border. So we shall be consulting the Irish Government on a coordinated approach.

It is through the political talks process that we wish to secure a lasting settlement. And I repeat today the promise I have given before: When these talks between the constitutional parties and the two Governments are over, we shall seek the approval of the people of Northern Ireland for the outcome as a whole in a referendum. Their consent is essential. . . .

Mr. Chairman, peace will give a massive boost to Northern Ireland's economy. Equally, the chance of more prosperity, more jobs, better security for families, must be the most powerful incentive for peace.

I know that the business community is already preparing for new opportunities. So is the Government, in partnership with you.

I can now announce that we shall be convening a large investment conference here in Belfast in December.

I hope that many of you will take part. We shall be asking the Institute of Directors and the CBI at national level to encourage their members to look at investment opportunities here. We shall invite senior figures from the City of London. And we shall also invite potential investors and business leaders from overseas—from Europe, the United States, and the Far East.

We are of course already in close touch with the European Commission. The President of the European Commission has established a special task force to look at a new European Community programme for Northern Ireland. This initiative aims to fund new projects to regenerate the inner cities. It will focus on action to cut long term unemployment, attract inward investment and stimulate tourism.

153

The details of the European Commission's initiative are still being worked out, in consultation with us and with others. From my latest contacts with Jacques Delors, I am confident that this initiative will result in a substantial package of new measures and new money.

I say new money. The European Union's programme will be in addition to the British Government's own expenditure plans for Northern Ireland. These, as you know, have long been supported by the EU's structural funds. The European Union has also increased its contribution to the International Fund for Ireland. . . .

Mr. Chairman, from this moment we are in a new phase of the peace process. A transitional phase which will lead to exploratory talks.

For twenty-five years violence has been the enemy of progress in Northern Ireland.

Think what opportunities have been lost, what could have been done to advance all areas of life here, were it not for the burden of terrorism.

Local democracy has been held back. A generation of politicians has been denied full responsibility.

In the community, walls have been going up where we should have spent the past twenty-five years breaking them down.

In the economy, for every million pounds of investment you have attracted, there should have been many millions. For every tourist there should have been thirty. For every hotel, factory or shop repaired after a bomb, we could have built a new one.

We cannot make up twenty-five lost years overnight. We shall have to make Herculean efforts. That is the purpose of the initiatives I have announced today. To begin to improve the lives of everyone in Northern Ireland as quickly as we can.

Above all, we must make the price of breaking the peace so high that there would be no shred of sympathy, no glimmer of support for anyone who contemplated using violence again. . . .

Let me speak directly to each and every person in Northern Ireland. If you want peace, say so now. Loudly. Don't sit back. Join the crusade for the future. Go to your friends. Go to your neighbours. Go to anyone you know who has ever supported violence.

You have not had this chance in years and you cannot afford to miss it. Let your voices be heard.

Ultimately you, and you alone, can ensure that Northern Ireland never goes backwards. And the benefits will be yours.

PRESIDENT CLINTON DENOUNCES ATTACK ON ABORTION CLINICS
December 30, 1994

By 1994 abortion clinics and their employees around the United States had become frequent targets of death threats and violence that ranged from bombings of clinic offices to murders of doctors who performed abortions. One of the most serious terrorist attacks occurred December 30, 1994, when two people were killed and five wounded in shootings at a pair of abortion clinics in a Boston suburb committed by John C. Salvi III, a twenty-two-year-old man from New Hampshire. In both cases Salvi walked into the clinic with a duffel bag, pulled out a rifle, and started shooting. The shootings brought to five the number of people who had been shot to death in clinic-related violence in the previous nineteen months.

In a statement released by the White House the day of the attacks, President Bill Clinton deplored the violence. "I am strongly committed to ending this form of domestic terrorism," Clinton said. Three days later Clinton made a second statement announcing that all U.S. attorneys had been instructed to immediately create task forces to develop security plans for clinics in their areas. Clinton also said that U.S. marshals had been ordered to consult with clinics in their areas to ensure that the clinics knew how to report potential threats to law enforcement officials.

Just twenty-five hours following the shootings outside Boston, police captured Salvi after he opened fire on an abortion clinic in Norfolk, Virginia. He was convicted of the two killings in Massachusetts and sentenced to two life terms in prison. He died in 1996 at a Massachusetts maximum security prison in what prison officials described as a suicide. Meanwhile, the violence against abortion clinics and providers continued. On November 9, 1998, Attorney General Janet Reno announced the creation of the National Task Force on Violence Against Health Care Providers. Her announcement came less than three weeks after Barnett Slepian, a well-known doctor in the Buffalo, New York, area who performed abortions, was killed by a rifle shot fired through the kitchen window of his home. (Task Force Created to Fight Antiabortion Violence, p. 267)

Following is a statement by President Bill Clinton released by the White House December 30, 1994, denouncing attacks on abortion clinics:

I strongly condemn the meaningless violence which abruptly ended the lives of two women and wounded five others in Massachusetts today.

Violence has no place in America. No matter where we stand on the issue of abortion, all Americans must stand together in condemning this tragic and brutal act. Nine years ago, President [Ronald] Reagan, a staunch foe of abortion, called for "a complete rejection of violence as a means of settling this issue." We would do well to heed those words today.

We must protect the safety and freedom of all our citizens. I am strongly committed to ending this form of domestic terrorism. I have called for a thorough investigation into this attack, and Attorney General [Janet] Reno and FBI Director [Louis] Freeh have already begun that task. I urge local officials to work closely with the Federal law enforcement community.

Hillary and I extend our deepest sympathy to the friends and families of those who were murdered. I speak for all Americans in expressing my hope for a full and complete recovery for those who were wounded.

BOMBING OF THE FEDERAL BUILDING IN OKLAHOMA CITY
April 23, 1995

During the 1970s, 1980s, and early 1990s the United States seemed almost invulnerable to the kinds of terrorist attacks that plagued other countries around the world. The February 1993 bombing of the World Trade Center in New York City by Islamic extremists had made it clear that terrorists could strike on American soil. Nonetheless, terrorism was still widely viewed as a problem that happened elsewhere. (The 1993 Bombing of the World Trade Center, p. 123)

The United States forever lost its sense of security on the morning of April 19, 1995, when a massive truck bomb blew up the Alfred P. Murrah Federal Building in Oklahoma City, Oklahoma. The explosion killed 168 people, including children attending a day care center on the building's second floor, and injured hundreds more. Most of the dead and injured were federal workers and visitors who had business at federal offices in the building. In the first hours and days following the explosion the nation watched on television as firefighters, rescue crews, medical teams, police, and volunteers risked their lives as they searched for survivors and bodies in the still crumbling building. On April 23 more than 10,000 people gathered at the state fairgrounds for a prayer service for the bombing victims and their families that included speeches by Governor Frank Keating and President Bill Clinton.

Much of the speculation immediately following the bombing focused on Islamic extremists as the most likely perpetrators. However, only days after the bombing federal agents arrested two army buddies, Timothy J. McVeigh and Terry L. Nichols, in the attack. The exact motive for the bombing was unclear, but both men were thought to have a deep-seated hatred of the federal government. Authorities identified McVeigh as the driver of the rental truck that exploded outside the Murrah Building and said that Nichols had bought the ammonium nitrate fertilizer and fuel oil that were the bomb's key ingredients. In separate trials in 1997, juries convicted the two men of planning and carrying out the bombing. Nichols was sentenced to life in prison on the federal charges, but still faced state charges in June 2002 that could bring the death penalty. McVeigh, the plot's alleged mastermind, was sentenced to death. On April 11, 2001, a still defiant McVeigh was executed by lethal injection, becoming the first federal prisoner executed in thirty-eight years.

Following are remarks by Governor Frank Keating of Oklahoma and President Bill Clinton at a prayer service at the Oklahoma State Fair Arena in Oklahoma City on April 23, 1995:

GOVERNOR KEATING'S REMARKS

The tragedy of April 19th shocked America. Its unspeakable evil sickened the world. Never in the history of our country have Americans witnessed such senseless barbarism. It has been suggested that those who committed this act of mass murder chose us as their victims because we were supposedly immune—the heartland of America.

Well, we are the heartland of America. Today we stand before the world, and before our God, together—our hearts and hands linked in a solidarity these criminals can never understand. We stand together in love.

We have seen the terrifying images and read the heart-touching stories. Some of us have lived them.

- The firefighter clutching the body of a sweet, innocent child.
- The policeman reaching through rubble to grasp an outstretched hand.
- The volunteer stretcher bearers—some black, some white, some brown, all linked in courage and compassion—rushing aid to the wounded.
- The healers embracing life. . . the mourners lamenting death.
- The endless lines of donors and helpers and givers—giving their labor, their hopes, their treasure, their very blood.

Through all of this—through the tears, the righteous anger, the soul-rending sorrow of immeasurable loss—we have sometimes felt alone. But we are never truly alone. We have God, and we have each other.

Today we have our neighbors—more than 3 million Oklahomans, and never have we drawn so close. There is something special about Oklahoma. We have always known that; now, so does America, and the world.

Today, we have our fellow Americans—from the power of our federal relief and investigative agencies to the prayers of millions. They will bring us justice as they have already brought us hope, and we will be forever grateful for this wonderful outpouring of love and support.

Today we have our families—so many of them torn by sorrow and hurt, but families still, strong through the generations, stronger yet through this terrible ordeal.

Today we have our heroes and heroines—saints in gray and blue and white and khaki—the rescuers and the healers. They have labored long and nobly. And they have cried with us.

Today we have our leaders: Mister President, Reverend [Billy] Graham, we are moved by your presence. The warmth of our welcome may be dimmed by tears, but it is one of deep gratitude. Thank you for coming to touch our lives.

Today we have our children—Oklahoma is still a young state, and our young people are very special to us. We have been brutally reminded of how precious they are by the events of the last few days. For them we reserve our warmest hugs and gentlest touch.

Today we have our God. He is not a God of your religion or mine, but of all people, in all times. He is a God of love, but He is also a God of justice. Today He assures us once again that good is stronger than evil, that love is greater than hate, that each of us is His special child, embraced by the Father's love.

Our pain is vast. Our loss is beyond measure. We cannot fathom this act, but we can reach beyond its horrible consequences.

The thousands of us gathered here today are multiplied by God's love, anointed by His gentle mercy. Today we are one with Him, and with one another.

It is right for us to grieve. We have all been touched by an immense tragedy, and our sorrow is part of the healing process. For some of us stricken with intense personal losses, it will be a long and tortured path. For all of us it is a journey through darkness.

But darkness ends in morning light. That is God's promise, and it is our hope.

There is a lovely parable of a man who looked back on his life and saw it as an endless series of footprints in the sand. At times there were two sets of footprints, side by side, and he remembered these times as happy. At others there was but one set of prints—the times of sadness and pain.

He confronted God and asked why He had ceased to walk beside him when he most needed that support. Why, he wondered, had God abandoned him?

And God answered: BUT MY SON, THOSE WERE THE TIMES I WAS CARRYING YOU.

He carries us today, cupped gently in His loving hands.

PRESIDENT CLINTON'S REMARKS

Thank you very much. Governor Keating and Mrs. Keating, Reverend Graham, to the families of those who have been lost and wounded, to the people of Oklahoma City, who have endured so much, and the people of this wonderful state, to all of you who are here as our fellow Americans.

I am honored to be here today to represent the American people. But I have to tell you that Hillary and I also come as parents, as husband and wife, as people who were your neighbors for some of the best years of our lives.

Today our Nation joins with you in grief. We mourn with you. We share your hope against hope that some may still survive. We thank all those who have worked so heroically to save lives and to solve this crime, those here in Oklahoma and those who are all across this great land and many who left their own lives to come here to work hand in hand with you.

We pledge to do all we can to help you heal the injured, to rebuild this city, and to bring to justice those who did this evil.

This terrible sin took the lives of our American family, innocent children in that building, only because their parents were trying to be good parents as well as good workers; citizens in the building going about their daily business and many there who served the rest of us—who worked to help the elderly and the disabled, who worked to support our farmers and our veterans, who worked to enforce our laws and to protect us. Let us say clearly, they served us well, and we are grateful.

But for so many of you they were also neighbors and friends. You saw them at church or the PTA meetings, at the civic clubs, at the ball park. You know them in ways that all the rest of America could not.

And to all the members of the families here present who have suffered loss, though we share your grief, your pain is unimaginable, and we know that. We cannot undo it. That is God's work.

Our words seem small beside the loss you have endured. But I found a few I wanted to share today. I've received a lot of letters in these last terrible days. One stood out because it came from a young widow and a mother of three whose own husband was murdered with over 200 other Americans when Pan Am 103 was shot down.* Here is what that woman said I should say to you today:

> The anger you feel is valid, but you must not allow yourselves to be consumed by it. The hurt you feel must not be allowed to turn into hate, but instead into the search for justice. The loss you feel must not paralyze your own lives. Instead, you must try to pay tribute to your loved ones by continuing to do all the things they left undone, thus ensuring they did not die in vain.

Wise words from one who also knows.

You have lost too much, but you have not lost everything. And you have certainly not lost America, for we will stand with you for as many tomorrows as it takes.

If ever we needed evidence of that, I could only recall the words of Governor and Mrs. Keating. If anybody thinks that Americans are mostly mean and selfish, they ought to come to Oklahoma. If anybody thinks Americans have lost the capacity for love and caring and courage, they ought to come to Oklahoma.

To all my fellow Americans beyond this hall, I say, one thing we owe those who have sacrificed is the duty to purge ourselves of the dark forces which gave rise to this evil. They are forces that threaten our common peace, our freedom, our way of life.

Editor's note: It was actually brought down by a bomb.

Let us teach our children that the God of comfort is also the God of righteousness. Those who trouble their own house will inherit the wind. Justice will prevail. Let us let our own children know that we will stand against the forces of fear. When there is talk of hatred, let us stand up and talk against it. When there is talk of violence, let us stand up and talk against it. In the face of death, let us honor life. As St. Paul admonished us, let us not be overcome by evil, but overcome evil with good.

Yesterday Hillary and I had the privilege of speaking with some children of other Federal employees—children like those who were lost here. And one little girl said something we will never forget. She said, we should all plant a tree in memory of the children. So this morning before we got on the plane to come here, at the White House, we planted that tree in honor of the children of Oklahoma. It was a dogwood with its wonderful spring flower and its deep, enduring roots. It embodies the lesson of the Psalms: that the life of a good person is like a tree whose leaf does not wither.

My fellow Americans, a tree takes a long time to grow, and wounds take a long time to heal. But we must begin. Those who are lost now belong to God. Some day we will be with them. But until that happens, their legacy must be our lives.

Thank you all, and God bless you.

CLINTON ANNOUNCES CLOSING
OF PENNSYLVANIA AVENUE
May 20, 1995

The April 19, 1995, terrorist bombing of the Alfred P. Murrah Federal Building in Oklahoma City, which killed 168 people, focused new concerns on the security of federal buildings and other facilities. The day after the bombing, President Bill Clinton asked Attorney General Janet Reno to review security measures at all federal buildings and recommend improvements. Approximately two months later Clinton ordered all federal agencies to start implementing the fifty-two minimum security standards that the Justice Department recommended. These included tighter identification for clearing employees into buildings, greater television monitoring and security at entrances and exits, better lighting, and shatterproof windows. (Bombing of the Federal Building in Oklahoma City, p. 157)

Clinton took another major step May 20 when he announced in his weekly radio address that the two blocks of Pennsylvania Avenue in front of the White House were being closed immediately to all vehicular traffic. By all accounts the president was reluctant to close the two blocks of Pennsylvania Avenue, which was known as "America's Main Street" because it ran in front of the White House. Security analysts, however, convinced the president that detonation of a large bomb in a truck parked up to 150 feet from the White House could inflict lethal damage, injuring or killing not only the president and his family but also White House personnel, visitors, and tourists. In his radio address, Clinton noted that Pennsylvania Avenue had been open to traffic for the nation's entire history: "Through four Presidential assassinations and eight unsuccessful attempts on the lives of Presidents, it's been open; through a civil war, two world wars and the Gulf War, it was open. And now it must be closed. . . .Clearly, this closing is necessary because of the changing nature and scope of the threat of terrorist actions."

The closing of Pennsylvania Avenue helped set off a massive effort in Washington to surround federal buildings and memorials with concrete barriers, chain-link fences, cast-iron posts, and other large objects that could block a truck carrying a bomb. Residents and visitors alike lamented that Washington was becoming uglier and less open with each new barrier.

In December 2001 Washington Post *reporter Fred Hiatt wrote: "Though the new urbanscape is meant to enhance security, many places look as though a small bomb already had gone off. Ditches, concrete barriers, unsightly guard huts, hastily erected fences, barricaded streets: The message is fear." Security measures tightened even more after the September 11, 2001, terrorist attacks on Washington and New York City. All public tours of the White House were immediately canceled, and new security barriers cropped up all over Washington. Officials also started focusing more attention on building underground centers, where visitors could be carefully screened before being allowed to enter the White House, the Capitol, the Washington Monument, and other major buildings and monuments.*

Following is President Bill Clinton's radio address on May 20, 1995, announcing the closure of Pennsylvania Avenue to all vehicular traffic:

Today, the Secretary of the Treasury, who oversees the Secret Service, will announce that from now on the two blocks of Pennsylvania Avenue in front of the White House will be closed to motor vehicle traffic.

Pennsylvania Avenue has been routinely open to traffic for the entire history of our Republic. Through four Presidential assassinations and eight unsuccessful attempts on the lives of Presidents, it's been open; through a civil war, two world wars and the Gulf War, it was open.

And now, it must be closed. This decision follows a lengthy review by the Treasury Department, the Secret Service and independent experts, including distinguished Americans who served in past administrations of both Democratic and Republican Presidents.

This step is necessary in the view of the Director of the Secret Service and the panel of experts to protect the President and his family, the White House itself, all the staff and others who work here, and the visitors and distinguished foreign and domestic guests who come here every day.

The Secret Service risk their lives to protect the President and his family. For 130 years they have stood watch over the people and the institutions of our Democracy. They are the best in the world at what they do. Though I am reluctant to accept any decision that might inconvenience the people who work in or visit our nation's capital, I believe it would be irresponsible to ignore their considered opinion, or to obstruct their decisions about the safety of our public officials, especially given the strong supporting voice of the expert panel.

Clearly, this closing is necessary because of the changing nature and scope of the threat of terrorist actions. It should be seen as a responsible security step necessary to preserve our freedom, not part of a long-term restriction of our freedom.

First, let me make it clear that I will not in any way allow the fight against domestic and foreign terrorism to build a wall between me and the American people. I will be every bit as active and in touch with ordinary American citizens as I have been since I took office.

Pennsylvania Avenue may be closed to cars and trucks but it will remain open to the people of America. If you want to visit the White House you can still do that just as you always could, and I hope you will. If you want to have your picture taken out in front of the White House, please do so. If you want to come here and protest our country's policies, you are still welcome to do that as well. And now you will be more secure in all these activities because it will be less likely that you could become an innocent victim of those who would do violence against symbols of our Democracy.

Closing Pennsylvania Avenue to motor vehicles is a practical step to protect against the kind of attack we saw in Oklahoma City, but I won't allow the people's access to the White House and their President to be curtailed.

The two blocks of Pennsylvania Avenue in front of the White House will be converted into a pedestrian mall. Free and public tours will continue as they always have. For most Americans this won't change much beyond the traffic patterns here in Washington.

For people who work in Washington, D.C., we will work hard to reroute the traffic in cooperation with local officials in the least burdensome way possible.

Now let's think for a minute about what this action says about the danger terrorism poses to the openness of our society, or to any free society. The fact that the Secret Service feels compelled to close Pennsylvania Avenue is an important reminder that we have to come together as a people and hold fast against the divisive tactics of violent extremists.

We saw in the awful tragedy of Oklahoma City and the bombing of the World Trade Center that America, as an open and free society, is not immune from terrorists from within and beyond our borders who believe they have a right to kill innocent civilians to pursue their own political ends, or to protest other policies. Such people seek to instill fear in our citizens, in our whole people. But when we are all afraid to get on a bus, or drive to work, or open an envelope or send our children off to school; when our children are fixated on the possibility of terrorist action against them, or other innocent children, we give terrorists a victory. That kind of corrosive fear could rust our national spirit, drain our will and wear away our freedom.

These are the true stakes in our war against terrorism. We cannot allow ourselves to be frightened or intimidated into a bunker mentality. We cannot allow our sacred freedoms to wither or diminish. We cannot allow the paranoia and conspiracy theories of extreme militants to dominate our society.

What we do today is a practical step to preserve freedom and peace of mind. It should be seen as a step in a long line of efforts to improve security in the modern world, that began with the installation of airport metal detectors. I remember when that started, and a lot of people thought that it might be seen as a restriction on our freedom, but most of us take it for granted now and after all, hijackings have gone way down. The airport metal detectors increased the freedom of the American people and so can this.

But more must be done to reduce the threat of terrorism—to deter terrorism. First, Congress must pass my anti-terrorism legislation. We mustn't let our country fight the war against terrorism ill-armed or ill-prepared. I want us to be armed with 1,000 more FBI agents. I want the ability to monitor high-tech communications among far-flung terrorists. I want to be able to have our people learn their plans before they strike. That's the key. Congress can give us these tools by passing the anti-terrorism bill before them. And they should do it now. Congressional leaders pledged to pass this bill by Memorial Day, in the wake of the terrible bombing in Oklahoma City. This is a commitment Congress must keep.

On a deeper level, we must all fight terrorism by fighting the fear that terrorists sow. Today, the Secret Service is taking a necessary precaution, but let no one mistake, we will not relinquish our fundamental freedoms. We will secure the personal safety of all Americans to live and move about as they please; to think and to speak as they please; to follow their beliefs and their conscience, as our founding fathers intended.

Thanks for listening.

NEW PRESIDENTIAL DIRECTIVE
ON TERRORISM POLICY
June 21, 1995

The first attempt to formalize U.S. terrorism policy came in 1986, when President Ronald Reagan signed National Security Decision Directive 207. The document made it clear that the United States would make no concessions to terrorists and said that the State Department would take the lead role in responding to foreign incidents and the Justice Department, through the Federal Bureau of Investigation, would take the lead role in responding to domestic incidents. (National Security Directive on Terrorism, p. 76)

President Bill Clinton reaffirmed the lead roles in an updated national terrorism policy he signed June 21, 1995, known as Presidential Decision Directive 39. The document, much of which remains classified, increased the number of federal agencies assigned roles in responding to terrorist incidents and ordered the heads of numerous federal agencies and departments to take specific steps to reduce U.S. vulnerabilities to terrorist attacks. The directive also emphasized the importance of preventing terrorists from using nuclear, biological, or chemical weapons. "The acquisition of weapons of mass destruction by a terrorist group, through theft or manufacture, is unacceptable," it said. "There is no higher priority than preventing the acquisition of this capability or removing this capability from terrorist groups potentially opposed to the U.S."

Clinton signed yet another update to national terrorism policy in May 1998, known as Presidential Decision Directive 62, that confirmed the policies established in the 1995 document. It also created the position of national coordinator for terrorism within the National Security Council. However, in a report released only days after the terrorist attacks of September 11, 2001, the General Accounting Office (GAO) said the duties of the national coordinator had never been specified. The GAO, the investigative arm of Congress, also said the national coordinator was not given many of the "overall leadership and coordination" functions needed to combat terrorism, leading to "a fragmented approach" by federal agencies. "Based upon numerous evaluations, the identification of recurring problems in the overall leadership and coordination of programs, and an analysis of various proposals, GAO believes a single focal point, with all critical functions and responsibilities, should be assigned to lead and coordinate these [terrorism] programs," the GAO said.

Following is the declassified version of Presidential Decision Directive 39, "U.S. Policy on Counterterrorism," dated June 21, 1995:

It is the policy of the United States to deter, defeat and respond vigorously to all terrorist attacks on our territory and against our citizens, or facilities, whether they occur domestically, in international waters or airspace or on foreign territory. The United States regards all such terrorism as a potential threat to national security as well as a criminal act and will apply all appropriate means to combat it. In doing so, the U.S. shall pursue vigorously efforts to deter and preempt, apprehend and prosecute, or assist other governments to prosecute, individuals who perpetrate or plan to perpetrate such attacks.

We shall work closely with friendly governments in carrying out our counterterrorism policy and will support Allied and friendly governments in combating terrorist threats against them.

Furthermore, the United States shall seek to identify groups or states that sponsor or support such terrorists, isolate them and extract a heavy price for their actions.

It is the policy of the United States not to make concessions to terrorists.

To ensure that the United States is prepared to combat domestic and international terrorism in all its forms, I direct the following steps be taken.

1. Reducing Our Vulnerabilities

The United States shall reduce its vulnerabilities to terrorism, at home and abroad.

It shall be the responsibility of all Department and Agency heads to ensure that their personnel and facilities, and the people and facilities under their jurisdiction, are fully protected against terrorism. With regard to ensuring security:

— The Attorney General, as the chief law enforcement officer, shall chair a Cabinet Committee to review the vulnerability to terrorism of government facilities in the United States and critical national infrastructure and make recommendations to me and the appropriate Cabinet member or Agency head;

— The Director, FBI, as head of the investigative agency for terrorism, shall reduce vulnerabilities by an expanded program of counterterrorism;

— The Secretary of State shall reduce vulnerabilities affecting the security of all personnel and facilities at non-military U.S. Government installations abroad and affecting the general safety of American citizens abroad;

— The Secretary of Defense shall reduce vulnerabilities affecting the security of all U.S. military personnel (except those assigned to diplomatic missions) and facilities;

— The Secretary of Transportation shall reduce vulnerabilities affecting the security of all airports in the U.S. and all aircraft and passengers and all maritime shipping under U.S. flag or registration or operating within the territory of the United States and shall coordinate security measures for rail, highway, mass transit and pipeline facilities;

— The Secretary of State and the Attorney General, in addition to the latter's overall responsibilities as the chief law enforcement official, shall use all legal means available to exclude from the United States persons who pose a terrorist threat and deport or otherwise remove from the United States any such aliens;

— The Secretary of the Treasury shall reduce vulnerabilities by preventing unlawful traffic in firearms and explosives, by protecting the President and other officials against terrorist attack and through enforcement of laws controlling movement of assets, and export from or import into the United States of goods and services, subject to jurisdiction of the Department of the Treasury;

— The Director, Central Intelligence shall lead the efforts of the Intelligence Community to reduce U.S. vulnerabilities to international terrorism through an aggressive program of foreign intelligence collection, analysis, counterintelligence and covert action in accordance with the National Security Act of 1947 and E. O. [Executive Order] 12333.

2. Deterring Terrorism

The United States shall seek to deter terrorism through a clear public position that our policies will not be affected by terrorist acts and that we will act vigorously to deal with terrorists and their sponsors. Our actions will reduce the capabilities and support available to terrorists.

[Section withheld from public release]

Within the United States, we shall vigorously apply U.S. laws and seek new legislation to prevent terrorist groups from operating in the United States or using it as a base for recruitment, training, fund raising or other related activities.

- *Return of Indicted Terrorists to the U.S. for Prosecution:* We shall vigorously apply extraterritorial statutes to counter acts of terrorism and apprehend terrorists outside of the United States. When terrorists wanted for violation of U.S. law are at large overseas, their return for prosecution shall be a matter of the highest priority and shall be a continuing central issue in bilateral relations with any state that harbors or assists them. Where we do not have adequate arrangements, the Departments of State and Justice shall work to resolve the problem, where possible and appropriate, through negotiation and conclusion of new extradition treaties.

If we do not receive adequate cooperation from a state that harbors a terrorist whose extradition we are seeking, we shall take appropriate measures to induce cooperation. Return of suspects by force may be effected without the cooperation of the host government, consistent with the procedures outlined in NSD-77 [National Security Directive 77], which shall remain in effect.

- *State Support and Sponsorship:* Foreign governments assist terrorists in a variety of ways.

[Section withheld from public release]

C. Enhancing Counterterrorism Capabilities

The Secretaries of State, Defense, Treasury, Energy and Transportation, the Attorney General, the Director of Central Intelligence and the Director, FBI shall ensure that their organizations' counterterrorism capabilities within their present areas of responsibility are well managed, funded and exercised.

[Section withheld from public release]

3. Responding to Terrorism

We shall have the ability to respond rapidly and decisively to terrorism directed against us wherever it occurs, to protect Americans, arrest or defeat the perpetrators, respond with all appropriate instruments against the sponsoring organizations and governments and provide recovery relief to victims, as permitted by law.

[Section withheld from public release]

D. Lead Agency Responsibilities

This directive validates and reaffirms existing lead agency responsibilities for all facets of the United States counterterrorism effort. Lead agencies are those that have the most direct role in and responsibility for implementation of U.S. counterterrorism policy, as set forth in this Directive. Lead agencies will normally be designated as follows:

The Department of State is the lead agency for international terrorist incidents that take place outside of U.S. territory, other than incidents on U.S. flag vessels in international waters. The State Department shall act through U.S. ambassadors as the on-scene coordinators for the U.S. Government. Once military force has been directed, however, the National Command Authority shall exercise control of the U.S. military force.

[Section withheld from public release]

F. Interagency Support

To ensure that the full range of necessary expertise and capabilities are available to the on-scene coordinator, there shall be a rapidly deployable interagency Emergency Support Team (EST). The State Department shall be responsible for leading and managing the Foreign Emergency Support Team (FEST) in foreign incidents. The FBI shall be responsible for the Domestic Emergency Support Team (DEST) in domestic incidents. The DEST shall consist only of those agencies needed to respond to the specific requirements of the incident. Membership in the two teams shall include modules for specific types of incidents such as nuclear, biological or chemical threats. The Defense Department shall provide timely transportation for ESTs.

G. Transportation-related Terrorism

The Federal Aviation Administration has exclusive responsibility in instances of air piracy for the coordination of any law enforcement activity affecting the safety of persons aboard aircraft within the special aircraft jurisdiction of the U.S. as defined in public law. The Department of Justice, acting through the FBI, shall establish and maintain procedures, in coordination with the Departments of State, Defense, and Transportation, to ensure the efficient resolution of terrorist hijackings. These procedures shall be based on the principle of lead agency responsibility for command, control and rules of engagement.

H. Consequence Management

The Director of the Federal Emergency Management Agency shall ensure that the Federal Response Plan is adequate to respond to the consequences of terrorism directed against large populations in the United States, including terrorism involving weapons of mass destruction. FEMA shall ensure that States' response plans are adequate and their capabilities are tested. The State Department shall develop a plan with the Office of Foreign Disaster Assistance and DOD to provide assistance to foreign populations so victimized.

[Section withheld from public release]

K. Costs

Agencies directed to participate in the resolution of terrorist incidents or conduct of counterterrorist operations shall bear the costs of their participation, unless otherwise directed by me.

4. Weapons of Mass Destruction

The United States shall give the highest priority to developing effective capabilities to detect, prevent, defeat and manage the consequences of nuclear, biological or chemical (NBC) materials or weapons use by terrorists.

The acquisition of weapons of mass destruction by a terrorist group, through theft or manufacture, is unacceptable. There is no higher priority than preventing the acquisition of this capability or removing this capability from terrorist groups potentially opposed to the U.S.

[Remaining text withheld from public release]

William J. Clinton

As of June 14, 2002, the full text of the declassified version of Presidential Decision Directive 39, "U.S. Policy on Counterterrorism," was available by searching the National Archives and Records Administration's Archival Research Catalog (http://arcweb.archives.gov/arc/basic_search.jsp)

IRAN ACCUSED OF SUPPORTING TERRORISM IN LATIN AMERICA
September 28, 1995

On July 18, 1994, a truck bomb blew up the Jewish community center in the heart of Buenos Aires, Argentina, killing 86 and wounding hundreds more. The attack came just over two years after a car bomb destroyed the Israeli embassy in Buenos Aires, killing 29 and wounding more than 250. Intelligence officials from Argentina, Israel, and the United States blamed the bombings on Hizballah, a Lebanon-based terrorist group supported by Iran. According to American officials, Iran hoped that its backing of Hizballah would help derail the Middle East peace process. In 1996 USA Today *reported that Iran gave Hizballah up to $100 million annually.* (U.S. on the Bombing of the Israeli Embassy in Argentina, p. 116)

Philip Wilcox Jr., coordinator for counterterrorism at the U.S. State Department, testified at a congressional hearing September 28, 1995, that Hizballah was the most active international terrorist group in Latin America. "Their pursuit of terrorism in our hemisphere and in many other parts of the world demonstrates that terrorism arising from conflicts in the Middle East is now a global phenomenon," Wilcox said. He added that Iran probably knew about and provided support for the two Buenos Aires bombings. "We believe that Hizballah has not committed terrorist acts abroad without Iranian consent," he said. "And Hizballah cells in Latin America and elsewhere in the world depend on guidance and logistical support from Iranian intelligence officers assigned to Iranian embassies in the region."

In 1998 Argentine authorities announced they had solid proof that Iran masterminded the two bombings and expelled all but one of Iran's diplomats. Iran denied the charge. In September 2001 twenty people—fifteen of them former local police officers—went on trial in Buenos Aires for allegedly playing relatively minor roles in the 1994 bombing. That trial was expected to stretch well into 2002. But in perhaps the most startling development, in January 2002 Swiss authorities started investigating an allegation that former Argentine president Carlos Menem received a $10 million bribe from Iran in return for covering up its role in the 1994 bombing. Argentine authorities requested the investigation. Menem, the son of Syrian *immigrants, denied accepting any bribe. Meanwhile, by June 2002 no one had ever been charged in the 1992 bombing, and no major figures had been charged in the 1994 attack.*

Following are excerpts from testimony by Philip Wilcox Jr., coordinator for counterterrorism at the U.S. State Department, at a September 28, 1995, hearing of the House Committee on International Relations concerning terrorism in Latin America:

I appreciate this opportunity to testify on the subject of terrorism in Latin America and the bombing of the AMIA Jewish Cultural Center in Buenos Aires on July 18, 1994. These subjects are of great concern to the United States, and we have intensified our focus on terrorism in Latin America and the need to bring the bombers of the AMIA center to justice.

The tragic bombing of the AMIA building, the almost identical bombing of the Israeli Embassy in Buenos Aires in 1992, the bombing of the World Trade Center, and the related plot to blow up various public areas and government facilities in New York, which is now before a federal court, brought home to us the truth that our hemisphere is also vulnerable to international terrorism.

The perpetrators of these savage crimes are or are believed to be extremists who abuse the Islamic faith in whose name they claim to act. Dedicated to the destruction of the Arab-Israeli peace process and the State of Israel, these groups are also steeped in hatred of the West and its culture. Their pursuit of terrorism in our hemisphere and in many other parts of the world demonstrates that terrorism arising from conflicts in the Middle East is now a global phenomenon.

The Lebanon-based, Iran-backed Hizballah, which has waged a campaign of terror in the Middle East for many years, including many suicide car bombings, is now the major international terrorist threat in Latin America. The suicide bombing of the Israeli Embassy in 1992, which killed twenty-nine, was Hizballah's first terrorist act in Latin America. Hizballah denied responsibility for the crime, but Islamic Jihad, a clandestine terrorist wing of Hizballah, claimed to have carried out the suicide bombing, and authenticated its claim with a videotape of the Embassy before the bombing—a Hizballah trademark. The Government of Argentina has not yet charged any suspect for the 1994 AMIA bombing, but the evidence points to Hizballah as the bomber. The operation was a virtual duplicate of the 1992 suicide bombing, in which a vehicle carrying a massive explosives charge detonated in front of the Israeli Embassy. Ansar Allah, a clandestine subgroup of Hizballah, issued a statement expressing support for the bombing of the AMIA Center after it happened.

Another act of terrorism, the bombing of a commuter aircraft in Panama in July 1994, one day after the AMIA disaster, is still unsolved. Evidence gathered so far suggests it may also have been a Hizballah suicide bombing. Of the 21 passengers who were killed, twelve were Jews, and three of the twelve were dual national Panamanian-Americans. Ansar Allah also issued a press release supporting the attack. The apparent suicide bomber used a Middle Eastern name, but has not been otherwise identified. He had traveled the commuter plane route several times before the bombing, and no one claimed his remains.

We believe that Hizballah activities, which include narcotics and smuggling as well as terrorism, are supported in the tri-border area of Argentina, Brazil, and Paraguay. The organization is known to have cells in Colombia and Venezuela as well. Hizballah cells are concealed amidst the large Shia' Muslim population of Lebanese origin which has settled in the tri-border area. Like the great majority of Latin America's large Shia' and Sunni Muslim communities, who emigrated from the Middle East, most of the Muslims in the tri-border area are peaceful, patriotic citizens who want nothing to do with terrorism. Nevertheless, Hizballah has used this area for fund raising and recruitment and for clandestine support for terrorism, narcotics and other illegal activities. Central government control is weak in this area; borders are porous and often unpatrolled; and it is a favorable environment for such operations.

Hizballah's chief patron is Iran, and it is likely that Iran was aware of and provided support to the two Buenos Aires bombings. We believe that Hizballah has not committed terrorist acts abroad without Iranian consent. And Hizballah cells in Latin America and elsewhere in the world depend on guidance and logistical support from Iranian intelligence officers assigned to Iranian embassies in the region.

Mr. Chairman, Hizballah is only one of various international terrorist threats in Latin America affecting U.S. interests. Through August 1995, there were 53 acts of international terrorism in the region, of which 35 were directed against U.S. interests. Forty-two of these were in Colombia, where there have been repeated bombing attacks against multinational-owned oil property, and an epidemic of kidnappings.

In 1994, there were nearly 1,400 reported kidnappings in Colombia, a 35 percent increase over 1993, but the actual number may be even higher, since families and employers prefer to settle cases quietly by paying ransom. As of today, at least four U.S. citizens are being held for ransom by Colombia guerrillas, and two American hostages were killed on June 19 during a shootout between the terrorists and government forces. We have urged the Colombian government to redouble its efforts to free these hostages. But since they are being held in remote areas where the government's control is weak, and since the terrorists are intent on extorting large ransoms, the prospect for voluntary release of these hostages is limited. Two groups, the Revolutionary Armed Forces of Colombia (FARC), and the National Liberation Army (ELN) were responsible for many of these terrorist acts. These and other guerrilla groups also have ties to Colombian narcotraffickers. . . .

Turning to the investigation of the AMIA bombing, Argentine leaders have emphasized to us their strong commitment to solve the AMIA bombing and the bombing of the Israeli Embassy, and to prevent any recurrence of such acts in their country. Also, Argentina's leadership in hemispheric councils to promote greater counterterrorism cooperation has been impressive.

Large suicide bombings of this kind, which create massive destruction, are extraordinarily difficult challenges for investigators. We are concerned, nevertheless, that neither of these major crimes has been solved, and to our knowledge there has been no breakthrough in the AMIA investigation. I believe there are various reasons for this:

— Argentina's laws and its investigative and judicial systems do not provide all the tools and resources that are needed to deal aggressively and intensively with such major crimes. We understand the Argentine Congress is now examining ways to strengthen its anti-terrorism laws that will enhance the government's capabilities without endangering human rights. We have encouraged this effort.

— In the past, Argentina's borders have been porous, and the government lacked an adequate system for monitoring immigration. Recently, President Menem's government has adopted a new program to prevent the use of fraudulent travel documents by terrorists or other criminal elements seeking to enter the country, and to tighten border controls against hostile elements.

— In the past, Argentina's investigative, security and intelligence services have suffered from inadequate interagency coordination. Recently, steps have been taken to provide greater cohesion. We believe this holds promise.

— Argentina also needs to improve the effectiveness of officials working in lower levels of its law enforcement agencies. The Government of Argentina realizes that to deal with major acts of terrorism like the 1992 and 1994 bombings, improved law enforcement machinery is needed.

The Buenos Aires bombings have created a sense of urgency in the hemisphere, galvanizing the states of the region into new cooperation. After the AMIA disaster, Secretary [of State Warren] Christopher announced that he would send me, as his Coordinator for Counterterrorism, to Latin America to consult with the most concerned governments on a concrete plan to combat terrorism. He also announced that "as host for the 1994 Summit of the Americas, the United States will move to make terrorism in our hemisphere a priority item on our agenda."

The United States has learned in other parts of the world that close consultation and cooperation among the law enforcement, intelligence, and diplomatic security services of friendly states is critical to fighting international terrorism. Spreading this approach of cooperation among the states of our own hemisphere has been one of this Administration's foremost counterterrorism goals during the past year. Following up on Secretary Christopher's announcement, in early September 1994 I led an interagency team to Buenos Aires, Asuncion, Brasilia, and Caracas, to discuss operative measures. . . .

The AMIA bombing was an especially heinous act of terrorism. Aimed at the very heart of Argentina's large and vibrant Jewish community, it imposed a dreadful cost in human life, and destroyed priceless archives as well. But out of this tragedy has come a greater awareness of the international terrorist threat to Argentina and the hemisphere.

The Argentine Government and people have rallied to denounce this evil and to express solidarity with the victims. And Argentina and the other states of Latin America are now working more closely together in the kinds of cooperative activities that are indispensable to fighting international terrorism.

This Administration is doing all it can to strengthen this trend, and to continue to assist Argentina, especially, to resolve the two bombings it has suffered and to prevent any recurrence of these terrible acts.

As of June 23, 2002, the full text of Wilcox's testimony was available by searching the State Department's Public Diplomacy Query (PDQ) database at http://pdq.state.gov

HEARING ON THE THREAT POSED BY RIGHT-WING MILITIAS
November 2, 1995

The deadly bombing of the federal building in Oklahoma City on April 19, 1995, suddenly focused national attention on militias within U.S. borders because the two suspects, Timothy McVeigh and Terry Nichols, had attended some militia meetings in Michigan. In addition, the Oklahoma City bombing occurred on the second anniversary of the confrontation between federal agents and Branch Davidians in Waco, Texas, that ended with a fire that killed seventy-two of the religious cultists. Militias had used the Waco tragedy as a rallying cry ever since it happened. (Bombing of the Federal Building in Oklahoma City, p. 157)*

Six months after the Oklahoma City bombing, a subcommittee of the House Judiciary Committee held a hearing about militias. Chairman Bill McCollum, R-Fla., opened the meeting by noting it was not about political doctrines, the free association of people, or guns. "This hearing is about violent behavior that threatens civil order," he said. Rep. Charles E. Schumer, D-N.Y., denounced militias as "a sickness of hate, paranoia, and violence." Rep. Peter T. King, R-N.Y., dismissed claims by militia members that they were patriots. "They are not 'patriots'—they are pathetic individuals for whom the imagined existence of some nebulous conspiracy and the compulsion to dress-up and play 'army' on the weekends provide some sad meaning to their lives," he said. Rep. Jerrold Nadler, D-N.Y., compared the militias to terrorist groups in the Middle East. "These private armies," he said, "are the lawless siblings of Hamas and every other criminal band that believes they have the right to bomb, kill and terrorize the public as a means to win the political debate."

The FBI emphasized the militia threat in its annual report about domestic terrorism for 1996. Militias also were mentioned prominently in the FBI domestic terrorism report for 1999. "Militias present U.S. law enforcement with a particularly difficult challenge," the report said, "given their documented proclivity for paramilitary training, their stockpiling of weapons, and their intense hatred for the federal government and for law enforcement."

Yet as the decade ended, the numbers of militias and militia members were in steep decline.

Following are excerpts from statements on militias by Reps. Bill McCollum, R-Fla.; Charles E. Schumer, D-N.Y.; Peter T. King, R-N.Y.; and Jerrold Nadler, D-N.Y., at a November 2, 1995, hearing of the House Judiciary Committee's Subcommittee on Crime:

McCOLLUM STATEMENT

. . . Since the shocking and despicable bombing in Oklahoma City last April, there have been many media stories about various anti government groups, generally referred to as "militias." Some accounts have involved alarming reports of violent attacks against unsuspecting government officials performing their lawful duties. These incidents should concern us all.

But let me begin by making three important points.

First I want to clearly state what this hearing is *not* about.

Today's hearing is not about ideologies, political doctrines or mindsets that are odd or troubling or even detestable. Government cannot and should not try to restrict the thoughts of its citizens. This hearing is also not about undesirable speech such as hate filled rhetoric or bigotry—the First Amendment to the Constitution is the final word on that subject.

It is not about the free association of people, no matter how much we may dislike the interests that draw them together.

Moreover, this hearing is not about guns. Gun ownership is guaranteed by the Constitution; it's a critical part of crime prevention; and it's a widely cherished part of America's heritage.

You might ask then, "What IS this hearing about?" The answer is simple. This hearing is about violent behavior that threatens civil order. It is about people who have physically harmed, or have threatened to harm, government officials who are simply trying to do their jobs. It is about those who refuse to live by the rule of law and who use force and intimidation to advance their cause. . . .

America's greatness and liberty are inseparable. Our founders understood that a free people will only live in freedom if they are capable of governing themselves. The use of force or intimidation against another person, particularly someone who is charged with the responsibility of administering laws, is intolerable in our civil order. If citizens are afraid to speak their thoughts, or to participate in lawful activities, and if public officials are afraid to perform their duties, then the very foundation of the American experiment in ordered liberty is endangered. . . .

SCHUMER STATEMENT

. . . Make no mistake. America is at risk. The armed radical groups we will hear about today are a sickness of hate, paranoia, and violence. Their angry germs are contaminating America's lifeblood.

This sickness threatens our future as a free country—a country whose democracy is the envy of the world.

These armed extremists assault democracy by choosing the bomb and the bullet over the ballot box. They claim to love liberty. In fact they love the bully's bludgeon—the same bludgeon used by Hitler's Gestapo, Stalin's KGB, and the secret police of scores of petty tyrants.

Their "liberty" is simple: disagree with me and I will beat your brains in. Oppose me and I will kill you.

These armed extremists are strangling the public dialogue upon which democracy depends. They are dragging debate down into a cramped, narrow-minded space of fear and suspicion. They claim to love America. But they insult it with a lunatic paranoia.

That paranoia—an imagined world of black helicopters, worldwide conspiracies, and microchips secretly planted in our bodies—is bottomless in its ignorance. This paranoia is smothering the ingenuity of Thomas Jefferson, choking the rationality of Alexander Hamilton, and smearing the heritage of centuries of political enlightenment. It distorts our Constitution beyond all recognition.

Finally, these armed militant groups—and their allies—are pouring a steady stream of ethnic, racial, and religious hatred into America. The history of such hatred is long and sad. It teaches us that hatred can never be taken lightly.

Left unchecked, hatred like this has spilled over the banks of even the most civilized nations. And it has left unspeakable violence and unimaginable horrors in its wake.

We must not let the fruits of such sickness ripen into violence in America. . . .

If we do not stand up to these dark forces of hatred and violence—mark my words—they will not simply kill and maim hundreds more innocent Americans.

They will destroy America.

KING STATEMENT

. . . As the first Republican Member of Congress to call for hearings on this highly controversial issue, I am very pleased to have this opportunity to offer testimony. . . .

Of all the issues I have been identified with since coming to Congress in 1993, none has triggered so vehement a response from those opposed to my position as my stand against the so-called citizen militia movement. The hate mail I have received since calling on the members of my party to repudiate this dangerous fringe element is of an intensity not even approached by those writing to take issue with my views on such controversial issues as abortion, making English the official national language, or my support for Irish nationalism.

My pro-militia mail has ranged in content from barely legible, obscenity filled scrawls to carefully typed, grammatical and seemingly logical treatises detailing the "New World Order" conspiracy. It is hard to say which type of communication is more disturbing. Some are vaguely threatening in nature. Some are clearly racist. And although I am a Roman Catholic of Irish extraction, more than one letter has contained anti-Semitic remarks directed at me. . . .

The conspiracy theories revolving around plots to foist the sinister "New World Order" upon the American people are the common thread running among the various, disparate and anything but well regulated militias. Anyone who denies the existence of the conspiracy must be part of the conspiracy.

Disaffected groups and individuals on the far ends of the political spectrum are often overtaken by a deep-seated paranoia giving birth to wild conspiracy theories. Imagined conspiracies involving the federal government offer a very handy political excuse for why things may not be going one's way.

Conspiracy theories have always held a special fascination for those with severely under-developed intellectual and emotional faculties. . . .

The members of the so-called militias have nothing to fear from the government—perhaps the only government in the history of the world that would permit their organizations to exist at all. They are not "patriots"—they are pathetic individuals for whom the imagined existence of some nebulous conspiracy and the compulsion to dress-up and play "army" on the weekends provide some sad meaning to their lives. While most may indeed be harmless eccentrics, those militia members who threaten government and law enforcement officials with violence are dangerous and should be treated accordingly.

The political reaction to the militias has been somewhat puzzling. Most vocal critics of the militias have been liberal Democrats so closely identified with gun control legislation that their condemnation is of course viewed by the movement as proof of the conspiracy against them. To me, this is not a partisan issue—being opposed to heavily armed lunatics is a common sense position, not a political one.

What possible logical or political gain is there in appearing sympathetic to this radical movement? Why are a handful of politicians carrying water for these wackos? Why are hundreds more lending implicit support via their silence?

The so-called "citizens militia" movement threatens the very fabric of a democratic society. Shouldn't we be concerned by scores of heavily-armed private armies being fueled by a steady diet of screwball conspiracy theories, heavily laced with xenophobic and racist elements? I think so.

I also think that the failure of conservative Republicans to completely disassociate ourselves from these radical extremists threatens the very viability of our party. I say this as one who has been active in conservative politics since the Goldwater movement in the early 1960s. (Unlike some of my GOP contemporaries, I was never a Rockefeller Republican.)

The Democratic Party has yet to recover from its takeover by radical liberal elements in the late sixties. I believe the GOP faces similar long-term political damage unless we denounce the militias in no uncertain terms. Until we do that, the Republican Party runs the risk of marginalizing itself and being perceived as a party of lunatics. . . .

NADLER STATEMENT

. . . Plainly, all individuals have the right to disagree with other citizens and with the actions of government. We all have the right to speak, organize, associate with others of a like mind. They have the right to use highly charged, vulgar speech. They have the right to demonstrate their dissatisfaction by marching, or by deriding others. The Supreme Court has even said we can demonstrate our outrage by burning our American flag or defiling the religious symbols I was raised to revere.

But the idea that anyone should be permitted to take up arms against the government or any private citizen to express their views is inimical to the very principles upon which this great nation was founded and for which our flag has stood for over 200 years.

This Subcommittee will hear testimony today about how these armed bands of terrorists have organized themselves into private armies for the purpose of coercing duly elected public officials and private individuals. No reasonable person can condone these terrorist tactics. These private armies are the lawless siblings of Hamas and every other criminal band that believes they have the right to bomb, kill and terrorize the public as a means to win the political debate.

I speak as one who knows all too well the human cost of violent terrorism. As many of the members of this Subcommittee will recall, the World Trade Center is in my district. That terrible day when the World Trade Center was bombed is forever etched in my mind. In fact, we had several uneasy hours in my Washington office as a member of my staff waited for word of her father who worked in one of the Twin Towers. . . .

We should all think about what kind of country we want to live in. To be truly patriotic means recognizing our responsibilities to uphold the democratic principles that make this the freest nation on Earth. It is important to remember that the opening words of the Constitution are "We the People," not "I the People." Being a citizen in a democracy means that you cannot organize your own private army because you disagree with the actions of the democratically elected government or because you do not like the color or religion or beliefs of your neighbors. If you settle political differences with bullets instead of ballots, you don't live in a democracy, you live in Beirut or Bosnia. . . .

THE ASSASSINATION OF ISRAELI PRIME MINISTER RABIN
November 6, 1995

Following decades of battles and terrorist attacks, in 1993 Prime Minister Yitzhak Rabin of Israel and the Palestine Liberation Organization (PLO) started secret talks. Those negotiations led to a historic peace declaration that Rabin and PLO leader Yasir Arafat signed at the White House in November 1993. Rabin, Arafat, and Israeli foreign minister Shimon Peres won the 1994 Nobel Peace Prize for their steps toward peace. Rabin negotiated a peace agreement with Jordan in 1994 and in November 1995 signed a new agreement with Arafat that gave the Palestinians control over much of the West Bank of the Jordan River, which Israel had occupied since 1967. More than any previous agreement, the West Bank accord provoked cries of outrage from Israeli rightists, who said God meant for the territory to be under Jewish control. (Remarks on Peace Agreement Between Israel and the PLO, p. 127)

As Rabin walked away after addressing a giant peace rally in Tel Aviv on November 4, a former Israeli soldier, Yigal Amir, gunned him down. Amir said the prime minister had betrayed Israel by making peace concessions to Arabs. At a November 6 court hearing, Amir said that killing Rabin "was my obligation according to religious law." That same day Rabin was buried in Jerusalem after a memorial service attended by leaders from eighty nations. Jordan's King Hussein, who just the previous year had signed a peace agreement with Rabin after nearly forty years of leading a country officially at war with Israel, shed tears as Rabin was laid to rest. Ironically, the assassination of Rabin—a Jew who was killed because he sought peace with the Arabs—came fourteen years after the assassination of President Anwar al-Sadat of Egypt, an Arab who was killed because he sought peace with the Jews. (The Assassination of Egyptian President Anwar al-Sadat, p. 47)

The assassination sparked an intense period of soul searching in Israel, which was sharply divided on all questions concerning peace with the Arabs. Nonetheless, the government continued the peace policies that Rabin had championed, including the peace agreement with the Palestinians.

Following are excerpts from remarks by acting Israeli prime minister Shimon Peres, King Hussein of Jordan, and President Hosni Mubarak of Egypt during memorial services for Yitzhak Rabin at Mount Herzl cemetery in Jerusalem on November 6, 1995:

REMARKS BY PERES

Yitzhak, the youngest of Israel's generals, and Yitzhak, the greatest of peacemakers: the suddenness of your passing illuminated the abundance of your accomplishments.

You resembled no one; nor did you seek to emulate anyone. You were not one of the "joyous and merry."

You were one who made great demands—first of yourself, and therefore also of others.

You refused to accept failures, and you were not intimidated by pinnacles.

You knew every detail, and you grasped the overall picture. You shaped the details one by one to form great steps, great decisions.

All your life, you worked hard, day and night. But the last three years were unparalleled in their intensity. You promised to change priorities. Indeed, a new order has arrived, a priority of openness.

New crossroads have been opened, new roads paved; unemployment has declined; immigrants have been absorbed; exports have increased and investments expanded; the economy is flourishing; education has doubled; and science has advanced.

And above all, perhaps at the root of it all, the mighty winds of peace have begun to blow.

Two agreements with our neighbors the Palestinians will enable them to hold democratic elections, and will free us from the necessity of ruling another people—as you promised.

A warm peace with Jordan invited the great desert between us to become a green promise for both peoples.

The Middle East has reawakened, and a coalition of peace is taking shape: a regional coalition supported by a world coalition, to which the leaders of America and Europe, of Asia and Africa, of Australia and of our region standing alongside your fresh grave bear witness.

They came, as we did, to salute you, and to declare that the course that you began will continue.

This time, Leah [Rabin's wife] is here without you. But the whole nation is with her, and with the family.

I see our people in profound shock, with tears in their eyes. But also a people who know that the bullets that [slew] you could not slay the idea which you embraced. You did not leave us a last will, but you left us a path on which we will march with conviction and faith. The nation today is shedding tears. But these are also tears of unity and of spiritual uplifting.

I see our Arab neighbors, and to them I say: the course of peace is irreversible. Neither for us, nor for you. Neither we nor you can stop, delay or hesitate when it comes to peace—a peace that must be full and comprehensive, for young and old, for all the peoples.

From here, from Jerusalem, where you were born, the birthplace of the three great religions, let us say in the words of the lamentation for Rachel, who passed away on the very day you were slain:

"Refrain thy voice from weeping, and thine eyes from tears for thy work shall be rewarded, and there is hope for thy future, saith the Lord" (Jeremiah 31:16–17).

Goodbye, my older brother, hero of peace. We shall continue to bear this great peace, near and far, as you sought during your lifetime, as you charge us with your death.

REMARKS BY KING HUSSEIN

My sister, Mrs. Leah Rabin, my friends, I had never thought that the moment would come like this when I would grieve the loss of a brother, a colleague and a friend—a man, a soldier who met us on the opposite side of a divide whom we respected as he respected us. A man I came to know because I realized, as he did, that we have to cross over the divide, establish a dialogue, get to know each other and strive to leave for those who follow us a legacy that is worthy of them. And so we did. And so we became brethren and friends.

I've never been used to standing, except with you next to me, speaking of peace, speaking about dreams and hopes for generations to come that must live in peace, enjoy human dignity, come together, work together, to build a better future which is their right. Never in all my thoughts would it have occurred to me that my first visit to Jerusalem and response to your invitation, the invitation of the Speaker of the Knesset, the invitation of the president of Israel, would be on such an occasion.

You lived as a soldier, you died as a soldier for peace and I believe it is time for all of us to come out, openly, and to speak our piece, but here today, but for all the times to come. We belong to the camp of peace. We believe in peace. We believe that our one God wishes us to live in peace and wishes peace upon us, for these are His teachings to all the followers of the three great monotheistic religions, the children of Abraham.

Let's not keep silent. Let our voices rise high to speak of our commitment to peace for all times to come, and let us tell those who live in darkness who are the enemies of life, and through faith and religion and the teachings of our one God, this is where we stand. This is our camp. May God bless you with the realization that you must join it and we pray that He will, but otherwise we are not ashamed, nor are we afraid, nor are we anything but determined to fulfill the legacy for which my friend fell, as did my grandfather in this very city when I was with him and but a young boy. He was a man of courage, a man of vision, and he was endowed with one of the greatest virtues that any man can have. He was endowed with humility. He felt with those around him and in a position of responsibility, he placed himself, as I do and have done, often, in the place of the other partner to achieve a worthy goal. And we achieved peace, an honorable peace and a lasting peace. He had courage, he had vision, and he had a commitment to peace, and standing here, I commit before you, before my people in Jordan, before the world, myself to continue with our utmost, to ensure that we leave a similar legacy. And when my time comes, I hope it will be like my grandfather's and like Yitzhak Rabin's.

The faces in my country amongst the majority of my people and our armed forces and people who once were your enemies are somber today and their hearts are heavy. Let's hope and pray that God will give us all guidance, each in his respective position to do what he can for the better future that Yitzhak Rabin sought with determination and courage. As long as I live, I'll be proud to have known him, to have worked with him, as a brother and as a friend, and as a man, and the relationship of friendship that we had is something unique and I am proud of that.

On behalf of the people of Jordan, my large Jordanian family, my Hashemite family, all those who belong to the camp of peace, our deepest sympathies, our deepest condolences as we share together this moment of remembrance and commitment, to continue our struggle for the future of generations to come, as did Yitzhak Rabin, and to fulfill his legacy. Thank you.

REMARKS BY MUBARAK

. . . [I]t is with deep regret that we assemble here today to pay our last respects to Prime Minister Yitzhak Rabin, a courageous leader and a recognized statesman. His earnest efforts to achieve peace in the Middle East are a testament to his vision, which we share, to end the suffering of all the peoples of our region.

He defied the prejudices of the past to tackle the most complicated of problems, namely the Palestinian problem, in a forthright manner. The success he achieved in this regard has firmly laid the foundations of peaceful coexistence between Palestinians and the Israelis in a climate of trust and a mutual respect. These achievements have undoubtedly established him as a true hero of peace.

The untimely loss of Prime Minister Yitzhak Rabin at this important juncture in the history of the Middle East has dealt a severe blow to our noble cause. We must, therefore, redouble our efforts and reaffirm our obligation to continue the sacred mission to achieve a just and lasting peace. We must deprive those treacherous hands hostile towards our goal from reaping the rewards of their vile actions. Only through our unwavering commitment to this objective can we truly honor the memory of this fallen hero of peace.

And I could say that the message memorial for Yitzhak Rabin is to continue what he started, which is the peace process and, of course, as we mentioned several times, peace is so precious for the whole people all over the world. On this sad occasion, ladies and gentlemen, I extend the condolences of the people and the government [of] Egypt, and my personal condolences, to the government and the people of Israel and the family of Mr. Yitzhak Rabin. Thank you.

TERRORIST PLOT TO BLOW UP AMERICAN PLANES IN FLIGHT
Undated [1996]

On December 11, 1994, a small bomb exploded underneath a passenger's seat on Philippine Airlines Flight 434 as it flew to Tokyo. The passenger was killed and ten others injured, but the pilot was able to make an emergency landing. That incident turned out to be a test run for a terrorist plot to blow up a dozen U.S. jumbo jets in a two-day period as they flew over the Pacific Ocean on their way from the Far East to Los Angeles, San Francisco, Honolulu, and New York. The only thing that stopped the plot, which could have killed up to 4,000 people, was sheer luck.

That luck came when two terrorists—both with strong ties to Osama bin Laden's al Qaeda terrorist network—made a mistake while mixing chemicals for the bombs in a Manila apartment on January 6, 1995. Their error caused a fire that drew the attention of local authorities. Police captured one of the terrorists, along with notebooks and a laptop computer filled with documents. During a long interrogation, the terrorist—Abdul Hakim Murad— provided details about the plot to place bombs made with liquid explosives on a dozen planes operated by Northwest, Delta, and United Airlines. The sophisticated bombs, which would have been almost impossible to detect during airport screenings, were concocted by Ramzi Ahmed Yousef, who escaped during the fire and also was the mastermind of the 1993 bombing of the World Trade Center in New York. The terrorists planned to place the bombs on planes in the Far East and set timers so the bombs would go off when the planes were over the Pacific Ocean on their way to the United States. Murad said the bombings, which would have occurred only days after the fire was detected, were intended to protest American support of Israel. Yousef was captured later in the year in Pakistan, and a New York jury convicted him, Murad, and a third man in September 1996 of planning the bombing. (The 1993 Bombing of the World Trade Center, p. 123)

After the September 11, 2001, hijackings in which terrorists flew passenger jets into the World Trade Center and the Pentagon, investigators were haunted by a statement that Murad made during his 1995 interrogation.

Murad, who had a commercial pilot's license he obtained after studying at several American flight schools, said he had also planned to hijack a commercial plane and crash it into Central Intelligence Agency headquarters in Virginia. The terrorists had additionally discussed flying hijacked planes into the Pentagon, the U.S. Capitol, the White House, and skyscrapers. All they needed, he said, was more trained pilots. Filipino authorities reportedly shared the information immediately with the FBI, but the FBI apparently focused most of its attention on the plot to blow up the dozen jets. The plan to turn planes into bombs was noted in a widely circulated 1999 report that the Library of Congress prepared for the National Intelligence Council. "Suicide bomber(s) belonging to al Qaeda's Martyrdom Battalion could crash-land an aircraft packed with high explosives (C-4 and semtex) into the Pentagon, the headquarters of the Central Intelligence Agency (CIA), or the White House," said the report, which was made public on the Internet. "Ramzi Yousef had planned to do this against the CIA headquarters." (Bush on Terrorist Attacks Against the United States, p. 351)

Following is an excerpt from "Terrorism in the United States 1995," a 1996 FBI report that discusses the arrests of Ramzi Ahmed Yousef and Abdul Hakim Murad and their plot to blow up a dozen U.S. jumbo jets:

Ramzi Ahmed Yousef Apprehended

On February 7, 1995, FBI Agents and State Department Diplomatic Security Officers apprehended Top Ten Fugitive Ramzi Ahmed Yousef, also known as Abdul Basit Mahmoud Abdul Karim, in Islamabad, Pakistan. Officials transported Yousef to the United States the following day where he was arraigned in the Southern District of New York on charges relating to his alleged involvement in the February 26, 1993, World Trade Center bombing. On April 12, 1995, Yousef was also indicted for conspiring to bomb Philippine Airlines Flight 434 on December 11, 1994, and to bomb several other U.S. air carriers transiting the Far East.

Yousef's trial began on May 13, 1996. On September 5, 1996, he and two associates were convicted of plotting to bomb U.S. airliners in the Far East. Yousef's trial for his alleged role in the World Trade Center bombing is expected to begin in early 1997.

Ramzi Yousef Associate Apprehended

On April 22, 1995, FBI Agents took custody of Abdul Hakim Murad from Philippine authorities. Philippine police arrested Murad after a fire broke in a Manila apartment in which Murad, Ramzi Yousef, and another associate were living. Inside the apartment, Philippine officials found explosives and bomb making materials.

Murad was returned to the United States and arraigned in the Southern District of New York. He, along with Ramzi Yousef and Wali Khan Amin Shah, was charged with conspiring to bomb U.S. civil aircraft transiting the Far East.

On September 5, 1996, Murad was convicted of plotting to bomb the U.S. airliners. He will be sentenced in December 1996.

ATTEMPT TO ASSASSINATE EGYPTIAN PRESIDENT MUBARAK
January 31, 1996

As Egyptian president Hosni Mubarak's four-car motorcade started driving from the airport at Addis Ababa, Ethiopia, into the city for a summit of the Organization of African Unity on June 26, 1995, a car suddenly pulled from a side street to block its path. Men in that car and two others behind it jumped out and opened fire on the motorcade with AK-47 assault rifles. Numerous bullets hit the president's limousine, but its armor plating saved his life. Two policemen and two terrorists died in the attack; the rest of the terrorists escaped. Terrorists from the Egyptian Islamic Jihad assassinated Mubarak's predecessor, Anwar al-Sadat, in 1981, and Muslim extremists were quickly suspected in the attack on Mubarak as well. (The Assassination of Egyptian President Anwar al-Sadat, p. 47)

Mubarak charged that the attackers came from neighboring Sudan, a country that the United States in 1993 had placed on its list of countries sponsoring terrorism. Sudanese officials denied any involvement. On January 31, 1996, the United Nations Security Council passed a resolution ordering Sudan to extradite three suspects in the attack and to stop assisting and giving shelter to terrorists. One of the terrorists that Sudan sheltered for many years was Osama bin Laden, the leader of the al Qaeda terrorist network. Sudan failed to comply, and the Security Council ultimately imposed sanctions that included a requirement that nations around the world reduce the number of Sudanese diplomats in their countries.

Even though Sudan continued refusing to extradite the suspects, at the end of 1999 Egypt and Sudan agreed to normalize their relations. On September 28, 2001, the Security Council voted to lift the sanctions based on Sudan's cooperation in the U.S. war on terrorism and its belief that the three suspects were no longer in Sudan. In late March 2002 Sudan suddenly announced it was sending a suspect in the Mubarak assassination attempt to Egypt to stand trial. Sudanese and American officials said the man was a member of Egyptian Islamic Jihad, the same group that killed Sadat in 1981. Despite Sudan's action and its continuing overtures to Washington, as of June 2002 Sudan remained on the U.S. list of nations that sponsor terrorism.

Following is the text of Resolution 1044, which the United Nations Security Council approved on January 31, 1996:

The Security Council,

Deeply disturbed by the world-wide persistence of acts of international terrorism in all its forms which endanger or take innocent lives, have a deleterious effect on international relations and jeopardize the security of States,

Recalling the statement made by the President of the Security Council on 31 January 1992 (S/23500) when the Council met at the level of Heads of State and Government in which the members of the Council expressed their deep concern over acts of international terrorism and emphasized the need for the international community to deal effectively with all such acts,

Recalling also the Convention on the Prevention and Punishment of Crimes against Internationally Protected Persons, including Diplomatic Agents, opened for signature at New York on 14 December 1973,

Stressing the imperative need to strengthen international cooperation between States in order to make and adopt practical and effective measures to prevent, combat and eliminate all forms of terrorism that affect the international community as a whole,

Convinced that the suppression of acts of international terrorism, including those in which States are involved, is an essential element for the maintenance of international peace and security,

Gravely alarmed at the terrorist assassination attempt on the life of the President of the Arab Republic of Egypt, in Addis Ababa, Ethiopia, on 26 June 1995, and *convinced* that those responsible for that act must be brought to justice,

Taking note that the Third Extraordinary Session of the Organization of African Unity (OAU) Mechanism for Conflict Prevention, Management and Resolution of 11 September 1995, considered that attack as aimed, not only at the President of the Arab Republic of Egypt, and not only at the sovereignty, integrity and stability of Ethiopia, but also at Africa as a whole,

Taking note also of the statements of the Central Organ of the OAU Mechanism of 11 September 1995 and of 19 December 1995 and *supporting* the implementation of the requests contained therein,

Regretting the fact that the Government of the Sudan has not yet complied with the requests of the Central Organ of the OAU set out in those statements,

Noting the letter from the Permanent Representative of Ethiopia of 9 January 1996 (S/1996/10) to the President of the Security Council,

Noting also the letters from the Permanent Representative of the Sudan of 11 January 1996 (S/1996/22) and 12 January 1996 (S/1996/25) to the President of the Council,

1. *Condemns* the terrorist assassination attempt on the life of the President of the Arab Republic of Egypt in Addis Ababa, Ethiopia, on 26 June 1995;
2. *Strongly deplores* the flagrant violation of the sovereignty and integrity of Ethiopia and the attempt to disturb the peace and security of Ethiopia and the region as a whole;
3. *Commends* the efforts of the Government of Ethiopia to resolve this issue through bilateral and regional arrangements;
4. *Calls upon* the Government of the Sudan to comply with the requests of the Organization of African Unity without further delay to:
   (a) Undertake immediate action to extradite to Ethiopia for prosecution the three suspects sheltering in the Sudan and wanted in connection with the assassination attempt on the basis of the 1964 Extradition Treaty between Ethiopia and the Sudan;
   (b) Desist from engaging in activities of assisting, supporting and facilitating terrorist activities and from giving shelter and sanctuaries to terrorist elements and act in its relations with its neighbours and with others in full conformity with the Charter of the United Nations and with the Charter of the Organization of African Unity;
5. *Urges* the international community to encourage the Government of the Sudan to respond fully and effectively to the OAU requests;
6. *Welcomes* the efforts of the Secretary-General of the OAU aimed at the implementation of the relevant provisions of the statements of the Central Organ of the OAU Mechanism of 11 September 1995 and of 19 December 1995, and *supports* the OAU in its continued efforts to implement its decisions;
7. *Requests* the Secretary-General in consultation with the OAU to seek the cooperation of the Government of the Sudan in the implementation of this resolution and to report to the Council within 60 days;
8. *Decides* to remain seized of the matter.

THE PROLIFERATION OF WEAPONS OF MASS DESTRUCTION
April 11, 1996

Fearful that a large quantity of highly enriched uranium stored in a poorly guarded warehouse in the former Soviet republic of Kazakhstan could end up in the hands of terrorists or two states that sponsored them— Iran and Iraq—in 1994 the United States embarked on a secret effort to move the uranium to the nuclear complex at Oak Ridge, Tennessee. The warehouse contained enough uranium to make at least twenty nuclear bombs. The Kazakhstan government agreed to the transfer in return for a payment from the United States. This incident was only one more indication of the growing fear that terrorists might obtain weapons of mass destruction—and of increasing efforts to prevent the proliferation of such weapons.

Among various groups that might obtain and use chemical, biological, or nuclear weapons, terrorists posed the greatest threat to the United States and its interests, according to a report released April 11, 1996, by the U.S. Department of Defense. "Most terrorist groups do not have the financial and technical resources necessary to acquire nuclear weapons, but could gather materials to make radiological dispersion devices and some biological and chemical agents," the report said. It also said some countries that sponsored terrorist groups either had or could obtain weapons of mass destruction, although none had passed along such weapons to terrorists so far.

More than three years later, on October 20, 1999, a senior official at the General Accounting Office testified before Congress that terrorist groups would have great difficulties creating and using biological or chemical weapons—unless they had help from a nation that sponsored terrorism. "According to the experts we consulted, in most cases terrorists would have to overcome significant technical and operational challenges to successfully make and release chemical agents of sufficient quality and quantity to kill or injure large numbers of people without substantial assistance from a state sponsor," said Assistant Comptroller General Henry L. Hinton Jr.
(GAO on Threats Posed by Weapons of Mass Destruction, p. 291)

Following are excerpts from "Proliferation: Threat and Response," a report issued April 11, 1996, by the U.S. Department of Defense:

The New Threat from Nuclear, Biological, and Chemical Weapons

During the height of the Cold War, the Russian physicist Andre Sakharov said, "Reducing the risk of annihilating humanity in a nuclear war carries an absolute priority over all other considerations." The end of the Cold War has reduced the threat of global nuclear war, but today a new threat is rising from the global spread of nuclear, biological, and chemical [NBC] weapons. Hostile groups and nations have tried—or have been able—to obtain these weapons, the technology, and homegrown ability to make them or ballistic missiles that can deliver the massive annihilation, poison, and death of these weapons hundreds of miles away. For rogue nations, these weapons are a ticket to power, stature, and confidence in regional war.

We received a wake-up call with [Iraqi president] Saddam Hussein's use of SCUD missiles during Operation Desert Storm and new information on his ambitious nuclear, biological, and chemical weapons programs. The proliferation of these horrific weapons presents a grave and urgent risk to the United States and our citizens, allies, and troops abroad. Reducing this risk is an absolute priority of the United States.

The way we reduce the risk from weapons of mass destruction has changed dramatically. During the Cold War, the United States and the Soviet Union lived under a doctrine known as Mutually Assured Destruction, commonly known as "MAD." MAD was essentially a balance of terror that assumed neither nuclear power would launch an attack and risk nuclear retaliation. This nuclear stand-off has ended. Instead, the United States and Russia are working together to reduce and dismantle our nuclear arsenals, and to prevent the export and sale of those weapons and related technology throughout the world.

Our progress is good news. The bad news is that in this era the simple threat of retaliation that worked during the Cold War may not be enough to deter terrorists or aggressive regimes from using nuclear, biological, and chemical weapons. Terrorists operate in a shadowy world in which they can detonate a device and disappear, as the poison gas attack in Tokyo illustrates. Rogue regimes may try to use these devastating weapons as blackmail, or as a relatively inexpensive way to sidestep the U.S. military's overwhelming conventional military superiority. Aggressors may also actually use these weapons in an attempt to gain a decisive edge in a regional war. The bottom line is, unlike during the Cold War, those who possess nuclear, biological, and chemical weapons may actually come to use them. . . .

The Transnational Threat: Dangers from Terrorism, Insurgencies, Civil Wars, and Organized Crime

Transnational groups of proliferation concern include terrorists, insurgents, opposing factions in civil wars, and members of organized criminal groups. Such groups are not generally bound by the same constraints and mores or motivated by the same factors as are nation-states, but pose significant threats to the interests of the United States and our allies and friends worldwide. Terrorist acts pose an especially potent threat to U.S. interests. When carried out by small, close-knit groups, these attacks are difficult to detect in advance, despite diligent intelligence efforts.

This category of proliferation threat is truly a global problem, cutting across all regions. The threat has been starkly demonstrated by the 1995 nerve gas attack in Japan, the bombing of the New York World Trade Center, and the increased involvement of criminal groups in the smuggling of nuclear materials. Furthermore, with numerous ongoing insurgencies and civil wars worldwide, there are additional dangers for escalation should NBC weapons or missiles be introduced to the conflict. Finally, there is an increased potential for leakage of NBC weapons or missile technology, or individuals with technological know-how. Such leakage would most likely occur between states that have reduced or dismantled their programs and states with programs under development.

Terrorist Groups

Terrorist groups that acquire NBC weapons and stridently oppose U.S. policies could pose significant potential dangers to U.S. interests. Terrorists armed with these weapons can gain leverage for their demands because of the weapons' nature.

Terrorists might wish to obtain NBC weapons for a variety of motives. Such groups might threaten using NBC weapons as "saber rattlers" to raise the ante in response to Western political or military actions or to achieve a specific objective, but would risk losing its base of support.

Most terrorist groups do not have the financial and technical resources necessary to acquire nuclear weapons, but could gather materials to make radiological dispersion devices and some biological and chemical agents. Some groups have state sponsors that possess or can obtain NBC weapons. Nations such as Iran and Libya have backed numerous groups over the years, but no sponsor has yet demonstrated a willingness to provide such groups with NBC weapons, perhaps a testament to the looming and certain threat of retaliation should the state be identified as the supplier.

Terrorist acts involving NBC weapons represent a particularly dangerous threat that must be countered. The ability of terrorists to take the initiative in the choice of targets and timing of attacks significantly complicates our ability to combat this threat. U.S. policy in countering terrorism is four-fold: make no concessions to terrorists, use political and economic instruments to pressure states that sponsor terrorism, exploit fully all available legal mechanisms to punish international terrorists, and help other governments improve their capabilities to combat terrorism.

Insurgents and Civil War Factions

Insurgent groups and separatist movements, should they acquire NBC weapons or missiles, pose another potential threat to U.S. interests. Presently, there are dozens of insurgencies ongoing throughout the world. Insurgent groups aim to overthrow existing governments, thus destabilizing regional balances of power. In some cases, such groups have kidnapped U.S. citizens or conducted economic retaliation against U.S. commercial interests abroad. For the most part, these groups operate with unsophisticated weapons, receive little financial backing, and lack an industrial base to develop or produce NBC weapons or missiles.

The primary proliferation concern about insurgent groups is that they might capture such weapons, acquire them from sympathizers in the government's forces, or purchase them, possibly from organized criminal groups. Insurgents might also attract sympathizers among knowledgeable scientists and technicians who might aid in developing weapons. Acquisition of such weapons could alter the regional balance of power and change the terms of conflict, if not its outcome, decisively.

Opposing factions in civil wars also could have access to NBC weapons and missiles. Such factions might be motivated to use these weapons as force multipliers to achieve quick and decisive victories. Factions could threaten or actually use the weapons against civilians for psychological and strategic effect. Tactically, the weapons might be used against a larger conventional force to disrupt staging or resupply efforts, thus prompting an evacuation of noncombatants.

Recently, opposing factions in two civil wars acquired and employed ballistic missiles with conventional warheads. After the Soviets withdrew from Afghanistan, Afghan rebel factions acquired a number of SCUD missiles, some of which the rebel groups fired at government forces in Kabul in January 1994. The second instance involved the Yemen civil war. During the spring of 1994, the southern faction launched SCUD missiles against civilians in the northern cities of Sana and Tai'z. None of the strikes in these two cases caused significant damage or casualties or affected the fighting significantly.

Organized Criminal Groups

The potential for international organized criminal groups to obtain, use, or sell NBC weapons has grown in the last few years. In the wake of the Cold War, some of these groups have emerged as a growing threat to U.S. interests. This situation is particularly critical in the former Soviet Union.

A careful distinction must be made, however, between material the criminal groups claim to offer for sale and what they can deliver. For example, numerous criminal elements throughout Europe have been implicated in scams involving the sale of what was advertised as weapons grade nuclear materials. To date, those materials seized by law enforcement officials have been well below enrichment or quantity levels suitable for weapons. Most appear to have come from research facilities rather than from weapons-related facilities.

Over the past several years, organized criminal groups and smugglers have become increasingly involved in trafficking illegal nuclear materials. The growing number and sophistication of groups attempting to acquire these materials or weapons is an increasingly crucial concern for international law enforcement.

Beginning in 1991, multiple incidents involving criminal activity and the theft of nuclear material surfaced in Europe. During a 1994 appearance before the Permanent Subcommittee on Investigations, the head of the German Federal Criminal Police (the Federal Bureau of Investigation's German counterpart) offered his insight into criminal trafficking of nuclear material. He reported that the number of incidents involving nuclear materials within Germany was increasing over time: from 41 in 1991, to 158 in 1992, to 241 in 1993, and to 267 in 1994. In late 1994, responding to the incidents involving nuclear material smuggled into Germany in August 1994, Moscow and Bonn agreed to new bilateral security measures.

Implications for Regional Security

Controlling or containing proliferation involving transnational groups is particularly difficult because these groups evade or defy recognized export controls or nonproliferation regimes. Should these groups acquire NBC weapons or missiles, they may be more inclined to employ them in order to achieve their goals than would a member in good standing of the international community of nations. Countering the transfer of these weapons and related technologies to or from these groups has become increasingly difficult. Furthermore, the sophistication of some of the groups—especially organized crime—involved in the smuggling of NBC-related materials has complicated the related problems of locating stolen materials and disabling weapons. In some cases, the difficulty is further complicated by the dual-use nature and availability of the raw materials associated with biological or chemical agents.

Of the transnational groups discussed above, the greatest dangers to U.S. interests stem from terrorists and, to a lesser extent, organized criminal groups. One of the most volatile and frightening scenarios for U.S. defense planning posits a terrorist group, whose actions are directed principally against the United States, with nuclear material or an actual NBC weapon. Though direct U.S. interests are always exposed to some risks, it is unlikely that attacks from insurgents or opposing sides in a civil war that involved such weapons would focus their main attacks on U.S. interests specifically.

As of June 17, 2002, the full text of the U.S. Department of Defense report was available at http://www.defenselink.mil/pubs/prolif

CIA DIRECTOR WARNS OF
CYBER ATTACKS BY TERRORISTS
June 25, 1996

Between April 1990 and May 1991 Internet-accessible computer systems at thirty-four Department of Defense (DoD) facilities were penetrated by foreign hackers, according to testimony at a congressional hearing on November 20, 1991, by Jack Brock Jr., the top expert on government information at the General Accounting Office (GAO), the investigative arm of Congress. "The hackers exploited well-known security weaknesses—many of which were exploited in the past by other hacker groups," he testified. Nearly five years later, little had changed—except the number of attacks. "Unknown and unauthorized individuals are increasingly attacking and gaining access to highly sensitive unclassified information on the Department of Defense's computer systems," the GAO said in a report released May 22, 1996. DoD computers might have suffered 250,000 attacks in the previous year, the GAO said—and 65 percent were successful. "The potential for catastrophic damage is great," said the congressional watchdog. "Organized foreign nations or terrorists could use 'information warfare' techniques to disrupt military operations by harming command and control systems, the public switch network, and other systems or networks Defense relies on."

Those information warfare attacks could extend well beyond Defense Department computers, warned John M. Deutch, director of the Central Intelligence Agency, at a hearing June 25, 1996, before the Senate Permanent Subcommittee on Investigations. Deutch said he was concerned that terrorists, hackers, or other nations could launch information warfare attacks that would disrupt electric power distribution, air traffic control, international commerce, or deployed military forces. He especially emphasized the threat posed by terrorists. "International terrorist groups clearly have the capability to attack the information infrastructure of the United States," Deutch said, "even if they use relatively simple means." In response to a question, Deutch said he considered computer attacks the second most serious national security threat, topped only by the worldwide proliferation of nuclear, chemical, and biological weapons.

More than five years later, security problems "with potentially devastating consequences" remained widespread in government computer systems, according to congressional testimony on November 9, 2001, by Robert F. Dacey, director of information security issues for the GAO. A recent GAO review of computer systems at twenty-four federal agencies found major security problems at every agency, he said. (Federal Computer Systems Face Severe Security Risk, p. 374)

Following are excerpts from the prepared statement of John M. Deutch, director of the Central Intelligence Agency, for a June 25, 1996, hearing of the Senate Permanent Subcommittee on Investigations:

I wish to thank you for inviting me to appear before you this morning and speak about foreign information warfare activities against the United States. Protecting our critical information systems and information-based infrastructures is a subject that is worthy of considerable attention and is an issue that I am deeply concerned about.

Over the past 20 years, our nation has witnessed and contributed greatly to a technology revolution. As a result, our government, business, and citizens have become increasingly dependent on an interconnected network of telecommunications and computer-based information systems. These systems, such as the ones comprising the public switched telephone network, serve as a critical backbone for the entire U.S. public and private sectors. U.S. military logistic and operational elements increasingly rely on computer databases and the public telephone network for their classified, as well as unclassified, activities. In addition, the U.S. civil sector increasingly depends on the uninterrupted and trusted flow of digital information. Day-to-day operations of U.S. banking, energy distribution, air traffic control, emergency medical services, transportation, and many other industries all depend on reliable telecommunications and an increasingly complex network of computers, information databases, and computer driven control systems. The Internet has created a global information network that will be an enabler for an exciting new opportunity for digital commerce. This connectivity will create a seemingly seamless world of commerce without borders.

I, like many others in this room, am concerned that this connectivity and dependency make us vulnerable to a variety of information warfare attacks. While attention is focused on computer based "cyber" attacks, we should not forget that key nodes and facilities that house critical systems and handle the flow of digital data can also be attacked with conventional high-explosives. These information attacks, in whatever form, could not only disrupt our daily lives, but also seriously jeopardize our national or economic security. Without sufficient planning as we build these systems, I am also concerned that the potential for damage could grow in the years ahead.

I welcome the efforts of this subcommittee to increase public awareness about these important issues. I believe steps need to be taken to address information system vulnerabilities and efforts to exploit them. We must think carefully about the kinds of attackers that might use information warfare techniques, their targets, objectives, and methods. . . .

My greatest concern is that hackers, terrorist organizations, or other nations might use information warfare techniques as part of a coordinated attack designed to seriously disrupt:

- infrastructures such as electric power distribution, air traffic control, or financial sectors;
- international commerce; and
- deployed military forces in time of peace or war.

Virtually any "bad actor" can acquire the hardware and software needed to attack some of our critical information-based infrastructures. Hacker tools are readily available on the Internet, and hackers themselves are a source of expertise for any nation or foreign terrorist organization that is interested in developing an information warfare capability. In fact, hackers, with or without their full knowledge, may be supplying advice and expertise to rogue states such as Iran and Libya.

It is important to keep in mind, however, that computer-based tools are only one part of an information warfare capability. An adversary also needs highly detailed information about the target and its vulnerabilities, access to the target, and some way to judge how effective the attack will be. While some key U.S. infrastructure targets may be vulnerable to both physical destruction and "cyber" attacks, others are more secure.

Last summer, the National Intelligence Council, with help from a number of Intelligence Community agencies, produced a classified report compiling our knowledge of foreign information warfare plans and programs. Produced at the request of the Pentagon, it focused on foreign efforts to attack the U.S. public switched telephone network and so-called Supervisory Control and Data Acquisition (or SCADA) systems—the computers that control electric power distribution, oil refineries, and other similar utilities. This Intelligence Community publication was the first of its kind on this topic, and served as a vehicle for organizing the Intelligence Community's collection and analysis on this subject.

While the details are classified and cannot be discussed here, we have evidence that a number of countries around the world are developing the doctrine, strategies, and tools to conduct information attacks. At present, most of these efforts are limited to information dominance on the battlefield; that is, crippling an enemy's military command and control centers, or disabling an air defense network prior to launching an air attack. However, I am convinced that there is a growing awareness around the world that advanced societies, especially the U.S., are increasingly dependent on open, and potentially vulnerable information systems.

The Intelligence Community is on the lookout for information that would indicate whether any of the "rogue" states have plans and programs underway to develop an offensive information warfare capability. These countries are very difficult intelligence targets and such programs, by their nature, are almost certainly highly covert and difficult to uncover. In virtually all of them we see advances in computer connectivity and information systems technology that would contribute to an offensive capability. We are alert for any evidence that these technologies are being applied to offensive information warfare programs, as well as information that suggests they may be sponsoring hacker activities. International terrorist groups clearly have the capability to attack the information infrastructure of the United States, even if they use relatively simple means. Since the possibilities for attacks are not difficult to imagine, I am concerned about the potential for such attacks in the future. The methods used could range from such traditional terrorist methods as a vehicle-delivered bomb—directed in this instance against, say, a telephone switching center or other communications node—to electronic means of attack. The latter methods could rely on paid hackers. The ability to launch attacks, however, is likely to be within the capabilities of a number of terrorist groups, which themselves have increasingly used the Internet and other modern means for their own communications. The groups concerned include such well-known, long-established organizations as the Lebanese Hizballah, as well as nameless and less well-known cells of international terrorists such as those who attacked the World Trade Center [in 1993].

As I noted earlier, many of the tools and technologies needed to penetrate computer systems and launch information warfare attacks are readily available to foreign adversaries. However, we need to remember that a threat is comprised not only of a capability, but also the intent to conduct an attack.

There are a number of activities underway designed to improve our ability to quantify the information system threat to our critical information systems.

First, we have initiated new collection activities designed to uncover evidence of foreign intent to attack our systems. Some of these initiatives involve traditional intelligence resources such as HUMINT [human intelligence] and SIGINT [signals intelligence]. Unfortunately, obtaining additional information on foreign information warfare plans and programs will take some time.

Second, we are working closely with the FBI and Department of Justice on this issue. I recognize that information warfare threat analysis is a non-traditional intelligence problem requiring non-traditional sources of data. Our effort looks for foreign sponsorship of U.S.-based computer hacking activities as well as for evidence of organized crime involvement.

Third, both the law enforcement and Intelligence Communities are attempting to forge working relationships with the private sector, including U.S. corporations and academic institutions. As we all know, the private sector is being "hit" every day by hackers. I believe that foreign organized crime is behind some of these events and we are eliciting the private sector's help in looking for evidence of foreign involvement and sponsorship. However, obtaining computer intrusion data from U.S. banks, telecommunications companies, and other institutions has been difficult. Although the situation is improving, many firms are still reluctant to share information on intrusions for fear of losing consumer confidence. I know the subcommittee witnessed this problem firsthand several weeks ago at your last hearing. We are working hard to develop a relationship with industry based on trust and confidentiality.

Fourth, the intelligence agencies are devoting additional resources to information system threat analysis. For example, analysts at CIA are developing methods to assess the status of foreign information warfare programs. At DIA [Defense Intelligence Agency], analysts are working on ways to understand the warning indicators signaling that a major information warfare attack against the United States is planned or imminent.

Fifth, in order to provide an increased Intelligence Community information warfare focus, the Deputy Secretary of Defense and I are looking to reorganize existing efforts and create a new center at the National Security Agency.

Finally, the National Intelligence Council is preparing a National Intelligence Estimate on this subject. . . .

I am convinced that the organized information warfare threat from both state and non-state actors will grow over the next decade as the technology proliferates. I am encouraged by the steps we have taken over the past year to improve our collection and analytic posture on this issue.

However, intelligence and threat analysis are only part of the infrastructure protection process. We also need to determine which systems are most important for the functioning of our society and which are most vulnerable to attack. . . .

BOMBING AT THE 1996 OLYMPICS IN ATLANTA, GEORGIA
July 27, 1996

After Black September terrorists killed eleven Israeli athletes at the 1972 Olympics in Munich, West Germany, Olympic organizers dramatically increased security at future events. They succeeded in preventing further terrorist attacks until the 1996 Olympics in Atlanta, Georgia. In Atlanta a terrorist planted a pipe bomb in a green knapsack at Centennial Olympic Park that went off at 1:25 A.M. on July 27 as 100,000 people enjoyed a rock concert. The explosion killed one person and injured more than one hundred others, and a Turkish television cameraman died of a heart attack as he rushed to the scene. (Murder of Israeli Athletes at the Munich Olympic Games, p. 7)

The morning after the explosion, Olympic officials met and decided to continue the games. Canceling the games would represent a victory for the bomber, they said. President Bill Clinton endorsed the decision that same morning in a statement to the press. "We cannot be intimidated by acts of terror," Clinton said.

The bombing investigation initially focused on a security guard who spotted the suspicious knapsack, alerted police, and after they determined it contained a bomb helped shoo people from the scene just before the explosion. But in February 1998 federal authorities announced that physical evidence from the Atlanta bomb matched evidence from a bombing a month earlier at an abortion clinic in Birmingham, Alabama, that killed an off-duty police officer and severely injured a nurse. Eric Robert Rudolph, a former carpenter, had been charged in the Birmingham bombing. In October 1998 federal authorities charged Rudolph with the Olympics bombing and with the 1997 bombings of an abortion clinic and a gay nightclub in Atlanta. But by then Rudolph was thought to have vanished into the Nantahala National Forest, a 516,000-acre park in western North Carolina that contained dense mountains and vegetation. By June 2002 the government had spent more than $24 million searching the park for Rudolph, but he had not been found.

Following is a statement made by President Bill Clinton on July 27, 1996, in reaction to a bombing at the 1996 Olympics in Atlanta, Georgia:

Good morning. The bombing at Centennial Olympic Park this morning was an evil act of terror. It was aimed at the innocent people who were participating in the Olympic games and in the spirit of the Olympics; an act of cowardice that stands in sharp contrast to the courage of the Olympic athletes.

On behalf of all Americans, let me extend my condolences to the families of those who lost their lives and our prayers to those who were injured.

I want to thank the brave security personnel who were on the scene. They saw the package. They alerted the bomb squad. They cleared the crowd. They prevented a much greater loss of life.

I also want to compliment the medical personnel at all the hospitals, those who were operating the ambulances. They and the volunteers who were helping people who were down at the scene, those of us who watched it throughout the night last night could not have been failed to be impressed by their courage, their confidence, their real heroism under pressure.

Last night I was awakened by Mr. Panetta [White House Chief of Staff Leon Panetta] shortly after the explosion, and I continued to receive reports and follow events until the press conference early this morning. Then this morning, the vice president and I spoke to the president of the International Olympic Committee, the president of the Atlanta Committee for the Games, the governor of Georgia, the mayor of Atlanta, the attorney general and the director of the FBI.

I want to make clear our common determination. We will spare no effort to find out who was responsible for this murderous act. We will track them down. We will bring them to justice. We will see that they are punished. In the meanwhile, we are all agreed the games will go on.

We will take every necessary step to protect the athletes and those who are attending the games.

I know that the people who've worked so hard to put on these Olympics—the people of Atlanta, the thousands and thousands of volunteers—are more determined than ever to see them to a successful conclusion.

Already we see the spirit at work this morning. The mayor spoke about the significant numbers of people in the streets in Atlanta. [International Olympic Committee] President [Juan Antonio] Samaranch reported to me on the events that are already taking place and said there were large crowds of spectators at them and that the people were clearly determined to go forward and attend the games and follow them.

Let me say, finally, that an act of vicious terror like this is clearly directed at the spirit of our own democracy. It seeks to rip also at the spirit of the Olympics. We are doing everything in our power to prevent these attacks.

There has been an enormous effort made to establish security at the sites of all the events.

At the park itself, the investigation will continue today, and then there will be additional security measures taken there. But we must not let these attacks stop us from going forward.

We cannot let terror win. That is not the American way. The Olympics will continue. The games will go on. The Olympic spirit will prevail. We must be firm in this.

We cannot be intimidated by acts of terror. Thank you very much.

STATE DEPARTMENT FACT SHEET ABOUT OSAMA BIN LADEN
August 14, 1996

Osama bin Laden was on the radar of U.S. officials long before the September 11, 2001, terrorist attacks on the United States, which he is accused of directing. But initially, the government pegged the extremely wealthy bin Laden as a financier of extremist activities instead of a more active participant.

For example, a fact sheet about bin Laden issued by the U.S. State Department on August 14, 1996, called him "one of the most significant financial sponsors of Islamic extremist activities in the world today." It did not note his leadership of Arab volunteers in the 1980s who fought against the Soviets in Afghanistan, a job that greatly increased his stature among Islamic extremists and won him thousands of followers. The fact sheet did, however, describe his funding and organization of numerous training camps for terrorists.

Only two weeks after the State Department issued the fact sheet, bin Laden formally called for a guerrilla war against U.S. troops based in Saudi Arabia. On March 3, 1998, the State Department noted that bin Laden and several other radical leaders had issued a "fatwa," or religious ruling, calling on Muslims to launch terrorist attacks on Americans and their allies — civilians as well as military personnel — around the world, but it still called him a "terrorist financier." That view abruptly changed with the August 7, 1998, bombings of U.S. embassies in Kenya and Tanzania, which U.S. officials accused bin Laden of masterminding. In retaliation for the embassy bombings, on August 20, 1998, the United States launched a cruise missile attack against bin Laden training camps in Afghanistan and a Sudanese factory that U.S. officials said was linked to bin Laden and was developing chemical weapons. On November 4, 1998, the same day that bin Laden was indicted for the embassy bombings, the State Department announced a $5 million reward for information leading to his arrest or conviction. And on June 7, 1999, the FBI added bin Laden to its "Ten Most Wanted Fugitives" list. Despite intensive efforts to locate and capture bin Laden—especially after the September 11, 2001 terrorist attacks—as of August 2002 his *whereabouts remained unknown.* (U.S. Fires Cruise Missiles at Sites Linked to Bin Laden, p. 253)

Following is a fact sheet titled "Usama Bin Ladin: Islamic Extremist Financier," issued August 14, 1996, by the U.S. State Department:

Usama bin Muhammad bin Awad Bin Ladin is one of the most significant financial sponsors of Islamic extremist activities in the world today. One of some 20 sons of wealthy Saudi construction magnate Muhammad Bin Ladin— founder of the Kingdom's Bin Ladin Group business empire—Usama joined the Afghan resistance movement following the 26 December 1979 Soviet invasion of Afghanistan. "I was enraged and went there at once," he claimed in a 1993 interview. "I arrived within days, before the end of 1979."

Bin Ladin gained prominence during the Afghan war for his role in financing the recruitment, transportation, and training of Arab nationals who volunteered to fight alongside the Afghan mujahedin. By 1985, Bin Ladin had drawn on his family's wealth, plus donations received from sympathetic merchant families in the Gulf region, to organize the Islamic Salvation Foundation, or al-Qaida, for this purpose.

— A network of al-Qaida recruitment centers and guesthouses in Egypt, Saudi Arabia, and Pakistan has enlisted and sheltered thousands of Arab recruits. This network remains active.
— Working in conjunction with extremist groups like the Egyptian al-Gama'at al-Islamiyyah, also known as the Islamic Group, al-Qaida organized and funded camps in Afghanistan and Pakistan that provided new recruits paramilitary training in preparation for the fighting in Afghanistan.
— Under al-Qaida auspices, Bin Ladin imported bulldozers and other heavy equipment to cut roads, tunnels, hospitals, and storage depots through Afghanistan's mountainous terrain to move and shelter fighters and supplies.

After the Soviets withdrew from Afghanistan in 1989, Bin Ladin returned to work in the family's Jeddah-based construction business. However, he continued to support militant Islamic groups that had begun targeting moderate Islamic governments in the region. Saudi officials held Bin Ladin's passport during 1989–1991 in a bid to prevent him from solidifying contacts with extremists whom he had befriended during the Afghan war.

Bin Ladin relocated to Sudan in 1991, where he was welcomed by National Islamic Front (NIF) leader Hasan al-Turabi. In a 1994 interview, Bin Ladin claimed to have surveyed business and agricultural investment opportunities in Sudan as early as 1983. He embarked on several business ventures in Sudan in 1990, which began to thrive following his move to Khartoum. Bin Ladin also formed symbiotic business relationships with wealthy NIF members by undertaking civil infrastructure development projects on the regime's behalf:

—Bin Ladin's company, Al-Hijrah for Construction and Development, Ltd., built the Tahaddi (challenge) road linking Khartoum with Port Sudan, as well as a modern international airport near Port Sudan.

—Bin Ladin's import-export firm, Wadi al-Aqiq Company, Ltd., in conjunction with his Taba Investment Company, Ltd., secured a near monopoly over Sudan's major agricultural exports of gum, corn, sunflower, and sesame products in cooperation with prominent NIF members. At the same time, Bin Ladin's Al-Themar al-Mubarakah Agriculture Company, Ltd. grew to encompass large tracts of land near Khartoum and in eastern Sudan.

—Bin Ladin and wealthy NIF members capitalized Al-Shamal Islamic Bank in Khartoum. Bin Ladin invested $50 million in the bank.

Bin Ladin's work force grew to include militant Afghan war veterans seeking to avoid a return to their own countries, where many stood accused of subversive and terrorist activities. In May 1993, for example, Bin Ladin financed the travel of 300 to 480 Afghan war veterans to Sudan after Islamabad launched a crackdown against extremists lingering in Pakistan. In addition to safehaven in Sudan, Bin Ladin has provided financial support to militants actively opposed to moderate Islamic governments and the West:

—Islamic extremists who perpetrated the December 1992 attempted bombings against some 100 U.S. servicemen in Aden (billeted there to support U.N. relief operations in Somalia) claimed that Bin Ladin financed their group.

—A joint Egyptian-Saudi investigation revealed in May 1993 that Bin Ladin business interests helped funnel money to Egyptian extremists, who used the cash to buy unspecified equipment, printing presses, and weapons.

—By January 1994, Bin Ladin had begun financing at least three terrorist training camps in northern Sudan (camp residents included Egyptian, Algerian, Tunisian and Palestinian extremists) in cooperation with the NIF. Bin Ladin's Al-Hijrah for Construction and Development works directly with Sudanese military officials to transport and provision terrorists training in such camps.

—Pakistani investigators have said that Ramzi Ahmed Yousef, the alleged mastermind of the February 1993 World Trade Center bombing, resided at the Bin Ladin-funded Bayt Ashuhada (house of martyrs) guesthouse in Peshawar during most of the three years before his apprehension in February 1995.

—A leading member of the Egyptian extremist group al-Jihad claimed in a July 1995 interview that Bin Ladin helped fund the group and was at times witting of specific terrorist operations mounted by the group against Egyptian interests.

—Bin Ladin remains the key financier behind the "Kunar" camp in Afghanistan, which provides terrorist training to al-Jihad and al-Gama'at al-Islamiyyah members, according to suspect terrorists captured recently by Egyptian authorities.

Bin Ladin's support for extremist causes continues despite criticisms from regional governments and his family. Algeria, Egypt, and Yemen have accused

Bin Ladin of financing militant Islamic groups on their soil (Yemen reportedly sought INTERPOL's assistance to apprehend Bin Ladin during 1994). In February 1994, Riyadh revoked Bin Ladin's Saudi citizenship for behavior that "contradicts the Kingdom's interests and risks harming its relations with fraternal countries." The move prompted Bin Ladin to form the Advisory and Reformation Committee, a London-based dissident organization that by July 1995 had issued over 350 pamphlets critical of the Saudi Government. Bin Ladin has not responded to condemnation leveled against him in March 1994 by his eldest brother, Bakr Bin Ladin, who expressed, through the Saudi media, his family's "regret, denunciation, and condemnation" of Bin Ladin's extremist activities.

VULNERABILITIES IN THE AVIATION SECURITY SYSTEM
September 11, 1996

On September 9, 1996, the White House Commission on Aviation Safety and Security—chaired by Vice President Al Gore—presented an interim report that called for greatly expanding the federal role in safeguarding security at airports. The commission recommended a wide variety of measures, ranging from requiring background checks on airport employees who could reach secure areas to establishing a computer system that would allow airlines to check passenger information against government criminal records. The Gore report was the latest in a long line of studies recommending substantial improvements in aviation security, especially in light of the growing terrorist threat. (GAO on the Risk of Terrorist Attacks on Aviation, p. 142)

Two days after the Gore panel issued its interim report, a top official with the General Accounting Office—the investigative arm of Congress—testified before a House subcommittee that protecting aviation against terrorism was an "urgent national issue" that required greater attention and funding than it had received. "Nearly every major aspect of the system—ranging from the screening of passengers, checked and carry-on baggage, mail, and cargo as well as access to secured areas within airports and aircraft—has weaknesses that terrorists could exploit," said Keith O. Fulz, assistant comptroller general.

Fulz testified on September 11, 1996—exactly five years before a total of nineteen hijackers successfully passed through security systems at several airports, took control of four commercial airliners, and crashed them into the World Trade Center in New York City, the Pentagon outside Washington, D.C., and a field in Pennsylvania, killing more than 3,000 people. (Bush on Terrorist Attacks Against the United States, p. 351)

Following are excerpts from testimony given September 11, 1996, by Keith O. Fulz, assistant comptroller general in the General Accounting Office's Resources, Community, and

Economic Development Division, before the Subcommittee on Aviation of the House Committee on Transportation and Infrastructure:

Protecting civil aviation from a terrorist attack is an urgent national issue. We appreciate the opportunity to testify before this Committee on the serious vulnerabilities that exist within the nation's air transportation system and ways to address them. Experts on terrorism within the government intelligence agencies believe that the threat to civil aviation is increasing. The threat from concealed explosive devices remains a high concern. The 1988 terrorist bombing of Pan Am flight 103, which killed 270 people, and the more recent, but as yet unexplained, explosion of TWA flight 800 have shaken the public's confidence in the safety and security of air travel. . . .

The following is our summary:

- The threat of terrorism against the United States has increased. Aviation is and will remain an attractive target for terrorists.
- The Federal Aviation Administration (FAA) has mandated additional security procedures as the threat has increased. Currently, aviation security relies on a mix of procedures and technology. However, the domestic and international aviation system has serious vulnerabilities. For example, conventional X-ray screening of checked baggage has performance limitations and offers little protection against a moderately sophisticated explosive device.
- Explosives detection devices that could improve security are commercially available for checked and carry-on baggage, but all of the devices have some limitations. Some of these devices are being tested domestically and are already in use at overseas locations. The Gore Commission has recommended that the federal government purchase some of this equipment for use in airports. Other devices are under development and may be available in a few years for screening baggage and passengers, but technologies for screening cargo and mail at airports are not as far along. Other security methods that could be expanded upon—and that have been recommended by the Gore Commission—include matching passengers with their bags and identifying passengers for additional security screening (profiling). A mix of technology and procedures will likely be needed to improve security.
- To improve aviation security, the Congress, the administration—specifically FAA and the intelligence community, among others—and the aviation industry need to agree and take action on what needs to be done to meet the threat of terrorism and who will pay for it. Several initiatives are under way to address this issue; they include two presidential commissions and an FAA working group. We have made recommendations to strengthen these initiatives. The Gore Commission's report provides opportunities for agreement on steps that could be taken in the short term;

however, the issue of how to finance security over the long term still needs to be addressed. Given the urgent need to improve aviation security and FAA's problems in addressing long-standing safety and security concerns, once steps are agreed upon, it will be important for the Congress to monitor their implementation. Therefore, we believe that the Congress should establish goals and performance measures and require periodic reports from FAA and other federal agencies on the progress and effectiveness of efforts to improve aviation security.

The Threat of Terrorists' Attacks on U.S. Civil Aviation Has Increased

. . . Until the early 1990s, the threat of terrorism was considered far greater overseas than in the United States. However, the threat of international terrorism within the United States has increased. Events such as the World Trade Center bombing have revealed that the terrorists' threat in the United States is more serious and extensive than previously believed.

Terrorists' activities are continually evolving and present unique challenges to FAA and law enforcement agencies. We reported in March 1996 that the bombing of Philippine Airlines flight 434 in December 1994 illustrated the potential extent of terrorists' motivation and capabilities as well as the attractiveness of aviation as a target for terrorists. According to information that was accidentally uncovered in January 1995, this bombing was a rehearsal for multiple attacks on specific U.S. flights in Asia.

Aviation Security System and Its Vulnerabilities

Even though FAA has increased security procedures as the threat has increased, the domestic and international aviation system continues to have numerous vulnerabilities. According to information provided by the intelligence community, FAA makes judgments about the threat and decides which procedures would best address the threat. The airlines and airports are responsible for implementing the procedures and paying for them. For example, the airlines are responsible for screening passengers and property, and the airports are responsible for the security of the airport environment. FAA and the aviation community rely on a multifaceted approach that includes information from various intelligence and law enforcement agencies, contingency plans to meet a variety of threat levels, and the use of screening equipment, such as conventional X-ray devices and metal detectors.

For flights within the United States, basic security measures include the use of walk-through metal detectors for passengers and X-ray screening of carry-on baggage—measures that were primarily designed to avert hijackings during the 1970s and 1980s, as opposed to the more current threat of attacks by terrorists that involve explosive devices. These measures are augmented by additional procedures that are based on an assessment of risk. Among these procedures are passenger profiling and passenger-bag matching.

Because the threat of terrorism had previously been considered greater overseas, FAA mandated more stringent security measures for international flights. Currently, for all international flights, FAA requires U.S. carriers, at a minimum, to implement the International Civil Aviation Organization's standards that include the inspection of carry-on bags and passenger-bag matching. FAA also requires additional, more stringent measures—including interviewing passengers that meet certain criteria, screening every checked bag, and screening carry-on baggage—at all airports in Europe and the Middle East and many airports elsewhere.

In the aftermath of the 1988 bombing of Pan Am flight 103, a Presidential Commission on Aviation Security and Terrorism was established to examine the nation's aviation security system. This commission reported that the system was seriously flawed and failed to provide the flying public with adequate protection. FAA's security reviews, audits prepared by the Department of Transportation's Office of the Inspector General, and work we have conducted show that the system continues to be flawed.

Providing effective security is a complex problem because of the size of the U.S. aviation system, the differences among airlines and airports, and the unpredictable nature of terrorism. In our previous reports and testimonies on aviation security, we highlighted a number of vulnerabilities in the overall security system, such as checked and carry-on baggage, mail, and cargo. We also raised concerns about unauthorized individuals gaining access to critical parts of an airport and the potential use of sophisticated weapons, such as surface-to-air missiles, against commercial aircraft. According to FAA officials, more recent concerns include smuggling bombs aboard aircraft in carry-on bags and on passengers themselves.

Specific information on the vulnerabilities of the nation's aviation security system is classified and cannot be detailed here, but we can provide you with unclassified information. Nearly every major aspect of the system—ranging from the screening of passengers, checked and carry-on baggage, mail, and cargo as well as access to secured areas within airports and aircraft—has weaknesses that terrorists could exploit. FAA believes that the greatest threat to aviation is explosives placed in checked baggage. For those bags that are screened, we reported in March 1996 that conventional X-ray screening systems (comprising the machine and operator who interprets the image on the X-ray screen) have performance limitations and offer little protection against a moderately sophisticated explosive device. In our August 1996 classified report, we provided details on the detection rates of current systems as measured by numerous FAA tests that have been conducted over the last several years.

In 1993, the Department of Transportation's Office of the Inspector General also reported weaknesses in security measures dealing with (1) access to restricted airport areas by unauthorized persons and (2) carry-on baggage. A follow-up review in 1996 indicated that these weaknesses continue to persist and have not significantly improved. . . .

Initiatives to Address Vulnerabilities
Should Be Coordinated

Addressing the vulnerabilities in the nation's aviation security system is an urgent national issue. Although the Gore Commission made recommendations on September 9, no agreement currently exists among all the key players, namely, the Congress, the administration—specifically FAA and the intelligence community, among others—and the aviation industry, on the steps necessary to improve security in the short and long term to meet the threat. In addition, who will be responsible in the long term for paying for new security initiatives has not been addressed. While FAA has increased security at domestic airports on a temporary basis, FAA and Department of Transportation officials believe that more permanent changes are needed. Furthermore, the cost of these changes will be significant, may require changes in how airlines and airports operate, and will likely have an impact on the flying public. To achieve these permanent changes, three initiatives that are under way may assist in developing a consensus among all interested parties on the appropriate direction and response to meet the ever-increasing threat. . . .

In our August 1, 1996, testimony before the Senate Committee on Commerce, Science, and Transportation, we emphasized the importance of informing the American public of and involving them in this effort. Furthermore, we recommended that the following steps be taken immediately:

- Conduct a comprehensive review of the safety and security of all major domestic and international airports and airlines to identify the strengths and weaknesses of their procedures to protect the traveling public.
- Identify vulnerabilities in the system.
- Establish priorities to address the system's identified vulnerabilities.
- Develop a short-term approach with immediate actions to correct significant security weaknesses.
- Develop a long-term and comprehensive national strategy that combines new technology, procedures, and better training for security personnel. . . .

Given the persistence of long-standing vulnerabilities and the increased threat to civil aviation, we believe corrective actions need to be undertaken immediately. These actions need a unified effort from the highest levels of the government to address this national issue. . . .

As of June 23, 2002, the full text of the testimony was available at http://www.gao.gov/archive/1996/rc96251t.pdf

STATE DEPARTMENT ON TRENDS IN INTERNATIONAL TERRORISM
September 12, 1996

A number of high-profile terrorist attacks outside the United States in 1995 and early 1996 drew increased attention to the problem of international terrorism. In March 1995 members of the Japanese cult Aum Shinrikyo killed 12 and injured 5,500 when they released the chemical nerve agent sarin in the Tokyo subway system; in June 1995 a group of terrorists attempted to assassinate Egyptian president Hosni Mubarak when he visited Ethiopia; a November 1995 car bomb explosion in Saudi Arabia killed 7 people, including 5 Americans; also in November 1995, a Jewish extremist assassinated Israeli prime minister Yitzhak Rabin; a series of suicide bombings in Israel by Palestinian extremists in early 1996 killed more than 60; and a June 1996 truck bombing in Saudi Arabia killed 19 American airmen.

Philip C. Wilcox Jr., coordinator for counterterrorism at the U.S. State Department, discussed trends in international terrorism during a speech September 12, 1996, before the Denver Council on Foreign Relations. Wilcox said the United States had taken many steps to specifically combat international terrorism but added that cuts in the overall foreign affairs budget increased the threat to the United States and its interests. "We can't rely just on tough, focussed counterterrorism efforts if we are to reduce the threat of terrorism," Wilcox said. "We need a larger, comprehensive effort to maintain U.S. foreign policy leadership and engagement, across the board—and this I emphasize—we also need the resources needed to sustain it."

There were 296 international terrorism attacks in 1996, according to an annual report released by the State Department in April 1997; this was the lowest number in twenty-five years. But the report noted that despite their decline in number, the attacks were becoming increasingly lethal. "The death toll from acts of international terrorism rose from 163 in 1995 to 311 in 1996," the report said, "as the trend continued toward more ruthless attacks on mass civilian targets and the use of more powerful bombs."

Following are excerpts from a speech September 12, 1996, by Philip C. Wilcox Jr., coordinator for counterterrorism at

the U.S. State Department, before the Denver Council on Foreign Relations:

. . . It is a paradox that although terrorism kills relatively few people, compared to other forms of violence, and although the statistical probability of any of us being killed by terrorists is minuscule, we are preoccupied by terrorism, and our government and others pay extraordinary attention to combatting it. Let me suggest some reasons why.

First, terrorism provokes deep fear and insecurity—more than other forms of violence. Terrorists strike innocent civilians, often randomly, and without warning. We think we can protect ourselves against other forms of violence, but we feel defenseless against terrorists.

Terrorists know this, and they seek to use intimidation to impose their political or other agendas. Killing is only a means to that end. By creating fear and panic, terrorists try to extort concessions or to weaken and discredit governments by showing they are unable to protect their citizens.

Terrorism is also used as low cost strategic warfare, sometimes by rogue states using surrogates, and sometimes by groups motivated by ideology, religion or ethnicity, to overthrow governments and change the course of history.

Terrorists also use violence in a less focused way to express protest and rage, to advance messianic and fanatic religious agendas, and for even more obscure pathological reasons.

One can argue that terrorism has failed historically, as a strategic weapon. But that's no cause for comfort. There is no doubt that it has caused great damage to American interests and those of our friends around the world. For example, terrorism has prolonged the Israeli-Palestinian conflict and the Northern Ireland conflict for decades. Real progress toward peace making in these struggles has come only when terrorism has been renounced and its practitioners marginalized.

Terrorism also has a high economic cost. The U.S. government alone spends about $5 billion a year to guard against terrorism, at home and abroad, and these costs will doubtless rise. And the cost to governments for security against terrorism is probably dwarfed by the cost to Americans, here and abroad. Terrorism can also cripple entire economies. For example, in Egypt two years ago by targeting a few tourists, terrorists almost shut down the vitally important tourist industry for many months.

Technology has also added to the terrorist threat. In 1605, the terrorist Guy Fawkes planted 29 barrels of explosives in a plot to blow up King James and the British Parliament. Today, a small explosive device in a purse could achieve the same effect. And bomb making recipes are readily available on the Internet.

Terrorists use computers, cellular phones, and encryption software to evade detection, and they have sophisticated means for forging passports and documents. Ramzi Ahmed Yousef and his gang, who were recently convicted for a plot to blow up twelve U.S. airliners over the Pacific, used all these tools.

Even more dangerous is the specter that terrorists will turn to materials of mass destruction—chemical, biological or nuclear—to multiply casualties far beyond traditional levels. The sarin gas attack by Aum Shinrikyo, the apocalyptic Japanese sect, in the Tokyo subway last year showed that the threat of chemical terrorism is now a reality.

And the willingness of some fanatic or crazed terrorists to commit suicide while carrying out attacks makes terrorism using weapons of mass destruction an even more sinister threat.

Finally, terrorism today is far more devastating than in the past because of the mass media. No story plays better, or longer, than a terrorist attack. Today's media, especially television, multiply the fear effect of terrorism by vividly conveying its horror. And this greatly increases our collective sense of vulnerability. The terrorists, of course, know this. And they seek to exploit media coverage to put us and our governments on the psychological defensive.

Now let's look at the current trend in terrorism. Who are today's terrorists? And what is the U.S. Government doing to combat them, and put them on the defensive, where they belong?

I'll focus on international terrorism, for which the State Department is the lead agency, whereas the FBI takes the lead on domestic terrorism.

First, the trend. There is good news and bad. The actual number of international terrorist incidents has declined in recent years, from a high of 665 in 1987 to an average between three and four hundred in recent years.

There are various reasons for this positive trend:

— The Soviet Union and almost all of the many revolutionary terrorist groups it supported are now history;
— After fifty years of war and terrorism, Arabs and Palestinians are struggling for peace. The PLO [Palestine Liberation Organization] has renounced terrorism, and most Arab states have also condemned it unequivocally;
— Only a few rogue states continue to sponsor or support terrorism;
— There is a growing international consensus today that killing innocents for political reasons is absolutely unacceptable, whatever the motivation or cause; and
— There is a corresponding willingness by the majority of states to crack down on terrorists by all means available, especially by using the law to combat terrorism.

But there is also a negative side of the ledger.

Notwithstanding the commitment of the Palestinian and Arab mainstream to peace in the Middle East, groups like HAMAS and the Palestinian Islamic Jihad last year carried out a vicious rear guard campaign of bombings in Israel in an effort to defeat the peace process.

— And an Israeli terrorist assassinated Prime Minister Rabin for the same purpose;
— Iran, notwithstanding U.S. efforts to contain it through sanctions, continues to use terrorism as a weapon of foreign policy to kill dissidents and disrupt the peace process;

—And Libya, although UN [United Nations] sanctions have curtailed its terrorism abroad, still defies the UN's mandate to deliver two suspects in the bombing of Pan Am 103 at Lockerbie to a British or U.S. court for trial;

—Exploitation of religion by terrorists may also be on the upsurge. In previous decades most terrorist groups were secular, but more and more terrorists today claim to act on behalf of religion, especially Islam. Some are part of organized groups such as HAMAS, the Lebanese Hizballah, and the Egyptian Gamaat. Others are ad hoc Islamic elements, such as Ramzi Ahmed Yousef's gang, many of whom received training in Afghanistan. . . .

Finally, let me say a few words about what the United States is doing to combat terrorism. I'm happy to confirm that we are doing a lot.

—First, our policy is to seek out relentlessly and punish terrorists wherever they may be, using the combined assets of U.S. law enforcement, diplomacy, and intelligence. . . .

—Second, we make no concessions to terrorists. We refuse to bow to demands for political concessions or ransom.

—Third, we designate states who sponsor terrorism, impose economic sanctions, and ask our friends to do likewise. . . .

—Fourth, we stress the rule of law in dealing with terrorists, and insist that terrorism is an unmitigated crime, whatever its motives or causes. By strengthening U.S. laws against terrorism, as President Clinton has done, and aggressively promoting international treaties and conventions against terror, of which there are now ten, we have led a worldwide trend to use the law as our most effective tool against terrorists.

—Fifth, we have superb military assets for use, when in rare cases the situation demands.

—Sixth, since terrorists operate in the dark, we are investing heavily in collection and analysis of intelligence. . . .

We can be proud of the successes we've achieved, using these policies and tools. But we can't be complacent, since terrorism is a dynamic, moving target.

Also, and perhaps most important, we can't rely just on tough, focussed counterterrorism efforts if we are to reduce the threat of terrorism. We need a larger, comprehensive effort to maintain U.S. foreign policy leadership and engagement, across the board—and this I emphasize—we also need the resources needed to sustain it.

Terrorism often emerges from the breeding grounds of political, economic and ideologic conflict. And it is often a product of poverty and despair. In the past half-century, the United States has led the way in addressing these problems around the world. But our leadership, and our ability to mobilize international support to resolve conflicts, reduce threats of all kinds, and build confident relationships, has required resources.

Today, I'm sorry to say, the resources we commit for our international affairs are in sharp decline. Spending for non-defense foreign affairs has been cut by 51% in real terms since 1984, while the need to protect our interests abroad has grown. Today we spend only 1.2 percent of our entire federal budget on all aspects of international affairs, about 1/125th of what the U.S. public spends on gambling. We rank 21st among the wealthiest countries in the world in the percentage of our wealth we give to foreign aid. By trying to pursue our foreign affairs on the cheap, we are risking U.S. leadership and compromising our interests. I fear we are living off capital, and if this trend continues, U.S. interests, including our ability to reduce the threat of violence and terrorism, are bound to suffer.

America's overall security interests require, therefore, not just the policies and activities we have in place to put terrorists out of business and behind bars, and not just the superb military forces we have, but adequate resources to support a vigorous, engaged foreign policy leadership role, across the board.

As of June 23, 2002, the full text of the speech was available at http://www.state.gov/www/global/terrorism/960912.html

NINETEEN AMERICAN AIRMEN DIE IN SAUDI ARABIA BOMBING
September 16, 1996

A car bombing in Riyadh, Saudi Arabia, on November 13, 1995, that killed 5 Americans and 2 Indians heightened concerns among U.S. military officials in Saudi Arabia about the threat of terrorism. After the bombing the military improved security measures at all U.S. installations in the country—including the giant Khobar Towers apartment complex in Dhahran, which was home to about 3,000 air force personnel who were enforcing the no-fly zone over Iraq. Early in 1996 U.S. intelligence agencies detected numerous warnings about additional terrorist attacks, and they specifically cited the Khobar Towers complex as a vulnerable "soft target." Nonetheless, on the night of June 25, 1996, terrorists were able to park a tanker truck filled with explosives just outside the compound's fence, about eighty feet from the apartment buildings. The truck blew up only minutes later, killing 19 Americans and wounding 500.

On September 16, 1996, a Department of Defense task force that investigated the bombing under orders from President Bill Clinton issued a report that criticized virtually every aspect of the military's defense against terrorism in Saudi Arabia. In particular, it found numerous security lapses that made the Dhahran apartment building vulnerable to terrorist attack. The strongly worded report held the military chain of command—including the local commander, Air Force Brigadier General Terryl Schwalier—responsible for failing to take adequate steps to thwart an attack. However, a separate investigation by the air force determined that no U.S. officials, including Schwalier, should be punished.

The Saudis and the FBI clashed throughout the lengthy criminal investigation, which nearly five years after the explosion resulted in the indictment of fourteen people by a U.S. federal grand jury on June 21, 2001. U.S. officials said that thirteen of those charged were members of the Saudi branch of the pro-Iranian terrorist organization Hizballah; the other person was linked to the Lebanese faction of Hizballah. The motive for the bombing, they said, was to drive U.S. forces out of Saudi Arabia. The indictment mentioned Iran dozens of times but did not specifically charge any Iranian officials. None of those indicted were in U.S. custody at the time, and Saudi Arabia refused to extradite the eleven who were in custody at Saudi prisons. In June 2002 Saudi Arabia's deputy interior minister was quoted as saying that some of the men had been sentenced for their roles in the bombing, but he did not say how many were sentenced or what penalties they received. Meanwhile, reports surfaced in early 2002 that Saudi Arabia's rulers would soon ask the United States to withdraw its military forces. Relations between the two countries had already been strained by the fact that fifteen of the nineteen hijackers who took over U.S. airliners on September 11, 2001, were from Saudi Arabia. (Bush on Terrorist Attacks Against the United States, p. 351)

Following are excerpts from the executive summary and the major findings section of the report, "Assessment of the Khobar Towers Bombing," written by a Department of Defense task force and released September 16, 1996:

Executive Summary

On June 25, 1996, a terrorist truck bomb estimated to contain the equivalent of 3,000 to 8,000 pounds of TNT exploded outside the northern perimeter of Khobar Towers, Dhahran, Saudi Arabia, a facility housing U.S. and allied forces supporting the coalition air operation over Iraq, Operation SOUTHERN WATCH. There were 19 fatalities and approximately 500 wounded. The perpetrators escaped.

This bomb attack marked the second terrorist strike at U.S. forces in Saudi Arabia within eight months. On November 13, 1995, a 220-pound car bomb exploded in a parking lot adjacent to an office building housing the Office of the Program Manager, Saudi Arabian National Guard in Riyadh, causing five U.S. and two Indian fatalities. A Department of State Accountability Review Board investigated this attack and made recommendations to improve U.S. security in the region. The DoD [Department of Defense] also conducted a Department-wide review of antiterrorism readiness following the November 1995 bombing. The Antiterrorism Task Force report made recommendations concerning enhancements to the security posture of deployed forces, education and training, intelligence sharing, and interagency coordination. The Department of State recommendations were being addressed, and the DoD actions were approved and being implemented at the time of the second bombing. . . .

Major Findings and Recommendations

. . . **A Comprehensive Approach to Force Protection Is Required.** The Assessment Task Force recommended that the Department of Defense take a range of actions to deter, prevent, or mitigate the effects of future terrorist attacks on servicemen and women overseas. None will—in and of themselves—provide an environment secure from all potential threats. However, the Task

Force strongly believes that to assure an acceptable level of security for U.S. forces worldwide, commanders must aggressively pursue an integrated systems approach to force protection that combines awareness and training, physical security measures, advanced technology systems, and specific protection measures tailored to each location. A comprehensive approach using common guidance, standards, and procedures will correct the inconsistent force protection practices observed in the theater. The Task Force believes that the designation of a single Department of Defense element responsible for force protection, to include antiterrorism and counter terrorism, is required. This entity would have policy, resource, and research and development responsibilities, as well as a capability to assist commanders in the field with implementation of force protection measures.

DoD Must Establish Force Protection Standards. The Department of Defense must establish realistic standards for force protection that provide commanders and staff guidance for construction and hardening of facilities and other overseas sites against the terrorist threat. Basically, the Department of Defense uses State Department standards for physical security. For the threat level, Building 131 at Khobar Towers required no stand-off distance from the perimeter according to State Department standards. Actionable standards will allow commanders to plan and program for the appropriate resources to protect troops and installations. While all U.S. commanders in the Gulf thought they had sufficient resources for force protection, they were not knowledgeable of technologies to enhance protection or how to develop an integrated systems approach to security. Consequently, they underestimated true requirements.

U.S. Central Command Requires an Empowered Chain of Command in the Region. The joint chain of command must have the authority to execute force protection measures. The command relationships in the Gulf were designed to support a short term contingency operation, Operation SOUTHERN WATCH, and enhance the transition of U.S. Central Command to war. The retention of operational control of forces in the theater by service component headquarters located over 7,000 miles away and the assignment of tactical control and oversight to a small, functional Joint Task Force headquarters located in the theater did not support the intensive, day-to-day command attention required to ensure force protection of service members assigned to the Command. The issue of inadequate organization and structure of Joint Task Force Headquarters for peacetime command and control was addressed in the assessment of the Joint Task Force-PROVIDE COMFORT following the shoot-down of two U.S. Army helicopters by U.S. Air Force F-15s in April 1994. The DoD must clarify command relationships in U.S. Central Command to ensure that all commanders have the requisite authority to accomplish their assigned responsibilities. Further, review of temporary Joint Task Force organization and structure must occur frequently to allow adaptation to changing threats and missions.

Command Emphasis on and Involvement in Force Protection Are Crucial. While committees at all levels in the theater and in the United States were active in discussing force protection policies and practices, this did not contribute materially to the security of military people and facilities. Committees are not effective without the emphasis and personal attention of commanders. In part, the inconsistent, and sometimes inadequate, force protection practices among service forces, joint headquarters, and different countries resulted from insufficient command involvement.

The Intelligence Community Provided Warning of the Potential for a Terrorist Attack. U.S. intelligence did not predict the precise attack on Khobar Towers. Commanders did have warning that the terrorist threat to U.S. service members and facilities was increasing. DoD elements in the theater had the authority, but were not exploiting all potential sources of information. Human intelligence (HUMINT) is probably the only source of information that can provide tactical details of a terrorist attack. The U.S. intelligence community must have the requisite authorities and invest more time, people, and funds into developing HUMINT against the terrorist threat.

The Chain of Command Was Responsible for Protecting the Forces at Khobar Towers. The chain of command of the 4404th Wing (Provisional) did not take all measures possible to protect the forces at Khobar Towers. The command relationships established in the region did not support unity of effort in force protection. There were no force protection or training standards provided by U.S. Central Command to forces assigned or deploying to the theater. The rotation and manning policies established by the U.S. Air Force did not support complete, cohesive units, especially Security Police, who were capable of coping with a viable terrorist threat. The Commander, 4404th Wing (Provisional) focused the force protection efforts of the command on preventing a bomb from penetrating the compound at Khobar Towers. Other vulnerabilities were not addressed adequately. Intelligence indicated that Khobar Towers was a potential terrorist target, and incidents from April through June 1996 reflected possible surveillance of the facility. Combined with the November 1995 attack in Riyadh, this should have triggered enhanced force protection measures, regardless of their impact on workload or quality of life. The 4404th Wing commander was ill-served by the intelligence arrangement within his command which focused almost exclusively on the air threat for Operation SOUTHERN WATCH. His senior headquarters, U.S. Air Forces Central Command and U.S. Central Command, did not provide sufficient guidance, assistance, and oversight to the 4404th Wing (Provisional) to avert or mitigate the attack on Khobar Towers. Their location 7,000 miles away contributed to this shortcoming. Placing all forces in Saudi Arabia and the Gulf region under the command of a single commander in the theater will help resolve the force protection problems identified during the Task Force assessment.

Host Nations Share in the Responsibility for Force Protection. Host nations have responsibility for the security of U.S. service members and installations in their country. The option of locating forces in isolated areas may not always exist. U.S. commanders and staffs must appreciate the importance of positive, working relationships with their host nation counterparts for force protection. Through these relationships, they can influence selection of locations of installations, allocation of host nation guard forces and priorities, and enhancement of host nation security as threat conditions escalate.

Department of State/Department of Defense Division of Responsibility Does Not Provide U.S. Forces Adequate Force Protection. The division of responsibility for force protection in the Department of State and the Department of Defense Memorandum of Understanding does not adequately support U.S. forces in countries with a large military presence. In Saudi Arabia, the Chief of Mission did not have sufficient resources to fully execute the force protection mission. Further, not all forces were under the Chief of Mission or combatant commander, creating a seam where certain units did not benefit from active oversight. The Secretary of Defense has the authority to assign forces to the combatant commander to redress this shortfall.

During its visits, the Task Force was impressed with the magnificent work being performed by Americans throughout the region. The 4404th Wing (Provisional) was especially notable. The reaction of these men and women to the bombing on the night of June 25th saved many lives. The care accorded to the more than 500 injured by both their comrades and U.S. and Saudi medical teams was remarkable. The Wing reconstituted and began flying combat missions over Iraq within 48 hours of the tragedy, a testament to the professionalism and fortitude we observed throughout the command. This same quality and professionalism were evident in the men and women of all services everywhere we visited in southwest Asia. . . .

As of June 23, 2002, the full text of the Defense Department report was available at http://www.defenselink.mil/pubs/downing_rpt/ prefuncl.html

DOMESTIC AND FOREIGN THREATS TO THE UNITED STATES
Undated [1997]

Until the mid-1990s it was widely believed that only foreign terrorists posed a real danger to the United States. That belief changed abruptly in April 1995 when two army buddies, Timothy McVeigh and Terry L. Nichols, blew up the federal building in Oklahoma City, Oklahoma. (Bombing of the Federal Building in Oklahoma City, p. 157)

In its annual report reviewing terrorism incidents and threats in the United States in 1995, the FBI noted that right-wing extremist groups continued to attract supporters. "Many of these recruits feel displaced by rapid changes in the U.S. culture and economy, or are seeking some form of personal affirmation," the report said. "As American society continues to change, the potential for hate crimes by extremist right wing groups is an increasing concern."

In its report for 1996 the FBI focused special attention on militias. "The current domestic terrorist threat stems in part from the rise of the militia movement in the United States," the report said. It followed upon testimony at a congressional hearing that warned of the dangers posed by militias. Partially in response to the growth of militias, the FBI in 1996 established its Domestic Counterterrorism Center. The FBI report for 1996 also noted the continuing threat to the United States posed by international terrorism perpetrated by state sponsors such as Iran and Syria, formalized terrorist groups such as the Lebanese Hizballah, and loosely affiliated radical extremists such as Ramzi Yousef. (Hearing on the Threat Posed by Right-Wing Militias, p. 177)

The next year, the FBI recorded only two terrorist incidents in the United States, neither of which caused injuries, and two suspected incidents. However, the agency said that twenty-one potential terrorist acts were prevented in 1997. These included a planned armored car robbery and bombings in Texas by four members of the True Knights of the Ku Klux Klan and a planned attack by a militia group on the U.S. Army base at Fort Hood, Texas.

Following is the chapter about terrorist threats to the United States from "Terrorism in the United States 1996," a report published by the Federal Bureau of Investigation in 1997:

The terrorist threat in the United States is composed of two separate components: domestic terrorists and foreign terrorists. Each presents a separate and distinct threat.

The current domestic terrorist threat stems in part from the rise of the militia movement in the United States. Several factors have contributed to the growth of this movement, including gun-control legislation, fears of increased United Nations involvement in domestic affairs, and several recent clashes between right-wing groups and law enforcement.

Concurrently, the FBI has seen an increase in activities among extremists associated with right-wing groups and special interest organizations. Right-wing terrorists are usually guided by racist or anti-Semitic philosophy and are concerned with ensuring the survival of the white race and/or the United States.

Traditional left-wing domestic extremism has continued to decline from the levels seen in previous years.

Domestic Terrorism

Domestic terrorism involves groups or individuals who are based and operate entirely within the United States and its territories, and are directed at elements of the U.S. Government or population, without foreign influence. Domestic terrorist groups represent right-wing, left-wing, and special interest beliefs. Their causes spring from issues relating to American political and social concerns. Domestic terrorism investigations are conducted in accordance with the *Attorney General Guidelines on General Crimes, Racketeering Enterprises, and Domestic Security/Terrorism Investigations*. These guidelines govern the justification, elements, and duration of FBI investigations.

Right-Wing Terrorism

The major themes espoused today by right-wing groups are conspiracies, such as the New World Order and gun-control laws, apocalyptic views stemming from the approach of the millennium, and white supremacy. Many right-wing extremist groups also articulate antigovernment and/or anti-taxation and anti-abortion sentiments, and engage in survivalist and/or paramilitary training to ensure the survival of the United States as a white, Christian nation. A convergence of ideas has occurred among right-wing white supremacist groups. Efforts have been made by these groups to reduce openly racist views in order to appeal to a broader segment of the population and to focus more attention on antigovernment rhetoric and resistance to anti-Christian court decisions.

Many extremist right-wing organizations generally operate through political involvement within the established system. Most activity is verbal and is protected by the First Amendment right of free speech. Adherents of extremist organizations are generally law-abiding citizens who have become intolerant of what they perceive to be violations of their constitutional rights. Certain extremists, however, such as members of the "militia" or "patriot" movement are unable to work within existing structures of government. These activists wish to remove federal involvement from a host of issues. For example, some militia members do not identify themselves as U.S. citizens and refuse to pay federal income taxes.

Membership in a militia organization is not an illegal activity in the United States. FBI interest in the militia movement is based upon the rise of violence or potential for violence or criminal activity stemming from the militia movement.

Militias are typically loose knit in nature. Adherents often are members of multiple groups, and because leaders of these groups tend to greatly inflate membership levels, actual group size is difficult to determine.

The most ominous aspect of the militias is the conviction, openly expressed by many members, that an impending armed conflict with the federal government necessitates paramilitary training and the stockpiling of weapons. Some militia members believe that federal authorities are enacting gun-control legislation in order to make it impossible for the people to resist the imposition of a "tyrannical regime" or a "one-world dictatorship." Many militia supporters believe that the conspiracy involves the United Nations as well as federal authorities.

The growth of the militia movement is traced, in part, to an effective communications system. Organizers promote their ideology not only at militia meetings, but at gun shows, patriot rallies, and gatherings of various other groups espousing antigovernment sentiments. Video tapes, computer bulletin boards, and networks such as the Internet are used with great effectiveness by militia sympathizers. Exploiting yet another medium, pro-militia fax networks disseminate material from well-known hate-group figures and conspiracy theorists.

Another phenomenon related to militias is the establishment of so-called "Common Law Courts." These courts, which have no legitimate legal basis, have self-appointed judges and juries, and have issued nonbinding "indictments" or "warrants" against law enforcement and government officials who have investigated or served them legal papers.

Left-Wing Terrorism

The United States still faces a threat from some leftist extremists, including Puerto Rican terrorist groups. Although Puerto Rico voted in 1993 to remain within the U.S. Commonwealth, some extremists are still willing to plan and conduct terrorist acts in order to draw attention to their desire for independence.

Left-wing groups generally profess a revolutionary socialist doctrine and view themselves as protectors of the American people against capitalism and imperialism. They aim to bring about a change in the United States and believe that this can only be accomplished through revolution, such as well-orchestrated criminal actions rather than participation in the established political process.

In the past, left-wing terrorist groups have claimed credit for numerous bombing attacks in the United States and Puerto Rico. These attacks have targeted military facilities, corporate offices, and federal buildings. Such groups believe that bombings alone will not result in change, but they are tools to gain publicity for their cause and thereby earn the support of the masses.

Over the last three decades, leftist-oriented extremist groups posed the predominant domestic terrorist threat in the United States. In the 1980s, the FBI dismantled many of these groups by arresting key members who were conducting criminal activity. The dissolution of the Soviet Union also deprived many leftist groups of a coherent ideology or spiritual patron. As a result, membership and support for these groups has waned, and the threat has diminished.

Special Interest Terrorism

"Special Interest" terrorism differs from traditional left-wing and right-wing terrorism since specific interest resolutions are sought, rather than widespread political changes. Some of the special interests of these groups include animal rights, environmental issues, and Hawaiian independence.

While the causes special interest groups represent can be understandable or even noteworthy in nature, they are separated from traditional law-abiding special interest groups by the conduct of criminal activity. These terrorist groups are attempting through their violent criminal actions to force various segments of society, including the general public, to change attitudes about issues considered important to them. Therefore, special interest groups will continue to present a threat that could surface at any time.

International Terrorism

International terrorism against the United States is foreign based and/or directed by countries or groups outside the United States. The activities of these countries or groups transcend national boundaries. The current international terrorist threat to U.S. persons and interests continues from years past and can be divided into three categories: state sponsors of international terrorism, formalized terrorist groups, and loosely affiliated international radical extremists.

The first threat to Americans comes from the activities of state sponsors of international terrorism. State sponsors include Iran, Iraq, Syria, Sudan, Libya, Cuba, and North Korea. In recent years, terrorist activities of Cuba and North Korea have declined due primarily to the deteriorating economic situations in both countries. However, the activities of Iran, Iraq, Syria, Sudan, and Libya have continued.

State sponsors continue to view terrorism as a tool of foreign policy. Past activities included direct terrorist support and operations by official state agents. Following successful investigations which have identified their involvement in terrorism, state sponsors now generally seek to conceal their support of terrorism by relying on surrogates to conduct actual operations. State sponsors, however, continue to engage in anti-Western terrorist activities by funding, organizing, networking, and providing other support and infrastructure to many extremists. A classic example of state-sponsored terrorism is the attack on Pan Am Flight 103 in 1988, which killed 270 people. Two Libyan intelligence operatives were indicted for their role in the attack.

The second terrorist threat to U.S. interests is posed by formalized terrorist groups. These autonomous organizations have their own infrastructures, personnel, financial arrangements, and training facilities. They are able to plan and mount terrorist campaigns overseas and support terrorist operations inside the United States. Extremist groups such as Lebanese Hizballah, the Egyptian Al-Gama'a Al-Islamiyya, and the Palestinian HAMAS have supporters inside the United States who could be used to support an act of terrorism here. Hizballah is one of the most dangerous of these groups. Hizballah has staged numerous anti-U.S. terrorist attacks, including the suicide truck bombing of the U.S. Embassy and the U.S. Marine barracks in Lebanon in 1983 and the U.S. Embassy annex in Lebanon in 1984. Elements of the group were also responsible for the kidnapping and detention of U.S. hostages in Lebanon.

Other formalized terrorist groups include the Irish Republican Army and Sikh terrorist elements. These groups have committed criminal activities in the United States over the years, including weapons acquisition, illegal immigration, and provision of safe haven to fugitives.

The final terrorist threat to U.S. interests stems from loosely affiliated international radical extremists, such as Ramzi Ahmed Yousef, and the other World Trade Center bombers. These extremists are neither surrogates of, nor strongly influenced by, any one nation. They have the ability to tap into a variety of official and private resource bases in order to facilitate terrorist acts against U.S. interests.

As of June 16, 2002, the full text of the report "Terrorism in the United States 1996" was available at http://www.fbi.gov/publications/ terror/terroris.pdf

JUSTICE DEPARTMENT ON EASE OF OBTAINING BOMB-MAKING PLANS
April 1997

According to prosecutors, Timothy McVeigh learned how to build the fertilizer bomb that he used to blow up the federal building in Oklahoma City in April 1995 by reading two books: The Turner Diaries, *a fictional book popular among right-wing extremists, and* Homemade C-4: A Recipe for Survival, *a how-to book published by Paladin Press in Colorado about making the military explosive. In 1996 Congress passed the Antiterrorism and Effective Death Penalty Act, one section of which instructed the Justice Department to determine just how easy it was for terrorists and others to find bomb-making instructions.*

In its April 1997 report to Congress, the Justice Department said bomb-making instructions are readily available in libraries, in bookstores, and on the Internet. ". . . [A]nyone interested in manufacturing a bomb, dangerous weapon, or a weapon of mass destruction can easily obtain detailed instructions from readily accessible sources, such as legitimate reference books, the so-called underground press, and the Internet," the report said. It even cited a case where a suspect in Topeka, Kansas, built pipe bombs based on information in an August 1993 Reader's Digest *article about a murder investigation.*

Concerns about the easy accessibility of information useful to terrorists arose again after the September 11, 2001, attacks on the World Trade Center and the Pentagon. Within hours after the planes crashed, federal agencies such as the Nuclear Regulatory Commission, the Environmental Protection Agency, and the U.S. Geological Survey started shutting down entire Web sites or removing selected documents from their sites that they believed might be useful to terrorists planning attacks on the United States. Some of the sites and documents were later restored, but many others were not.

Following are excerpts from "1997 Report on the Availability of Bombmaking Information," a report released by the U.S. Department of Justice in April 1997:

Introduction and Summary

. . . [A]nyone interested in manufacturing a bomb, dangerous weapon, or a weapon of mass destruction can easily obtain detailed instructions from readily accessible sources, such as legitimate reference books, the so-called underground press, and the Internet. Circumstantial evidence suggests that, in a number of crimes involving the employment of such weapons and devices, defendants have relied upon such material in manufacturing and using such items. Law enforcement agencies believe that, because the availability of bombmaking information is becoming increasingly widespread (over the Internet and from other sources), such published instructions will continue to play a significant role in aiding those intent upon committing future acts of terrorism and violence. . . .

Background

. . . On May 11, 1995, less than one month after the Oklahoma City terrorist bombing, in testimony before the Subcommittee on Terrorism, Technology and Government Information of the Senate Judiciary Committee, Deputy Assistant Attorney General Robert Litt, of the Justice Department's Criminal Division, explained that "how to" guides for the manufacture of explosives are readily available on the Internet, in bookstores and even in public libraries. To illustrate the point, he observed that, according to a news article, only hours after the Oklahoma City bombing, someone posted on the Internet directions—including a diagram—explaining how to construct a bomb of the type that was used in that tragic act of terrorism. Another Internet posting offered not only information concerning how to build bombs, but also instructions as to how the device used in the Oklahoma City bombing could have been improved. . . .

I. The Public Availability of Information on the Manufacture of Bombs, Destructive Devices, and Weapons of Mass Destruction

The first question that section 709 [of the Antiterrorism and Effective Death Penalty Act] required the Attorney General to study concerns the availability of instructional information describing the fabrication of explosives, destructive devices and other weapons of mass destruction. Our study confirms that any member of the public who desires such information can readily obtain it.

A. Books, Pamphlets and Other Printed Material

Most strikingly, a cursory search of the holdings of the Library of Congress located at least 50 publications substantially devoted to such information, all readily available to any member of the public interested in reading them and copying their contents. The titles of a number of these publications are indicative of their contents. They include:

—*Guerrilla's Arsenal: Advanced Techniques for Making Explosives and Time-delay Bombs* (Paladin Press, 1994);
—*The Anarchist Arsenal* (Harber, 1992);
—*Deadly Brew: Advanced Improvised Explosives* (Paladin Press, 1987);

—*The Anarchist's Handbook* (J. Flores, 1995);
—*Improvised Explosives: How To Make Your Own* (Paladin Press, 1985); and
—*Ragnar's Guide to Home and Recreational Use of High Explosives* (Paladin Press, 1988).

Other texts, intended for military training, agricultural and engineering use, contain information equally useful to individuals bent upon constructing bombs and other dangerous weapons. Publications in this category include:

—*Explosives in Roadworks: User's Guide* (Assoc. of Australian State Road Authorities, 1982);
—*Explosives and Blasting Procedures Manual* (U.S. Bureau of Mines, 1982);
—*Military Chemical and Biological Agents: Chemical and Toxicological Properties* (Telford Press, 1987); and
—*Clearing Land of Rocks for Agricultural and Other Purposes* (Institute of Makers of Explosives, 1918).

Another collection of some 48 different "underground publications" dealing with bombmaking, contained in the library of the FBI Explosives Unit, reflects a similar diversity of such published material. All of this literature was easily obtainable from commercial sources.

The ready accessibility of such literature is further illustrated by reference to a single page in a recent 70-page catalog of Delta Press, Ltd., of El Dorado, Arizona, captioned "Homemade Explosives." Among the texts featured on that page are *Improvised Shape Charges*, *Two Component High Explosive Mixtures*, *Improvised Radio Detonation Techniques*, and the *Anarchists Handbook Series*. Another page, captioned "poisons," advertises *The Poisoner's Handbook*, which it touts as "a complete handbook of poisons, both natural and manmade," including poisonous gases, lethal drugs, poisonous explosive compounds and a "list of sources and some additional chemistry." A number of the titles featured in this publication are commonly featured, along with firearms publications, at local gun shows.

With respect to weapons of mass destruction, there are a number of readily available books, pamphlets, and other printed materials that purport to provide information relating to the manufacture, design and fabrication of nuclear devices. The Department is aware of many publications that claim to provide some fundamentals necessary for the understanding of nuclear weapons, e.g., physics, design, manufacture, or fabrication. They include:

—*The Curve of Binding Energy* (J. McPhee, 1974);
—*U.S. Nuclear Weapons: The Secret History* (C. Hansen, 1966); and
—*The Swords of Armageddon* (C. Hansen, 1986).

Stories of crimes contained in popular literature and magazines also constitute a rich source of bombmaking information. For example, the August 1993 edition of *Reader's Digest* contains an account of efforts by law enforcement officers to track down the killer of United States Court of Appeals Judge Robert S. Vance and attorney Robert Robinson. That article contained a detailed description of the explosive devices used by the bomber in committing the murders, including such information as the size of the pipe bombs, how the bombs were constructed, and what type of smokeless powder was used in their construction. According to the Arson and Explosives Division of the Bureau of Alcohol, Tobacco and Firearms, in a bombing case originating in Topeka, Kansas, the devices were patterned after the bomb used to kill Judge Vance. Upon questioning, the suspect admitted to investigators that he constructed the bomb based on information contained in the *Reader's Digest* article.

B. The Internet

Bombmaking information is literally at the fingertips of anyone with access to a home computer equipped with a modem. To demonstrate such availability, a member of the DOJ Committee accessed a single website on the World Wide Web and obtained the titles to over 110 different bombmaking texts, including "Calcium Carbide Bomb," "Jug Bomb," "How To Make a CO_2 Bomb," "Cherry Bomb," "Mail Grenade," and "Chemical Fire Bottle." The user could access and print the text of each of the listed titles.

One of the texts, captioned "Nifty Things That Go Boom," appears to be a computer adaptation of *The Terrorist's Handbook* (purportedly edited at Michigan State University). The publication contains chapters that describe and address the procurement (legal and otherwise) of necessary explosives, chemicals and other ingredients, the preparation of chemicals, techniques for transforming such substances into bombs and explosives, and the manufacture of fuses and other ignition systems.

Another of the accessed texts purports to consist of the "Bomb Excerpts" from *Anarchy Cookbook*. This text explains in minute detail how to construct dozens of different types of bombs and explosive devices, including fertilizer bombs, dynamite and other explosives made with chemicals and other substances that "can be bought at Kmart, and various hardware supply shops." The text also details the ways that such devices can be employed following their fabrication. . . .

Our review of material accessible on the Internet also reveals the frequent use of "Usenet" newsgroups to facilitate the exchange of information concerning the fabrication and use of explosives and other dangerous weapons. For example, on August 28, 1996, one participant of a Usenet newsgroup inquired whether anyone had a recipe for C-4 and detonation techniques. The following day, someone responded to the inquiry by posting a detailed formula, explaining that "[t]he production of C-4 is probably beyond what can [be] done in the kitchen, but here is something to get you started. . . ."

Summary

It is readily apparent from our cursory examination that anyone interested in manufacturing a bomb, dangerous weapon or weapon of mass destruction can easily obtain detailed instructions for fabricating and using such a device. Available sources include not only publications from the so-called underground press but also manuals written for legitimate purposes, such as military, agricultural, industrial and engineering purposes. Such information is also readily available to anyone with access to a home computer equipped with a modem.

II. The Extent to Which Published Bombmaking Information Has Facilitated the Manufacture and Use of Explosives in Acts of Terrorism and Other Criminal Activity

Recent law enforcement experience demonstrates that persons who attempt or plan acts of terrorism often possess literature that describes the construction of explosive devices and other weapons of mass destruction (including biological weapons). Although in some cases there is no hard evidence demonstrating that such individuals actually employed such information in furtherance of their crimes, possession of such information is strong circumstantial evidence from which such usage can be inferred. . . .

As of June 20, 2002, the full text of the report was available at http://www.usdoj.gov/criminal/cybercrime/bombmakinginfo.html

JAPANESE PRIME MINISTER ON HOSTAGE RESCUE IN PERU
April 23, 1997

Peru's long history of terrorist violence did not end with the September 1992 capture of the leader of the Shining Path, a guerrilla movement that frequently engaged in terrorist acts. One of the most significant terrorist attacks started December 17, 1996, when fourteen armed members of the Tupac Amaru Revolutionary Movement, like the Shining Path a guerrilla group that often resorted to terrorism, burst into the Japanese ambassador's residence in Lima during a cocktail party. The guerrillas, who took more than 500 diplomats, Peruvian government officials, business leaders, and others hostage, threatened to kill the captives systematically unless the government released other Tupac Amaru rebels who were in prison. The government refused. Efforts to resolve the crisis diplomatically over the next four months were inconclusive, although the guerrillas released all but six dozen of the captives.

As the guerrillas were relaxing on the afternoon of April 22, 1997, Peruvian commandos set off plastic explosives beneath the building and stormed inside. They killed all fourteen guerrillas, many of whom were senior Tupac Amaru leaders, and rescued the hostages. Two soldiers died in the raid, and one hostage died later from complications resulting from a gunshot wound. At a press conference the day after the raid, Japanese prime minister Ryutaro Hashimoto thanked Peru's president, Alberto K. Fujimori, for the successful rescue. Hashimoto noted, however, that his government had not been notified in advance of the military action as Peru had promised.

In 2001 the rebels' bodies were exhumed in response to continuing claims that some of the guerrillas had been executed after they surrendered. According to media reports in May 2002, a forensic study found that at least eight of the rebels were executed at close range with shots in the neck. Based on the study, a judge ordered the arrests of twelve officers who participated in the raid. Prosecutors also were exploring the possibility of charging Fujimori, who was forced from office in November 2000 by a corruption scandal, with crimes against humanity in connection with the raid. However, it

235

was unlikely Fujimori would ever face trial because he had fled to Japan, where he held dual citizenship.

Following is the transcript of a press conference by Japanese prime minister Ryutaro Hashimoto on April 23, 1997, announcing the rescue of hostages being held in Peru:

Special forces of the Peruvian military stormed the Japanese Ambassador's Residence in the Republic of Peru at 3:23 P.M. yesterday Peru time.

The Cabinet immediately called for a meeting of the Headquarters and gathered information while keeping a close watch on the developments of the situation at the Ambassador's Residence. At 6:43 this morning Japan time Ambassador Aoki was able to speak directly with me on the phone after being rescued. All of the Japanese hostages were safely rescued, and a few of them have sustained light injuries. However, none of those are serious. Right now we are in the process of confirming everyone, one-by-one, and determining the degree of their injuries.

Unfortunately, Japan was not informed prior to the initiation of this rescue operation.

While I must say that it is regrettable that Japan did not learn of the action in advance, I would like once again to express my gratitude to President Alberto Fujimori and the other members of the Government of Peru who seized the opportunity and carried out this remarkable rescue operation.

Among the media reports that have come out, there are some reports that some of the Peruvian military personnel involved have been killed and wounded. My heart grieves for the dead and wounded and for their bereaved families.

Ambassador Aoki, and Mrs. Aoki, whom I also spoke with on the phone, were in extremely good spirits. It seems that Ambassador Aoki has a slight injury to his elbow, but he sounded great and told me that "it is just a slight scratch."

The Ambassador said that he intends personally to visit all of the hospitals where the injured are. At any rate, efforts to confirm the safety of all involved have already begun.

The Government of Japan has decided to dispatch Foreign Minister Ikeda to Lima today in order to take any measures which will be necessary following what has happened.

If the situation is as it seems to be, there probably is no need for the medical team which we prepared in advance. Still, considering that those hostages who were held for such a long time may be prone to fatigue after they are relieved, I have given instructions that preparations be made to dispatch the medical team as well. Also, I have instructed the Chairman of the National Public Safety Commission and the Director-General of the National Police Agency to prepare to send their staff members to Lima to investigate and confirm everything that has occurred since the incident broke out.

I have given you a report on the situation as it is and I am glad to be able to share with you the joyous news that the hostages are all right. Furthermore, although the reports are still not confirmed, if it is true that some of the members of the Peruvian military who participated in this rescue operation have been killed or injured, then I would like to express my heartfelt condolences and prayers that their injuries are light ones.

We will be reporting on the situation to the countries who have been so generous with assistance during this incident and to thank them. I would like to express my deep gratitude to the many individuals who, in this extremely difficult situation, showed their goodwill and gave us their cooperation. That is all that I have to tell you now.

Press: Earlier just now you said that there was no prior notification. How did you learn of the storming by the Peruvian military forces?

As of 5:30 A.M., I had not yet heard, but I received a phone call immediately after the reports of the storming came through.

Press: Who called you?

I received calls from several of my assistants and from the Headquarters. I will take only one more question.

Press: You stated that you hoped to see a peaceful solution. However, in fact the military forces stormed the residence. What are your thoughts on that?

We truly hoped that this situation would end without incident and not through a forced storming of the Residence. Still, those were the thoughts of people in a location separated by 14 time zones from those who were there watching the situation. It is natural that there was a difference. I wonder if there is anyone who could criticize President Fujimori for the use of force now that the hostages have been safely rescued, whether or not there was prior notification.

REPORT BY THE NATIONAL CHURCH ARSON TASK FORCE
June 6, 1997

During the civil rights movement of the 1960s, black churches in the South were frequent targets of bombings and arson attacks by terrorists. A new wave of attacks on churches, most noticeably on black churches around the time of the annual Martin Luther King Jr. holiday in January 1996, caused renewed concern. Congress passed the Church Arson Prevention Act of 1996, which broadened federal jurisdiction over church arsons and increased the maximum prison term in federal arson cases from ten to twenty years. In a June 1996 radio address, President Bill Clinton said: "We do not now have evidence of a national conspiracy, but it is clear that racial hostility is the driving force behind a number of these incidents." Clinton ordered the Justice and Treasury Departments to form a task force to investigate church arson cases and help communities rebuild burned churches.

In a report to Clinton one year later, on June 6, 1997, the task force said it had investigated 429 cases involving arsons, bombings, and other attacks on churches between January 1, 1995, and May 27, 1997, and had found "a wide array" of motivations for the attacks. Some cases involved "blatant racism" or racial hatred, including a case where four former members of the Ku Klux Klan pleaded guilty to federal charges in connection with the burning of two black churches in South Carolina in June 1995. However, the task force reported that, in many cases, factors other than racism appeared to have motivated the attackers. Burglars often set fire to churches to cover up their crimes, some attackers were seeking revenge for perceived slights, and in numerous cases juveniles set fire to churches either accidentally or deliberately but with no clear motivations.

In its annual report three years later, on September 15, 2000, the task force reported that the number of arsons, bombings, and attempted bombings at churches had steadily decreased since its formation. There were 297 incidents in 1996, 209 in 1997, 165 in 1998, and 140 in 1999. The task force said it had opened 945 investigations since 1996, resulting in the ar-

rests of 431 suspects in connection with 342 cases. The arrest rate was more than twice the national average for arson cases. The 2000 report, unlike the first report in 1997, did not discuss the attackers' motivations.

Following are excerpts from the "First Year Report for the President," dated June 6, 1997, from the National Church Arson Task Force:

Overview

In early 1996, federal officials detected a sharp rise in the number of reported attacks on our nation's houses of worship, especially African American churches in the South. This trend troubled communities, challenged law enforcement agencies, and stirred the nation's conscience.

In June 1996, President Clinton formed the National Church Arson Task Force ("NCATF" or "Task Force"), made the investigation of these fires a top priority of federal law enforcement, and called on all Americans to come together in a spirit of respect and reconciliation.

The President directed his Administration to implement a strategy to (1) identify and prosecute the arsonists; (2) help communities rebuild the burned houses of worship; and (3) offer assistance in preventing more fires. Working with state and local law enforcement and private groups, federal officials achieved great success on these fronts. Significantly, many Americans came together as a result of these arsons, often independent of the federal effort, to lend assistance in many ways.

Prosecutions

- 429 Investigations Launched—The NCATF has opened 429 investigations into arsons, bombings or attempted bombings that have occurred at houses of worship between January 1, 1995, and May 27, 1997.
- 199 Arrested—Federal, state and local authorities have arrested 199 suspects since January 1995, in connection with 150 of the 429 investigations.
- 35% Solved—The 35% rate of arrest in NCATF cases is more than double the 16% rate of arrest for arsons in general.
- 110 Convicted—Federal and state prosecutors have successfully convicted 110 individuals in connection with fires at 77 houses of worship.

Rebuilding

- The Department of Housing and Urban Development (HUD) is working closely with the National Council of Churches, the Congress of National Black Churches, Habitat for Humanity and other organizations in the rebuilding effort.
- As a result of this cooperation, 25 houses of worship have been rebuilt and 65 are undergoing construction.

- HUD is administering a $10 million Federal Loan Guarantee Fund—established by Congress as part of the 1996 Church Arson Prevention Act—to assist with the rebuilding effort.

Prevention

- Arson prevention efforts continue across the nation. The U.S. Department of Justice awarded $3 million in grants to counties in 13 states to intensify their enforcement and surveillance efforts around vulnerable houses of worship, and the Federal Emergency Management Agency (FEMA) awarded approximately $1.5 million in arson prevention and training grants.
- FEMA established a Clearinghouse for arson prevention resources that has received over 15,000 telephone inquiries from all 50 states and the District of Columbia.
- FEMA has distributed more than 500,000 arson prevention packets, including the NCATF Church Threat Assessment Guide.
- FEMA efforts also include a four-city pilot project in Nashville, TN, Charlotte, NC, Macon, GA, and Utica, NY, to develop grass-roots arson prevention programs. . . .

Prosecuting Defendants

Arrests

The partnership among various enforcement agencies has produced a significant number of state and federal arrests.

Since January 1995, federal, state and local authorities have arrested 199 suspects in connection with 150 of the 429 investigations that the Task Force has launched. This 35% rate of arrest is more than double the general arrest rate for arsons, which is approximately 16%, according to Justice Department statistics.

Of the 199 persons arrested, 160 are white, 34 are African American, and 5 are Hispanic. Eighty-three people arrested were juveniles. Of the 81 suspects arrested for arsons at African American churches, 55 are white, 25 are African American and 1 is Hispanic. Of the 123 suspects arrested for arsons at non-African American houses of worship, 110 are white, 9 are African American, and 4 are Hispanic. Five of the white suspects were arrested for arsons at both African American and non-African American churches.

Convictions

Since January 1, 1995, 110 defendants have been convicted in federal and state prosecutions in connection with fires at 77 houses of worship. These successes include the first convictions under provisions of the Church Arson Prevention Act of 1996. Of the 25 defendants who have been convicted of federal charges, 14 have been convicted of criminal civil rights charges.

Federal charges are also pending in a number of other cases, and grand jury investigations are ongoing as well. The Task Force has found that only a few of the fires are linked by common defendants. Conspiracy charges have been filed in a limited number of cases. These conspiracies, though, have tended to be confined to the small geographic areas where the arsons have occurred. Investigators continue to pursue the question of whether broader conspiracies were responsible for some of the fires, but to date the evidence has not established the existence of a national conspiracy.

In still other cases, state prosecutions have been initiated in consultation with federal prosecutors or investigators. The NCATF actively monitors these prosecutions to ensure that any federal interest is vindicated and to ensure that accurate information is compiled regarding law enforcement's response to attacks on houses of worship. . . .

Drawing Preliminary Conclusions

Although the investigations of most of the fires continue, the charges filed and the convictions obtained to date enable the Task Force to offer some preliminary conclusions. These conclusions are not based on cases that have not been completed or where evidence is not sufficient to support additional charges. As a result, the Task Force cannot answer all of the questions raised by the fires.

- *Damage.* Hundreds of houses of worship burned, congregations were temporarily displaced, and many people were left wondering how this could happen in the 1990s. These arsons destroyed rural wooden churches, ruined 100-year-old Bibles, and caused tens of millions of dollars in damage. But those communities which suffered a burned house of worship came to realize that thousands of Americans really care. The arsonists may have sought to divide our communities by burning our houses of worship, but in the end they only helped bring them closer together.

- *Multiple Motives.* The arsons at African American churches raised significant fears about an increase in racially motivated crimes. As a result of our efforts to date, we have determined that the arsons—at both African American and other houses of worship—were motivated by a wide array of factors, including not only blatant racism or religious hatred, but also financial profit, burglary, and personal revenge. The Task Force continues to investigate many cases. When sufficient evidence of racial motive is developed, we will continue to seek and obtain criminal civil rights convictions, as we have against 14 of the 25 defendants convicted of federal charges in Alabama, Nevada, North Carolina, South Carolina, Tennessee and Texas.

- *National Conspiracy.* While the Task Force continues to explore the question whether there are connections between the fires across the nation, the cases closed to date and the charges that have been filed do not support the theory that these fires were the product of a nationwide conspiracy. For instance, the Task Force has found that only a few of the fires are linked by common defendants. Conspiracy charges have been filed in a limited number of cases. These conspiracies, though, have tended to be confined to the small geographic areas where the arsons have occurred.

- *Hate Group Involvement.* While there have been a handful of cases in which members and former members of hate groups, such as the Ku Klux Klan, have been convicted for arsons at houses of worship, most of the defendants were not found to be members of hate groups. Prosecutors need not show, however, that a defendant belongs to a particular hate group in order to gain a conviction.
- *Investigations Continue.* The Task Force continues to investigate and prosecute those responsible for burning our nation's houses of worship. It is, therefore, too soon for the task force to speak conclusively about the motivation behind many of the fires at churches and other houses of worship. While it was the number of fires at African American churches that brought these crimes to national attention, the NCATF will continue to investigate and prosecute attacks on all houses of worship, regardless of their denomination or racial composition. . . .

COMMISSION REPORT ON NEED TO PROTECT INFRASTRUCTURE
October 20, 1997

When it became apparent in the early and mid-1990s that terrorists could and would strike targets within the United States, protecting the nation's infrastructure—roads, bridges, pipelines, water supplies, electrical grids, computer systems, and other essential elements of everyday life—took on new importance. With the increasing reliance on computers to control everything from nuclear power plants to the air traffic system, experts were becoming increasingly concerned that simple cyber attacks launched by hackers, terrorists, a hostile nation, or others could cripple the United States. In July 1996 President Bill Clinton appointed the President's Commission on Critical Infrastructure Protection to study the issue. He appointed the panel partly in response to several incidents in which computer hackers gained access to and damaged computer systems operated by several government agencies, including the Department of Defense.

In a report released October 20, 1997, the commission concluded that there was little immediate threat of a massive attack on the nation's physical and electronic lifelines. Nonetheless, it said the prospect of serious damage was rapidly increasing, and more planning to head off attacks was urgently needed. The commission recommended that the government and private business join together to develop protections against threats to the infrastructure that could cripple the economy and damage national security.

In a report released almost a year later, on September 23, 1998, the General Accounting Office (GAO), the investigative arm of Congress, found "widespread and serious weaknesses" in the security of federal government computer systems. The weaknesses "place critical government operations, such as national defense, tax collection, law enforcement, and benefit payments, as well as the assets associated with these operations, at great risk of fraud, disruption, and inappropriate disclosures," the GAO said. "In addition, many intrusions or other potentially malicious acts could be occurring but going undetected because agencies have not implemented effective controls to identify suspicious activity on their networks and computer systems."

Following are excerpts from the summary of "Critical Foundations: Protecting America's Infrastructures," a report released October 20, 1997, by the President's Commission on Critical Infrastructure Protection:

Introduction

The United States is in the midst of a tremendous cultural change—a change that affects every aspect of our lives. The cyber dimension promotes accelerating reliance on our infrastructures and offers access to them from all over the world, blurring traditional boundaries and jurisdictions. National defense is not just about government anymore, and economic security is not just about business. The critical infrastructures are central to our national defense and our economic power, and we must lay the foundations for their future security on a new form of cooperation between the private sector and the federal government.

The federal government has an important role to play in defense against cyber threats—collecting information about tools that can do harm, conducting research into defensive technologies, and sharing defensive techniques and best practices. Government also must lead and energize its own protection efforts, and engage the private sector by offering expertise to facilitate protection of privately owned infrastructures.

In the private sector, the defenses and responsibilities naturally encouraged and expected as prudent business practice for owners and operators of our infrastructures are the very same measures needed to protect against the cyber tools available to terrorists and other threats to national security. . . .

Venues for Change

Terrorist bombings of U.S. forces in Saudi Arabia, the World Trade Center in New York City, and the federal building in Oklahoma City remind us that the end of the Cold War has not eliminated threats of hostile action against the United States. . . .

We Found

Increasing Dependence on Critical Infrastructures

The development of the computer and its astonishingly rapid improvements have ushered in the Information Age that affects almost all aspects of American commerce and society. Our security, economy, way of life, and perhaps even survival, are now dependent on the interrelated trio of electrical energy, communications, and computers.

Increasing Vulnerabilities

Classical Physical Disruptions

A satchel of dynamite or a truckload of fertilizer and diesel fuel have been frequent terrorist tools. The explosion and the damage are so certain to draw attention that these kinds of attacks continue to be among the probable threats to our infrastructures.

New, Cyber Threats

Today, the right command sent over a network to a power generating station's control computer could be just as effective as a backpack full of explosives, and the perpetrator would be harder to identify and apprehend.

The rapid growth of a computer-literate population ensures that increasing millions of people possess the skills necessary to consider such an attack. The wide adoption of public protocols for system interconnection and the availability of "hacker tool" libraries make their task easier.

While the resources needed to conduct a physical attack have not changed much recently, the resources necessary to conduct a cyber attack are now commonplace. A personal computer and a simple telephone connection to an Internet Service Provider anywhere in the world are enough to cause a great deal of harm.

System Complexities and Interdependencies

The energy and communications infrastructures especially are growing in complexity and operating closer to their designed capacity. This creates an increased possibility of cascading effects that begin with a rather minor and routine disturbance and end only after a large regional outage. Because of their technical complexity, some of these dependencies may be unrecognized until a major failure occurs. . . .

Lack of Awareness

We have observed that the general public seems unaware of the extent of the vulnerabilities in the services that we all take for granted, and that within government and among industry decision-makers, awareness is limited. Several have told us that there has not yet been a cause for concern sufficient to demand action.

We do acknowledge that this situation seems to be changing for the better. The public news media seem to be carrying relevant articles more frequently; attendance at conferences of security professionals is up; and vendors are actively introducing new security products.

The Commission believes that the actions recommended in this report will increase sensitivity to these problems and reduce our vulnerabilities at all levels.

No National Focus

Related to the lack of awareness is the need for a national focus or advocate for infrastructure protection. Following up on our report to the President, we need to build a framework of effective deterrence and prevention.

This is not simply the usual study group's lament that "no one is in charge." These infrastructures are so varied, and form such a large part of this nation's economic activity, that no one person or organization can be in charge. We do not need, and probably could not stand, the appointment of a Director of Infrastructures. We do need, and recommend, several more modest ways to create and maintain a national focus on the issues.

Protection of our infrastructures will not be accomplished by a big federal project. It will require continuous attention and incremental improvement for the foreseeable future.

We Concluded

Life on the information superhighway isn't much different from life on the streets; the good guys have to hustle to keep the bad guys from getting ahead.

Rules Change in Cyberspace—New Thinking Is Required

It is not surprising that infrastructures have always been attractive targets for those who would do us harm. In the past we have been protected from hostile attacks on the infrastructures by broad oceans and friendly neighbors. Today, the evolution of cyber threats has changed the situation dramatically. In cyberspace, national borders are no longer relevant. Electrons don't stop to show passports.

Potentially serious cyber attacks can be conceived and planned without detectable logistic preparation. They can be invisibly reconnoitered, clandestinely rehearsed, and then mounted in a matter of minutes or even seconds without revealing the identity and location of the attacker.

Formulas that carefully divide responsibility between foreign defense and domestic law enforcement no longer apply as clearly as they used to. With the existing rules, you may have to solve the crime before you can decide who has the authority to investigate it.

We Should Act Now to Protect Our Future

The Commission has not discovered an imminent attack or a credible threat sufficient to warrant a sense of immediate national crisis. However, we are quite convinced that our vulnerabilities are increasing steadily while the costs associated with an effective attack continue to drop. What is more, the investments required to improve the situation are still relatively modest, but will rise if we procrastinate.

We should attend to our critical foundations before the storm arrives, not after: Waiting for disaster will prove as expensive as it is irresponsible.

Infrastructure Assurance Is a Shared Responsibility

National security requires much more than military strength. Our world position, our ability to influence others, our standard of living, and our own self-image depend on economic prosperity and public confidence. Clear distinctions between foreign and domestic policy no longer serve our interests well.

At the same time, the effective operation of our military forces depends more and more on the continuous availability of infrastructures, especially communications and transportation, that are not dedicated to military use.

While no nation state is likely to attack our territory or our armed forces, we are inevitably the target of ill will and hostility from some quarters. Disruption of the services on which our economy and well-being depend could have significant effects, and if repeated frequently could seriously harm public confidence. Because our military and private infrastructures are becoming less and less separate, because the threats are harder to differentiate as from local criminals or foreign powers, and because the techniques of protection, mitigation, and restoration are largely the same, we conclude that responsibility for infrastructure protection and assurance can no longer be delegated on the basis of who the attacker is or where the attack originates. Rather, the responsibility should be shared cooperatively among all of the players. . . .

BETTER COORDINATION URGED FOR FEDERAL TERRORISM SPENDING
December 1, 1997

Federal spending on antiterrorism programs soared during the 1990s, especially during the decade's second half. For example, terrorism funding for the Federal Aviation Administration tripled between 1994 and 1997, and FBI terrorism funding jumped fivefold during the same period. By 1997 more than forty federal departments, agencies, bureaus, and offices had terrorism-related programs—everyone from the Department of State to the U.S. Postal Service.

But in a report released December 1, 1997, the General Accounting Office (GAO)—the investigative arm of Congress—said no one knew how much the federal government spent on antiterrorism efforts overall. In addition, no one had an overall picture of whether the money was being spent wisely or whether some critical areas were being ignored. The reason, the GAO said, was that each agency developed its terrorism program independently, with little or no coordination between agencies. "No governmentwide spending priorities for the various aspects of combating terrorism have been set," the GAO said, "and no federal entity manages the crosscutting program to channel resources where they are most needed in consideration of the threat and the risk of terrorist attack and to prevent wasteful spending that might occur from unnecessary duplication of efforts."

Federal efforts to protect homeland security remained fragmented well after the September 11, 2001, terrorist attacks, according to congressional testimony on April 2, 2002, by Patricia Dalton, director of strategic issues for the GAO. Dalton said this lack of federal coordination particularly hurt state and local police departments, fire departments, public health agencies, and others that would be the first responders to any new attacks. For example, she said that the Federal Emergency Management Agency, the Department of Justice, the Centers for Disease Control and Prevention, and the Department of Health and Human Services all offered separate programs providing assistance to state and local governments in planning for emergencies. Two months after Dalton testified, President George W. Bush pro-

posed creating a Department of Homeland Security to better coordinate federal terrorism efforts. Under Bush's proposal, the cabinet-level department would be created by integrating twenty-two existing agencies and programs that employed 170,000 people. At a congressional hearing on July 17, 2002, Comptroller General David Walker, the GAO's director, cautioned against rushing into anything too quickly. "It is clear that fixing the wrong problems, or even worse, fixing the right problems poorly, could cause more harm than good in our efforts to defend our country against terrorism," he told the House Select Committee on Homeland Security. (Watchdog Urges Caution on Homeland Security Plan, p. 426)

Following are excerpts from "Combating Terrorism: Spending on Governmentwide Programs Requires Better Management and Coordination," a report released December 1, 1997, by the General Accounting Office:

Background

Under Presidential Decision Directive (PDD) 39 (U.S. Policy on Counterterrorism, June 1995), the National Security Council (NSC) is to coordinate interagency terrorism policy issues and review ongoing crisis operations and activities concerning foreign terrorism and domestic terrorism with significant foreign involvement. An NSC-chaired coordinating group is to ensure the PDD is implemented but does not have authority to direct agencies' activities.

Among its general mission responsibilities, the Office of Management and Budget (OMB) is to evaluate the effectiveness of agency programs, policies, and procedures; assess competing funding demands among agencies; set funding priorities; and develop better performance measures and coordinating mechanisms. Further, according to PDD 39, OMB is to analyze the adequacy of funding for terrorism-related programs and ensure the adequacy of funding for research, development, and acquisition of counterterrorism-related technology and systems on an ongoing basis.

Under PDD 39, the State Department and the Department of Justice, through the Federal Bureau of Investigation (FBI), have lead federal agency responsibility for dealing with terrorist incidents overseas and domestically, respectively. Numerous federal departments, agencies, bureaus, and offices also have terrorism-related programs and activities that are funded through annual and supplemental appropriations. . . .

The Government Performance and Results Act (Results Act) of 1993 is intended to improve the management and accountability of federal agencies. The Results Act seeks to shift the focus of federal management and decision-making from activities that are undertaken to the results of activities as reflected in citizens' lives. Specifically, it requires federal agencies to prepare multiyear strategic plans and annual performance plans, establish program performance measures and goals, and provide annual performance reports to the Congress. Agencies submitted the first strategic plans to OMB and the Congress by September 30, 1997; the first annual performance plans, covering fiscal year 1999, are to be submitted to the Congress after the President's budget submission in 1998.

In recent years, several efforts have been undertaken to coordinate federal programs that cut across agencies to help ensure that national needs are being effectively targeted. These efforts have shown that coordinating crosscutting programs takes time and sustained attention and, because of the statutory bases of crosscutting programs, may require congressional involvement to integrate the federal response to national needs. With the large number of government entities involved, the federal effort to combat terrorism is one example of a crosscutting program to which Results Act principles and measures might be applied.

Results in Brief

The amount of federal funds being spent on programs and activities to combat terrorism is unknown and difficult to determine. Identifying and tracking terrorism-related governmentwide spending with precision is difficult for several reasons, such as the lack of a uniform definition of terrorism and the inclusion of these expenditures within larger categories that do not readily allow separation. For example, building security measures protect against criminals as well as terrorists. Some agencies maintain data on their spending for efforts to combat terrorism, while others have only fragmented information or estimates. Information from key agencies involved in combating terrorism shows that nearly $7 billion was spent for unclassified terrorism-related programs and activities during fiscal year 1997. The Department of Defense (DoD)—which plays a key supporting role to the lead federal agencies in combating terrorism and is also responsible for protecting its personnel and facilities from terrorist attack worldwide—budgeted about $3.7 billion in fiscal year 1997, or about 55 percent of the estimated spending.

Although NSC is to coordinate counterterrorism policy issues and OMB is to assess competing funding demands, neither agency is required to regularly collect, aggregate, and review funding and spending data relative to combating terrorism on a crosscutting, governmentwide basis. Further, neither agency establishes funding priorities for terrorism-related programs across agencies' budgets or ensures that individual agencies' stated requirements have been validated against threat and risk criteria before budget requests are submitted to the Congress. Because governmentwide priorities for combating terrorism have not been established and funding requirements have not necessarily been validated based on an analytically sound assessment of the threat and risk of terrorist attack, there is no basis to have reasonable assurance that

- agencies' requests are funded through a coordinated and focused approach to implement national policy and strategy,
- the highest priority requirements are being met,

- terrorism-related activities and capabilities are not unnecessarily duplicative or redundant, and
- funding gaps or misallocations have not occurred.

The Results Act principles and framework can provide guidance and opportunities for the many federal agencies involved in the crosscutting program to combat terrorism to develop coordinated goals, objectives, and performance measures and to enhance the management of individual agency and overall federal efforts related to combating terrorism. In the next phase of Results Act implementation, agencies are to develop annual performance plans that are linked to their strategic plans. These plans are to contain annual performance goals, performance measures to gauge progress toward achieving the goals, and the resources agencies will need to meet their goals. The development of annual plans may provide the many federal agencies involved in combating terrorism the next opportunity to develop coordinated goals, objectives, and performance measures for programs and activities that combat terrorism and to articulate how they plan to manage this crosscutting program area. . . .

Total Terrorism-Related Spending Is Uncertain

Federal agencies are not required to account separately for their terrorism-related programs and activities. Because most federal agencies do not isolate or account specifically for terrorism-related funding, it is difficult to determine how much the government budgets and spends to combat terrorism. Key agencies provided us their estimates of terrorism-related spending, using their own definitions. These estimates totaled nearly $7 billion for unclassified programs and activities for fiscal year 1997, and should be considered a minimum estimate of federal spending for unclassified terrorism-related programs and activities.

The amounts for governmentwide terrorism-related funding and spending are uncertain because (1) definitions of antiterrorism and counterterrorism vary from agency to agency; (2) in most cases agencies do not have separate budget line items for terrorism-related activities; (3) some agency functions serve more than one purpose, and it is difficult to allocate costs applicable to terrorism alone (e.g., U.S. embassy security measures protect not only against terrorism but also against theft, compromise of classified documents, and violent demonstrations); (4) some agencies, such as the Departments of Energy and Transportation, have decentralized budgeting and accounting functions and do not aggregate terrorism-related funding agencywide; (5) programs and activities may receive funding from more than one appropriation within a given agency, which makes it difficult to track collective totals; and (6) appropriations legislation often is not clear regarding which amounts are designated to combat terrorism. . . .

Key Interagency Management Functions Are Not Clearly Required or Performed

There is no interagency mechanism to centrally manage funding requirements and requests to ensure an efficient, focused governmentwide application of federal funds to numerous agencies' programs designed to combat terrorism. Given the high national priority and magnitude of this nearly $7-billion federal effort, sound management principles dictate that (1) governmentwide requirements be prioritized to meet the objectives of national policy and strategy and (2) spending and program data be collected from the federal agencies involved to conduct annual, crosscutting evaluations of their funding requests based on the threat and risk of terrorist attack and to avoid duplicated efforts or serious funding gaps. Neither NSC nor OMB currently performs these functions for the governmentwide program to combat terrorism. Rather, each agency is responsible for identifying and seeking funding for its priorities within its own budget allocation, and OMB reviews the budget requests on an agency-by-agency basis. Because individual agencies continue to propose new programs, activities, and capabilities to combat terrorism, annual cross-cutting evaluations of agency budget requests for such programs would be prudent to help avoid duplicated efforts.

Under PDD 39, NSC is to ensure the federal policy and strategy for combating terrorism is implemented. Although PDD 39 establishes interagency coordinating and working groups under the auspices of NSC to handle policy and operational issues related to combating terrorism, these groups operate on a consensus basis, do not have decision-making authority, and do not establish governmentwide resource priorities for combating terrorism. Moreover, PDD 39 does not assign responsibility to NSC to ensure that terrorism-related requirements and related funding proposals (1) are analyzed and reviewed to ensure they are based on a validated assessment of the terrorism threat and risks of terrorist attack, (2) provide a measured and appropriate level of effort across the federal government, (3) avoid duplicative efforts and capabilities, and (4) are prioritized governmentwide in a comprehensive strategy to combat the terrorist threat. . . .

Conclusions

Billions of dollars are being spent by numerous agencies with roles or potential roles in combating terrorism, but because no federal entity has been tasked to collect such information across the government, the specific amount is unknown. Further, no governmentwide spending priorities for the various aspects of combating terrorism have been set, and no federal entity manages the crosscutting program to channel resources where they are most needed in consideration of the threat and the risk of terrorist attack and to prevent wasteful spending that might occur from unnecessary duplication of effort. . . .

As of June 28, 2002, the full text of the GAO report was available at http://www.gao.gov/archive/1998/ns98039.pdf

U.S. FIRES CRUISE MISSILES AT SITES LINKED TO BIN LADEN
August 20, 1998

In almost simultaneous attacks on August 7, 1998, truck bombs blew up the American embassies in Nairobi, Kenya, and Dar Es Salaam, Tanzania. The Kenya blast killed 247 people, including 12 Americans, and wounded more than 4,000 others. The Tanzania bombing killed 12, none of them Americans, and wounded 85. U.S. officials quickly pinned blame for the bombings on Osama bin Laden, a wealthy Saudi Arabian exile who had financed terrorist activities for years. (State Department Fact Sheet About Osama bin Laden, p. 206)

In a nationally televised speech on August 20 President Bill Clinton announced that he had ordered cruise missile attacks against sites in Afghanistan and Sudan that were linked to the terrorists who committed the embassy bombings. The missiles struck three camps in Afghanistan that U.S. officials said the terrorists used as training facilities and a factory in Sudan that U.S. officials said was linked to bin Laden and produced precursor chemicals for a deadly nerve gas. The Sudanese government insisted that the factory produced medicines.

The missile attacks caused heavy damage to buildings at the three camps in Afghanistan, and Afghan officials estimated that anywhere from twenty-one to more than fifty people were killed. The attacks did little to deter terrorism, however, since the damaged buildings were repaired or replaced and the camps were quickly back in business. The attacks also failed in their unstated goal of killing bin Laden, who reportedly left one of the camps shortly before the missiles hit. Twenty-two men were eventually charged in connection with the embassy bombings. One pled guilty in October 2000 and a federal jury convicted four others in May 2001. However, bin Laden and most of the others remained at large. According to U.S. officials, bin Laden's freedom gave him the opportunity to plan the September 11, 2001, attacks on the World Trade Center and the Pentagon. (Bush on Terrorist Attacks Against the United States, p. 351)

Following is the text of a nationally televised speech by President Bill Clinton on August 20, 1998, announcing that he had ordered cruise missile attacks against terrorist sites in Afghanistan and Sudan:

Good afternoon. Today I ordered our Armed Forces to strike at terrorist-related facilities in Afghanistan and Sudan because of the imminent threat they presented to our national security.

I want to speak with you about the objective of this action and why it was necessary. Our target was terror. Our mission was clear—to strike at the network of radical groups affiliated with and funded by Osama bin Laden, perhaps the preeminent organizer and financier of international terrorism in the world today.

The groups associated with him come from diverse places, but share a hatred for democracy, a fanatical glorification of violence, and a horrible distortion of their religion to justify the murder of innocents. They have made the United States their adversary precisely because of what we stand for and what we stand against.

A few months ago, and again this week, bin Laden publicly vowed to wage a terrorist war against America, saying—and I quote—"We do not differentiate between those dressed in military uniforms and civilians. They're all targets. Their mission is murder and their history is bloody."

In recent years, they killed American, Belgian and Pakistani peacekeepers in Somalia. They plotted to assassinate the President of Egypt and the Pope. They planned to bomb six* United States 747s over the Pacific. They bombed the Egyptian embassy in Pakistan. They gunned down German tourists in Egypt.

The most recent terrorist events are fresh in our memory. Two weeks ago, 12 Americans and nearly 300 Kenyans and Tanzanians lost their lives, and another 5,000 were wounded when our embassies in Nairobi and Dar es Salaam were bombed. There is convincing information from our intelligence community that the bin Laden terrorist network was responsible for these bombings.

Based on this information, we have high confidence that these bombings were planned, financed, and carried out by the organization bin Laden leads.

America has battled terrorism for many years. Where possible, we've used law enforcement and diplomatic tools to wage the fight. The long arm of American law has reached out around the world and brought to trial those guilty of attacks in New York and Virginia and in the Pacific. We have quietly disrupted terrorist groups and foiled their plots. We have isolated countries that practice terrorism. We've worked to build an international coalition against terror.

But there have been, and will be, times when law enforcement and diplomatic tools are simply not enough, when our very national security is challenged, and when we must take extraordinary steps to protect the safety of

---

Editor's note: The actual number was twelve.

our citizens. With compelling evidence that the bin Laden network of terrorist groups was planning to mount further attacks against Americans and other freedom-loving people, I decided America must act.

And so, this morning, based on the unanimous recommendation of my national security team, I ordered our Armed Forces to take action to counter an immediate threat from the bin Laden network. Earlier today, the United States carried out simultaneous strikes against terrorist facilities and infrastructure in Afghanistan. Our forces targeted one of the most active terrorist bases in the world. It contained key elements of the bin Laden network's infrastructure and has served as a training camp for literally thousands of terrorists from around the globe. We have reason to believe that a gathering of key terrorist leaders was to take place there today, thus underscoring the urgency of our actions.

Our forces also attacked a factory in Sudan associated with the bin Laden network. The factory was involved in the production of materials for chemical weapons.

The United States does not take this action lightly. Afghanistan and Sudan have been warned for years to stop harboring and supporting these terrorist groups. But countries that persistently host terrorists have no right to be safe havens.

Let me express my gratitude to our intelligence and law enforcement agencies for their hard, good work. And let me express my pride in our Armed Forces who carried out this mission while making every possible effort to minimize the loss of innocent life.

I want you to understand, I want the world to understand, that our actions today were not aimed against Islam, the faith of hundreds of millions of good, peace-loving people all around the world, including the United States. No religion condones the murder of innocent men, women and children. But our actions were aimed at fanatics and killers who wrap murder in the cloak of righteousness; and in so doing, profane the great religion in whose name they claim to act.

My fellow Americans, our battle against terrorism did not begin with the bombing of our embassies in Africa; nor will it end with today's strike. It will require strength, courage and endurance. We will not yield to this threat. We will meet it, no matter how long it may take. This will be a long, ongoing struggle between freedom and fanaticism; between the rule of law and terrorism. We must be prepared to do all that we can for as long as we must.

America is and will remain a target of terrorists precisely because we are leaders; because we act to advance peace, democracy and basic human values; because we're the most open society on Earth; and because, as we have shown yet again, we take an uncompromising stand against terrorism.

But of this I am also sure. The risks from inaction to America and the world would be far greater than action, for that would embolden our enemies, leaving their ability and their willingness to strike us intact. In this case, we knew before our attack that these groups already had planned further actions against us and others.

I want to reiterate: The United States wants peace, not conflict. We want to lift lives around the world, not take them. We have worked for peace—in Bosnia, in Northern Ireland, in Haiti, in the Middle East and elsewhere. But in this day, no campaign for peace can succeed without a determination to fight terrorism. Let our actions today send this message loud and clear: There are no expendable American targets. There will be no sanctuary for terrorists. We will defend our people, our interests and our values. We will help people of all faiths, in all parts of the world, who want to live free of fear and violence. We will persist and we will prevail.

Thank you. God bless you, and may God bless our country.

"REAL IRA" CLAIMS CREDIT FOR OMAGH BLAST
September 2, 1998

After thirty years of terrorist violence in Northern Ireland by paramilitary Protestant and Catholic forces that had killed more than 3,200 people, in early 1998 there was reason to believe that peace might finally be within reach. The previous July the Irish Republican Army (IRA) had declared a ceasefire, and complicated negotiations over the future of Northern Ireland were under way among the province's various factions. On April 10, 1998— Good Friday—negotiators finally reached an agreement. A little more than a month later, voters in both Northern Ireland and the Republic of Ireland overwhelmingly approved the agreement in referendums. (Talks with IRA Promised If Ceasefire Continued, p. 151)

Then shortly after 3 P.M. on August 15, 1998, as adults and children swarmed the main shopping district in the small town of Omagh on a Saturday afternoon, a parked car exploded. Twenty-nine people—a mixture of Protestants and Catholics, of men, women, and children—died in the blast, and more than 200 were wounded, some of whom lost limbs. It was the most deadly act of violence in the thirty-year history of the "troubles" in Northern Ireland. A splinter group from the Irish Republican Army calling itself the "Real IRA" claimed credit for the car bomb, which it said was aimed at blocking implementation of the peace agreement. The bombing was almost universally condemned—even by Gerry Adams, president of Sinn Fein, the IRA's political wing, who had never before criticized an IRA attack. In a speech September 2, 1998, to the British House of Commons, Prime Minister Tony Blair called the attack "a deliberate attempt, by a small group of extremists, with no moral or political support anywhere, to wreck the Good Friday Agreement and the foundation for a lasting and peaceful Northern Ireland which the Agreement offers. It was a cynical attempt to provoke a violent reaction from others."

Ironically, the Omagh bombing seemed to have the opposite effect from that intended. Instead of derailing the peace process and leading to renewed violence, the brutal murder of civilians horrified the population and gave new determination to the leaders who signed the agreement. Efforts to implement the pact moved forward, albeit in fits and starts. Within days of the bombing, both the British and Irish governments passed tough laws giving them new powers to fight terrorists. Nevertheless, the bombing investigation languished. In a scathing report released in December 2001, the new ombudsman for police in Northern Ireland said officers had bungled the investigation so badly that the bombing might never be solved. The report, which caused an uproar in Northern Ireland, also said that police intelligence officers had received two tips in the days before the bombing, but they had violated procedure and failed to pass them along to local police in Omagh. Police representatives attacked the report as inaccurate and said they knew who the bombers were but lacked the evidence to charge them. Finally, in January 2002 a forty-nine-year-old man was found guilty of conspiring in the bombing and sentenced to fourteen years in prison. Evidence showed he only played a minor role, though, and by June 2002 no one else had ever been charged. Meanwhile, the families of those killed at Omagh were trying to raise enough money to file civil suits against five men suspected in the bombing.

Following is the text of a speech by Prime Minister Tony Blair to the British House of Commons on September 2, 1998, in reaction to the August 15 bombing in Omagh, Northern Ireland:

Madam Speaker, with permission, I will make a statement on the bomb in Omagh.

At 3:10 P.M. on 15 August a car bomb, consisting of 2–300 pounds of homemade explosive, blew up in Market Street in the centre of Omagh, as a community festival was in progress. The explosion brought devastation and tragedy to the heart of the town. Twenty-eight people were killed*—the highest death toll in any single incident in Northern Ireland. Seventeen were Roman Catholic. Eleven were Protestant. Eleven were under the age of eighteen. The dead included three from the Republic [of Ireland] and two from Spain. Over two hundred people were injured, many very seriously. More than fifty continue to receive medical treatment in hospitals around the country. The whole House will want to join me in our disgust, outrage and condemnation of those responsible.

There was a telephone warning at 2:30 P.M. to Ulster TV. It spoke of a bomb close to the Court House in Main Street. The RUC [Royal Ulster Constabulary, the local police] responded accordingly and moved people away from the Court House down Market Street. The bomb went off 400 yards from the Court House in Market Street, in the very area to which people had been directed. The bomb was in a car in the street outside busy shops at a busy time of a busy

---

Editor's note: The final death toll was actually twenty-nine.

day. The resulting carnage was inevitable. We reject the excuses of those who have tried to explain it away.

The atrocity was later admitted by the so-called Real IRA, a renegade republican group. All the political parties in Northern Ireland condemned the attack unequivocally.

Honourable Members from Northern Ireland, and those of us who have been to Omagh, including myself, the Deputy Prime Minister and the Secretary of State, have seen the terrible pain and grief inflicted and the trauma which has resulted for many. No one can fail to have been moved by the procession of coffins which we saw on our television screens as those killed in the explosion were buried. We extend our deepest sympathies to the victims of this wicked attack, and to all their families and friends.

We should also take this opportunity to appreciate — once again — the magnificent work carried out by the emergency and health services. In dreadfully difficult and distressing circumstances, they did their utmost to rescue the victims of this outrage, to tend to the injured, and to comfort the shocked. They went through experiences no one should have to face. Their courage and dedication were remarkable. They are remarkable people and we, in this House today, salute them.

When I visited the Royal Victoria Hospital the following day, I saw for myself not only the professional skill of the medical staff but also the hugely important comforting and counselling role they play. They have my wholehearted admiration and respect.

The RUC also deserve the highest praise. On many occasions in the past their skill and courage have prevented similar scenes of carnage, but perhaps as a result warning times have been shortening. On this occasion they were helpless in the face of the misleading warning given by the cowards who carried out this attack. The RUC's subsequent actions attracted deserved gratitude from all sides of the Community.

Madam Speaker, we have known tragedy in Northern Ireland many times before. But this was an indiscriminate attack on a whole community, bringing nothing but further grief to the long-suffering people of Northern Ireland. It was a deliberate attempt, by a small group of extremists, with no moral or political support anywhere, to wreck the Good Friday Agreement and the foundation for a lasting and peaceful Northern Ireland which the Agreement offers. It was a cynical attempt to provoke a violent reaction from others.

These aims have not succeeded and will not be allowed to succeed. That has been the response not only of the two governments and the political parties, but also, overwhelmingly, of the people of Omagh and elsewhere in Northern Ireland and the Republic. It was on the lips of virtually all those to whom I spoke, even those who had suffered most, when I visited Omagh just over a week ago.

The aim of the bombers was not just to kill innocent people but was to strike at the heart of the peace process. The best response we can give is not therefore to abandon the Good Friday Agreement but to carry it forward vigorously, to deny them the very objective they seek, and to continue to work for a better future for Northern Ireland that puts the past behind us.

The Agreement reached on Good Friday was emphatically endorsed in referendums north and south. The election in June underlined the wish of the majority of people in Northern Ireland to reach for a new and peaceful future. Those who continue with terror have no support, no votes, no mandate from any part of any community in the island of Ireland.

Both we and the Irish Government are fully committed to implementing the will of the people of Ireland north and south. Further political progress is by far the best answer to violence. As I have said, it is what the people of Northern Ireland demand, and deserve.

Madam Speaker, I therefore welcome the efforts to achieve this of David Trimble and Seamus Mallon, the First Minister and First Deputy Minister designate of the new Northern Ireland Assembly, and of other politicians in Northern Ireland. I welcome yesterday's statement by Sinn Fein [the political arm of the Irish Republican Army] making clearer than ever their rejection of violence and commitment to peaceful means, and the initiative of David Trimble and Seamus Mallon in calling a meeting of the leaders of all the political parties next week.

I welcome too the latest announcement of the appointment of Martin McGuinness to work with the Independent Commission on Decommissioning, to facilitate the process of decommissioning [IRA weapons]. This is practical evidence to underpin what Sinn Fein said yesterday, and a further important step forward in the implementation of all aspects of the Good Friday Agreement. Under that Agreement, the decommissioning of paramilitary weapons within two years is a vital part of a lasting settlement.

Madam Speaker, this is a difficult process. There will be many more difficulties along the way. But I have no doubt things are on the move, and we are moving in the right direction. In the wake of Omagh, people of both communities are determined as never before to overcome past divisions and build new confidence and trust. We are doing all we can to help this process.

But we must also take strong and decisive steps to deal with the unrepresentative minority who want to use violence to undermine this peaceful future. Amid what I believe to be unprecedented cooperation between governments and police forces, we continue to provide maximum support to the RUC and the Garda Siochana as they hunt for those responsible for the Omagh bomb and other outrages. I can assure the House that the investigation to bring to justice those responsible is being pursued with the utmost intensity, and with complete unity of purpose between the British and Irish authorities.

To complement and reinforce these security operations, both we and the Government of the Republic propose to strengthen our anti-terrorist laws to help bring to justice those still dedicated to violence. I am grateful to you, Madam Speaker, for agreeing to this recall of Parliament to enable early action to be taken. The Irish Parliament is also meeting today to discuss a wide range of new proposals designed to strengthen their anti-terrorist legislation, and in many cases bring it into line with our own.

This House will shortly be debating our own proposals. My RHF [Right Honourable Friend] the Home Secretary will explain the full details, but they are a proportionate and targeted response to deal with small and evil groups of violent men who seek to wreck the hopes for peace which the great majority yearn for and have voted for. Our basic aim is to make it easier to achieve convictions for membership of the organisations concerned, in particular by changing the rules of evidence in a way that is tough but fully thought through and fully in line with the rule of law and our commitments under the European Convention on Human Rights.

Madam Speaker, this House is also well aware that terrorism is an increasing threat worldwide. The horrific bomb attacks on the US Embassies in Kenya and Tanzania in early August brought this home yet again, as did the more recent bomb in a restaurant in South Africa. As I know from my own discussions with other leaders, not least in Europe, the international community is determined to respond uncompromisingly to this.

Britain must play an active part in this international battle against terrorism, and avoid becoming any kind of haven for international terrorists and their supporters. We are therefore taking the opportunity of Parliament's recall to put into law long-held plans to make a criminal offence of conspiracy to commit offences outside the UK.

Madam Speaker, we will not forget the horror of Omagh. But I say this to the bombers.

You sought to wreck the Agreement, and you failed.

You sought to divide the community, and you failed.

You sought to win new support, and you failed.

You failed because violence and terror represent the past in Northern Ireland, and democracy and peace represent the future.

There are few more important challenges to democracy, and therefore to this House, than terrorism in all its forms. We must fight it vigorously wherever it appears, while holding fast to our democratic principles and the rule of law. We must also redouble our efforts to carry through the political settlement in Northern Ireland which alone can bring lasting peace. That is the approach I commend to this House.

CLINTON URGES UNITED NATIONS TO FOCUS ON TERRORISM
September 21, 1998

The air strikes that President Bill Clinton ordered August 20, 1998, against suspected terrorist targets in Afghanistan and Sudan drew mixed reactions around the world. Some countries—most notably Israel, Great Britain, and Germany—said the air strikes were a reasonable response to terrorist bombings earlier in the month of U.S. embassies in Kenya and Tanzania. But others—mostly in the Middle East—said the United States had no right to bomb countries with which it was not at war. Anti-American street demonstrations took place throughout the Arab world. (U.S. Fires Cruise Missiles at Sites Linked to Bin Laden, p. 253)

Despite this mixed reaction, Clinton received a warm standing ovation a month later when he spoke about terrorism at the annual opening session of the United Nations General Assembly on September 21, 1998. Clinton urged the assembled heads of state, ambassadors, and other dignitaries to put terrorism at the top of the world agenda. Clinton said terrorism was not just an American problem, calling it "a clear and present danger to tolerant and open societies and innocent people everywhere." He also emphasized that the harm caused by terrorism extended far beyond the people killed or injured in a particular attack. "In the Middle East, in Asia, in South America, how many agreements have been thwarted after bombs blew up?" he asked. "How many businesses will never be created in places crying out for investments of time and money? How many talented young people in countries represented here have turned their backs on public service?"

Less than three months after his speech Clinton ordered new air strikes, this time against Iraq. The bombing campaign, which also included British ships and planes, was retaliation for Iraqi president Saddam Hussein's repeated blocking of United Nations weapons inspectors. The UN officials were attempting to locate and destroy any chemical, biological, or nuclear weapons in Iraq, a country that the United States officially listed as a sponsor of terrorism.

Following are excerpts from a speech by President Bill Clinton at the opening session of the Fifty-third United Nations General Assembly in New York City on September 21, 1998:

. . . Today, I would like to talk to you about why all nations must put the fight against terrorism at the top of our agenda.

Obviously this is a matter of profound concern to us. In the last 15 years our citizens have been targeted over and over again—in Beirut, over Lockerbie, in Saudi Arabia, at home in Oklahoma City by one of our own citizens, and even here in New York in one of our most public buildings, and most recently on August 7th in Nairobi and Dar cs Salaam, where Americans who devoted their lives to building bridges between nations, people very much like all of you, died in a campaign of hatred against the United States.

Because we are blessed to be a wealthy nation with a powerful military and a worldwide presence active in promoting peace and security, we are often a target. We love our country for its dedication to political and religious freedom, to economic opportunity, to respect for the rights of the individual. But we know many people see us as a symbol of a system and values they reject, and often they find it expedient to blame us for problems with deep roots elsewhere.

But we are no threat to any peaceful nation, and we believe the best way to disprove these claims is to continue our work for peace and prosperity around the world. For us to pull back from the world's trouble spots, to turn our backs on those taking risks for peace, to weaken our own opposition to terrorism, would hand the enemies of peace a victory they must never have.

Still, it is a grave misconception to see terrorism as only, or even mostly, an American problem. Indeed, it is a clear and present danger to tolerant and open societies and innocent people everywhere. No one in this room, nor the people you represent, are immune.

Certainly not the people of Nairobi and Dar es Salaam. For every American killed there, roughly 20 Africans were murdered and 500 more injured— innocent people going about their business on a busy morning. Not the people of Omagh in Northern Ireland, where the wounded and killed were Catholics and Protestants alike, mostly children and women, and two of them pregnant, people out shopping together, when their future was snuffed out by a fringe group clinging to the past.

Not the people of Japan who were poisoned by sarin gas in the Tokyo subway. Not the people of Argentina who died when a car bomb decimated a Jewish community center in Buenos Aires. Not the people of Kashmir and Sri Lanka killed by ancient animosities that cry out for resolution. Not the Palestinians and Israelis who still die year after year for all the progress toward peace. Not the people of Algeria enduring the nightmare of unfathomable terror with still no end in sight. Not the people of Egypt, who nearly lost a second

President to assassination. Not the people of Turkey, Colombia, Albania, Russia, Iran, Indonesia, and countless other nations where innocent people have been victimized by terror.

Now, none of these victims are American, but every one was a son or a daughter, a husband or wife, a father or mother, a human life extinguished by someone else's hatred, leaving a circle of people whose lives will never be the same. Terror has become the world's problem. Some argue, of course, that the problem is overblown, saying that the number of deaths from terrorism is comparatively small, sometimes less than the number of people killed by lightning in a single year. I believe that misses the point in several ways.

First, terrorism has a new face in the 1990s. Today terrorists take advantage of greater openness and the explosion of information and weapons technology. The new technologies of terror and their increasing availability, along with the increasing mobility of terrorists, raise chilling prospects of vulnerability to chemical, biological, and other kinds of attacks, bringing each of us into the category of possible victim. This is a threat to all humankind.

Beyond the physical damage of each attack, there is an even greater residue of psychological damage—hard to measure, but slow to heal. Every bomb, every bomb threat has an insidious effect on free and open institutions, the kinds of institutions all of you in this body are working so hard to build.

Each time an innocent man or woman or child is killed, it makes the future more hazardous for the rest of us. For each violent act saps the confidence that is so crucial to peace and prosperity. In every corner of the world, with the active support of UN agencies, people are struggling to build better futures, based on bonds of trust connecting them to their fellow citizens and with partners and investors from around the world.

The glimpse of growing prosperity in Northern Ireland was a crucial factor in the Good Friday Agreement. But that took confidence—confidence that cannot be bought in times of violence. We can measure each attack and the grisly statistics of dead and wounded, but what are the wounds we cannot measure?

In the Middle East, in Asia, in South America, how many agreements have been thwarted after bombs blew up? How many businesses will never be created in places crying out for investments of time and money? How many talented young people in countries represented here have turned their backs on public service?

The question is not only how many lives have been lost in each attack, but how many futures were lost in their aftermath. There is no justification for killing innocents. Ideology, religion, and politics, even deprivation and righteous grievance do not justify it. We must seek to understand the roiled waters in which terror occurs; of course we must.

Often, in my own experience, I have seen where peace is making progress, terror is a desperate act to turn back the tide of history. The Omagh bombing came as peace was succeeding in Northern Ireland. In the Middle East, whenever we get close to another step toward peace, its enemies respond with terror. We must not let this stall our momentum.

The bridging of ancient hatreds is, after all, a leap of faith, a break with the past, and thus a frightening threat to those who cannot let go of their own hatred. Because they fear the future, in these cases terrorists seek to blow the peacemakers back into the past.

We must also acknowledge that there are economic sources of this rage as well. Poverty, inequality, masses of disenfranchised young people are fertile fields for the siren call of the terrorists and their claims of advancing social justice. But depravation cannot justify destruction, nor can inequity ever atone for murder. The killing of innocents is not a social program.

Nevertheless, our resolute opposition to terrorism does not mean we can ever be indifferent to the conditions that foster it. The most recent UN human development report suggests the gulf is widening between the world's haves and have-nots. We must work harder to treat the sources of despair before they turn into the poison of hatred. Dr. Martin Luther King once wrote that the only revolutionary is a man who has nothing to lose. We must show people they have everything to gain by embracing cooperation and renouncing violence. This is not simply an American or a Western responsibility; it is the world's responsibility.

Developing nations have an obligation to spread new wealth fairly, to create new opportunities, to build new open economies. Developed nations have an obligation to help developing nations stay on the path of prosperity and to spur global economic growth. A week ago I outlined ways we can build a stronger international economy to benefit not only all nations, but all citizens within them.

Some people believe that terrorism's principal fault line centers on what they see as an inevitable clash of civilizations. It is an issue that deserves a lot of debate in this great hall. Specifically, many believe there is an inevitable clash between Western civilization and Western values, and Islamic civilizations and values. I believe this view is terribly wrong. False prophets may use and abuse any religion to justify whatever political objectives they have— even cold-blooded murder. Some may have the world believe that almighty God himself, the merciful, grants a license to kill. But that is not our understanding of Islam.

A quarter of the world's population is Muslim—from Africa to the Middle East to Asia and to the United States, where Islam is one of our fastest growing faiths. There are over 1,200 mosques and Islamic centers in the United States, and the number is rapidly increasing. The 6 million Americans who worship there will tell you there is no inherent clash between Islam and America. Americans respect and honor Islam.

As I talked to Muslim leaders in my country and around the world, I see again that we share the same hopes and aspirations: to live in peace and security, to provide for our children, to follow the faith of our choosing, to build a better life than our parents knew and pass on brighter possibilities to our own children. Of course, we are not identical. There are important differences that cross race and culture and religion which demand understanding and deserve respect.

But every river has a crossing place. Even as we struggle here in America, like the United Nations, to reconcile all Americans to each other and to find

265

greater unity in our increasing diversity, we will remain on a course of friendship and respect for the Muslim world. We will continue to look for common values, common interests, and common endeavors. I agree very much with the spirit expressed by these words of Mohammed: rewards for prayers by people assembled together are twice those said at home.

When it comes to terrorism there should be no dividing line between Muslims and Jews, Protestants and Catholics, Serbs and Albanians, developed societies and emerging countries. The only dividing line is between those who practice, support, or tolerate terror, and those who understand that it is murder, plain and simple. . . .

In closing, let me urge all of us to think in new terms on terrorism, to see it not as a clash of cultures or political action by other means, or a divine calling, but a clash between the forces of the past and the forces of the future, between those who tear down and those who build up, between hope and fear, chaos and community.

The fight will not be easy. But every nation will be strengthened in joining it, in working to give real meaning to the words of the Universal Declaration on Human Rights we signed 50 years ago. It is very, very important that we do this together.

Eleanor Roosevelt was one of the authors of the Universal Declaration. She said in one of her many speeches in support of the United Nations, when it was just beginning, "All agreements and all peace are built on confidence. You cannot have peace and you cannot get on with other people in the world unless you have confidence in them."

It is not necessary that we solve all the world's problems to have confidence in one another. It is not necessary that we agree on all the world's issues to have confidence in one another. It is not even necessary that we understand every single difference among us to have confidence in one another. But it is necessary that we affirm our belief in the primacy of the Universal Declaration on Human Rights, and, therefore, that together we say terror is not a way to tomorrow, it is only a throwback to yesterday. And together—together—we can meet it and overcome its threats, its injuries, and its fears with confidence.

Thank you very much.

As of June 22, 2002, the full text of President Clinton's speech was available at http://clinton2.nara.gov/WH/New/html/19980921-29469. html

TASK FORCE CREATED TO FIGHT ANTIABORTION VIOLENCE
November 9, 1998

Following the shooting deaths of two people at abortion clinics in a Boston suburb in December 1994, President Bill Clinton ordered U.S. attorneys and federal marshals around the country to step up their efforts to prevent antiabortion violence. Yet the terrorist attacks continued. A bomb that exploded at an abortion clinic in Birmingham, Alabama, on January 29, 1998, killed an off-duty police officer employed as a security guard and severely wounded a clinic nurse. Then Barnettt Slepian, a well-known doctor in the Buffalo, New York, area who performed abortions, was killed by a rifle shot fired through the kitchen window of his home on the evening of October 23, 1998. (President Clinton Denounces Attack on Abortion Clinics, p. 155)

Largely in response to Slepian's murder, Attorney General Janet Reno on November 9, 1998, announced the creation of the National Task Force on Violence Against Health Care Providers. The task force, which included representatives from the Justice Department, the FBI, the Bureau of Alcohol, Tobacco, and Firearms (ATF), and other federal agencies, was formed to investigate possible connections between clinic attacks, help local officials in their investigations of clinic violence, and coordinate efforts to prevent violence against abortion clinics.

After Slepian's murder, federal marshals guarded doctors who volunteered to perform abortions at his clinic. Slepian's shooting was the fifth sniper attack in four years on doctors who performed abortions in upstate New York and across the border in Canada, attacks that law enforcement officials said were very similar. The suspect in Slepian's murder, an anti-abortion activist named James Kopp, eluded an international manhunt for more than two years until his capture in France in March 2001. In June 2002 Kopp was extradited to the United States, where he faced federal and state charges in Slepian's killing.

Following are excerpts from statements by Attorney General Janet Reno and Robert Bryant, deputy director of the

FBI, at a news conference on November 9, 1998, announcing the creation of the National Task Force on Violence Against Health Care Providers:

ATTORNEY GENERAL'S STATEMENT

Last month, Americans everywhere were outraged over the death of Dr. Barnett Slepian. While standing in his kitchen in Amherst, New York, Dr. Slepian was shot by a high-powered rifle fired through his window. Sadly, this was not the first such shooting. There were others. And it was just one more act of violence in a series of savage attacks against providers of reproductive health care.

Over the summer, about 20 clinics in Florida, Louisiana and Texas were attacked with acid. This fall, two clinics in North Carolina were the victims of arson and attempted bombings. And just last week, clinics in Indiana, Tennessee, Kansas and Kentucky were sent letters falsely claiming to contain anthrax.

These attacks and others seek to undermine a woman's basic constitutional right—the right to reproductive health care. And while some people may oppose that right, no one should ever use violence to impede it.

Since I became attorney general, I have been very concerned about this issue. That's why in 1994 I established a task force to investigate whether a national conspiracy existed. While that task force developed several successful criminal cases, it did not develop evidence sufficient to prosecute a national conspiracy.

Two years later, the efforts of the task force were taken over by the Civil Rights Division, which continued the work of prosecuting clinic violence cases. In addition, local working groups were set up by U.S. attorneys across the country.

To date, these efforts have made a difference. Since 1994, we have brought 27 criminal cases and 17 civil cases. But in light of the recent increase in clinic violence, we are taking new steps.

Today I am announcing the creation of the National Task Force on Violence Against Health Care Providers. Its mission is very important. First, it will lead a national investigative effort, focusing on connections that may exist between individuals engaged in these acts.

Secondly, it will assist local officials in the investigation and prosecution of clinic violence.

Third, it will identify at-risk clinics and develop ways to make those clinics more secure.

Fourth, it will establish a centralized national database for all information on clinic violence.

Fifth, it will assist the many working groups already hard at work across the country.

And sixth, it will oversee a program to train law enforcement on the best ways to handle clinic cases. Two training sessions are already scheduled for December.

As part of our stepped-up effort, today I have also directed all U.S. attorneys to convene their local working groups to assess the security needs of clinics in their communities.

The National Clinic Violence Task Force will be led by the head of the Civil Rights Division, Bill Lann Lee. It will be staffed by attorneys from the Civil Rights and Criminal Divisions, as well as agents from the FBI, ATF, U.S. Marshal Service and the U.S. Postal Service. And it will work closely with state and local officials in deciding how best to proceed with each incident.

Treasury Secretary Robert Rubin will be represented on the task force by Assistant Secretary Elizabeth Bresee. And Mr. Lee will consult with her concerning his oversight of the task force.

Today I am announcing a reward of $500,000 for information leading to the arrest and conviction of the person or persons responsible for the murder of Dr. Slepian. Anyone with information or tips in that shooting should call 1-800-281-1184. That's 1-800-281-1184.

One thing must be very, very clear: There is no excuse for this violence. And working together with state and local law enforcement, we will do everything we can to prevent it. . . .

FBI STATEMENT

America cannot tolerate violence, whether it is violence on the street, violence in the workplace or violence to health care providers. America has seen over the last several months buteric acid attacks in the South—from Florida to Texas. In middle America, anthrax threat letters have been received from Ohio to Kansas. And doctors have been shot at and wounded in Canada and the United States.

The attorney general just announced a task force to address this violence, which will not be tolerated.

This task force is set up to prevent and stop violence. The FBI will be joining the Department of Justice, and our federal, state and local agencies and our Canadian colleagues to ensure that all Americans have safe access to health service providers as well as any other lawfully protected activity.

FBI special agents and analysts—including those experienced in criminal and civil investigations of the Freedom of Access to Clinic Entrances, or better known as the FACE Act—also experienced in domestic terrorism matters and in matters involving weapons of mass destruction as they relate to abortion clinics will join with the attorney general's task force.

The concrete steps that will be taken—the FBI personnel will oversee ongoing FBI investigations of violence directed against abortion providers and/or threats of violence directed toward the same, and it will integrate all FBI intelligence information together with details from investigations, including the FACE and other databases.

I would just like to say in closing that this task force and the FBI are dedicated to the prevention of violence and to ensure the protection of constitutional rights.

CLINTON ORDER BLOCKS TRADE WITH THE TALIBAN
July 4, 1999

By 1999 the United States was intent on catching or killing Osama bin Laden, leader of the al Qaeda terrorist network. The August 1998 U.S. air strikes on bin Laden training camps in Afghanistan, which were retaliation for the bombing weeks earlier of U.S. embassies in Kenya and Tanzania, were aimed at killing bin Laden. When those air strikes failed—bin Laden reportedly left one of the camps shortly before the missiles fell—the U.S. State Department announced a $5 million reward for information leading to his arrest or conviction. On June 7, 1999, the FBI added the Saudi exile to its "Ten Most Wanted Fugitives" list. But he remained in Afghanistan, where the Taliban militia that ruled most of the country gave him refuge—reportedly in exchange for large contributions of money and fighters. Repeated U.S. efforts aimed at persuading the Taliban to hand over bin Laden to a third country for trial went nowhere. (State Department Fact Sheet About Osama bin Laden, p. 206; U.S. Fires Cruise Missiles at Sites Linked to Bin Laden, p. 253)

On July 4, 1999, President Bill Clinton increased the pressure on the Taliban to stop harboring bin Laden by signing an executive order that froze Taliban assets in the United States, blocked all U.S. trade with the Taliban, and barred U.S. citizens from contributing money to the group. In a letter notifying Congress of the order, Clinton wrote: "The measures taken in this order will immediately demonstrate to the Taliban the seriousness of our concern over its support for terrorists and terrorist networks, and increase the international isolation of the Taliban."

The United States next turned to the United Nations to ratchet up international pressure on the Taliban. On October 15, 1999, the UN Security Council passed a resolution imposing limited economic sanctions on the Taliban if they did not hand over bin Laden within thirty days. (UN Threatens Sanctions Against Taliban, p. 286)

Following is the text of a letter dated July 4, 1999, from President Bill Clinton to congressional leaders reporting the signing of Executive Order 13129:

271

Pursuant to section 204(b) of the International Emergency Economic Powers Act, 50 U.S.C. 1703(b) and section 301 of the National Emergencies Act, 50 U.S.C. 1631, I hereby report that I have exercised my statutory authority to declare a National emergency with respect to the threat to the United States posed by the actions and policies of the Afghan Taliban and have issued an executive order to deal with this threat.

The actions and policies of the Afghan Taliban pose an unusual and extraordinary threat to the national security and foreign policy of the United States. The Taliban continues to provide safe haven to Usama bin Ladin allowing him and the Al-Qaida organization to operate from Taliban-controlled territory a network of terrorist training camps and to use Afghanistan as a base from which to sponsor terrorist operations against the United States.

Usama bin Ladin and the Al-Qaida organization have been involved in at least two separate attacks against the United States. On August 7, 1998, the U.S. embassies in Nairobi, Kenya, and in Dar es Salaam, Tanzania, were attacked using powerful explosive truck bombs. The following people have been indicted for criminal activity against the United States in connection with Usama bin Ladin and/or the Al-Qaida organization: Usama bin Ladin, his military commander Muhammed Atef, Wadih El Hage, Fazul Abdullah Mohammed, Mohammed Sadeek Odeh, Mohamed Rashed Daoud Al-Owhali, Mustafa Mohammed Fadhil, Khalfan Khamis Mohamed, Ahmed Khalfan Ghailani, Fahid Mohommed Ally Msalam, Sheikh Ahmed Salim Swedan, Mamdouh Mahmud Salim, Ali Mohammed, Ayman Al-Zawahiri, and Khaled Al Fawwaz. In addition, bin Ladin and his network are currently planning additional attacks against U.S. interests and nationals.

Since at least 1998 and up to the date of the Executive order, the Taliban has continued to provide bin Ladin with safe haven and security, allowing him the necessary freedom to operate. Repeated efforts by the United States to persuade the Taliban to expel bin Ladin to a third country where he can be brought to justice for his crimes have failed. The United States has also attempted to apply pressure on the Taliban both directly and through frontline states in a position to influence Taliban behavior. Despite these efforts, the Taliban has not only continued, but has also deepened its support for, and its relationship with, Usama bin Ladin and associated terrorist networks.

Accordingly, I have concluded that the actions and policies of the Taliban pose an unusual and extraordinary threat to the national security and foreign policy of the United States. I have, therefore, exercised my statutory authority and issued an Executive order which, except to the extent provided for in section 203 (b) of IEEPA (50 U.S.C. 1072(b)) and regulations, orders, directives or licenses that may be issued pursuant to this order, and notwithstanding any contract entered into or any license or permit granted prior to the effective date:

—blocks all property and interests in property of the Taliban, including the Taliban leaders listed in the annex to the order that are in the United States or that are or hereafter come within the possession or control of United States persons;

— prohibits any transaction or dealing by United States persons or within the United States in property or interests in property blocked pursuant to the order, including the making or receiving of any contribution of funds, goods, or services to or for the benefit of the Taliban;

— prohibits the exportation, re-exportation, sale, or supply, directly or indirectly, from the United States, or by a United States person, wherever located, of any goods, software, technology (including technical data), or services to the territory of Afghanistan under the control of the Taliban or to the Taliban; and prohibits the importation into the United States of any goods, software, technology, or services owned or controlled by the Taliban or from the territory of Afghanistan under the control of the Taliban.

The Secretary of the Treasury, in consultation with the Secretary of State, is directed to authorize commercial sales of agricultural commodities and products, medicine and medical equipment, for civilian end use in the territory of Afghanistan controlled by the Taliban under appropriate safeguards to prevent diversion to military, paramilitary, or terrorist end-users or end-use or to political end-use. This order and subsequent licenses will likewise allow humanitarian, diplomatic, and journalistic activities to continue.

I have designated in the Executive order, Mullah Mohhamad Omar, the leader of the Taliban, and I have authorized the Secretary of State to designate additional persons as Taliban leaders in consultation with the Secretary of the Treasury and the Attorney General.

The Secretary of the Treasury is further authorized to designate persons or entities, in consultation with the Secretary of State and the Attorney General, that are owned or controlled, or are acting for or on behalf of the Taliban or that provide financial, material, or technical support to the Taliban. The Secretary of the Treasury is also authorized to issue regulations in the exercise of my authorities under the International Emergency Economic Powers Act to implement these measures in consultation with the Secretary of State and the Attorney General. All Federal agencies are directed to take actions within their authority to carry out the provisions of the Executive order.

The measures taken in this order will immediately demonstrate to the Taliban the seriousness of our concern over its support for terrorists and terrorist networks, and increase the international isolation of the Taliban. The blocking of the Taliban's property and the other prohibitions imposed under this executive order will further limit the Taliban's ability to facilitate and support terrorists and terrorist networks. It is particularly important for the United States to demonstrate to the Taliban the necessity of conforming to accepted norms of international behavior.

I am enclosing a copy of the Executive order I have issued. This order is effective at 12:01 A.M. Eastern Daylight Time on July 6, 1999.

Sincerely,

WILLIAM J. CLINTON

REPORT ON POSSIBLE TERRORIST ATTACKS USING AIRPLANES
September 1999

On January 6, 1995, a terrorist mixing bomb chemicals in a Manila apartment as part of a plot to blow up twelve American airliners while they flew over the Pacific made a mistake. A fire erupted, drawing the attention of local authorities. During a long interrogation, Abdul Hakim Murad— who was working with Ramzi Ahmed Yousef, the mastermind of the 1993 World Trade Center bombing—said the plot also called for him to crash a plane into the Central Intelligence Agency headquarters in Virginia. Murad had a commercial pilot's license he obtained after studying at several American flight schools. Murad said the terrorists had also discussed flying hijacked planes into the Pentagon, the Capitol Building, the White House, and skyscrapers. Filipino authorities shared the information with the FBI, but the FBI reportedly dropped the matter after agents visited two of the flight schools Murad had attended. (Terrorist Plot to Blow Up American Planes in Flight, p. 187)

The plot received renewed attention in a September 1999 report prepared by researchers from the Library of Congress at the request of the CIA. The executive summary of the unclassified report, which was widely circulated, warned that Osama bin Laden "most likely will retaliate in a spectacular way" for the 1998 U.S. air strikes on his terrorist training camps in Afghanistan. In briefly reviewing how bin Laden might attack Washington, D.C., the report said: "Suicide bomber(s) belonging to al Qaeda's Martyrdom Battalion could crash-land an aircraft packed with high explosives (C-4 and semtex) into the Pentagon, the headquarters of the Central Intelligence Agency (CIA), or the White House. Ramzi Yousef had planned to do this against the CIA headquarters."

Following the September 11, 2001, attacks in which terrorists flew airliners into the Pentagon and the World Trade Center, several members of the Bush administration said no one had ever imagined that terrorists would crash planes into buildings. "I don't think anybody could have predicted that these people would take an airplane and slam it into the World Trade Center, take another one and slam it into the Pentagon, that they would try to use an airplane as a missile," said Condoleezza Rice, Bush's national security adviser, on May 16, 2002. Two days later, on May 18, numerous media outlets reported on the existence of the 1999 document, prompting renewed calls in Congress for a full investigation of what the government knew before September 11. At a press briefing that day, White House press secretary Ari Fleischer said the administration had only learned of the report in the morning. He added that the document was "not a piece of intelligence information suggesting that we had information about a specific plan." The Library of Congress posted the full text of the report on its Web site on December 14, 2001.

> ***Following are excerpts from the executive summary of "The Sociology and Psychology of Terrorism: Who Becomes a Terrorist and Why," a report written by the Federal Research Division of the Library of Congress and published in September 1999:***

New Types of Post-Cold War Terrorists

...When the conventional terrorist groups and individuals of the early 1970s are compared with terrorists of the early 1990s, a trend can be seen: the emergence of religious fundamentalist and new religious groups espousing the rhetoric of mass-destruction terrorism. In the 1990s, groups motivated by religious imperatives, such as Aum Shinrikyo, Hizballah, and al-Qaida, have grown and proliferated. These groups have a different attitude toward violence—one that is extranormative and seeks to maximize violence against the perceived enemy, essentially anyone who is not a fundamentalist Muslim or an Aum Shinrikyo member. Their outlook is one that divides the world simplistically into "them" and "us." With its sarin attack on the Tokyo subway system on March 20, 1995, the doomsday cult Aum Shinrikyo turned the prediction of terrorists using WMD [weapons of mass destruction] into reality.

Beginning in the early 1990s, Aum Shinrikyo engaged in a systematic program to develop and use WMD. It used chemical or biological WMD in about a dozen largely unreported instances in the first half of the 1990s, although they proved to be no more effective—actually less effective—than conventional weapons because of the terrorists' ineptitude. Nevertheless, it was Aum Shinrikyo's sarin attack on the Tokyo subway on March 20, 1995, that showed the world how dangerous the mindset of a religious terrorist group could be. The attack provided convincing evidence that Aum Shinrikyo probably would not hesitate to use WMD in a U.S. city, if it had an opportunity to do so. These religiously motivated groups would have no reason to take "credit" for such an act of mass destruction, just as Aum Shinrikyo did not take credit for its attack on the Tokyo subway, and just as Osama bin Laden did not take credit for various acts of high-casualty terrorism against U.S. targets in the 1990s. Taking credit means asking for retaliation. Instead, it is enough for these groups to simply take private satisfaction in knowing that they have dealt a harsh blow to what they perceive to be the "Great Satan." Groups unlikely to be deterred by fear of public disapproval, such as Aum Shinrikyo, are the ones who seek chaos as an end in itself. . . .

New breeds of increasingly dangerous religious terrorists emerged in the 1990s. The most dangerous type is the Islamic fundamentalist. A case in point is Ramzi Yousef, who brought together a loosely organized, ad hoc group, the so-called Liberation Army, apparently for the sole purpose of carrying out the WTC [World Trade Center] operation on February 26, 1993. Moreover, by acting independently the small self-contained cell led by Yousef prevented authorities from linking it to an established terrorist organization, such as its suspected coordinating group, Osama bin Laden's al-Qaida, or a possible state sponsor. . . .

Aum Shinrikyo is representative of the other type of religious terrorist group, in this case a cult. Shoko Asahara adopted a different approach to terrorism by modeling his organization on the structure of the Japanese government rather than an ad hoc terrorist group. Accordingly, Aum Shinrikyo "ministers" undertook a program to develop WMD by bringing together a core group of bright scientists skilled in the modern technologies of the computer, telecommunications equipment, information databases, and financial networks. They proved themselves capable of developing rudimentary WMD in a relatively short time and demonstrated a willingness to use them in the most lethal ways possible. Aum Shinrikyo's sarin gas attack in the Tokyo subway system in 1995 marked the official debut of terrorism involving WMD. Had a more lethal batch of sarin been used, or had the dissemination procedure been improved slightly, the attack might have killed thousands of people, instead of only a few. Both of these incidents—the WTC bombing and the Tokyo subway sarin attack—had similar casualty totals but could have had massive casualties. Ramzi Yousef's plot to blow up the WTC might have killed an estimated 50,000 people had his team not made a minor error in the placement of the bomb. In any case, these two acts in Manhattan and Tokyo seem an ominous foretaste of the WMD terrorism to come in the first decade of the new millennium.

Increasingly, terrorist groups are recruiting members with expertise in fields such as communications, computer programming, engineering, finance, and the sciences. Ramzi Yousef graduated from Britain's Swansea University with a degree in engineering. Aum Shinrikyo's Shoko Asahara recruited a scientific team with all the expertise needed to develop WMD. Osama bin Laden also recruits highly skilled professionals in the fields of engineering, medicine, chemistry, physics, computer programming, communications, and so forth. Whereas the skills of the elite terrorist commandos of the 1960s and 1970s were often limited to what they learned in training camp, the terrorists of the 1990s who have carried out major operations have included biologists, chemists, computer specialists, engineers, and physicists.

New Forms of Terrorist-Threat Scenarios

The number of international terrorist incidents has declined in the 1990s, but the potential threat posed by terrorists has increased. The increased threat level, in the form of terrorist actions aimed at achieving a larger scale of destruction than the conventional attacks of the previous three decades of terrorism, was dramatically demonstrated with the bombing of the WTC. The WTC bombing illustrated how terrorists with technological sophistication are increasingly being recruited to carry out lethal terrorist bombing attacks. The WTC bombing may also have been a harbinger of more destructive attacks of international terrorism in the United States.

Although there are not too many examples, if any, of guerrilla groups dispatching commandos to carry out a terrorist operation in the United States, the mindsets of four groups discussed herein—two guerrilla/terrorist groups, a terrorist group, and a terrorist cult—are such that these groups pose particularly dangerous actual or potential terrorist threats to U.S. security interests. The two guerrilla/terrorist groups are the Liberation Tigers of Tamil Ealam (LTTE) and Hizballah, the terrorist group is al-Qaida, and the terrorist cult is Aum Shinrikyo.

The LTTE is not known to have engaged in anti-U.S. terrorism to date, but its suicide commandos have already assassinated a prime minister of India, a president of Sri Lanka, and a former prime minister of Sri Lanka. In August 1999, the LTTE reportedly deployed a 10-member suicide squad in Colombo to assassinate Prime Minister Chandrika Kumaratunga and others. It cannot be safely assumed, however, that the LTTE will restrict its terrorism to the South Asian subcontinent. [LTTE leader Velupillai] Prabhakaran has repeatedly warned the Western nations providing military support to Sri Lanka that they are exposing their citizens to possible attacks. The LTTE, which has an extensive international network, should not be underestimated in the terrorist threat that it could potentially pose to the United States, should it perceive this country as actively aiding the Sri Lankan government's counterinsurgency campaign. Prabhakaran is a megalomaniac whose record of ordering the assassinations of heads of state or former presidents, his meticulous planning of such actions, his compulsion to have the acts photographed and chronicled by LTTE members, and the limitless supply of female suicide commandos at his disposal add a dangerous new dimension to potential assassination threats. His highly trained and disciplined Black Tiger commandos are far more deadly than Aum Shinrikyo's inept cultists. There is little protection against the LTTE's trademark weapon: a belt-bomb suicide commando.

Hizballah is likewise quite dangerous. Except for its ongoing terrorist war against Israel, however, it appears to be reactive, often carrying out terrorist attacks for what it perceives to be Western military, cultural, or political threats to the establishment of an Iranian-style Islamic republic in Lebanon.

The threat to U.S. interests posed by Islamic fundamentalist terrorists in particular was underscored by al-Qaida's bombings of the U.S. Embassies in Kenya and Tanzania in August 1998. With those two devastating bombings, Osama bin Laden resurfaced as a potent terrorist threat to U.S. interests worldwide. Bin Laden is the prototype of a new breed of terrorist—the private entrepreneur who puts modern enterprise at the service of a global terrorist network.

With its sarin attack against the Tokyo subway system in March 1995, Aum

Shinrikyo has already used WMD, and very likely has not abandoned its quest to use such weapons to greater effect. The activities of Aum's large membership in Russia should be of particular concern because Aum Shinrikyo has used its Russian organization to try to obtain WMD, or at least WMD technologies.

The leaders of any of these groups—Prabhakaran, bin Laden, and Asahara—could become paranoid, desperate, or simply vengeful enough to order their suicide devotees to employ the belt-bomb technique against the leader of the Western World. Iranian intelligence leaders could order Hizballah to attack the U.S. leadership in retaliation for some future U.S. or Israeli action, although Iran may now be distancing itself from Hizballah. Whether or not a U.S. president would be a logical target of Asahara, Prabhakaran, or bin Laden is not a particularly useful guideline to assess the probability of such an attack. Indian Prime Minister Rajiv Gandhi was not a logical target for the LTTE, and his assassination had very negative consequences for the LTTE. In Prabhakaran's "psycho-logic," to use Post's term, he may conclude that his cause needs greater international attention, and targeting a country's top leaders is his way of getting attention. Nor does bin Laden need a logical reason, for he believes that he has a mandate from Allah to punish the "Great Satan." Instead of thinking logically, Asahara thinks in terms of a megalomaniac with an apocalyptic outlook. Aum Shinrikyo is a group whose delusional leader is genuinely paranoid about the United States and is known to have plotted to assassinate Japan's emperor. Shoko Asahara's cult is already on record for having made an assassination threat against President Clinton.

If Iran's mullahs or Iraq's Saddam Hussein decide to use terrorists to attack the continental United States, they would likely turn to bin Laden's al-Qaida. Al-Qaida is among the Islamic groups recruiting increasingly skilled professionals, such as computer and communications technicians, engineers, pharmacists, and physicists, as well as Ukrainian chemists and biologists, Iraqi chemical weapons experts, and others capable of helping to develop WMD. Al-Qaida poses the most serious terrorist threat to U.S. security interests, for al-Qaida's well-trained terrorists are actively engaged in a terrorist jihad against U.S. interests worldwide.

These four groups in particular are each capable of perpetrating a horrific act of terrorism in the United States, particularly on the occasion of the new millennium. Aum Shinrikyo has already threatened to use WMD in downtown Manhattan or in Washington, D.C., where it could attack the Congress, the Pentagon's Concourse, the White House, or President Clinton. The cult has threatened New York City with WMD, threatened to assassinate President Clinton, unsuccessfully attacked a U.S. naval base in Japan with biological weapons, and plotted in 1994 to attack the White House and the Pentagon with sarin and VX [a nerve gas]. If the LTTE's serial assassin of heads of state were to become angered by President Clinton, Prabhakaran could react by dispatching a Tamil "belt-bomb girl" to detonate a powerful semtex bomb after approaching the President in a crowd with a garland of flowers or after jumping next to his car.

Al-Qaida's expected retaliation for the U.S. cruise missile attack against al-Qaida's training facilities in Afghanistan on August 20, 1998, could take several forms of terrorist attack in the nation's capital. Al-Qaida could detonate a Chechen-type building-buster bomb at a federal building. Suicide bomber(s) belonging to al-Qaida's Martyrdom Battalion could crash-land an aircraft packed with high explosives (C-4 and semtex) into the Pentagon, the headquarters of the Central Intelligence Agency (CIA), or the White House. Ramzi Yousef had planned to do this against the CIA headquarters. In addition, both al-Qaida and Yousef were linked to a plot to assassinate President Clinton during his visit to the Philippines in early 1995. Following the August 1998 cruise missile attack, at least one Islamic religious leader called for Clinton's assassination, and another stated that "the time is not far off" for when the White House will be destroyed by a nuclear bomb. A horrendous scenario consonant with al-Qaida's mindset would be its use of a nuclear suitcase bomb against any number of targets in the nation's capital. Bin Laden allegedly has already purchased a number of nuclear suitcase bombs from the Chechen Mafia. Al-Qaida's retaliation, however, is more likely to take the lower-risk form of bombing one or more U.S. airliners with time-bombs. Yousef was planning simultaneous bombings of 11 U.S. airliners prior to his capture. Whatever form an attack may take, bin Laden will most likely retaliate in a spectacular way for the cruise missile attack against his Afghan camp in August 1998. . . .

As of July 2, 2002, the full text of the report was available at http://www.loc.gov/rr/frd/Sociology-Psychology%20of%20Terrorism.htm

REPORT ON U.S. VULNERABILITY TO TERRORIST ATTACKS
September 15, 1999

The numerous terrorist attacks in the 1990s on the United States and its interests—including the 1993 bombing of the World Trade Center, the 1995 bombing of the federal building in Oklahoma City, and the 1996 bombing in Saudi Arabia of an apartment building housing American military personnel—made it clear that the definition of "national security" was changing as the twentieth century came to an end. During the cold war, American military power was so strong that it deterred other countries from attacking the United States. But as the twentieth century ended, the greatest threat to national security did not necessarily come from other nations attacking with conventional armies.

In a look forward to the first quarter of the twenty-first century, the United States Commission on National Security/21st Century came to a chilling conclusion in a report released September 15, 1999: "America will become increasingly vulnerable to hostile attack on our homeland, and our military superiority will not entirely protect us." The panel, appointed by the Department of Defense and consisting of influential Washington insiders and national security experts from both parties, was chaired by former senators Gary Hart, D-Colo., and Warren Rudman, R-N.H. One of the biggest threats to the United States in the twenty-first century, the commission said, would come from terrorists or other groups that acquired biological, chemical, or nuclear weapons. "States, terrorists, and other disaffected groups will acquire weapons of mass destruction and mass disruption, and some will use them," the commission said. "Americans will likely die on American soil, possibly in large numbers."

As the twentieth century closed, national security officials were slowly shifting some of their attention to the types of threats outlined in the commission's report. That shift roared forward following the September 11, 2001, terrorist attacks on the World Trade Center and the Pentagon that killed more than 3,000 people.

*Following are excerpts from the "Major Themes and Impli-
cations" section of "New World Coming: American Security
in the 21st Century," a report issued September 15, 1999,
by the United States Commission on National Security/
21st Century:*

1. America will become increasingly vulnerable to hostile attack on our homeland, and our military superiority will not entirely protect us.

The United States will be both absolutely and relatively stronger than any other state or combination of states. Although a global competitor to the United States is unlikely to arise over the next 25 years, emerging powers— either singly or in coalition—will increasingly constrain U.S. options regionally and limit its strategic influence. As a result, we will remain limited in our ability to impose our will, and we will be vulnerable to an increasing range of threats against American forces and citizens overseas as well as at home. American influence will increasingly be both embraced and resented abroad, as U.S. cultural, economic, and political power persists and perhaps spreads. States, terrorists, and other disaffected groups will acquire weapons of mass destruction and mass disruption, and some will use them. Americans will likely die on American soil, possibly in large numbers.

2. Rapid advances in information and biotechnologies will create new vulnerabilities for U.S. security.

Governments or groups hostile to the United States and its interests will gain access to advanced technologies. They will seek to counter U.S. military advantages through the possession of these technologies and their actual use in non-traditional attacks. . . .

3. New technologies will divide the world as well as draw it together.

In the next century people around the world in both developed and developing countries will be able to communicate with each other almost instantaneously. New technologies will increase productivity and create a transnational cyberclass of people. We will see much greater mobility and emigration among educated elites from less to more developed societies. We will be increasingly deluged by information, and have less time to process and interpret it. We will learn to cure illnesses, prolong and enrich life, and routinely clone it, but at the same time, advances in biotechnology will create moral dilemmas. An anti-technology backlash is possible, and even likely, as the adoption of emerging technologies creates new moral, cultural, and economic divisions.

4. The national security of all advanced states will be increasingly affected by the vulnerabilities of the evolving global economic infrastructure.

The economic future will be more difficult to predict and to manage. The emergence or strengthening of significant global economic actors will cause realignments of economic power. Global changes in the next quarter-century will produce opportunities and vulnerabilities. Overall global economic growth will continue, albeit unevenly. At the same time, economic integration and fragmentation will co-exist. Serious and unexpected economic downturns, major disparities of wealth, volatile capital flows, increasing vulnerabilities in global electronic infrastructures, labor and social disruptions, and pressures for increased protectionism will also occur. . . .

5. Energy will continue to have major strategic significance.

Although energy distribution and consumption patterns will shift, we are unlikely to see dramatic changes in energy technology on a world scale in the next quarter century. Demand for fossil fuel will increase as major developing economies grow, increasing most rapidly in Asia. American dependence on foreign sources of energy will also grow over the next two decades. In the absence of events that alter significantly the price of oil, the stability of the world oil market will continue to depend on an uninterrupted supply of oil from the Persian Gulf, and the location of all key fossil fuel deposits will retain geopolitical significance.

6. All borders will be more porous; some will bend and some will break.

New technologies will continue to stretch and strain all existing borders—physical and social. Citizens will communicate with and form allegiances to individuals or movements anywhere in the world. Traditional bonds between states and their citizens can no longer be taken for granted, even in the United States. Many countries will have difficulties keeping dangers out of their territories, but their governments will still be committed to upholding the integrity of their borders. Global connectivity will allow "big ideas" to spread quickly around the globe. Some ideas may be religious in nature, some populist, some devoted to democracy and human rights. . . .

7. The sovereignty of states will come under pressure, but will endure.

The international system will wrestle constantly over the next quarter century to establish the proper balance between fealty to the state on the one hand, and the impetus to build effective transnational institutions on the other. This struggle will be played out in the debate over international institutions to regulate financial markets, international policing and peace-making agencies, as well as several other shared global problems. Nevertheless, global forces, especially economic ones, will continue to batter the concept of national sovereignty. The state, as we know it, will also face challenges to its sovereignty under the mandate of evolving international law and by disaffected groups, including terrorists and criminals. Nonetheless, the principle of national sovereignty will endure, albeit in changed forms.

8. Fragmentation or failure of states will occur, with destabilizing effects on neighboring states.

Global and regional dynamics will normally bind states together, but events in major countries will still drive whether the world is peaceful or violent. States will differ in their ability to seize technological and economic opportunities, establish the social and political infrastructure necessary for economic growth, build political institutions responsive to the aspirations of their citizens, and find the leadership necessary to guide them through an era of uncertainty and risk. Some important states may not be able to manage these challenges and could fragment or fail. The result will be an increase in the rise of suppressed nationalisms, ethnic or religious violence, humanitarian disasters, major catalytic regional crises, and the spread of dangerous weapons.

9. Foreign crises will be replete with atrocities and the deliberate terrorizing of civilian populations.

Interstate wars will occur over the next 25 years, but most violence will erupt from conflicts internal to current territorial states. As the desire for self-determination spreads, and many governments fail to adapt to new economic and social realities, minorities will be less likely to tolerate bad or prejudicial government. In consequence, the number of new states, international protectorates, and zones of autonomy will increase, and many will be born in violence. The major powers will struggle to devise an accountable and effective institutional response to such crises.

10. Space will become a critical and competitive military environment.

The U.S. use of space for military purposes will expand, but other countries will also learn to exploit space for both commercial and military purposes. . . .

11. The essence of war will not change.

Despite the proliferation of highly sophisticated and remote means of attack, the essence of war will remain the same. There will be casualties, carnage, and death; it will not be like a video game. What will change will be the kinds of actors and the weapons available to them. While some societies will attempt to limit violence and damage, others will seek to maximize them, particularly against those societies with a lower tolerance for casualties.

12. U.S. intelligence will face more challenging adversaries, and even excellent intelligence will not prevent all surprises.

Micro-sensors and electronic communications will continue to expand intelligence collection capabilities around the world. As a result of the proliferation of other technologies, however, many countries and disaffected groups will develop techniques of denial and deception in an attempt to thwart U.S.

283

intelligence efforts—despite U.S. technological superiority. In any event, the United States will continue to confront strategic shocks, as intelligence analysis and human judgments will fail to detect all dangers in an ever-changing world.

13. The United States will be called upon frequently to intervene militarily in a time of uncertain alliances and with the prospect of fewer forward-deployed forces.

Political changes abroad, economic considerations, and the increased vulnerability of U.S. bases around the world will increase pressures on the United States to reduce substantially its forward military presence in Europe and Asia. In dealing with security crises, the 21st century will be characterized more by episodic "posses of the willing" than the traditional World War II-style alliance systems. The United States will increasingly find itself wishing to form coalitions but increasingly unable to find partners willing and able to carry out combined military operations.

14. The emerging security environment in the next quarter century will require different military and other national capabilities.

The United States must act together with its allies to shape the future of the international environment, using all the instruments of American diplomatic, economic, and military power. The type of conflict in which this country will generally engage in the first quarter of the 21st century will require sustainable military capabilities characterized by stealth, speed, range, unprecedented accuracy, lethality, strategic mobility, superior intelligence, and the overall will and ability to prevail. It is essential to maintain U.S. technological superiority, despite the unavoidable tension between acquisition of advanced capabilities and the maintenance of current capabilities. The mix and effectiveness of overall American capabilities need to be rethought and adjusted, and substantial changes in non-military national capabilities will also be needed. Discriminating and hard choices will be required.

Seeking an American National Security Strategy

In many respects, the world ahead seems amenable to basic American interests and values. A world pried open by the information revolution is a world less hospitable to tyranny and more friendly to human liberty. A more prosperous world is, on balance, a world more conducive to democracy and less tolerant of fatalism and the dour dogmas that often attend it. A less socially rigid, freer, and self-regulating world also accords with our deepest political beliefs and our central political metaphors—the checks and balances of our Constitution, the "invisible hand" of the market, our social creed of E Pluribus Unum, and the concept of federalism itself.

Nevertheless, a world amenable to our interests and values will not come into being by itself. Much of the world will resent and oppose us, if not for . . . our preeminence, then for the fact that others often perceive the United States as exercising its power with arrogance and self-absorption. There will also be much apprehension and confusion as the world changes. National leaderships will have their hands full, and some will make mistakes.

As a result, for many years to come Americans will become increasingly less secure, and much less secure than they now believe themselves to be. That is because many of the threats emerging in our future will differ significantly from those of the past, not only in their physical but also in their psychological effects. . . .

As of June 29, 2002, the full text of the report was available at http://www.nssg.gov/Reports/New_World_Coming/new_world_coming.htm

UN THREATENS SANCTIONS AGAINST TALIBAN
October 15, 1999

President Bill Clinton signed an executive order July 4, 1999, imposing economic sanctions against the Taliban rulers of Afghanistan because they continued to harbor accused terrorist Osama bin Laden. U.S. officials next sought broad international support for their efforts to persuade the Taliban to expel bin Laden so he could face trial for the 1998 bombings of U.S. embassies in Kenya and Tanzania. (Clinton Order Blocks Trade with the Taliban, p. 271)

On October 15, 1999, the fifteen-member United Nations Security Council unanimously approved a resolution demanding that the Taliban turn over bin Laden, who had lived in Afghanistan since 1996. If the Taliban did not act within thirty days, the resolution ordered countries around the world to impose limited economic sanctions. These included freezing all Taliban funds and other assets, barring investments that could benefit the Taliban, and banning international flights by planes controlled by the strict Islamic movement. To the surprise of some diplomats, the two Islamic nations on the Security Council—Bahrain and Malaysia—voted in favor of the measure.

The sanctions took effect in November when Taliban leaders refused to oust bin Laden. "We will never hand over Osama bin Laden, and we will not force him out," the Taliban's foreign minister was quoted as saying by the Washington Post. *"He will remain free in defiance of America. . . . We will not hand him to an infidel nation." Crowds angry about the sanctions attacked UN humanitarian relief offices throughout Afghanistan. A year later, after the UN withdrew all its aid workers from the country because of fears for their safety, the Security Council passed a resolution December 19, 2000, imposing new sanctions on the Taliban, including an arms embargo. The Taliban continued ignoring the UN resolutions and were driven from power after the United States and Great Britain invaded Afghanistan in October 2001. But bin Laden and most of his al Qaeda followers managed to escape during the fighting.* (United States, Britain Launch War in Afghanistan, p. 366)

Following is the text of Resolution 1267, which the United Nations Security Council adopted October 15, 1999:

The Security Council,

Reaffirming its previous resolutions, in particular resolutions 1189 (1998) of 13 August 1998, 1193 (1998) of 28 August 1998 and 1214 (1998) of 8 December 1998, and the statements of its President on the situation in Afghanistan,

Reaffirming its strong commitment to the sovereignty, independence, territorial integrity and national unity of Afghanistan, and its respect for Afghanistan's cultural and historical heritage,

Reiterating its deep concern over the continuing violations of international humanitarian law and of human rights, particularly discrimination against women and girls, and over the significant rise in the illicit production of opium, and stressing that the capture by the Taliban of the Consulate-General of the Islamic Republic of Iran and the murder of Iranian diplomats and a journalist in Mazar-e-Sharif constituted flagrant violations of established international law,

Recalling the relevant international counter-terrorism conventions and in particular the obligations of parties to those conventions to extradite or prosecute terrorists,

Strongly condemning the continuing use of Afghan territory, especially areas controlled by the Taliban, for the sheltering and training of terrorists and planning of terrorist acts, and *reaffirming* its conviction that the suppression of international terrorism is essential for the maintenance of international peace and security,

Deploring the fact that the Taliban continues to provide safe haven to Usama bin Laden and to allow him and others associated with him to operate a network of terrorist training camps from Taliban-controlled territory and to use Afghanistan as a base from which to sponsor international terrorist operations,

Noting the indictment of Usama bin Laden and his associates by the United States of America for, *inter alia*, the 7 August 1998 bombings of the United States embassies in Nairobi, Kenya, and Dar es Salaam, Tanzania and for conspiring to kill American nationals outside the United States, and noting also the request of the United States of America to the Taliban to surrender them for trial (S/1999/1021),

Determining that the failure of the Taliban authorities to respond to the demands in paragraph 13 of resolution 1214 (1998) constitutes a threat to international peace and security,

Stressing its determination to ensure respect for its resolutions,

Acting under Chapter VII of the Charter of the United Nations,

1. *Insists* that the Afghan faction known as the Taliban, which also calls itself the Islamic Emirate of Afghanistan, comply promptly with its previous resolutions and in particular cease the provision of sanctuary and

training for international terrorists and their organizations, take appropriate effective measures to ensure that the territory under its control is not used for terrorist installations and camps, or for the preparation or organization of terrorist acts against other States or their citizens, and cooperate with efforts to bring indicted terrorists to justice;

2. *Demands* that the Taliban turn over Usama bin Laden without further delay to appropriate authorities in a country where he has been indicted, or to appropriate authorities in a country where he will be returned to such a country, or to appropriate authorities in a country where he will be arrested and effectively brought to justice;

3. *Decides* that on 14 November 1999 all States shall impose the measures set out in paragraph 4 below, unless the Council has previously decided, on the basis of a report of the Secretary-General, that the Taliban has fully complied with the obligation set out in paragraph 2 above;

4. *Decides further* that, in order to enforce paragraph 2 above, all States shall:

   (a) Deny permission for any aircraft to take off from or land in their territory if it is owned, leased or operated by or on behalf of the Taliban as designated by the Committee established by paragraph 6 below, unless the particular flight has been approved in advance by the Committee on the grounds of humanitarian need, including religious obligation such as the performance of the Hajj;

   (b) Freeze funds and other financial resources, including funds derived or generated from property owned or controlled directly or indirectly by the Taliban, or by any undertaking owned or controlled by the Taliban, as designated by the Committee established by paragraph 6 below, and ensure that neither they nor any other funds or financial resources so designated are made available, by their nationals or by any persons within their territory, to or for the benefit of the Taliban or any undertaking owned or controlled, directly or indirectly, by the Taliban, except as may be authorized by the Committee on a case-by-case basis on the grounds of humanitarian need;

5. *Urges* all States to cooperate with efforts to fulfill the demand in paragraph 2 above, and to consider further measures against Usama bin Laden and his associates;

6. *Decides* to establish, in accordance with rule 28 of its provisional rules of procedure, a Committee of the Security Council consisting of all the members of the Council to undertake the following tasks and to report on its work to the Council with its observations and recommendations:

   (a) To seek from all States further information regarding the action taken by them with a view to effectively implementing the measures imposed by paragraph 4 above;

   (b) To consider information brought to its attention by States concerning violations of the measures imposed by paragraph 4 above and to recommend appropriate measures in response thereto;

(c) To make periodic reports to the Council on the impact, including the humanitarian implications, of the measures imposed by paragraph 4 above;

(d) To make periodic reports to the Council on information submitted to it regarding alleged violations of the measures imposed by paragraph 4 above, identifying where possible persons or entities reported to be engaged in such violations;

(e) To designate the aircraft and funds or other financial resources referred to in paragraph 4 above in order to facilitate the implementation of the measures imposed by that paragraph;

(f) To consider requests for exemptions from the measures imposed by paragraph 4 above as provided in that paragraph, and to decide on the granting of an exemption to these measures in respect of the payment by the International Air Transport Association (IATA) to the aeronautical authority of Afghanistan on behalf of international airlines for air traffic control services;

(g) To examine the reports submitted pursuant to paragraph 9 below;

7. *Calls upon* all States to act strictly in accordance with the provisions of this resolution, notwithstanding the existence of any rights or obligations conferred or imposed by any international agreement or any contract entered into or any licence or permit granted prior to the date of coming into force of the measures imposed by paragraph 4 above;

8. *Calls upon* States to bring proceedings against persons and entities within their jurisdiction that violate the measures imposed by paragraph 4 above and to impose appropriate penalties;

9. *Calls upon* all States to cooperate fully with the Committee established by paragraph 6 above in the fulfillment of its tasks, including supplying such information as may be required by the Committee in pursuance of this resolution;

10. *Requests* all States to report to the Committee established by paragraph 6 above within 30 days of the coming into force of the measures imposed by paragraph 4 above on the steps they have taken with a view to effectively implementing paragraph 4 above;

11. *Requests* the Secretary-General to provide all necessary assistance to the Committee established by paragraph 6 above and to make the necessary arrangements in the Secretariat for this purpose;

12. *Requests* the Committee established by paragraph 6 above to determine appropriate arrangements, on the basis of recommendations of the Secretariat, with competent international organizations, neighbouring and other States, and parties concerned with a view to improving the monitoring of the implementation of the measures imposed by paragraph 4 above;

13. *Requests* the Secretariat to submit for consideration by the Committee established by paragraph 6 above information received from Governments and public sources on possible violations of the measures imposed by paragraph 4 above;

14. *Decides* to terminate the measures imposed by paragraph 4 above once the Secretary-General reports to the Security Council that the Taliban has fulfilled the obligation set out in paragraph 2 above;
15. *Expresses* its readiness to consider the imposition of further measures, in accordance with its responsibility under the Charter of the United Nations, with the aim of achieving the full implementation of this resolution;
16. *Decides* to remain actively seized of the matter.

GAO ON THREATS POSED BY WEAPONS OF MASS DESTRUCTION
October 20, 1999

In an April 1996 look at the various groups that might obtain and use chemical, biological, or nuclear weapons, the U.S. Department of Defense (DoD) concluded that terrorists posed the greatest threat to the United States. The DoD said most terrorist groups lacked the money and technical skill needed to acquire nuclear weapons, but it warned that they could make "dirty bombs" that dispersed radiation and could build some types of chem-ical and biological weapons. (The Proliferation of Weapons of Mass Destruc-tion, p. 193)

More than three years later, however, a senior official at the General Ac-counting Office testified before Congress that terrorist groups would have great difficulties creating and using biological weapons—unless they had lots of help from a nation that sponsored terrorism. On October 20, 1999, Assistant Comptroller General Henry L. Hinton Jr. told Congress that ter-rorists would have to overcome "significant technical and operational chal-lenges" to make and release large enough quantities of chemical or biological agents to inflict mass casualties.

In a report less than two months later, the Congressional Research Service said a number of factors had previously constrained terrorist use of biologi-cal, chemical, and nuclear weapons. "However, the increasing casualty count of terrorist attacks is a cause of worry," the report said, "and some have ar-gued that the growing fanaticism and erosion of traditional constraints may lead to a departure from pragmatic calculations and override the stigma attached to use of WMD [weapons of mass destruction]. As a consequence, although WMD terrorism remains rare, the Central Intelligence Agency es-timates that terrorist interest in WMD is growing, as is the number of po-tential perpetrators." The report closed by noting that Osama bin Laden had been seeking biological, chemical, and nuclear weapons for years, and that his "motivation to use weapons of mass destruction appears unmistakable."

Following are excerpts from testimony by Henry L. Hinton Jr., assistant comptroller general at the General Accounting

Office, before the Subcommittee on National Security, Veterans Affairs, and International Relations of the House Committee on Government Reform on October 20, 1999:

Summary

According to the experts we consulted, in most cases terrorists would have to overcome significant technical and operational challenges to successfully make and release chemical or biological agents of sufficient quality and quantity to kill or injure large numbers of people without substantial assistance from a state sponsor. With the exception of toxic industrial chemicals such as chlorine, specialized knowledge is required in the manufacturing process and in improvising an effective delivery device for most chemical and nearly all biological agents that could be used in terrorist attacks. Moreover, some of the required components of chemical agents and highly infective strains of biological agents are difficult to obtain. Finally, terrorists may have to overcome other obstacles for a successful attack, such as unfavorable environmental conditions and personal safety risks.

The President's fiscal year 2000 budget proposes $10 billion for counterterrorism programs—an increase of more than $3 billion over the requested funding of $6.7 billion for fiscal year 1999. To assess whether the government is spending appropriate levels on counterterrorism and spending these funds on the most appropriate programs, policymakers need the best estimates of the specific threats the U.S. faces. The intelligence community has recently produced estimates of the foreign-origin terrorist threat involving chemical and biological weapons. However, the intelligence community has not produced comparable estimates of the domestic threat. In our report we recommended that the FBI prepare these estimates and use them in a national-level risk assessment that can be used to identify and prioritize the most effective programs to combat terrorism. The FBI agreed.

Production and Delivery of Chemical and Biological Agents Generally Requires Specialized Knowledge

Terrorists face serious technical and operational challenges at different stages of the process of producing and delivering most chemical and all biological agents. The Special Assistant to the Director of Central Intelligence for Nonproliferation testified in March 1999 that "the preparation and effective use of BW [biological weapons] by both potentially hostile states and by non-state actors, including terrorists, is harder than some popular literature seems to suggest." We agree. A number of obstacles exist for terrorists. . . .

Some chemical agents are commercially available and require little sophistication or expertise to obtain or use, but other chemical agents are technically challenging to make and deliver. Toxic industrial chemicals such as chlorine, phosgene, and hydrogen cyanide are used in commercial manufacturing and could be easily acquired and adapted as terrorist weapons. In contrast, most chemical nerve agents such as tabun (GA), sarin (GB), soman (GD), and VX are difficult to produce. To begin with, developing nerve agents requires the synthesis of multiple chemicals that, according to the experts we consulted, are very difficult to obtain in large quantities due to the provisions of the 1993 Chemical Weapons Convention, which has been in force since April 1997. In addition, a 1993 Office of Technology Assessment report on the technologies underlying weapons of mass destruction indicated that some steps in the production process of these nerve agents are difficult and hazardous. For example, although tabun is one of the easier chemical agents to make, containment of the highly toxic hydrogen cyanide gas that is produced during the process is a technical challenge. In general, production of chemical nerve agents could be technically unfeasible for terrorists without a sophisticated laboratory infrastructure because their production requires the use of high temperatures and generates corrosive and dangerous by-products. On the other hand, chemical blister agents such as sulfur mustard, nitrogen mustard, and lewisite can be manufactured with little to moderate difficulty; but again, according to experts, purchasing large quantities of certain chemicals needed to make blister agents is difficult due to the Chemical Weapons Convention. Even if chemical agents can be produced successfully, they must be released effectively as a vapor, or aerosol, for inhalation exposure, or they need to be in a spray of large droplets or liquid for skin penetration. To serve as terrorist weapons, chemical agents require high toxicity and volatility (tendency of a chemical to vaporize), and need to maintain their strength during storage and release.

Causing mass casualties with biological agents also presents extraordinary technical and operational challenges for terrorists without the assistance of a state-sponsored program. For example, highly infectious seed stock for nearly all biological agents is difficult to obtain, particularly since controls over the stocks have improved. The only known sources of the smallpox virus, for example, are within government-controlled facilities in the United States and Russia. Ricin, a biological toxin, is easy to obtain and produce but requires such large quantities to cause mass casualties that the risk of arousing suspicion or detection prior to dissemination would be great.

Although most biological agents are easy to grow if the seed stock can be obtained, they are difficult to process into a lethal form and successfully deliver to achieve large scale casualties. Processing biological agents into the right particle size and delivering them effectively requires expertise in a wide range of scientific disciplines. Since the most effective way to deliver a biological agent is by aerosol (to allow the simultaneous respiratory infection of a large number of people), the particles need to be small enough to reach the small air sacs in the lungs and bypass the body's natural filtering and defense mechanisms. Terrorists can try to process biological agents into liquid or dry forms for release, but both forms pose difficult technical challenges. Experts told us that although liquid agents are easy to produce, it is difficult to effectively deliver them in the right particle size without reducing the strength of the mixture. Further, a liquid agent requires larger quantities, which can increase the possibility of raising suspicion and detection. Dry biological agents are easier to deliver, but they are more difficult to manufacture than liquid agents, are less stable, and are dangerous to work with. Other important technical hurdles include obtaining the right equipment to generate properly sized aerosols, calculating the correct output rate (i.e., speed at which the equipment operates), and having the required liquid composition.

Terrorists have additional hurdles to overcome. For example, outdoor delivery of chemical and biological agents can be disrupted by environmental (e.g., pollution) and meteorological (e.g., sun, rain, mist, and wind) conditions. Once released, an aerosol cloud gradually dissipates over time and as a result of exposure to oxygen, pollutants, and ultraviolet rays. If wind conditions are too erratic or strong, the agent might dissipate too rapidly or fail to reach the desired area. Indoor dissemination of an agent could be affected by the air exchange rate of the building. In addition, terrorists risk capture and personal safety in acquiring and processing materials, disposing byproducts, and releasing the agent. Many agents are dangerous to handle. In some cases the lack of an effective vaccine, antibiotic/antiviral treatment, or antidote poses the same risk to the terrorist as it does to a targeted population.

National-Level Assessment of the Risk of Chemical and Biological Terrorism Is Needed to Focus Resources

A national-level assessment of the risk of chemical and biological terrorism, based on analyses of both the foreign- and domestic-origin threats, could help determine the requirements and priorities for combating terrorism and target resources where most needed. Much of the intelligence information that can be incorporated into a national-level risk assessment already exists. The U.S. foreign intelligence community has issued classified National Intelligence Estimates and Intelligence Community Assessments that discuss the foreign-origin chemical and biological terrorist threat in some detail. These intelligence assessments identify the agents that would more likely be used by foreign-origin terrorists.

The FBI is responsible for assessing domestic-origin threats. However, FBI analysts' judgments concerning the more likely chemical and biological agents that may be used by domestic-origin terrorists have not been captured in a formal assessment. The FBI has not specified or ranked individual chemical or biological agents as threats, but instead ranked groups of agents according to the likelihood that a category of chemical or biological agent would be used. The FBI analysis was based on law enforcement cases where chemical or biological agents were used or their use was threatened, including hoaxes. . . .

By combining an FBI estimate of the domestic-origin threat with existing intelligence estimates and assessments of the foreign-origin threat, analysts could provide policymakers with a better understanding of the threat from terrorists' use of chemical or biological weapons. A national-level risk assessment based in part on the threat estimates would better enable federal agencies to establish soundly defined program requirements and prioritize and focus the nation's investments to combat terrorism. For example, in March 1999 we testified that the Department of Health and Human Services is establishing a national pharmaceutical and vaccine stockpile to prepare medical responses for possible terrorist use of chemical or biological weapons. We pointed out that the Department's effort was initiated without the benefit of a sound threat and risk assessment process. We also found that some of the items the Department plans to procure do not match intelligence agencies' judgments of the more likely chemical and biological agents that terrorists might use and seem to be based on worst-case scenarios. We questioned whether stockpiling for the items listed in the Department's plan was the best approach for investing in medical preparedness. . . .

As of June 28, 2002, the full text of the testimony was available at http://www.gao.gov/archive/2000/ns00050t.pdf

CLINTON GRANTS CLEMENCY TO PUERTO RICAN TERRORISTS
September 21 and December 10, 1999

When President Jimmy Carter commuted the prison sentences of four Puerto Rican terrorists in 1979, there was little public reaction. But when President Bill Clinton offered clemency to sixteen Puerto Rican terrorists in August 1999, a storm of controversy erupted. The sixteen were members of two allied groups—Los Macheteros and the Armed Forces for National Liberation, commonly known by its Spanish initials FALN—that sought independence for Puerto Rico, a commonwealth of the United States. Law enforcement officials blamed the FALN for a wave of more than 130 bombings in the 1970s and 1980s that killed six people, wounded eighty, and caused more than $3.5 million in damage in New York, Chicago, Washington, D.C., and other cities. The sixteen terrorists had been convicted of crimes such as seditious conspiracy, possession of an unregistered firearm, interstate transportation of firearms with intent to commit a crime, and interstate transportation of a stolen vehicle, and they had received sentences ranging from thirty-five to ninety years in jail. By the time Clinton offered them clemency, most of the prisoners had served nineteen years. (President Carter Commutes Sentences for 1950s Attacks, p. 32)

In response to harsh criticism of his offer from both Democratic and Republican members of Congress, Clinton on September 21, 1999, sent a letter to Rep. Henry Waxman, D-Calif., saying he offered clemency because the prisoners' sentences "were out of proportion to their crimes." He said the sixteen "were not convicted of crimes involving the killing or maiming of any individuals," and noted that he had received letters requesting their release on humanitarian grounds from Carter, South African Archbishop Desmond Tutu, Coretta Scott King, Cardinal John O'Connor of the Archdiocese of New York, and many others. Critics, on the other hand, charged that Clinton made the offers to help his wife, Hillary, win New York's large Puerto Rican vote when she ran for senator in the state the following year. They also noted that every federal law enforcement agency that was asked to review the clemency petition—including the Federal Bureau of Investigation, the Bureau of Prisons, and United States Attorneys in Illinois and

Connecticut—strongly opposed it. The Senate passed a nonbinding resolution condemning the offer by a 95–2 vote, and the House passed a similar measure 311–41. Three congressional committees conducted investigations, and at one hearing Neil Gallagher, assistant director of national security for the FBI, said of the sixteen: "These are criminals and they are terrorists and they represent a threat to the United States." In December the House Committee on Government Reform issued a report saying the White House repeatedly misrepresented facts during the clemency controversy.

Fourteen of those offered clemency accepted it. Eleven were released from prison immediately, one had to serve five more years before being paroled, and two who had previously been released had their outstanding fines eliminated. Those who received clemency had to agree to renounce violence, to end their relationships with the FALN, and to never associate with one another. Two of the FALN prisoners rejected the deal.

Following are excerpts from a letter sent by President Bill Clinton to Rep. Henry Waxman on September 21, 1999, and from a report by the House Government Reform Committee released December 10, 1999:

PRESIDENT CLINTON'S LETTER

. . . For the last six years various Members of Congress, religious and civic leaders, as well as others have urged me to grant clemency to a group of Puerto Rican prisoners, most of whom have been in prison between 16 and 19 years as a result of convictions for offenses arising out of their participation in organizations supporting Puerto Rican independence.

The question of clemency for these prisoners was a very difficult one. I did what I believe equity and fairness dictated. I certainly understand, however, that other people could review the same facts I did and arrive at a different decision. In making my decision, I did not minimize the serious criminal conduct in which these men and women engaged. I recognize and appreciate that there are victims of FALN-related violence who feel strongly that these individuals, although not directly convicted of crimes involving bodily harm to anyone, should serve the full sentences imposed.

Before making my decision, I sought and considered the views of the Department of Justice. Press reports note that certain Federal Bureau of Investigation and Justice Department officials, including the U.S. Attorneys in Chicago and Connecticut, were opposed to clemency. I did not dismiss those concerns as some have implied. Rather, I carefully weighed them in making this difficult decision.

On the other hand, the prisoners were serving extremely lengthy sentences—in some cases, 90 years—which were out of proportion to their crimes. (In contrast, Jose Solis Jordan, who was prosecuted and convicted in July in Chicago of conspiring to place explosive devices at a Marine recruiting center, received a sentence of 51 months.)

The petitioners received worldwide support on humanitarian grounds from numerous quarters. President Jimmy Carter wrote in 1997 that granting clemency to these men and women "would be a significant humanitarian gesture and would be viewed as such by much of the international community, a concern that was relevant in 1979 and I believe is today."

He noted that each individual had "spent many years in prison and no legitimate deterrent or correctional purpose is served by continuing their incarceration. . . ."

Bishop Tutu and Coretta Scott King all wrote to seek clemency for the petitioners since they had received "virtual life sentences" and "have spent over a decade in prison while their children have grown up without them."

In addition, various Members of Congress, a number of religious organizations, labor organizations, human rights groups and Hispanic civic and community groups supported clemency. The petitioners also received widespread support across the political spectrum within Puerto Rico.

We have recently provided Congress more than 14,000 pages of materials that the White House received in connection with this clemency matter, including thousands of letters seeking clemency for the prisoners. Many of those who supported unconditional clemency for the prisoners argued that they were political prisoners who acted out of sincere political beliefs. I rejected this argument. No form of violence is ever justified as a means of political expression in a democratic society based on the rule of law.

Our society believes, however, that a punishment should fit the crime. Whatever the conduct of other FALN members may have been, these petitioners, while convicted of serious crimes, were not convicted of crimes involving the killing or maiming of any individuals. For me the question, therefore, was whether the prisoners' sentences were unduly severe and whether their continuing incarceration served any meaningful purpose. I considered clemency for each of them on an individual basis. . . .

The timing of my decision was dictated by the fact that my former counsel, Charles Ruff, committed to many of those interested in this issue that he would consult with the Department of Justice and make a recommendation to me before he left the counsel position. Pursuant to this commitment, I received his recommendation in early August. As he recently indicated to the *New York Times*, his recommendation and my decision were based on our view of the merits of the requests—political considerations played no role in the process.

As you know, last week I asserted executive privilege in the face of Chairman Burton's subpoena seeking memoranda and testimony concerning the decision process. I did so after receiving the opinion of the Attorney General that such assertion was proper, as the demand clearly intruded on areas reserved to the President under the Constitution.

Grants of clemency generate passionate views. In vesting the pardon power in the President alone, the framers of our Constitution ensured that clemency could be given even in cases that might be unpopular or controversial. The history of our country is full of examples of clemency with which many disagreed, sometimes fervently. When Theodore Roosevelt granted amnesty to Filipino nationals who attempted to overthrow U.S. control of the Philippines, when Harry Truman commuted the death sentence of Oscar Collazo, and when Jimmy Carter commuted the sentence of Collazo and other Puerto Rican nationalists who had fired upon the House of Representatives, they exercised the power vested them by the Constitution to do what they believed was right even in the face of great controversy. I have done the same. . . .

Government Reform Committee Report

. . . Some Within the White House Saw Political Benefit in the Release of these Terrorists. One of the key White House staff members during the clemency process wrote that the release of the sixteen terrorists would "have a positive impact among strategic Puerto Rican communities in the U.S. (read, voters)." Other notes produced to the Committee indicate that White House personnel believed that certain Congressmen would not vote with the President unless he committed to releasing the terrorists. Jeffrey Farrow, a key Presidential adviser on this issue, wrote in an e-mail:

> We should think about a meeting soon with Reps. Gutierrez, Velazquez, and Serrano on the Puerto Rico independence crimes prisoners issue. They have requested one with the POTUS but the options include the VP and John as well. The issue should be resolved soon—the petitions have been before us for a long time. The VP's Puerto Rican position would be helped: The issue is Gutierrez's [sic] top priority as well as of high constituent importance to Serrano and Velazquez.

The Sentences Imposed Upon the FALN and Macheteros Prisoners Were Fair. The President and his spokesmen represented that the sixteen offered clemency had served sentences in excess of what they would now receive under the sentencing guidelines. This is not true. According to the United States Sentencing Commission, which analyzed this matter specifically, "the federal sentencing guidelines generally would call for sentences as long as or longer than those actually imposed, if the defendants had been sentenced under current law." Furthermore, less than nine months before the President and his spokesman made these statements, a senior Justice Department official informed a Member of Congress, in writing, "[t]he sentences are in line with sentences imposed in other cases for similar terrorist activity. . . ."

The President and His Spokesman Misrepresented Facts Concerning the Terrorists. The President communicated that the sixteen terrorists offered clemency were being held in prison "in effect for guilt by association." In fact, they were incarcerated because they had committed serious crimes and had been sentenced for those crimes. The individuals in question were not the non-violent wing of the FALN or Macheteros. They built bombs, were engaged in a wide-ranging conspiracy, and committed crimes that justified lengthy prison terms. There has been no suggestion that there were errors in the sentencing process.

Those Offered Clemency were Violent Offenders. In the days after the clemency offers were made, the President made an effort, through his surrogates, to convince the American people that those offered clemency were non-violent offenders. For example, National Security Adviser Sandy Berger, appearing on national television at a time when this issue was headline news (and therefore likely to be the subject of contemporaneous briefings), said "[t]hey're not individuals who personally were involved in violence." Below are some examples of the "non-violent" offenders offered clemency by the President:

Oscar López: An individual so "non-violent" that he wouldn't renounce violence to get out of prison. In addition to crimes committed in furtherance of FALN goals, he plotted two escapes from federal prison. One was from Leavenworth Penitentiary and, according to a Victim Impact Statement, he "planned to blow up Fort Leavenworth with the most powerful plastic explosives known to the military, riddle guard towers with rounds from automatic weapons, and throw grenades in the path of those who pursued them. . . ."

Juan Segarra-Palmer: In 1987, the U.S. Court of Appeals for the Second Circuit found that: "The [federal] district judge also found that [Juan] Segarra-Palmer had organized and taken part in the attack in Puerto Rico on a United States Navy bus taking sailors to a radar station, on December 3, 1979, in which two sailors were killed and nine wounded. . . ."

Finally, the seditious conspiracy counts in the indictments of fourteen of the individuals offered clemency included the construction and planting of explosive and incendiary devices (bombs) at 28 separate locations.

Those Offered Clemency Were Very Unlikely Candidates for Clemency. Prior to the offer of clemency to the sixteen FALN and Macheteros terrorists, President Clinton had received 3,229 requests for clemency. He had acted favorably on only three of these requests. The sixteen terrorists appear to be most unlikely candidates. They did not personally request clemency. They did not admit to wrongdoing and they had not renounced violence before such a renunciation had been made a quid pro quo for their release. They expressed no contrition for their crimes, and were at times openly belligerent about their actions. . . .

The White House Seemed to Want Clemency More than the Terrorists. Notwithstanding the fact that the sixteen did not express enough personal interest in the clemency process to file their own applications, the White House appeared eager to assist throughout the process. Meetings were held with supporters, and some senior staff even suggested ways to improve the likelihood of the President granting the clemency. Overall, the White House appears to have exercised more initiative than the terrorists themselves. . . .

Some White House Employees Thought the Sixteen Terrorists Were Political Prisoners. At least one White House employee consistently referred to the sixteen as "political prisoners." Given the crimes committed by the sixteen terrorists, it is disturbing that anyone, let alone a White House aide whose salary is paid by the American people, would deem these individuals to be "political prisoners. . . ."

Law Enforcement Organizations Were Not Adequately Consulted Prior to the President's Decision. The FBI was not aware that the President was seriously entertaining the petitions for clemency. In addition, the Bureau of Prisons was not consulted. Had the White House asked for a review of the prisoners' recent telephone conversations, it would have found that several prisoners made remarks advocating violence.

The Victims Were Ignored. Victims were unable to get meetings with the White House or Department of Justice. Some had tried to schedule meetings; they were simply rebuffed. Activists seeking clemency did get such meetings. Furthermore, while clemency supporters were updated regularly on the progress of the petition, victims were not even informed of the clemency decisions. . . .

The Clemency Decision Undermines the United States' Position in the International Fight Against Terrorism. The decision to grant clemency to the FALN and Macheteros terrorists sends a clear message that our demands for severe punishment, and our willingness to mete out severe punishment for terrorism, can be hollow. . . .

The Clemency Decision Empowered Two Dangerous Terrorist Organizations. As the FBI made clear in a written statement prepared for the Committee's September 21, 1999, hearing: "The FALN and Macheteros terrorist groups continue to pose a danger to the U.S. Government and to the American people, here and in Puerto Rico. . . . The challenge before us is the potential that the release of these individuals will psychologically and operationally enhance the ongoing violent and criminal activities of terrorist groups, not only in Puerto Rico, but throughout the world. . . ."

As of June 28, 2002, the full text of President Bill Clinton's letter was available as part of a congressional hearing transcript at http://commdocs.house.gov/committees/gro/hgo60935.000/hgo60935_0.htm#14, and the full text of the House Government Reform Committee's report was available at http://frwebgate.access.gpo.gov/cgi-bin/getdoc.cgi?dbname=106_cong_reports&docid=f:hr488.pdf

PANEL REPORT ON ANTITERRORISM PRIORITIES
December 15, 1999

By 1998 President Bill Clinton's terrorism policy emphasized the threat from attacks with biological or chemical weapons that could kill thousands or tens of thousands of people. Spending soared on programs to thwart or respond to terrorist attacks using such weapons. The threat was reinforced in a September 1999 report by an expert panel appointed by the Defense Department, which said that "states, terrorists, and other disaffected groups" would acquire and use weapons of mass destruction. "Americans will likely die on American soil, possibly in large numbers," the panel said. (Report on U.S. Vulnerability to Terrorist Attacks, p. 280)

But some experts contended that the threat of terrorists using biological or chemical weapons to kill massive numbers of people was overblown. Terrorists were far more likely to use conventional explosives than biological, chemical, or nuclear weapons, according to a report released December 15, 1999, by a federal commission formed to look at the nation's vulnerability to weapons of mass destruction. Even if terrorists did use such weapons, it was highly unlikely an attack would result in mass casualties, said the panel, which was commonly called the "Gilmore commission" because it was chaired by Virginia governor James Gilmore. The panel agreed that some money and planning should be devoted to the threat of terrorists using biological or chemical weapons to inflict mass casualties, but it warned that more attention should be paid to efforts aimed at smaller-scale attacks with conventional explosives, biological weapons, or chemical weapons.

In a follow-up report a year later, the Gilmore commission said the United States needed to develop a comprehensive national strategy aimed at all types of terrorism threats. "The United States has no coherent, functional national strategy for combating terrorism," the panel said.

Following are excerpts from the executive summary of "Assessing the Threat," a report issued December 15, 1999, by the Advisory Panel to Assess Domestic Response Capabilities for Terrorism Involving Weapons of Mass Destruction:

The possibility that terrorists will use "weapons of mass destruction (WMD)" in this country to kill and injure Americans, including those responsible for protecting and saving lives, presents a genuine threat to the United States. As we stand on the threshold of the twenty-first century, the stark reality is that the face and character of terrorism are changing and that previous beliefs about the restraint on terrorist use of chemical, biological, radiological, and nuclear (CBRN) devices may be disappearing. Beyond the potential loss of life and the infliction of wanton casualties, and the structural or environmental damage that might result from such an attack, our civil liberties, our economy, and indeed our democratic ideals could also be threatened. The challenge for the United States is first to deter and, failing that, to be able to detect and interdict terrorists before they strike. Should an attack occur, we must be confident that local, state, and Federal authorities are well prepared to respond and to address the consequences of the entire spectrum of violent acts.

In recent years, efforts have clearly been focused on more preparations for such attacks. The bombings of the World Trade Center in New York and Alfred P. Murrah Federal Building in Oklahoma City, coupled with the 1995 sarin nerve gas attack in Tokyo and the U.S. embassy bombings this past summer, have heightened American concern and have already prompted an array of responses across all levels of government. At the same time, the country's seeming inability to develop and implement a clear, comprehensive, and truly integrated national domestic preparedness strategy means that we may still remain fundamentally incapable of responding effectively to a serious terrorist attack.

The vast array of CBRN weapons conceivably available to terrorists today can be used against humans, animals, crops, the environment, and physical structures in many different ways. The complexity of these CBRN terrorist threats, and the variety of contingencies and critical responses that they suggest, requires us to ensure that preparedness efforts are carefully planned, implemented, and sustained among all potential responders, with all levels of government operating as partners. These threats, moreover, will require new ways of thinking throughout the entire spectrum of local, state, and Federal agencies. Effecting true change in the culture of a single government agency, much less achieving fundamental changes throughout and among all three, presents formidable hurdles. Nonetheless, the nature of these threats and their potential consequences demands the full commitment of officials at all levels to achieve these goals. . . .

. . . CBRN terrorism has emerged as a U.S. national security concern for several reasons:

- There has been a trend toward increased lethality in terrorism in the past decade.
- There is an increasing focus on the apparent dangers posed by potential CBRN terrorism.
- Terrorists may now feel less constrained to use a CBRN device in an attempt to cause mass casualties, especially following the precedent-setting attack in 1995 by the Aum Shinrikyo.

The reasons terrorists may perpetrate a WMD attack include a desire to kill as many people as possible as a means "to annihilate their enemies," to instill fear and panic to undermine a governmental regime, to create a means of negotiating from a position of unsurpassed strength, or to cause great social and economic impact.

Given any of those potential motives, the report identifies the "most likely terrorists groups" to use CBRN as fundamentalist or apocalyptic religious organizations, cults, and extreme single-issue groups but suggests that such a group may resort to a smaller-scale attack to achieve its goal. The analysis, however, indicates two additional possibilities:

- A terrorist attack against an agricultural base.
- A terrorist use of a CBRN device with the assistance of state sponsorship.

In the latter case, nevertheless, the Panel concludes that several reasons work against state sponsorship, including the prospect of significant reprisals by the United States against the state sponsor, the potential inability of the state sponsor to control its surrogate, and the prospect that the surrogate cannot be trusted, even to the point of using the weapon against its sponsor.

The Panel concludes that the Nation must be prepared for the entire spectrum of potential terrorist threats—both the unprecedented higher-consequence attack, as well as the historically more frequent, lesser-consequence terrorist attack, which the Panel believes is more likely in the near term. Conventional explosives, traditionally a favorite tool of the terrorist, will likely remain the terrorist weapon of choice in the near term as well. Whether smaller-scale CBRN or conventional, any such lower-consequence event—at least in terms of casualties or destruction—could, nevertheless, accomplish one or more terrorist objectives: exhausting response capabilities, instilling fear, undermining government credibility, or provoking an overreaction by the government. With that in mind, the Panel's report urges a more balanced approach, so that not only higher-consequence scenarios will be considered, but that increasing attention must now also be paid to the historically more frequent, more probable, lesser-consequence attack, especially in terms of policy implications for budget priorities or the allocation of other resources, to optimize local response capabilities. A singular focus on preparing for an event potentially affecting thousands or tens of thousands may result in a smaller, but nevertheless lethal attack involving dozens failing to receive an appropriate response in the first critical minutes and hours.

While noting that the technology currently exists that would allow terrorists to produce one of several lethal CBRN weapons, the report also describes the current difficulties in acquiring or developing and in maintaining, handling, testing, transporting, and delivering a device that truly has the capability to cause "mass casualties." Those difficulties include the requirement, in almost all cases, for highly knowledgeable personnel, significant financial resources, obtainable but fairly sophisticated production facilities and equipment, quality control and testing, and special handling. In many cases, the personnel of a terrorist organization run high personal safety risks, in producing, handling, testing, and delivering such a device. Moreover, the report notes, the more sophisticated a device, or the more personnel, equipment, facilities, and the like involved, the greater the risk that the enterprise will expose itself to detection and interdiction by intelligence and law enforcement agencies—particularly in light of the increasing attention focused on terrorism today. . . .

The report contains several conclusions and recommendations, as a result of the threat analysis and other information provided to the Panel and the collective expertise and experience of its members:

- The conclusion that the United States needs to have a viable national strategy to guide the development of clear, comprehensive, and truly integrated national domestic preparedness plans to combat terrorism, one that recognizes that the Federal role will be defined by the nature and severity of the incident but will generally be supportive of state and local authorities, who traditionally have the fundamental responsibility for response, and the recommendation for promulgation of a national-level strategy, with a "bottom-up" perspective—a strategy that clearly delineates and distinguishes Federal, state, and local roles and responsibilities and articulates clear direction for Federal priorities and programs to support local responders; and a comprehensive, parallel public education effort.

- The conclusion that initial and continuing, comprehensive and articulate assessments of potential, credible, terrorist threats within the United States, and the ensuing risk and vulnerability assessments are critical for policymakers and the recommendation that more attention be paid to assessments of the higher-probability/lower-consequence threats—not at the expense of, but in addition to, assessments of the lower-probability/higher-consequence threats.

- The conclusion that the complex nature of current Federal organizations and programs makes it very difficult for state and local authorities to obtain Federal information, assistance, funding, and support; that a Federal focal point and "clearinghouse" for related preparedness information and for directing state and local entities to appropriate Federal agencies, is needed; and that the *concept* behind the National Domestic Preparedness Office is fundamentally sound.

- The conclusion that congressional decisions for authority and funding to address the issue appear to be uncoordinated, and the recommendation that Congress consider forming an *ad hoc* Joint Special or Select Committee, to provide more efficiency and effectiveness in Federal efforts.

- The conclusion that much more needs to be and can be done to obtain and share information on potential terrorist threats at all levels of government, to provide more effective deterrence, prevention, interdiction, or response, using modern information technology.

- The conclusion that many definitions and terms in this arena are ambiguous or confusing (e.g., "weapons of mass destruction" and "mass casualties"), and the recommendation that there be a revision and codification of universal and easily understood terms.

- The conclusion that national standards for responders at all levels, particularly for planning, training, and equipment, are critical, and the recommendation that more emphasis be placed on research, development, testing, and evaluation in the adoption of such standards.
- The conclusion that, despite recent improvements, too much ambiguity remains about the issue of "who's in charge" if an incident occurs, and the recommendation that efforts be accelerated to develop and to test agreed-on templates for command and control under a wide variety of terrorist threat scenarios. . . .

As of June 29, 2002, the full text of the report was available at http://purl.access.gpo.gov/GPO/LPS16552

STUDY EXAMINES TRENDS IN INTERNATIONAL TERRORISM
Undated [2000]

Events in 1999 illustrated the changing nature of the international terrorist threat to the United States and its interests around the world. Although state-sponsored terrorism and formal terrorist organizations continued to threaten the United States, the FBI claimed that the largest threat came from "loosely affiliated extremists and rogue international terrorists." The leading example was Osama bin Laden, leader of the al Qaeda terrorist network and the alleged mastermind of the 1998 bombings of U.S. embassies in Kenya and Tanzania. The FBI placed bin Laden on its "Ten Most Wanted List" in June 1999, and the next month President Bill Clinton blocked all trade with the Taliban, which ruled most of Afghanistan, because it sheltered bin Laden. The United Nations Security Council imposed economic sanctions of its own on the Taliban in November, again because it harbored bin Laden. (Clinton Order Blocks Trade with the Taliban, p. 271; UN Threatens Sanctions Against Taliban, p. 286)

The FBI reviewed trends in international terrorism over the previous three decades in a report titled "Terrorism in the United States: 1999." Attacks from the late 1960s through the 1980s were primarily committed by formal terrorist groups such as Black September and the Abu Nidal Organization, the FBI said, although in the 1980s countries such as Libya and Iran also sponsored attacks. In the 1980s the largest threat came from Hizballah, an Iranian-backed group that wanted to create an Islamic government in Lebanon and to drive out any non-Islamic influences, the FBI said. But by the 1990s formal terrorist groups and state-sponsored efforts had faded, replaced by loosely affiliated international terrorists. The report also noted that international terrorists had changed their tactics over the years. Popular tactics in the 1970s included hijacking airplanes and taking hostages, but by the 1990s international extremists increasingly focused on large-scale attacks that caused as many casualties as possible.

This change in tactics was exemplified by Ahmed Ressam, an Algerian who was arrested on December 14, 1999, as he attempted to drive a car loaded with explosives and other bomb components across the border from

Canada into the United States at Port Angeles, Washington. Ressam was headed for Los Angeles International Airport—not to hijack a plane, but to blow up the airport itself during millennium celebrations. Ressam, who trained in camps in Afghanistan run by bin Laden, was convicted on nine counts in April 2001 and faced up to 140 years in prison. But his sentencing was repeatedly delayed—finally until March 2003—as he started cooperating with authorities, including testifying against several other Algerian Islamic extremists who helped him. In May 2002 a British judge ordered the extradition to the United States of Amar Makhlulif, who Ressam said directed an al Qaeda cell in London and helped him plan the Los Angeles attack.

Following are excerpts from "Terrorism in the United States: 1999," a report published in 2000 by the Federal Bureau of Investigation:

. . . During the past 25 years, the threat posed by international terrorism has changed dramatically and will undoubtedly continue to evolve in the years to come.

In recent years, the U.S. Intelligence Community has identified several important trends in international terrorism. Among these has been an apparent shift in operational intensity from traditional sources of terrorism—state sponsors and formalized terrorist organizations—to rogue and loosely affiliated extremists. This trend has been paralleled by a general shift in tactics among international terrorists.

From State Sponsors and Formal Groups to International Radical Fundamentalism

From the late 1960s through the 1980s, formal terrorist groups, such as 17 November, Black September, the Abu Nidal Organization, the Popular Front for the Liberation of Palestine-General Command (PFLP-GC), the Palestinian Islamic Jihad (PIJ), Sendero Luminoso (Shining Path), and Hizballah, perpetrated the vast majority of international terrorist attacks worldwide. In the 1980s, a number of countries were identified as the sometimes overt, but generally covert, sponsors of terrorism. In some cases, these countries used formal terrorist organizations as their surrogates to carry out terrorist acts while providing the state sponsor with a degree of "plausible deniability." Libya, for example, has provided support to various terrorist organizations, including the PFLP-GC and the PIJ. The extremist Shiite Lebanese organization Hizballah continues to take strategic and operational direction from Iran, as it has done since its inception in the early 1980s. . . .

The U.S. Department of State currently designates seven nations—Cuba, Iran, Iraq, Libya, North Korea, Sudan, and Syria—as state sponsors of terrorism. Several of these countries continue to target dissidents, both within and outside their borders, harbor terrorists, and provide safe haven to terrorist organizations. However, with the exception of Iran, none of these countries is known to have participated directly in a terrorist act since the unsuccessful attempt of the Iraqi Intelligence Service (IIS) to assassinate former President George Bush on a visit to Kuwait in April 1993. . . .

Among formal terrorist organizations, Iranian-backed Hizballah emerged as the greatest international terrorist threat to U.S. interests in the 1980s. Dedicated to creating an Iranian-style Islamic theocracy in Lebanon, the group seeks the removal of all non-Islamic influences from the area. Hizballah carried out the truck bombings of the U.S. Embassy and the U.S. Marine barracks in Beirut in October 1983 and the U.S. Embassy Annex in Beirut in September 1984. Members of the group also were responsible for the kidnapping of U.S. and Western hostages in Lebanon throughout the 1980s. Combined, Hizballah attacks have resulted in the deaths of at least 270 Americans, more than any other terrorist group in the world.

Other organized groups, such as 17 November in Greece, the Red Army Faction in Germany, the Red Brigades in Italy, the Manuel Rodriguez Patriotic Front-Dissident (FPMR/D) in Chile, the National Liberation Army (ELN) in Colombia, and the Revolutionary Armed Forces of Colombia (FARC), have targeted U.S. persons and interests. Several of these groups continue to represent a serious threat to U.S. and other Western interests. The group 17 November, for example, is believed to be responsible for a large share of the 20 anti-U.S. terrorist attacks that occurred in Greece in 1999; the group also carried out several attacks against third-country targets in Greece during the year. Other groups thought to be rendered largely inactive have proven that extremist fervor is often difficult to extinguish. The Tupac Amaru Revolutionary Movement in Peru, for example, was believed to be nearly defunct when it staged the takeover of the Japanese Ambassador's residence in Lima in 1996. Still, the operational activity of other groups generally diminished throughout the 1990s. In some cases, this decreased activity resulted from successful counterterrorism/counterinsurgency efforts by the countries in which these organizations operate. Enhanced international cooperation on counterterrorism issues also weakened many of these groups. The vitality of some groups was further eroded by the loss of Soviet patronage after the Cold War.

The general decline in overt operational activities among state sponsors and some formalized terrorist organizations during the 1990s, however, did not signal an end to international terrorism. In the 1990s, the United States was introduced to a form of international extremism that poses challenges different in many ways from those posed by state sponsors and formalized terrorist organizations.

The phenomenon of loosely affiliated international extremists first came to the attention of the U.S. law enforcement and intelligence communities in the direct aftermath of the February 1993 World Trade Center (WTC) bombing. Through its investigation of the WTC bombing, the FBI uncovered a subsequent plot to attack various landmarks throughout New York City during the summer of 1993. While these two plots were only tangentially related, many of the participants shared similar backgrounds. Ramzi Yousef, the operational mastermind of the WTC bombing (as well as a subsequent thwarted plot to bomb U.S. air carriers transiting the Far East in 1995) had assembled a transnational group of extremists specifically to carry out the bombing. All of these individuals adhered to a virulently anti-Western ideology; most had fought in Afghanistan as *mujahedin* (holy warriors) in the successful struggle against the Soviet-backed regime. Likewise, extremists representing various ethnicities formed around Shaykh Omar Abdel Rahman to plot the series of attacks against New York landmarks.

Investigation into these two plots revealed basic commonalities among the loosely affiliated groups that were quickly emerging as a significant threat to U.S. and Western interests. Often, these ideologically driven extremists form loose-knit groups that carry out specific operational objectives. These groups are generally transnational and multi-ethnic in nature and made up of individuals who fought or trained in Afghanistan or other areas, such as Bosnia; groups generally may form on an ad hoc basis to carry out a specific operational objective and plan to disperse once this objective is met or when their plots are uncovered by law enforcement. These extremists may receive funding from various sources.

While Ramzi Yousef is currently serving a life-plus sentence in the United States for his roles in the WTC bombing and the thwarted plot to bomb U.S. airliners, an even more menacing rogue extremist, Usama Bin Laden, continues to pose a serious threat to U.S. interests. His organization, Al-Qaeda (the "base" or the "root"), is much larger and more structured than the groups assembled by Yousef and other rogue international extremists; there are indications that Al-Qaeda has a presence in dozens of countries, including the United States. Bin Laden's personal wealth, his ties to existing terrorist organizations, and his prominent standing among the *mujahedin* and other disaffected populations have established him as a type of de facto state sponsor of terrorism. However, his position as the head of a large, but loosely affiliated, terrorist network allows him the flexibility to operate more freely than traditional state sponsors. It also allows him to operate with relative impunity from many of the countermeasures that have been applied to state sponsors.

Bin Laden's objectives—driving U.S. and Western forces from the Arabian Peninsula, removing Saudi Arabia's ruling family from power, "liberating" Palestine, and overthrowing "Western-oriented" governments in predominately Muslim countries—have established him as a leading figure among extremists who share a similar ideological orientation. While Bin Laden is one of the most recognized proponents and a key financier of this broad movement, he does not control or direct all such extremism. Should either he or Al-Qaeda cease to exist this international movement would, in all likelihood, continue.

Changing Tactics

The general shift in focus from state sponsors and formalized terrorist organizations to loosely affiliated extremists has in many ways paralleled a similar transition in terrorist tactics during the past three decades. Incidents of aircraft hijackings and hostage taking—two hallmarks of international terrorism in the 1970s and 1980s—fell dramatically during the 1990s. . . . In lieu of these types of attacks, international extremists have increasingly focused on attacks that yield maximum destruction, casualties, and impact. . . .

Conclusion

State sponsors of terrorism (most notably Iran) and formalized terrorist organizations continue to represent significant threats to U.S. national security and interests; however, during the 1990s a new type of terrorist threat emerged emanating from loosely affiliated extremists. As the 21st Century dawns, the most direct threat to U.S. interests may stem from Usama Bin Laden, his organization Al-Qaeda, and sympathetic groups. . . .

The last decade also witnessed a general shift in tactics among international terrorists away from numerous direct, but limited attacks, such as hijackings and hostage taking, toward fewer indiscriminate, high-impact attacks, such as large-scale vehicle bombings. The trend toward high-casualty, indiscriminate attacks served to spark public anxiety regarding terrorism even as the overall number of terrorist attacks generally declined during the decade (there were 392 international terrorist attacks worldwide in 1999, compared to 565 in 1991). Concern over the potential for large-scale WMD [weapon of mass destruction] attacks also fueled public concerns as the potential for extremist groups to successfully deploy such weapons appeared to grow increasingly plausible as the decade proceeded.

Whether these trends endure into the new Millennium remains to be seen. It does appear that international terrorists will continue to focus on attacks that yield significant destruction and high casualties, thus maximizing worldwide media attention and public anxiety. It also appears likely that as governments "harden" (or make more secure) official targets, terrorists will increasingly seek out more vulnerable "softer" targets, such as high-profile offices of multinational firms and Americans traveling and working abroad. One factor seems certain to endure: as the influence of the United States continues to shape world events, U.S. interests—both official and nonofficial—will continue to be targets of terrorist attack. . . .

As of July 5, 2002, the full text of the report was available at http://www.fbi.gov/publications/terror/terror99.pdf

GAO CITES ONGOING PROBLEMS WITH AIRPORT SCREENERS
March 16, 2000

Only six years after American airports were first required to have secu-rity checkpoints to screen passengers and their bags, in 1979 a joint study by the Federal Aviation Administration and the airline industry found nu-merous problems with screeners who ran the checkpoints. The problems found then—high turnover, low wages, and inadequate training—were re-peatedly documented over subsequent years in reports by the General Ac-counting Office (GAO), the Department of Transportation's inspector general, and others. (Testimony on Ineffective Airport Passenger Screening, p. 92)

The latest round of reports and congressional hearings came in March 2000. At a hearing March 16 by the House Aviation Subcommittee, the GAO's associate director for transportation issues had trouble con-cealing his frustration. "The message I bring here today is not new," said Gerald R. Dillingham. "The performance problems affecting airport screen-ers are longstanding." The high turnover rates identified since 1979 were getting even worse, he said, with rates exceeding 100 percent annually at most major airports and topping 400 percent at one. A major reason for turnover was the wages screeners received, which were often lower than those received by workers at airport fast-food restaurants. Dillingham also noted that screening practices in five other countries examined by the GAO were more stringent than those in the United States.

In a follow-up report about screener problems issued three months after the hearing, the GAO seemed eerily prescient. The first paragraph of the re-port said:

> *The threat of attacks on aircraft by terrorists or others remains a persistent and growing concern for the United States. According to the Federal Bureau of In-vestigation, the trend in terrorism against U.S. targets is toward large-scale in-cidents designed for maximum destruction, terror, and media impact—exactly what terrorists intended in a 1995 plot to blow up 12 U.S. airliners in a single day. That plot, uncovered by police in the Philippines, focused on U.S. airliners operating in the Pacific region, but concerns are growing about the potential for attacks within the United States.*

The next major round of reports and congressional hearings about problems in aviation security started on September 20, 2001—slightly more than a week after nineteen hijackers cleared security checkpoints at three major airports, seized control of four airliners, and crashed them into the World Trade Center, the Pentagon, and a field in Pennsylvania, killing more than 3,000 people. (September 11 Attacks Affirm Aviation Security Concerns, p. 356)

Following are excerpts from testimony by Gerald L. Dillingham, associate director of transportation issues for the General Accounting Office, before the House Committee on Transportation and Infrastructure's Aviation Subcommittee on March 16, 2000:

. . . Events over the past decade have shown that the threat of terrorism against the United States is an ever-present danger. Aviation is an attractive target for terrorists, and because the air transportation system is critical to the nation's well-being, protecting it is an important national issue. . . .

. . . Concerns have been raised for many years by GAO and others about the effectiveness of screeners and the need to improve their performance. Two Presidential commissions—established after the bombing of Pan Am Flight 103 in 1988 and the then-unexplained crash of TWA Flight 800 in 1996—as well as numerous GAO and Department of Transportation Inspector General reports have highlighted problems with screening and the need for improvements. This situation still exists. . . .

Background

Screening checkpoints and the screeners who operate them are a key line of defense against the introduction of a dangerous object into the aviation system. Over 2 million passengers and their baggage must be checked each day for weapons, explosives, or other dangerous articles that could pose a threat to the safety of an aircraft and those aboard it. The FAA and air carriers share this responsibility. FAA prescribes screening regulations and establishes basic standards for screeners, equipment, and procedures to be used. It monitors the performance of the screeners by periodically testing their ability to detect potentially dangerous objects carried by FAA special agents posing as passengers. The air carriers are responsible for screening passengers and their baggage before they are permitted into the secure areas of an airport or onto an aircraft. Air carriers can use their own employees to conduct screening activities, but for the most part air carriers hire security companies to do the screening.

Screeners use metal detectors, X-ray machines, and physical bag searches to identify dangerous objects. However, because equipment at checkpoints does not automatically detect threats, the effectiveness of the screening depends heavily on the performance of the screeners themselves. It can be a difficult, stressful, yet monotonous job, requiring sustained attention to the task of identifying faint indications of infrequently appearing targets. The screeners detect thousands of dangerous objects each year. Over the last 5 years, screeners detected nearly 10,000 firearms being carried through checkpoints. Nevertheless, screeners do not identify all threats—instances occur each year in which weapons were discovered to have passed through a checkpoint.

Screener Performance Problems Are Attributed to Rapid Turnover and Inattention to Human Factors

There is no single reason why screeners fail to identify dangerous objects. Two conditions—rapid screener turnover and inadequate attention to human factors—are believed to be important causes. The rapid turnover among screeners has been a long-standing problem, having been singled out as a concern in FAA and GAO reports dating back to at least 1979. We reported in 1987 that turnover among screeners was about 100 percent a year at some airports, and today, the turnover is considerably higher. From May 1998 through April 1999, screener turnover averaged 126 percent at the nation's 19 largest airports, with five airports reporting turnover of 200 percent or more and one reporting turnover of 416 percent. . . .

Both FAA and the aviation industry attribute the rapid turnover to the low wages screeners receive, the minimal benefits, and the daily stress of the job. Generally, screeners get paid at or near the minimum wage. We found that some of the screening companies at 14 of the nation's 19 largest airports paid screeners a starting salary of $6.00 an hour or less and, at 5 of these airports, the starting salary was the minimum wage—$5.15 an hour. It is common for the starting wages at airport fast-food restaurants to be higher than the wages screeners receive. . . .

Human factors associated with screening—those work-related issues that are influenced by human capabilities and constraints—have also been noted by FAA as problems affecting performance for over 20 years. Screening duties require repetitive tasks as well as intense monitoring for the very rare event when a dangerous object might be observed. Too little attention has been given to factors such as (1) individuals' aptitudes for effectively performing screener duties, (2) the sufficiency of the training provided to the screeners and how well they comprehend it, and (3) the monotony of the job and the distractions that reduce the screeners' vigilance. As a result, screeners are being placed on the job who do not have the necessary abilities, do not have adequate knowledge to effectively perform the work, and who then find the duties tedious and unstimulating.

FAA Is Making Efforts to Address Causes of Screeners' Performance Problems, but Progress Has Been Slow

FAA has demonstrated that it is aware of the need to improve the screeners' performance by conducting efforts intended to address the turnover and human factors problems and establishing goals with which to measure the agency's success in improving screener performance. . . .

The Threat Image Projection System

FAA is deploying an enhancement to the X-ray machines used at the checkpoints called the threat image projection (TIP) system. As screeners routinely scan passengers' carry-on bags, TIP occasionally projects images of threat objects like guns and explosives on the X-ray machines' screens. Screeners are expected to spot the threat objects and signal for the bags to be manually searched. Once prompted, TIP indicates whether an image is of an actual object in a bag or was generated by the system and also records the screeners' responses, providing a measure of their performance while keeping them more alert. By frequently exposing screeners to what a variety of threat images look like on screen, TIP will also provide continuous on-the-job training.

FAA is behind schedule in deploying this system. . . .

The Certification of Screening Companies

In response to a mandate in the Federal Aviation Reauthorization Act of 1996 and a recommendation from the 1997 White House Commission on Aviation Safety and Security, FAA is creating a program to certify the security companies that staff the screening checkpoints. The agency plans to establish performance standards—an action we recommended in 1987—that the screening companies will have to meet in order to earn and retain certification. It will also require that all screeners pass automated readiness tests after training and that all air carriers have TIP units on the X-ray machines at their checkpoints so that screeners' performance can be measured to ensure FAA's standards are met. FAA believes that the need to meet certification standards will give the security companies a greater incentive to retain their best screeners longer and so will indirectly reduce turnover by raising the screeners' wages and improving training. Most of the air carrier, screening company, and airport representatives we contacted said they believe certification has the potential to improve screeners' performance.

The agency plans to use data from the TIP system to guide it in setting its performance standards, but because the system will not be at all airports before the end of fiscal year 2003, the agency is having to explore additional ways to set standards. FAA plans to issue the regulation establishing the certification program by May 2001, over 2 years later than its original deadline. According to FAA, it has needed more time to develop performance standards and to develop and process a very complex regulation. The first certification of screening companies is expected to take place in 2002. . . .

Screening Practices in Five Other Countries Differ from U.S. Practices

We visited five countries—Belgium, Canada, France, the Netherlands, and the United Kingdom—viewed by FAA and industry as having effective screening operations to identify screening practices that differ from those in the United States. . . .

First, screening operations in some countries are more stringent. For example, Belgium, the Netherlands, and the United Kingdom routinely touch or "pat down" passengers in response to metal detector alarms. Additionally, all five countries allowed only ticketed passengers through the screening checkpoints, thereby allowing the screeners to more thoroughly check fewer people. Some countries also had a greater police or military presence near checkpoints. . . .

Second, the screeners' qualifications are usually more extensive. In contrast to the United States, Belgium requires screeners to be citizens; France requires screeners to be citizens of a European Union country. In the Netherlands, screeners do not have to be citizens, but they must have been residents of the country for 5 years. Four of the countries we visited had greater training requirements for screeners. While FAA requires that screeners in this country have 12 hours of classroom training, Belgium, Canada, France, and the Netherlands require more. For example, France requires 60 hours of training and Belgium requires at least 40 hours of training with an additional 16 to 24 hours for each activity, such as X-ray machine operations, the screener will conduct.

Third, screeners receive relatively better pay and benefits in most of these countries. While in the United States screeners receive wages that are at or slightly above minimum wage, screeners in some countries receive wages that are viewed as being at the "middle income" level by screeners. In the Netherlands, for example, screeners receive at least the equivalent of about $7.50 per hour. This wage is about 30 percent higher than wages at fast-food restaurants. In Belgium, screeners receive about $14 per hour. Not only is pay higher, but the screeners in some countries receive some benefits, such as health care or vacations—in large part because it is required under the laws of these countries.

Finally, the responsibility for screening in most of these countries is placed with the airport or with the government, not with the air carriers as it is in the United States. . . .

Summary

The message I bring here today is not new. The performance problems affecting airport screeners are longstanding. Yet, as we enter the new millennium, not only do the same problems continue to exist but in the case of turnover among the screeners, it is even getting worse. . . .

As of July 6, 2002, the full text of the testimony was available at http://www.gao.gov/archive/2000/rc00125t.pdf

SECURITY FAILS AT FEDERAL AGENCIES AND AIRPORTS
May 25, 2000

By 2000 just about everything imaginable could be purchased on the Internet—including fake police badges and credentials. Some members of Congress worried that terrorists, foreign intelligence agents, and criminals could use the bogus items to enter secure federal buildings and airports. To see whether this was possible, they asked the General Accounting Office (GAO)—the investigative arm of Congress—to outfit undercover agents with phony badges and credentials and see if they could enter restricted areas at federal facilities.

The agents were spectacularly successful, according to testimony at a congressional hearing on May 25, 2000, by Robert H. Hast, head of special investigations for the GAO. Undercover agents tested nineteen federal buildings and two airports, Hast told the House Subcommittee on Crime—and in every case they gained access with the bogus IDs, which were never challenged. Not once did the agents have to undergo X-ray screenings or other security checks. At each site the agents "could have carried in weapons, listening devices, explosives, chemical/biological agents," and other hazardous materials, Hast said. The headquarters for the Central Intelligence Agency, the Federal Bureau of Investigation, the Pentagon, the Justice Department, the State Department, and the Federal Aviation Administration were just some of the buildings where agents gained entrance and, in most cases, were allowed to wander unimpeded.

On February 1, 2002, the Los Angeles Times *reported that U.S. personnel in Afghanistan had found a copy of Hast's testimony on a computer linked to al Qaeda, raising concerns that terrorists were studying the document to plan new attacks. The testimony, like virtually all GAO reports, had been available on the agency's Web site. GAO removed the document from its site, presumably because of security concerns, although paper copies were available to people who sent requests to the GAO, and the document was available in libraries across the United States. Ironically, the testimony remained available online at some nongovernmental Web sites, and it also could be found at a federal Web site in a transcript of the congressional hearing where it was presented. Meanwhile, in late April 2002 the GAO reported that, in a similar test, its undercover investigators fooled guards at four federal buildings in Atlanta, Georgia, and gained unauthorized access. They bypassed X-ray machines and metal detectors, the GAO said, and in one case were even given a security code that would have allowed them to enter a building after working hours.*

Following are excerpts from testimony by Robert H. Hast, assistant comptroller general for investigations in the Office of Special Investigations at the General Accounting Office, at a May 25, 2000, hearing of the House Judiciary Committee's Subcommittee on Crime:

I am pleased to be here today to discuss our findings with respect to the Subcommittee's request that we investigate the potential security risk to the United States posed by the use of stolen or counterfeit law enforcement badges and credentials. Specifically, you expressed concerns that such badges and credentials are readily available for purchase on the Internet and from other public sources and could be used by criminals, terrorists, and foreign intelligence agents to gain access to secure government buildings and airports.

To address these concerns, you asked us to acquire fictitious law enforcement badges currently available to the public and to create fictitious identification to accompany the badges. You also asked that our special agents, in an undercover capacity, attempt to gain access to secure facilities in such a manner that they could have introduced weapons, explosives, chemical/biological agents, listening devices, or other hazardous material.

Scope and Methodology

In conducting our investigation, we collected background information from public sources on various federal government sites in the Washington, D.C., area and other geographical areas. We established a list of potential target locations based upon the sites' involvement in national security, intelligence, and criminal justice and their symbolic or historic significance. We also included major commercial airports. All sites require screening of visitors. All sites appeared to have magnetometers and X-ray machines at the security checkpoints for screening visitors and valises, e.g., briefcases and baggage.

We visited some of these sites as private citizens, i.e., members of the "general public," to observe the screening procedures and conduct surveillance from public areas. We set out to determine if some sites employed additional security measures, such as outer-perimeter checkpoints, roving patrols, or countersurveillance teams.

We also developed information about each site based on public source information, the Internet, and pretext telephone calls.

We acquired the counterfeit and/or unauthorized law enforcement badges that you asked us to obtain from public sources. We created multiple counterfeit sets of credentials representing local and federal law enforcement agencies.

In April and May 2000, we performed our undercover work at 19 federal facilities and 2 major commercial airports.

Results in Brief

Our undercover agents were 100 percent successful in penetrating 19 federal sites and 2 commercial airports. We were able to enter 18 of the 21 sites on the first attempt. The remaining 3 required a second visit before we were able to penetrate the sites.

At no time during the undercover visits were our agents' bogus credentials or badges challenged by anyone. At the 21 sites that our undercover agents successfully penetrated, they could have carried in weapons, listening devices, explosives, chemical/biological agents, devices, and/or other such items/materials. . . .

Background

We acquired badges from public sources to use in this case. The badges included a movie prop of a police department badge, which is in similitude to genuine badges. In addition, we acquired a counterfeit federal badge not in similitude to a genuine federal badge and a drug task force badge that is in similitude to a genuine badge.

We created counterfeit law enforcement identification using commercially available software packages or information downloaded from the Internet. We used a standard computer graphics program, an ink-jet color printer, and photographs. After we printed the identifications, we laminated them. The credentials we created bear no likeness to any genuine law enforcement credentials.

Sites Penetrated

We penetrated 21 sites—19 federal departments/agencies and 2 commercial airports. We were successful at each site and our agents' bogus credentials and badges were not challenged by security. The sites were selected on the basis of their involvement in national security, intelligence, and criminal justice, and in their symbolic or historic significance. All sites require screening of visitors. All sites appeared to have magnetometers and X-ray machines at the security checkpoints for screening visitors and valises, e.g., briefcases and baggage.

How Penetration Was Accomplished

At all but two agencies, our undercover team consisted of two agents. Three agents worked undercover at the other two agencies. In all cases, upon entering the federal facilities, our undercover agents

- "declared" themselves as law enforcement officers,
- stated the name of their purported agency,

- stated that they were armed, and
- in most cases, displayed both a bogus badge and a bogus credential.

In some cases, only one agent had to show a badge, and the other agent was waved in by a security guard. At least one agent always carried a valise. In all cases, our agents were able to enter the facility by being waved around or through a magnetometer, without their person or valise being screened.

We were able to enter 18 of the 21 sites on the first attempt. The remaining 3 required a second visit before we were able to penetrate the sites.

In all but three sites, escorts were not required and our agents wandered through the buildings without being stopped. At the three sites that required escorts, our undercover agents were permitted to "keep" their declared fire-arms and carry their unscreened valises. Indeed, at all three of the sites, our agents were able to enter a rest room carrying a valise without the escort. At one of the sites, our agents later separated from their escort and walked through the building for about 15 minutes without being challenged.

At 15 of the 16 locations that contained the offices of cabinet secretaries or agency heads, our agents were able to stand immediately outside the suite of the cabinet secretary or agency head. At the 5 locations at which our agents attempted entry into such suites, they were successful. At 15 sites, our agents entered a rest room in the vicinity of these offices and could have left a valise containing weapons, explosives, and/or other such items/materials without being detected.

In all but two of the agencies we penetrated, the suite numbers of the cabinet head or agency head were listed in public documents.

Examples of Sites Penetrated

- Our agents drove a rented minivan into the courtyard entrance of a department and only one agent showed identification. They and the vehicle were permitted entry without being screened. They parked the van in the courtyard and proceeded to the department head's office. They entered the office and asked a receptionist whether the head of the department was in and told the receptionist that they were friends of the department head, with whom they had previously worked. They were told that the department head was not in. The agents then requested and received a tour of the agency head's suite and conference room.
- Three agents drove a sedan to a site and only the driver showed identification. They were issued a VIP parking pass and parked a few yards from the building entrance. The vehicle was not screened. The agents then walked into the building, avoided the magnetometer, and verbally declared themselves as law enforcement officers. Only one agent showed identification. All three were issued "No Escort Required" visitor passes. Two agents carried valises, which were also not checked. They then proceeded to the hallway outside the Secretary's office. Two agents briefly entered the Secretary's suite, before excusing themselves. All three agents were able to enter the Secretary's conference room and other offices without being challenged.

- Our agents, one of whom carried a valise, entered a historic site posing as police detective sergeants and were waved past the magnetometer. After a few minutes, they were approached by a uniformed police officer. He said that because they were local police officers, not federal, they would have to check their firearms in a lock box in the basement. Our agents stated that they did not have the time to stay and left the building.

At the two airports we visited, our agents had tickets issued in their undercover names on commercial flights. These agents declared themselves as armed police detective sergeants, displayed their spurious badges and identification, and were issued "law enforcement" boarding passes by the airline representative at the ticket counter. The procedure after checking in at the ticket counter varied at each airport.

- At one airport, our agents walked unescorted to the airport's security checkpoint, showed their badges to a contract security guard, and were waved around the magnetometer. A contract guard supervisor was then called to examine the undercover agents' credentials and law enforcement boarding passes. The agents then "logged" themselves in a book kept behind the security checkpoint. Neither the agents nor their valises were screened and they walked unescorted to their departure gate. At no time were they required to present themselves to an airport police officer.
- At the second airport, our undercover agents were required to show identification to an airline contract security guard. The airline contract security guard then escorted our undercover agents from the ticket counter to the security checkpoint and called for a local police officer. The contract security guard waited with our agents for about 10 minutes until the police officer arrived.

The police officer then examined our agents' credentials and escorted them around the magnetometer. Neither the agents nor their valises were screened. They then proceeded unescorted to their departure gate. . . .

As of July 6, 2002, the full text of the testimony was available at http://www.msnbc.com/modules/legal_docs/020201gaoreport.pdf

PANEL URGES MORE SPENDING
TO COUNTER TERROR THREAT
June 5, 2000

In the second half of the 1990s, a variety of commissions, committees, and other expert panels were appointed by the president, Congress, and the Defense Department to examine the nation's counterterrorism program and recommend improvements. Although mandates for the various groups differed somewhat, they generally examined U.S. efforts to prevent terrorist attacks and to respond to any that might occur. Overall, the committees reached the same broad conclusion: Although the United States was spending a skyrocketing amount of money on counterterrorism, the program lacked coordination and suffered from serious gaps.

On June 5, 2000, the National Commission on Terrorism, a group mandated by Congress, weighed in with a report titled "Countering the Changing Threat of International Terrorism." It said the government needed to spend even more money on counterterrorism and also to loosen restrictions on federal agencies that investigated terrorists. Perhaps the commission's most controversial recommendation was that the Clinton administration drop restrictions on the Central Intelligence Agency recruiting informants who might have committed serious crimes, such as human rights abuses. The reasoning was simple: Terrorists are not upstanding citizens, and people who would be close enough to them to provide useful information likely would not be nice people, either. The panel also emphasized the need to do a better job of collecting intelligence and—equally important—analyzing it for useful information.

On December 15, 2000, another commission mandated by Congress recommended the creation of a single high-level agency to coordinate federal counterterrorism efforts that were spread across dozens of agencies and departments. The previous year the same group, the Congressional Advisory Panel to Assess Domestic Response Capabilities for Terrorism Involving Weapons of Mass Destruction, recommended that the nation devote more resources to the threat of terrorists engaging in small-scale attacks with conventional explosives, biological weapons, or chemical weapons. The group said small-scale attacks were far more likely than large-scale efforts involving mass casualties. (Panel Report on Antiterrorism Priorities, p. 302)

Following are the foreword and executive summary from "Countering the Changing Threat of International Terrorism," a report issued June 5, 2000, by the National Commission on Terrorism:

Foreword

Six months ago, the National Commission on Terrorism began its Congressionally mandated evaluation of America's laws, policies, and practices for preventing and punishing terrorism directed at American citizens. After a thorough review, the Commission concluded that, although American strategies and policies are basically on the right track, significant aspects of implementation are seriously deficient. Thus, this report does not attempt to describe all American counterterrorism activities, but instead concentrates on problem areas and recommended changes. We wish to note, however, that in the course of our assessment we gained renewed confidence in the abilities and dedication of the Americans who stand on the front lines in the fight against terrorism.

Each of the 10 commissioners approached these issues from a different perspective. If any one commissioner had written the report on his or her own, it might not be identical to that which we are presenting today. However, through a process of careful deliberation, we reached the consensus reflected in this report.

Throughout our deliberations, we were mindful of several important points:

- The imperative to find terrorists and prevent their attacks requires energetic use of all the legal authorities and instruments available.
- Terrorist attacks against America threaten more than the tragic loss of individual lives. Some terrorists hope to provoke a response that undermines our Constitutional system of government. So U.S. leaders must find the appropriate balance by adopting counterterrorism policies which are effective but also respect the democratic traditions which are the bedrock of America's strength.
- Combating terrorism should not be used as a pretext for discrimination against any segment of society. Terrorists often claim to act on behalf of ethnic groups, religions, or even entire nations. These claims are false. Terrorists represent only a minuscule faction of any such group.
- People turn to terrorism for various reasons. Many terrorists act from political, ideological, or religious convictions. Some are simply criminals for hire. Others become terrorists because of perceived oppression or economic deprivation. An astute American foreign policy must take into

account the reasons people turn to terror and, where appropriate and feasible, address them. No cause, however, justifies terrorism.

Terrorists attack American targets more often than those of any other country. America's pre-eminent role in the world guarantees that this will continue to be the case, and the threat of attacks creating massive casualties is growing. If the United States is to protect itself, if it is to remain a world leader, this nation must develop and continuously refine sound counterterrorism policies appropriate to the rapidly changing world around us.

Executive Summary

International terrorism poses an increasingly dangerous and difficult threat to America. This was underscored by the December 1999 arrests in Jordan and at the U.S./Canadian border of foreign nationals who were allegedly planning to attack crowded millennium celebrations. Today's terrorists seek to inflict mass casualties, and they are attempting to do so both overseas and on American soil. They are less dependent on state sponsorship and are, instead, forming loose, transnational affiliations based on religious or ideological affinity and a common hatred of the United States. This makes terrorist attacks more difficult to detect and prevent.

Countering the growing danger of the terrorist threat requires significantly stepping up U.S. efforts. The government must immediately take steps to reinvigorate the collection of intelligence about terrorists' plans, use all available legal avenues to disrupt and prosecute terrorist activities and private sources of support, convince other nations to cease all support for terrorists, and ensure that federal, state, and local officials are prepared for attacks that may result in mass casualties. The Commission has made a number of recommendations to accomplish these objectives:

Priority one is to prevent terrorist attacks. U.S. intelligence and law enforcement communities must use the full scope of their authority to collect intelligence regarding terrorist plans and methods.

- CIA guidelines adopted in 1995 restricting recruitment of unsavory sources should not apply when recruiting counterterrorism sources.
- The Attorney General should ensure that FBI is exercising fully its authority for investigating suspected terrorist groups or individuals, including authority for electronic surveillance.
- Funding for counterterrorism efforts by CIA, NSA [National Security Agency], and FBI must be given higher priority to ensure continuation of important operational activity and to close the technology gap that threatens their ability to collect and exploit terrorist communications.
- FBI should establish a cadre of reports officers to distill and disseminate terrorism-related information once it is collected.

U.S. policies must firmly target all states that support terrorists.

- Iran and Syria should be kept on the list of state sponsors until they stop supporting terrorists.

- Afghanistan should be designated a sponsor of terrorism and subjected to all the sanctions applicable to state sponsors.
- The President should impose sanctions on countries that, while not direct sponsors of terrorism, are nevertheless not cooperating fully on counterterrorism. Candidates for consideration include Pakistan and Greece.

Private sources of financial and logistical support for terrorists must be subjected to the full force and sweep of U.S. and international laws.

- All relevant agencies should use every available means, including the full array of criminal, civil, and administrative sanctions to block or disrupt nongovernmental sources of support for international terrorism.
- Congress should promptly ratify and implement the International Convention for the Suppression of the Financing of Terrorism to enhance international cooperative efforts.
- Where criminal prosecution is not possible, the Attorney General should vigorously pursue the expulsion of terrorists from the United States through proceedings which protect both the national security interest in safeguarding classified evidence and the right of the accused to challenge that evidence.

A terrorist attack involving a biological agent, deadly chemicals, or nuclear or radiological material, even if it succeeds only partially, could profoundly affect the entire nation. The government must do more to prepare for such an event.

- The President should direct the preparation of a manual to guide the implementation of existing legal authority in the event of a catastrophic terrorist threat or attack. The President and Congress should determine whether additional legal authority is needed to deal with catastrophic terrorism.
- The Department of Defense must have detailed plans for its role in the event of a catastrophic terrorist attack, including criteria for decisions on transfer of command authority to DoD in extraordinary circumstances.
- Senior officials of all government agencies involved in responding to a catastrophic terrorism threat or crisis should be required to participate in national exercises every year to test capabilities and coordination.
- Congress should make it illegal for anyone not properly certified to possess certain critical pathogens and should enact laws to control the transfer of equipment critical to the development or use of biological agents.
- The President should establish a comprehensive and coordinated long-term research and development program for catastrophic terrorism.
- The Secretary of State should press for an international convention to improve multilateral cooperation on preventing or responding to cyber attacks by terrorists.

The President and Congress should reform the system for reviewing and funding departmental counterterrorism programs to ensure that the activities and programs of various agencies are part of a comprehensive plan.

- The executive branch official responsible for coordinating counterterrorism efforts across the government should be given a stronger hand in the budget process.
- Congress should develop mechanisms for a comprehensive review of the President's counterterrorism policy and budget.

As of July 5, 2002, the full text of the report was available at http://www.fas.org/irp/threat/commission.html

ARRESTS MADE IN 1985 BOMBING THAT KILLED 329 PEOPLE
October 27, 2000

Terrorist attacks by Sikh religious extremists killed hundreds of people in India in the early 1980s. The extremists wanted to create a separate Sikh state in the Punjab region of northern India. Nearly 600 extremists were killed in June 1984 when, under orders from Prime Minister Indira Gandhi, troops stormed the Golden Temple of Armistar. The extremists had been using the temple, Sikhism's holiest shrine, as a base for terrorist operations. In revenge for the raid, on October 31, 1984, two of Gandhi's trusted Sikh bodyguards assassinated her. (The Assassination of Indian Prime Minister Indira Gandhi, p. 65)

In what investigators quickly determined was further revenge for the raid, on June 23, 1985, Air India Flight 182 from Montreal to London blew up as it flew at 31,000 feet off the coast of Ireland. All 329 people aboard the Boeing 747 died, some apparently from drowning after they survived the explosion and crash into the Atlantic Ocean. Less than an hour before the Air India plane exploded, a suitcase bomb meant for another Air India flight exploded prematurely at Tokyo's Narita airport, killing two baggage handlers and injuring four others. Both suitcase bombs originated with flights from Vancouver, Canada, according to investigators. In 1991 a Sikh named Inderjit Singh Reyat was convicted of manslaughter in Canada for the deaths of the two Tokyo baggage handlers and sentenced to ten years in prison. But in the longest and costliest investigation in Canadian history, more than fifteen years elapsed between the explosion of Air India Flight 182 and any arrests in the case. Finally, on October 27, 2000, the Royal Canadian Mounted Police announced the arrest and indictment of two Vancouver-area Sikhs, Ripudaman Singh Malik and Ajaib Singh Bagri, for the crime. Bagri was also separately indicted for the 1988 attempted murder of Tara Singh Hayer, publisher of the Indo-Canadian Times *newspaper. Two days before Reyat was to be released from prison for the Tokyo airport bombing, he also was charged in the bombing of Air India Flight 182. Another man suspected in the case, Talwinder Singh Parmar, was killed in a gun battle with Bombay police in 1992.*

After multiple delays, in May 2002 the trial of the three men charged in the Air India bombing was scheduled to begin in March 2003. The trial was expected to last months or even years, eventually becoming one of the longest and most complex in Canadian history.

Following is a press release issued by the Royal Canadian Mounted Police on October 27, 2000, announcing charges in the June 23, 1985, bombing of Air India Flight 182:

The RCMP [Royal Canadian Mounted Police] has laid charges in connection with the Air India bombing off the coast of Ireland on June 23, 1985, which killed 329 people. Included in the Information are charges relating to the 1985 suitcase bomb which exploded at the New Tokyo International Airport in Narita Japan, killing two men and injuring four others. A separate charge has also been laid in the 1988 murder attempt against the life of *Indo-Canadian Times* Publisher Tara Singh HAYER.

At approximately 12:00 P.M. today, members of the Air India Task Force arrested 53-year-old, Ripudaman Singh MALIK of Vancouver and 51-year-old, Ajaib Singh BAGRI of Kamloops. They have been jointly charged with the following offences:

1). Unlawfully conspiring with Talwinder Singh PARMAR and Inderjit Singh REYAT, who are unindicted co-conspirators, to commit the murder of 177 passengers and the crew on board Air India Flight 301 from Narita, Japan to Bangkok, Thailand, and the 329 passengers and crew on board Air India Flight 182 from Montreal to London, England, contrary to Section 423(1)(a) of the Criminal Code.

2). First degree murder of the 329 passengers and crew of Air India Flight 182, contrary to Section 218 of the Criminal Code.

3). Attempted murder of the passengers and crew of Air India Flight 301 by seeking to place a bomb on board the aircraft, with the intent that it would detonate and cause the aircraft's destruction and the death of its occupants, contrary to Section 222 of the Criminal Code.

4). First degree murder in the deaths of Hideo ASANO and Hideharu KODA contrary to Section 218 of the Criminal Code.

5). On or about the 22nd of June, 1985, they did conspire with Talwinder Singh PARMAR to cause bombs to be placed on board
    a). CP Air Flight 003 from Vancouver, BC to Narita, Japan
    b). Air India Flight 301 from Narita, Japan to Bangkok, Thailand
    c). CP Air Flight 060 from Vancouver, BC to Toronto, ON
    d). Air India Flight 181 from Toronto, ON, to Montreal, PQ, where the flight was renamed Air India Flight 182 contrary to Sections 76.2(c) and 423(1)(d) of the Criminal Code.

6). On or about the 22nd of June, 1985, they did cause a bomb to be placed on board CP Air Flight 003, a bomb that would likely cause damage to the aircraft, render it incapable of flight or endanger the safety of the aircraft, contrary to Section 76.2 of the Criminal Code.

7). On or about the 22nd of June, 1985, they did cause a bomb to be placed on board CP Air Flight 060, a bomb that would likely cause damage to the aircraft, render it incapable of flight or endanger the safety of the aircraft, contrary to Section 76.2 of the Criminal Code.

8). On or about the 22nd of June, 1985, they did cause a bomb to be placed on board Air India Flight 181, a bomb that was likely to cause damage to the aircraft, render it incapable of flight or endanger the safety of the aircraft, contrary to Section 76.2 of the Criminal Code.

The RCMP is not prepared to release any information regarding the individual involvement of each accused in this case. That information will be presented to the courts at the appropriate time. We are also not prepared to discuss any direct evidence in this case as this may affect the integrity of the investigation.

Although arrests have been made, this does not mark the conclusion of the police investigation. We are continuing to receive information which is being followed up and which we consider beneficial to our case. The Air India Task Force investigators believe there are some people who will come forward with information now that arrests have been made. Anyone who has information about this investigation is asked to phone 264-3331.

In a separate Information sworn today, Ajaib Singh BAGRI has also been charged with attempting to commit the murder of Tara Singh HAYER on August 26, 1988, contrary to Section 222 of the Criminal Code. These charges have no connection to the ongoing investigation of Mr. HAYER's murder in November 1998 and any questions regarding that investigation should be forwarded to Surrey RCMP.

The Air India Task Force has attempted to contact as many of the victims' families as possible, to inform them of today's arrests and charges. Over the years, unfortunately, we have lost contact with many of the next of kin. We are encouraging any of the victims' family members to contact the task force at 604-264-3015 or 264-2385.

SEVENTEEN KILLED IN SUICIDE ATTACK ON USS *COLE*
January 9, 2001

As the USS Cole, a 505-foot destroyer, made a brief refueling stop at the port of Aden, Yemen, on October 12, 2000, a small skiff with two men pulled up about midship on the port side. Almost immediately a massive explosion erupted, blowing a forty-foot-by-forty-foot hole in the Cole at the waterline. Seventeen sailors died in the blast and thirty-nine others were wounded. For days after the explosion, which flooded several compartments, the surviving sailors worked frantically to keep their ship from sinking. They succeeded, and the Cole was eventually lifted aboard a massive Norwegian transport ship, which took it back to the United States for $250 million in repairs and upgrades.

A Pentagon panel that investigated the attack, the USS Cole Commission, determined that the entire military chain of command—not any single individual—should be held responsible for security lapses that may have contributed to the Cole's vulnerability. The panel's full report was classified, but an unclassified executive summary released January 9, 2001, said the military needed to be more proactive in detecting and stopping terrorist threats. In the past, the report said, the military had been in a "purely defensive mode" in reacting to terrorism. The report also made a strong pitch for the military services to devote more attention to training their forces to combat terrorism.

Meanwhile, U.S. and Yemeni officials repeatedly clashed during the criminal investigation. Officials in Yemen, a longtime hotbed of Islamic radicalism, would not let U.S. FBI agents interview suspects they had arrested, but they suddenly became much more cooperative after the September 11, 2001, terrorist attacks on the United States. The Yemenis wanted to put an undisclosed number of people on trial for the Cole attack, but delayed the trials at the request of U.S. investigators. U.S. officials asked for the delay so they could focus on identifying and capturing the masterminds behind the attack, who were believed to be connected to Osama bin Laden's al Qaeda terrorist network.

Following are excerpts from the findings and recommendations section from the unclassified executive summary of the "DoD USS Cole *Commission Report," released January 9, 2001:*

Organizational

Finding: Combating terrorism is so important that it demands complete unity of effort at the level of the Office of the Secretary of Defense.

- *Recommendation:* Secretary of Defense develop an organization that more cohesively aligns policy and resources within DoD to combat terrorism and designate an Assistant Secretary of Defense (ASD) to oversee these functions.

Finding: The execution of the engagement element of the National Security Strategy lacks an effective, coordinated interagency process, which results in a fragmented engagement program that may not provide optimal support to in-transit units.

- *Recommendation:* Secretary of Defense support an interagency process to provide overall coordination of U.S. engagement.

Finding: DoD needs to spearhead an interagency, coordinated approach to developing non-military host nation security efforts in order to enhance force protection for transiting U.S. forces.

- *Recommendation:* Secretary of Defense coordinate with Secretary of State to develop an approach with shared responsibility to enhance host nation security capabilities that result in increased security for transiting U.S. forces.

Antiterrorism/Force Protection (AT/FP)

Finding: Service manning policies and procedures that establish requirements for full-time Force Protection Officers and staff billets at the Service Component level and above will reduce the vulnerability of in-transit forces to terrorist attacks.

- *Recommendation:* Secretary of Defense direct the Services to provide Component Commanders with full-time force protection officers and staffs that are capable of supporting the force protection requirements of transiting units.

Finding: Component Commanders need the resources to provide in-transit units with temporary security augmentation of various kinds.

- *Recommendation:* Secretary of Defense direct the Services to resource Component Commanders to adequately augment units transiting through higher-threat areas.

Finding: Service AT/FP programs must be adequately manned and funded to support threat and physical vulnerability assessments of ports, airfields and inland movement routes that may be used by transiting forces.

- *Recommendation:* Secretary of Defense direct the Chairman of the Joint Chiefs of Staff, the CINCs and the Services to identify and resource manning and funding requirements to perform quality assessments of routes and sites used by transiting forces in support of Component Commanders. . . .

Finding: More responsive application of currently available military equipment, commercial technologies, and aggressive research and development can enhance the AT/FP and deterrence posture of transiting forces.

- *Recommendation:* Secretary of Defense direct the Services to initiate a major unified effort to identify near-term AT/FP equipment and technology requirements, field existing solutions from either military or commercial sources, and develop new technologies for remaining requirements. . . .

Finding: We need to shift transiting units from an entirely reactive posture to a posture that more effectively deters terrorist attacks.

- *Recommendation:* Secretary of Defense direct the CINCs and Services to have Component Commanders identify proactive techniques and assets to deter terrorists.

Finding: The amount of AT/FP emphasis that units in-transit receive prior to or during transfer between CINCs can be improved.

- *Recommendation:* Secretary of Defense direct the CINCs and Services to have Component Commanders ensure unit situational awareness by providing AT/FP briefings to transiting units prior to entry into higher threat level areas in the gaining Geographic CINC's AOR.

Finding: Intra-theater transiting units require the same degree of attention as other transiting units to deter, disrupt and mitigate acts of terrorism.

- *Recommendation:* Secretary of Defense direct Geographic CINCs and Component Commanders to reassess current procedures to ensure that AT/FP principles enumerated in this Report are applied to intra-theater transiting units.

Finding: Using operational risk management standards as a tool to measure engagement activities against risk to in-transit forces will enable commanders to determine whether to suspend or continue engagement activities.

- *Recommendation:* Secretary of Defense direct the CINCs to adopt and institutionalize a discrete operational risk management model to be used in AT/FP planning and execution.

Finding: Incident response must be an integral element of AT/FP planning.

- *Recommendation:* Secretary of Defense direct the Geographic CINCs to identify theater rapid incident response team requirements and integrate their utilization in contingency planning for in-transit units, and the Services to organize, train, and equip such forces.

Intelligence

Finding: In-transit units require intelligence support tailored to the terrorist threat in their immediate area of operations. This support must be dedicated from a higher echelon (tailored production and analysis).

- *Recommendation:* Secretary of Defense reprioritize intelligence production to ensure that in-transit units are given tailored, focused intelligence support for independent missions.

Finding: If the Department of Defense is to execute engagement activities related to the National Security Strategy with the least possible level of risk, then Services must reprioritize time, emphasis, and resources to prepare the transiting units to perform intelligence preparation of the battlespace–like processes and formulate intelligence requests for information to support operational decision points.

- *Recommendation:* Secretary of Defense direct the Services to ensure forces are adequately resourced and trained to make maximum use of intelligence processes and procedures, including priority information requests and requests for information to support intelligence preparation of the battlespace for in-transit unit antiterrorism/force protection.

Finding: DoD does not allocate sufficient resources or all-source intelligence analysis and collection in support of combating terrorism.

Recommendations:
- Secretary of Defense reprioritize all-source intelligence collection and analysis personnel and resources so that sufficient emphasis is applied to combating terrorism. Analytical expertise must be imbedded, from the national, CINC, and Component Command levels, to the joint task force level.
- Secretary of Defense reprioritize terrorism-related human intelligence and signals intelligence resources.
- Secretary of Defense reprioritize resources for the development of language skills that support combating terrorism analysis and collection.

Finding: Service counterintelligence programs are integral to force protection and must be adequately manned and funded to meet the dynamic demands of supporting in-transit forces.

- *Recommendation:* Secretary of Defense ensure DoD counterintelligence organizations are adequately staffed and funded to meet counterintelligence force protection requirements.

Finding: Clearer DoD standards for threat and vulnerability assessments, must be developed at the joint level and be common across Services and commands.

Recommendations:
- Secretary of Defense standardize counterintelligence assessments and increase counterintelligence resources.
- Secretary of Defense direct DoD-standard requirements for the conduct of threat and vulnerability assessments for combating terrorism.
- Secretary of Defense direct the production of a DoD-standard Counterintelligence Collection Manual for combating terrorism.

Logistics

Finding: While classifying the diplomatic clearance and logistics requirement process may improve the operational security of transiting units, it is not practical due to the commercial nature of the process.

- *Recommendation:* None. Implementing proactive AT/FP measures identified in this report mitigate the effect of public knowledge of U.S. military ship and aircraft visits. . . .

Finding: Local providers of goods, services, and transportation must be employed and evaluated in ways that enhance the AT/FP posture of the in-transit unit.

- *Recommendation:* Secretary of Defense direct the Defense Logistics Agency and the Services to incorporate AT/FP concerns into the entire fabric of logistics support.

Training

Finding: Military Services must accomplish AT/FP training with a degree of rigor that equates to the unit's primary mission areas.

Recommendations:
- Secretary of Defense direct the Services to develop rigorous tactics, techniques, and procedures with measurable standards for AT/FP training and develop training regimens that will integrate AT/FP into unit-level training plans and pre-deployment exercises.
- Secretary of Defense direct the Services to elevate AT/FP training to the equivalent of a primary mission area and provide the same emphasis afforded combat tasks in order to instill a force protection mindset into each Service.

Finding: Better force protection is achieved if forces in transit are trained to demonstrate preparedness to deter acts of terrorism.

Recommendations:
- Secretary of Defense direct the Services to develop and resource credible deterrence standards, deterrence-specific tactics, techniques, and procedures and defensive equipment packages for all forms of transiting forces.

- Secretary of Defense direct the Services to ensure that pre-deployment training regimes include deterrence tactics, techniques, and procedures and AT/FP measures specific to the area of operation and equipment rehearsals.

Finding: DoD must better support commanders' ability to sustain their antiterrorism/force protection program and training regimens.

Recommendations:
- Secretary of Defense direct the Chairman of the Joint Chiefs of Staff to publish a single source document that categorizes all of the existing AT/FP training literature, plans and tactics, techniques, and procedures for use by the Services (on both classified and unclassified versions) (short term).
- Secretary of Defense direct the Chairman of the Joint Chiefs of Staff to consolidate and develop a single repository for all AT/FP lessons learned. This database should be accessible to unit commanders in the classified and unclassified mode (long term).
- Secretary of Defense direct the Chairman of the Joint Chiefs of Staff to continually update training tools, capture lessons and trends and aid Commanders in sustaining meaningful AT/FP training programs. . . .

As of July 5, 2002, the full text of the unclassified summary from the report was available at http://www.defenselink.mil/pubs/cole20010109.html

VERDICT IN THE 1988 BOMBING OF PAN AM FLIGHT 103
January 31, 2001

The bombing of Pan American World Airways Flight 103 on Decem-
ber 21, 1988, as it flew over Lockerbie, Scotland, on its way from London to
New York still ranks as one of the most horrific acts of international terror-
ism. The explosion at 30,000 feet killed all 259 people on board the plane—
including 189 Americans—and 11 people on the ground. The massive
international investigation that ensued initially focused on Palestinian
groups backed by Iran as the most likely culprits. However, scientific exam-
ination of evidence from the explosion eventually turned the criminal focus
toward Libyan operatives. (The Bombing of Pan Am Flight 103 over Scotland,
p. 102)

On November 14, 1991, the United States and Scotland indicted two
Libyan nationals for the bombing. When Libya refused to hand over the sus-
pects for trial, the United States and later the United Nations Security Coun-
cil imposed economic sanctions. Finally, in April 1999 the Libyan, British,
and U.S. governments reached an agreement for the two men to be tried in
the Netherlands by a Scottish court consisting of three judges. The trial be-
gan on May 3, 2000, and lasted eight months. On January 31, 2001, the
judges convicted Abdelbaset Ali Al Megrahi in the bombing and sentenced
him to life in prison with parole possible after twenty years. The judges said
that Megrahi was a high-ranking officer in one of Libya's intelligence ser-
vices. "The clear inference which we draw from this evidence is that the con-
ception, planning and execution of the plot which led to the planting of the
explosive device was of Libyan origin," they wrote. Megrahi's codefendant,
Al Amin Khalifa Fhimah, was found not guilty and freed from custody.
Fhimah was the former manager of Libyan Arab Airlines in Malta, where
prosecutors said the bomb originated.

Libya apparently hoped that handing over the suspects for trial would
help end its international isolation as a pariah state that sponsored terror-
ism. In January 2002 the Wall Street Journal *reported that senior U.S. and*
Libyan officials had held several secret meetings in recent years in England
and Switzerland to discuss improving relations between the two countries.

336

However, the newspaper also said that an unclassified CIA report found that Libya still had biological and chemical weapons programs and wanted to acquire long-range ballistic missiles. In May 2002 the Libyan government offered to pay $2.7 billion to the families of the Pan Am victims, but only if the United States and United Nations lifted their sanctions. The U.S. State Department said that in order for the sanctions to be lifted, Libya had to comply with UN requirements to compensate the families, admit responsibility for the bombing, and renounce terrorism. Meetings between the U.S., British, and Libyan governments in an attempt to resolve the issues were continuing in June 2002. Meanwhile, some families of British victims said what they really wanted was a government inquiry to determine exactly who ordered the bombing. Many Western intelligence officials believed it was ordered by Libyan leader Muammar Qadaffi, although he denied involvement.

Following is a statement by Robin Cook, the British foreign secretary, to the House of Commons on January 31, 2001, announcing that the British government accepts the Scottish court verdict that convicts one Libyan national and acquits the other:

Almost two years ago, I announced that we had secured the agreement of the Libyan Government to the surrender of the two men charged with the Lockerbie bombing. That agreement brought an end to almost a decade of diplomatic stalemate. It was made possible by a unique legal innovation—a trial before Scottish judges under Scotch law in a third country.

I want to record our gratitude to the Government of the Netherlands and to their local authorities for their ready and full cooperation in making available the excellent facilities at Camp Zeist. Their cooperation has confirmed the reputation of the Netherlands as a seat of international justice. I have today written to the Dutch Foreign Minister formally recording our thanks.

The whole House will wish to express its appreciation of the work of the police in what has been one of the longest and widest investigations in British history. Dumfries and Galloway police and the other police forces who cooperated in the inquiry can take credit for the evidence brought before the court.

The trial has been open and its proceedings have been punctilious. It is widely agreed that it has proved the fair trial, which we promised.

The panel of Scottish judges has now returned their verdict. They unanimously found guilty Mr. Al Megrahi, an official of the Libyan Intelligence Service. They acquitted Mr. Fhimah.

We accept the verdicts of the court. Mr. Al Megrahi is reported to intend to appeal. The House will understand that in the circumstances I will not comment on the substance of the legal arguments. However, the House will wish to know what international action the Government intends to take in the light of these verdicts.

The initiative to hold the trial at Camp Zeist was taken by Britain and secured by agreement with the Governments of the Netherlands, the United States and Libya. But we made those arrangements in accordance with a resolution of the United Nations Security Council, which is binding on all Member States.

Libya has complied with some of the requirements of the Security Council, such as handing over the two suspects. In the light of the guilty verdict, we will expect the Libyan Government to fulfil the remaining requirements. We therefore require Libya to accept responsibility for the act of their official who has been convicted. We also require Libya to pay compensation to the relatives of the victims.

Before coming to the House, I spoke by phone to Colin Powell, the U.S. Secretary of State. We both are clear that Libya must now fulfill the requirements in full of the Security Council. And we both committed our Governments to close cooperation to achieve that objective. I will be able to continue that consultation with Colin Powell when I meet him in Washington next week.

It is also in Libya's own interests to be seen to cooperate fully with the Security Council. In the light of the conviction of one of their senior intelligence officials, Libyan leaders need to take every opportunity to prove to the international community that they have definitively renounced terrorism and they will abide by international law.

Mr. Speaker,

The Lockerbie bombing stands among the most brutal acts of mass murder. The community of Lockerbie suffered a sudden and devastating tragedy. I spoke after the verdicts to my Hon. Friend for Dumfries, who is today with the local people who have borne their tragedy with dignity.

Every passenger and crew member of Pan Am 103 was killed. That night, more than 400 parents lost a child. Seventy-six women and men lost husbands or wives. And seven children lost both parents.

Nothing can repair the loss of those who were murdered that night or remove the grief of their relatives. But today at last those relatives know that in a fair trial in an open court justice has been done.

REPORT EXAMINES ORIGIN OF CURRENT MIDEAST VIOLENCE
May 21, 2001

In September 2000 a cycle of attacks and counterattacks by Israelis and Palestinians started that, by the end of 2001, had killed more than 800 people and wounded thousands more. The vast majority of those killed were Palestinians, but repeated suicide bombings by Palestinian militants struck fear into the hearts of Israelis. International diplomatic efforts failed to stop the seemingly singular fixation by both sides on exacting revenge for the latest attack by the other.

An eloquent warning of the long-term dangers faced by both Israelis and Palestinians came from an international commission, the Sharm el-Sheikh Fact-Finding Commission, which President Bill Clinton had appointed to investigate why violence broke out in September 2000. "Fear, hate, anger, and frustration have risen on both sides," the commission, headed by former U.S. senator George Mitchell, D-Maine, said in a report released May 21, 2001. "The greatest danger of all is that the culture of peace, nurtured over the previous decade, is being shattered. In its place there is a growing sense of futility and despair, and a growing resort to violence." Mitchell's panel also offered suggestions for restarting the peace process that became the basis for U.S. policy.

But neither the Palestinians nor the Israelis seemed inclined toward peace. On the Palestinian side, Palestine Liberation Organization leader Yasir Arafat ceded the initiative to Hamas and Islamic Jihad, two radical groups that used the Islamic religion to appeal to young, disaffected Palestinians. The two groups had initiated much of the violence against Israel during the first Palestinian uprising, or Intifada, from 1987 to 1991, and both were successful in recruiting suicide bombers willing to destroy themselves, along with as many Israelis as possible, for the rewards of heaven as promised by the Koran. On the Israeli side, the government became increasingly aggressive. Since late 2000 Israel had used helicopter-launched missiles and other high-tech military weapons to assassinate senior Palestinian figures who, the government said, helped direct the violence. Israel also used its overwhelming military force to attack Palestinian civilian areas in retaliation for terrorist bombings and other killings of Israeli civilians. Yet the suicide bombings continued. (Eyewitness Report Describing Sbarro Suicide Bombing, p. 346)

> ***Following are excerpts from the report released May 21, 2001, by the Sharm el-Sheikh Fact-Finding Commission that President Bill Clinton had appointed in September 2000 to investigate the latest round of violence in the Middle East. In the report, quotations attributed to the government of Israel (GOI), the Palestine Liberation Organization (PLO), and the Palestinian Authority (PA) refer to written submissions that those organizations gave the commission:***

Introduction

. . . Despite their long history and close proximity, some Israelis and Palestinians seem not to fully appreciate each other's problems and concerns. Some Israelis appear not to comprehend the humiliation and frustration that Palestinians must endure every day as a result of living with the continuing effects of occupation, sustained by the presence of Israeli military forces and settlements in their midst, or the determination of the Palestinians to achieve independence and genuine self-determination. Some Palestinians appear not to comprehend the extent to which terrorism creates fear among the Israeli people and undermines their belief in the possibility of co-existence, or the determination of the GOI [Government of Israel] to do whatever is necessary to protect its people.

Fear, hate, anger, and frustration have risen on both sides. The greatest danger of all is that the culture of peace, nurtured over the previous decade, is being shattered. In its place there is a growing sense of futility and despair, and a growing resort to violence. . . .

What Happened?

. . . In late September 2000, Israeli, Palestinian, and other officials received reports that Member of the Knesset (now Prime Minister) Ariel Sharon was planning a visit to the Haram al-Sharif/Temple Mount in Jerusalem. Palestinian and U.S. officials urged then Prime Minister Ehud Barak to prohibit the visit. Mr. Barak told us that he believed the visit was intended to be an internal political act directed against him by a political opponent, and he declined to prohibit it.

Mr. Sharon made the visit on September 28 accompanied by over 1,000 Israeli police officers. Although Israelis viewed the visit in an internal political context, Palestinians saw it as highly provocative to them. On the following day, in the same place, a large number of unarmed Palestinian demonstrators and a large Israeli police contingent confronted each other. According to the

U.S. Department of State, "Palestinians held large demonstrations and threw stones at police in the vicinity of the Western Wall. Police used rubber-coated metal bullets and live ammunition to disperse the demonstrators, killing 4 persons and injuring about 200." According to the GOI, 14 Israeli policemen were injured.

Similar demonstrations took place over the following several days. Thus began what has become known as the "Al-Aqsa Intifada" (Al-Aqsa being a mosque at the Haram al-Sharif/Temple Mount).

The GOI asserts that the immediate catalyst for the violence was the breakdown of the Camp David negotiations on July 25, 2000 and the "widespread appreciation in the international community of Palestinian responsibility for the impasse." In this view, Palestinian violence was planned by the PA [Palestinian Authority] leadership, and was aimed at "provoking and incurring Palestinian casualties as a means of regaining the diplomatic initiative."

The Palestine Liberation Organization (PLO) denies the allegation that the intifada was planned. It claims, however, that "Camp David represented nothing less than an attempt by Israel to extend the force it exercises on the ground to negotiations," and that "the failure of the summit, and the attempts to allocate blame on the Palestinian side only added to the tension on the ground. . . ."

From the perspective of the PLO, Israel responded to the disturbances with excessive and illegal use of deadly force against demonstrators; behavior which, in the PLO's view, reflected Israel's contempt for the lives and safety of Palestinians. For Palestinians, the widely seen images of the killing of 12-year-old Muhammad al Durra in Gaza on September 30, shot as he huddled behind his father, reinforced that perception.

From the perspective of the GOI, the demonstrations were organized and directed by the Palestinian leadership to create sympathy for their cause around the world by provoking Israeli security forces to fire upon demonstrators, especially young people. For Israelis, the lynching of two military reservists, First Sgt. Vadim Novesche and First Cpl. Yosef Avrahami, in Ramallah on October 12, reflected a deep-seated Palestinian hatred of Israel and Jews.

What began as a series of confrontations between Palestinian demonstrators and Israeli security forces, which resulted in the GOI's initial restrictions on the movement of people and goods in the West Bank and Gaza Strip (closures), has since evolved into a wider array of violent actions and responses. There have been exchanges of fire between built-up areas, sniping incidents and clashes between Israeli settlers and Palestinians. There have also been terrorist acts and Israeli reactions thereto (characterized by the GOI as counter-terrorism), including killings, further destruction of property and economic measures. Most recently, there have been mortar attacks on Israeli locations and IDF [Israel Defense Forces] ground incursions into Palestinian areas.

From the Palestinian perspective, the decision of Israel to characterize the current crisis as "an armed conflict short of war" is simply a means "to justify its assassination policy, its collective punishment policy, and its use of lethal force." From the Israeli perspective, "The Palestinian leadership have instigated, orchestrated and directed the violence. It has used, and continues to use, terror and attrition as strategic tools."

In their submissions, the parties traded allegations about the motivation and degree of control exercised by the other. However, we were provided with no persuasive evidence that the Sharon visit was anything other than an internal political act; neither were we provided with persuasive evidence that the PA planned the uprising.

Accordingly, we have no basis on which to conclude that there was a deliberate plan by the PA to initiate a campaign of violence at the first opportunity; or to conclude that there was a deliberate plan by the GOI to respond with lethal force.

However, there is also no evidence on which to conclude that the PA made a consistent effort to contain the demonstrations and control the violence once it began; or that the GOI made a consistent effort to use non-lethal means to control demonstrations of unarmed Palestinians. Amid rising anger, fear, and mistrust, each side assumed the worst about the other and acted accordingly.

The Sharon visit did not cause the "Al-Aqsa Intifada." But it was poorly timed and the provocative effect should have been foreseen; indeed it was foreseen by those who urged that the visit be prohibited. More significant were the events that followed: the decision of the Israeli police on September 29 to use lethal means against the Palestinian demonstrators; and the subsequent failure, as noted above, of either party to exercise restraint.

Why Did It Happen?

The roots of the current violence extend much deeper than an inconclusive summit conference. Both sides have made clear a profound disillusionment with the behavior of the other in failing to meet the expectations arising from the peace process launched in Madrid in 1991 and then in Oslo in 1993. Each side has accused the other of violating specific undertakings and undermining the spirit of their commitment to resolving their political differences peacefully.

Divergent Expectations

We are struck by the divergent expectations expressed by the parties relating to the implementation of the Oslo process. Results achieved from this process were unthinkable less than 10 years ago. During the latest round of negotiations, the parties were closer to a permanent settlement than ever before.

Nonetheless, Palestinians and Israelis alike told us that the premise on which the Oslo process is based—that tackling the hard "permanent status" issues be deferred to the end of the process—has gradually come under serious pressure. The step-by-step process agreed to by the parties was based on the assumption that each step in the negotiating process would lead to enhanced trust and confidence. To achieve this, each party would have to implement agreed upon commitments and abstain from actions that would be seen by the other as attempts to abuse the process in order to predetermine the shape of the final outcome. If this requirement is not met, the Oslo road map cannot successfully lead to its agreed destination. Today, each side blames the other for having ignored this fundamental aspect, resulting in a crisis in confidence. This problem became even more pressing with the opening of permanent status talks.

The GOI has placed primacy on moving toward a Permanent Status Agreement in a nonviolent atmosphere, consistent with commitments contained in the agreements between the parties. "Even if slower than was initially envisaged, there has, since the start of the peace process in Madrid in 1991, been steady progress towards the goal of a Permanent Status Agreement without the resort to violence on a scale that has characterized recent weeks." The "goal" is the Permanent Status Agreement, the terms of which must be negotiated by the parties.

The PLO view is that delays in the process have been the result of an Israeli attempt to prolong and solidify the occupation. Palestinians "believed that the Oslo process would yield an end to Israeli occupation in five years," the timeframe for the transitional period specified in the Declaration of Principles. Instead there have been, in the PLO's view, repeated Israeli delays culminating in the Camp David summit, where, "Israel proposed to annex about 11.2% of the West Bank (excluding Jerusalem) . . ." and offered unacceptable proposals concerning Jerusalem, security and refugees. "In sum, Israel's proposals at Camp David provided for Israel's annexation of the best Palestinian lands, the perpetuation of Israeli control over East Jerusalem, a continued Israeli military presence on Palestinian territory, Israeli control over Palestinian natural resources, airspace and borders, and the return of fewer than 1 per cent of refugees to their homes."

Both sides see the lack of full compliance with agreements reached since the opening of the peace process as evidence of a lack of good faith. This conclusion led to an erosion of trust even before the permanent status negotiations began.

Divergent Perspectives

During the last seven months, these views have hardened into divergent realities. Each side views the other as having acted in bad faith; as having turned the optimism of Oslo into the suffering and grief of victims and their loved ones. In their statements and actions, each side demonstrates a perspective that fails to recognize any truth in the perspective of the other.

The Palestinian Perspective

For the Palestinian side, "Madrid" and "Oslo" heralded the prospect of a State, and guaranteed an end to the occupation and a resolution of outstanding matters within an agreed time frame. Palestinians are genuinely angry at the continued growth of settlements and at their daily experiences of humiliation and disruption as a result of Israel's presence in the Palestinian territories. Palestinians see settlers and settlements in their midst not only as violating the spirit of the Oslo process, but also as an application of force in the form of Israel's overwhelming military superiority, which sustains and protects the settlements. . . .

The PLO alleges that Israeli political leaders "have made no secret of the fact that the Israeli interpretation of Oslo was designed to segregate the Palestinians in non-contiguous enclaves, surrounded by Israeli military-controlled borders, with settlements and settlement roads violating the territories' integrity." According to the PLO, "In the seven years since the [Declaration of Principles], the settler population in the West Bank, excluding East Jerusalem and the Gaza Strip, has doubled to 200,000, and the settler population in East Jerusalem has risen to 170,000. Israel has constructed approximately 30 new settlements, and expanded a number of existing ones to house these new settlers."

The PLO also claims that the GOI has failed to comply with other commitments such as the further withdrawal from the West Bank and the release of Palestinian prisoners. In addition, Palestinians expressed frustration with the impasse over refugees and the deteriorating economic circumstances in the West Bank and Gaza Strip.

The Israeli Perspective

From the GOI perspective, the expansion of settlement activity and the taking of measures to facilitate the convenience and safety of settlers do not prejudice the outcome of permanent status negotiations. . . .

Indeed, Israelis point out that at the Camp David summit and during subsequent talks the GOI offered to make significant concessions with respect to settlements in the context of an overall agreement.

Security, however, is the key GOI concern. The GOI maintains that the PLO has breached its solemn commitments by continuing the use of violence in the pursuit of political objectives. "Israel's principal concern in the peace process has been security. This issue is of overriding importance. . . . [S]ecurity is not something on which Israel will bargain or compromise. The failure of the Palestinian side to comply with both the letter and spirit of the security provisions in the various agreements has long been a source of disturbance in Israel."

According to the GOI, the Palestinian failure takes several forms: institutionalized anti-Israel, anti-Jewish incitement; the release from detention of terrorists; the failure to control illegal weapons; and the actual conduct of violent operations, ranging from the insertion of riflemen into demonstrations to terrorist attacks on Israeli civilians. The GOI maintains that the PLO has explicitly violated its renunciation of terrorism and other acts of violence, thereby significantly eroding trust between the parties. The GOI perceives "a thread, implied but nonetheless clear, that runs throughout the Palestinian submissions. It is that Palestinian violence against Israel and Israelis is somehow explicable, understandable, legitimate. . . ."

Recommendations

The GOI and the PA must act swiftly and decisively to halt the violence. Their immediate objectives then should be to rebuild confidence and resume negotiations. What we are asking is not easy. Palestinians and Israelis—not just their leaders, but two publics at large—have lost confidence in one another. We are asking political leaders to do, for the sake of their people, the politically difficult: to lead without knowing how many will follow. . . .

As of July 13, 2002, the full text of the report was available at http:// usinfo.state.gov/regional/nea/mitchell.htm

EYEWITNESS REPORT DESCRIBING SBARRO SUICIDE BOMBING

August 10, 2001

During 2001 news stories from the Middle East regularly reported the carnage as Palestinians and Israelis engaged in seemingly endless rounds of attacks and counterattacks. The stories made clear that neither party was interested in the suggestions by the Sharm el-Shikh Fact-Finding Commission for restarting the peace process. On the Palestinian side the primary weapon was disaffected young men who strapped bombs around their waists, traveled the short distance into Israel, and blew themselves up in markets or on buses, attempting to kill as many Israelis as possible. On the Israeli side the primary weapons were helicopter gunships and tanks. Yet the news accounts, which usually dryly stated the facts about the latest atrocity and toted up the number of new casualties, muted the true horror of what was happening. (Report Examines Origin of Current Mideast Violence, p. 339)

Then came August 9, 2001, when a twenty-three-year-old Palestinian blew himself up inside a crowded Sbarro pizzeria in downtown Jerusalem during the lunch hour. The blast killed fifteen people and injured at least ninety, making it one of the most deadly suicide attacks since the latest round of violence began in September 2000. Veteran USA Today *reporter Jack Kelley was thirty yards down the street when the pizzeria exploded, only moments after he and a source had given up their plan to eat at Sbarro because it was so crowded. "Three men, who had been eating pizza inside, were catapulted out on the chairs they had been sitting on," Kelley wrote in his graphic and harrowing eyewitness account of the attack. "When they hit the ground, their heads separated from their bodies and rolled down the street." Kelley's story helped earn him honors as a Pulitzer Prize finalist.*

Palestinian militants said the Sbarro bombing was revenge for the Israeli government's official policy of assassinating Palestinian leaders who it believed were behind the violence. Israel responded to the attack within hours by seizing nine Palestinian offices in East Jerusalem, including the headquarters of the Palestine Liberation Organization; firing missiles from F-16 fighter planes at a Palestinian police headquarters in Ramallah, de-

stroying the building; and moving tanks into Palestinian-controlled areas in the West Bank. Yet the cycle of violence continued, and there was no apparent end in sight by the summer of 2002.

Following is the newspaper account by USA Today *reporter Jack Kelley of the August 9, 2001, bombing of a Sbarro pizzeria in Jerusalem, published in the newspaper August 10, 2001:*

JERUSALEM—It was a scene out of a war movie.

The blast was so powerful it blew out the front of the Sbarro pizza restaurant on Jaffa Street. It knocked down people up to 30 yards away and sent flesh onto 2nd-story balconies on the next block.

Traumatized women, some with nails from the bomb embedded in their faces, arms and chests, huddled on the street corner and cried. Men stood motionless in shock. Children, their faces burned, walked around screaming, "Mom, mom, where are you?" Blood splattered the walls and dripped onto sidewalks.

Thursday's suicide bombing, which killed at least 15 people and injured nearly 90, struck downtown Jerusalem at the busiest time of the day—as the lunch hour was ending, at 2 P.M. I happened to be walking near the restaurant when the bomber struck.

It was the deadliest attack in Israel since the suicide bombing of a Tel Aviv disco June 1 that claimed the lives of 21 young Israelis. With so many people critically injured, it threatens to become the most deadly attack since violence erupted here in late September.

Officials warned that the death toll could rise. At least 10 people were in critical condition, including a 4-month-old child.

An entire family—a couple and their three children—were killed, relatives said. The family had lived in a settlement in the West Bank.

Two foreign tourists were among the dead, Israeli public radio reported. The radio identified them as Judith Greenbaum, 31, from New Jersey and Giora Balach, 60, from Brazil.

Hanna Tova Nachemberg, 31, of Riverdale, N.Y., was critically wounded with shrapnel in her chest, according to Rabbi Avi Weiss of the Hebrew Institute of Riverdale.

Three French tourists also were injured.

"The bomber knew what he was doing," Jerusalem Mayor Ehud Olmert said as he helped teams of Orthodox rabbis gather pieces of flesh from the street. Under Jewish law, people's bodies must be placed in their graves whole, or with all parts accounted for.

"This is a massacre," Olmert said.

The militant Muslim group Islamic Jihad, in a telephone interview with *USA Today*, claimed responsibility for the attack. It identified the suicide bomber as Hussein Omar Abu Naaseh, 23, of the West Bank town of Jenin.

The militant Muslim group Hamas also claimed credit for the bombing.

"We want this successful operation to prove to the terrorist (Israeli Prime Minister Ariel) Sharon that we can, and we will continue to, get him and his fellow pigs and monkeys where it hurts the most," senior Islamic Jihad official Abdallah al-Shami said.

Sharon convened an emergency meeting of his Security Cabinet immediately after the bombing and vowed to carry out a retaliatory attack against militant Muslim leaders. Israel has been targeting Palestinian extremists and assassinating them. It says they direct the terrorism.

Soon after the bombing, Palestinian Television reported Israeli tanks were shelling homes in Gaza.

Later in the day, Israeli soldiers took over a Palestinian security building in Abu Dis, which is next to Jerusalem.

The Israeli military sealed the entire West Bank and was moving troops into Jenin, the suicide bomber's hometown.

Palestinian Flag Comes Down

The Israelis also closed nine Palestinian Authority offices in East Jerusalem, including Orient House, the unofficial Palestinian foreign ministry. Seven Palestinian officials were brought out of Orient House early today and taken into custody by the Israeli military. Soldiers took down the Palestinian flag and replaced it with the Israeli flag.

Also, Israeli F-16 warplanes fired missiles at a Palestinian police building near Ramallah in the West Bank early today, Palestinians said. There were no casualties, but the building was destroyed. It was the first F-16 attack since May. Until now, Israel had confined its retaliation for Palestinian attacks to tank and helicopter strikes on Palestinian police positions.

"We hold (Palestinian Authority Chairman Yasser) Arafat responsible for this madness," Israeli government spokesman Danny Naveh said. "He has given the green light to Islamic Jihad, Hamas and the other terrorists."

But Palestinian Authority spokesman Yasser Abed Rabbo, who denounced the bombing, blamed Sharon for carrying out "Mafia-style" assassinations of nearly 60 militant Muslim leaders since September. "Sharon has inflamed the Palestinian people with his terrorist, gangland-style assassinations," Rabbo said.

The popular Sbarro restaurant, like other shops and eating places along Jaffa Street, was packed at lunchtime, so I and an Israeli official I was scheduled to interview decided not to eat there.

Several customers, including three mothers and their infants in strollers, stood outside on the sidewalk, eating their pizza and plates of spaghetti. Dozens of pedestrians pushed their way around the women or were forced to walk along the busy street next to the crowded buses.

Among those I could see fighting their way into the restaurant was a young man, wearing a white T-shirt and dark sport jacket. A black pouch, similar to a small camera case, was attached to his waist. He appeared to be Palestinian.

Once inside, he stared at the fluorescent menu board and at the red, green and white tiles, as if to survey his surroundings, one of the restaurant workers said later. He then asked the restaurant clerk how long he would have to wait for a plate of take-out spaghetti. As the clerk answered, witnesses said, the man reached inside his pouch and calmly detonated what turned out to be a bomb.

The explosion was deafening and sent out a burst of heat that could be felt far down the street. It blew out windows and threw tables and chairs into the air. Victims' arms and legs rained down onto the street.

Three men, who had been eating pizza inside, were catapulted out on the chairs they had been sitting on. When they hit the ground, their heads separated from their bodies and rolled down the street. Dozens of men, women and children, their bodies punctured by nails from the bomb, began dropping in pain. One woman had six nails in her neck. Another had a nail in her left eye.

Two men, one with a 6-inch piece of glass in his right temple, the other with glass shards in his calf, fell to the ground bleeding. A passerby tried to comfort them but broke down crying. As he walked away, he tripped on a decapitated body and fell.

Next to them, a man groaned in pain. "Help me, please. I'm dying," he said. His legs had been blown off. Blood poured from where his genitals had been. An Israeli soldier, upon seeing him, gasped "Oh, God," dropped his gun and vomited. The man bled to death less than a minute later.

"There Could Be Another Bomb!"

Police officers began arriving, yelling into their handheld walkie-talkies and shouting instructions for bystanders to leave. "There could be another bomb! There could be another bomb!" a police officer yelled into a megaphone. He began to cordon off the area.

Few could hear him over the screams of the injured, the sirens of approaching ambulances and the shrill blare of dozens of car alarms set off by the explosion.

Suddenly, a Palestinian man ran up to an injured Israeli as if to help. An Israeli soldier butted the Palestinian in the chest with his rifle, knocking him to the ground. "I'm a nurse! I'm a nurse," the Palestinian yelled. As he got up, another Israeli soldier threw him against a wall, grabbed him by the neck and placed him under arrest. Two other soldiers hauled him off, hitting him in the head as they walked.

"Terrorist!" a nearby police officer yelled, pointing at the man.

Meanwhile, yards away, a little girl about 3 years old, her face covered with glass, walked among the bodies, calling out her mother's name. Seconds later, she found her. The girl told her mother to get up. But the mother, apparently already dead, didn't respond. The girl, still unaware of what had happened, was led away, in hysterics, by an Israeli policewoman.

Inside the blackened shell of the restaurant, a policeman pointed to what he said was the top of the head of the suicide bomber, which was lying on the floor. The nose and mouth were missing. The teeth appeared to be lying nearby.

"You've killed us all, you bastard," the officer said, pointing to the head.

He then tried to kick the head, but was stopped by another officer. The man spat at the head as he was led away.

349

Dozens of ambulances arrived over the next thirty minutes to cart off the dead and injured as relatives begin arriving. Rabbis, with white gloves, raced around the street picking up pieces of flesh. One rabbi found a small hand splattered against a white Subaru parked outside the restaurant.

"It's of a girl," Rabbi Moshe Aaron said. "She was probably 5 or 6, the same age as my daughter." He gently put it into a bag.

"I wish I could say there won't be anything like this tragedy again," Aaron said. "But it's just a matter of time until another bomber kills more of us. It'll be like this until the end of time."

BUSH ON TERRORIST ATTACKS AGAINST THE UNITED STATES
September 11 and 14, 2001

The terrorists who blew up a massive truck bomb in the parking garage underneath the World Trade Center in February 1993 hoped that the blast would cause one of the famous 110-story twin towers to topple onto the other, killing 50,000 people or even more. The bombing killed six people, injured more than 1,000 others, and caused hundreds of millions of dollars in damage, but the twin towers remained standing. (The 1993 Bombing of the World Trade Center, p. 123)

Just over eight years later, a second band of terrorists succeeded in the original goal of destroying the World Trade Center. On the morning of September 11, 2001, groups of terrorists wielding box-cutter knives hijacked four airliners on the East Coast, killed or incapacitated pilots and flight attendants, took over the controls, and deliberately flew three of the planes into buildings that represented American financial and military might: the two towers of the World Trade Center in New York City and the Pentagon, just outside Washington, D.C. The planes were loaded with 10,000 gallons of fuel each, and they exploded in massive fireballs when they hit their targets. The first plane struck the north tower of the World Trade Center at 8:46 A.M., and it collapsed at 10:29 A.M. The second plane hit the south tower at 9:03 A.M., and it collapsed at 9:50 A.M. As flames that reached 2,000 degrees Fahrenheit consumed the buildings, some people trapped on upper floors jumped from windows to their death. More than 25,000 people managed to escape the two buildings before they collapsed. The fourth plane, which was reportedly headed for the White House, crashed in a field in Pennsylvania after passengers fought with the hijackers. Authorities intent on preventing more attacks shut down the nation's air traffic system, ordering all planes in the air to land at the nearest airport, and mobilized fighter jets to patrol the skies over the nation's largest cities. Less than a dozen hours after the attacks began in New York City, President George W. Bush went on television to reassure a stunned nation and world. "These acts of mass murder were intended to frighten our nation into chaos and retreat, but they have failed," the president said. Three days later, on September 14, Bush addressed the nation again at a ceremony at Washington's National Cathedral marking what he had declared as a National Day of Prayer and Remembrance. "War has been waged against us by stealth and deceit and murder," Bush said. "This nation is peaceful, but fierce when stirred to anger. This conflict was begun on the timing and terms of others. It will end in a way, and at an hour, of our choosing."

Law enforcement officials quickly tied the nineteen hijackers, all from the Middle East, with the al Qaeda terrorist network run by Osama bin Laden. On October 7 U.S. and British forces launched an enormous military campaign in Afghanistan that, within weeks, led to the overthrow of the Taliban regime that had allowed bin Laden to base his operations in that country. Meanwhile, the process of cleanup began at home. Within less than nine months workers at the World Trade Center site, dubbed Ground Zero, removed 108,342 truckloads of debris before officially ending their task with a solemn ceremony on May 30, 2002. Two months later employees at the city medical examiner's office were still continuing their grim task of attempting to identify nearly 20,000 body parts recovered at the scene, but it was estimated that no remains would be identified for about 800 victims. And in Washington, construction workers at the Pentagon raced to finish repairs by the one-year anniversary of the attack. The final death toll, not including the hijackers, was believed to be 3,025 people: 2,801 in New York City, 184 in Washington, and 40 in Pennsylvania. In New York, the dead included 343 firefighters. (United States, Britain Launch War in Afghanistan, p. 366)

Following are the texts of a televised address by President George W. Bush on September 11, 2001, and a statement by Bush at Washington's National Cathedral marking a National Day of Prayer and Remembrance on September 14, 2001:

SEPTEMBER 11 ADDRESS

Good evening. Today, our fellow citizens, our way of life, our very freedom came under attack in a series of deliberate and deadly terrorist acts. The victims were in airplanes, or in their offices; secretaries, businessmen and women, military and federal workers; moms and dads, friends and neighbors. Thousands of lives were suddenly ended by evil, despicable acts of terror.

The pictures of airplanes flying into buildings, fires burning, huge structures collapsing, have filled us with disbelief, terrible sadness, and a quiet, unyielding anger. These acts of mass murder were intended to frighten our nation into chaos and retreat. But they have failed; our country is strong.

A great people has been moved to defend a great nation. Terrorist attacks can shake the foundations of our biggest buildings, but they cannot touch the foundation of America. These acts shattered steel, but they cannot dent the steel of American resolve.

America was targeted for attack because we're the brightest beacon for freedom and opportunity in the world. And no one will keep that light from shining.

Today, our nation saw evil, the very worst of human nature. And we responded with the best of America—with the daring of our rescue workers, with the caring for strangers and neighbors who came to give blood and help in any way they could.

Immediately following the first attack, I implemented our government's emergency response plans. Our military is powerful, and it's prepared. Our emergency teams are working in New York City and Washington, D.C. to help with local rescue efforts.

Our first priority is to get help to those who have been injured, and to take every precaution to protect our citizens at home and around the world from further attacks.

The functions of our government continue without interruption. Federal agencies in Washington which had to be evacuated today are reopening for essential personnel tonight, and will be open for business tomorrow. Our financial institutions remain strong, and the American economy will be open for business, as well.

The search is underway for those who are behind these evil acts. I've directed the full resources of our intelligence and law enforcement communities to find those responsible and to bring them to justice. We will make no distinction between the terrorists who committed these acts and those who harbor them.

I appreciate so very much the members of Congress who have joined me in strongly condemning these attacks. And on behalf of the American people, I thank the many world leaders who have called to offer their condolences and assistance.

America and our friends and allies join with all those who want peace and security in the world, and we stand together to win the war against terrorism. Tonight, I ask for your prayers for all those who grieve, for the children whose worlds have been shattered, for all whose sense of safety and security has been threatened. And I pray they will be comforted by a power greater than any of us, spoken through the ages in Psalm 23: "Even though I walk through the valley of the shadow of death, I fear no evil, for You are with me."

This is a day when all Americans from every walk of life unite in our resolve for justice and peace. America has stood down enemies before, and we will do so this time. None of us will ever forget this day. Yet, we go forward to defend freedom and all that is good and just in our world.

Thank you. Good night, and God bless America.

SEPTEMBER 14 STATEMENT

We are here in the middle hour of our grief. So many have suffered so great a loss, and today we express our nation's sorrow. We come before God to pray for the missing and the dead, and for those who love them.

On Tuesday, our country was attacked with deliberate and massive cruelty. We have seen the images of fire and ashes, and bent steel.

Now come the names, the list of casualties we are only beginning to read. They are the names of men and women who began their day at a desk or in an airport, busy with life. They are the names of people who faced death, and in their last moments called home to say, be brave, and I love you.

They are the names of passengers who defied their murderers, and prevented the murder of others on the ground. They are the names of men and women who wore the uniform of the United States, and died at their posts.

They are the names of rescuers, the ones whom death found running up the stairs and into the fires to help others. We will read all these names. We will linger over them, and learn their stories, and many Americans will weep.

To the children and parents and spouses and families and friends of the lost, we offer the deepest sympathy of the nation. And I assure you, you are not alone.

Just three days removed from these events, Americans do not yet have the distance of history. But our responsibility to history is already clear: to answer these attacks and rid the world of evil.

War has been waged against us by stealth and deceit and murder. This nation is peaceful, but fierce when stirred to anger. This conflict was begun on the timing and terms of others. It will end in a way, and at an hour, of our choosing.

Our purpose as a nation is firm. Yet our wounds as a people are recent and unhealed, and lead us to pray. In many of our prayers this week, there is a searching, and an honesty. At St. Patrick's Cathedral in New York on Tuesday, a woman said, "I prayed to God to give us a sign that He is still here." Others have prayed for the same, searching hospital to hospital, carrying pictures of those still missing.

God's signs are not always the ones we look for. We learn in tragedy that His purposes are not always our own. Yet the prayers of private suffering, whether in our homes or in this great cathedral, are known and heard, and understood.

There are prayers that help us last through the day, or endure the night. There are prayers of friends and strangers, that give us strength for the journey. And there are prayers that yield our will to a will greater than our own.

This world He created is of moral design. Grief and tragedy and hatred are only for a time. Goodness, remembrance, and love have no end. And the Lord of life holds all who die, and all who mourn.

It is said that adversity introduces us to ourselves. This is true of a nation as well. In this trial, we have been reminded, and the world has seen, that our fellow Americans are generous and kind, resourceful and brave. We see our national character in rescuers working past exhaustion; in long lines of blood donors; in thousands of citizens who have asked to work and serve in any way possible.

And we have seen our national character in eloquent acts of sacrifice. Inside the World Trade Center, one man who could have saved himself stayed until the end at the side of his quadriplegic friend. A beloved priest died giving the last rites to a firefighter. Two office workers, finding a disabled stranger, carried her down sixty-eight floors to safety. A group of men drove through the night from Dallas to Washington to bring skin grafts for burn victims.

In these acts, and in many others, Americans showed a deep commitment to one another, and an abiding love for our country. Today, we feel what Franklin Roosevelt called the warm courage of national unity. This is a unity of every faith, and every background.

It has joined together political parties in both houses of Congress. It is evident in services of prayer and candlelight vigils, and American flags, which are displayed in pride, and wave in defiance.

Our unity is a kinship of grief, and a steadfast resolve to prevail against our enemies. And this unity against terror is now extending across the world.

America is a nation full of good fortune, with so much to be grateful for. But we are not spared from suffering. In every generation, the world has produced enemies of human freedom. They have attacked America, because we are freedom's home and defender. And the commitment of our fathers is now the calling of our time.

On this national day of prayer and remembrance, we ask almighty God to watch over our nation, and grant us patience and resolve in all that is to come. We pray that He will comfort and console those who now walk in sorrow. We thank Him for each life we now must mourn, and the promise of a life to come.

As we have been assured, neither death nor life, nor angels nor principalities nor powers, nor things present nor things to come, nor height nor depth, can separate us from God's love. May He bless the souls of the departed. May He comfort our own. And may He always guide our country.

God bless America.

SEPTEMBER 11 ATTACKS AFFIRM AVIATION SECURITY CONCERNS
September 20, 2001

Since at least 1987, investigators from the General Accounting Office (GAO) have repeatedly warned about major weaknesses in aviation security in public reports and testimony before Congress. Over the years several federal commissions, the Transportation Department inspector general, and others have also expressed strong concerns about security problems at America's airports. Some problems were eventually corrected, but many others were not. Then came September 11, 2001, when nineteen terrorists passed through security checkpoints at three major airports, seized control of four airliners, and crashed them into the World Trade Center, the Pentagon, and a field in Pennsylvania. (Bush on Terrorist Attacks Against the United States, p. 351)

The attacks quickly led to yet another round of congressional hearings about troubles with aviation security. At an unusual joint meeting of House and Senate Appropriations subcommittees on September 20, 2001, Gerald L. Dillingham, director of physical infrastructure issues for the GAO, ticked off the biggest problems that remained unresolved. Dillingham said the FAA's computerized air traffic control system was "susceptible to intrusion and malicious attacks," airports and airlines were doing a poor job of controlling access to supposedly secure areas, and turnover rates for security screeners at most airports continued to exceed 100 percent annually. "In recent years, we and others have often demonstrated that significant weaknesses continue to plague the nation's aviation security," Dillingham said.

Public confidence in aviation security was further shaken in December when Richard C. Reid passed through airport security in Paris and allegedly attempted to ignite explosives packed in his shoes aboard an American Airlines flight to Miami. Alert crew members and passengers subdued Reid, who turned out to have links to the al Qaeda terrorist network. Then in March 2002, USA Today reported that undercover tests by the Transportation Department's inspector general in the months after September 11 still found massive weaknesses in aviation security. In tests at security checkpoints at numerous airports, the newspaper said that screeners failed to spot guns in 30 percent of the tests, missed simulated explosive devices in 60 percent, and failed to detect knives in 70 percent. Overall, they missed dangerous items 48 percent of the time. Investigators also tried secretly boarding aircraft or gaining access to the airport tarmac, the newspaper said. They succeeded in 48 percent of their attempts.

Following are excerpts from testimony by Gerald L. Dillingham, director of physical infrastructure issues at the General Accounting Office, at a September 20, 2001, hearing of the transportation subcommittees of the House and Senate appropriations committees:

Background

Some context for my remarks is appropriate. The threat of terrorism was significant throughout the 1990s; a plot to destroy 12 U.S. airliners was discovered and thwarted in 1995, for instance. Yet the task of providing security to the nation's aviation system is unquestionably daunting, and we must reluctantly acknowledge that any form of travel can never be made totally secure. The enormous size of U.S. airspace alone defies easy protection. Furthermore, given this country's hundreds of airports, thousands of planes, tens of thousands of daily flights, and the seemingly limitless ways terrorists or criminals can devise to attack the system, aviation security must be enforced on several fronts. Safeguarding airplanes and passengers requires, at the least, ensuring that perpetrators are kept from breaching security checkpoints and gaining access to secure airport areas or to aircraft. Additionally, vigilance is required to prevent attacks against the extensive computer networks that FAA uses to guide thousands of flights safely through U.S. airspace. FAA has developed several mechanisms to prevent criminal acts against aircraft, such as adopting technology to detect explosives and establishing procedures to ensure that passengers are positively identified before boarding a flight. Still, in recent years, we and others have often demonstrated that significant weaknesses continue to plague the nation's aviation security.

Potential for Unauthorized Access to Aviation Computer Systems

Our work has identified numerous problems with aspects of aviation security in recent years. One such problem is FAA's computer-based air traffic control (ATC) system. The ATC system is an enormous, complex collection of interrelated systems, including navigation, surveillance, weather, and automated information processing and display systems that link hundreds of ATC facilities and provide information to air traffic controllers and pilots. Failure to adequately protect these systems could increase the risk of regional or nationwide disruption of air traffic—or even collisions.

In five reports issued from 1998 through 2000, we pointed out numerous weaknesses in FAA's computer security. FAA had not (1) completed background checks on thousands of contractor employees, (2) assessed and accredited as secure many of its ATC facilities, (3) performed appropriate risk assessments to determine the vulnerability of the majority of its ATC systems, (4) established a comprehensive security program, (5) developed service continuity controls to ensure that critical operations continue without undue interruption when unexpected events occur, and (6) fully implemented an intrusion detection capability to detect and respond to malicious intrusions. Some of these weaknesses could have led to serious problems. For example, as part of its Year 2000 readiness efforts, FAA allowed 36 mainland Chinese nationals who had not undergone required background checks to review the computer source code for eight mission-critical systems.

To date, we have made nearly 22 recommendations to improve FAA's computer security. FAA has worked to address these recommendations, but most of them have yet to be completed. For example, it is making progress in obtaining background checks on contractors and accrediting facilities and systems as secure. However, it will take time to complete these efforts.

Weaknesses in Airport Access Controls

Control of access to aircraft, airfields, and certain airport facilities is another component of aviation security. Among the access controls in place are requirements intended to prevent unauthorized individuals from using forged, stolen, or outdated identification or their familiarity with airport procedures to gain access to secured areas. In May 2000, we reported that our special agents, in an undercover capacity, obtained access to secure areas of two airports by using counterfeit law enforcement credentials and badges. At these airports, our agents declared themselves as armed law enforcement officers, displayed simulated badges and credentials created from commercially available software packages or downloaded from the Internet, and were issued "law enforcement" boarding passes. They were then waved around the screening checkpoints without being screened. Our agents could thus have carried weapons, explosives, chemical/biological agents, or other dangerous objects onto aircraft. In response to our findings, FAA now requires that each airport's law enforcement officers examine the badges and credentials of any individual seeking to bypass passenger screening. FAA is also working on a "smart card" computer system that would verify law enforcement officers' identity and authorization for bypassing passenger screening.

The Department of Transportation's Inspector General has also uncovered problems with access controls at airports. The Inspector General's staff conducted testing in 1998 and 1999 of the access controls at eight major airports and succeeded in gaining access to secure areas in 68 percent of the tests; they were able to board aircraft 117 times. After the release of its report describing its successes in breaching security, the Inspector General conducted additional testing between December 1999 and March 2000 and found that, although improvements had been made, access to secure areas was still gained more than 30 percent of the time.

Inadequate Detection of Dangerous Objects by Screeners

Screening checkpoints and the screeners who operate them are a key line of defense against the introduction of dangerous objects into the aviation system. Over 2 million passengers and their baggage must be checked each day for articles that could pose threats to the safety of an aircraft and those aboard it. The air carriers are responsible for screening passengers and their baggage before they are permitted into the secure areas of an airport or onto an aircraft. Air carriers can use their own employees to conduct screening activities, but mostly air carriers hire security companies to do the screening. Currently, multiple carriers and screening companies are responsible for screening at some of the nation's larger airports.

Concerns have long existed over screeners' ability to detect and prevent dangerous objects from entering secure areas. Each year, weapons were discovered to have passed through one checkpoint and have later been found during screening for a subsequent flight. FAA monitors the performance of screeners by periodically testing their ability to detect potentially dangerous objects carried by FAA special agents posing as passengers. In 1978, screeners failed to detect 13 percent of the objects during FAA tests. In 1987, screeners missed 20 percent of the objects during the same type of test. Test data for the 1991 to 1999 period show that the declining trend in detection rates continues. [Information on FAA tests results is now designated as sensitive security information and cannot be publicly released. Consequently, we cannot discuss the actual detection rates for the 1991–1999 period.] Furthermore, the recent tests show that as tests become more realistic and more closely approximate how a terrorist might attempt to penetrate a checkpoint, screeners' ability to detect dangerous objects declines even further. . . .

Differences in the Screening Practices of Five Other Countries and the United States

We visited five countries—Belgium, Canada, France, the Netherlands, and the United Kingdom—viewed by FAA and the civil aviation industry as having effective screening operations to identify screening practices that differ from those in the United States. We found that some significant differences exist in four areas: screening operations, screener qualifications, screener pay and benefits, and institutional responsibility for screening.

First, screening operations in some of the countries we visited are more stringent. . . .

Second, screeners' qualifications are usually more extensive. In contrast to the United States, Belgium requires screeners to be citizens; France requires screeners to be citizens of a European Union country. In the Netherlands, screeners do not have to be citizens, but they must have been residents of the country for 5 years. Training requirements for screeners were also greater in four of the countries we visited than in the United States. While FAA requires that screeners in this country have 12 hours of classroom training before they can begin work, Belgium, Canada, France, and the Netherlands require more. . . .

Third, screeners receive relatively better pay and benefits in most of these countries. Whereas screeners in the United States receive wages that are at or slightly above minimum wage, screeners in some countries receive wages that are viewed as being at the "middle income" level in those countries. . . .

Finally, the responsibility for screening in most of these countries is placed with the airport authority or with the government, not with the air carriers as it is in the United States. In Belgium, France, and the United Kingdom, the responsibility for screening has been placed with the airports, which either hire screening companies to conduct the screening operations or, as at some airports in the United Kingdom, hire screeners and manage the checkpoints themselves. In the Netherlands, the government is responsible for passenger screening and hires a screening company to conduct checkpoint operations, which are overseen by a Dutch police force. We note that, worldwide, of 102 other countries with international airports, 100 have placed screening responsibility with the airports or the government; only 2 other countries—Canada and Bermuda—place screening responsibility with air carriers. . . .

As of July 8, 2002, the full text of the testimony was available at http://www.gao.gov/new.items/d011166t.pdf

CASTRO ACCUSES UNITED STATES OF INCONSISTENCY ON TERRORISM
October 6, 2001

On October 6, 1976, a bomb exploded aboard a Cubana Airlines DC8 as it flew from Barbados to Cuba, killing all seventy-three people aboard. Authorities in Venezuela, where the flight originated, arrested Orlando Bosch, a well-known Cuban exile and anti-Castro militant who previously lived in Florida, and charged him with masterminding the crime. Bosch spent eleven years in jail despite being acquitted twice. Upon his release he flew to Miami on February 16, 1988, where he was immediately arrested for violating parole. Many members of Miami's Cuban exile community considered Bosch a hero because of his ceaseless battle against Cuban president Fidel Castro. The U.S. Justice Department disagreed, labeling Bosch a terrorist who should be deported. In June 1989 Acting Associate Attorney General Joe Whitley, citing classified FBI and CIA files, wrote in a deportation order that Bosch directed the 1976 Cubana Airlines bombing and had participated in more than thirty other acts of sabotage and violence. Whitley said Bosch "has been resolute and unwavering in his advocacy of terrorist violence. . . . Appeasement of those who would use force will only breed more terrorists. We must look on terrorism as a universal evil, even if it is directed toward those with whom we have no political sympathy." But a year later, after extensive lobbying of President George H. Bush's administration by Miami's Cuban community and Florida politicians, including the president's son Jeb, the Justice Department suddenly announced that Bosch would be paroled into the community because no other country would take him. Time *magazine headlined its story about Bosch's release "Victory for a Terrorist."*

At a huge rally in Havana on October 6, 2001, marking the twenty-fifth anniversary of the airliner bombing, Castro asked why Bosch and others he accused of terrorist acts against Cuba were allowed to remain free in the United States. "It is not too much to ask that justice be done," Castro said, "for these professional terrorists, acting from inside the very territory of the United States, have not ceased to apply their despicable methods against our people to sow terror and to destroy the economy. . . ." In his speech Castro also condemned the terrorist attacks on the World Trade Center and the Pentagon that had occurred less than a month earlier.

Only months before Castro spoke, on June 8, 2001, a federal jury in Miami convicted five men of spying for Cuba. The men—three of whom were agents of Cuba's intelligence service—had spent most of their time infiltrating anti-Castro groups in Miami. The defendants said their spying was necessary to prevent terrorist attacks against Cuba. The men received sentences ranging from ten years to life in prison. The next dust-up over terrorism between the United States and Cuba came in May 2002, when a State Department official accused Cuba of developing biochemical weapons and providing them to other countries. Castro called the claim an "infamous and slanderous lie." Former president Jimmy Carter, who toured Cuba only days afterward, said he saw no evidence to back up the State Department's accusation. In July 2002 Bosch's case was again in the news when Governor Jeb Bush of Florida appointed Raoul Cantero III as the first Hispanic member of the state's Supreme Court. Cantero, a Cuban-American, had represented Bosch when he was threatened with deportation.

Following are excerpts from a speech by Cuban president Fidel Castro at a rally in Havana on October 6, 2001:

Fellow countrymen:

History can be unpredictable and move along strange labyrinths. Twenty-five years ago, in this very same square, we bid a final farewell to a small number of coffins. They contained tiny fragments of human remains and personal belongings of some of the 57 Cubans, 11 Guyanese—most of them students on scholarships in Cuba—and five North Korean cultural officials who were the victims of a brutal and inconceivable act of terrorism. What was particularly moving was the death of almost the entire Cuban juvenile fencing team, both women and men, coming home with every single one of the gold medals awarded in this sport at a Central American and Caribbean tournament.

A million of our fellow countrymen, with tears filling their eyes and running down their cheeks, gathered here to bid a more symbolic than actual farewell to our brothers and sisters whose bodies rested on the ocean floor.

Nobody, except for a group of friendly personalities and institutions, shared our pain and sorrow. There was no upheaval around the world, no acute political crises, no United Nations meetings, nor the imminent threat of war.

Perhaps, few people in the world understood the terrible significance of that event. How important could it be that a Cuban jetliner was blown up in mid-flight with 73 people aboard? It was almost a common occurrence. Thousands of Cubans had already died in La Coubre, the Escambray Mountains, the Bay of Pigs, and in hundreds of other terrorist acts, pirate attacks and similar actions, had they not? Who could pay any attention to the denunciations of this tiny country? All that was needed, apparently, was a simple denial from the powerful neighbor and their media, which inundate the world, and the matter was forgotten.

Who could have predicted that almost exactly 25 years later, a war with totally unpredictable consequences would be on the verge of breaking out as a result of an equally heinous terrorist attack, which claimed the lives of thousands of innocent people in the United States? Back then, in what now appears to be a tragic omen, innocent people from various countries died; this time, there were victims from 86 nations. . . .

Dramatic events like the assassination of President Kennedy led to in-depth investigations, like that carried out by an U.S. Senate Committee. The embarrassing situations and major scandals that resulted forced a change in tactics, although there was never really any change in the policy towards Cuba. As a consequence, after periods of relative calm, new waves of terrorism have continued to break out.

This is exactly what happened in late 1975. The Church Commission had presented its famous report on assassination plots against the leaders of Cuba and other countries on November 20 of that year, therefore, the Central Intelligence Agency could not continue assuming direct responsibility for assassination plots and terrorist acts against Cuba. The solution was simple: their most trustworthy and best-trained terrorist personnel would adopt the form of independent groups, which would act on their own behalf and under their own responsibility. This led to the sudden emergence of a bizarre coordinating organization, called the CORU [Command of United Revolutionary Organizations], and made up by the main terrorist groups in operation, which as a rule were fiercely divided, due to leadership ambitions and personal interests. A wave of violent terrorist actions was then unleashed. . . .

The groups that made up the CORU, which began to operate in the first months of 1976, although it was not officially founded until June of that year, issued public statements in the United States claiming responsibility for every one of the terrorist acts they perpetrated. They sent their war dispatches— as they themselves called them—from Costa Rica to the Miami press. One of their publications printed an article entitled "War Dispatch" recounting the destruction of a Cuban embassy. That was the day they did not hesitate in publishing a particularly significant communiqué signed by the five terrorist groups that made up the CORU: "Very soon we will attack airplanes in mid-flight."

To carry out their attacks, the CORU terrorists freely used as the main bases for their operations the territories of the United States, Puerto Rico, Somoza's Nicaragua, and Pinochet's Chile.

Only eight weeks later, the Cuban jetliner would be blown up in mid-flight off the coasts of Barbados with 73 people aboard.

Hernán Ricardo and Freddy Lugo were the two Venezuelan mercenaries who planted the bomb during the Trinidad and Tobago-Barbados leg of the flight. They got off the plane in Barbados and returned to Trinidad, where they were arrested and immediately confessed to their involvement.

The Barbados police commissioner declared before an investigative committee that Ricardo and Lugo had confessed that they were working for the CIA. He added that Ricardo had pulled out a CIA card and another one where the rules for the use of C-4 plastic explosives were described.

On October 24, 1976, The *New York Times* indicated that "the terrorists who launched a wave of attacks in seven countries during the last two years were the product and instruments of the CIA."

The *Washington Post* noted that confirmed contacts with the U.S. embassy in Venezuela "cast doubt" on the statement issued on October 15 by U.S. Secretary of State Henry Kissinger, with regard to the claim that "no one related to the U.S. government had anything to do with the sabotage of the airplane" from Cuba.

A correspondent from the Mexican daily *Excelsior* commented from Port of Spain that "with the confession made by Hernán Ricardo Lozano, the Venezuelan detained here in Trinidad, about his responsibility in the attack on a Cubana aircraft that crashed off the coast of Barbados with 73 people aboard, a major anti-Castro terrorist network that is somehow linked with the CIA is on the verge of exposure."

Le Monde wrote that the CIA connection with Cuban-born terrorist groups that moved about freely on U.S. soil was public knowledge.

Many of the world's most respected news publications expressed the same view. . . .

The cold figure of 73 innocent people murdered in Barbados could not possibly express the significance and magnitude of the tragedy.

Certainly, Americans will better understand by comparing the population of Cuba 25 years ago with that of the United States on September 11, 2001. The death of 73 people aboard a Cuban jetliner blown up in mid-flight is to the U.S. people as if seven American jetliners, with over 300 passengers each, had been destroyed in full flight the same day, at the same time, by a terrorist conspiracy.

We could still go further and say that if we were to consider the 3,478 Cubans who have perished in over four decades as a result of acts of aggression—including the invasion by the Bay of Pigs as well as all the other terrorist acts sustained by Cuba, which originated in the United States—it would be as if 88,434 people had died in that country, that is, a figure almost similar to the number of Americans who died in the Korean and Vietnam wars combined.

This denunciation we are making here today is not inspired in either hate or rancor. I understand that American officials do not even want to hear us raise these embarrassing issues. They say that we simply should look ahead.

However, it would be senseless not to look back at the sources of errors whose repetition should be avoided, and at the causes of major human tragedies, wars and other calamities that, perhaps, could have been prevented. There should not be innocent deaths anywhere in the world.

This massive demonstration against terrorism has been called to pay homage and tribute to the memory of our brothers and sisters who died off the coast of Barbados 25 years ago, but also to express our solidarity with the thousands of innocent people who died in New York and Washington. We are here to condemn the brutal crime committed against them while supporting the search for ways conducive to a real and lasting eradication of terrorism, to the prevalence of peace and against the development of a bloody and open-ended war.

I am deeply convinced that relations between the terrorist groups created by the United States in the first 15 years of the Revolution, to act against Cuba, and the U.S. authorities have never been severed.

In a day such as this, it is only right that we ask what will be done about Posada Carriles and Orlando Bosch, the main culprits of the obnoxious terrorist act perpetrated in Barbados; and what about those who planned and financed the bombs that were set up in hotels of the country's capital and have been restlessly trying, for over four decades, to murder Cuban leaders.

It is not too much to ask that justice be done, for these professional terrorists, acting from inside the very territory of the United States, have not ceased to apply their despicable methods against our people to sow terror and to destroy the economy of a harassed and blockaded nation, one from which terrorist devices have never come—not even a gram of explosives—to blast in the United States. Never has an American been injured or killed, nor has a facility big or small in that large and rich country ever suffered the least damage from any action coming from Cuba.

As we are involved in the worldwide struggle against terrorism—committed to take part alongside the United Nations and the rest of the international community—we have the full moral authority and the right to demand the end of terrorism against Cuba. . . .

As of July 22, 2002, the full text of Castro's speech was available at http://www.cubaminrex.cu/versioningles/25BARBADOS-ING.htm

UNITED STATES, BRITAIN LAUNCH WAR IN AFGHANISTAN
October 7, 2001

In 1999 first the United States and then the United Nations Security Council imposed sanctions on the Taliban rulers of Afghanistan because they refused to hand over Osama bin Laden, who had been indicted for the August 1998 bombings of U.S. embassies in Kenya and Tanzania, and because they continued to harbor other terrorists as well. But the September 11, 2001, terrorist attacks, which the United States quickly blamed on bin Laden and his al Qaeda terrorist network, immeasurably escalated the stakes. In a speech to a joint session of Congress on September 20, 2001, President George W. Bush said that if the Taliban did not turn over bin Laden and other terrorists, "they will share in their fate." Still the Taliban refused, fully aware that their decision would lead to military action by the United States and its allies. (Clinton Order Blocks Trade with the Taliban, p. 271; UN Threatens Sanctions Against Taliban, p. 286)

That action started on October 7, 2001, when the United States and Great Britain launched a large-scale war in Afghanistan. In a televised speech shortly after the attack began, Bush said the "carefully targeted actions are designed to disrupt the use of Afghanistan as a terrorist base of operations, and to attack the military capability of the Taliban regime." Speaking shortly after Bush, British prime minister Tony Blair said the objective was "to eradicate Osama bin Laden's network of terror and to take action against the Taliban regime that is sponsoring it." The U.S. and British allies—with substantial logistical, intelligence, and other forms of help from about two dozen countries—quickly achieved their initial goals. The Taliban, who had imposed their extreme interpretation of Islamic law on Afghanistan, fell from power two months after the war began. The U.S. and British forces faced limited resistance as thousands of Taliban and al Qaeda fighters simply melted back into the general population or fled the country, most heading for neighboring Pakistan. Under United Nations sponsorship, Afghan leaders in December created an interim government.

Yet despite these successes, Bush and his allies were frustrated by their failure to capture or kill bin Laden, his senior associates, and large numbers of Taliban and al Qaeda fighters. Their best chance came late in the year when it was believed that bin Laden, other al Qaeda leaders, and hundreds of fighters had taken refuge in an enormous cave complex in the rugged Tora Bora mountains of eastern Afghanistan. U.S. bombers dropped heavy "bunker-buster" bombs on the caves during much of November. Following the bombing, U.S. commanders relied on Afghan warlords to undertake the labor-intensive work of searching the Tora Bora caves and patrolling the border regions to prevent escapes into Pakistan. But the warlords, who were known for regularly switching sides, apparently allowed bin Laden and his trapped followers to escape. As of mid-July 2002, bin Laden and most of his senior associates remained at large.

Following are excerpts from statements made October 7, 2001, by President George W. Bush and by British prime minister Tony Blair on launching war in Afghanistan:

BUSH STATEMENT

Good afternoon. On my orders, the United States military has begun strikes against al Qaeda terrorist training camps and military installations of the Taliban regime in Afghanistan. These carefully targeted actions are designed to disrupt the use of Afghanistan as a terrorist base of operations, and to attack the military capability of the Taliban regime.

We are joined in this operation by our staunch friend, Great Britain. Other close friends, including Canada, Australia, Germany and France, have pledged forces as the operation unfolds. More than 40 countries in the Middle East, Africa, Europe and across Asia have granted air transit or landing rights. Many more have shared intelligence. We are supported by the collective will of the world.

More than two weeks ago, I gave Taliban leaders a series of clear and specific demands: Close terrorist training camps; hand over leaders of the al Qaeda network; and return all foreign nationals, including American citizens, unjustly detained in your country. None of these demands were met. And now the Taliban will pay a price. By destroying camps and disrupting communications, we will make it more difficult for the terror network to train new recruits and coordinate their evil plans.

Initially, the terrorists may burrow deeper into caves and other entrenched hiding places. Our military action is also designed to clear the way for sustained, comprehensive and relentless operations to drive them out and bring them to justice.

At the same time, the oppressed people of Afghanistan will know the generosity of America and our allies. As we strike military targets, we'll also drop food, medicine and supplies to the starving and suffering men and women and children of Afghanistan.

The United States of America is a friend to the Afghan people, and we are the friends of almost a billion worldwide who practice the Islamic faith. The United States of America is an enemy of those who aid terrorists and of the barbaric criminals who profane a great religion by committing murder in its name.

This military action is a part of our campaign against terrorism, another front in a war that has already been joined through diplomacy, intelligence, the freezing of financial assets and the arrests of known terrorists by law enforcement agents in 38 countries. Given the nature and reach of our enemies, we will win this conflict by the patient accumulation of successes, by meeting a series of challenges with determination and will and purpose.

Today we focus on Afghanistan, but the battle is broader. Every nation has a choice to make. In this conflict, there is no neutral ground. If any government sponsors the outlaws and killers of innocents, they have become outlaws and murderers, themselves. And they will take that lonely path at their own peril.

I'm speaking to you today from the Treaty Room of the White House, a place where American Presidents have worked for peace. We're a peaceful nation. Yet, as we have learned, so suddenly and so tragically, there can be no peace in a world of sudden terror. In the face of today's new threat, the only way to pursue peace is to pursue those who threaten it.

We did not ask for this mission, but we will fulfill it. The name of today's military operation is Enduring Freedom. We defend not only our precious freedoms, but also the freedom of people everywhere to live and raise their children free from fear.

I know many Americans feel fear today. And our government is taking strong precautions. All law enforcement and intelligence agencies are working aggressively around America, around the world and around the clock. At my request, many governors have activated the National Guard to strengthen airport security. We have called up Reserves to reinforce our military capability and strengthen the protection of our homeland. . . .

I recently received a touching letter that says a lot about the state of America in these difficult times—a letter from a 4th-grade girl, with a father in the military: "As much as I don't want my Dad to fight," she wrote, "I'm willing to give him to you."

This is a precious gift, the greatest she could give. This young girl knows what America is all about. Since September 11, an entire generation of young Americans has gained new understanding of the value of freedom, and its cost in duty and in sacrifice.

The battle is now joined on many fronts. We will not waver; we will not tire; we will not falter; and we will not fail. Peace and freedom will prevail.

Thank you. May God continue to bless America.

BLAIR STATEMENT

. . . No country lightly commits forces to military action and the inevitable risks involved but we made it clear following the attacks upon the United States on September 11th that we would take part in action once it was clear who was responsible.

There is no doubt in my mind, nor in the mind of anyone who has been through all the available evidence, including intelligence material, that these attacks were carried out by the al Qaeda network masterminded by Osama bin Laden. Equally it is clear that his network is harbored and supported by the Taliban regime inside Afghanistan.

It is now almost a month since the atrocity occurred, it is more than two weeks since an ultimatum was delivered to the Taliban to yield up the terrorists or face the consequences. It is clear beyond doubt that they will not do this. They were given the choice of siding with justice or siding with terror and they chose to side with terror.

There are three parts all equally important to the operation of which we're engaged: military, diplomatic and humanitarian. The military action we are taking will be targeted against places we know to be involved in the operation of terror or against the military apparatus of the Taliban. This military plan has been put together mindful of our determination to do all we humanly can to avoid civilian casualties. . . .

On the diplomatic and political front in the time I've been Prime Minister I cannot recall a situation that has commanded so quickly such a powerful coalition of support and not just from those countries directly involved in military action but from many others in all parts of the world. The coalition has, I believe, strengthened not weakened in the twenty-six days since the atrocity occurred. And this is in no small measure due to the statesmanship of President Bush to whom I pay tribute tonight.

The world understands that whilst, of course, there are dangers in acting the dangers of inaction are far, far greater. The threat of further such outrages, the threat to our economies, the threat to the stability of the world.

On the humanitarian front we are assembling a coalition of support for refugees in and outside Afghanistan which is as vital as the military coalition. Even before September 11th four million Afghans were on the move. There are two million refugees in Pakistan and one and a half million in Iran. We have to act for humanitarian reasons to alleviate the appalling suffering of the Afghan people and deliver stability so that people from that region stay in that region. Britain, of course, is heavily involved in this effort.

So we are taking action therefore on all those three fronts: military, diplomatic and humanitarian. I also want to say very directly to the British people why this matters so much directly to Britain. First let us not forget that the attacks of the September 11th represented the worst terrorist outrage against British citizens in our history. The murder of British citizens, whether it happens overseas or not, is an attack upon Britain. But even if no British citizen had died it would be right to act.

This atrocity was an attack on us all, on people of all faiths and people of none. We know the al Qaeda network threaten Europe, including Britain, and, indeed, any nation throughout the world that does not share their fanatical views. So we have a direct interest in acting in our own self defence to protect British lives. It was also an attack not just on lives but on livelihoods. We can see since the 11th of September how economic confidence has suffered with all that means for British jobs and British industry. Our prosperity and standard of living, therefore, require us to deal with this terrorist threat.

We act also because the al Qaeda network and the Taliban regime are funded in large part on the drugs trade. Ninety per cent of all the heroin sold on British streets originates from Afghanistan. Stopping that trade is, again, directly in our interests.

I wish to say finally, as I've said many times before, that this is not a war with Islam. It angers me, as it angers the vast majority of Muslims, to hear bin Laden and his associates described as Islamic terrorists. They are terrorists pure and simple. Islam is a peaceful and tolerant religion and the acts of these people are wholly contrary to the teachings of the Koran.

These are difficult and testing times therefore for all of us. People are bound to be concerned about what the terrorists may seek to do in response. I should say there is at present no specific credible threat to the UK that we know of and that we have in place tried and tested contingency plans which are the best possible response to any further attempts at terror.

This, of course, is a moment of the utmost gravity for the world. None of the leaders involved in this action want war. None of our nations want it. We are a peaceful people. But we know that sometimes to safeguard peace we have to fight. Britain has learnt that lesson many times in our history. . . .

As of July 18, 2002, the full text of Bush's statement was available at http://www.whitehouse.gov/news/releases/2001/10/20011007-8.html; the full text of Blair's statement was available at http://www.pm.gov. uk/news.asp?NewsId=2712&SectionId=32

THE IRISH REPUBLICAN ARMY DESTROYS WEAPONS
October 23, 2001

The fragile agreement of April 1998 aimed at resolving the political future of Northern Ireland and ending three decades of terrorist violence by paramilitary Protestant and Catholic forces clung to life as the 1990s ended and the next decade began, despite efforts by opponents to kill it. Even a car bombing on August 15, 1998, in Omagh that killed twenty-nine people—the most deadly act of violence in the thirty-year history of the "troubles"—did not destroy the peace process, as the Irish Republican Army (IRA) splinter group behind the attack had hoped. ("Real IRA" Claims Credit for Omagh Blast, p. 257)

As the peace process continued teetering between life and death, the British government and Northern Ireland's Protestant leaders stepped up their pressure on the Irish Republican Army, the Catholic paramilitary group, to destroy its weapons as a sign that it would actually abide by the peace agreement. The pressure on the IRA increased in August 2001 when three men closely tied to the group were arrested in Colombia, where they reportedly were training members of a leftist guerrilla group that sought to overthrow the government. The pressure grew even stronger after the September 11 terrorist attacks on the United States, which according to press reports caused some Irish Americans who had long supplied the IRA with money to buy weapons to withdraw their support for paramilitary actions. Finally, on October 23, 2001, an independent international commission announced that its members had witnessed the IRA destroying some weapons. The British government responded by withdrawing some of its military presence from the province.

In early April 2002 the IRA destroyed a second cache of weapons, but it was widely accused of duplicity after a series of events later in the month. These included a report in the Sunday Telegraph *newspaper that the IRA was rearming with powerful Russian assault rifles, accusations that the IRA stole top-secret intelligence files from a Belfast police station, the thwarting by police of IRA dissidents when they attempted to drive a van carrying a large gasoline bomb into Belfast, and an attempted bombing by suspected*

371

IRA dissidents of Northern Ireland's main prison. Also in April, Gerry Adams, leader of the IRA's political arm, Sinn Fein, declined to testify at a hearing by a U.S. congressional committee about allegations that the IRA was training terrorists in Colombia. Three months later the Northern Ireland Affairs Committee in the British House of Commons released a report saying that Catholic and Protestant paramilitary groups raised millions of dollars annually for their terrorist activities through armed robbery, protection rackets, drug sales, and smuggling. The most startling event, however, occurred July 16 when the IRA issued an apology for all the civilians it killed during nearly three decades of attacks.

Following are statements issued October 23, 2001, by the Independent International Commission on Decommissioning and by the Irish Republican Army:

COMMISSION STATEMENT

1. On 6th August 2001 the [Independent International] Commission [on Decommissioning] reported that agreement had been reached with the IRA on a method to put IRA arms completely and verifiably beyond use. This would be done in such a way as to involve no risk to the public and avoid the possibility of misappropriation by others.

2. We have now witnessed an event—which we regard as significant—in which the IRA has put a quantity of arms completely beyond use. The materiel in question includes arms, ammunition and explosives.

3. We are satisfied that the arms in question have been dealt with in accordance with the scheme and regulations. We are also satisfied that it would not further the process of putting all arms beyond use were we to provide further details of this event.

4. We will continue our contact with the IRA representative in the pursuit of our mandate.

IRA STATEMENT

The IRA is committed to our republican objectives and to the establishment of a united Ireland based on justice, equality and freedom.

In August 1994, against a background of lengthy and intensive discussions involving the two governments and others, the leadership of the IRA called a complete cessation of military operations in order to create the dynamic for a peace process.

Decommissioning was no part of that. There was no ambiguity about this. Unfortunately, there are those within the British establishment and the leadership of Unionism who are fundamentally opposed to change. At every opportunity they have used the issue of arms as an excuse to undermine and frustrate progress.

It is for this reason that decommissioning was introduced to the process by the British Government. It has been used since to prevent the changes that a lasting peace requires.

In order to overcome this and to encourage the changes necessary for a lasting peace, the leadership of Oglaigh na hEireann (IRA) has taken a number of substantial initiatives. These include our engagement with the IICD (Independent International Commission on Decommissioning) and the inspection of a number of arms dumps by the two international inspectors, Cyril Ramaphosa and Martti Ahtisaari.

No one should doubt the difficulties these initiatives cause for us, our volunteers and our supporters.

The political process is now on the point of collapse. Such a collapse would certainly, and eventually, put the overall peace process in jeopardy. There is a responsibility upon everyone seriously committed to a just peace to do our best to avoid this.

Therefore, in order to save the peace process, we have implemented the scheme agreed with the IICD in August.

Our motivation is clear. This unprecedented move is to save the peace process and to persuade others of our genuine intentions.

FEDERAL COMPUTER SYSTEMS FACE SEVERE SECURITY RISK
November 9, 2001

In June 1996 John M. Deutch, director of the Central Intelligence Agency, warned a Senate subcommittee that terrorists, hackers, or other nations could launch cyber attacks against the United States that would disrupt electric power distribution, air traffic control, international commerce, or deployed military forces. Three months later the General Accounting Office (GAO), the congressional watchdog, issued the first of numerous reports warning that poor security of government computer systems was "a widespread federal problem with potentially devastating consequences." Some of the security weaknesses were as basic as not requiring passwords to access federal systems or using "password" as the password. In response to the warnings, in May 1998 President Bill Clinton signed Presidential Decision Directive 63, which said that by 2003 the government and the private sector should have in place "a reliable, interconnected, and secure information system infrastructure." (CIA Director Warns of Cyber Attacks by Terrorists, p. 198)

Testimony at a congressional hearing on November 9, 2001, made it clear that the United States had little chance of meeting Clinton's goal. Robert F. Dacey, director of information security issues for the GAO, told members of a House subcommittee that security weaknesses remained pervasive across federal computer systems. A recent GAO review of computer systems at twenty-four federal agencies found major security problems at every agency, he said.

The month before the hearing, Richard A. Clarke assumed the new position of White House adviser on cyberspace security issues. Clarke spent his early months on the job pushing companies to beef up their efforts at protecting the nation's electronic infrastructure from terrorists and other potential attackers. His efforts came none too soon, according to a story published June 27, 2002, in the Washington Post. *"Unsettling signs of al Qaeda's aims and skills in cyberspace have led some government experts to conclude that terrorists are at the threshold of using the Internet as a direct instrument of bloodshed," wrote reporter Barton Gellman. As one example, he cited recent FBI monitoring of Internet traffic routed through Saudi Arabia, Indonesia, and Pakistan that seemed aimed at conducting surveillance of emergency telephone systems, nuclear power plants, electrical transmission systems, and other parts of the nation's infrastructure. Federal experts told Gellman their greatest fear was that terrorists would combine a cyber attack with a simultaneous conventional attack. In one possible scenario, terrorists might try to knock out a city's emergency communications system at the same time that they bombed buildings, bridges, or other structures.*

Following are excerpts from testimony by Robert F. Dacey, director of information security issues for the General Accounting Office, at a hearing by the House Subcommittee on Government Efficiency, Financial Management, and Intergovernmental Relations on November 9, 2001:

Background

Dramatic increases in computer interconnectivity, especially in the use of the Internet, are revolutionizing the way our government, our nation, and much of the world communicate and conduct business. The benefits have been enormous. Vast amounts of information are now literally at our fingertips, facilitating research on virtually every topic imaginable; financial and other business transactions can be executed almost instantaneously, often 24 hours a day; and electronic mail, Internet web sites, and computer bulletin boards allow us to communicate quickly and easily with virtually an unlimited number of individuals and groups.

In addition to such benefits, however, this widespread interconnectivity poses significant risks to our computer systems and, more important, to the critical operations and infrastructures they support. For example, telecommunications, power distribution, public health, national defense (including the military's warfighting capability), law enforcement, government, and emergency services all depend on the security of their computer operations. Likewise, the speed and accessibility that create the enormous benefits of the computer age, if not properly controlled, allow individuals and organizations to inexpensively eavesdrop on or interfere with these operations from remote locations for mischievous or malicious purposes, including fraud or sabotage.

Reports of attacks and disruptions are growing. The number of computer security incidents reported to the CERT® Coordination Center rose from 9,859 in 1999 to 21,756 in 2000 and 34,754 for just the first 9 months of 2001. And these are only the *reported* attacks. The CERT® Coordination Center estimates that as much as 80 percent of actual security incidents go unreported, in most cases because the organization was unable to recognize that its systems had been penetrated or because there were no indications of penetration or attack. As the number of individuals with computer skills has increased, more intrusion or "hacking" tools have become readily available and relatively easy to use. A potential hacker can literally download tools from the Internet and "point and click" to start a hack. According to a recent National Institute of Standards and Technology (NIST) publication, hackers post 30 to 40 new tools to hacking sites on the Internet every month.

Experts also agree that there has been a steady advance in the sophistication and effectiveness of attack technology. Intruders quickly develop attacks to exploit vulnerabilities discovered in products, use these attacks to compromise computers, and share them with other attackers. In addition, they can combine these attacks with other forms of technology to develop programs that automatically scan the network for vulnerable systems, attack them, compromise them, and use them to spread the attack even further.

Attacks over the past several months illustrate the risks. As we reported to this Subcommittee in August 2001, the attacks referred to as Code Red, Code Red II, and SirCam have affected millions of computer users, shut down web sites, slowed Internet service, and disrupted business and government operations, and have reportedly caused billions of dollars in damage. More recently, the Nimda worm appeared using some of the most significant attack profile aspects of Code Red II and 1999's infamous Melissa virus, allowing it to spread widely in a short amount of time.

As greater amounts of money are transferred through computer systems, as more sensitive economic and commercial information is exchanged electronically, and as the nation's defense and intelligence communities increasingly rely on commercially available information technology, the likelihood increases that information attacks will threaten vital national interests. Government officials have long been concerned about attacks from individuals and groups with malicious intent, such as crime, terrorism, foreign intelligence gathering, and acts of war. According to the Federal Bureau of Investigation (FBI), terrorists, transnational criminals, and intelligence services are quickly becoming aware of and using information exploitation tools such as computer viruses, worms, Trojan horses, logic bombs, and eavesdropping sniffers that can destroy, intercept, or degrade the integrity of and deny access to data. In addition, the disgruntled organization insider is a significant threat, since such individuals with little knowledge about computer intrusions often have knowledge that allows them to gain unrestricted access and inflict damage or steal assets. Examples of such attacks already exist:

- In October 2000, the FBI's National Infrastructure Protection Center (NIPC) issued an advisory concerning an increased level of cyber activity against web sites related to Israel and pro-Palestinian organizations. This advisory noted that due to the credible threat of terrorist acts in the Middle East region, and the conduct of these web attacks, increased vigilance should be exercised to the possibility that U.S.-government and private-sector web sites may become potential targets. In less than a month, a group of hackers calling itself Gforce Pakistan defaced more than 20 web sites and posted threats to launch an Internet attack against AT&T. Further, in October 2001, this same group attacked a government web server operated by the National Oceanic and Atmospheric Adminis tration, defacing a web site and threatening to release some highly confidential data unless the United States met several demands.

- According to recent Defense Intelligence Agency and Central Intelligence Agency estimates, at least 20 countries are known to be developing information warfare strategies that specifically target U.S. military and private-sector data networks. The fear is that computer viruses and worms unleashed by foreign hackers could wreak havoc on the U.S. infrastructure in the event of a military conflict.

- In his April 2001 written statement for the House Energy and Commerce Committee on intrusions into government computer networks, the director of the NIPC noted that terrorist groups are increasingly using new information technology and the Internet to formulate plans, raise funds, spread propaganda, and communicate securely. Citing the example of convicted terrorist Ramzi Yousef, who masterminded the 1993 World Trade Center bombing and stored detailed plans to destroy U.S. airliners in encrypted files on his laptop computer, the director concluded that while we have not yet seen terrorist groups employ cyber tools as a weapon against critical infrastructures, the reliance of these groups on information technology and acquisition of computer expertise are clear warning signs.

After the September 11, 2001, attacks, the NIPC warned of an expected upswing in incidents and encouraged system administrators to follow best practices to limit the potential damage from any cyber attacks. In particular, it warned that political events and international situations would likely lead to increasing cyber protests and that such attacks were expected to now target the information infrastructure more often and exploit opportunities to disrupt or damage it. On November 2, the NIPC updated its warning, noting that hacking groups have formed and participated in pro-U.S. and anti-U.S. cyber activities, which have mainly taken the form of web defacements. The NIPC went on to say that while there has been minimal activity in the form of denial-of-service attacks, it has reason to believe that the potential for such attacks in the future is high and that infrastructure support systems must take a defensive posture and remain at a higher state of alert.

Finally, while the warning of a potential "digital Pearl Harbor" has been raised in the past, the events of September 11, 2001, further underscored the need to protect America's cyberspace against potentially disastrous cyber attacks. In his September 2001 testimony before this Subcommittee on cyber attacks, the former NIPC director warned that a cyber attack by terrorists or nation-states using multiple-attack scenarios could have disastrous effects on infrastructure systems and could also be coordinated to coincide with physical terrorist attacks to maximize the impact of both. Further, in his October congressional testimony, Governor James Gilmore, Governor of the Commonwealth of Virginia and Chairman of the Advisory Panel to Assess Domestic Response Capabilities for Terrorism Involving Weapons of Mass Destruction (commonly known as the "Gilmore Commission"), cautioned that our critical information and communication infrastructures are targets for terrorists because of the broad economic and operational consequences of a shutdown. He warned that systems and services critical to the American economy and the health of our citizens—such as banking and finance, "just-in-time" delivery system for goods, hospitals, and state and local emergency services—can all be shut down or severely handicapped by a cyber attack or a physical attack against computer hardware.

Weaknesses in Federal Systems Remain Pervasive

Since September 1996, we have reported that poor information security is a widespread federal problem with potentially devastating consequences. Our analyses of information security at major federal agencies have shown that federal systems were not being adequately protected from computer-based threats, even though these systems process, store, and transmit enormous amounts of sensitive data and are indispensable to many federal agency operations. . . .

As of July 22, 2002, the full text of the testimony was available at http://www.gao.gov/new.items/d02231t.pdf

TWELVE DIE IN ATTACK ON INDIAN PARLIAMENT
December 18, 2001

India and Pakistan have fought over Kashmir, a territory that both countries claim, ever since Britain gave up its control of the Indian subcontinent in 1947. Several wars left India with control over about two-thirds of Kashmir, but the Islamic state of Pakistan insisted that Kashmir's inhabitants—most of whom were Muslim—should have the right to join Pakistan instead of being governed by India, which was dominated by Hindus. Pro-Pakistan militants, armed and aided by the government of Pakistan, launched a guerrilla war against Indian control of Kashmir in 1989 that resulted in nearly 40,000 deaths over the next decade, according to India's official estimate. During the late 1990s India said the fighting had escalated to a more dangerous level because many of the guerrillas came from Arab countries and Central Asia, were associated with Islamic terrorist groups, and had the full support of Pakistan. Pakistan denied these charges and insisted that the guerrillas were Kashmiri "freedom fighters."

Yet another escalation occurred on December 13, 2001, when five heavily armed terrorists attacked India's parliament building with assault rifles and grenades. Guards managed to keep the terrorists from entering the building, but in a gun battle that lasted more than thirty minutes two guards, four policemen, and all five terrorists were killed, as was a gardener caught in the crossfire. On December 18 India's home minister, L. K. Advani, told parliament that two groups based in Pakistan—Jaish-i-Muhammad and Lashkar-e-Tayyaba—had carried out the attack with support from Pakistan's intelligence service. Advani called the attack "undoubtedly the most audacious, and also the most alarming, act of terrorism in the two-decade-long history of Pakistan-sponsored terrorism in India." Pakistan's government hotly denied any connection with the attack.

As the war of words over the attack continued, both countries started moving thousands of troops up to their borders. Pakistan president Pervez Musharraf on December 28 quietly ordered the arrests of four dozen leaders of the two groups that India blamed for the attack. Yet tensions remained high, especially since both countries had developed nuclear weapons. On

June 6, 2002, with about one million troops massed along the border be-
tween Pakistan and India, Britain's Foreign Office advised all British citi-
zens to leave the two countries because of the growing threat of war. Within
a week, however, intense diplomatic efforts by the United States, Britain,
and other countries had cooled tensions. The key was the United States ob-
taining a pledge from Musharraf that he would permanently end terror-
ist incursions into the Indian-held part of Kashmir. In return, the United
States promised to help resolve the Kashmir conflict. The number of terror-
ist incursions and attacks fell after Musharraf made the promise, but by
early July Indian officials said they had risen again—and both countries
still had their troops massed on the border.

Following is a statement to the parliament of India by L. K. Advani, the country's home secretary, on December 18, 2001:

The ghastly attack on Parliament House on 13th December, 2001 has shocked the entire nation. This terrorist assault on the very bastion of our democracy was clearly aimed at wiping out the country's top political leadership. It is a tribute to our security personnel that they rose to the occasion and succeeded in averting what could have been a national catastrophe. In so doing they made the supreme sacrifice for which the country would always remain indebted to them.

It is now evident that the terrorist assault on the Parliament House was executed jointly by Pak-based [Pakistan] and supported terrorist outfits, namely, Lashkar-e-Taiba and Jaish-e-Mohmmad. These two organizations are known to derive their support and patronage from Pak ISI [the Pakistani intelligence service]. The investigation so far carried out by the police shows that all the five terrorists who formed the suicide squad were Pakistani nationals. All of them were killed on the spot and their Indian associates have since been nabbed and arrested.

The investigation at this stage indicates that the five Pakistani terrorists entered the Parliament House Complex at about 11:40 A.M. in an Ambassador Car bearing registration No. DL-3CJ-1527 and moved towards Building Gate No. 12 when it encountered the carcade of Vice President of India which was parked at Gate No. 11. One of the members of the Parliament House Watch and Ward Staff, Shri Jagdish Prasad Yadav, became suspicious about the identity of the car and immediately ran after it. The car was forced to turn backward and in the process it hit the Vice President's car. When challenged by the security personnel present on the spot all the five terrorists jumped out of the car and started firing indiscriminately. The Delhi Police personnel attached with the Vice-President's security as also the personnel of CRPF and ITBP on duty immediately took their positions and returned the fire. It was at this point that another member of Parliament House Watch and Ward Staff, Shri Matbar Singh, sustained bullet injuries. He rushed inside Gate No. 11 and closed it. An alarm was raised and all the gates in the building were immediately closed.

The terrorists ran towards Gate No. 12 and then to Gate No. 1 of the Parliament House Building. One terrorist was shot dead by the security forces at Gate No. 1 and in the process the explosives wrapped around his body exploded. The remaining four terrorists turned back and reached Gate No. 9 of the Building. Three of them were gunned down there. The fifth terrorist ran towards Gate No. 5 where he also was gunned down.

During the exchange of fire, four Delhi Police personnel, namely, Shri Nanak Chand, Assistant Sub-Inspector, Shri Rampal, Assistant Sub-Inspector, Shri Om Prakash, Head Constable and Shri Ghanshyam, Head Constable attached with the Vice President's security lost their lives on the spot. The other three persons who were also killed were Smt. Kamlesh Kumari, a Woman Constable of CRPF, Shri Jagdish Prasad Yadav, a Security Assistant of Watch and Ward Staff of the Parliament House, who had rushed after the terrorists' car and a civilian employee of CPWD, Shri Desh Raj—18 other persons were injured and they were immediately rushed to Dr. Ram Manohar Lohia Hospital for medical treatment. These included Shri Matbar Singh, Security Assistant, Watch and Ward Staff of the Parliament House who later succumbed to his injuries. The scene of the crime was cordoned off and Investigation Teams including Forensic Experts and Bomb Detection Squads were pressed into service. A number of hand grenades were recovered from the site of the incident and defused. A large quantity of arms and ammunition including explosives was also recovered.

The break-through in the investigation of the case was achieved with the arrest of Syed Abdul Rehman Gilani, a Lecturer in a local College, whose interrogation led to the identification of two other accomplices, Afzal and Shaukat Hussain Guru. The wife of the latter disclosed that her husband and Afzal had in the afternoon of 13th December, 2001 left for Srinagar. This information was immediately conveyed to the J&K [Jammu and Kashmir] Police who apprehended both of them. A laptop computer and Rs.10 lakhs in cash were recovered from them. They were later brought to Delhi by a Special Team deputed for the purpose by Delhi Police.

Interrogation of the accused persons has revealed that Afzal was the main coordinator who was assigned this task by a Pakistani national, Gazi Baba of Jaish-e-Mohmmad. Afzal had earlier been trained in a camp run by Pak ISI at Muzaffarabad in Pak Occupied Kashmir. The hideouts for the five Pak terrorists were arranged by Shaukat Hussain Guru, two in Mukherjee Nagar and one in Timarpur area in North Delhi. During the subsequent raids, the police recovered from two of these hideouts a lot of incriminating material including a large quantity of Ammonium Nitrate and other ingredients used in preparing Improvised Explosive Devices; a map of Delhi; a sheet of paper carrying a map of Chankyapuri drawn in hand; and three police uniforms. In all, four persons have so far been arrested in connection with this case.

This incident once again establishes that terrorism in India is the handiwork of Pakistan-based terrorist outfits known to derive their support and sustenance from Pak ISI. The hijacking of IC-814 Flight to Kandahar, the terrorist intrusion into the Red Fort and attack on J&K Legislative Assembly Complex at Srinagar on 1st October this year were master minded and executed by militant outfits at the behest of the ISI. Lashkar-e-Taiba and Jaish-e-Mohmmad in particular have been in the forefront in organizing terrorist violence in our country. The Pakistan High Commissioner in India was summoned to the Ministry of External Affairs and issued a verbal demarche demanding that Islamabad take action against the two terrorist outfits involved in the attack on the Parliament House.

Last week's attack on Parliament is undoubtedly the most audacious, and also the most alarming, act of terrorism in the nearly two-decades-long history of Pakistan-sponsored terrorism in India. This time the terrorists and their mentors across the border had the temerity to try to wipe out the entire political leadership of India, as represented in our multi-party Parliament. Naturally, it is time for all of us in this august House, and all of us in the country, to ponder why the terrorists and their backers tried to raise the stakes so high, particularly at a time when Pakistan is claiming to be a part of the international coalition against terrorism.

The only answer that satisfactorily addresses this query is that Pakistan— itself a product of the indefensible Two-Nation Theory, itself a theocratic State with an extremely tenuous tradition of democracy—is unable to reconcile itself with the reality of a secular, democratic, self-confident and steadily progressing India, whose standing in the international community is getting inexorably higher with the passage of time.

The Prime Minister in his address to the nation on the 13th December, 2001 has declared that the fight against terrorism had reached a decisive phase. The supreme sacrifice made by the security personnel who lost their lives in this incident will not be allowed to go in vain. Those behind the attack on Parliament House should know that the Indian people are united and determined to stamp out terrorism from the country.

FBI EXPERT DESCRIBES RISE
OF BIN LADEN AND AL QAEDA
December 18, 2001

Before the September 11, 2001, terrorist attacks on the United States, many Americans had never heard of Osama bin Laden or his al Qaeda terrorist network. They were suddenly filled with basic questions: Who was Osama bin Laden? Where did al Qaeda come from? Was it tied to other terrorist groups? And why did bin Laden and other Islamic terrorists hate the United States so much that they had devoted their lives to killing as many Americans as possible?

An FBI expert answered many of the questions at a hearing on December 18, 2001, by a subcommittee of the Senate Committee on Foreign Relations. J. T. Caruso, acting assistant director of the FBI's counterterrorism division, told lawmakers that bin Laden and others originally created al Qaeda in the early 1980s to help drive Soviet troops out of Afghanistan, an effort that was supported by the United States. When the Soviets withdrew, bin Laden and his followers decided to launch a jihad, or holy war, against the United States and its allies because of their anger over U.S. troops being stationed in Saudi Arabia while they fought to drive Iraq out of Kuwait during Operation Desert Shield. Caruso described al Qaeda's early efforts to create terrorist cells around the world, including in the United States, and its ties to a variety of other terrorist groups.

Apparently, members of the American public were not the only ones in the dark about bin Laden and al Qaeda. American intelligence agencies were largely unaware of al Qaeda's scope until its 1998 bombings of U.S. embassies in Kenya and Tanzania, according to a lengthy article by New York Times *reporters Judith Miller and Don Van Natta Jr. that was published June 9, 2002. Attributing the information to lawmakers and investigators, the reporters wrote: "A re-examination of years of terrorist plots and attacks around the world, including the 1993 World Trade Center bombing, suggests that American intelligence agencies profoundly underestimated Al Qaeda's reach and aspirations for more than a decade as it grew from obscurity into a global terrorist threat." Only a few months earlier George Tenet, director of the Central Intelligence Agency, testified before Congress that despite U.S. efforts in Afghanistan and elsewhere to destroy al Qaeda, it remained "the most immediate and serious" threat faced by the United States.* (CIA Director Says al Qaeda Remains a Serious Threat, p. 388)

> ***Following are excerpts from the prepared statement of J. T. Caruso, acting assistant director of the FBI's counterterrorism division, for a December 18, 2001, hearing of the Subcommittee on International Operations and Terrorism of the Senate Committee on Foreign Relations:***

"Al-Qaeda" ("The Base") was developed by Usama Bin Laden and others in the early 1980s to support the war effort in Afghanistan against the Soviets. The resulting "victory" in Afghanistan gave rise to the overall "Jihad" (Holy War) movement. Trained Mujahedin fighters from Afghanistan began returning to such countries as Egypt, Algeria, and Saudi Arabia, with extensive "jihad" experience and the desire to continue the "jihad." This antagonism began to be refocused against the U.S. and its allies.

Sometime in 1989, Al-Qaeda dedicated itself to further opposing non-Islamic governments in this region with force and violence. The group grew out of the "mekhtab al khidemat" (the Services Office) organization which maintained offices in various parts of the world, including Afghanistan, Pakistan and the United States. Al-Qaeda began to provide training camps and guesthouses in various areas for the use of Al-Qaeda and its affiliated groups. They attempted to recruit U.S. citizens to travel throughout the Western world to deliver messages and engage in financial transactions for the benefit of Al-Qaeda and its affiliated groups and to help carry out operations. By 1990 Al-Qaeda was providing military and intelligence training in various areas including Afghanistan, Pakistan and the Sudan, for the use of Al-Qaeda and its affiliated groups, including the Al-Jihad (Islamic Jihad) organization.

One of the principal goals of Al-Qaeda was to drive the United States armed forces out of Saudi Arabia (and elsewhere on the Saudi Arabian peninsula) and Somalia by violence. Members of Al-Qaeda issued fatwahs (rulings on Islamic law) indicating that such attacks were both proper and necessary.

Al-Qaeda opposed the United States for several reasons. First, the United States was regarded as an "infidel" because it was not governed in a manner consistent with the group's extremist interpretation of Islam. Second, the United States was viewed as providing essential support for other "infidel" governments and institutions, particularly the governments of Saudi Arabia and Egypt, the nation of Israel and the United Nations organization, which were regarded as enemies of the group. Third, Al-Qaeda opposed the involvement of the United States armed forces in the Gulf War in 1991 and in Operation Restore Hope in Somalia in 1992 and 1993, which were viewed by Al-Qaeda as pretextual preparations for an American occupation of Islamic countries. In particular, Al-Qaeda opposed the continued presence of American military forces in Saudi Arabia (and elsewhere on the Saudi Arabian peninsula) following the Gulf War. Fourth, Al-Qaeda opposed the United States Government because of the arrest, conviction and imprisonment of persons belonging to Al-Qaeda or its affiliated terrorist groups or with whom it worked, including Sheik Omar Abdel Rahman, who was convicted in the first World Trade Center bombing.

From its inception until approximately 1991, the group was headquartered in Afghanistan and Peshawar, Pakistan. Then in 1991, the group relocated to the Sudan where it was headquartered until approximately 1996, when Bin Laden, Mohammed Atef and other members of Al-Qaeda returned to Afghanistan. During the years Al-Qaeda was headquartered in Sudan the network continued to maintain offices in various parts of the world and established businesses which were operated to provide income and cover to Al-Qaeda operatives.

Al-Qaeda Ties to Other Terrorist Organizations

Although Al-Qaeda functions independently of other terrorist organizations, it also functions through some of the terrorist organizations that operate under its umbrella or with its support, including: the Al-Jihad, the Al-Gamma Al-Islamiyya (Islamic Group—led by Sheik Omar Abdel Rahman and later by Ahmed Refai Taha, a/k/a "Abu Yasser al Masri"), Egyptian Islamic Jihad, and a number of jihad groups in other countries, including the Sudan, Egypt, Saudi Arabia, Yemen, Somalia, Eritrea, Djibouti, Afghanistan, Pakistan, Bosnia, Croatia, Albania, Algeria, Tunisia, Lebanon, the Philippines, Tajikistan, Azerbaijan, the Kashmiri region of India, and the Chechen region of Russia. Al-Qaeda also maintained cells and personnel in a number of countries to facilitate its activities, including in Kenya, Tanzania, the United Kingdom, Canada and the United States. By banding together, Al-Qaeda proposed to work together against the perceived common enemies in the West—particularly the United States, which Al-Qaeda regards as an "infidel" state which provides essential support for other "infidel" governments. Al-Qaeda responded to the presence of United States armed forces in the Gulf and the arrest, conviction and imprisonment in the United States of persons belonging to Al-Qaeda by issuing fatwahs indicating that attacks against U.S. interests, domestic and foreign, civilian and military, were both proper and necessary. Those fatwahs resulted in attacks against U.S. nationals in locations around the world including Somalia, Kenya, Tanzania, Yemen, and now in the United States. Since 1993, thousands of people have died in those attacks.

The Fatwahs of Al-Qaeda

At various times from about 1992 until about 1993, Usama Bin Laden, working together with members of the fatwah committee of Al-Qaeda, disseminated fatwahs to other members and associates of Al-Qaeda which directed that the United States forces stationed in the Horn of Africa, including Somalia, should be attacked. Indeed, Bin Laden has claimed responsibility for the deaths of 18 U.S. servicemen killed in "Operation Restore Hope" in Somalia in 1994.

On February 22, 1998, Bin Laden issued a fatwah stating that it is the duty of all Muslims to kill Americans. This fatwah read, in part, that "in compliance with God's order, we issue the following fatwah to all Muslims: the ruling to kill the Americans and their allies, including civilians and military, is an individual duty for every Muslim who can do it in any country in which it is possible to do it." This fatwah appears to have provided the religious justification for, and marked the start of logistical planning for, the U.S. Embassy bombings in Kenya and Tanzania. . . .

The Trial in New York City

As was revealed at the trial that took place in New York earlier this year, a former member of Bin Laden's Al-Qaeda network began working with the United States government in 1996. That witness revealed that Bin Laden had a terrorist group, Al-Qaeda, which had privately declared war on America and was operating both on its own and as an umbrella for other terrorist groups. The witness revealed that Al-Qaeda had a close working relationship with the aforementioned Egyptian terrorist group known as Egyptian Islamic Jihad. The witness recounted that Bin Laden and Al-Qaeda were seeking to obtain nuclear and chemical weapons and that the organization engaged in sophisticated training. He also revealed that Al-Qaeda obtained specialized terrorist training from and worked with Iranian government officials and the terrorist group Hizballah. . . .

On August 7, 1998, the bombings of the embassies in Nairobi, Kenya, and Dar es Salaam, Tanzania, occurred roughly simultaneously. The persons who carried out the attacks in Kenya and Tanzania have since been identified publicly: the principal participants were members of Al-Qaeda and/or the affiliated terrorist group EIJ [Egyptian Islamic Jihad]. Indeed, Mohamed Rashed Daoud al-Owhali, a Saudi who admitted he was in the bomb truck used in Nairobi, confessed that he had been trained in Al-Qaeda camps, fought with the Taliban in Afghanistan (with the permission of Usama Bin Laden), had asked Bin Laden for a mission and was thereafter dispatched by others to East Africa after undergoing extensive specialized training at camps in Afghanistan. Another defendant, Mohamed Sadeek Odeh, in whose residence was found a sketch of the area where the bomb was to be placed, admitted he was a member of Al-Qaeda and identified the other principal participants in the bombing as Al-Qaeda members. Odeh admitted that he was told the night prior to the bombings that Bin Laden and the others he was working with in Afghanistan had relocated from their camps because they expected the American military to retaliate.

There was independent proof of the involvement of Bin Laden, Al-Qaeda and EIJ in the bombings. First, the would-be suicide bomber, al-Owhali, ran away from the bomb truck at the last minute and survived. However, he had no money or passport or plan by which to escape Kenya. Days later, he called a telephone number in Yemen and thus arranged to have money transferred to him in Kenya. That same telephone number in Yemen was contacted by Usama Bin Laden's satellite phone on the same days that al-Owhali was arranging to get money. . . .

Additional proof of the involvement of Al-Qaeda and EIJ in the East Africa bombings came from a search conducted in London of several residences and business addresses belonging to Al-Qaeda and EIJ members. . . .

In short, the trial record left little doubt that the East Africa embassy bombings were carried out as a joint operation of Al-Qaeda and EIJ. The testimony in the trial confirmed that:

- Al-Qaeda has access to the money, training, and equipment it needs to carry out successful terrorist attacks.
- They plan their operations well in advance and have the patience to wait to conduct the attack at the right time.
- Prior to carrying out the operation, Al-Qaeda conducts surveillance of the target, sometimes on multiple occasions, often using nationals of the target they are surveilling to enter the location without suspicion. The results of the surveillance are forwarded to Al-Qaeda HQ as elaborate "ops plans" or "targeting packages" prepared using photographs, CADCAM (computer assisted design/computer assisted mapping) software, and the operative's notes. . . .

As of July 18, 2002, the full text of the statement was available at http://www.fbi.gov/congress/congress01/caruso121801.htm

CIA DIRECTOR SAYS AL QAEDA REMAINS A SERIOUS THREAT
February 6, 2002

Osama bin Laden and his al Qaeda terrorism network posed the greatest threat to U.S. national security of any foe, CIA director George Tenet testified February 7, 2001, before the Senate Select Committee on Intelligence. "The threat from terrorism is real, it is immediate, and it is evolving," Tenet said in his annual assessment of security threats facing the United States.

In his next assessment a year later, Tenet reflected on the accuracy of his earlier forecast in light of the September 11, 2001, attacks on the United States, which law enforcement officials blamed on bin Laden and al Qaeda. In testimony February 6, 2002, before the same Senate committee, Tenet said bin Laden and al Qaeda remained the largest threat to the United States despite efforts in Afghanistan and elsewhere to disrupt the terrorist network. "Al-Qa'ida has not yet been destroyed," Tenet said. "It and other like-minded groups remain willing and able to strike us." He emphasized that the terrorist threat to the United States extended well beyond al Qaeda to other groups in the Middle East, Colombia, Turkey, and elsewhere. Tenet also urged senators to look past the immediate danger of terrorist attacks to the underlying conditions of poverty, alienation, and ethnic tensions that contribute to the spread of terrorism. "These conditions are no less threatening to U.S. national security than terrorism itself," Tenet said.

In June 2002 the Washington Post *reported that al Qaeda was increasingly joining with Hizballah, one of the foremost terrorist groups in the Middle East and previously a rival, on logistics and training for terrorist operations. In early July a key al Qaeda spokesman issued a new threat against the United States. "Al-Qaida will organize more attacks inside American territory and outside, at the moment we choose, at the place we choose, and with the objectives that we want," said Sulaiman Abu Ghaith in an audio recording. On July 11, Attorney General John Ashcroft told a House committee that al Qaeda continued to have a strong network of "sleeper" cells within the United States and was trying to enlarge the network by smuggling more terrorists into the country.*

Following are excerpts from the prepared testimony of George Tenet, director of the Central Intelligence Agency, at a February 6, 2002, hearing of the Senate Select Committee on Intelligence:

Mr. Chairman, I appear before you this year under circumstances that are extraordinary and historic for reasons I need not recount. Never before has the subject of this annual threat briefing had more immediate resonance. Never before have the dangers been more clear or more present.

September 11 brought together and brought home—literally—several vital threats to the United States and its interests that we have long been aware of. It is the convergence of these threats that I want to emphasize with you today: the connection between terrorists and other enemies of this country; the weapons of mass destruction they seek to use against us; and the social, economic, and political tensions across the world that they exploit in mobilizing their followers. September 11 demonstrated the dangers that arise when these threats converge—and it reminds us that we overlook at our own peril the impact of crises in remote parts of the world.

This convergence of threats has created the world I will present to you today—a world in which dangers exist not only in those places where we have most often focused our attention, but also in other areas that demand it:

In places like Somalia, where the absence of a national government has created an environment in which groups sympathetic to al-Qa'ida have offered terrorists an operational base and potential haven.

In places like Indonesia, where political instability, separatist and ethnic tensions, and protracted violence are hampering economic recovery and fueling Islamic extremism.

In places like Colombia, where leftist insurgents who make much of their money from drug trafficking are escalating their assault on the government—further undermining economic prospects and fueling a cycle of violence.

And finally, Mr. Chairman, in places like Connecticut, where the death of a 94-year-old woman in her own home of anthrax poisoning can arouse our worst fears about what our enemies might try to do to us.

These threats demand our utmost response. The United States has clearly demonstrated since September 11 that it is up to the challenge. But make no mistake: despite the battles we have won in Afghanistan, we remain a nation at war.

Last year I told you that Usama Bin Ladin and the al-Qa'ida network were the most immediate and serious threat this country faced. This remains true today despite the progress we have made in Afghanistan and in disrupting the network elsewhere. We assess that Al-Qa'ida and other terrorist groups will continue to plan to attack this country and its interests abroad. Their modus operandi is to have multiple attack plans in the works simultaneously, and to have al-Qa'ida cells in place to conduct them.

- We know that terrorists have considered attacks in the U.S. against high-profile government or private facilities, famous landmarks, and U.S. infrastructure nodes such as airports, bridges, harbors, and dams. High profile events such as the Olympics or last weekend's Super Bowl also fit the terrorists' interest in striking another blow within the United States that would command worldwide media attention.
- Al-Qa'ida also has plans to strike against U.S. and allied targets in Europe, the Middle East, Africa, and Southeast Asia. American diplomatic and military installations are at high risk—especially in East Africa, Israel, Saudi Arabia, and Turkey.
- Operations against U.S. targets could be launched by al-Qa'ida cells already in place in major cities in Europe and the Middle East. Al-Qa'ida can also exploit its presence or connections to other groups in such countries as Somalia, Yemen, Indonesia, and the Philippines.

Although the September 11 attacks suggest that al-Qa'ida and other terrorists will continue to use conventional weapons, one of our highest concerns is their stated readiness to attempt unconventional attacks against us. As early as 1998, Bin Ladin publicly declared that acquiring unconventional weapons was "a religious duty."

- Terrorist groups worldwide have ready access to information on chemical, biological, and even nuclear weapons via the Internet, and we know that al-Qa'ida was working to acquire some of the most dangerous chemical agents and toxins. Documents recovered from al-Qa'ida facilities in Afghanistan show that Bin Ladin was pursuing a sophisticated biological weapons research program.
- We also believe that Bin Ladin was seeking to acquire or develop a nuclear device. Al-Qa'ida may be pursuing a radioactive dispersal device—what some call a "dirty bomb."
- Alternatively, al-Qa'ida or other terrorist groups might also try to launch conventional attacks against the chemical or nuclear industrial infrastructure of the United States to cause widespread toxic or radiological damage.

We are also alert to the possibility of cyber warfare attack by terrorists. September 11 demonstrated our dependence on critical infrastructure systems that rely on electronic and computer networks. Attacks of this nature will become an increasingly viable option for terrorists as they and other foreign adversaries become more familiar with these targets, and the technologies required to attack them.

The terrorist threat goes well beyond al-Qa'ida. The situation in the Middle East continues to fuel terrorism and anti-U.S. sentiment worldwide. Groups like the Palestine Islamic Jihad (PIJ) and HAMAS have escalated their violence against Israel, and the intifada has rejuvenated once-dormant groups like the Popular Front for the Liberation of Palestine. If these groups feel that

U.S. actions are threatening their existence, they may begin targeting Americans directly—as Hizballah's terrorist wing already does.

- The terrorist threat also goes beyond Islamic extremists and the Muslim world. The Revolutionary Armed Forces of Colombia (FARC) poses a serious threat to U.S. interests in Latin America because it associates us with the government it is fighting against.
- The same is true in Turkey, where the Revolutionary People's Liberation Party/Front has publicly criticized the United States and our operations in Afghanistan.
- We are also watching states like Iran and Iraq that continue to support terrorist groups.
- Iran continues to provide support—including arms transfers—to Palestinian rejectionist groups and Hizballah. Tehran has also failed to move decisively against al-Qa'ida members who have relocated to Iran from Afghanistan.
- Iraq has a long history of supporting terrorists, including giving sanctuary to Abu Nidal.

The war on terrorism has dealt severe blows to al-Qa'ida and its leadership. The group has been denied its safehaven and strategic command center in Afghanistan. Drawing on both our own assets and increased cooperation from allies around the world, we are uncovering terrorists' plans and breaking up their cells. These efforts have yielded the arrest of nearly 1,000 al-Qa'ida operatives in over 60 countries, and have disrupted terrorist operations and potential terrorist attacks.

Mr. Chairman, Bin Ladin did not believe that we would invade his sanctuary. He saw the United States as soft, impatient, unprepared, and fearful of a long, bloody war of attrition. He did not count on the fact that we had lined up allies that could help us overcome barriers of terrain and culture. He did not know about the collection and operational initiatives that would allow us to strike—with great accuracy—at the heart of the Taliban and al-Qa'ida. He underestimated our capabilities, our readiness, and our resolve.

That said, I must repeat that al-Qa'ida has not yet been destroyed. It and other like-minded groups remain willing and able to strike us. Al-Qa'ida leaders still at large are working to reconstitute the organization and to resume its terrorist operations. We must eradicate these organizations by denying them their sources of financing and eliminating their ability to hijack charitable organizations for their terrorist purposes. We must be prepared for a long war, and we must not falter.

Mr. Chairman, we must also look beyond the immediate danger of terrorist attacks to the conditions that allow terrorism to take root around the world. These conditions are no less threatening to U.S. national security than terrorism itself. The problems that terrorists exploit—poverty, alienation, and ethnic tensions—will grow more acute over the next decade. This will especially be the case in those parts of the world that have served as the most fertile recruiting grounds for Islamic extremist groups.

- We have already seen—in Afghanistan and elsewhere—that domestic unrest and conflict in weak states is one of the factors that create an environment conducive to terrorism.
- More importantly, demographic trends tell us that the world's poorest and most politically unstable regions—which include parts of the Middle East and Sub-Saharan Africa—will have the largest youth populations in the world over the next two decades and beyond. Most of these countries will lack the economic institutions or resources to effectively integrate these youth into society. . . .

As of July 20, 2002, the full text of Tenet's prepared testimony was available at http://www.cia.gov/cia/public_affairs/speeches/ dci_speech_02062002.html

FBI OFFICIAL DESCRIBES THREAT FROM ECOTERRORISTS
February 12, 2002

*As the domestic threat from traditional left-wing and right-wing ter-
rorists continued declining in the late 1990s, the FBI focused increased
attention on "special interest" terrorists—especially ecoterrorists. Acts of
ecoterrorism range from releasing animals at fur farms to burning down
corporate offices of timber companies, all in the name of protecting animals
and the environment. In the United States, most ecoterrorist acts have been
carried out by small cells of the Animal Liberation Front (ALF) and the
Earth Liberation Front (ELF), two seemingly connected groups that have no
official leaders or formal structures. The largest act of ecoterrorism in the
United States was an arson in October 1998 at the Vail ski resort in Colorado that caused $12 million in damage. In an e-mail message sent to a ra-
dio station, the ELF said it set the fire because the resort planned to expand
into national forest lands that were prime lynx habitat. The expansion proceeded despite the fire, for which no one had been arrested as of July 2002.*

*At a congressional hearing on February 12, 2002, James Jarboe, domes-
tic terrorism section chief in the FBI's counterterrorism division, said that
ALF and ELF had carried out more than 600 attacks since 1996 that caused
more than $43 million in damage. Although he listed several recent convic-
tions for ecoterrorist acts, Jarboe admitted that law enforcement has great
difficulties investigating the groups because of their lack of structure.*

*One conviction that Jarboe mentioned twice in his testimony raised
questions about exactly how closely the FBI tracks ecoterrorism. The case
involved arson fires in 2000 and 2001 at eight luxury homes being built in
a Phoenix suburb next to a nature preserve. Notes to local news outlets
claimed the fires were aimed at stopping sprawl and were set by a group of
mountain bikers called the Coalition to Save the Preserves (CSP), setting off
fears that a group of ecoterrorists was at work. In his testimony, Jarboe
noted the fires and said no direct connection had been made between CSP
and ALF or ELF. "However," he said, "the stated goal of CSP to stop development of previously undeveloped lands, is similar to that of the ELF." He
failed to mention that the CSP did not really exist—it was simply a cover*

created by Mark Warren Sands, who was arrested for the arsons in June 2001 and pleaded guilty the following November. Sands, a church usher, youth soccer referee, former spokesman for the Arizona Department of Education, and laid-off marketing consultant, lived in the suburb where the houses were being built. He told the New York Times *that he torched the first house because it blocked access to his favorite jogging trail. Delighted by the media attention his act received, he set the other fires "seemingly to prove something to himself: that he still knew how to run a campaign," the newspaper said. It quoted Sands as saying: "My drug was the news media coverage. There was the excitement of waiting for the media coverage to come out. There was a sense of power."*

Following are excerpts from a statement by James F. Jarboe, domestic terrorism section chief in the FBI's counterterrorism division, at a February 12, 2002, hearing of the House Resources Committee's Subcommittee on Forests and Forest Health:

. . . During the past decade we have witnessed dramatic changes in the nature of the terrorist threat. In the 1990s, right-wing extremism overtook left-wing terrorism as the most dangerous domestic terrorist threat to the country. During the past several years, special interest extremism, as characterized by the Animal Liberation Front (ALF) and the Earth Liberation Front (ELF), has emerged as a serious terrorist threat. Generally, extremist groups engage in much activity that is protected by constitutional guarantees of free speech and assembly. Law enforcement becomes involved when the volatile talk of these groups transgresses into unlawful action. The FBI estimates that the ALF/ELF have committed more than 600 criminal acts in the United States since 1996, resulting in damages in excess of 43 million dollars.

Special interest terrorism differs from traditional right-wing and left-wing terrorism in that extremist special interest groups seek to resolve specific issues, rather than effect widespread political change. Special interest extremists continue to conduct acts of politically motivated violence to force segments of society, including the general public, to change attitudes about issues considered important to their causes. These groups occupy the extreme fringes of animal rights, pro-life, environmental, anti-nuclear, and other movements. Some special interest extremists—most notably within the animal rights and environmental movements—have turned increasingly toward vandalism and terrorist activity in attempts to further their causes.

Since 1977, when disaffected members of the ecological preservation group Greenpeace formed the Sea Shepherd Conservation Society and attacked commercial fishing operations by cutting drift nets, acts of "eco-terrorism" have occurred around the globe. The FBI defines eco-terrorism as the use or threatened use of violence of a criminal nature against innocent victims or property by an environmentally-oriented, subnational group for environmental-political reasons, or aimed at an audience beyond the target, often of a symbolic nature.

In recent years, the Animal Liberation Front (ALF) has become one of the most active extremist elements in the United States. Despite the destructive aspects of ALF's operations, its operational philosophy discourages acts that harm "any animal, human and nonhuman." Animal rights groups in the United States, including the ALF, have generally adhered to this mandate. The ALF, established in Great Britain in the mid-1970s, is a loosely organized movement committed to ending the abuse and exploitation of animals. The American branch of the ALF began its operations in the late 1970s. Individuals become members of the ALF not by filing paperwork or paying dues, but simply by engaging in "direct action" against companies or individuals who utilize animals for research or economic gain. "Direct action" generally occurs in the form of criminal activity to cause economic loss or to destroy the victims' company operations. The ALF activists have engaged in a steadily growing campaign of illegal activity against fur companies, mink farms, restaurants, and animal research laboratories.

Estimates of damage and destruction in the United States claimed by the ALF during the past ten years, as compiled by national organizations such as the Fur Commission and the National Association for Biomedical Research (NABR), put the fur industry and medical research losses at more than 45 million dollars. The ALF is considered a terrorist group, whose purpose is to bring about social and political change through the use of force and violence.

Disaffected environmentalists, in 1980, formed a radical group called "Earth First!" and engaged in a series of protests and civil disobedience events. In 1984, however, members introduced "tree spiking" (insertion of metal or ceramic spikes in trees in an effort to damage saws) as a tactic to thwart logging. In 1992, the ELF was founded in Brighton, England, by Earth First! members who refused to abandon criminal acts as a tactic when others wished to mainstream Earth First!. In 1993, the ELF was listed for the first time along with the ALF in a communiqué declaring solidarity in actions between the two groups. This unity continues today with a crossover of leadership and membership. It is not uncommon for the ALF and the ELF to post joint declarations of responsibility for criminal actions on their websites. In 1994, founders of the San Francisco branch of Earth First! published in *The Earth First! Journal* a recommendation that Earth First! mainstream itself in the United States, leaving criminal acts other than unlawful protests to the ELF.

The ELF advocates "monkeywrenching," a euphemism for acts of sabotage and property destruction against industries and other entities perceived to be damaging to the natural environment. "Monkeywrenching" includes tree spiking, arson, sabotage of logging or construction equipment, and other types of property destruction. Speeches given by Jonathan Paul and Craig Rosebraugh at the 1998 National Animal Rights Conference held at the University of Oregon, promoted the unity of both the ELF and the ALF movements. The ELF posted information on the ALF website until it began its own website in January 2001, and is listed in the same underground activist publications as the ALF.

The most destructive practice of the ALF/ELF is arson. The ALF/ELF members consistently use improvised incendiary devices equipped with crude but effective timing mechanisms. These incendiary devices are often constructed based upon instructions found on the ALF/ELF websites. The ALF/ELF criminal incidents often involve pre-activity surveillance and well-planned operations. Members are believed to engage in significant intelligence gathering against potential targets, including the review of industry/trade publications, photographic/video surveillance of potential targets, and posting details about potential targets on the internet.

The ALF and the ELF have jointly claimed credit for several raids including a November 1997 attack on the Bureau of Land Management wild horse corrals near Burns, Oregon, where arson destroyed the entire complex resulting in damages in excess of four hundred and fifty thousand dollars, and the June 1998 arson attack of a U.S. Department of Agriculture Animal Damage Control Building near Olympia, Washington, in which damages exceeded two million dollars. The ELF claimed sole credit for the October 1998 arson of a Vail, Colorado, ski facility in which four ski lifts, a restaurant, a picnic facility and a utility building were destroyed. Damage exceeded $12 million. On 12/27/1998, the ELF claimed responsibility for the arson at the U.S. Forest Industries Office in Medford, Oregon, where damages exceeded five hundred thousand dollars. Other arsons in Oregon, New York, Washington, Michigan, and Indiana have been claimed by the ELF. Recently, the ELF has also claimed attacks on genetically engineered crops and trees. The ELF claims these attacks have totaled close to $40 million in damages.

The name of a group called the Coalition to Save the Preserves (CSP), surfaced in relation to a series of arsons that occurred in the Phoenix, Arizona, area. These arsons targeted several new homes under construction near the North Phoenix Mountain Preserves. No direct connection was established between the CSP and ALF/ELF. However, the stated goal of CSP to stop development of previously undeveloped lands, is similar to that of the ELF. The property damage associated with the arsons has been estimated to be in excess of $5 million. . . .

The FBI and our law enforcement partners have made a number of arrests of individuals alleged to have perpetrated acts of eco-terrorism. Several of these individuals have been successfully prosecuted. Following the investigation of the Phoenix, Arizona, arsons noted earlier, Mark Warren Sands was indicted and arrested on 6/14/2001. On 11/07/2001, Sands pleaded guilty to ten counts of extortion and using fire in the commission of a federal felony. . . .

Currently, more than 26 FBI field offices have pending investigations associated with ALF/ELF activities. Despite all of our efforts (increased resources allocated, JTTFs [Joint Terrorism Task Forces], successful arrests and prosecutions), law enforcement has a long way to go to adequately address the problem of eco-terrorism. Groups such as the ALF and the ELF present unique challenges. There is little if any hierarchical structure to such entities. Ecoterrorists are unlike traditional criminal enterprises which are often structured and organized.

The difficulty investigating such groups is demonstrated by the fact that law enforcement has thus far been unable to effect the arrests of anyone for some recent criminal activity directed at federal land managers or their offices. However, there are several ongoing investigations regarding such acts. Current investigations include the 10/14/2001 arson at the Bureau of Land Management Wild Horse and Burro Corral in Litchfield, California, the 7/20/2000 destruction of trees and damage to vehicles at the U.S. Forestry Science Laboratory in Rhinelander, Wisconsin, and the 11/29/1997 arson at the Bureau of Land Management Corral in Burns, Oregon.

Before closing, I would like to acknowledge the cooperation and assistance rendered by the U.S. Forest Service in investigating incidents of eco-terrorism. Specifically, I would like to recognize the assistance that the Forest Service is providing with regard to the ongoing investigation of the 7/20/2000 incident of vandalism and destruction that occurred at the U.S. Forestry Science Laboratory in Rhinelander, Wisconsin.

The FBI and all of our federal, state, and local law enforcement partners will continue to strive to address the difficult and unique challenges posed by eco-terrorists. Despite the recent focus on international terrorism, we remain fully cognizant of the full range of threats that confront the United States.

As of July 16, 2002, the full text of the testimony was available at http://www.fbi.gov/congress/congress02/jarboe021202.htm

PAKISTANI TERRORISTS KILL
WALL STREET JOURNAL REPORTER
February 22 and March 14, 2002

During a period of less than three weeks in November 2001, eight foreign journalists covering the war against terrorism in Afghanistan were killed. Three died when Northern Alliance troops they were accompanying were ambushed by Taliban fighters, four died when their convoy was stopped by unknown men who executed them, and the last was killed by masked gunmen who invaded the house he was sharing with other journalists. During the same period no U.S. soldiers were killed in combat.

The danger faced by journalists covering the Afghanistan war and related events was brought home to Americans when thirty-eight-year-old Wall Street Journal *reporter Daniel Pearl was kidnapped by Islamic militants in Karachi, Pakistan, on January 23, 2002. The kidnappers lured Pearl into a trap by promising him a meeting with a prominent Islamic cleric. Four days later, a previously unknown group sent e-mail messages to the* Wall Street Journal *and other media with pictures of Pearl tied up, in one picture with a gun to his head. The kidnappers made a number of demands, including that the United States immediately release all Pakistani nationals that it had in custody overseas and in the United States as part of the fight against terrorism. The United States refused. On February 21, 2002, the U.S. embassy in Pakistan received a gruesome videotape that showed Pearl being decapitated. The next day President George W. Bush made a brief statement condemning the murder. Less than a month later, on March 14, 2002, Attorney General John Ashcroft announced the indictment of Ahmed Omar Saeed Sheikh, a British citizen who was being held by Pakistani authorities, for allegedly masterminding Pearl's murder.*

U.S. authorities asked their Pakistani counterparts to extradite Saeed to the United States for trial. The Pakistanis refused, saying they wanted to try Saeed themselves. He and three other men went on trial April 22, 2002, and a Pakistani judge convicted all four on July 15, 2002. The judge sentenced Saeed to death by hanging and the three others to twenty-five years in prison. After his sentencing Saeed threatened death to anyone who harmed him. All four men appealed, and their chances for overturning the convic-

tions were bolstered by the fact that during the trial Pakistani authorities had arrested a second group of men in connection with Pearl's death. On May 17 the second group led police to a shallow grave containing a badly decomposed body, chopped into nine pieces, that turned out to be Pearl. Eleven days later Pearl's widow, Mariane, a freelance journalist living in Paris, gave birth to the couple's first child.

Following are a statement by President George W. Bush on February 22, 2002, and excerpts from a statement by Attorney General John Ashcroft on March 14, 2002, concerning the death of journalist Daniel Pearl:

BUSH STATEMENT

Laura and I, and the American people, are deeply saddened to learn about the loss of Daniel Pearl's life. And we're really sad for his wife and his parents, and his friends and colleagues, who have been clinging to hope for weeks that he be found alive. We are especially sad for his unborn child, who will now know his father only through the memory of others.

All Americans are sad and angry to learn of the murder. All around the world, American journalists and humanitarian aid workers and diplomats and others do important work in places that are sometimes dangerous. Those who would threaten Americans, those who would engage in criminal, barbaric acts, need to know that these crimes only hurt their cause and only deepen the resolve of the United States of America to rid the world of these agents of terror.

May God bless Daniel Pearl.

ASHCROFT STATEMENT

Today I'm announcing a grand jury's indictment of Ahmed Omar Saeed Sheikh, a British citizen currently in custody of Pakistani authorities, for acts of terrorism against two United States citizens. Saeed is charged with the kidnapping and murder of Daniel Pearl and the 1994 kidnapping of a United States citizen in India. A grand jury in the district of New Jersey has returned an indictment charging Saeed with hostage-taking and conspiracy to commit hostage-taking, resulting in the death of Daniel Pearl.

In addition, we are today unsealing an indictment filed in November of last year, charging Saeed with the 1994 armed kidnapping of Bela J. Nuss, an American tourist, in India. If Saeed is found guilty of the crimes he is charged with committing against Daniel Pearl, he could receive the death penalty. Conviction in the Nuss case carries the maximum penalty of life in prison.

It has now been three weeks since the mystery of Daniel Pearl's disappearance was resolved tragically by the news of his brutal murder. In this time, in the face of this tragedy, Mariane Pearl, Daniel's widow, has refused to concede defeat to terrorists. She has instead rallied Americans and citizens of all nations to unite against the evil that took the life of the father of her unborn son. She has been an eloquent and forceful reminder to all of us that what is at stake in the fight against terrorism is nothing less than the values of free speech and open inquiry that Daniel cherished, the values that protect and undergird the freedom we enjoy.

This morning I had the opportunity to meet with Mrs. Pearl, and I thank her and I commend her for her courage and the resolve that she has shown. With today's indictment, I'm honored to be able to offer to Mariane Pearl a measure of solace and this pledge: The United States has not forsaken your husband nor the values that he embodied and cherished. The story of Daniel Pearl— that he died trying to tell—will be told, and justice will be done. . . .

The indictment in the Pearl case announced today states that Ahmed Omar Saeed Sheikh is affiliated with radical militant organizations. The indictment charges further that Saeed trained in military camps in Afghanistan and, in or about September and October 2001, fought in Afghanistan with Taliban and al Qaeda forces.

The grand jury charges that in the opening weeks of 2002, Saeed led a ring of co-conspirators who carefully and methodically set a death trap for Daniel Pearl, lured him into it with lies, and savagely ended his life. The indictment states that Saeed and his co-conspirators purposefully set out to take hostage an acclaimed journalist from an influential United States newspaper in order to change U.S. policies in the war against terrorism and to achieve other goals.

Using the Internet to communicate, Saeed assumed a false identity to lure Daniel Pearl to a meeting in Karachi with a fictitious source. It was from this meeting that Pearl was abducted.

In the captivity of his kidnappers the indictment charges that Daniel Pearl was kept in seclusion under the use and threat of violence. His kidnappers communicated their demands to various media outlets by e-mail, beginning with a message sent on January the 26th that included a photograph of Pearl with a gun pointed at his head. In a second e-mail sent January 30th, Daniel Pearl's kidnappers threatened to execute him if their demands were not met and threatened the lives of other American journalists in Pakistan. But before that message was sent, the indictment charges the conspirators had already brutally killed Daniel Pearl and videotaped the mutilation of his body.

The additional indictment against Ahmed Omar Saeed Sheikh, being unsealed today, makes clear that Daniel Pearl was not the first American to fall victim to terror at the hands of Saeed. In October 1994, the indictment charges, Saeed met Bela J. Nuss, an American tourist, at a restaurant in New Delhi while scouting areas of the city known to be frequented by U.S. citizens and other Westerners. As in the case of Daniel Pearl, Saeed carefully selected Nuss, used lies to befriend him, and lured him to an isolated place where he was kidnapped at gunpoint. Also like the case of Daniel Pearl, Nuss was held in brutal isolation and photographed with a gun pointed at his head while Saeed and his co-conspirators communicated their demands to the media.

At the time of the 1994 kidnapping, the indictment states that Saeed was a member of the Harakat ul-Ansar, which was implicated in several terrorist acts against United States citizens in India during the 1990s. The indictment charges Saeed with hostage-taking and conspiracy to commit hostage-taking.

The United States has worked in cooperation with Pakistani and other authorities to build the case for the indictment of Ahmed Omar Saeed Sheikh announced today.

But we pursue this case, and we continue this investigation not merely to bring Daniel Pearl's killers to justice or to provide closure to Bela Nuss. We pursue this case to uphold and protect the values Daniel Pearl cherished and the freedoms he died exercising.

The men who conspired to kill Daniel Pearl and kidnap Bela Nuss did not act at random but carefully chose their targets, their methods and their words. By killing Daniel Pearl and threatening other Americans, terrorists hoped to send a message of defiance. But what survives is an unmistakable message of their fear. Stunted by their hatred, imprisoned in their lies, even terrorists understand, as we understand, that unfettered speech and open inquiry are the bedrock upon which freedom stands—what George Mason called "the bulwark of liberty" and Thomas Jefferson included in the creed of our political faith, the text of our civil instruction, the touchstone by which we try the services of those we trust.

Where freedom is feared, men and women like Daniel Pearl will always be hunted. But where freedom is cherished, they will be forever defended. With today's indictments, we begin the process of securing justice for Daniel Pearl and Bela Nuss, solace for their families and vindication for the values they and all civilized people share. The department's investigation of this case is an ongoing one. And we will not rest until we do everything possible to complete bringing to justice the entirety of the individuals involved. . . .

As of July 19, 2002, the full text of Ashcroft's statement was available at http://www.usdoj.gov/ag/speeches/2002/ 031402newsconferenceindictmentindanielpearlcase.htm

TESTIMONY ON DRUG TRADE AS SOURCE OF TERRORISM FUNDING
March 13, 2002

The U.S.-led war to topple the Taliban leaders of Afghanistan focused renewed attention on narcoterrorism, in which terrorist groups or related individuals raise money by participating directly or indirectly in the drug trade, because the Taliban financed much of their military operations from taxes imposed on opium production and drug movements. A December 2000 report by a United Nations committee said that "funds raised from the production and trade of opium and heroin are used by the Taliban to buy arms and war materials and to finance the training of terrorists and support the operation of extremists in neighboring countries and beyond." There also were allegations that Osama bin Laden, the terrorist sheltered by the Taliban, was personally involved in drug trafficking to help finance his al Qaeda terrorist network, according to an October 2001 report by the Congressional Research Service.

Terrorists were increasingly turning to drug trafficking to replace money they previously received from state sponsors of terrorism, said two senior State Department officials in a joint statement prepared for a March 13, 2002, congressional hearing on narcoterrorism. Rand Beers, assistant secretary for international narcotics and law enforcement affairs, and Francis X. Taylor, ambassador-at-large for counterterrorism, said that for some terrorists drug trafficking had a two-fold purpose. "Not only does it provide funds, but it also furthers the strategic objectives of the terrorists," they told a subcommittee of the Senate Judiciary Committee. "Some terrorist groups believe they can weaken their enemies by flooding their societies with addictive drugs."

As they spoke, the destructive impact of narcoterrorism was nowhere more apparent than in Colombia. Three major groups—funded by hundreds of millions of dollars annually in drug profits and each labeled a terrorist organization by the U.S. State Department—regularly carried out guerrilla operations and terrorist attacks against the government, each other, and civilians, with 3,500 people killed annually. In late May 2002 Alvaro Uribe Velez was elected president largely based on his promise to step up military action against the three groups. In that same month the U.S. Congress held hearings about whether it should allow Colombia to use military aid that was restricted to fighting drug trafficking to also fight the terrorist groups. The debate was complicated by the fact that, in March, Colombian authorities had charged three men closely tied to the Irish Republican Army with teaching bombmaking to members of the largest rebel group, the Revolutionary Armed Forces of Colombia, which is known by its Spanish acronym FARC. In July FARC ordered all state governors, mayors, judges, and other local officials in Colombia to resign or face being declared "military targets," and the group backed up its threat by murdering one mayor and kidnapping three others. Also in July, Colombia's secret police announced they had thwarted a plot by FARC to crash a plane into either the Congress building or the presidential palace. Meanwhile, one of the terrorist groups—the right-wing United Self-Defense Forces of Colombia, known as AUC—splintered after internal disputes about whether it should be involved in drug trafficking.

Following are excerpts from the prepared joint testimony of State Department officials Rand Beers, assistant secretary for international narcotics and law enforcement affairs, and Francis X. Taylor, ambassador-at-large for counterterrorism, for a March 13, 2002, hearing of the Senate Judiciary Committee's Subcommittee on Technology, Terrorism, and Government Information:

. . . There often is a nexus between terrorism and organized crime, including drug trafficking. Links between terrorist organizations and drug traffickers take many forms, ranging from facilitation—protection, transportation, and taxation—to direct trafficking by the terrorist organization itself in order to finance its activities. Traffickers and terrorists have similar logistical needs in terms of material and the covert movement of goods, people and money. . . .

Similarity of Methods

Terrorist groups and drug trafficking organizations increasingly rely on cell structures to accomplish their respective goals. While there may be a strong central leadership, day-to-day operations are carried out by members of compartmentalized cells. This structure enhances security by providing a degree of separation between the leadership and the rank-and-file. In addition, terrorists and drug traffickers use similar means to conceal profits and fundraising. They use informal transfer systems such as "hawala," and also rely on bulk cash smuggling, multiple accounts, and front organizations to launder money. Both groups make use of fraudulent documents, including passports and other identification and customs documents to smuggle goods and weapons. They both fully exploit their networks of trusted couriers and contacts to conduct business. In addition, they use multiple cell phones and are careful about what they say on the phone to increase communications security.

The methods used for moving and laundering money for general criminal purposes are similar to those used to move money to support terrorist activities. It is no secret which countries and jurisdictions have poorly regulated banking structures, and both terrorist organizations and drug trafficking groups have made use of online transfers and accounts that do not require disclosure of owners. . . .

From State-Sponsorship to Drug Trafficking

In the past, state sponsors provided funding for terrorists, and their relationships with terrorist organizations were used to secure territory or provide access to gray arms networks. Lately, however, as state sponsorship of terrorism has come under increased scrutiny and greater international condemnation, terrorist groups have looked increasingly at drug trafficking as a source of revenue. But trafficking often has a two-fold purpose for the terrorists. Not only does it provide funds, it also furthers the strategic objectives of the terrorists. Some terrorist groups believe that they can weaken their enemies by flooding their societies with addictive drugs.

Growing pressure on state sponsors of terrorism has increased the likelihood that terrorists will become involved in the drug trade. Interdiction of terrorist finances and shutdowns of "charitable" and other non-governmental front organizations have also contributed to their convergence. Terrorist groups are increasingly able to justify their involvement in illicit activity to their membership and have largely abandoned the belief that it can damage the moral basis for their cause.

Listed below, by geographic region, are terrorist organizations that are known to have connections to drug-trafficking. Most of these organizations have been officially designated as Foreign Terrorist Organizations (FTOs) by the Secretary of State.

Latin America

In the Western Hemisphere, there is an historic link between various terrorist groups and narcotics trafficking. . . .

The Andean region is the source of virtually all the world's cocaine. Colombia, Peru and Bolivia, in that order, are the primary producers of coca and the final products. The presence of terrorist organizations in Colombia and Peru—and their need to finance operations—establishes a natural symbiotic relationship to exploit drugs as a revenue source.

The linkage between drugs and terrorism in Colombia is one that particularly concerns us and one that we watch carefully. In the 1990s, the international drug cartels operating in Colombia embarked on a campaign of violence that severely challenged the authority and even the sovereignty of the Colombian state. The September 11 attacks illustrate in graphic detail the serious threat posed by forces hostile to the United States operating under the cover and protection of a narco-terrorist state. In light of recent events in Colombia, the potential for increased violence between the government and terrorist groups, and the growing linkage between terrorism and drug trafficking, we are reviewing our policy options there. At present, there are three terrorist groups operating in Colombia including the FARC, ELN, and AUC.

Revolutionary Armed Forces of Colombia (FARC)—Although the FARC-controlled safe haven, or "despeje"—which is situated between two of Colombia's largest coca cultivation areas—is not considered a major area for coca cultivation or drug trafficking, many FARC units throughout southern Colombia raise funds through the extortion ("taxation") of both legal and illegal businesses, the latter including the drug trade. Similarly, in return for cash payments, or possibly in exchange for weapons, some FARC units protect cocaine laboratories and clandestine airstrips in southern Colombia. In addition, some FARC units may be independently involved in limited cocaine laboratory operations. Some FARC units in southern Colombia are more directly involved in local drug trafficking activities, such as controlling local cocaine base markets. At least one prominent FARC commander has served as a source of cocaine for a Brazilian trafficking organization. There are strong indications that the FARC has established links with the Irish Republican Army to increase its capability to conduct urban terrorism. In July 2001, the Colombian National Police arrested three members of the IRA who are believed to have used the demilitarized zone to train the FARC in the use of explosives.

National Liberation Army (ELN)—The ELN operates primarily along Colombia's northeastern border with Venezuela and in central and northwestern Colombia. The territories under ELN influence include cannabis and opium poppy growing areas. Some ELN units raise funds through extortion or by protecting laboratory operations. Some ELN units may be independently involved in limited cocaine laboratory operations, but the ELN appears to be much less dependent than the FARC on coca and cocaine profits to fund its operations. The ELN expresses a disdain for illegal drugs, but does take advantage of the profits available where it controls coca producing areas.

United Self-Defense Groups of Colombia (AUC)—The AUC umbrella group, which includes many Colombian paramilitary forces, admittedly uses the cocaine trade to finance its counterinsurgency campaign. The head of the AUC, Carlos Castano, stated in 2000 that "70 percent" of AUC operational funding was from drug money and described it as an undesired but necessary evil. AUC elements appear to be directly involved in processing cocaine and exporting cocaine from Colombia. In 2001, the AUC claimed publicly that it was getting out of the drug business, but it will be very difficult for this umbrella group to keep its many semi-autonomous units from continuing in the lucrative drug business.

Shining Path (Sendero Luminoso SL) (Peru)—The SL historically has operated in remote areas of Peru where central government authority is least prevalent—a condition conducive to drug producers, drug traffickers and terrorists. The geographic coincidence and reliance on violence to protect safe havens made the SL a natural to engage in protection and extortion rackets involving coca and cocaine. The SL cut a brutal swath through Peru from the 1980s to the mid-1990s, largely funded by levies it imposed on cocaine trafficking. As the SL waned in the late 1990s, so did its influence on the drug trade.

But in 2001, the SL had a slight resurgence in areas like the Huallaga and Apurimac valleys where coca is cultivated and processed, indicating that the remnants of the group are probably financing operations with drug profits from security and taxation "services."

Tri-Border Islamic Groups—In Ciudad del Este, Paraguay, and along the loosely controlled region that it borders with Brazil and Argentina, members of radical Islamic groups are reported to be engaged in drug trafficking, money laundering, intellectual property rights piracy, alien smuggling and arms trafficking. One such individual is Said Hassan Ali Mohamed Mukhlis, a suspected member of the Egyptian Islamic Group with possible ties to Osama bin Laden. This group is linked to the murder of 58 tourists in Luxor, Egypt, and Mukhlis himself was arrested in 1999 by Uruguayan authorities in connection with foiled plots to bomb the U.S. embassies in Paraguay and Uruguay.

South Asia and Former Soviet Union

Throughout this region, proximity to cultivation and production, combined with the infrastructure provided by the traffickers, has encouraged mutually beneficial relationships between terrorist groups and drug trafficking organizations.

Al-Qaida—Since it transferred its base of operations to Afghanistan, al-Qaida has been sustained by a government that earned a substantial part of its revenue through taxes on opium production and trafficking. Afghanistan's opiate trafficking, which accounts for more than 70 percent of the world's supply, was reportedly advocated by Osama bin Ladin as a way to weaken the West.

Kashmiri militant groups—These groups likely take part in the drug trade to finance their activities given their proximity to major production and refining sites and trafficking routes.

Liberation Tigers of Tamil Eelam [LTTE] (Sri Lanka)—Individual members and sympathizers worldwide traffic drugs—principally heroin—to raise money for their cause, but there is no evidence of official LTTE involvement in the drug trade. The LTTE reportedly has close ties to drug trafficking networks in Burma, and Tamil expatriates may carry drugs in exchange for training from Burma, Pakistan and Afghanistan.

Islamic Movement of Uzbekistan (IMU)—The IMU has reportedly profited from the drug trade out of Afghanistan and trafficking through Central Asia to Russia and Europe.

Middle East

Hizballah—The Lebanese "Hizballah" group smuggles cocaine from Latin America to Europe and the Middle East and has in the past smuggled opiates out of Lebanon's Bekaa valley, although poppy cultivation there has dwindled in recent years. Its involvement in drug trafficking and other illicit activity may expand as state sponsorship declines. . . .

As of July 24, 2002, the full text of the testimony was available at http://www.state.gov/g/inl/rls/rm/8743pf.htm

UNITED STATES INDICTS LAWYER FOR CONVICTED TERRORIST
April 9, 2002

In 1995 Sheik Omar Abdel-Rahman, the spiritual leader of an Egyptian terrorist organization called the Islamic Group, was convicted of conspiring with nine other men to blow up a number of New York tunnels, bridges, and buildings—including the United Nations—on a single day in 1993. The blind Egyptian cleric, who was believed to have masterminded the plan, was sentenced to life in prison without parole. Federal authorities were concerned that the sheik would continue to direct the Islamic Group from his prison cell, so in 1997 they issued an order that basically forbade him from communicating with anyone in the outside world except his attorneys. The order was expanded in 1999 to bar Abdel-Rahman from communicating with the news media either personally or through his attorneys. Each of his attorneys signed statements saying they would abide by the order.

But on April 9, 2002, Attorney General John Ashcroft announced the indictment of Lynne F. Stewart, a sixty-two-year-old defense attorney for the sheik, for violating the order and otherwise helping Abdel-Rahman continue directing the Islamic Group from his cell. The indictment alleged that Stewart, while visiting her client in the Minnesota federal prison hospital where he was incarcerated, had distracted prison guards so that an interpreter with her—speaking Arabic—could pass messages between Abdel-Rahman and his followers in Egypt about terrorist activities. It also alleged that Stewart had violated the order by announcing to the news media that Abdel-Rahman had withdrawn his support for a ceasefire by the Islamic Group, in effect sending instructions to the group's members. The interpreter and two other men were indicted along with Stewart. The attorney-client privilege normally bars law enforcement authorities from listening to conversations between lawyers and their clients. However, federal authorities had obtained a judge's approval to listen to Abdel-Rahman's conversations under the Foreign Intelligence Surveillance Act, which permits the government to monitor conversations by spies and terrorists.

At her arraignment Stewart, a grandmother, former librarian, and prominent attorney known for frequently representing terrorists and other *controversial clients, pleaded "emphatically not guilty" and was released on $500,000 bond. She faced a sentence of up to forty years in prison if convicted. When he announced the indictment, Ashcroft said all of Abdel-Rahman's future conversations with his attorneys would be monitored under a new rule allowing the Bureau of Prisons to listen in on such communications by inmates who might commit "future acts of violence or terrorism." In June 2002 an FBI affidavit filed in the case alleged that terrorists who bombed the USS* Cole *in October 2000 did so at least partially to pressure the United States into releasing the sheik from prison.* (Seventeen Killed in Suicide Attack on USS *Cole,* p. 330)

Following is a statement prepared for an April 9, 2002, press conference by Attorney General John Ashcroft announcing the indictment of Lynne F. Stewart, an attorney for Sheik Abdel-Rahman, and three other people:

This afternoon, I am announcing the indictment of four associates of Sheik Abdel-Rahman, a leader of the designated terrorist organization the Islamic Group. Since 1995, Sheik Rahman has been serving life in prison for conspiring to wage a war of terrorism against the United States, including the plot that resulted in the 1993 bombing of the World Trade Center and a conspiracy to destroy several New York landmarks, including the United Nations. Today's indictment charges four individuals—including Rahman's lawyer, a United States citizen—with aiding Sheik Abdel-Rahman in continuing to direct the terrorist activities of the Islamic Group from his prison cell in the United States.

The United States charges the following individuals:

- Lynne Stewart, who was Sheik Abdel-Rahman's attorney during his 1995 conviction for the World Trade Center bombing and has continued to act as one of his attorneys since he has been in prison;
- Mohammed Yousry, the Arabic language interpreter for communications between Stewart and the imprisoned Sheik Rahman;
- Ahmed Abdel Sattar, a resident of Staten Island, New York and an active Islamic Group leader, whom the indictment describes as a "surrogate" for Rahman; and
- Yassir Al-Sirri, the former head of the London-based Islamic Observation Center, currently in custody in the United Kingdom, who is charged with facilitating communications among Islamic Group members and providing financing for their activities.

The indictment charges that these defendants worked in concert with Sheik Abdel-Rahman—in violation of Special Administrative Measures restricting Rahman's communications with the outside world—to provide material support and resources to the Islamic Group. The indictment charges that Rahman used communications with Stewart, translated by Yousry, to pass messages to and receive messages from Sattar, Al-Sirri and other Islamic Group members.

The terrorist movement at the center of the facts alleged in this indictment, the Islamic Group, has as its credo a message of hate that is now tragically familiar to Americans: to oppose by whatever means necessary the nations, governments, and individuals who do not share its radical interpretation of Islamic law. The Islamic Group is a global terrorist organization that has forged alliances with other terrorist groups, including al Qaeda. It has an active membership in the United States, concentrated in the New York City metropolitan area.

Since at least the early 1990s, Sheik Abdel-Rahman has been one of the principal leaders of the Islamic Group, and has directed its terrorist operations, defined its goals, and recruited its membership in the United States. In 1997, following his 1995 imprisonment, Special Administrative Measures were imposed on Sheik Abdel-Rahman. Among other restrictions, these measures prohibited Rahman "from passing or receiving any written or recorded communications to or from other inmates, visitors, attorney(s), prison staff or anyone else." In 1999, these restrictions were amended to prohibit Rahman from communicating with any member of the news media in person or through his attorneys. Before being allowed access to Rahman, his attorneys, including Lynne Stewart, were required to sign and did sign an affirmation acknowledging that they would abide by these measures and would be accompanied by translators only to communicate with Sheik Rahman regarding legal matters.

Today's indictment charges that Lynne Stewart and Mohammed Yousry repeatedly and willfully violated these orders in order to maintain Sheik Abdel-Rahman's influence over the terrorist activities of the Islamic Group. Among other overt acts, the indictment charges that during a May 2000 visit to Sheik Abdel-Rahman, Stewart allowed Yousry to read letters from Ahmed Abdel Sattar regarding whether the Islamic Group should continue to comply with a cease-fire in terrorist activities against Egyptian authorities that had been in place following the shooting and stabbing of 58 tourists and four Egyptians visiting an archeological site in Luxor, Egypt in 1997—a terrorist attack for which the Islamic Group claimed credit. The indictment charges that, because these communications violated the Special Administrative Measures placed on Sheik Rahman, Stewart took affirmative steps to conceal the conversation from prison guards, making extraneous comments in English to mask the Arabic conversation between Rahman and Yousry. Following the meeting, and in further violation of the Special Administrative Measures to which she had agreed, Stewart is charged with announcing to the news media that Rahman had withdrawn his support for the cease-fire.

The indictment further alleges that in a January 2001 phone call, Ahmed Abdel Sattar informed Stewart that prison administrators had pleaded with Rahman's wife to tell Rahman to take his medicine. The indictment charges that although they knew Rahman was voluntarily refusing to take insulin for his diabetes, Sattar and Stewart agreed to issue a public statement falsely claiming that Rahman was being denied medical treatment. The indictment charges that Stewart stated that this misrepresentation was "safe" because no one on the "outside" would know the truth.

Shortly after terrorists attacked the United States on September 11, 2001, the Department of Justice promulgated a rule creating the authority to monitor the attorney-client communications of federal inmates whom we suspected of facilitating acts of terrorism. At the time, we attempted to make clear that of the 158,000 inmates in the federal system, this authority would apply only to the 16 inmates who, like Sheik Abdel-Rahman, were already under Special Administrative Measures. The authority was carefully circumscribed to preserve inmates' rights while preventing acts of terrorism. Each prisoner would be told in advance his conversations would be monitored. None of the information that is protected by attorney-client privilege would be used for prosecution. Information would only be used to stop impending terrorist acts and save American lives.

The Department of Justice announced this authority back in October with the knowledge—which could not be publicly shared for fear of exposing Americans to greater risk—that inmates such as Sheik Abdel-Rahman were attempting to subvert our system of justice for terrorist ends. In fact, the training manual for al Qaeda terrorists offers detailed instructions to recruits on how to continue their terrorist operations in the event they get caught. Imprisoned terrorists are instructed to take advantage of any contact with the outside world to "communicate with brothers outside prison and exchange information that may be helpful to them in their work. The importance of mastering the art of hiding messages is self-evident here."

As today's indictment sets forth, Sheik Abdel-Rahman has learned al Qaeda's lessons well. Sheik Rahman is determined to exploit the rights guaranteed him under the United States system of justice to pursue the destruction of that very system. The United States cannot and will not stand by and allow this to happen. Accordingly, today I am announcing that the Department of Justice is invoking for the first time the authority to monitor the communications between Sheik Abdel-Rahman and his attorneys under the new regulations.

Since our country was attacked over six months ago, I have sought to reassure the American people that the actions of the Department of Justice are carefully designed to target terrorists and to protect American rights and freedoms.

Today's actions pursue the same objectives with the same protections in mind. We will not look the other way when our institutions of justice are subverted. We will not ignore those who claim rights for themselves while they seek their destruction for others.

We will, in the President's words, defend freedom—and justice—no matter what the cost.

LAST MAJOR SUSPECT CONVICTED
IN 1963 CHURCH BOMBING
May 14, 2002

By 1963, Birmingham, Alabama, was a hotbed of racial tension. Civil rights protests and marches were frequent—as was violence aimed at squelching the civil rights movement. Birmingham's schools were integrated for the first time on September 10, 1963, by a court order. That was the last straw for some white supremacists. On Sunday morning, September 15, 1963, a dynamite bomb exploded just outside the 16th Street Baptist Church, where civil rights activists frequently rallied. The blast killed four black girls as they prepared for the morning service: Denise McNair, 11; Addie Mae Collins, 14; Cynthia Wesley, 14; and Carole Robertson, 14. The terrorist bombing, the most deadly attack of the civil rights era, earned the city the nickname "Bombingham." Police and FBI agents quickly identified the main suspects in the crime, but efforts to prosecute the men were repeatedly derailed. For example, a May 1965 FBI memo to then-director J. Edgar Hoover named four former members of the Ku Klux Klan as the bombers. Hoover said the chances for conviction were "remote" and ordered agents not to share their information with state and local authorities. Over the next four decades two of the men named in the memo were convicted of the crime, and another died without being charged. Robert E. Chambliss, known as "Dynamite Bob" because of his participation in many bombings, was convicted in November 1977 and died in prison in 1985; Herman Frank Cash, another prime suspect, died in 1994 without being prosecuted; and Thomas E. Blanton was convicted in May 2001 and sentenced to life in prison.

That left Bobby Frank Cherry, whose trial began in May 2002 when he was seventy-one years old. In his opening statement at the trial, Assistant U.S. Attorney Robert Posey said Cherry frequently boasted about his role in the bombing. "Over the years, this defendant has hung this crime on his chest like a badge of honor, like a Klan medal, like a hero," Posey said. A jury of nine whites and three blacks deliberated for less than a day before finding Cherry guilty of murder. He was automatically sentenced to life in prison.

Prosecutors said Cherry would be the last person prosecuted for the

Birmingham bombing, even though other men likely played smaller roles in the crime. Cherry's conviction left the June 1964 slayings of three civil rights workers in Mississippi as the last major terrorist act of the civil rights era still unsolved. Previously, another major case from the civil rights era had been closed when Byron De La Beckwith was convicted in 1994 in Mississippi of the 1963 murder of civil rights leader Medgar Evers. (Trial Remarks on the Murder of Civil Rights Leader Evers, p. 146)

Following is the opening statement of Assistant U.S. Attorney Robert Posey on May 14, 2002, at the trial of Bobby Frank Cherry in Birmingham, Alabama:

Bobby Frank Cherry is charged with the bombing of the 16th Street Baptist Church on a Sunday morning in September 1963. He's charged with the murder of four of the children of that church, four children of Birmingham. I'd like to take a few minutes this morning to tell you what I expect the evidence will be, and I'd like to start by taking you back to 1963.

In 1963, John F. Kennedy was President of the United States. George Wallace became Governor of Alabama for the first time in January of 1963. In his inaugural speech Wallace promised "segregation now, segregation tomorrow and segregation forever."

In the spring of 1963, Dr. Martin Luther King, Jr. and the Southern Christian Leadership Conference initiated a non-violent direct action program in Birmingham, to protest segregation of public facilities. Dr. King was arrested and put in jail. His famous "Letter from the Birmingham Jail" was dated April 16.

The 16th Street Baptist Church became a fixture of the civil rights movement. Dr. King spoke at the church. Marches sometimes originated from the church. In May we had the Children's Marches, where children joined the protests, marching from the 16th Street Baptist Church to Kelly Ingram Park.

In June of 1963, George Wallace made his stand in the schoolhouse door to oppose the admission of black students to the University of Alabama. In August, Dr. King gave his "I Have a Dream" speech on the Capitol steps in Washington, D.C.

And then in September 1963, in Birmingham, black children were admitted to previously all-white schools for the first time. The last time that desegregation had been attempted in Birmingham was when a black preacher named Fred Shuttlesworth tried to enroll his children in Phillips High School. They were met by a mob of Klansmen who beat Shuttlesworth to the ground. One of the men in the Klan mob was the defendant, Bobby Frank Cherry, and Cherry would later brag about how he hit Shuttlesworth in the face with a set of brass knuckles.

The desegregation of Birmingham schools happened on September 10, 1963. Five days later, on September 15, the bomb exploded at the 16th Street Baptist Church that killed the four children.

I expect the evidence will be that it was not a coincidence that this deadly

412

bombing occurred at the moment schools were opened to all races. It was designed as an instrument of terror to force back the tide of civil rights progress. It was done by Ku Klux Klansmen who could not stand the thought of black children going to school with white children.

Like other Klan activities, carried out under the shroud of a hooded robe, this bombing was carried out in secret. The bomb was made in secret, and it was put down at the church at a time when nobody was around to see. But as this trial progresses, I expect that the evidence will remove the shroud, will lift up that white hood, and allow this jury to see who committed this crime.

I expect the evidence will be that the week before the bombing, a boy named Bobby Birdwell was playing at Bobby Frank Cherry's house in Birmingham with the defendant's son Frank. As the boys ran back and forth through the house, from the front yard to the back yard, Birdwell noticed a white hooded robe laid out in the living room. As he went through the kitchen, he saw the defendant sitting at the kitchen table with three other men. In fragments of conversation, he heard one of the men say "the bomb is ready" and "16th Street" and "church." And when the bomb exploded at the church a few days later, the image of that scene in Cherry's kitchen was burned into Birdwell's memory.

September 15, 1963, was a Sunday morning. Schools had just started back after the summer break. It was Youth Sunday at the 16th Street Baptist Church, and the youth of the church were planning to participate in the leadership of the worship service. Among the children at the church that morning were:

Carole Robertson. Carole was 14 years old. Both of her parents were teachers. She played clarinet in her school band, and was looking forward to playing at her first football game the next day.

Denise McNair was 11 years old. She was the only child of Mr. and Mrs. Chris McNair. Her parents were both teachers.

Cynthia Wesley was 14 years old. She was an only child. Her father was an elementary school principal and her mother was a teacher. She sang in the church choir.

Addie Mae Collins was 14 years old. She had come to church that day with her younger sister Sara.

Around 10:20 that morning, these five girls left their Sunday School room and went down to the ladies' lounge to freshen up and get ready for their parts in the special service. The ladies' lounge was in the basement of the church, partly below ground level. On one wall there was a window that looked out onto 16th Street. There were concrete stairs outside the window. The girls could stand in the light of the window to adjust their ribbons and sashes. Sara Collins walked to a sink at the back of the lounge, and glanced back to see Denise McNair adjusting the sash on Addie's dress.

Just then, a powerful explosion rocked the church. A bomb, placed just outside the window of the ladies' lounge, blew a huge crater into the foundation of the church, and filled the lounge with flying glass and brick. The force of the explosion blew out the masonry wall opposite the window, and splintered the wood panels and stairs.

Sara Collins somehow survived the blast. As she lay in the rubble of the ladies' lounge, blinded by glass in both eyes, she called out for her sister Addie. But she got no answer. Sara couldn't see that just a few feet away, her sister Addie, and Denise, and Carole and Cynthia were all dead.

In the sanctuary, the blast shattered stained glass windows, and a number of the adults were injured by flying glass. Parents were crying and searching for their children. The pastor, Rev. Haywood Cross, told them to get out of the church. One of the members, Sam Rutledge, tried to leave the church the same way he had come in that morning, by the stairs on the 16th Street side of the building. But when he came to the door at the top of the stairs, the stairs were gone. So he jumped. And then he saw that the '58 Oldsmobile he drove to church that morning had been mangled by the force of the blast.

Firemen from Station Number One, a few blocks away, felt the shock and heard the blast and came to help. Jack Crews was the lieutenant in charge of Station One's engine. When he and his men got to the church, Lt. Crews climbed down into the crater and saw the bodies, and saw that it was bad. Cynthia Wesley's body could only be identified by the shoes she was wearing.

As rescue workers uncovered the bodies of the four girls, the families of Cynthia, Carole, Denise and Addie learned the horrible news that their children had been taken from them, that someone had bombed their church on a Sunday morning.

After the bombing, the FBI and local law enforcement launched an intensive investigation. Bobby Frank Cherry became a suspect. He was interviewed by FBI agents on a number of occasions, beginning shortly after the bombing and continuing over a period of years. Cherry talked about his involvement in the Ku Klux Klan. He was a member of Eastview Klavern 13, a group that included Thomas Blanton and Robert Chambliss. He talked about a splinter group of Klansmen who met under the Cahaba River Bridge on Highway 280.

He told the FBI that he knew how to use explosives, and he described in detail the chemical ingredients for making a time-delay detonator for a bomb.

He said that the only reason he didn't bomb the church was that somebody else beat him to it.

Cherry talked a lot about the bombing. I expect the evidence to be that, over the years, the bombing of the 16th Street Baptist Church became Bobby Frank Cherry's claim to fame. He was proud of it, and he talked about it. He boasted to others that he was responsible for this bombing.

At Cherry family gatherings the bombing was a frequent topic of conversation. It was understood by most of the family that Bobby Frank Cherry was responsible. His children knew the story.

His granddaughter, Teresa, growing up in Texas, heard her grandfather brag about how he put a bomb at a church in Birmingham.

Cherry's brother-in-law, Wayne Brogdon, visited him frequently while they were both living in Chicago. Brogdon listened on many occasions to Cherry tell about how he had bombed a church in Birmingham, and about the children who were killed. Sometimes Cherry even cried when he talked about the four little girls, but then he would recover, and make some vulgar remark about their deaths.

One of Cherry's wives, named Willadean, remembers how he drove her to the church to show her where it happened.

In 1982, in Dallas, Texas, Cherry was installing carpet in an apartment building, and the son of the building manager was there working on the same apartment. As they talked they discovered that they were both from Birmingham, and Cherry proceeded to tell this man the story of how he bombed the church where four little girls were killed. The man didn't think much of it at the time. But in 1997, he saw the defendant on TV, and heard that this investigation had been reopened, and he called the FBI. And I expect that man, Wayne Gowins, will testify in this trial.

I expect that the testimony of Wayne Gowins and others will make it clear to you that, over the years, this defendant has hung this crime on his chest like a badge of honor, like a Klan medal, like a hero. He boasted of what he and his Klan buddies did about integration in Birmingham. He boasted about the deaths of the four little girls. He boasted about bombing a church on a Sunday morning. He said that his only regret was that more people had not been killed. Ladies and gentlemen, I submit to you that his own words convict him of this crime.

I expect that you will hear evidence from eyewitnesses to this bombing, and from explosives experts. You will hear tape recordings of conversations between this defendant and others. You'll hear statements made by this defendant to the FBI, to his family members and to others. You will hear that Bobby Frank Cherry was a part of the group of Klansmen who bombed this church. He was in the thick of it, aiding and abetting the others in the planning and execution of this crime. The judge will tell you that a person who helps in any way is guilty. The driver of the getaway car, the man who's just there ready to help if needed is guilty.

I ask you to listen carefully to the evidence, to notice how the pieces of the puzzle fit together. And at the conclusion of the evidence, we will ask you to find this defendant guilty as charged.

U.S. EFFORTS TO HALT
NUCLEAR SMUGGLING FAULTED
May 16, 2002

The arrest on May 8, 2002, of Abdullah al Muhajir when he arrived in Chicago after a flight from Zurich added new urgency to efforts to stop the smuggling of nuclear and other radioactive materials. The following month Attorney General John Ashcroft said that Muhajir, a U.S. citizen, had learned in al Qaeda terrorist camps how to wire bombs and researched how to build "dirty bombs," which are conventional bombs that disperse radioactive materials. "We have captured a known terrorist who was exploring a plan to build and explode a radiological dispersion device, or 'dirty bomb,' in the United States," Ashcroft said. Muhajir had discussed the bomb plot with top al Qaeda leaders in Pakistan and Afghanistan, but he had not yet obtained the components to build the bomb, according to sources the New York Times *identified as "senior government officials."*

Eight days after Muhajir's arrest, the U.S. General Accounting Office (GAO) issued a report sharply criticizing a group of U.S. programs aimed at helping countries stop radioactive smuggling at their borders. Six federal agencies gave countries equipment such as radiation detection monitors and trained border guards in how to use the devices, the GAO said. Between them the agencies had spent $86 million from 1992 to 2001 to help about thirty countries, mostly in the former Soviet Union and Central and Eastern Europe. But the GAO, the investigative arm of Congress, said there was little coordination among the programs, leaving some borders less protected than others. In addition, the GAO said there was little follow-up to see whether the equipment was installed, used, and worked properly. "The current multiple-agency approach to providing U.S. assistance to combat nuclear smuggling is not, in our view, the most effective way to deliver this assistance," the GAO concluded.

In June 2002 the International Atomic Energy Agency (IAEA), which is part of the United Nations, warned that countries around the world needed to take urgent measures to improve the security of radioactive materials used in everything from medicine to nuclear power plants. "The radioactive materials needed to build a 'dirty bomb' can be found in almost any coun-

416

try in the world," the agency said, "and more than 100 countries may have inadequate control and monitoring programs necessary to prevent or even detect the theft of these materials." It implied that the United States was one of those countries, noting that the U.S. Nuclear Regulatory Commission reported that American firms had "lost track" of nearly 1,500 radio- active sources since 1996. The IAEA said more than half of the lost ra- dioactive sources were never recovered.

Following are excerpts from "Nuclear Nonproliferation: U.S. Efforts to Help Other Countries Combat Nuclear Smug- gling Need Strengthened Coordination and Planning," a report released May 16, 2002, by the U.S. General Account- ing Office:

Illicit trafficking in or smuggling of nuclear and other radioactive materials occurs worldwide and has reportedly increased in recent years. According to the International Atomic Energy Agency (IAEA), as of December 31, 2001, there had been 181 confirmed cases of illicit trafficking of nuclear material since 1993. A significant number of the cases reported by IAEA involved ma- terial that could be used to produce a nuclear weapon or a device that uses conventional explosives with radioactive material ("dirty bomb") to spread ra- dioactive contamination over a wide area. Nuclear material can be smuggled across a country's border through a variety of means: it can be hidden in a car, train, or ship, carried in personal luggage through an airport, or walked across an unprotected border.

Many nuclear smuggling cases have been traced to nuclear material that originated in the countries of the former Soviet Union. The United States, through the Department of Energy's Material Protection, Control, and Ac- counting (MPC&A) program, has helped these countries secure nuclear mate- rial at civilian and defense facilities—this effort is considered the first line of defense against potential theft and/or diversion of nuclear materials. To ad- dress the threat posed by nuclear smuggling, the United States is helping these countries improve their border security—a second line of defense—but these assistance efforts face daunting challenges. For example, Russia alone has al- most 12,500 miles of borders with 14 countries, including North Korea. It is also in close geographical proximity to Afghanistan, Iran, and Iraq. . . .

Results in Brief

U.S. assistance efforts to combat nuclear smuggling are divided among six federal agencies—the Departments of Energy, State, and Defense; the U.S. Customs Service; the Federal Bureau of Investigation (FBI); and the U.S. Coast Guard. From fiscal year 1992 through fiscal year 2001, the six agencies spent about $86 million to help about 30 countries, mostly in the former Soviet Union and Central and Eastern Europe, combat the threat of smuggling of nuclear and other materials that could be used in weapons of mass destruction. The

417

agencies have provided a range of assistance, including radiation detection equipment and training, technical exchanges to promote the development and enforcement of laws and regulations governing the export of nuclear-related equipment and technology, and other equipment and training to generally improve countries' ability to interdict nuclear smuggling. The Department of Energy (DOE) has two programs to combat nuclear smuggling and primarily focuses on Russia. Energy has installed radiation detection monitors at eight border crossings, including at an airport in Moscow, and plans to install similar equipment at close to 60 sites in Russia. The State Department has provided radiation detection monitors, mobile vans equipped with radiation detectors, handheld radiation detectors, and other assistance to about 30 countries through two separate programs. The Department of Defense (DoD) has two programs that have provided radiation detection monitors, handheld detectors, and other assistance to about 20 countries. With funding provided by the Departments of State and Defense, the U.S. Customs Service, the Federal Bureau of Investigation, and the U.S. Coast Guard have provided a variety of training and equipment to customs, border guard, and law enforcement officials in numerous countries.

U.S. assistance is not effectively coordinated and lacks an overall governmentwide plan to guide it. Although an interagency group, chaired by the State Department, exists to coordinate U.S. assistance efforts, the six agencies that are providing assistance do not always coordinate their efforts through this group. As a result, the Departments of Energy, State, and Defense have pursued separate approaches to installing radiation detection equipment at other countries' border crossings; consequently, some countries' border crossings are more vulnerable to nuclear smuggling than others. Specifically, the Department of Energy is installing equipment at border sites in Russia and the Department of Defense is installing equipment in another country that is better able to detect weapons-usable nuclear material, while the State Department has installed less sophisticated radiation detection monitors in other countries. Coordination problems also exist within agencies. For example, the Department of Energy's Second Line of Defense program does not coordinate its efforts with another office within the Department that also provides radiation detection equipment because that office receives funding from and installs equipment on behalf of the State Department. Officials of the Departments of State, Energy, and Defense have acknowledged that U.S. assistance efforts lack adequate planning and need better coordination among all the agencies. In addition, these officials told us that the roles and responsibilities of each agency in the overall U.S. assistance effort should be better clarified. . . .

While U.S. assistance is generally helping countries combat the smuggling of nuclear and other radioactive materials, serious problems with installing, using, and maintaining radiation detection equipment have undermined U.S. efforts. Representatives of 17 recipient countries told us that U.S. assistance has provided needed radiation detection equipment at border sites and training for border security guards and other law enforcement personnel. Without U.S. assistance, some countries would not have any radiation detection equipment at their borders or training in how to inspect vehicles, luggage, and people and investigate nuclear smuggling cases. In other countries, U.S. assistance has bolstered existing nuclear smuggling detection programs. We observed at border sites in countries we visited that U.S.-provided equipment was working and was being used for the purposes intended. However, we also found serious problems with some of the equipment provided to various countries. For example, about one-half of the stationary radiation detection monitors funded by the Department of Defense to one country in the former Soviet Union was never installed; numerous portable radiation detectors could not be accounted for; and radiation detection equipment provided by the State Department to Lithuania was stored in the basement of the U.S. embassy for about 2 years because of a disagreement between the department and the recipient country about the need for a power supply line costing $12,600. These and other problems are largely a result of the lack of oversight and follow-up by the agencies providing the assistance. U.S. officials are attempting to correct some of these problems by, among other things, stationing advisors in countries receiving U.S. assistance. Another problem affecting U.S. assistance efforts is that recipient countries do not systematically report incidents of nuclear material detected at their borders, which limits the ability of U.S. agencies to measure the effectiveness of the equipment they are providing. . . .

Background

Over the past decade, the United States has paid increased attention to the threat that unsecured weapons-usable nuclear material in the countries of the former Soviet Union, particularly Russia, could be stolen and fall into the hands of terrorists or countries seeking weapons of mass destruction.

By some estimates, the former Soviet Union had about 30,000 nuclear weapons and over 600 metric tons of weapons-usable material when it collapsed about 10 years ago. Several cases of illicit trafficking in nuclear material in Germany and the Czech Republic in the early to mid-1990s underscored the proliferation threat. The United States responded to the threat by providing assistance to increase security at numerous nuclear facilities in the former Soviet Union, particularly in Russia, in order to prevent weapons-usable nuclear material from being stolen. In addition, the United States has provided portal monitors (stationary equipment designed to detect radioactive materials carried by pedestrians or vehicles) and smaller, portable radiation detectors at border crossings in many countries of the former Soviet Union and Central and Eastern Europe. The equipment, which is installed at car and truck crossings, railroad crossings, seaports, and airports, can serve two purposes: deterring smugglers from trafficking in nuclear material and detecting cases of actual nuclear smuggling.

Radiation detection equipment can detect radioactive materials used in medicine and industry, patients who have recently had radiological treatment, commodities that are sources of naturally occurring radiation such as fertilizer, and—of primary concern in terms of nonproliferation—nuclear material that could be used in a nuclear weapon. Nuclear material includes radioactive source materials—such as natural uranium, low enriched uranium used as fuel in commercial nuclear power reactors, and plutonium and highly enriched uranium—that are key components of nuclear weapons. . . .

Conclusions

The current multiple-agency approach to providing U.S. assistance to combat nuclear smuggling is not, in our view, the most effective way to deliver this assistance. To date, the efforts of the six U.S. agencies participating in these programs and activities have not been well coordinated, and there is no single agency that leads the effort to effectively establish funding priorities and thoroughly assess recipient country requirements. Coordination is also a problem within agencies providing assistance. We question why, for example, there are two offices within the Department of Energy that are providing radiation detection equipment and two offices within the Department of State that have funded similar types of equipment for various countries. To ensure the efficient and effective delivery of assistance and the timely and effective expenditure of program funds, we believe that the development of a governmentwide plan is needed. Such a plan could identify a unified set of program goals and priorities and define agency roles and responsibilities; determine program cost estimates; establish time frames for effectively spending program funds; develop strategies to maintain and sustain the operation of equipment; and develop exit strategies for each country receiving assistance, including a plan for transferring responsibility for equipment maintenance to the countries.

We are also concerned about how U.S. equipment is being used by the recipient countries. While foreign officials told us that U.S.-provided equipment had improved their ability to detect radioactive material, some equipment has not been well maintained, adequately accounted for, or installed on a timely basis. A fundamental issue surrounding nuclear smuggling is the sharing of information about incidents that occur in each country. Currently, the agencies that are providing the equipment have limited access to this type of information. There is currently no systematic effort to obtain this data, and the United States depends on the willingness of the countries to voluntarily provide information. It is difficult to assess the impact and effectiveness of the U.S.-supplied equipment unless data are routinely obtained and analyzed. . . .

As of July 25, 2002, the full text of the report was available at http://www.gao.gov/new.items/d02426.pdf

FBI GETS EXPANDED AUTHORITY TO MONITOR AMERICANS
May 30, 2002

In April 1976 a U.S. Senate committee issued a stinging report documenting widespread abuses of the constitutional rights of Americans by intelligence agencies such as the Federal Bureau of Investigation and the Central Intelligence Agency. The committee, headed by Sen. Frank Church, D-Idaho, said intelligence agencies had done everything from creating files on thousands of people and groups whose only crime was disagreeing with government policy to conducting illegal wiretaps and break-ins. "We have seen a consistent pattern in which programs initiated with limited goals, such as preventing criminal violence or identifying foreign spies, were expanded to what witnesses characterized as 'vacuum cleaners,' sweeping in information about lawful activities of American citizens," the committee said. The abuses it described resulted in restrictions being placed on the FBI's power to conduct domestic surveillance. FBI abuses made headlines again in 1990 when it was learned that the agency had opened files on thousands of individuals and groups during a massive investigation of the Committee in Solidarity with the People of El Salvador (CISPES), an investigation that resulted in no prosecutions and that CISPES claimed was politically motivated. (Intelligence Activities and the Rights of Americans, p. 22; FBI Admits Terrorism Probe Violated First Amendment, p. 107)

On May 30, 2002, Attorney General John Ashcroft announced new investigative guidelines for the FBI that, among other things, largely overturned the restrictions on domestic surveillance imposed in the 1970s. He said the old rules hampered agents' abilities to prevent terrorism. For example, the previous rules generally did not allow FBI agents to visit political meetings, churches, mosques, libraries, and similar public places unless they had evidence that a crime was being committed. The new rule states: "For the purpose of detecting or preventing terrorist activities, the FBI is authorized to visit any place and attend any event that is open to the public, on the same terms and conditions as members of the public generally." Ashcroft said the new rules were aimed at helping agents prevent terrorist attacks rather than just investigating attacks after they occurred. "Our philosophy today is not to wait and sift through the rubble following a terrorist attack," he said.

But critics, including the American Civil Liberties Union and some leading members of Congress, said the changes could pave the way to resuming past abuses of constitutional rights. Critics also said the new powers would flood the FBI with largely irrelevant information, further hampering its ability to zero in on clues to terrorist threats. To improve the FBI's ability to fight terrorism, the critics said, what the agency really needed were internal changes, such as updates to its antiquated computer system that prevented agents from even sending e-mail messages, increased sharing of intelligence information both inside and outside the FBI, and an overhaul of its rigid, risk-averse culture. Meanwhile, in mid-2002 Congress delayed its planned reorganizations of the FBI and the CIA until the Department of Homeland Security was established, likely delaying any major changes in the agencies until at least early 2003. (Watchdog Urges Caution on Homeland Security Plan, p. 426)

Following are the prepared remarks for a May 30, 2002, press conference by Attorney General John Ashcroft on new guidelines for the FBI:

In its 94-year history, the Federal Bureau of Investigation has been many things—the defender of the nation from organized crime, the guardian of our security from international espionage, and the tireless protector of civil rights and civil liberties for all Americans.

On September 11, a stunned nation turned once again to the brave men and women of the FBI, and they, once again, answered the call. I spent the hours, days, and most of the first weeks after the attack in the FBI's Strategic Information and Operations Center with Director Mueller. Even today, eight months later, it is difficult to convey the professionalism, dedication and quiet resolve I witnessed in those first, 24-hour days. I saw men and women work themselves beyond fatigue to prevent new terrorist attacks. I witnessed individuals put aside their personal lives, personal agendas and personal safety to answer our nation's call.

From the first moments we spent together, launching the largest investigation in history, we understood that the mission of American justice and law enforcement had changed. That day, in those early hours, the prevention of terrorist acts became the central goal of the law enforcement and national security mission of the FBI. And from that time forward, we in the leadership of the FBI and the Department of Justice began a concerted effort to free the field agents—the brave men and women on the front lines—from the bureaucratic, organizational, and operational restrictions and structures that hindered them from doing their jobs effectively.

As we have heard recently, FBI men and women in the field are frustrated because many of our own internal restrictions have hampered our ability to fight terrorism. The current investigative guidelines have contributed to that frustration. In many instances, the guidelines bar FBI field agents from taking the initiative to detect and prevent future terrorist acts unless the FBI learns of possible criminal activity from external sources.

Under the current guidelines, FBI investigators cannot surf the web the way you or I can. Nor can they simply walk into a public event or a public place to observe ongoing activities. They have no clear authority to use commercial data services that any business in America can use. These restrictions are a competitive advantage for terrorists who skillfully utilize sophisticated techniques and modern computer systems to compile information for targeting and attacking innocent Americans.

That is why the Attorney General's guidelines and procedures relating to criminal investigations and national security were high on the list of action items for reform. Beginning in the 1970s, guidelines have been developed to inform agents of the circumstances under which investigations may be opened, the permissible scope of these investigations, the techniques that may be used, and the objectives that should be pursued. These guidelines provide limitations and guidance over and above all requirements and safeguards imposed by the Constitution and beyond the legal framework established by federal statutes enacted by Congress. Promulgated for different purposes and revised at various times, the guidelines currently cover FBI investigations, undercover operations, the use of confidential informants, and consensual monitoring of verbal communications.

The guidelines defining the general rules for FBI investigations, for example, were first issued over 20 years ago. They derive from a period in which Soviet communism was the greatest threat to the United States, in which the Internet did not exist, and in which concerns over terrorist threats to the homeland related mainly to domestic hate groups.

Shortly after September 11, I took two steps to free FBI field agents to prevent additional terrorist attacks. First, I authorized the FBI to waive the guidelines, with headquarters approval, in extraordinary cases to prevent and investigate terrorism. That authority has been used, but I am disappointed that it was not used more widely. This experience over the past few months reinforces my belief that greater authority to investigate more vigorously needs to be given directly to FBI field agents.

Second, I directed a top-to-bottom review of the guidelines to ensure that they provide front-line field agents with the legal authority they need to protect the American people from future terrorist attacks. That comprehensive review showed that the guidelines mistakenly combined timeless objectives—the enforcement of the law and respect for civil rights and liberties—with outdated means.

Today, I am announcing comprehensive revisions to the Department's investigative guidelines. As revised, the guidelines reflect four overriding principles.

First, the war against terrorism is the central mission and highest priority of the FBI. This principle is stated explicitly in the revised guidelines, and it is facilitated and reinforced through many specific reforms. The guidelines emphasize that the FBI must not be deprived of using all lawful authorized methods in investigations, consistent with the Constitution and statutory authority, to pursue and prevent terrorist actions.

Second, terrorism prevention is the key objective under the revised guidelines. Our philosophy today is not to wait and sift through the rubble following a terrorist attack. Rather, the FBI must intervene early and investigate aggressively where information exists suggesting the possibility of terrorism, so as to prevent acts of terrorism. The new guidelines advance this strategy of prevention by strengthening investigative authority at the early stage of preliminary inquiries. Also, even absent specific investigative predicates, FBI agents under the new guidelines are empowered to scour public sources for information on future terrorist threats.

Third, unnecessary procedural red tape must not interfere with the effective detection, investigation, and prevention of terrorist activities. To this end, the revised guidelines allow Special Agents in Charge of FBI field offices to approve and renew terrorism enterprise investigations, rather than having to seek and wait for approval from headquarters. I believe this responds to a number of concerns we have heard from our field agents. The guidelines expand the scope of those investigations to the full range of terrorist activities under the USA Patriot Act. These major changes will free field agents to counter potential terrorist threats swiftly and vigorously without waiting for headquarters to act.

Fourth, the FBI must draw proactively on all lawful sources of information to identify terrorist threats and activities. It cannot meet its paramount responsibility to prevent acts of terrorism if FBI agents are required, as they were in the past, to blind themselves to information that everyone else is free to see. Under the revised guidelines, the FBI can identify and track foreign terrorists by combining its investigative results with information obtained from other lawful sources, such as foreign intelligence and commercial data services. To detect and prevent terrorist activities, the FBI under the revised guidelines will also be able to enter and observe public places and forums just as any member of the public might.

Let me pause here for a moment. What I am saying is this: FBI field agents have been inhibited from attending public events, open to any other citizen—not because they are barred by the U.S. Constitution, or barred by any federal law enacted by Congress, but because of the lack of clear authority under administrative guidelines issued decades ago. Today, I am clarifying that, for the specific purpose of detecting or preventing terrorist activities, FBI field agents may enter public places and attend events open to other citizens, unless they are barred from attending by the Constitution or federal law.

Our new guideline reads, "For the purpose of detecting or preventing terrorist activities, the FBI is authorized to visit any place and attend any event that is open to the public, on the same terms and conditions as members of the public generally."

I believe in the principle of community policing, in which an active, visible law enforcement presence is linked to communities and neighborhoods. Local police can enter public places and attend public events in their communities, and they detect and prevent crime by doing so. To protect our communities from terrorism, the FBI must be free to do the same.

The revised guidelines will take effect immediately and will be incorporated into the training of FBI agents. These guidelines will also be a resource to inform the American public and demonstrate that we seek to protect life and liberty from terrorism and other criminal violence with a scrupulous respect for civil rights and personal freedoms. The guidelines are available on the internet at http://www.usdoj.gov/olp/index.html#agguide.

The campaign against terrorism is a campaign to affirm the values of freedom and human dignity that transcend national boundaries, racial classifications, and religious differences. Called to the service of our nation, we are called to the defense of liberty for all men and women. On behalf of the Department of Justice and the people of this great nation, I thank Director Mueller and the FBI for their hard work to defend freedom. And I thank Deputy Attorney General Larry Thompson, and Assistant Attorneys General Michael Chertoff and Viet Dinh, for their efforts in revising the guidelines to honor these values.

WATCHDOG URGES CAUTION ON HOMELAND SECURITY PLAN
July 17, 2002

In December 1997 the General Accounting Office (GAO), the investigative arm of Congress, reported that although the United States was spending billions of dollars annually to fight terrorism, no one was in overall charge of the effort. More than forty federal departments, agencies, bureaus, and offices had terrorism programs of some sort, but there was little or no coordination. The result, according to the GAO, was that no one knew whether the money was being spent wisely or whether critical areas were being missed. Three years later, in December 2000 the creation of a single high-level agency to coordinate federal counterterrorism efforts was recommended by the Congressional Advisory Panel to Assess Domestic Response Capabilities for Terrorism Involving Weapons of Mass Destruction. (Better Coordination Urged for Federal Terrorism Spending, p. 248)*

The issue took on new urgency following the terrorist attacks on September 11, 2001. Although President George W. Bush initially rejected calls to create a federal Department of Homeland Security, he proposed just such a department on June 6, 2002. Under the president's plan, the cabinet-level department would be created by integrating twenty-two existing agencies and programs that employed 170,000 people. Supporters billed the effort as the biggest government reorganization in half a century. But at a congressional hearing on July 17, 2002, Comptroller General David Walker, the GAO's director, cautioned against rushing into anything too quickly. "It is clear that fixing the wrong problems, or even worse, fixing the right problems poorly, could cause more harm than good in our efforts to defend our country against terrorism," he told the House Select Committee on Homeland Security. Walker urged the committee members to carefully consider which agencies should be merged into the new department, keeping in mind that some agencies proposed for merger had significant duties unrelated to homeland security. He also cautioned that fully implementing the reorganization would take years, making it critical to carefully plan the transition so that domestic preparedness did not falter.

One of the biggest criticisms of Bush's plan was that it did not merge the Federal Bureau of Investigation and the Central Intelligence Agency, the two agencies most responsible for protecting the nation from terrorists, into the new Department of Homeland Security. Instead, it called for creating a division within the new department that would analyze reports from the two agencies. Congress was investigating both agencies to determine whether intelligence failures, including failures by the FBI and CIA to share information with each other, had allowed the September 11 attacks to occur. Meanwhile, a week before Bush unveiled his plan, Attorney General John Ashcroft announced that he was expanding the FBI's authority to conduct domestic surveillance. (FBI Gets Expanded Authority to Monitor Americans, p. 421)

> ***Following are excerpts from testimony by Comptroller General David Walker at a July 17, 2002, hearing of the House Select Committee on Homeland Security:***

. . . In my testimony today, I will focus on two major issues that we believe the Congress should consider in creating a new cabinet department principally dedicated to homeland security: (1) the national strategy and criteria needed to guide any reorganization of homeland security activities and to help evaluate which agencies and missions should be included in or left out of the new DHS [Department of Homeland Security]; and (2) key issues related to the successful implementation of, and transition to, a new department, including leadership, cost and phasing, and other management challenges. Our testimony is based largely on our previous and ongoing work on national preparedness issues, as well as a review of the proposed legislation.

In response to global challenges the government faces in the coming years, we have a unique opportunity to create an extremely effective and performance-based organization that can strengthen the nation's ability to protect its borders and citizens against terrorism. There is likely to be considerable benefit over time from restructuring some of the homeland security functions, including reducing risk and improving the economy, efficiency, and effectiveness of these consolidated agencies and programs. Sorting out those programs and agencies that would most benefit from consolidation versus those in which dual missions must be balanced in order to achieve a more effective fit in DHS is a difficult but critical task. Moreover, the magnitude of the challenges that the new department faces will clearly require substantial time and effort, and will take institutional continuity and additional resources to make it fully effective. Numerous complicated issues will need to be resolved in the short term, including a harmonization of the communication systems, information technology systems, human capital systems, the physical location of people and other assets, and many other factors. Implementation of the new department will be an extremely complex task and will ultimately take years to achieve. Given the magnitude of the endeavor, not everything can be achieved at the same time and a deliberate phasing of some operations will be necessary. As a result, it will be important for the new department to focus on: articulating a clear overarching mission and core values; establishing a short list of initial critical priorities; assuring effective communication and information systems; and developing an overall implementation plan for the new national strategy and related reorganization. Further, effective performance and risk management systems must be established, and work must be completed on threat and vulnerability assessments. . . .

Need for Criteria and Reorganization

Often it has taken years for the consolidated functions in new departments to effectively build on their combined strengths, and it is not uncommon for these structures to remain as management challenges for decades. It is instructive to note that the 1947 legislation creating DoD [Department of Defense] was further changed by the Congress in 1949, 1953, 1958, and 1986 in order to improve the department's structural effectiveness. Despite these and other changes made by DoD, GAO has consistently reported over the years that the department—more than 50 years after the reorganization—continues to face a number of serious management challenges. In fact, DoD has 8 of 24 government-wide high-risk areas based on GAO's latest list, including the governmentwide high-risk areas of human capital and computer security. This note of caution is not intended to dissuade the Congress from seeking logical and important consolidations in government agencies and programs in order to improve homeland security missions. Rather, it is meant to suggest that reorganizations of government agencies frequently encounter start-up problems and unanticipated consequences that result from the consolidations, are unlikely to fully overcome obstacles and challenges, and may require additional modifications in the future to effectively achieve our collective goals for defending the country against terrorism.

The Congress faces a challenging and complex job in its consideration of DHS. On the one hand, there exists a certain urgency to move rapidly in order to remedy known problems relating to intelligence and information sharing and leveraging like activities that have in the past and even today prevent the United States from exercising as strong a homeland defense as emerging and potential threats warrant. Simultaneously, that same urgency of purpose would suggest that the Congress be extremely careful and deliberate in how it creates a new department for defending the country against terrorism. The urge to "do it quickly" must be balanced by an equal need to "do it right." This is necessary to ensure a consensus on identified problems and needs, and to be sure that the solutions our government legislates and implements can effectively remedy the problems we face in a timely manner. It is clear that fixing the wrong problems, or even worse, fixing the right problems poorly, could cause more harm than good in our efforts to defend our country against terrorism. . . .

Homeland Security Reorganization and Missions

The President's proposal for the new department indicates that DHS, in addition to its homeland security responsibilities, will also be responsible for carrying out all other functions of the agencies and programs that are transferred to it. In fact, quite a number of the agencies proposed to be transferred to DHS have multiple functions. Agencies or programs that balance multiple missions present the Congress with significant issues that must be evaluated in order to determine how best to achieve all of the goals and objectives for which the entity was created. While we have not found any missions that would appear to be in fundamental conflict with the department's primary mission of homeland security, as presented in the President's proposal, the Congress will need to consider whether many of the non-homeland security missions of those agencies transferred to DHS will receive adequate funding, attention, visibility, and support when subsumed into a department that will be under tremendous pressure to succeed in its primary mission. As important and vital as the homeland security mission is to our nation's future, the other non-homeland security missions transferred to DHS for the most part are not small or trivial responsibilities. Rather, they represent extremely important functions executed by the federal government that, absent sufficient attention, could have serious implications for their effective delivery and consequences for sectors of our economy, health and safety, research programs and other significant government functions. Some of these responsibilities include:

- maritime safety and drug interdiction by the Coast Guard,
- collection of commercial tariffs by the Customs Service,
- public health research by the Department of Health and Human Services,
- advanced energy and environmental research by the Lawrence Livermore and Environmental Measurements labs,
- responding to floods and other natural disasters by the Federal Emergency Management Agency (FEMA), and
- authority over processing visas by the State Department's consular officers.

These examples reveal that many non-homeland security missions could be integrated into a cabinet department overwhelmingly dedicated to protecting the nation from terrorism. Congress may wish to consider whether the new department, as proposed, will dedicate sufficient management capacity and accountability to ensure the execution of non-homeland security missions, as well as consider potential alternatives to the current framework for handling these important functions. . . .

As the proposal to create DHS demonstrates, the terrorist events of last fall have provided an impetus for the government to look at the larger picture of how it provides homeland security and how it can best accomplish associated missions. Yet, even for those agencies that are not being integrated into DHS, there remains a very real need and possibly a unique opportunity to rethink approaches and priorities to enable them to better target their resources to address our most urgent needs. In some cases, the new emphasis on homeland security has prompted attention to longstanding problems that have suddenly become more pressing. For example, we've mentioned in previous testimony the overlapping and duplicative food safety programs in the federal government. While such overlap and duplication has been responsible for poor coordination and inefficient allocation of resources, these issues assume a new, and potentially more foreboding, meaning after September 11th given the threat from bio-terrorism. In another example, we have recommended combining the Department of Justice's Office of Domestic Preparedness with FEMA to improve coordination. A consolidated approach to many of these issues can facilitate a concerted and effective response to new threats and mission performance. . . .

DHS Transition Issues

The creation of the Department of Homeland Security will be one of the largest reorganizations ever undertaken and the difficulty of this task should not be underestimated. Under the President's proposal, 22 existing agencies and programs and 170,000 people would be integrated into the new department in order to strengthen the country's defense against terrorism. With an estimated budget authority of the component parts of the new department of $37.45 billion, successfully transitioning the government in an endeavor of this scale will take considerable time and money. Careful and thorough planning will be critical to the successful creation of the new department. While national needs suggest a rapid reorganization of homeland security functions, the transition of agencies and programs into the new department is likely to take time to achieve. At the same time, the need for speed to get the new department up and running must be balanced with the need to maintain readiness for new and existing threats during the transition period. Moreover, the organizational transition of the various components will simply be the starting point—as implementation challenges beyond the first year should be expected in building a fully integrated department. As I stated earlier, it could take 5 to 10 years to fully implement this reorganization in an effective and sustainable manner. . . .

As of July 23, 2002, the full text of the testimony was available at http://www.gao.gov/new.items/d02957t.pdf

REPORT CITES TERROR FAILURES BY U.S. INTELLIGENCE AGENCIES
July 17, 2002

Almost as soon as the first plane hit the World Trade Center on September 11, 2001, questions arose about whether failures by U.S. intelligence agencies contributed to the terrorist attacks. Leaders of the various agencies initially said their agents had no evidence that would have pointed them toward the September 11 plot, but they had to backpedal in the face of new revelations. In early May 2002 it was revealed that on July 10, 2001, an FBI counterterrorism agent in Arizona reported to Washington headquarters that several Middle Eastern men affiliated with Muslim extremist groups were training at a flight school in Arizona. He urged that the FBI instruct agents nationwide to contact local flight schools regarding any Arab students, but the checks ended up being conducted after the September 11 attacks. Only weeks after the first revelation, it was disclosed that in August 2001 Minneapolis FBI agents had arrested Zacarias Moussaoui, the alleged "twentieth hijacker," on immigration violations after the agency was contacted by the flight school where he was training. The agents believed Moussaoui had terrorism ties and requested permission from headquarters to search his computer and other possessions, but their efforts were blocked. The Minneapolis agents were so frustrated that they went outside channels and sent their concerns to the CIA.

Congress launched three separate investigations of the September 11 attacks, and the first results were released July 17, 2002, in a report by the House Subcommittee on Terrorism and Homeland Security. The panel's full report of more than one hundred pages was classified, but a ten-page executive summary released to the public sharply criticized three of the nation's leading intelligence agencies: the CIA, the FBI, and the National Security Agency. "The failure of the Intelligence Community (IC) to provide adequate forewarning was affected by resource constraints and a series of questionable management decisions related to funding priorities," the subcommittee said in the executive summary. The panel criticized the agencies for responding to events instead of anticipating them, devoting insufficient attention to terrorism, failing to share information, and lacking sufficient employees with the needed foreign language skills, among other problems.

In late August the New York Times *reported that in September the Senate Judiciary Committee would issue a report attacking FBI officials in Washington for bungling the Moussaoui case. By the beginning of September it was unclear when results from the biggest congressional investigation of them all, an unusual joint probe by the House and Senate intelligence committees, would be released.*

Following are excerpts from the executive summary of "Counterterrorism Intelligence Capabilities and Performance Prior to 9-11," a report released July 17, 2002, by the Subcommittee on Terrorism and Homeland Security of the House Permanent Select Committee on Intelligence:

The principal objective of this report and the work of the Subcommittee has been to review the counterterrorism [CT] capabilities and performance of the Intelligence Community before 9-11 in order to assess intelligence deficiencies and reduce the risks from acts of terrorism in the future.

The terrorist attacks perpetrated on September 11, 2001 constituted a significant strategic surprise for the United States. The failure of the Intelligence Community (IC) to provide adequate forewarning was affected by resource constraints and a series of questionable management decisions related to funding priorities. Prophetically, IC leadership concluded at a high-level offsite on September 11, 1998 that "failure to improve operations management, resource allocation, and other key issues within the [IC], including making substantial and sweeping changes in the way the nation collects, analyzes, and produces intelligence, will likely result in a catastrophic systemic intelligence failure."

The Subcommittee has found that practically every agency of the United States Government (USG) with a counterterrorism mission uses a different definition of terrorism. All USG agencies charged with the counterterrorism mission should agree on a single definition, so that it would be clear what activity constitutes a terrorist act and who should be designated a terrorist. Without a standard definition, terrorism might be treated no differently than other crimes. The Subcommittee supports a standard definition as follows: *"Terrorism is the illegitimate, premeditated use of politically motivated violence or the threat of violence by a sub-national group against persons or property with the intent to coerce a government by instilling fear amongst the populace. . . ."*

CIA

The summary finding regarding CIA is that CIA needs to institutionalize its sharp reorientation toward going on the offensive against terrorism. This report also arrived at the findings and recommendations that follow.

- **Keep HUMINT Mission Central.** CIA is the government's national HUMINT [human intelligence] organization—it has to keep this mission at its center. CIA did not sufficiently penetrate the al-Qa'ida organization before September 11th. Because of the perceived reduction in the threat environment in the early to mid 1990s, and the concomitant reduction in resources for basic human intelligence collection, there were fewer operations officers, fewer stations, fewer agents, and fewer intelligence reports produced. This likely gave CIA fewer opportunities for accessing agents useful in the counterterrorism campaign and eroded overall capabilities. Several management decisions also likely degraded CIA's CT capabilities by, for example, redirecting funds earmarked for core field collection and analysis to headquarters; paying insufficient attention to CIA's unilateral CT capability; relying too much on liaison for CT; and neglecting sufficient investment of foreign language training and exploitation. The dramatic increase in resources for intelligence since 9-11 improves the outlook for CIA's CT capabilities, but only if CIA management acknowledges and deals with the systemic problems outlined in this report. . . .
- **Forewarning of Terrorist Intentions.** There were a number of pre-9-11 successes, including a number of takedowns during the Millennium. There was also, however, intelligence acquired prior to 9-11 that, in retrospect, proved to be directly relevant to 9-11. The ability to watchlist terrorist suspects by CIA and in other agencies proved inadequate. Fixing some of the structural issues identified in this report might have put CIA in a better position to make use of such warning information. . . .
- **Additional Attention to Foreign Language Training and Document Exploitation.** CIA has paid insufficient attention to foreign language training and document exploitation efforts requiring linguists. In the most recent class of new case officers in training, less than one-third had any language expertise. . . .
- **Balance CIA's No Threshold Terrorist Threat Reporting Policy.** It has been increasingly difficult for consumers to determine the reliability of source reporting amidst the large volumes of reporting provided. One example of a CTC summer 2001 threat report, entitled "Threat of Impending al-Qa'ida Attack to Continue Indefinitely" illustrates the point. . . .
- **Recruiting Assets.** The availability and allocation of resources, including the redirection by CIA managers of funds earmarked for core field collection and analysis to headquarters, likely negatively impacted CIA's CT capabilities. The excessive caution and burdensome vetting process resulting from the guidelines on the recruitment of foreign assets and sources issued in 1995 undermined the CIA's ability and willingness to recruit assets, especially those who would provide insights into terrorist organizations and other hard targets. Despite a statutory requirement in December 2001 to rescind the 1995 guidelines the DCI still had not done so at the time this report was completed. . . .

433

- CIA's problems require more than just expressed commitment from senior CIA managers. . . .
- CIA may not be capable of providing information useful in preventing every 9-11 type incident, but it can certainly manage its resources more efficiently and effectively to enhance its CT capabilities and thereby reduce the likelihood that future 9-11s will occur. HUMINT is one of our best hopes. We must not squander this historic opportunity to effect lasting positive change.

FBI

The summary finding regarding FBI is that FBI's main problem going forward is to overcome its information sharing failures. This report also arrived at the findings and recommendations that follow.

- **Enhance FBI's Prevention Mission.** The Subcommittee has found that FBI focus has been investigating terrorist acts, but it has placed less emphasis on preventing such acts. FBI identified many of its CT program shortcomings prior to 9-11, but was slow to implement necessary changes. FBI's policy to decentralize investigations was inefficient for CT operations, especially against the international terrorist target. FBI's CT Program was most negatively impacted by the reticence of senior FBI managers to institute broader information-sharing initiatives; a failure to leverage FBI's ability to perform joint financial operations with other U.S. government agencies against terrorists until after 9-11; an ineffective FBI headquarters-based CT analytical capability prior to 9-11; the failure to share field office CT expertise with the FBI community-at-large; and critical staffing shortages of translators, interpreters, and Special Agents with proficiency in languages native to most terrorists. Since accepting the position as FBI Director just a few days prior to the 9-11 attacks, Robert Mueller has mandated positive, substantive changes in the modus operandi of the FBI's CT Program. . . .
- **Improve Intelligence Gathering and Analytical Capabilities.** Significant changes in law were made in the October 2001 USA Patriot Act and the May 2001 changes to the Attorney General's guidelines. While these may improve intelligence gathering, FBI's analytical capabilities remain insufficient, pending the establishment of the new Office of Intelligence.
- **Address Foreign Language Shortfalls.** A January 2002 report noted that FBI projected shortages of permanent translators and interpreters in FY 2002 and 2003, and reported backlogs of thousands of unreviewed and untranslated materials. In key counterterrorism languages, FBI reported having in June 2001 a critical shortage of special agents with some proficiency, and FBI had very few translators and interpreters with native language skills in those languages.
- **Fixing Information Technology Challenges.** The Webster Commission in March 2002 noted in detail many of the information technology

challenges of the FBI. FBI has made concerted efforts to implement change to improve technology. . . .

NSA

The summary finding regarding NSA is that NSA needs to change from a passive gatherer to a proactive hunter—a revolution in how it conducts its work. This report also arrived at the findings and recommendations that follow.

- **Ensure Appropriate Intelligence Collection Priorities.** The Subcommittee found it troubling that more SIGINT [signals intelligence] resources were not devoted by NSA to CT prior to 9-11, given the prior terrorist attacks against U.S. interests starting in 1983. Also of concern is the fact that NSA hired virtually no new employees for an extended period of time prior to 9-11, resulting in a negative impact in overall capabilities, including CT. . . .
- **Address Analyst and Linguist Shortfalls.** In April 2000, the GAO [General Accounting Office] reported a significant shortfall in linguists at NSA. After the 9-11 attacks, this shortfall actually increased slightly and was well below additional requirements identified since 9-11. . . .
- **Support Signals Research and Target Development.** In the art of finding new targets, before 9-11 NSA did not have a comprehensive, focused, counter-terrorism target development effort. Although there were numerous analysts conducting the mission across NSA and its collection sites, NSA claims there were insufficient resources to conduct a focused CT-specific target development effort. . . .
- **Need for Worldwide Collection Across the Global Communications Network.** The global communications network is increasingly digital, high-volume fiber optic cable rather than radio frequency, internal rather than telephone, and packet-switched rather than circuit-switched, with customer instruments moving from fixed to mobile. NSA has been unable to organize itself to define and implement an integrated system that can follow the target across the global intelligent network, beyond high-level goals and plans. NSA also needs to develop methodologies to find nongovernmental radical extremists who are associated with international terrorist organizations but might not be in direct contact with them. . . .

As of August 29, 2002, the full text of the report's executive summary was available at http://intelligence.house.gov/Word/ THSReport071702.doc

COURT OVERTURNS ORDER
REQUIRING SECRET HEARINGS
August 26, 2002

In the weeks and months following the terrorist attacks on September 11, 2001, law enforcement officials around the country rounded up more than 1,200 people—almost all of Middle Eastern or South Asian descent—on suspicions they were terrorists or were witnesses to terrorist activities. The Bush administration refused to say how many people had been detained, to release their names, or to make any information about their cases public. Administration officials said the secrecy was necessary to keep terrorists from gaining valuable information. Some detainees were held for months before being cleared of any connection with terrorism. Once cleared, most of the detainees were deported for immigration violations. In August 2002 two different federal courts blasted the administration's secrecy policy, saying it violated the U.S. Constitution. On August 2 U.S. District Judge Gladys Kessler ruled in Washington, D.C., that the Justice Department had to release the names of all the people detained. Kessler wrote that the names had to be released "to ensure that our government always operates within the statutory and constitutional constraints which distinguish a democracy from a dictatorship."

On August 26 a three-judge panel of the U.S. Court of Appeals for the Sixth Circuit used equally strong language in a related case. It involved a Lebanese native living in Michigan who was arrested in December on a visa violation. His deportation hearings, like those of all the others rounded up in the post-September 11 sweep, were held in secret under a blanket order issued by the nation's chief immigration judge, Michael J. Creppy. Four newspapers and Rep. John Conyers Jr., a Democrat from Michigan, sued to open the man's hearings. In April a federal district judge in Detroit ruled that the blanket closure of all hearings was unconstitutional, and in August the Sixth Circuit panel agreed. "Democracies die behind closed doors," Judge Damon J. Keith wrote for the panel. The judges said that the government could still ask immigration judges to close particular cases because of specific security concerns—it just could not close all of them with a blanket order shutting out the public and the press. "A government operating in the shadow of secrecy stands in complete opposition to the society envisioned by the Framers of our Constitution," the judges said.

By the beginning of September the Justice Department had not decided whether to appeal the Sixth Circuit ruling. However, the government did appeal the earlier ruling requiring it to release the names of all the people who had been detained. The judge in that case stayed her order that the names be released until the appeal could be decided, a process that was expected to take months.

Following are excerpts from the August 26, 2002, decision of the U.S. Court of Appeals for the Sixth Circuit in the case of Detroit Free Press vs. John Ashcroft:

The primary issue on appeal in this case, is whether the First Amendment to the United States Constitution confers a public right of access to deportation hearings. If it does, then the Government must make a showing to overcome that right.

No one will ever forget the egregious, deplorable, and despicable terrorist attacks of September 11, 2001. These were cowardly acts. In response, our government launched an extensive investigation into the attacks, future threats, conspiracies, and attempts to come. As part of this effort, immigration laws are prosecuted with increased vigor. The issue before us today involves these efforts.

. . . Since the end of the 19th Century, our government has enacted immigration laws banishing, or deporting, non-citizens because of their race and their beliefs. . . . While the Bill of Rights jealously protects citizens from such laws, it has never protected non-citizens facing deportation in the same way. In our democracy, based on checks and balances, neither the Bill of Rights nor the judiciary can second-guess government's choices. The only safeguard on this extraordinary governmental power is the public, deputizing the press as the guardians of their liberty. . . .

Today, the Executive Branch seeks to take this safeguard away from the public by placing its actions beyond public scrutiny. Against non-citizens, it seeks the power to secretly deport a class if it unilaterally calls them "special interest" cases. The Executive Branch seeks to uproot people's lives, outside the public eye, and behind a closed door. Democracies die behind closed doors. The First Amendment, through a free press, protects the people's right to know that their government acts fairly, lawfully, and accurately in deportation proceedings. When government begins closing doors, it selectively controls information rightfully belonging to the people. Selective information is misinformation. . . .

On September 21, 2001, Chief Immigration Judge Michael Creppy issued a directive (the "Creppy directive") to all United States Immigration Judges requiring closure of special interest cases. The Creppy directive requires that all proceedings in such cases be closed to the press and public, including family members and friends. The Record of the Proceeding is not to be disclosed to anyone except a deportee's attorney or representative, "assuming the file does not contain classified information." "This restriction on information includes confirming or denying whether such a case is on the docket or scheduled for a hearing."

On December 19, 2001, Immigration Judge Elizabeth Hacker conducted a bond hearing for Rabih Haddad ("Haddad"), one such special interest case. Haddad was subject to deportation, having overstayed his tourist visa. The Government further suspects that the Islamic charity Haddad operates supplies funds to terrorist organizations. Haddad's family, members of the public, including Congressman John Conyers, and several newspapers sought to attend his deportation hearing. Without prior notice to the public, Haddad, or his attorney, courtroom security officers announced that the hearing was closed to the public and the press. Haddad was denied bail, detained, and has since been in the government's custody. Subsequent hearings, conducted on January 2 and 10, 2002, were also closed to the public and the press. Haddad has been transferred to Chicago for additional proceedings. . . .

While we sympathize and share the Government's fear that dangerous information might be disclosed in some of these hearings, we feel that the ordinary process of determining whether closure is warranted on a case-by-case basis sufficiently addresses their concerns. Using this stricter standard does not mean that information helpful to terrorists will be disclosed, only that the Government must be more targeted and precise in its approach. Given the importance of the constitutional rights involved, such safeguards must be vigorously guarded lest the First Amendment turn into another balancing test. In the words of Justice Black:

> The word "security" is a broad, vague generality whose contours should not be invoked to abrogate the fundamental law embodied in the First Amendment. The guarding of military and diplomatic secrets at the expense of informed representative government provides no real security for our Republic. . . .

Next, we turn to the "logic" prong, which asks "whether public access plays a significant positive role in the functioning of the particular process in question." Public access undoubtedly enhances the quality of deportation proceedings. . . .

First, public access acts as a check on the actions of the Executive by assuring us that proceedings are conducted fairly and properly. . . . In an area such as immigration, where the government has nearly unlimited authority, the press and the public serve as perhaps the only check on abusive government practices.

Second, openness ensures that government does its job properly; that it does not make mistakes. . . . Moreover, "[t]he natural tendency of government officials is to hold their meetings in secret. They can thereby avoid criticism and proceed informally and less carefully. They do not have to worry before they proceed with the task that a careless remark may be splashed across the next day's headlines."

These first two concerns are magnified by the fact that deportees have no right to an attorney at the government's expense. Effectively, the press and the public may be their only guardian.

Third, after the devastation of September 11 and the massive investigation that followed, the cathartic effect of open deportations cannot be overstated. They serve a "therapeutic" purpose as outlets for "community concern, hostility, and emotions." As the district court stated:

> It is important for the public, particularly individuals who feel that they are being targeted by the Government as a result of the terrorist attacks of September 11, to know that even during these sensitive times the Government is adhering to immigration procedures and respecting individuals' rights.... And if in fact the Government determines that Haddad is connected to terrorist activity or organizations, a decision made openly concerning his deportation may assure the public that justice has been done....

... the blanket closure rule mandated by the Creppy directive is not narrowly tailored. The Government offers no persuasive argument as to why the Government's concerns cannot be addressed on a case-by-case basis....

Finally, the Government seeks to protect from disclosure the bits and pieces of information that seem innocuous in isolation, but when pieced together with other bits and pieces aid in creating a bigger picture of the Government's anti-terrorism investigation, i.e., the "mosaic intelligence." Mindful of the Government's concerns, we must nevertheless conclude that the Creppy directive is over-inclusive. While the risk of "mosaic intelligence" may exist, we do not believe speculation should form the basis for such a drastic restriction of the public's First Amendment rights....

Furthermore, there seems to be no limit to the Government's argument. The Government could use its "mosaic intelligence" argument as a justification to close any public hearing completely and categorically, including criminal proceedings. The Government could operate in virtual secrecy in all matters dealing, even remotely, with "national security," resulting in a wholesale suspension of First Amendment rights. By the simple assertion of "national security," the Government seeks a process where it may, without review, designate certain classes of cases as "special interest cases" and, behind closed doors, adjudicate the merits of these cases to deprive non-citizens of their fundamental liberty interests.

This, we simply may not countenance. A government operating in the shadow of secrecy stands in complete opposition to the society envisioned by the Framers of our Constitution....

Lastly, the public's interests are best served by open proceedings. A true democracy is one that operates on faith—faith that government officials are forthcoming and honest, and faith that informed citizens will arrive at logical conclusions. This is a vital reciprocity that America should not discard in these troubling times. Without question, the events of September 11, 2001, left an indelible mark on our nation, but we as a people are united in the wake of the destruction to demonstrate to the world that we are a country deeply committed to preserving the rights and freedoms guaranteed by our democracy.

Today, we reflect our commitment to those democratic values by ensuring that our government is held accountable to the people and that First Amendment rights are not impermissibly compromised. Open proceedings, with a vigorous and scrutinizing press, serve to ensure the durability of our democracy. . . .

As of August 29, 2002, the full text of the court's opinion was available at http://pacer.ca6.uscourts.gov/cgi-bin/getopn.pl?OPINION= 02a0291p.06

CHRONOLOGY

1972

January 30: In an incident dubbed "Bloody Sunday," British troops shoot and kill 14 civilians during a protest march by 10,000 people in Londonderry, Northern Ireland.

February 22: A bomb planted by the Irish Republican Army (IRA) explodes in the British Parachute Regiment Officers club in Aldershot, England, killing seven people.

March 4: Protestant terrorists bomb a restaurant in Belfast, Northern Ireland, killing two people and injuring 130.

May 8: At Ben Gurion Airport in Israel, commandos storm a Belgian Sabena airliner that has been hijacked by four terrorists from the Palestinian group Black September. They free the hostages, but five Israeli soldiers, one passenger, and all four terrorists die in the assault.

May 30: At Lod Airport in Israel, Japanese terrorists acting for the Popular Front for the Liberation of Palestine attack the passenger terminal with automatic weapons and hand grenades, killing 26 people and wounding nearly 80.

June 19: In a case involving the 1968 bombing of the Central Intelligence Agency's recruiting office in Ann Arbor, Michigan, the U.S. Supreme Court rules unanimously that law enforcement officials cannot conduct electronic surveillance without a court order. *(Electronic Surveillance in Domestic Security Cases, p. 1)*

July 21: In response to the January 1972 "Bloody Sunday" shootings of civilians by British soldiers, the Irish Republican Army detonates nearly two dozen bombs around Belfast in just over one hour, killing nine people and wounding 130. *(The "Bloody Friday" Attacks in Northern Ireland, p. 5)*

September 5: Just before dawn, eight members of the Palestinian group Black September invade the quarters of Israeli athletes at the 1972 Olympic Games in Munich, West Germany, killing two and taking nine others hostage. A botched rescue attempt by German authorities results in the deaths of all the Israeli athletes, five terrorists, and a policeman. The incident becomes known as the Munich Massacre.

September 8: In retaliation for the Munich Massacre three days earlier, dozens of Israeli warplanes attack suspected Arab guerrilla bases and naval installations in Syria and Lebanon.

September 10: U.S. ambassador George H. Bush vetoes a resolution by the United Nations Security Council condemning Israeli's attacks two days earlier in Syria and Lebanon. *(Murder of Israeli Athletes at the Munich Olympic Games, p. 7)*

October: In Rome, Israeli agents assassinate Wael Zuwaiter, a Palestinian writer who Israeli officials believe is a Black September commander.

October 29: Two members of Black September hijack a West German airliner over Turkey. The hijackers demand that West Germany free the three Black September terrorists who were captured the previous month during the Munich Massacre. West Germany complies, and the three are flown to Tripoli, Libya. In subsequent years, Israeli agents track down and assassinate two of the three.

December 8: Mahmoud Hamshari, the Paris representative of the Palestine Liberation Organization (PLO), dies in an explosion at his apartment. Agents of the Mossad, the Israeli secret service, planted the bomb because of Hamshari's alleged involvement in planning and organizing the Munich Massacre earlier in the year.

1973

March 1: Black September terrorists storm a diplomatic reception at the Saudi Arabian embassy in Khartoum, Sudan. When their demands to various countries are not met, they kill U.S. ambassador Cleo A. Noel, U.S. charge d'affaires Curtis Moore, and a Belgian diplomat. The terrorists are eventually released to the custody of the Palestine Liberation Organization.

April 10: Israeli commandos assassinate three top leaders of the Palestine Liberation Organization in their Beirut apartments. Israeli officials believe the three were involved in the Munich Massacre the previous September.

July: In Norway, Israeli agents murder a Moroccan waiter in the mistaken belief he is Ali Hassan Salameh, a Black September leader who masterminded the attack on Israeli athletes at the Munich Olympics in 1972. In January 1979 Israeli agents kill Salameh in Beirut, Lebanon, and in January 1996 the Israeli government agrees to compensate the family of the waiter who was mistakenly killed in 1973.

August 5: Black September terrorists attack the passenger terminal at the airport in Athens, Greece, killing three people and wounding more than 50.

November 6: Members of the Symbionese Liberation Army, a small group of black convicts and white radicals, assassinate Marcus Foster, the superintendent of schools in Oakland, California.

December 17: Firing guns and tossing hand grenades, five Palestinian terrorists kill 32 people and injure 50 at Rome's airport. They take hostages and hijack a plane, which eventually flies to Kuwait. The hijackers surrender to Kuwaiti authorities and release their hostages in exchange for a promise of safe conduct.

December 20: A bomb attack in Madrid kills Admiral Luis Carrero Blanco, prime minister of Spain. The attack is carried out by members of Basque Fatherland and Liberty, a Basque nationalist group.

1974

February 4: The Irish Republican Army bombs a British Army bus as it travels down a highway in Yorkshire, England, killing nine soldiers and three civilians.

February 5: In California the Symbionese Liberation Army kidnaps 19-year-old newspaper heiress Patty Hearst, granddaughter of the late newspaper magnate William Randolph Hearst.

April 3: In a tape recording Patty Hearst says she has chosen to join the Symbionese Liberation Army, which kidnapped her in February. (*Messages by Patty Hearst Following Her Kidnapping, p. 9*)

May: Six core members of the Symbionese Liberation Army die in a confrontation with police, but there is no sign of kidnapped newspaper heiress Patty Hearst.

May 15: Palestinian terrorists take 90 children hostage at a school in Maalot, Israel, and demand that the government release Palestinians held in Israeli jails. Israeli troops storm the school and 21 children are killed and 70 wounded.

May 17: A pair of car bomb attacks in Dublin and Monaghan, Ireland, kill 33 people. Protestant paramilitary groups are blamed for the attacks.

August 14: The U.S. ambassador to Cyprus and an American embassy secretary are shot and killed.

September 8: A Trans World Airlines flight from Tel Aviv to New York crashes into the Ionian Sea after a bomb goes off in the plane's rear cargo compartment, killing all 88 people aboard.

November 13: In a speech before the United Nations General Assembly, Yasir Arafat, leader of the Palestine Liberation Organization, calls for eliminating Israel and replacing it with a Palestinian state comprised of Muslims, Christians, and Jews. *(Arafat's Speech Before the UN General Assembly, p. 13)*

November 22: The United Nations General Assembly passes Resolution 3237, which grants the Palestine Liberation Organization permanent status to observe its meetings.

1975

January 24: A bomb explodes in a New York City bar, killing four people and injuring more than 50 others. The Armed Forces for National Liberation, a Puerto Rican nationalist group commonly known by its Spanish initials FALN, claims responsibility.

June 10: A presidential panel, the Commission on CIA Activities Within the United States, issues a study largely confirming newspaper reports that the CIA had engaged in a wide range of illegal acts while investigating Vietnam War protesters and others who it believed threatened domestic security. *(Rockefeller Report on the CIA's Domestic Activities, p. 17)*

September 18: The FBI captures Patty Hearst and three other Symbionese Liberation Army members in San Francisco, ending the group's activities.

December 21: The notorious terrorist Carlos the Jackal and five other members of the Popular Front for the Liberation of Palestine storm a meeting of the Organization of Petroleum Exporting Countries (OPEC) in Vienna, Austria. They kill three people and take 70 others hostage, including the oil ministers from several Middle Eastern countries, but eventually release them after receiving a ransom variously described as being in the tens or hundreds of millions of dollars.

December 23: The left-wing Greek terrorist group 17 November shoots to death CIA station chief Richard Welch outside his home in Athens.

December 29: A bomb explodes in the TWA terminal at LaGuardia Airport in New York, killing 11 people and wounding 80. Investigators suspect that members of a Croatian nationalist group are responsible, but no one is ever charged with the crime.

1976

March 21: Newspaper heiress Patty Hearst, who was kidnapped by the Symbionese Liberation Army in 1974 but later claimed to have joined the group, is convicted of bank robbery and sentenced to seven years in prison.

April 26: A Senate committee issues a report documenting widespread abuses of the rights of Americans by the FBI, the CIA, and other agencies during domestic intelligence investigations conducted in the name of protecting national security. *(Intelligence Activities and the Rights of Americans, p. 22)*

June 16: In Beirut, Lebanon, terrorists kidnap and murder U.S. ambassador Francis E. Meloy, economic counselor Robert O. Waring, and their Lebanese driver.

July 3: Israeli commandos swoop down on the Entebbe Airport in Uganda to rescue about 100 hostages being held by hijackers from the Popular Front for the Liberation of Palestine and Germany's Baader-Meinhof terrorist group. Three hostages, one commando leader, and all the terrorists die in the raid. *(Israeli Prime Minister Rabin on the Entebbe Airport Raid, p. 27)*

September 21: A car bomb planted by agents of the Chilean government kills exiled Chilean foreign minister Orlando Letelier and an American associate in Washington, D.C.

October 6: A bomb explodes aboard a Cubana Airlines DC8 as it flies from Barbados to Havana, killing all 73 people aboard.

1977

March 15: In a directive aimed at normalizing relations with Cuba, President Jimmy Carter implicitly acknowledges that terrorists based in the United States had attacked Cuba. *(Presidential Directive/NSC-6 on Relations with Cuba, p. 30)*

October 13: Four Palestinian terrorists hijack a Lufthansa airliner as it flies from the Spanish island of Majorca to Frankfurt, West Germany. They order the pilot to fly to various Middle East destinations over the next four days. After the plane lands in Mogadishu, Somalia, the hijackers kill the pilot. German counterterrorist troops then storm the aircraft, rescuing all 90 passengers and killing three of the hijackers.

December 4: A Malaysian airliner that is hijacked 10 minutes after taking off from Kuala Lampur crashes while approaching to land in Singapore, killing 93 people.

December 16: The United Nations General Assembly passes Resolution 32/147, in which it expresses "deep concern over increasing acts of international terrorism" but also reaffirms "the inalienable right to self-determination and independence of all peoples under colonial and racist regimes and other forms of alien domination, and upholds the legitimacy of their struggle, in particular the struggle of national liberation movements. . . ."

1978

February 17: Twelve people die and 23 are injured in a bomb attack by the Irish Republican Army at a restaurant near Belfast, Northern Ireland.

March 11: Arab guerrillas who infiltrate Israel from the sea attack a bus and other vehicles on a highway, killing 37 people and wounding more than 80.

March 16: In Italy, members of the left-wing Red Brigades kidnap Premier Aldo Moro and kill five security personnel accompanying him. They kill Moro after holding him for 55 days.

June 3: A bomb explosion aboard a bus in Jerusalem kills six people.

1979

January: Agents of Mossad, Israel's secret service, assassinate Ali Hassan Salameh with a remote-controlled car bomb in Beirut, Lebanon. Israeli officials believe that

Salameh, a Black September leader, masterminded the attack on Israeli athletes at the 1972 Munich Olympics.

January: President Jimmy Carter commutes the prison sentence of Patty Hearst, the kidnapped newspaper heiress who was convicted of helping the Symbionese Liberation Army rob a bank, after she serves 21 months of her seven-year sentence.

February 14: Armed terrorists kidnap the U.S. ambassador to Afghanistan in Kabul. They kill him when Afghan police storm the hotel room where he is being held.

August 27: In a pair of attacks, the Irish Republican Army kills Lord Earl Mountbatten on his boat and 18 British soldiers at Warrenpoint, Northern Ireland.

September 6: President Jimmy Carter commutes the sentences of four Puerto Rican terrorists who were convicted in the 1950s of shooting members of Congress and attempting to assassinate President Harry Truman. *(President Carter Commutes Sentences for 1950s Attacks, p. 32)*

October 22: The Carter administration allows Shah Mohammad Raza Pahlavi, the former ruler of Iran who fled his country in January, to enter the United States for medical treatment.

November 4: Angered by the Carter administration's decision to admit the Shah of Iran to the United States, Iranian militants seize the U.S. embassy in Tehran and take everyone inside hostage. After releasing several groups of hostages, the militants continue holding 52 Americans. *(The Beginning of the Iran Hostage Crisis, p. 34)*

November 12: In response to Iranian militants taking American diplomats hostage eight days earlier, President Jimmy Carter embargoes oil shipments from Iran to the United States.

November 20: Two hundred Islamic terrorists seize the Grand Mosque in Mecca, Saudi Arabia, the holiest site in the Islamic world, and take hundreds of people hostage. An attack by Saudi and French security forces succeeds in retaking the shrine, but 250 people are killed and 600 wounded.

December 17: The United Nations General Assembly adopts Resolution 34/146, which establishes the International Convention Against the Taking of Hostages. The convention takes effect June 3, 1983.

1980

February 27: Timing their attack to coincide with a diplomatic reception, members of the 19th of April Movement take over the Dominican Republic embassy in Bogota, Colombia, and seize 57 hostages, including ambassadors from 11 countries. The terrorists release the last hostages 61 days later, in exchange for a $2 million ransom and safe passage to Cuba.

April 24: Eight American soldiers are killed and five injured during a botched effort to rescue the American hostages being held in Iran. *(Rescue Attempt and Release of U.S. Hostages in Iran, p. 40)*

April 30: Five terrorists seize the Iranian embassy in London, capturing 26 hostages. They demand autonomy for an Arab province in Iran and the release of 91 prisoners. When their demands are not met they kill two hostages, precipitating an assault on the embassy by British Army antiterrorist commandos. The commandos rescue the remaining hostages, kill three terrorists, and capture two terrorists.

August 2: A massive bomb explodes at the railway station in Bologna, Italy, killing 85 people and injuring hundreds more. The right-wing Revolutionary Armed Nuclei group is blamed for the attack.

October 26: Neo-Nazi terrorists set off a bomb at a beer festival in Munich, West Germany, killing 12 people and wounding 200.

November: President Jimmy Carter loses the presidential election to Ronald Reagan. Many political analysts say a major factor in Carter's defeat is his failure to gain release of the hostages in Iran.

1981

January 20: In the final minutes of the Carter administration, a complex deal is reached for release of the 52 Americans who have been held hostage in Iran for 444 days. Minutes after the presidency passes from Carter to Ronald Reagan, planes carrying the hostages lift off from Tehran's airport.

May: Citing "Libyan provocations and misconduct, including support for international terrorism," the United States government orders Libya to close its embassy in Washington, D.C.

May 5: Bobby Sands, a member of the Irish Republican Army who is serving a 14-year sentence for a firearms offense in the Maze Prison near Belfast, Northern Ireland, dies after 66 days on a hunger strike. He started the strike in an effort to force the British government to treat him as a political prisoner. Nine other imprisoned IRA members die in hunger strikes before the action is called off October 3 after family members intervene.

May 13: In Saint Peter's Square in Vatican City, Turkish prison escapee Mehmet Ali Agca shoots Pope John Paul II. The pope is seriously wounded but recovers after two surgeries and a lengthy recuperation period. *(The Attempted Assassination of Pope John Paul II, p. 45)*

July 22: An Italian court convicts Turkish fugitive Mehmet Ali Agca of attempting to kill Pope John Paul II and two women who were wounded in the attack two months earlier and sentences him to life in prison.

October 2: Members of two left-wing terrorist groups, the Weather Underground and the Black Liberation Army, kill two police officers and a guard during a botched robbery of a Brink's armored truck in Nyack, New York.

October 6: Members of al-Jihad, also known as Egyptian Islamic Jihad, assassinate President Anwar al-Sadat of Egypt during a military parade. Many Arabs view Sadat as a traitor because he sought peace with Israel. *(The Assassination of Egyptian President Anwar al-Sadat, p. 47)*

December 4: President Ronald Reagan signs Executive Order 12333, which loosens restrictions on U.S. intelligence agencies that President Jimmy Carter had imposed. The order permits the CIA and other agencies besides the FBI to collect "significant foreign intelligence" within the United States, provided the effort is not aimed at monitoring domestic activities of American citizens and corporations.

1982

June 3: In London, terrorists from the Abu Nidal organization attempt to assassinate Israeli ambassador Shlomo Argov, who survives but is crippled for life. Three days later Israeli troops invade Lebanon to attack Palestinian guerrillas; Israeli officials cite the assassination attempt as a reason for the action.

July: David Dodge, president of the American University of Beirut, becomes the first American kidnapped by Islamic militants and held hostage in Lebanon.

July 20: Eleven British soldiers die in a pair of bomb attacks by the Irish Republican Army in London.

August 7: In Ankara, Turkey, two terrorists from the Armenian Secret Army for the

Liberation of Armenia attack the airport with bombs and machine guns, killing nine people.

September 14: A bomb kills President-elect Bashir Gemayel of Lebanon in Beirut. To avenge the crime, Christian militiamen slaughter hundreds of unarmed civilians in two Palestinian camps.

November 11: A suicide truck bombing of Israeli military headquarters in Tyre, Lebanon, kills 75 people, most of them Israeli soldiers. The Palestinian group Hizballah claims responsibility for the attack.

December 6: A bomb attack by the Irish National Liberation Army at a bar in Ballykelly, Northern Ireland, kills 11 British soldiers and six civilians.

1983

February 13: In Medina, North Dakota, federal marshals attempt to arrest Gordon Kahl, a farmer and member of the right-wing Posse Comitatus, for violating probation. Kahl and others with him open fire, killing two U.S. marshals and wounding three other law enforcement officers. Kahl escapes but dies less than four months later in a confrontation with officers in Arkansas.

February 24: In a stinging 467-page report, a panel created by Congress to examine the internment of Japanese-Americans for security reasons during World War II concludes that the internees suffered a "grave injustice." *(The World War II Internment of Japanese-Americans, p. 52)*

April 18: A truck bomb blows up the U.S. embassy in Beirut, Lebanon, killing 63 people, including 17 Americans. Islamic Jihad claims responsibility.

June 3: Gordon Kahl, a 63-year-old North Dakota farmer and member of the Posse Comitatus, dies in a shootout with law enforcement officers in Smithville, Arkansas. A local sheriff also dies in the gunfight. Less than four months earlier, Kahl had killed two federal marshals and wounded three other law enforcement officers when they tried to arrest him in Medina, North Dakota.

July 15: A bomb explodes at Orly Airport in Paris, killing six people. Armenian terrorists are suspected in the attack.

September 23: An airliner explodes near Abu Dhabi, United Arab Emirates, killing all 111 people aboard. The Abu Nidal organization claims responsibility.

October 9: A bombing in Rangoon, Burma, kills five South Korean cabinet ministers and 16 other people. North Korean intelligence agents are blamed for the attack.

October 23: A suicide truck-bomb attack on the U.S. Marine Corps headquarters in Beirut, Lebanon, kills 241 soldiers. A nearly simultaneous suicide attack at a French military barracks only two miles away kills 58 soldiers. Islamic Jihad claims responsibility. *(Bombing of the U.S. Marine Headquarters in Lebanon, p. 57)*

October 24: President Ronald Reagan announces that, despite the terrorist attack the day before in Beirut, U.S. troops will remain in Lebanon until their mission is complete.

November 7: A bomb planted by left-wing terrorists explodes just outside the Senate chamber at the U.S. Capitol in Washington, D.C. The blast damages a wall, but no one is hurt.

November 15: The chief of the U.S. Naval Mission in Greece and his Greek driver are shot to death in Athens. The left-wing terrorist group 17 November claims responsibility.

December 17: A car bombing at Harrods department store in London, England, kills five people and injures more than 90 others. The Irish Republican Army claims responsibility.

December 19: A report issued by the Investigations Subcommittee of the House Armed Services Committee concludes that critical failures by Marine commanders led to the October 23, 1983, suicide attack in Beirut that killed 241 American soldiers.

1984

January 18: The president of the American University of Beirut is shot and killed in the school's administration building. Islamic Jihad claims responsibility.

February 7: With Lebanon's political situation sharply deteriorating, President Ronald Reagan orders all U.S. troops in Beirut to return to their ships offshore. This is widely viewed as an abrupt shift from Reagan's announcement October 24, 1983, that U.S. troops would remain in Lebanon despite a suicide bombing the day before.

March 16: Members of Islamic Jihad kidnap William Buckley, the CIA station chief in Beirut, Lebanon. Buckley is tortured and eventually executed.

March 16: Members of the neo-Nazi group The Order rob an armored car in Seattle, Washington. They escape with $40,000.

June: Members of the neo-Nazi group The Order rob an armored car in Ukiah, California, escaping with an estimated $3 million.

June: During a traffic stop Richard Wayne Snell, a member of the right-wing Covenant, Sword, & Arm of the Lord, shoots to death a black Arkansas state trooper. Snell is executed in April 1995.

June 5: Sikh terrorists seize the Golden Temple in Amritsar, India. At least 100 people die when Indian security forces retake the Sikh holy shrine.

June 18: Alan Berg, a Jewish radio talk-show host in Denver who frequently denounces right-wing groups on his program, is shot to death by members of The Order, a neo-Nazi group.

September 20: A car bomb explodes at a U.S. embassy annex in Beirut, Lebanon, killing 23 people and wounding dozens more. Islamic Jihad claims responsibility.

October 12: British prime minister Margaret Thatcher narrowly escapes death in an Irish Republican Army bombing of the Grand Hotel in Brighton, England, during the Conservative Party's annual conference. Five people are killed and more than 20 wounded in the attack.

October 25: In a speech to the Jewish Community Relations Council in Manhattan, Secretary of State George P. Shultz says the United States should make preemptive strikes against terrorists and retaliate for any attacks—even if the actions kill innocent people. *(Speech on Terrorism by Secretary of State Shultz, p. 61)*

October 31: Two trusted Sikh bodyguards assassinate Prime Minister Indira Gandhi of India. *(The Assassination of Indian Prime Minister Indira Gandhi, p. 65)*

December 7: Robert Mathews, founder of the neo-Nazi group The Order, dies during a siege by law enforcement authorities of his home on Whidbey Island, off the coast of Washington state.

December 18: The United Nations General Assembly passes Resolution A/RES/39/159, which expresses its "profound concern that State terrorism has lately been practiced ever more frequently" and calling on all nations to halt the practice.

1985

February 17: The Greek terrorist group 17 November shoots to death newspaper publisher Nikos Momferratos.

February 28: Nine members of the Royal Ulster Constabulary are killed in an Irish Republican Army attack on a police station in Newry, Northern Ireland.

March 8: In an effort to kill Sheik Mohammed Hussein Fadlallah, leader of the Hizballah terrorist group, Lebanese intelligence agents trained by the CIA detonate a car bomb near his home in Beirut, Lebanon. Fadlallah is not injured, but the blast kills 80 people and wounds 250. *Washington Post* reporter Bob Woodward later writes that the Saudi Arabian intelligence service organized the attack at the request of CIA director William Casey.

March 16: Terry Anderson, chief Middle East correspondent for the Associated Press, is kidnapped by Islamic radicals in Beirut, Lebanon. He is released in December 1991.

April 15: During a traffic stop, David Tate, a member of the neo-Nazi group The Order, shoots to death one Missouri highway patrolman and severely wounds another.

May 20: A bombing in Pretoria, South Africa, that authorities blame on the African National Congress kills 19 people and injures more than 200.

June 14: Two Lebanese Hizballah terrorists hijack Trans World Airlines Flight 847 as it flies from Cairo to Rome. They murder passenger Robert D. Stethem, a U.S. Navy diver, but after 17 days finally release the last 39 hostages. *(Release of the Hostages from TWA Flight 847, p. 68)*

June 23: A bomb explodes aboard Air India Flight 182 from Montreal to London, killing all 329 people aboard. Fifteen years later, three Sikhs living in Canada are charged with the crime.

July 8: In a speech at the American Bar Association's national convention, President Ronald Reagan accuses five nations—Libya, Iran, North Korea, Cuba, and Nicaragua—of engaging in terrorism. *(President Reagan Charges Five Nations with Terrorism, p. 71)*

September 14: Rev. Benjamin Weir, a Protestant missionary from the United States, is released after being kidnapped and held hostage in Beirut, Lebanon.

September 30: Terrorists from the Islamic Liberation Organization kidnap four Soviet diplomats in Beirut, Lebanon, and kill one. The other three hostages are released unharmed, reportedly after the Soviet KGB kidnaps and kills a relative of one of the terrorist group's leaders.

October 7: Four Palestinian terrorists hijack the Italian cruise ship Achille Lauro off the coast of Egypt and murder Leon Klinghoffer, a 69-year-old disabled passenger from the United States.

October 11: A pipe bomb explodes at the West Coast headquarters of the American-Arab Anti-Discrimination Committee in Santa Ana, California, killing regional director Alex Odeh and injuring seven others. The FBI suspects that the militant Jewish Defense League planted the bomb. In 1996 the U.S. Department of Justice offers a $1 million reward for any information that helps solve the case, but it remains open.

November 6: Terrorists from the left-wing guerrilla group M-19 take over the Palace of Justice in downtown Bogota, Colombia. About 100 people, including a dozen judges, die when Colombian forces storm the building.

November 23: Terrorists from the Abu Nidal organization hijack an EgyptAir plane as it flies from Athens to Malta, and kill one American. Egyptian commandos storm the plane in Malta and 60 more people die.

December 27: At airports in Rome and Vienna, gunmen from the Palestinian group Abu Nidal kill 14 people and wound more than 110 in attacks at the check-in counters of El Al, the national airline of Israel.

1986

January 17: President Ronald Reagan signs a secret executive order approving covert arms sales to Iran in the hope that they will lead to release of Americans held hostage in Lebanon—even though the United States has an embargo on such sales and Reagan frequently cites the U.S. policy of making no concessions to terrorists.

January 20: President Ronald Reagan signs National Security Decision Directive Number 207, which for the first time formalizes U.S. terrorism policy. *(National Security Directive on Terrorism, p. 76)*

February 12: FBI agents arrest Mutulu Shakur, alleged leader of the Black Liberation Army, in Los Angeles. Law enforcement authorities say Shakur masterminded the 1981 robbery of a Brink's armored car in New York during which two police officers and a Brink's guard were killed.

April 2: A bomb rips a hole in a TWA jetliner as it descends into Athens, killing four passengers.

April 5: An American soldier and a Turkish woman are killed and 200 others are wounded when a bomb explodes at a West Berlin discotheque frequented by U.S. military personnel. U.S. officials say the Libyan government ordered the attack.

April 14: President Ronald Reagan announces that American forces have launched military strikes against Libya. The action is at least partially in retaliation for Libya's role in the bombing nine days earlier of a West Berlin discotheque. *(President Reagan on Military Strikes Against Libya, p. 80)*

April 17: Three faculty members at the American University of Beirut—two British and one American—who were kidnapped earlier are found shot to death. A Palestinian group claims it killed the three in retaliation for the American attacks on Libya.

September: During a nine-day period, 10 people are killed and more than 160 wounded in a series of terrorist bombings at Paris stores, restaurants, and public buildings. In response, the French government initiates a strict antiterrorism plan aimed primarily at keeping terrorists out of France. *(Prime Minister Chirac on French Antiterrorist Laws, p. 84)*

September 5: In Karachi, Pakistan, four Arab terrorists seize Pan American Flight 73 when it arrives from Bombay and take the 389 people aboard hostage. When the plane's power supply fails after 16 hours on the ground the terrorists panic, thinking they are under attack, and start shooting passengers and tossing grenades. Twenty-two passengers die and more than 100 people are wounded before Pakistani special forces can storm the plane and free the hostages.

September 14: A bombing at Kimpo Airport in Seoul, South Korea, kills five people and injures 29. North Korean agents planted the bomb.

October: Based on "conclusive evidence" of ties between the Syrian government and a Palestinian who a British jury convicted of attempting to blow up an El Al airliner, the British government breaks diplomatic relations with Syria. The United States and Canada show their support by withdrawing their ambassadors from Syria.

November 13: After press reports disclose that the United States secretly sold weapons to Iran, President Ronald Reagan makes a nationally televised speech admitting the sales but denying that they were a trade for Americans held hostage in Lebanon by terrorists. *(President Reagan's Speech on the Iran-Contra Affair, p. 88)*

November 25: The Reagan administration reveals that profits from arms sales to Iran were diverted to U.S.-backed contra guerrillas who are attempting to overthrow the communist Sandinista government in Nicaragua.

1987

January 10: British church envoy Terry Waite, who has traveled to Beirut, Lebanon, in an effort to negotiate the release of Westerners held hostage by terrorists backed by Iran, is himself kidnapped and taken hostage. He is released on November 18, 1991.

March 4: In a nationally televised speech, President Ronald Reagan admits that secret U.S. arms sales to Iran were aimed at gaining the release of Americans held hostage in Lebanon.

May 20: Two bombs explode outside a downtown courthouse in Johannesburg, South Africa, killing three police officers and injuring 10 other people. Government officials blame the blasts on the African National Congress.

June 1: Prime Minister Rashid Karami of Lebanon is assassinated and 13 others injured when a bomb explodes aboard the government helicopter that is carrying them to Beirut from Karami's home town in northern Lebanon.

June 18: An expert from the General Accounting Office, the investigative arm of Congress, testifies before a congressional subcommittee that security screeners at major airports detected as few as 34 percent of weapons that inspectors tried to get past them. *(Testimony on Ineffective Airport Passenger Screening, p. 92)*

November 8: An Irish Republican Army bomb attack kills 11 people and injures 63 during a ceremony in Enniskillen, Northern Ireland.

November 29: A bomb explodes aboard Korean Airlines Flight 858 over the coast of Burma, killing all 115 people aboard. Two North Korean agents planted the bomb.

December: The *intifada*, or uprising, begins in the Israeli-occupied West Bank and Gaza Strip with Palestinian youths throwing stones at Israeli positions. About 300 Palestinians and 12 Israelis die in the uprising's first year.

1988

June 28: A car bomb kills the U.S. defense attaché in Athens, Greece. The left-wing group 17 November claims responsibility.

June 29: After Congress passes a bill labeling the Palestine Liberation Organization a terrorist group, a federal judge blocks government attempts to close the PLO's office at the United Nations. *(Court on Closing the PLO's Mission to the United Nations, p. 97)*

November 15: At a meeting in Algiers, the Palestine National Council declares the establishment of an independent Palestinian state.

November 26: The Reagan administration refuses to grant a visa to Palestine Liberation Organization leader Yasir Arafat so he can address the United Nations General Assembly, contending that Arafat "knows of, condones and lends support to" acts of terrorism.

December 13: The United Nations General Assembly holds a special session in Geneva to hear an address by Palestine Liberation Organization leader Yasir Arafat after the Reagan administration refuses to allow Arafat to enter the United States.

December 21: A bomb explodes aboard Pan American World Airways Flight 103 as it flies over Lockerbie, Scotland, killing all 259 people aboard and 11 people on the ground. In January 2001 a Scottish court convicts a Libyan intelligence officer in the bombing and sentences him to life in prison; the court acquits a codefendant in the case.

1989

July: Israeli military forces kidnap Sheikh Abdul Karim Obeid, a prominent Hizballah cleric from South Lebanon, apparently in an effort to trade him for Israeli hostages and prisoners of war held by various groups.

July 6: A Palestinian passenger on a bus from Jerusalem to Tel Aviv grabs the wheel, shouts "Allah Akbar" (God is great), and drives the bus into a ravine, killing 16 people.

August: In response to a string of political assassinations attributed to the Medellin drug cartel, the Colombian government launches a crackdown. The narcoterrorists respond with a violent campaign of bombings and assassinations of political figures and policemen.

September 19: A bomb explodes aboard a French UTA DC-10 as it flies over Niger, killing all 171 people aboard. In March 1999 a French court convicts six Libyan intelligence officers *in absentia* for the crime.

September 22: The Irish Republican Army bombs a British Army base in Kent, England, killing 11 soldiers.

September 26: The left-wing Colombian guerrilla group M-19 signs a peace accord with the government, ending more than a decade of violence that often included terrorist attacks. M-19 is best known for its November 1985 takeover of the Palace of Justice in Bogota, during which about 100 people were killed.

November 22: President Rene Moawad of Lebanon is assassinated.

November 27: An Avianca jetliner explodes over Bogota, Colombia, killing all 107 people aboard. In December 1994 a U.S. jury convicts a Colombian for the crime. Law enforcement officials describe him as the top hired assassin for the Medellin drug cartel.

November 30: The Red Army Faction assassinates Deutsche Bank chairman Alfred Herrhausen in Frankfurt, West Germany.

1990

May 15: In a 182-page report, the President's Commission on Aviation Safety and Terrorism calls the aviation security system "seriously flawed" and concludes that the bombing of Pan Am 103 "may well have been preventable" if luggage had been screened properly at airports in Frankfurt and London. *(The Bombing of Pan Am Flight 103 over Scotland, p. 102)*

September: The U.S. State Department returns Iraq to its official list of nations that sponsor terrorism.

September 7: A report by the General Accounting Office, the investigative arm of Congress, says its review of thousands of international terrorism investigations by the Federal Bureau of Investigation found that in about 12 percent of cases agents monitored activities protected by the First Amendment. The report was requested by a congressional committee investigating the FBI's massive three-year probe of the Committee in Solidarity with the People of El Salvador, which did not result in any criminal charges. *(FBI Admits Terrorism Probe Violated First Amendment, p. 107)*

October 12: Rif'at al Mahgoub, speaker of the People's Assembly in Egypt, is assassinated. His assassins are believed to be associated with Islamic extremists linked to the October 1981 assassination of President Anwar al-Sadat.

November: An Iranian-American dissident is murdered in Paris. French authorities believe a hit squad directed by the Iranian government is responsible.

November 5: Extremist leader Rabbi Meir Kahane, founder of the Jewish Defense League, is assassinated in New York City.

1991

March: Members of the Liberation Tigers of Tamil Eelam, a Sri Lankan separatist group, assassinate Deputy Defense Minister Ranjan Wijeratne in Colombo, Sri Lanka. Scores of bystanders are killed or wounded.

May 21: Former Indian prime minister Rajiv Gandhi is assassinated by a suicide bomber while campaigning in Madras, India; 17 other people also die in the bombing. The bomber is a young woman from the Liberation Tigers of Tamil Eelan who detonated explosives strapped to her waist as she approached and greeted Gandhi.

August: Shapour Bakhtiar, former prime minister of Iran, and an aide are murdered in Paris. Agents of the Iranian government are suspected in the attack.

October: A bomb planted by Sikh terrorists kills 55 people and wounds more than 125 others at a Hindu festival in Uttar Pradesh, India.

October: A record 422 Peruvians die in terrorist attacks during the month; at least 2,800 die in attacks during all of 1991.

November 18: British clergyman Terry Waite and American educator Thomas Sutherland, who had been kidnapped in Beirut and held hostage, are freed. *(Statements by Hostages Upon Their Release in Lebanon, p. 112)*

December 4: American Terry Anderson, chief Middle East correspondent for the Associated Press, is released in Lebanon after being held hostage for 2,454 days.

December 30: The bodies of two Americans who had been taken hostage in Lebanon and killed by their captors return to the United States. The two are William Buckley, the Central Intelligence Agency's station chief in Beirut, and William Higgins, a Marine Corps lieutenant colonel who was kidnapped while serving on a United Nations truce-observer team.

December 30: A car bomb in Beirut, Lebanon, kills 30 people and injures more than 100.

1992

February 16: In a helicopter attack in southern Lebanon, the Israeli Defense Forces kill Sheikh Abbas Musawi, the leader of the terrorist group Hizballah, as well as his wife and six-year-old child.

March 17: A car bomb destroys the Israeli embassy in Buenos Aires, Argentina, killing 29 people and wounding hundreds. Intelligence officials ultimately blame the attack on Hizballah, the radical Islamic group based in Lebanon. *(U.S. on the Bombing of the Israeli Embassy in Argentina, p. 116)*

April: Leaders of the left-wing Red Army Faction in Germany announce a ceasefire.

April 5: President Alberto Fujimori suspends constitutional government in Peru, largely because of frustration with the government's failure to contain terrorists.

April 10: The Irish Republican Army explodes a van bomb in London's financial district, killing three people and wounding more than 90 others. The attack causes more than $500 million in property damage.

June 17: Two German relief workers, the last Western hostages held in Lebanon, are freed.

September: In Berlin, the leader of the Kurdish Democratic Party of Iran and three of his followers are assassinated. Iranian intelligence agents are suspected in the attack.

September 12: Peruvian authorities capture Abimael Guzman Reynoso, founder of the guerrilla group Shining Path, and several other rebel leaders. *(Peruvian President on the Arrest of Terrorist Leaders, p. 118)*

December 24: Only weeks before leaving office, President George H. Bush pardons former defense secretary Caspar W. Weinberger and five other Reagan administration officials who are facing trial or sentencing for their involvement in the Iran-contra affair.

1993

January 25: Mir Aimal Kansi, a Pakistani national, opens fire outside CIA headquarters in Virginia, killing two employees and wounding three others. After being arrested abroad in June 1997, Kansi is convicted by a jury in November 1997 and sentenced to death.

February 26: Islamic terrorists detonate a truck bomb underneath the 110-story World Trade Center in New York City, killing six people and injuring more than 1,000. At the time, it is the worst international terrorist act ever committed in the United States. *(The 1993 Bombing of the World Trade Center, p. 123)*

March 10: David Gunn, a physician who performs abortions, is shot to death during an antiabortion protest at a clinic in Pensacola, Florida.

April 14: The Iraqi Intelligence Service attempts to assassinate former president George H. Bush when he visits Kuwait.

April 24: The Irish Republican Army sets off a huge bomb in London's financial district that kills one person, injures more than 30, and causes $1.5 billion in damage.

May 1: Former Sri Lankan president Ranasingle Premadasa and dozens of bystanders are killed in Colombo, Sri Lanka, by a suicide bomber from the Liberation Tigers of Tamil Eelam.

August: George Tiller, a physician who performs abortions, is shot in both arms outside an abortion clinic in Wichita, Kansas.

August: The U.S. State Department places Sudan on its official list of nations that sponsor terrorism.

September 9: Yasir Arafat, leader of the Palestine Liberation Organization, signs a letter that recognizes Israel and renounces terrorism.

September 13: Leaders of Israel and the Palestine Liberation Organization sign a "Declaration of Principles" in Washington, D.C., that promises limited self-government for Palestinians living in the occupied Gaza Strip and the West Bank town of Jericho. *(Remarks on Peace Agreement Between Israel and the PLO, p. 127)*

October 29: The British and Irish prime ministers issue a joint statement inferring that Sinn Fein, the political arm of the Irish Republican Army, would be allowed to join negotiations over the future of Northern Ireland if the IRA stopped its bombings and other terrorist acts. *(Prime Ministers on Bringing Peace to Northern Ireland, p. 132)*

November 29: The British government admits that emissaries of Prime Minister John Major and the Irish Republican Army have been conducting secret talks in an effort to end the violence in Northern Ireland.

December 2: After 17 months on the run following a prison escape, narcoterrorist Pablo Escobar, head of Colombia's Medellin drug cartel, dies in a gun battle with Colombian security forces.

1994

January 1: Three men found the right-wing Militia of Montana, which quickly becomes one of the most influential militia groups in the United States.

January 18: In a report on his investigation into the Iran-contra scandal, independent counsel Lawrence E. Walsh issues a report concluding that "Reagan administration officials deliberately deceived the Congress and the public about the level and extent of official knowledge of and support of these operations." *(Independent Counsel's Report on the Iran-Contra Affair, p. 137)*

January 27: The General Accounting Office, the investigative arm of Congress, issues a report urging the Federal Aviation Administration to pay closer attention to the threat posed by terrorists. *(GAO on the Risk of Terrorist Attacks on Aviation, p. 142)*

February 5: A Mississippi jury convicts Byron De La Beckwith, 73, of the June 1963 assassination of civil rights leader Medgar Evers. Beckwith dies in prison in January 2001. *(Trial Remarks on the Murder of Civil Rights Leader Evers, p. 146)*

February 25: Baruch Goldstein, a member of the Jewish right-wing extremist group Kach, opens fire with a machine gun on Muslim worshippers at a mosque in the West Bank town of Hebron, killing 29 people and wounding more than 200.

April 6: A car-bomb attack on a bus in Afula, Israel, kills eight people. The Islamic Resistance Movement (known as Hamas), which seeks to replace Israel with an Islamic Palestinian state, claims responsibility.

April 24: In Johannesburg, South Africa, a car bomb kills nine people and injures approximately 100. The bomb explodes only days before South Africans head to the polls to complete the historic transition from apartheid to a multiracial democracy. Right-wing racists are believed responsible.

July 18: In an attack widely blamed on Hizballah, a truck bomb blows up the Jewish community center in Buenos Aires, Argentina, killing 86 people and wounding hundreds. *(Iran Accused of Supporting Terrorism in Latin America, p. 172)*

July 19: A Panamanian commuter aircraft is bombed during flight, apparently by a suicide bomber. All 21 people aboard are killed, 12 of whom are Jewish.

July 29: Reverend Paul Hill, a well-known antiabortion advocate, shoots to death physician John Britton and his clinic escort, James H. Barnett, outside a reproductive health clinic in Pensacola, Florida.

August 4: Law enforcement agents arrest four members of the Minnesota Patriots Council for making ricin, a deadly toxin. The men are later convicted of conspiring to poison federal agents.

August 31: The Irish Republican Army issues a statement announcing "a complete cessation of military hostilities" in Northern Ireland; six weeks later the Protestant side announces its own ceasefire.

October: In Sri Lanka, the separatist group Liberation Tigers of Tamil Eelam is widely believed to be responsible for a suicide bombing attack that kills a leading presidential candidate and 56 other people.

October 19: A Hamas suicide bomber blows up a bus in the heart of the business and shopping district in Tel Aviv, Israel, killing 22 people and wounding nearly 50.

October 21: In a speech to a business group in Belfast, Northern Ireland, British prime minister John Major promises to open exploratory talks with Sinn Fein, the political arm of the Irish Republican Army, if the IRA continues its seven-week-old ceasefire. *(Talks with IRA Promised If Ceasefire Continued, p. 151)*

October 26: Israel and Jordan sign a peace agreement that commits them to cooperate against terrorism.

December 10: Representatives of the British government and Sinn Fein meet for historic talks in Belfast, Northern Ireland.

December 24: Terrorists from the Armed Islamic Group hijack an Air France plane in Algiers, murder three passengers, and order the plane to fly to Marseille. French commandos storm the plane, rescuing the 170 hostages and killing all four hijackers.

December 30: In shootings at two abortion clinics in the Boston suburbs, John C. Salvi III kills two people and wounds five. Police capture him 25 hours later when he opens fire on an abortion clinic in Norfolk, Virginia. *(President Clinton Denounces Attack on Abortion Clinics, p. 155)*

1995

January 6: A fire in a Manila apartment draws the attention of authorities and disrupts a plan by Ramzi Ahmed Yousef, the mastermind of the 1993 bombing of the World Trade Center, and other terrorists to blow up a dozen U.S. jumbo jets as they fly over the Pacific Ocean. *(Terrorist Plot to Blow Up American Planes in Flight, p. 187)*

February 7: U.S. agents apprehend Ramzi Ahmed Yousef, leader of the 1993 bombing of the World Trade Center, in Islamabad, Pakistan.

March 20: Members of the Japanese religious cult Aum Shinrikyo release the chemical nerve agent sarin in the Tokyo subway system, killing 12 people and injuring 5,500. The attack is the first major use of chemical weapons by terrorists.

April 19: A massive truck bomb built by right-wing extremists Timothy McVeigh and Terry Nichols destroys the Alfred P. Murrah Federal Building in Oklahoma City, Oklahoma, killing 168 and wounding hundreds. At the time, it is the deadliest terrorist attack ever on American soil. *(Bombing of the Federal Building in Oklahoma City, p. 157)*

April 19: Richard Wayne Snell, a member of the right-wing Covenant, Sword, & Arm of the Lord who killed a black Arkansas state trooper in June 1984, is executed.

May 20: In response to the April Oklahoma City bombing, President Bill Clinton announces that a two-block stretch of Pennsylvania Avenue in front of the White House will be closed to vehicular traffic. *(Clinton Announces Closing of Pennsylvania Avenue, p. 162)*

June 21: President Bill Clinton signs Presidential Decision Directive 39, which updates the federal government's terrorism policy. *(New Presidential Directive on Terrorism Policy, p. 166)*

June 26: In a carefully coordinated attack, Islamic terrorists attempt to assassinate President Hosni Mubarak of Egypt while he attends a meeting in Addis Ababa, Ethiopia. Mubarak is not harmed.

July 25: A bombing aboard a Paris subway kills seven people and wounds 86. Algerian extremists are suspected in the attack.

August: Spanish authorities break up a plot by the separatist group Basque Fatherland and Liberty to assassinate King Juan Carlos of Spain after it comes close to succeeding.

August 21: The Islamic Resistance Movement (Hamas) claims responsibility for detonating a bomb on a bus in Jerusalem that kills six people and injures more than 100.

October 1: Sheik Omar Abdel-Rahman, the spiritual leader of an Egyptian terrorist organization called the Islamic Group, is convicted of conspiring with nine other men in a failed plot to blow up a number of New York City tunnels, bridges, and buildings—including the United Nations—on a single day in 1993.

November 4: A former Israeli soldier assassinates Prime Minister Yitzhak Rabin of Israel. The assassin claims the prime minister betrayed Israel by making peace concessions to Arabs. *(The Assassination of Israeli Prime Minister Rabin, p. 182)*

November 13: A car bombing at a military compound in Riyadh, Saudi Arabia, kills five Americans and two Indians and wounds 42 other people.

November 19: An Islamic militant blows up the Egyptian embassy in Islamabad, Pakistan, killing 16 people and injuring 60.

1996

January 31: The United Nations Security Council passes Resolution 1044, which orders Sudan to extradite three suspects in the June 1995 assassination attempt on President Hosni Mubarak of Egypt and to stop assisting and sheltering terrorists. Sudan fails to comply, and the Security Council ultimately imposes sanctions. *(Attempt to Assassinate Egyptian President Mubarak, p. 190)*

January 31: Members of the Liberation Tigers of Tamil Eelan ram a truck carrying explosives into the Central Bank in downtown Colombo, Sri Lanka, killing 90 people and injuring more than 1,400.

February 9: The Irish Republican Army announces the end of the ceasefire it declared in August 1994, and sets off a bomb in London that kills two people and wounds more than 100 others.

February 25: A suicide bomber from the Islamic Resistance Movement (Hamas) blows up a bus in Jerusalem, killing 26 people and wounding more than 80.

March 3: Hamas claims credit for the suicide bombing of a bus in Jerusalem that kills 19 people and injures six others.

March 4: Both Hamas and the Palestine Islamic Jihad claim responsibility for a bombing outside Tel Aviv's largest shopping mall that kills 13 people and injures 75.

March 25: FBI agents arrest two members of the Montana Freemen, a group that files illegal liens on property, operates its own court system, offers rewards for the arrests of local and federal officials, and produces forged money orders. Following the arrests, other members of the Freemen barricade themselves on a ranch near Brusett, Montana. After an 81-day standoff, the remaining 16 Freemen surrender to the FBI.

April: The U.S. State Department expels a diplomat at the Sudanese UN Mission who has ties to 10 men convicted in October 1995 of conspiring to bomb a number of New York City landmarks, including the UN headquarters.

April 1: Members of the Phineas Priesthood, a right-wing white separatist group, bomb a newspaper office in Spokane, Washington, and 10 minutes later rob a Spokane bank of $50,000. The FBI arrests three suspects in October.

April 11: A Department of Defense report concludes that among various groups that might obtain and use chemical, biological, or nuclear weapons against the United States and its interests, terrorists pose the greatest threat. *(The Proliferation of Weapons of Mass Destruction, p. 193)*

April 18: In a shooting attack outside the Europa Hotel in Cairo, Egypt, members of the Islamic Group kill 18 Greek tourists and wound 14 other people.

May 18: Under pressure from the United States and the United Nations, Sudan expels terrorist leader Osama bin Laden. He moves to Afghanistan.

June 15: A fertilizer-based car bomb explodes near a shopping center in Manchester, England, injuring more than 200 people and causing an estimated $300 million in property damage. The Irish Republican Army planted the bomb.

June 25: A tanker truck packed with explosives blows up outside the Khobar Towers apartment complex in Dhahran, Saudi Arabia, where 3,000 U.S. Air Force personnel are housed. The blast, which is blamed on Hizballah, kills 19 Americans and wounds nearly 400. *(Nineteen American Airmen Die in Saudi Arabia Bombing, p. 220)*

June 25: John M. Deutch, director of the Central Intelligence Agency, testifies at a Senate hearing that terrorists, hackers, or other nations could launch information warfare attacks against the United States that could disrupt everything from electric power distribution to air traffic control. *(CIA Director Warns of Cyber Attacks by Terrorists, p. 198)*

July 24: In Sri Lanka, the Liberation Tigers of Tamil Eelam bomb a commuter train, killing 70 people and wounding hundreds more.

July 27: A pipe bomb explodes at the 1996 Olympics in Atlanta, Georgia, killing one person and injuring more than 100 others. In October 1998 federal authorities charge Eric Robert Rudolph with the bombing, along with the 1997 bombings of an abortion clinic in Birmingham, Alabama, and a gay nightclub in Atlanta, Georgia, but by then he has disappeared. *(Bombing at the 1996 Olympics in Atlanta, Georgia, p. 203)*

August 14: The U.S. State Department issues a fact sheet about Osama bin Laden, leader of the al-Qaida terrorist network, that calls him "one of the most significant financial sponsors of Islamic extremist activities in the world today." Two weeks later bin Laden formally calls for a guerrilla war against U.S. troops based in Saudi Arabia. *(State Department Fact Sheet About Osama Bin Laden, p. 206)*

September 9: The White House Commission on Aviation Safety and Security—chaired by Vice President Al Gore—presents an interim report that calls for greatly expanding the federal role in safeguarding security at airports.

September 11: A top official with the General Accounting Office, the investigative arm of Congress, testifies at a congressional hearing that protecting aviation against terrorism is an "urgent national issue" that requires greater attention and more funding. *(Vulnerabilities in the Aviation Security System, p. 210)*

December 3: A bomb explodes aboard a Paris commuter train during rush hour, killing four people and injuring more than 80. No one claims responsibility for the attack, but the Algerian Armed Islamic Group is suspected.

December 17: Fourteen members of the Tupac Amaru Revolutionary Movement burst into the Japanese ambassador's residence in Lima, Peru, during a cocktail party and take more than 500 people hostage. The terrorists quickly release all but about 70 hostages. Four months later Peruvian commandos storm the building and rescue the hostages, killing all their captors in the process.

December 29: Guatemala's 36-year insurgency formally ends with the signing of a peace accord between the government and the Guatemalan National Revolutionary Unity (URNG) guerrillas. The URNG is an umbrella group for four separate guerrilla/terrorist groups that joined together in 1982.

1997

January 16: Two bombs explode within a one-hour period at a women's health facility in Atlanta, Georgia, wounding several police officers and other emergency responders and causing major damage to the clinic.

April: A Justice Department report says instructions for making bombs are readily available to terrorists and others in libraries, in bookstores, and on the Internet. *(Justice Department on Ease of Obtaining Bomb-Making Plans, p. 230)*

April 22: Peruvian commandos storm the Japanese ambassador's residence in Lima, where 14 members of the Tupac Amaru Revolutionary Movement have been holding approximately 70 hostages since December. Two soldiers and all 14 guerrillas die in the raid, and one hostage who is wounded during the rescue dies later of complications. *(Japanese Prime Minister on Hostage Rescue in Peru, p. 235)*

April 22: Law enforcement officers in Texas arrest four members of the True Knights of the Ku Klux Klan who were allegedly planning to detonate bombs at a natural gas facility to divert attention from a simultaneous armored car robbery.

May 2: In Colorado law enforcement officers arrest three members of the Colorado First Light Infantry, a militia group, for possessing numerous illegal weapons. A search of their shared residence finds mortars, pipe bombs, ammunition, automatic weapons, grenades, and various explosive devices, according to the FBI.

June 2: Timothy McVeigh is convicted of the April 1995 bombing of the Alfred P. Murrah Federal Building in Oklahoma City, which killed 168 people. Later in the year he is sentenced to death.

June 12: Federal officials in Jacksonville, Florida, arrest Bradley James Orns for allegedly planning to rob an armored car of $20 million and to kill its three guards. Prosecutors say Orns planned to use money from the robbery to finance militia groups.

July: The FBI and law enforcement agencies in Texas, Colorado, Kansas, Indiana, and Wisconsin arrest 10 men who allegedly planned to attack the U.S. Army base at Fort Hood, Texas, in the mistaken belief that United Nations troops were stationed there.

July 30: Two suicide bombers attack a market in Jerusalem, killing 16 people and wounding 178. Hamas claims responsibility for the attack.

September 4: A bombing at the Copacabana Hotel in Havana, Cuba, kills an Italian tourist. The Cuban government alleges that groups based in the United States sponsored the attack, along with others on Cuban hotels.

September 4: Three suicide bombers from Hamas detonate bombs in the Ben Yehuda mall in Jerusalem, killing five people and wounding nearly 200.

September 18: Terrorists throw grenades at a bus parked in front of the Egyptian National Antiquities Museum in Cairo, killing nine German tourists and their Egyptian driver.

September 25: Agents of the Israeli government launch an unsuccessful attempt to assassinate Khalid Mishal, a top Hamas official, in Jordan. Jordanian security officials capture the agents and return them to Israel after the Israeli government releases the founder of Hamas and others from prison.

October 8: Under the new Antiterrorism and Effective Death Penalty Act, Secretary of State Madeline Albright designates 30 groups as foreign terrorist organizations. Groups on the list range from the Abu Nidal organization to the Tupac Amaru Revolutionary Movement. The new law makes it illegal to provide funds or other material support to listed groups and requires financial institutions to freeze their assets.

October 15: In Sri Lanka, a truck bombing by the Liberation Tigers of Tamil Eelam of the Colombo World Trade Center kills 18 people and injures more than 100.

November 12: Two gunmen shoot to death four U.S. employees of the Union Texas Petroleum Corporation and their Pakistani driver after they drive away from the Sheraton Hotel in Karachi, Pakistan. Two different groups claim responsibility for the attack.

November 17: In a shooting rampage, six gunmen from the Islamic Group kill 58 tourists and four Egyptians at the Hatsheput Temple near Luxor, Egypt, and wound 26 others. The gunmen escape in a commandeered tour bus, but Egyptian security forces pursue them and kill all six.

December: To settle a lawsuit filed against the Federal Bureau of Investigation and the Justice Department by the Committee in Solidarity with the People of El Salvador, the government agrees to improve training of FBI agents about respecting First Amendment activities and to pay the group's legal costs of $190,000.

December: A French court convicts the notorious terrorist Carlos the Jackal of the June 1975 murders of two French counterintelligence agents and an informer and sentences him to life in prison. *(The Capture of Carlos the Jackal, p. 149)*

December 1: A report by the General Accounting Office, the investigative arm of Congress, says no one knows how much money the federal government spends on antiterrorism efforts overall or whether the money is being spent properly. *(Better Coordination Urged for Federal Terrorism Spending, p. 248)*

1998

January 29: A bomb explodes at an abortion clinic in Birmingham, Alabama, killing an off-duty police officer working as a security guard and severely wounding a clinic nurse.

January 29: British prime minister Tony Blair announces that, because of "compelling new evidence," a new inquiry will be conducted into the January 1972 "Bloody Sunday" incident in which British troops shot and killed 14 civilians during a protest march in Londonderry, Northern Ireland.

February: Law enforcement authorities arrest several members of the white supremacist group The New Order in Illinois and Michigan and charge them with weapons violations. The group allegedly planned to rob an armored car in St. Louis, Missouri; kill the founder of the Southern Poverty Law Center; bomb the Simon Weisenthal Center in Los Angeles; and attack the New York office of the Jewish organization B'nai B'rith, among other crimes.

February 9: Chechen mercenaries and supporters of a deceased former Georgian president attack the motorcade of Georgian president Eduard Shevardnadze with automatic weapons and rocket-propelled grenades. Shevardnadze survives the attack—the second assassination attempt against him in three years.

February 22: Osama bin Laden, leader of the al-Qaida terrorist network, and allied groups issue a *fatwa*, or religious ruling, stating that it is the duty of all Muslims to kill Americans—both military and civilians—anywhere in the world.

February 26: The FBI establishes the National Infrastructure Protection Center at its headquarters in Washington, D.C.

April: In Germany, the Red Army Faction announces that it is dissolving. The RAF was once one of the world's most deadly terrorist groups.

April 10: Eight of the 10 political parties in Northern Ireland sign the "Good Friday" agreement aimed at ending violence by Catholic and Protestant terrorists and paving the way for the British province's political future.

April 13: Terrell P. Coon is sentenced to four years and three months in federal prison for his role in a 1996 plot to bomb an FBI fingerprint complex in Clarksburg, West Virginia. Four other men also are convicted in the case.

May 22: In referendums, voters in both Northern Ireland and the Republic of Ireland overwhelmingly support the "Good Friday" agreement reached the previous month concerning the future of Northern Ireland.

July 1: Federal, state, and local law enforcement authorities arrest three alleged members of the violent secessionist group the Republic of Texas in McAllen, Texas. Prosecutors allege that the men were constructing a device to infect selected government officials with toxic substances such as anthrax. In October a jury finds two of the men guilty of threatening to use a weapon of mass destruction against federal agents and their families and acquits the third man.

August: A Mississippi jury convicts Samuel Bowers, former Imperial Wizard of the Mississippi White Knights of the Ku Klux Klan, of murder for a January 1966 firebombing that killed Vernon Dahmer Sr., a black store keeper who was killed because he helped other blacks register to vote.

August: In Sapasoa, Peru, members of the Shining Path kill the mayor and three of his supporters at a rally.

August 7: In almost simultaneous attacks, truck bombs blow up the American embassies in Nairobi, Kenya, and Dar Es Salaam, Tanzania. The Kenya blast kills 213 people, including 12 Americans, and the Tanzania bombing kills 11, none of whom are Americans. Altogether, about 4,500 people are wounded in the two attacks. In November Osama bin Laden, leader of the al-Qaida terrorist network, is indicted in the United States for the bombings.

August 15: In the deadliest act of violence in the 30-year history of the "troubles" in Northern Ireland, a car bomb explosion in the small town of Omagh kills 29 people and wounds more than 200. The Real IRA, a splinter group from the Irish Republican Army, claims credit for the attack and says it is aimed at blocking implementation of the "Good Friday" peace agreement. *("Real IRA" Claims Credit for Omagh Blast, p. 257)*

August 20: President Bill Clinton announces in a nationally televised speech that he has ordered cruise missile attacks against sites in Afghanistan and Sudan that are linked to the terrorists who blew up two U.S. embassies in Africa on August 7. *(U.S. Fires Cruise Missiles at Sites Linked to Bin Laden, p. 253)*

September 21: In a speech at the opening session of the United Nations General Assembly, President Bill Clinton urges the assembled heads of state, ambassadors, and other dignitaries to put terrorism at the top of the world agenda. *(Clinton Urges United Nations to Focus on Terrorism, p. 262)*

September 23: A report by the General Accounting Office, the investigative arm of Congress, finds "widespread and serious weaknesses" in the security of federal government computer systems that leave them vulnerable to attack by terrorists, hackers, and others.

October 16: The Department of Justice and the FBI announce plans to establish the National Domestic Preparedness Office to integrate federal, state, and local resources to respond to threats and incidents involving weapons of mass destruction.

October 18: A bomb planted by the National Liberation Army explodes on Colombia's central oil pipeline, killing 71 people and injuring at least 100.

October 19: In the largest act of ecoterrorism in the United States, the Earth Liberation Front burns numerous buildings at the Vail ski resort in Colorado, causing $12 million in damage. *(FBI Official Describes Threat from Ecoterrorists, p. 393)*

October 23: Barnettt Slepian, a well-known doctor in the Buffalo, New York, area who performs abortions, is killed by a rifle shot fired through the kitchen window of his home.

November 4: Osama bin Laden, leader of the al-Qaida terrorist network, is indicted in the United States for the August 7, 1998, bombings of U.S. embassies in Kenya and Tanzania. The State Department announces a $5 million reward for information leading to his arrest or conviction.

November 9: Attorney General Janet Reno announces the creation of the National Task Force on Violence Against Health Care Providers, which is charged with coordinating efforts to prevent violence against abortion clinics and to investigate possible connections between clinic attacks. *(Task Force Created to Fight Antiabortion Violence, p. 267)*

December 27: The Earth Liberation Front burns down the U.S. Forest Industries office in Medford, Oregon, causing more than $500,000 in damage.

1999

February 16: Turkish security forces arrest Abdullah Ocalan, chairman of the Kurdistan Workers' Party, when he leaves his safehaven at the Greek ambassador's residence in Nairobi, Kenya. Kurdish sympathizers respond to his arrest with demonstrations—

many of them violent—throughout Europe. In late June the Turkish State Security Court sentences Ocalan to death for treason.

February 16: In the former Soviet republic of Uzbekistan, five coordinated car bombs targeting government facilities explode within a two-hour period in downtown Tashkent, killing 16 people and wounding more than 100. Government officials suspect that the Islamic Movement of Uzbekistan is responsible.

February 25: Members of the Revolutionary Armed Forces of Colombia kidnap and kill three Americans working in the country.

March: A French court convicts six Libyan intelligence officers *in absentia* for the September 1989 bombing of UTA Flight 772 over Niger, which killed all 171 people aboard. The court also orders the Libyan government to pay 211 million French francs to compensate the victims' families, and Libya pays within a few months.

April 5: Members of the Animal Liberation Front vandalize 12 animal research laboratories and steal research animals at the University of Minnesota in Minneapolis. According to the FBI, damage from the attack totals $2 million.

April 14: FBI agents in Cincinnati, Ohio, arrest Kale Todd Kelly, a member of the Aryan Nations who they allege was planning a terrorist attack on a federal building and the assassination of Morris Dees, chief defense counsel for the Southern Poverty Law Center.

May: In Italy, the left-wing Red Brigades claims responsibility for assassinating labor leader Massimo D'Antono, an adviser to Italy's labor minister.

June 7: The Federal Bureau of Investigation adds Osama bin Laden to its "Ten Most Wanted Fugitives" list.

June 16: Authorities in St. Paul, Minnesota, arrest Kathleen Ann Soliah, who allegedly committed crimes during the mid-1970s as a member of the Symbionese Liberation Army. Soliah had avoided capture by changing her name to Sara Jane Olson while raising a family.

July: Federal agents in Miami and Philadelphia arrest four men for allegedly smuggling nearly 100 weapons to the Irish Republican Army.

July 4: President Bill Clinton increases the pressure on the Taliban rulers of Afghanistan to stop harboring Osama bin Laden, leader of the al-Qaida terrorist network, by signing an executive order that freezes Taliban assets in the United States, blocks all U.S. trade with the Taliban, and bars U.S. citizens from contributing money to the group. *(Clinton Order Blocks Trade with the Taliban, p. 271)*

August 11: In a controversial move, President Bill Clinton offers clemency to 16 terrorists convicted years earlier of crimes committed in their effort to win independence for Puerto Rico, a commonwealth of the United States. *(Clinton Grants Clemency to Puerto Rican Terrorists, p. 296)*

September: A report prepared by the Library of Congress for the Central Intelligence Agency warns that terrorist leader Osama bin Laden could crash airplanes into the Pentagon, the White House, and the CIA headquarters. *(Report on Possible Terrorist Attacks Using Airplanes, p. 274)*

September: During a shootout in Vienna, Austrian police kill suspected German Red Army Faction terrorist Horst Ludwig-Mayer and arrest his accomplice, who is extradited to Germany to face numerous charges.

September 8 and 13: Powerful bombs explode in two Moscow apartment buildings, killing more than 200 people and wounding 200 others.

September 15: A federal commission predicts that terrorists or other groups that acquire biological, chemical, or nuclear weapons will pose one of the biggest threats to the United States in the twenty-first century. *(Report on U.S. Vulnerability to Terrorist Attacks, p. 280)*

October: Five gunmen attack Armenia's parliament building, killing the prime minister, the speaker of the national assembly, and six others.

October 15: The United Nations Security Council unanimously approves Resolution 1267, which threatens the Taliban rulers of Afghanistan with economic sanctions if they do not hand over Osama bin Leader, leader of the al-Qaida terrorist network, for trial within 30 days. The Taliban leaders refuse to oust bin Laden, and the sanctions take effect in November. *(UN Threatens Sanctions Against Taliban, p. 286)*

October 20: An expert from the General Accounting Office, the investigative arm of Congress, testifies before a congressional committee that terrorist groups would have great difficulties creating and using biological weapons unless they had lots of help from a nation that sponsored terrorism. *(GAO on Threats Posed by Weapons of Mass Destruction, p. 291)*

December: President Chandrika Kumaratunga of Sri Lanka narrowly escapes an assassination attempt by the Liberation Tigers of Tamil Eelam.

December 1: Leaders of the Japanese religious cult Aum Shinrikyo, which released the chemical nerve agent sarin in the Tokyo subway system in March 1995, admit responsibility for the sarin attack—which they had previously denied—and apologize publicly for it and other acts.

December 15: A federal commission concludes in a report that terrorists are far more likely to attack the United States with conventional explosives than with biological, chemical, or nuclear weapons, and urges federal antiterrorism programs to focus greater attention on conventional attacks. *(Panel Report on Antiterrorism Priorities, p. 302)*

December 19: Ahmed Ressam, an Algerian national, is arrested as he attempts to drive a car loaded with explosives and other bomb components across the border from Canada into the United States at Port Angeles, Washington. Law enforcement officials say Ressam planned to blow up Los Angeles International Airport.

December 24: Five Kashmiri militants hijack Indian Airlines Flight 814 as it flies from Nepal to New Delhi with 200 passengers and crew members. The hijackers order the plane to land at Kandahar Airport in Afghanistan, where they demand that India release 36 imprisoned Kashmiri militants. India ultimately frees three people in exchange for the hijackers releasing their hostages.

December 25: The Earth Liberation Front claims credit for burning down the Monmouth, Oregon, offices of Boise Cascade, a logging company.

2000

February: In Thailand, security forces kill Saarli Taloh-Mayaw, leader of a Muslim separatist group called the New Pattani United Liberation Organization.

March 21: In India, militants kill 35 Sikhs in Chadisinghpoora Village. Two major Muslim groups in Kashmir—Jaish-i-Muhammad and Lashkar-e-Tayyaba—are suspected in the massacre.

April 19: The bombing of a McDonald's restaurant in Quevert, France, kills one person and causes major damage. Authorities suspect the Breton Liberation Army is responsible.

May 1: In Makeni, Sierra Leone, members of the Revolutionary United Front surround and open fire on a facility operated by the United Nations Assistance Mission in Sierra Leone, killing five UN soldiers.

May 25: The head of special investigations for the General Accounting Office, the investigative arm of Congress, testifies before Congress that undercover agents using phony police badges and credentials breached security in every one of more than

20 tests of airports and major federal buildings in Washington, D.C. *(Security Fails at Federal Agencies and Airports, p. 317)*

June 5: The National Commission on Terrorism, a panel mandated by Congress, recommends in a report that the federal government increase spending on counterterrorism and loosen restrictions on federal agencies that investigate terrorists. *(Panel Urges More Spending to Counter Terror Threat, p. 322)*

June 8: In Athens, Greece, two unidentified gunmen kill British defense attaché Stephen Saunders in an ambush. The left-wing group 17 November claims responsibility.

August 2: Armed militants throw grenades and then open fire on a community kitchen in Rajwas, India, killing 30 people and injuring 47. The Muslim group Lashkar-e-Tayyaba claims responsibility.

August 10: In Srinagar, India, a remote-controlled car bomb kills nine people, including eight police officers, and wounds 25. No one claims responsibility for the attack.

September: A rocket attack causes minor damage to the headquarters of Britain's foreign intelligence service, MI6, in central London. The dissident Real IRA is believed to be responsible.

September 13: Ten people are killed when a car bomb explodes in the underground parking garage of the stock exchange in Jakarta, Indonesia.

September 29: A new *intifada*, or uprising, by Palestinians begins in territories occupied by Israel.

October 12: As the destroyer USS *Cole* refuels in Aden, Yemen, two terrorists in a small skiff pull alongside and detonate a large quantity of explosives that blast a gaping hole in the ship, killing 17 sailors and wounding 39. American officials blame the bombing on followers of Osama bin Laden, leader of the al-Qaida terrorist network. *(Seventeen Killed in Suicide Attack on USS* Cole, *p. 330)*

October 27: After a 15-year investigation, the Royal Canadian Mounted Police arrest two Sikhs living in Canada for the June 1985 bombing of Air India Flight 182 from Montreal to London, which killed all 329 people aboard. *(Arrests Made in 1985 Bombing That Killed 329 People, p. 327)*

December 15: The United States "has no coherent, functional national strategy for combating terrorism," according to a report by the Advisory Panel to Assess Domestic Response Capabilities for Terrorism Involving Weapons of Mass Destruction, a federal commission headed by Governor James Gilmore of Virginia. It recommends that the federal government create a single high-level agency to coordinate counterterrorism efforts that are spread across dozens of agencies and departments.

2001

January 19: United Nations Security Council Resolution 1333, which tightens sanctions against the Taliban leaders of Afghanistan, takes effect. The new sanctions ban weapons sales and military assistance to the Taliban. The sanctions are aimed at forcing the Taliban to comply with Security Council demands to turn over terrorist Osama bin Laden for prosecution, close terrorist training camps in Afghanistan, and stop providing sanctuary for international terrorists.

January 20: On his last day in office, President Bill Clinton pardons Susan L. Rosenberg, a former member of the left-wing Weather Underground terrorist group who was suspected of being involved in a 1981 armed robbery of a Brink's armored truck in Nyack, New York, during which a guard and two police officers were killed. He also pardons newspaper heiress Patty Hearst for her role in a 1975 bank robbery by the Symbionese Liberation Army.

January 24: In Turkey, Turkish Hizballah assassinates Diyarbakir police chief Gaffar Okkan and five policemen.

January 31: A Scottish court convicts Abdelbaset Ali Al Megrahi, a Libyan intelligence agent, in the 1988 bombing of Pan American World Airways Flight 103 as it flew over Lockerbie, Scotland, killing all 259 people aboard and 11 on the ground. The court acquits a codefendant in the case. *(Verdict in the 1988 Bombing of Pan Am Flight 103, p. 336)*

February 1: In Algeria, Islamic extremists massacre 26 people near Berrouaghia.

February 7: In his annual assessment of security threats facing the United States, CIA Director George Tenet testifies before the Senate Select Committee on Intelligence that Osama bin Laden and his al-Qaida terrorist network pose the greatest danger to national security of any foe.

March 15: Three Chechen separatists hijack a Russian charter jet carrying 175 passengers as it flies from Istanbul to Moscow, and the plane lands in Medina, Saudi Arabia, to be refueled. After Saudi authorities negotiate with the hijackers overnight, special forces storm the plane and capture two of the hijackers. The third hijacker, one crew member, and one passenger die during the rescue.

March 27: Militiamen loyal to a warlord in Mogadishu, Somalia, attack a Medecins Sans Frontieres (Doctors Without Borders) medical charity facility, killing 11 people and wounding 40.

April 11: Timothy McVeigh, convicted of the April 1995 bombing of the federal building in Oklahoma City, is executed by lethal injection. He is the first federal prisoner executed in 38 years.

May 21: A report by the Sharm el-Sheikh Fact-Finding Commission, appointed by President Clinton to investigate why a new round of violence broke out in the Middle East in September 2000, warns both Israelis and Palestinians of the long-term danger they face if the seemingly endless cycle of attacks and counterattacks continues. *(Report Examines Origin of Current Mideast Violence, p. 339)*

June 1: Hamas claims responsibility for a suicide bombing at a popular disco in Tel Aviv that kills 21 people and wounds 120.

June 8: A federal jury in Miami convicts five men—three of whom are agents of Cuba's intelligence service—of spying for Cuba. The men spent most of their time infiltrating anti-Castro groups in Miami and say their spying was necessary to prevent terrorist attacks against Cuba.

June 21: A federal grand jury in the United States indicts 14 people for the June 1996 bombing of the Khobar Towers apartment complex in Saudi Arabia, which killed 19 American servicemen and wounded nearly 400. Eleven of those indicted are in Saudi Arabian custody, but Saudi officials refuse to extradite them to the United States for trial.

July 24: In Colombo, Sri Lanka, the Liberation Tigers of Tamil Eelam claim responsibility for an attack on the international and military airports that kills six people and injures nine. The attackers also destroy five commercial planes, eight military aircraft, several ammunition dumps, and oil storage depots.

July 25: As part of Israel's campaign of "targeted killings" of Palestinian militants, Israeli forces assassinate a Hamas leader with antitank missiles near Nablus.

July 31: An Israeli helicopter fires rockets at the office of Hamas in Nablus, killing eight Palestinians. They include Jamal Mansour, the top Hamas leader on the West Bank, and two children.

August: In Angola unidentified militants ambush a train, killing 256 people and injuring 161. The National Union for the Total Independence of Angola is suspected in the attack.

August 9: A 23-year-old Palestinian suicide bomber blows up the crowded Sbarro pizzeria in Jerusalem during the lunch hour, killing 15 people and wounding about 130 others. *(Eyewitness Report Describing Sbarro Suicide Bombing, p. 346)*

August 11: Three men closely tied to the Irish Republican Army are arrested in Colombia, where they are allegedly teaching members of the Revolutionary Armed Forces of Colombia how to make bombs.

August 27: Israeli forces assassinate Abu Ali Mustafa, leader of the Popular Front for the Liberation of Palestine, with missiles fired from Apache helicopters.

September 1: In Nimule, Uganda, militants kill five people and wound two others during an ambush of a vehicle belonging to Catholic Relief Services. The Lord's Resistance Army is suspected in the attack.

September 9: A pair of suicide bombers pretending to be journalists kill Ahmad Shah Massoud, leader of the Northern Alliance in Afghanistan.

September 11: Nineteen hijackers take control of four airliners on the East Coast of the United States shortly after takeoff. They fly two of the planes into the twin towers of the World Trade Center in New York City, one into the Pentagon in Washington, D.C., and one into a field in southern Pennsylvania, killing slightly more than 3,000 people. Law enforcement officials quickly tie the hijackers, all of whom are from the Middle East, to the al-Qaida terrorist network run by Osama bin Laden. *(Bush on Terrorist Attacks Against the United States, p. 351)*

September 28: The United Nations Security Council adopts Resolution 1373, which requires member nations to cut off financing of terrorist groups and their activities, deny safe haven to terrorists and their supporters, prosecute and punish terrorists, and cooperate with other nations in investigating terrorist acts.

September 28: Partly because of Sudan's cooperation in the U.S. war on terrorism, the United Nations Security Council lifts sanctions it had imposed against the country years earlier.

October: Over an eight-day period, more than 250 abortion and family planning clinics across the United States receive letters that purport to contain anthrax.

October 1: A car bombing at the main entrance of the Jammu and Kashmir legislative assembly building in Srinagar, India, kills 31 people and injures 60. The Kashmiri separatist group Jaish e-Mohammed claims responsibility.

October 6: At a rally in Havana, Cuba, to mark the twenty-fifth anniversary of the bombing of a Cubana Airlines plane that killed 73 people, President Fidel Castro asks why the U.S. government has not prosecuted the bombing's alleged mastermind and other people in Florida who he accuses of committing terrorist acts against Cuba. *(Castro Accuses United States of Inconsistency on Terrorism, p. 361)*

October 7: The United States and Great Britain launch a large-scale war in Afghanistan, which President George W. Bush says in a televised speech is designed to "disrupt the use of Afghanistan as a terrorist base of operations, and to attack the military capability of the Taliban regime." The Taliban fall from power about two months after the war begins. *(United States, Britain Launch War in Afghanistan, p. 366)*

October 17: The Popular Front for the Liberation of Palestine assassinates Israeli cabinet minister Rehavam Zeevi in an East Jerusalem hotel.

October 23: An independent international commission announces that its members had witnessed the Irish Republican Army destroying some of its weapons. *(The Irish Republican Army Destroys Weapons, p. 371)*

November: Authorities in Peru announce they have thwarted a plan by the Shining Path to attack the U.S. embassy in Lima.

November: An attack in Sri Lanka by the Liberation Tigers of Tamil Eelam kills 14 policemen and wounds 14 other policemen and four civilians.

November 9: The director of information security issues for the General Accounting Office, the investigative arm of Congress, testifies before a congressional committee that security weaknesses remain pervasive across federal computer systems. *(Federal Computer Systems Face Severe Security Risk, p. 374)*

December: In a scathing report, the new ombudsman for police in Northern Ireland says officers have so badly bungled their investigation of the August 1998 car bombing in Omagh, which killed 29 people, that the case may never be solved.

December: Norway brokers a ceasefire between the government of Sri Lanka and the Liberation Tigers of Tamil Eelam.

December 1: Two suicide bombers kill 11 people and injure about 180 on a pedestrian mall in the center of Jerusalem. Hamas claims responsibility.

December 2: A suicide bombing on a bus in Haifa, Israel, kills 15 people and injures 40. Hamas claims responsibility.

December 12: Federal prosecutors in Los Angeles charge two leaders of the militant Jewish Defense League (JDL) with plotting to bomb the Muslim Public Affairs Council in Los Angeles, a mosque in Culver City, and the San Clemente office of an Arab-American member of Congress. The two charged are Irv Rubin, the JDL's national director, and Earl Krugel, the group's West Coast coordinator.

December 13: Five heavily armed terrorists attack India's parliament building with assault rifles and grenades, but guards and police officers kill them before they are able to get inside. Indian officials claim that two groups based in Pakistan carried out the attack with support from Pakistan's intelligence service, a charge that Pakistani officials hotly deny. *(Twelve Die in Attack on Indian Parliament, p. 379)*

December 22: Alert crew members and passengers subdue Richard C. Reid when he tries to ignite explosives hidden in his shoes aboard an American Airlines flight from Paris to Miami. Law enforcement officials say Reid has ties to Osama bin Laden's al-Qaida terrorist network.

2002

January 5: Israeli forces board a ship in the Red Sea and discover nearly 50 tons of Iranian arms that were apparently bound for Palestinian militants in the West Bank and Gaza Strip.

January 15: Israeli forces assassinate Raed al-Karmi, a leader in the al-Aqsa Brigades, who it says was involved in 10 murders.

January 23: Daniel Pearl, a reporter for the *Wall Street Journal*, is kidnapped in Karachi, Pakistan, by Islamic militants. Almost a month later the U.S. embassy in Pakistan receives a videotape that shows Pearl being decapitated. *(Pakistani Terrorists Kill* Wall Street Journal *Reporter, p. 398)*

January 24: Bakr Hamdan, a senior Hamas commander, and two associates are killed in his car by a missile fired from an Israeli helicopter.

February 6: CIA Director George Tenet testifies before the Senate Select Committee on Intelligence that Osama bin Laden and al-Qaida remain the biggest threat to U.S. security despite efforts in Afghanistan and elsewhere to disrupt the terrorist network. *(CIA Director Says al Qaeda Remains a Serious Threat, p. 388)*

March 9: A suicide bomber attacks a cafe in the center of Jerusalem, killing 11 people and injuring 54. Hamas claims responsibility.

March 18: Attorney General John Ashcroft announces the indictment of three members of the Revolutionary Armed Forces of Colombia (FARC) for conspiring to import cocaine into the United States. FARC is a guerrilla group included on the State Department's official list of foreign terrorist organizations.

March 19: An Italian economist working on controversial changes in the nation's labor laws is shot to death. An offshoot of the Red Brigades terrorist group claims responsibility.

March 20: A car bomb blows up across the street from the U.S. embassy in Lima, Peru, killing nine people and injuring 30. The attack, which is widely attributed to the Shining Path, comes just three days before President George W. Bush is to visit Peru.

March 27: A suicide bombing in the dining room of the Park Hotel in Netanya, Israel, during Passover kills 29 people and injures 140. Hamas claims responsibility for the attack.

April: Police in Northern Ireland thwart dissidents from the Irish Republican Army as they attempt to drive a van containing a large gasoline bomb into Belfast.

April 7: Two bombs explode in a provincial capital of Colombia, killing 12 people and wounding dozens. Police blame the attack on the Revolutionary Armed Forces of Colombia.

April 9: Attorney General John Ashcroft announces the indictment of the lawyer for Sheik Omar Abdel-Rahman, who was convicted in 1995 of conspiring to blow up New York City landmarks, and three other people for allegedly helping Abdel-Rahman continue running the Egyptian terrorist organization Islamic Group from his Minnesota prison cell. *(United States Indicts Lawyer for Convicted Terrorist, p. 407)*

April 10: The Islamic militant group Hamas claims responsibility for a suicide bombing on a bus near the Israeli city of Haifa that kills eight people.

April 11: A gas truck explodes outside a synagogue in Tunisia, killing 16 people. The al-Qaida terrorist network is suspected in the attack.

April 21: Three bombs explode in the Philippines city of General Santos, killing 14 people and injuring dozens. Muslim extremists are suspected in the blasts.

April 29: The first U.S. soldiers arrive in the former Soviet republic of Georgia to provide antiterrorism training to the Georgian military. Georgia's primary terrorism threat comes from Muslim extremists.

April 30: The General Accounting Office, the investigative arm of Congress, reports that undercover investigators fooled guards at four federal buildings in Atlanta, Georgia, and gained unauthorized access.

May: Alvaro Uribe Velez is elected president of Colombia based largely on his pledge to step up military action against three terrorist groups that have plagued Colombia for decades. *(Testimony on Drug Trade as Source of Terrorism Funding, p. 402)*

May 2: In the West Bank city of Ramallah, Israeli military forces lift a 34-day siege of the battered headquarters of Palestine Liberation Organization leader Yasir Arafat. The siege ends after the United States brokers a deal under which six Palestinian militants wanted by the Israelis and sheltered by Arafat are transferred to U.S. and British custody.

May 7: In London, a judge sentences three men to 30 years in prison after they plead guilty to trying to smuggle weapons from Slovakia for attacks on England. The three are members of the Real IRA, a splinter group from the Irish Republican Army.

May 7: In Rishon Lezion, Israel, a suicide bomber kills 16 people and wounds 55 at a club. Hamas claims responsibility.

May 10: More than 100 people, including several dozen armed Palestinian militants, leave the Church of the Nativity in Bethlehem after a 39-day siege by Israeli military forces. As part of the deal to end the standoff at the church, which Christians believe is the birthplace of Jesus, 13 Palestinian militants who Israeli officials call "senior terrorists" are exiled to foreign countries.

May 14: Three Islamic militants armed with automatic weapons kill 30 people and wound nearly 50 on the outskirts of Jammu, India.

May 21: In its annual report about international terrorism, the U.S. State Department lists seven nations as state sponsors of terrorism: Cuba, Iran, Iraq, Libya, North Korea, Sudan, and Syria.

May 22: A jury in Birmingham, Alabama, convicts former Ku Klux Klansman Bobby Frank Cherry in the September 1963 bombing of the 16th Street Baptist Church in which four young black girls were killed. *(Last Major Suspect Convicted in 1963 Church Bombing, p. 411)*

May 22: A California jury convicts two militia members of conspiring to blow up two huge propane storage tanks in a Sacramento suburb. Prosecutors say the men hoped the attack, which police thwarted, would lead to civil unrest and eventually topple the federal government.

May 30: Attorney General John Ashcroft announces that he is loosening restrictions on the FBI's ability to conduct domestic surveillance. *(FBI Gets Expanded Authority to Monitor Americans, p. 421)*

June: France extradites antiabortion activist James Kopp to the United States to stand trial for the October 1998 murder of Barnett Slepian, a doctor in the Buffalo, New York, area who performed abortions.

June: The *Washington Post* reports that the al-Qaida terrorist network is increasingly joining with Hizballah, one of the foremost terrorist groups in the Middle East and previously a rival, on logistics and training for terrorist operations.

June: The International Atomic Energy Agency warns that countries around the world need to take urgent measures to improve the security of radioactive materials that could be used to build a "dirty bomb." *(U.S. Efforts to Halt Nuclear Smuggling Faulted, p. 416)*

June 4: The city council in Belfast, Northern Ireland, elects Alex Maskey as mayor. In the 1970s Maskey was jailed twice on suspicion that he was a terrorist for the Irish Republican Army. Maskey ran for mayor as a candidate for Sinn Fein, the IRA's political arm.

June 5: A car packed with explosives strikes a bus near Afula, Israel, killing 17 people and wounding 38. Islamic Jihad claims responsibility for the attack.

June 18: A suicide bombing on a bus traveling from Gilo, Israel, to Jerusalem kills 19 people and injures 74.

June 21: A jury in Charlotte, North Carolina, convicts two brothers—Mohamad Hammoud and Chawki Hammoud—of smuggling cigarettes and sending some of the profits to the militant Islamic group Hizballah.

June 27: A story in the *Washington Post* reports that some government computer experts believe terrorists "are at the threshold of using the Internet as a direct instrument of bloodshed."

June 27: In an effort to stop terrorists from obtaining weapons of mass destruction, the Group of Eight nations announce at a summit meeting in Canada that they will contribute up to $20 billion over a 10-year period to help Russia secure its stockpiles of nuclear, biological, and chemical weapons.

June 29: A botched bombing in Athens, Greece, leads in the following months to the arrests of numerous members of the left-wing terrorist group 17 November. Members of the group, which claimed to have committed 23 murders, had eluded the authorities for more than a quarter-century.

July: A key al-Qaida spokesman issues a new threat against the United States. "Al-Qaida will organize more attacks inside American territory and outside, at the moment we choose, at the place we choose, and with the objectives that we want," says Sulaiman Abu Ghaith in an audio recording.

July: One of the three major terrorist organizations in Colombia, the right-wing United Self-Defense Forces of Colombia, splinters after internal disputes about whether it should be involved in drug trafficking.

July 1: During a raid Israeli special forces kill Muhaned Taher, the top bomb maker for Hamas.

July 4: A judge in Tokyo sentences a member of the Japanese Red Army terrorist group to 20 years in prison for her role in a series of bomb attacks in the 1970s.

July 5: During a celebration of Algeria's 40 years of independence from France, a bombing at an outdoor market in Larba, Algeria, kills 49 people. Islamic extremists are suspected in the attack.

July 11: Attorney General John Ashcroft testifies before a House committee that al-Qaida continues to have a strong network of "sleeper" cells within the United States and is trying to enlarge the network by smuggling more terrorists into the country.

July 16: In an unprecedented move, the Irish Republican Army apologizes for the deaths of "noncombatants" during its 30-year campaign to drive the British from Northern Ireland.

July 17: Comptroller General David Walker, director of the U.S. General Accounting Office, urges members of Congress to proceed cautiously in creating the new Department of Homeland Security, which is supposed to coordinate federal counterterrorism efforts. *(Watchdog Urges Caution on Homeland Security Plan, p. 426)*

July 17: In a report about its investigation of the attacks on September 11, 2001, a House subcommittee sharply criticizes three of the nation's leading intelligence agencies: the CIA, the FBI, and the National Security Agency. *(Report Cites Terror Failures by U.S. Intelligence Agencies, p. 431)*

July 22: In an attempt to kill Hamas military leader Salah Shehadeh, an Israeli F-16 fighter plane drops a bomb on a residential area in Gaza City. The bomb kills Shehadeh and 14 other people, nine of whom are children.

July 26: In Boston, a federal jury convicts a white-supremacist couple of conspiring to blow up black and Jewish landmarks around Boston. Prosecutors say the couple hoped to set off a "racial holy war."

July 31: An explosion in the cafeteria at Hebrew University in Jerusalem kills seven people and injures 85. Hamas claims responsibility and says the attack is revenge for Israel's July 22 killing of its military leader, Salah Shedadeh.

August 6: Israel's Supreme Court rules that the military may continue its policy of demolishing with no warning the homes of suspected Palestinian terrorists.

August 8: A mortar shell attack during the inauguration of Alvaro Uribe Velez as president of Colombia kills 19 people and wounds more than 30. Velez is not injured, and officials blame the attack on the Revolutionary Armed Forces of Colombia.

August 26: The federal government cannot automatically bar the public from all deportation hearings for hundreds of people rounded up by authorities following the attacks of September 11, 2001, according to a ruling by the U.S. Court of Appeals for the Sixth Circuit. The people detained almost all of them Middle Eastern or South Asian descent were held on suspicions they were terrorists or were witnesses to terrorist activities. *(Court Overturns Order Requiring Secret Hearings, p. 436)*

BIBLIOGRAPHY

Articles, Books, and Reports

Abanes, Richard. *American Militias: Rebellion, Racism & Religion*. Downers Grove, Ill.: InterVarsity Press, 1996.

Anderson, Sean K., and Stephen Sloan. *Historical Dictionary of Terrorism*. Lanham, Md.: Scarecrow Press, 2002.

Arquilla, John, and David Ronfeldt, eds. *Networks and Netwars: The Future of Terror, Crime, and Militancy*. Santa Monica, Calif.: RAND, 2001. http://www.rand.org/publications/MR/MR1382 (August 17, 2002).

Baird-Windle, Patricia, and Eleanor J. Bader. *Targets of Hatred: Anti-Abortion Terrorism*. New York: Palgrave (for St. Martin's Press), 2001.

Balz, Dan, and Bob Woodward. "Bush's Global Strategy Began to Take Shape in First Frantic Hours After Attack." Part 1 of "America's Chaotic Road to War," *Washington Post*, January 27, 2002. http://www.washingtonpost.com/ac2/wp-dyn?pagename=article&node=&contentId=A42754-2002Jan26 (August 16, 2002).

Barkun, Michael. *Religion and the Racist Right: The Origins of the Christian Identity Movement*. Chapel Hill: University of North Carolina Press, 1997.

Bell, J. Bowyer. *The IRA, 1968–2000: Analysis of a Secret Army*. London/Portland, Ore.: Frank Cass, 2000.

Bergen, Peter L. *Holy War, Inc.: Inside the Secret World of Osama bin Laden*. New York: The Free Press, 2001.

Bodansky, Yossef. *Bin Laden: The Man Who Declared War on America*. Roseville, Calif.: Prima Publishing, 2001.

Bremer, L. Paul III, and Edwin Meese III. *Defending the American Homeland: A Report of the Heritage Foundation Homeland Security Task Force*. Washington, D.C.: Heritage Foundation, 2002. http://www.heritage.org/homelanddefense/welcome.html (August 17, 2002).

Brennan, Richard. *Protecting the Homeland: Insights from Army Wargames*. Santa Monica, Calif.: RAND, 2002. http://www.rand.org/publications/MR/MR1490 (August 17, 2002).

Byman, Daniel. *Keeping the Peace: Lasting Solutions to Ethnic Conflicts*. Baltimore: Johns Hopkins University Press, 2001.

Byman, Daniel, Peter Chalk, Bruce Hoffman, William Rosenau, and David Brannan.

Trends in Outside Support for Insurgent Movements. Santa Monica, Calif.: RAND, 2001. http://www.rand.org/publications/MR/MR1405 (August 17, 2002).

Byman, Daniel, and Jerrold D. Green. *Political Violence and Stability in the States of the Northern Persian Gulf.* Santa Monica, Calif.: RAND, 1999. http://www.rand.org/publications/MR/MR1021 (August 17, 2002).

Byman, Daniel, and John R. Wise. *The Persian Gulf in the Coming Decade: Trends, Threats, and Opportunities.* Santa Monica, Calif.: RAND, 2002.

Canadian Security Intelligence Service. "Trends in Terrorism," *Perspectives,* December 18, 1999. http://www.fas.org/irp/threat/200001e.htm (April 16, 2002).

Coogan, Tim Pat. *The IRA.* New York: Palgrave (for St. Martin's Press), 2002.

Corbin, Jane. *Al Qaeda: In Search of the Terror Network That Shook the World.* New York: Thunder Mouth Press/Nation Books, 2002.

Corcoran, James. *Bitter Harvest: Gordon Kahl and the Posse Comitatus: Murder in the Heartland.* New York: Viking Penguin, 1990.

Council on Foreign Relations. "Terrorist, Guerrilla, Freedom Fighter: What's the Difference?" http://www.cfrterrorism.org/policy/guerrilla_print.html (August 15, 2002).

Dalglish, Lucy A., Gregg P. Leslie, and Phillip Taylor, eds. *Homefront Confidential: How the War on Terrorism Affects Access to Information and the Public's Right to Know.* Arlington, Va.: The Reporters Committee for Freedom of the Press, 2002. http://www.rcfp.org/homefrontconfidential (August 17, 2002).

Dees, Morris, and James Corcoran. *Gathering Storm: America's Militia Threat.* New York: HarperCollins, 1996.

Dobratz, Betty A., and Stephanie L. Shanks-Meile. *The White Separatist Movement in the United States: White Power, White Pride.* Baltimore: Johns Hopkins University Press, 2000.

Dyer, Joel. *Harvest of Rage: Why Oklahoma City Is Only the Beginning.* Boulder, Colo.: Westview Press, 1998.

Elliott, Michael. "Could 9/11 Have Been Prevented?" *Time,* August 12, 2002.

Emerson, Steven. *American Jihad: The Terrorists Living Among Us.* New York: The Free Press, 2002.

Falkenrath, Richard A., Robert D. Newman, and Bradley A. Thayer. *America's Achilles' Heel: Nuclear, Biological, and Chemical Terrorism and Covert Attack.* Cambridge, Mass.: MIT Press, 1998.

Friedman, Thomas L. *From Beirut to Jerusalem.* New York: Anchor Books, 1990.

Ganor, Boaz. "Terrorism: No Prohibition Without Definition" (October 7, 2001). http://www.ict.org.il/articles/articledet.cfm?articleid=393 (April 5, 2002).

———. "Defining Terrorism: Is One Man's Terrorist Another Man's Freedom Fighter?" http://www.ict.org.il/articles/define.htm (April 4, 2002).

Gellman, Barton. "Broad Effort Launched After '98 Attacks." Part 1 of "The Covert Hunt for bin Laden." *Washington Post,* December 19, 2001. http://www.washingtonpost.com/ac2/wp-dyn?pagename=article&node=&contentId=A62725-2001Dec18 (August 16, 2002).

———. "Cyber-Attacks by Al Qaeda Feared." *Washington Post,* June 27, 2002.

Gershman, John. "Is Southeast Asia the Second Front?" *Foreign Affairs,* July–August 2002.

Godson, Roy. *Dirty Tricks or Trump Cards: U.S. Covert Action & Counterintelligence.* New Brunswick, N.J.: Transaction, 2001.

Gunaratna, Rohan. "Suicide Terrorism: A Global Threat." *Jane's Intelligence Review,* October 20, 2000. http://www.janes.com/security/international_security/news/usscole/jir001020_1_n.shtml (August 17, 2002).

———. *Global Terror: Unearthing the Support Networks That Allow Terrorism to Survive and Succeed.* New York: New York University Press, 2002.

Hamm, Mark S. *In Bad Company: America's Terrorist Underground.* Boston: Northeastern University Press, 2001.

Hane, Paula J. "Removing Information From the Public Web." *Information Today,* May 2002. http://www.infotoday.com/it/may02/hane2.htm (August 15, 2002).

Harris, Elisa D. "Chemical and Biological Weapons: Prospects and Priorities After September 11." *Brookings Review,* Summer 2002.

Hersh, Seymour M. "Missed Messages: Why the Government Didn't Know What It Knew." *The New Yorker,* June 3, 2002. http://www.newyorker.com/printable/?fact/020603fa_FACT (August 15, 2002).

Hewitt, Christopher, and Tom Cheetham. *Encyclopedia of Modern Separatist Movements.* Santa Barbara, Calif.: ABC-CLIO, 2000.

Heymann, Philip B. *Terrorism and America: A Commonsense Strategy for a Democratic Society.* Cambridge, Mass.: MIT Press, 1998.

Hoffman, Bruce. *Inside Terrorism.* New York: Columbia University Press, 1998.

Huntington, Samuel P. *The Clash of Civilizations and the Remaking of World Order.* New York: Simon & Schuster, 1996.

Johnson, Loch K. *Bombs, Bugs, Drugs, and Thugs: Intelligence and America's Quest for Security.* New York: New York University Press, 2002.

Keller, Bill, and Fred R. Conrad. "Nuclear Nightmares: Experts on Terrorism and Proliferation Agree on One Thing—Sooner or Later, an Attack Will Happen Here." *New York Times Magazine,* May 26, 2002.

Kepel, Gilles. *Jihad: The Trail of Political Islam.* Anthony F. Roberts, trans. Cambridge, Mass.: Harvard University Press, 2002.

Laqueur, Walter. *The New Terrorism: Fanaticism and the Arms of Mass Destruction.* Oxford: Oxford University Press, 1999.

Lesser, Ian O., Bruce Hoffman, John Arquilla, David F. Ronfeldt, Michele Zanini, and Brian Michael Jenkins. *Countering the New Terrorism.* Santa Monica, Calif.: RAND, 1999. http://www.rand.org/publications/MR/MR989 (August 17, 2002).

Levitas, Daniel. "The Radical Right After 9/11: The Attacks Hardened the Resolve of Immigrant Bashers and Anti-Semites." *The Nation,* July 22, 2002.

———. *The Terrorist Next Door.* New York: Thomas Dunne Books/St. Martin's Press, 2002.

Lewis, Bernard. *The Middle East: A Brief History of the Last 2,000 Years.* New York: Scribner, 1995.

Lichtblau, Eric, and Charles Pillar. "War on Terrorism Highlights FBI's Computer Woes." *Los Angeles Times,* July 28, 2002. http://www.latimes.com/news/nationworld/nation/la-na-computer28jul28005104.story?coll=la%2Dheadlines%2Dnation (August 15, 2002).

Lipset, Seymour Martin, and Earl Raab. *The Politics of Unreason: Right-Wing Extremism in America, 1790–1970.* New York: Harper & Row, 1970.

Luft, Gal. "The Palestinian H-Bomb: Terror's Winning Strategy." *Foreign Affairs,* July–August 2002.

Mann, Charles C. "Homeland Insecurity." *Atlantic Monthly,* September 2002. http://www.theatlantic.com/issues/2002/09/mann.htm (August 15, 2002).

Miller, Judith, Jeff Gerth, and Don Van Natta Jr. "Many Say U.S. Planned for Terror but Failed to Take Action." *New York Times,* December 30, 2001. http://www.nytimes.com/2001/12/30/national/30TERR.html (July 30, 2002).

Miller, Judith, and Don Van Natta Jr. "In Years of Plots and Clues, Scope of Qaeda Eluded U.S." *New York Times,* June 7, 2002.

Moloney, Ed. *A Secret History of the IRA*. New York: W.W. Norton, 2002.

Nordland, Rod, Sami Yousafzai, and Babak Dehghanpisheh. "How Al Qaeda Slipped Away." *Newsweek*, August 19, 2002.

Pillar, Paul R. *Terrorism and U.S. Foreign Policy*. Washington, D.C.: Brookings Institution Press, 2001.

Quandt, William B. *Peace Process: American Diplomacy and the Arab-Israeli Conflict Since 1967*. Washington, D.C.: Brookings Institution Press; Berkeley: University of California Press, 2001.

Rabasa, Angel, and Peter Chalk. *Colombian Labyrinth: The Synergy of Drugs and Insurgency and Its Implications for Regional Stability*. Santa Monica, Calif.: RAND, 2001. http://www.rand.org/publications/MR/MR1339 (August 17, 2002).

Rashid, Ahmed. *Taliban: Militant Islam, Oil and Fundamentalism in Central Asia*. New Haven: Yale University Press, 2000.

———. *Jihad: The Rise of Militant Islam in Central Asia*. New Haven: Yale University Press, 2002.

Reeve, Simon. *The New Jackals: Ramzi Yousef, Osama bin Laden and the Future of Terrorism*. Boston: Northeastern University Press, 1999.

Reich, Walter, ed. *Origins of Terrorism: Psychologies, Ideologies, Theologies, States of Mind*. Washington, D.C.: Woodrow Wilson Center Press, 1998.

Reiter, Jerry. *Live from the Gates of Hell: An Insider's Look at the Anti-Abortion Movement*. Amherst, N.Y.: Prometheus Books, 2000.

Richelson, Jeffrey T. "Defusing Nuclear Terror." *Bulletin of the Atomic Scientists*, March/April 2002. http://www.thebulletin.org/issues/2002/ma02/ma02richelson.html (August 15, 2002).

Rubin, Elizabeth. "The Most Wanted Palestinian." *New York Times Magazine*, June 30, 2002.

Ruthven, Malise. *A Fury for God: The Islamist Attack on America*. London: Granta Books, 2002.

Said, Edward W. *Covering Islam: How the Media and the Experts Determine How We See the Rest of the World*. New York: Vintage Books, 1997.

Simon, Jeffrey D. *The Terrorist Trap: America's Experience with Terrorism*. 2d ed. Bloomington: Indiana University Press, 2001.

Sims, Patsy. *The Klan*. New York: Stein and Day, 1978.

Sweet, Kathleen M. *Terrorism and Airport Security*. Lewiston, N.Y.: Edwin Mellen Press, 2002.

Tanter, Raymond. *Rogue Regimes: Terrorism and Proliferation*. New York: St. Martin's Griffin, 1999.

Tessler, Mark A. *A History of the Israeli-Palestinian Conflict*. Bloomington: Indiana University Press, 1994.

Thomas, Gordon. *Gideon's Spies: The Secret History of the Mossad*. New York: St. Martin's Press, 1999.

Toolis, Kevin. *Rebel Hearts: Journeys Within the IRA's Soul*. New York: St. Martin's Press, 1996.

Treverton, Gregory F. *Reshaping National Intelligence in an Age of Information*. New York: Cambridge University Press, 2001.

U.S. Congress. House. Committee on the Judiciary. Subcommittee on Crime. *Nature and Threat of Violent Anti-Government Groups in America: Hearing Before the Subcommittee on Crime of the Committee on the Judiciary*. 104th Congress, 1st sess., Serial 51, November 2, 1995.

U.S. Congress. House. Committee on Transportation and Infrastructure. Subcommittee on Aviation. *Aviation Security (Focusing on Training and Retention of*

Screeners): Hearing Before the Subcommittee on Aviation of the Committee on Transportation and Infrastructure. 106th Congress, 2d sess., Serial 106-77, March 16, 2000.

U.S. Congress. House. Committee on International Relations. *Al-Qaeda and the Global Reach of Terrorism: Hearing Before the Committee on International Relations.* 107th Congress, 1st sess., Serial 107–50, October 3, 2001.

U.S. Congress. Senate. Committee on Governmental Affairs. *Vulnerability of the Nation's Electric Systems to Multi-Site Terrorist Attack: Hearing Before the Committee on Governmental Affairs.* 101st Cong., 2d sess., S. hrg. 101–959, June 28, 1990.

U.S. Congress. Senate. Committee on Foreign Relations. Subcommittee on Western Hemisphere, Peace Corps, Narcotics, and Terrorism. *An Overview of U.S. Counterterrorism Policy and President Clinton's Decision to Grant Clemency to FALN Terrorists: Hearing Before the Subcommittee on Western Hemisphere, Peace Corps, Narcotics and Terrorism of the Committee on Foreign Relations.* 106th Congress, 1st sess., S. hrg. 106–259, September 14, 1999. http://purl.access.gpo.gov/ GPO/LPS4456 (August 18, 2002).

U.S. Congress. Senate. Committee on the Judiciary. *Clemency for FALN Members: Hearings Before the Committee on the Judiciary.* 106th Congress, 1st sess., S. hrg. 106–779, September 15 and October 20, 1999. http://purl.access.gpo.gov/GPO/ LPS9560 (HTML); http://purl.access.gpo.gov/GPO/LPS9562 (PDF) (August 18, 2002).

U.S. Congress. Senate. Committee on the Judiciary. Subcommittee on Technology, Terrorism, and Government Information. *Domestic Response Capabilities For Terrorism Involving Weapons of Mass Destruction: Hearing Before the Subcommittee on Technology, Terrorism, and Government Information of the Committee on the Judiciary.* 107th Congress, 1st sess., S. hrg. 107–224, March 27, 2001. http://purl .access.gpo.gov/GPO/LPS17608 (HTML); http://purl.access.gpo.gov/GPO/LPS17609 (PDF) (August 17, 2002).

U.S. Congress. Senate. Committee on Governmental Affairs. *Weak Links: How Should the Federal Government Manage Airline Passenger and Baggage Screening? Hearing Before the Committee on Governmental Affairs.* 107th Congress, 1st sess., S. hrg. 107–208, September 25, 2001. http://purl.access.gpo.gov/GPO/LPS21053 (HTML); http://purl.access.gpo.gov/GPO/LPS21054 (PDF) (August 18, 2002).

U.S. Congress. Senate. Committee on Foreign Relations. *Strategies for Homeland Defense: A Compilation by the Committee on Foreign Relations.* 107th Congress, 1st sess., Committee Print 107–43, September 26, 2001. http://purl.access.gpo.gov/ GPO/LPS15541 (HTML); http://purl.access.gpo.gov/GPO/LPS15542 (PDF) (August 18, 2002).

U.S. Congress. Senate. Committee on Foreign Relations. Subcommittee on International Operations and Terrorism. *The Global Reach of Al-Qaeda: Hearing Before the Subcommittee on International Operations and Terrorism of the Committee on Foreign Relations.* 107th Congress, 1st sess., S. hrg. 107–390, December 18, 2001. http://purl.access.gpo.gov/GPO/LPS19421 (HTML); http://purl.access.gpo .gov/GPO/LPS19422 (PDF) (August 17, 2002).

U.S. Congress. Senate. Committee on Foreign Relations. *Dirty Bombs and Basement Nukes: The Terrorist Nuclear Threat: Hearing Before the Committee on Foreign Relations.* 107th Congress, 2d sess., S. hrg. 107–575, March 5, 2002. http://frweb gate.access.gpo.gov/cgi-bin/getdoc.cgi?dbname=107_senate_hearings&docid= f:80848.wais (HTML); http://frwebgate.access.gpo.gov/cgi-bin/getdoc.cgi?dbname= 107_senate_hearings&docid=f:80848.pdf (PDF) (August 18, 2002).

U.S. Department of State. *Patterns of Global Terrorism 2001*. May 21, 2002. http://www.state.gov/s/ct/rls/pgtrpt/2001 (July 28, 2002).

Wade, Wyn Craig. *The Fiery Cross: The Ku Klux Klan in America*. New York: Oxford University Press, 1998.

Wilkinson, Paul, and Brian Michael Jenkins, eds. *Aviation Terrorism and Security*. London; Portland, Ore.: Frank Cass, 1999.

Woodward, Bob. *Veil: The Secret Wars of the CIA 1981–1987*. New York: Simon and Schuster, 1987.

———. *Bush at War*. New York: Simon and Schuster, 2002.

Yeoman, Barry, and Bill Hogan. "Airline Insecurity." *Mother Jones*, January/February 2002. http://motherjones.com/magazine/JF02/airlines.html (August 15, 2002).

World Wide Web Sites

Air University Library Bibliographies
http://www.maxwell.af.mil/au/aul/bibs/bib97.htm

This site offers excellent bibliographies on topics such as homeland security and defense, the history and role of intelligence in American society, the Israeli-Palestinian conflict, the Middle East, narcoterrorism, terrorist and insurgent organizations, weapons of mass destruction, media coverage of 9/11, Islamic activism, the terrorism threat and post-9/11 trends, and nuclear, biological, and chemical weapons. The bibliographies vary in the types of materials they list, but they typically include Internet sites, books, government documents, and periodical articles. The bibliographies were created by librarians at the Air University Library at Maxwell Air Force Base in Alabama.

Alternative Resources on the U.S. "War Against Terrorism"
http://www.pitt.edu/~ttwiss/irtf/Alternative.html

This page provides briefly annotated links to an interesting assortment of Web sites that question or criticize U.S. efforts to fight terrorism. The page is provided by the International Responsibilities Task Force of the American Library Association's Social Responsibilities Round Table.

America Responds
http://www.refdesk.com/attack.html

Through this page, refdesk.com offers links to a wide range of sites that provide everything from breaking news about terrorism to information about anthrax.

America's War Against Terrorism
http://www.lib.umich.edu/govdocs/usterror.html

The Documents Center at the University of Michigan Library offers links to hundreds of Web sites about virtually every aspect of terrorism through this excellent page. The links are divided into seven major categories: September 11th attack, counterterrorism, post-September 11 attacks, previous attacks, other countries, background research, and related Web pages.

ANSER Institute for Homeland Security
http://www.homelandsecurity.org

Highlights at this site include links to many of the most important reports, treaties, executive orders, and other government documents about terrorism and links to current news stories about the subject from major publications. The site is operated by the ANSER Institute for Homeland Security, a nonprofit organization.

Anti-Castro Guerrillas
http://www.rose-hulman.edu/~delacova/belligerence.htm
> An eclectic assortment of valuable information about attacks on Cuba and President Fidel Castro, largely by Cuban exiles living in the United States, is available through this site. The site is operated by a professor in the Latin American Studies Program at the Rose-Hulman Institute of Technology in Indiana.

Attack on America: Osama bin Laden, al-Qa'ida, and Terrorism
http://www.lib.ecu.edu/govdoc/terrorism.html
> Librarians from the Joyner Library at East Carolina University put together this strong collection of links to Web sites and individual documents about Osama bin Laden, his al-Qaida terrorist network, radical Islam, and related topics.

CAIN Web Service
http://cain.ulst.ac.uk/index.html
> This site provides a huge assortment of valuable information about the conflict in Northern Ireland. It has background information, details about key events, descriptions of the most important issues, a bibliographic database containing more than 4,200 references to materials about the Northern Ireland conflict, and much more. The site is operated by the Centre for the Study of Conflict at the University of Ulster in Northern Ireland.

CDC: Public Health Emergency Preparedness and Response
http://www.bt.cdc.gov
> The federal Centers for Disease Control and Prevention operates this site, which offers extensive information for the public and health professionals about topics such as anthrax, smallpox, radiation contamination from "dirty bombs," and threats from other chemical and biological agents.

Centre for Defence and International Security
http://www.cdiss.org/terror.htm
> The key resource at this site is a collection of detailed chronologies of terrorist attacks around the world from 1945 to 1998.

Christian Science Monitor: A Changed World
http://www.csmonitor.com/specials/sept11
> This site's highlight is its daily updates about the war on terrorism that quote a wide range of media sources from around the world. It also provides free access to all articles the *Christian Science Monitor* has published about terrorism from September 12, 2001, to the present.

Defend AMERICA
http://www.defendamerica.mil
> Defend AMERICA is the official Department of Defense Web site about the war on terrorism. Its original content is mainly limited to news stories and photographs, but it also has links to lots of other government sites that provide information about terrorism.

Dudley Knox Library: Terrorism
http://library.nps.navy.mil/home/terrorism.htm
> Among the many excellent collections of links to terrorism information available on the Internet, this list from the Dudley Knox Library at the Naval Postgraduate School is among the best because the links have been carefully selected for their quality. The site has links to numerous terrorism bibliographies, presidential directives, terrorism chronologies, reports by the Congressional Research Service and other government agencies, and Web sites.

BIBLIOGRAPHY

Earth Liberation Front
http://www.earthliberationfront.com/main.shtml
   This site is operated by the Earth Liberation Front (ELF), one of the two major
   ecoterrorist groups in the United States (the other is the affiliated Animal Liberation
   Front). It has a manual about how to set arson fires, a publication titled *If an Agent
   Knocks: Federal Investigators and Your Rights*, an extensive list of "direct actions"
   undertaken by ELF members, and answers to frequently asked questions about
   the ELF.

The Electronic Intifada
http://electronicintifada.net
   The Electronic Intifada presents the Palestinian viewpoint on the Israeli-Palestinian
   conflict. The site primarily focuses on media coverage of the conflict, providing
   news articles from a large number of sources, an overview of media coverage, and
   articles about alleged media distortions and misrepresentations. The site is operated by the Middle East Cultural and Charitable Society, a tax-exempt organization.

Federation of American Scientists
http://www.fas.org
   Through its own publications and links to other sites, the Federation of American
   Scientists provides access to excellent resources about weapons of mass destruction, information security, arms transfers, domestic security, intelligence programs,
   and related topics.

Google Web Directory: Israel-Palestine Terrorism
http://directory.google.com/Top/Society/Issues/Warfare_and_Conflict/Specific_
Conflicts/Middle_East/Israel-Palestine/Terrorism
   This page at the Google Web Directory provides links to more than one hundred
   Web sites that offer information about terrorist attacks in the Middle East. Each link
   is briefly annotated.

Google Web Directory: Terrorism
http://directory.google.com/Top/Society/Issues/Terrorism
   Links to several thousand Web sites about terrorism are provided on this page at the
   Google Web Directory. Most of the links are organized into categories such as articles and reports, biological and chemical terrorism, cyber terrorism, incidents,
   and U.S. domestic terrorism.

Google Web Directory: Terrorist Organizations
http://directory.google.com/Top/Society/Issues/Terrorism/Terrorist_Organizations
   This page at the Google Web Directory is a good place to start a search for information about a particular terrorist group. It has links to more than one hundred
   sites either operated by or about various organizations. Most of the links are arranged by terrorist group.

Hizballah
http://www.hizballah.org/english/frames/frames_c.htm
   This is the official Web site of Hizballah, the Palestinian group that frequently conducts terrorist attacks against Israel and other countries. Whether because of internal technical problems or external cyber attacks, the site is often unavailable.

The International Policy Institute for Counter-Terrorism
http://www.ict.org.il
   The highlights at this site are two databases. One contains descriptions of selected
   international terrorist and guerrilla attacks from 1986 to the present; the other has
   descriptions of terrorist attacks related to the Arab-Israeli conflict from 1970 to the
   present. The site also offers articles, news updates, profiles of terrorist groups, and
   documents issued by various governments and terrorist organizations.

Internet Islamic History Sourcebook

http://www.fordham.edu/halsall/islam/islamsbook.html

> Through its own files and links to other sites, the Internet Islamic History Source-book provides access to a huge quantity of information about the history of Islam. One of the highlights is a collection of links to various translations of the Koran, the sacred text of Islam. A history professor at Fordham University in New York operates the site.

Islamic Studies

http://www.arches.uga.edu/~godlas/

> The careful selection of high-quality links and detailed annotations of those links make the Islamic Studies site stand out. Various sections of the site lead to information about the Koran, Islamic history, Islam and the modern world, Muslim women and women's rights, Islamic art and music, and many other topics. A religion professor at the University of Georgia operates the site.

Israeli Ministry of Foreign Affairs

http://www.mfa.gov.il

> Through thousands of documents, the Israeli Ministry of Foreign Affairs site presents the official views of the Israeli government regarding the Arab-Israeli conflict and Palestinian terrorism. The site has articles describing recent terrorist attacks, chronologies of terrorist attacks, indictments of terrorists, resolutions by the United Nations Security Council, and numerous documents about efforts to find peace in the Middle East.

Kashmir Virtual Library

http://www.clas.ufl.edu/users/gthursby/kashmir/

> Annotated links to dozens of Web sites and individual documents about Kashmir, the area disputed by India and Pakistan that is the frequent scene of terrorist attacks, are provided by the Kashmir Virtual Library. A religion professor at the University of Florida operates the site.

Liberation Movements, Terrorist Organizations, Substance Cartels, and Other Para-State Entities

http://www.fas.org/irp/world/para/index.html

> Background information about hundreds of terrorist groups and guerrilla movements is provided at this site from the Federation of American Scientists. The amount of information about each group varies, but it usually includes at least a basic description and links to any relevant Web sites.

Librarians' Index to the Internet: September 11 and Beyond

http://www.lii.org/search/file/attack_and_aftermath

> This page at the Librarians' Index to the Internet provides carefully annotated listings for about one hundred selected Web sites related to terrorism. Many of the listings are divided into categories such as Afghanistan, anthrax, Arab-Israeli conflict, Osama bin Laden, biological and chemical weapons, Islam, and national security.

The Middle East 1916–2001: A Documentary Record

http://www.yale.edu/lawweb/avalon/mideast/mideast.htm

> A huge assortment of primary source documents about the Middle East are available through this page at Yale Law School's Avalon Project site. The documents, which date from 1916 to the present, include United Nations resolutions, statements by leaders of various governments, the Israeli Declaration of Independence, peace agreements, the Palestinian National Charter, and the Covenant of the Islamic Resistance Movement (Hamas).

BIBLIOGRAPHY

Middle East Historical and Peace Process Documents
http://www.mideastweb.org/history.htm

The primary source documents about the Middle East offered at this site nicely complement those offered by Yale Law School's Avalon Project. They include the British mandate for Palestine, statements by the Arab League, United Nations documents, the Palestinian Declaration of Independence, numerous peace treaties and proposals, and speeches by leaders of various governments.

National Security Archive: The September 11th Sourcebooks
http://www.gwu.edu/~nsarchiv/NSAEBB/sept11

More than one hundred government documents related to terrorism—many of them previously classified and obtained under the Freedom of Information Act—are available at this site. The documents are divided into six collections: "Terrorism and U.S. Policy," "Afghanistan: Lessons from the Last War," "BIOWAR: The Nixon Administration's Decision to End U.S. Biological Warfare Programs," "The Once and Future King?: From the Secret Files on King Zahir's Reign in Afghanistan, 1970–1973," "Anthrax at Sverdlovsk, 1979: U.S. Intelligence on the Deadliest Modern Outbreak," and "The Hunt for Bin Laden: Background on the Role of Special Forces in U.S. Strategy." The site is operated by the National Security Archive, an independent research institute and library in Washington, D.C.

Newseum: America Under Attack
http://www.newseum.org/frontpages/

Stunning images of the front pages from more than 120 newspapers around the world published on September 12, 2001, are available at this site from the Newseum.

NewsTrove: Al Qaeda
http://alqaeda.NewsTrove.com

This site archives recent stories about al-Qaida, the terrorist network operated by Osama bin Laden, from a wide variety of news sources. They include CNN, ABC News, CBS News, Fox News, *Washington Post*, *DAWN* (Pakistan), *San Francisco Examiner*, *International Herald Tribune*, *Washington Times*, *Village Voice*, *Christian Science Monitor*, *National Review*, *Salon*, *Time*, and *Forbes*.

NewsTrove: Middle East
http://middleeast.newstrove.com

Newstrove's archive of recent stories about the Middle East is particularly strong in foreign sources. They include the *Globe and Mail* (Canada), *Arab News* (Saudi Arabia), *Pravda* (Russia), *Sydney Morning Herald* (Australia), *DAWN* (Pakistan), *Straits Times* (Singapore), *South China Morning Post* (Hong Kong), and the *International Herald Tribune* (France).

NewsTrove: Terrorism
http://terrorism.newstrove.com

American and foreign news sources are both well represented in NewsTrove's archive of recent articles about terrorism. The sources include the Associated Press, Reuters, Fox News, ABC News, CNN, Radio Free Europe, the *Chicago Tribune*, *Washington Post*, *Washington Times*, *Christian Science Monitor*, *Village Voice*, *National Review*, *Salon*, *DAWN* (Pakistan), *Sydney Morning Herald* (Australia), *International Herald Tribune* (France), *Economist* (United Kingdom), and the *Globe and Mail* (Canada).

Palestine at the United Nations
http://www.un.org/Depts/dpa/qpal/index.html

This site's highlight is a database containing more than three thousand United Nations documents about Palestine and the Arab-Israeli conflict from 1946 to the present. It also offers a history of efforts to determine the future of Palestine, a chronology of related events, maps, and details about upcoming UN meetings about the Middle East. The site is operated by the Division for Palestinian Rights, which is part of the UN.

Palestine Liberation Organization: Negotiations Affairs Department
http://www.nad-plo.org/index.html

The Palestine Liberation Organization (PLO) operates this site, which focuses on negotiations between the PLO and Israel. It has fact sheets about some of the major issues in the negotiations, the texts of agreements between Israel and the PLO, United Nations resolutions, speeches about the Palestinian-Israeli negotiations by PLO leader Yasir Arafat and leaders from numerous nations, and links to many related Web sites.

Remembering September 11, 2001
http://poynter.org/dj/shedden/091101.htm

Links to nearly two dozen media sites that offer extensive coverage about terrorism highlight this site by The Poynter Institute, a journalism organization in Florida. Best of all, the links take users directly to the section at each site devoted to terrorism instead of dumping them at the home page. The site also provides images of newspaper front pages from around the world published on September 11 and 12 and links to a few dozen general Web sites related to terrorism.

Response to Terrorism: U.S. Department of State
http://usinfo.state.gov/topical/pol/terror

This site is an excellent source for current press releases, speech transcripts, and reports about terrorism from a variety of federal agencies and departments. It also has an archive of similar materials dating back to 1995 and special sections about major terrorist attacks on the United States prior to September 11.

Revolutionary Armed Forces of Colombia (FARC)
http://www.farc-ep.org/pagina%5Fingles

The Revolutionary Armed Forces of Colombia (FARC), one of the major guerrilla/terrorist groups in Colombia, operates this site. It has a history of FARC, letters and communiqués from FARC, and related information.

The Search for Peace
http://www.usembassy-israel.org.il/publish/peace/peace1.htm

The U.S. embassy in Israel runs this site, which has press statements, transcripts of speeches by major U.S. officials, and other documents about U.S. policy in the Middle East dating back to 1996. The site also provides the texts of many Middle East peace agreements.

Separatist, Para-military, Military, Intelligence, and Political Organizations
http://www.cromwell-intl.com/security/netusers.html

Basic information about hundreds of terrorist, separatist, and guerrilla organizations is available at this site, along with separate files about the countries where they operate. For each group and country, the site also provides helpful links to further information.

September 11, 2001: Attack on America
http://www.yale.edu/lawweb/avalon/sept_11/sept_11.htm

Hundreds of primary source documents about the September 11 attacks are available from this page at Yale Law School's Avalon Project site. The documents, which are arranged by date, include speeches by U.S. and foreign leaders, congressional bills and resolutions, transcripts of press briefings by various federal agencies, transcripts of statements at congressional hearings, executive orders, statements by organizations such as NATO and the Organization of American States, and United Nations resolutions.

BIBLIOGRAPHY

September 11 Web Archive
http://september11.archive.org
>The Library of Congress has joined with several other organizations to create this archive of reactions to the September 11 attacks from Web sites operated by everyone from individuals to government institutions around the world.

Sinn Fein
http://www.sinnfein.ie/index2.html
>Sinn Fein, the political wing of the Irish Republican Army, operates this site. It has official documents and press releases from Sinn Fein and information about the party's political activities.

Strategic Intelligence
http://www.loyola.edu/dept/politics/intel.html
>This site provides extensive links to Web sites and specific documents about intelligence issues. The links lead to Web sites operated by U.S. and foreign intelligence agencies, numerous government documents about intelligence, laws and legislative reports, transcripts of congressional hearings, and historical documents. The political science department at Loyola College in Maryland operates the site.

Television Archive: A Library of World Perspectives Concerning September 11th, 2001
http://client.alexa.com/tvarchive/html
>Television news broadcasts from around the world on September 11 and the days immediately afterward are available at this site. It also has numerous papers about the quality of news coverage of the September 11 attacks and the war on terrorism.

Terrorism: Questions and Answers
http://cfrterrorism.org/home
>Anyone trying to research or just understand terrorism would do well to start at this site, which is provided by the Council on Foreign Relations in cooperation with the Markle Foundation. In question-and-answer format, it offers solid, readable information about different types of terrorism, individual terrorist groups, various weapons of mass destruction, Afghanistan, state sponsors of terrorism, terrorist havens, homeland security, possible causes of the September 11 attacks, and policy issues following the attacks. The site also provides a useful weekly roundup of events in the war on terrorism.

Terrorism Research Center
http://www.terrorism.com
>The Terrorism Research Center offers recent news stories about terrorism, profiles of terrorist groups, articles analyzing various terrorism issues, links to numerous reports and other documents about terrorism, and a database of information warfare incidents.

UN Action Against Terrorism
http://www.un.org/terrorism
>The United Nations operates this site to showcase actions it has taken against terrorism. The site has resolutions by the Security Council and the General Assembly, statements and reports by the secretary general, the texts of international terrorism conventions, links to key documents about terrorism produced by various UN agencies, and related information.

U.S. Department of State: Counterterrorism Office
http://www.state.gov/s/ct
>Highlights at this site operated by the U.S. Department of State include a list of groups designated as foreign terrorist organizations, chronologies of terrorist incidents, the annual report *Patterns of Global Terrorism*, and other reports and press releases about terrorism issued by the State Department.

U.S. General Accounting Office: Terrorism
http://www.gao.gov/terrorism.html
> This special page at the Web site of the U.S. General Accounting Office, the investigative arm of Congress, provides links to the full texts of nearly two hundred reports about various terrorism issues that the agency has published since 1981. The reports address topics such as aviation security, computer security, critical infrastructure protection, homeland security, national preparedness strategies, security threats, and weapons of mass destruction.

United States Intelligence Community
http://www.columbia.edu/cu/lweb/indiv/dsc/intell.html
> Librarians at Columbia University created this great list of Internet and print resources about the U.S. intelligence community. The list includes resources that provide background information, bibliographies and indexes, periodicals, publications about intelligence reform, congressional documents about intelligence, declassified intelligence documents, resources about specific agencies such as the CIA, and publications about the Freedom of Information Act.

Urban Legends Reference Pages: Rumors of War
http://www.snopes2.com/rumors/rumors.htm
> The war on terrorism has led to a flood of rumors. This site tackles more than a hundred of them, explaining their background and categorizing each one as true, false, of undetermined veracity, or of unclassifiable veracity. Private individuals operate this handy and reliable site, which is part of the Urban Legends Reference Pages.

Washington Post: America at War
http://www.washingtonpost.com/wp-dyn/nation/specials/attacked
> The *Washington Post* offers free access to several thousand of its articles about the September 11 attacks and the war on terrorism through this page.

Washington Post: Colombia's Civil War
http://www.washingtonpost.com/wp-dyn/world/issues/colombiareport
> Current and archived stories from the *Washington Post* about terrorist attacks and other events in Colombia are available through this page.

Washington Post: War and Peace in the Mideast
http://www.washingtonpost.com/wp-dyn/world/issues/mideastpeace
> Links to current and archived stories from the *Washington Post* about the Middle East peace process and individual Middle Eastern countries are provided on this page.

Yahoo! Directory: Militias
http://dir.yahoo.com/Society_and_Culture/Issues_and_causes/militia_movement/militias
> Links to Web sites operated by nearly two dozen militia groups from around the United States are provided through this Yahoo! page.

Yahoo! News Full Coverage: Kashmir Conflict
http://news.yahoo.com/fc?tmpl=fc&cid=34&in=world&cat=kashmir_dispute
> Thousands of current and archived news stories dating back to February 1998 about the conflict between India and Pakistan over Kashmir, which has included numerous terrorist attacks, are available through this Yahoo! page. Sources include newswires such as the Associated Press and Reuters; American media such as the *New York Times, Washington Post, Christian Science Monitor,* and CNN; and foreign media such as the BBC (United Kingdom), *London Times* (United Kingdom), *The Guardian* (United Kingdom), *The Independent* (United Kingdom), *The News* (Pakistan), *DAWN* (Pakistan), *Times of India* (India), and *Arab News* (Saudi Arabia).

BIBLIOGRAPHY

Yahoo! News Full Coverage: Terrorism
http://story.news.yahoo.com/fc?cid=34&tmpl=fc&in=US&cat=Terrorism
    This page at Yahoo! provides access to thousands of current and archived news sto-
    ries about terrorism from sources such as the *New York Times*, *Los Angeles Times*,
    Boston Globe, *Washington Post*, *San Francisco Chronicle*, *USA Today*, *Christian
    Science Monitor*, *Newsday*, *New York Daily News*, the Associated Press, Reuters,
    CNN, the BBC, *The Independent* (United Kingdom), and *The Guardian* (United
    Kingdom). It also has links to forty selected Web sites about terrorism.

484

INDEX

INDEX

Arms Export Control Act, 138, 141
Asahara, Shoko, Aum Shinirkyo leader, 276, 278
Ashcroft, John
  al Qaeda terrorist network, 388
  bomb plot with nuclear materials, 416
  FBI domestic spying, 23
  FBI investigation guidelines, 421–425
  Pearl kidnapping and murder, 398, 399–401
  Stewart indictment, 407–410
Assad, Hafez al-, Beirut hijacking negotiations, 68
Assassination attempts
  John Paul II (Pope), 45–46
  Mubarak, Hosni, 190–192, 215
  Truman, Harry, 32
Assassinations
  Foster, Marcus, 9
  Gandhi, Indira, 61–62, 65–67, 327
  Kumaratunga, Chandrika, 277
  Rabin, Yitzhak, 127, 182–186, 215
  al-Sadat, Anwar, 47–51
Atef, Mohammed, 385
AUC. See United Self-Defense Forces of Colombia
Aum Shinrikyo (Japanese terrorist cult), Tokyo
  subway nerve gas incident, 215, 275–278
Aviation Security and Terrorism, Presidential Com-
  mission on, 102–106, 143
Aviation Security Improvement Act, 143–144

B

Bagri, Ajaib Singh
  Air India flight bombing, 327
  murder of Tara Singh Hayer, 329
Beers, Rand, narcoterrorism, Congressional testi-
  mony on, 402–406
Bhindranwale, Jarnail Singh, 65
Bibliography on terrorism, selected, 471–484
bin Laden, Osama
  bombings in Argentina, 116
  escape from Afghanistan, 367
  FBI ten most wanted fugitives, 271, 307
  head of al Qaeda, 47, 187, 278
  sheltered in Sudan, 190
  State Department fact sheet on, 206–209
  State Department reward for, 271
  Taliban regime sheltering in Afghanistan, 286–
    288
  UN resolution for Taliban to turn over, 286, 287–
    288
  U.S. embassy bombings in Kenya and Tanzania,
    206, 253, 271, 277, 307, 386–387
  U.S. missile attacks on terrorist training sites in
    Afghanistan and Sudan, 253–256
  weapons of mass destruction, 291
  World Trade Center bombing, 123
  See also al Qaeda terrorist network
Biochemical/Biological weapons. See Weapons of
  mass destruction
Black Panther Party, 1
Black September (Palestinian group), 7–8
Blair, Tony
  Afghanistan war, 366, 369–370
  "Bloody Sunday" investigations, 5–6
  on Omagh, Northern Ireland car bombing, 258–
    261
Blanton, Thomas E., church bombing conviction,
  411
"Bloody Friday" (Northern Ireland), 5–6
"Bloody Sunday" (Northern Ireland), 5
Bombings
  Air India Flight 182, 71, 327–329
  "Bloody Friday" attacks (Northern Ireland,
    1972), 5–6

Central Intelligence Agency recruiting office
  (Ann Arbor, 1968), 1
  Cubana Airlines bombing, 361–365
  Israeli embassy in Argentina, 116–117
  Jewish community center (Buenos Aires), 116,
    172
  Northern Ireland, "Real IRA" Omagh bombing,
    257–261, 371
  Oklahoma City federal building, 157–161, 177
  Olympic games (Atlanta, 1996), 203–205
  Pan Am Flight 103 (Lockerbie, Scotland), 102–
    106, 142, 336–338
  Paris, France terrorist bombings, 84, 150
  Peru, car-bomb attacks, 118–122
  Saudi Arabia, car/truck bombing incidents, 215,
    220–224
  U.S. embassies in Kenya and Tanzania, 30, 206,
    253, 271, 277, 386–387
  U.S. embassy in Beirut (1983), 57
  U.S. Marine headquarters in Lebanon (1983),
    57–60
  USS Cole suicide bombing in Yemen, 330–335,
    408
  West Berlin discotheque, 103
  World Trade Center bombing, 123–126, 157,
    187–189, 274, 351
Bombmaking information, Justice Department on
  ease of obtaining, 230–234
Bosch, Orlando, anti-Castro militant, 361, 365
Bowers, Sam, 146
Branch Davidians (Waco, Texas), 177
Brock, Jack, Jr., on government computer security,
  198
Bryant, Robert, antiabortion violence, national
  task force against, 267, 269–270
Buckley, William, hostage murdered by captors,
  112
Bush administration
  anti-Castro terrorist groups in U.S., 361
  terrorist airline attacks
    predictions of, 274–275
    secret hearings order, 436–440
Bush, George H. W.
  counterterrorism policy, 61
  foreign policy
    Israeli air strikes, 7–8
    Middle East peace process, 7–8
    visit to Peru, 118
  Iran-Contra affair
    involvement in, 137, 141
    knowledge of, 138
Bush, George W.
  on Afghanistan war against Taliban regime, 366,
    367–368
  Homeland Security Department proposal, 248–
    249, 426
  Pearl kidnapping and murder in Pakistan, 398,
    399
  September 11 terrorist attacks, 351–355
Bush, Jeb (Florida governor), Cantero, Raoul III
  judicial appointment, 362

C

Canada, Air India flight bombing arrests, 327–
  329
Cantero, Raoul III, Florida Supreme Court appoint-
  ment, 362
Carlos the Jackal. See Ramirez Sanchez, Ilich
Carriles, Posada, anti-Castro militant, 365
Carter, Jimmy
  Cuba-U.S. relations, 30–31
  on Cuban biochemical weapons, 362

INDEX

I

Independent Counsel, Iran-Contra affair, 137–141

India
Air India Flight 182 bombing, 71, 327–329
Gandhi, Indira, assassination of, 61–62, 65–67, 327
Gandhi, Rajiv, assassination of, 278
Kashmir disputes, 379–380
terrorist attack on Indian Parliament, 379–382

Indonesia, Islamic extremists, 389

Infrastructure, protecting, 243–247

Intelligence agencies
counterterrorism intelligence failures, 431–435
and rights of Americans, 22–26, 421–425

Intelligence gathering
Cubans infiltrating anti-Castro terrorist groups in U.S., 362
failures of U.S. agencies, 431–435
government restrictions, Clinton administration, 322

International Atomic Energy Agency (IAEA), nuclear smuggling, 416–417

International terrorism
FBI report on trends, 307–311
FBI on threats to U.S., 228–229
State Department on trends in, 215–219

IRA. *See* Irish Republican Army

Iran
Reagan charges of terrorism, 71
terrorism in Latin America, support for, 172–176
terrorist support, 391
U.S. arms sales, 88–91
U.S embassy hostages
beginnings of crisis, 34–39
Carter statements on, 34–37, 40–44
release of hostages, 40–44
rescue attempt, 40, 41–42
U.S. relations, 88

Iran-Contra affair
Independent counsel on, 137–141
prosecutions, 139–140
Reagan speech on, 88–91

Iraq, U.S. air strikes, 262

Irish Republican Army (IRA)
"Bloody Friday" attacks, 5–6
ceasefire negotiations, 132
destroying weapons of, 371–373
"Real Ira" Omagh car bombing, 257–261, 371
secret talks and peace negotiations, 151–154

Islamic extremist groups
Sadat assassination, 47
threat to U.S., 276
World Trade Center bombing, 123

Islamic Group (Egypt), Rahman leader of, 407–410

Islamic Jihad
alliance with al Qaeda network, 47, 384, 385
Egyptian, bombings, 47, 386–387
Israeli embassy in Argentina bombing, 116–117
Palestine, 390
PLO support for, 339
Sbarro restaurant suicide bombing in Jerusalem, 346–350

Islamic Movement of Uzbekistan (IMU), 406

Israel
air strikes against Syria and Lebanon, 7–8
embassy in Argentina bombing, 116–117, 172
Entebbe airport raid (1976), 27–29
Middle East violence, 339–345
Palestinian extremist suicide bombings, 215
PLO peace agreement, 127–131, 182

Rabin assassination, 127, 182–186, 215
terrorism against Olympic athletes, 7–8, 203

J

Jacobsen, David, 90

Japan
hostage rescue in Peru, 235–237
Tokyo subway terrorist nerve gas incident (Aum Shinrikyo), 215, 275–278

Japanese American Evacuation Claims Act, 56

Japanese-Americans, World War II internment, 52–56

Jarboe, James, ecoterrorist threats, Congressional testimony on, 393–397

Jewish community center (Buenos Aires), bombing, 116, 172–176

Jewish Community Relations Council, Shultz speech on terrorism, 61–64

Jihad (Holy War) movement, 384
See also Islamic Jihad

John Paul II (Pope), assassination attempt, 45–46

Justice Department
bombmaking information, 230–234
closing of PLO observer mission to the UN, 97–101
federal agency security standards, 162

K

Kashmir, India-Pakistan disputes, 379–380

Katz v. U.S. (1967), 2

Keating, Frank (Oklahoma governor), Oklahoma City bombing incident, 158–159

Keith, Damon J., secret hearings order, 436

Kelley, Jack, on Sbarro restaurant suicide bombing in Jerusalem, 346–350

Kelly, Raymond, World Trade Center bombing, 123–126

Kenya, U.S. embassy bombing, 206, 253, 271, 277, 307, 386–387

Kessler, Gladys, secret hearings order, 436

Khomeini, Ayatollah Ruhollah
return to power, 34
U.S. embassy hostages in Iran, 36

Kidnappings
of Americans in Lebanon, 68
Hearst by Symbionese Liberation Army, 9–12
Pearl, Daniel, murder of, 398–401
of Westerners in Lebanon, 112

King, Peter T. (R-N.Y.), on militia groups, 177, 179–181

Kissinger, Henry A.
on Cubana airlines bombing, CIA involvement, 364
Middle East peace process, 13

Kopp, James, antiabortion activist arrested, 267

Ku Klux Klan
bombings in Texas averted, 225
burning of two churches in South Carolina, 238
church bombing (Birmingham, 1963), 411–415
murder of Medgar Evers, 146–148

Kumaratunga, Chandrika, assassination of, 277

L

Latin America
Iran support for terrorism in, 172–176
narcoterrorism, 404–406

Lebanese Armed Revolutionary Faction (FARL)
Paris terrorist bombings, 84
terrorist network, 150

Lebanon
hostages released, 112–115
Israeli air strikes, 7–8